and
usage

Punctuation

Other conventions of writing

Diction

Sentences and paragraphs

Composition

FLOSSIE HOUGH
11:10 Wednesday

Handbook of Current English

3rd edition

Porter G. Perrin
George H. Smith

Third edition revised by
Jim W. Corder
Texas Christian University

Scott, Foresman and Company

Library of Congress Catalog Card #68-19902

The sources of quotations used for illustrative purposes are indicated in the text. Acknowledgement is due the following publishers and authors for special permission to reproduce their materials.

American Historical Association: Selection from "Everyman His Own Historian" by Carl Becker in *American Historical Review.*
The American West: Selection from "The Eye of the Beholder" by Joseph Wood Krutch; by permission of the author and the publisher.
Appleton-Century-Crofts: Selection from *Spelling for the Millions* by Edna L. Furness; by permission of the Meredith Press.
The Atlantic Monthly: Selections from "A Ghost for Mark Twain" by Burgess Johnson; from "In Time of Trial" by Barbara Ward; and from "How Good Is Government Medical Care?" by Osler Peterson, M.D.
Miss Sonia Brownell and Secker & Warburg Ltd.: Selection from *The English People* by George Orwell.
Curtis Brown, Ltd.: Selection from "A Pontifical Splendor" by Sean O'Faolain, in *Holiday,* April 1960. Reprinted by permission of Curtis Brown, Ltd. Copyright © 1960 by The Curtis Publishing Company, Inc. British rights controlled by A. P. Watt and Sons, Ltd., London.
The Curtis Publishing Company: Selection from "A Capsule History of Rome" by Arnold Ehrlich, in *Holiday,* April 1960.
Doubleday & Company, Inc.: Selections from *Amy Vanderbilt's Complete Book of Etiquette.* Copyright 1958 by Amy Vanderbilt. Reprinted by permission of Doubleday & Company, Inc.
Lincoln Dryden: Selection from "How to Drive a Car" by Lincoln Dryden, in *Harper's Magazine,* June 1952.
Loren C. Eiseley: Selection from "The Time of Man" by Loren C. Eiseley, in *Horizon,* March 1962.
Farrar, Straus & Giroux, Inc.: Selection from *The Kandy-Kolored Tangerine-Flake Streamline Baby* by Tom Wolfe. Copyright © 1965 by Thomas K. Wolfe, Jr. Reprinted with permission of Farrar, Straus & Giroux, Inc. British rights controlled by Sterling Lord Agency, London.
Nathan Glazer: Selections from "The Wasted Classroom" by Nathan Glazer. Copyright © 1961 by Harper's Magazine, Inc. Reprinted from the October 1961 issue of *Harper's Magazine* by special permission.
Leo Gurko: Selections from *The Angry Decade* by Leo Gurko, published by Dodd, Mead & Co. Copyright 1947 by Leo Gurko.
Harcourt, Brace & World, Inc.: Selections from *The Modern Researcher* by Jacques Barzun and Henry Graff; from *Aspects of the Novel* by E. M. Forster; from *Introduction to Linguistic Structure* by Archibald A. Hill; from *Babbitt* by Sinclair Lewis (British rights controlled by Jonathan Cape Limited, London); from *Abraham Lincoln: The Prairie Years* by Carl Sandburg; from "A Piece of News" by Eudora Welty in *A Curtain of Green and Other Stories* (British rights controlled by A. M. Heath & Company, Ltd., London). Selections by George Orwell from "A Hanging" and (on page 249) "Politics and the English Language," both in *Shooting an Elephant and Other Essays;* from *Such, Such Were the Joys;* and from *The Orwell Reader* by permission of Harcourt, Brace & World, Inc., and also by permission of Miss Sonia Brownell and Secker & Warburg, Ltd., London.
Harper & Row, Publishers: Selections from pp. 249-250, 197, 231-232 in *Only Yesterday* by Frederick Lewis Allen. Copyright 1931 by Frederick Lewis Allen; renewed, 1959, by Agnes Rogers Allen. Reprinted by permission of Harper & Row, Publishers. Selections from "Crossing the Atlantic in a 13-Foot Sailboat" by Robert Manry, in *Harper's Magazine,* June 1966; adapted from Chapters 1 and 11 of *Tinkerbelle* by Robert Manry, Harper & Row, Publishers, 1966. British rights controlled by Wm. Collins & Sons, Ltd., London.

Harper's Magazine, Inc.: Selection from "Do Women's Colleges Turn Out Spinsters" by Lynn White, Jr.
Holt, Rinehart and Winston, Inc.: Selection from *Dissenter in a Great Society* by William Stringfellow.
Houghton Mifflin Company: Selection from *Silent Spring* by Rachel Carson.
Little, Brown and Company: Selection from *The Story of Maps* by Lloyd A. Brown; Copyright 1949 by Lloyd Arnold Brown; by permission of Little, Brown and Company. Selection from "Flying by Guess and by God" by Dean C. Smith, in *By the Seat of My Pants;* Copyright © 1961 by Dean C. Smith; by permission of Atlantic - Little, Brown and Company. British rights controlled by Harold Ober Associates, Inc.
Russell Lynes: Selection from "How Good Are the Junior Colleges?" by Russell Lynes; Copyright © 1966, by Harper's Magazine, Inc.; reprinted from the November 1966 issue of *Harper's Magazine* by permission of the author.
The Macmillan Company: Selections from *The Aims of Education* by Alfred North Whitehead, copyright © 1959 by The Macmillan Company; also by permission of Cambridge University Press.
Michigan Education Association: Selection from "Speling Is Strikly for the Burds" by Parm Mayer in the *Michigan Educational Journal* by permission of the author and the Michigan Education Association.
William Morris Agency, Inc.: Selection from "Good-By to Oedipus" by Helen Eustis; Copyright © 1953 by Harper's Magazine, Inc. Reprinted by permission of William Morris Agency, Inc.
Natural History: Selection from "Pin-Pointing the Past with the Cosmic Clock" by Richard Foster Flint.
The New York Review of Books: Selection from "We Won't Go" by Paul Goodman. Reprinted from *The New York Review of Books.* Copyright © 1967, The New York Review.
The New Yorker Magazine, Inc.: Selections from "Onward and Upward with the Arts" by Jacob Brackman; from "A Matter of Degree" by David Daiches; from "The Never-Ending Time" by Bertie Johnson; from "A Reporter at Large: China Notes" by Hans Koningsberger; from "The Sporting Scene" by Herbert Warren Wind.
W. W. Norton & Company, Inc.: Selection from *Arts and the Man* by Irwin Edman. Reprinted by permission of W. W. Norton & Company, Inc. Copyright 1928, 1939 by W. W. Norton & Company, Inc., Copyright renewed 1956 by Meta Markel.
Penguin Books Ltd.: Selection from *The Greeks* by H. D. F. Kitto.
Random House, Inc. - Alfred A. Knopf, Inc.: Selection from *The Dyer's Hand* by W. H. Auden, copyright 1956 by Random House, Inc. Selections from *Goodbye to a River* by John Graves, copyright 1960 by Alfred A. Knopf, Inc., by permission of John Graves and Alfred A. Knopf, Inc. Selection from *The Art of Teaching* by Gilbert Highet, copyright 1950 by Alfred A. Knopf, Inc. Selections from *Prejudices, Third Series* by H. L. Mencken. Copyright, 1922 by Alfred A. Knopf, Inc. Renewed, 1950 by H. L. Mencken. Reprinted by permission of the publisher.
Saturday Review: Selections from "The Coming Era of Ecumenopolis" by C. A. Doxiadis; from "Five Years of Change" by Richard P. Kleeman, by permission also of the author; from "The Dynamics of Education" by Lou LaBrant; from "The Glorious and the Terrible" by Allan Nevins; from "Plunder or Plenty?" by Samuel Ordway, Jr.; from "Perspective: The Future Without the Past" by J. H. Plumb; from "Facing the Music" by Peter Schrag; from "Our Perilous Population Implosion" by Stewart L. Udall.
Mrs. Bradford Smith: Selection from "We're Selling America Short" by Bradford Smith in *The American Scholar.*
Mrs. Helen Thurber: Selection from *Franklin Avenue, U.S.A.,* in *The Thurber Album,* published by Simon and Schuster. Copr. © 1952, James Thurber. Originally printed in *The New Yorker.* Selection from *The Psychosemanticist Will See You Now, Mr. Thurber,* in *Alarms and Diversions.* Copr. © 1957, James Thurber. Published by Harper and Row. Selection from *The Thirteen Clocks.* Copr. © 1950, James Thurber. Published by Simon and Schuster.
Time, Inc.: Selections from "A Cerfit of Riches," copyright © 1966 by Time, Inc.; from "Music to His Ears," copyright © 1967 by Time, Inc. Reprinted by courtesy of *Time, The Weekly Newsmagazine.*
Today's Health, published by the American Medical Association: Selection from 'Coronary Thrombosis" by William A. R. Thompson, M.D.

Preface

In a paper presented at the 1965 meeting of the National Council of Teachers of English, Professor Edward P. J. Corbett cited our need for men "of the stature of Porter Perrin" to continue their work in the preparation of modern rhetoric texts. Professor Perrin was a pioneer who opened a new territory and went further into it than most of his successors. Understanding that "good English" need not always be Formal English, he liberalized many of our conceptions about language by showing the varied ways it is used by contemporary writers and speakers. Yet he also understood the importance of being carefully selective in language use, and his texts for college students were designed to show them why some forms of expression are more effective—and, in the context of college writing, more appropriate—than others. Largely through his influence, the principle of *appropriateness* has become basic in other texts on composition and usage.

Content and organization of the handbook. Although this revision of the *Handbook of Current English* contains a substantial amount of new material on writing and has been geared more specifically than earlier editions to the special needs of students in beginning composition courses, it preserves much of Porter Perrin's plan and most of his philosophy. The first three parts of the *Handbook* summarize and illustrate the basic principles of current grammar and usage and the various conventions of writing. Whether or not these sections are taught systematically, students will refer to them often when writing, revising, and correcting their papers. The arrangement of content and the format make the *Handbook* a reference tool that students can use easily on their own.

Sections 1-10, *Grammar and Usage*, review the grammar of English sentences and the functions and uses of various kinds of words and word groups. The standards for judging "good English" are discussed in Section 1, which describes the main varieties of English usage and the principle of appropriateness. Students should read this material at the start of the course, since they will need it to interpret recommendations made throughout the text and should also have it in mind when writing and revising their papers.

Sections 11-15, *Punctuation and Mechanics*, discuss and illustrate the principles governing the use of end stops, commas, semicolons, colons, dashes, parentheses, quotation marks, brackets, ellipses, and italics. The sections on internal punctuation show how choice of punctuation can relate to meaning and effect.

Sections 16-18, *Other Conventions of Writing*, discuss spelling problems and the various conventions for using capital letters, hyphens, apostrophes, abbreviations, and numbers.

The sections in this first half of the *Handbook* treat single, definite topics. Grammatical definitions are included where they are relevant and necessary to the discussion rather than in a separate glossary. Similarly, particular matters of usage are discussed at the point where they relate to general principles. In cases of divided usage, students are directed clearly to the form or construction considered appropriate for college writing.

The second half of the *Handbook* serves both as a brief rhetoric and as a practical guide to college writing tasks:

Sections 19-21, *Diction*, deal with the correct and effective use of words. Here as elsewhere in the revision, fresh illustrations are used to foster an inductive understanding of good writing.

Sections 22-24, *Sentences and Paragraphs*, discuss the means by which these elements of composition can be controlled to shape meaning. The student is shown how to employ various sentence patterns and various patterns of paragraph development in effectively developing and supporting his ideas.

Sections 25-29, *Composition*, are concerned with the application of language skills to particular problems of writing. Recognizing the changing emphases in composition courses, they incorporate much material not included in earlier editions of the *Handbook*. A substantially new section called "Discovering and organizing material for writing" emphasizes the importance of pre-writing—the need for exploring the potential of a subject in order to find a real purpose in writing. The section on "Writing the first draft" draws on the new rhetoric of sentences and paragraphs to show the practical use of these elements in directing the development of an essay. A new section called "Writing in college and out" relates the basic principles of planning and composition to particular kinds of writing: exposition, argumentation, description, narration, answers to essay examinations, reports and critiques, literary analyses, and letters. The final section of the *Handbook* is devoted to the special problems of the research paper.

Exercises. The exercises at the end of each section reinforce and further develop the points made in the text by giving the student practice in applying the principles he has learned and by encouraging him to analyze particular writing practices. The vast majority of exercises in this edition are new, and many of them illustrate something more about good writing than the relatively straightforward matter of correctness. The exercises at the end of Section 2, for example, make use of aphorisms to provide practice in sentence construction; those for Section 12 illustrate the uses of irony while teaching the correct use of commas. Unlike many exercises on grammar and mechanics, these should keep students interested and make them alert to the ultimate relevance of their task. A key to the exercises is available to instructors.

Index and correction chart. An especially full index provides a quick means of referring to both general and particular points of discussion, and students should develop the habit of using it when they write and revise their papers. The marginal tabs on the text pages, giving both correction symbol and section number, are designed to increase the *Handbook's* usefulness as a reference tool.

Themes can be marked by using either the correction symbols or the section numbers; the two are coordinated in the correction chart on the back end papers as well as on the marginal tabs. In the text itself, correction symbols are printed in color together with specific instructions for revision. Students should study the text that follows each instruction whenever they are not sure why revision is necessary. Section 27.3, "Revising a corrected paper," illustrates the use of the correction symbols.

I wish to thank Eugene K. Garber for providing the exercises for the first eighteen sections of this revision. Valuable suggestions for revising the text itself were made by Kenneth E. Biddle, Wilma R. Ebbitt, William Holmes, Kenneth R. Johnston, Vernon L. Schonert, and many of the *Handbook's* users, all of whom deserve my gratitude. Finally, as first and always, I thank my wife for everything.

Jim W. Corder

Contents

Grammar and usage

1 What is good English?

1.1 The elements of language 1
Sounds 1. Words 1. Word forms 2. Constructions 2.
Writing practices 2.

1.2 Varieties of English usage 3
General English 5. Formal English 7. Informal
English 11. Nonstandard English 12.

1.3 The qualities of good English 13
Appropriateness to purpose and situation 14.
Appropriateness to listener or reader 15.
Appropriateness to speaker or writer 17.

Exercises 18

2 Grammar of sentences

2.1 Main sentence elements 23
The subject 23. The verb 24. The object 24. The
complement 25. Word order 25.

2.2 Secondary sentence elements 27
Adjectives and adverbs as modifiers 27. Other words
and word groups as modifiers 27. Appositives 29.
Modifiers of modifiers 29.

2.3 Phrases and clauses 29
Phrases 30. Clauses 30.

2.4 Sentences classified by clause structure 31
Simple sentences 31. Compound sentences 32.
Complex sentences 33. Compound-complex sentences 33.

2.5 Sentences classified by purpose 33

2.6 Minor sentence types 34
Subjectless sentences 34. Verbless sentences 35.

Exercises 36

3 Basic sentence faults

3.1 Fragmentary sentences 38
Joining a fragment to another sentence 39. Making a
fragment into a sentence 40. Rewriting a fragment 41.

3.2 **Comma faults** 41
Making two sentences 42. Using a semicolon 42. Revising the passage 43.

3.3 **Fused sentences** 44

3.4 **Mixed constructions** 44

Exercises 45

4 Subordinate clauses and connectives

4.1 **Adjective clauses** 48
Clauses without relative words 49. *and which* 49.

4.2 **Adverb clauses** 49

4.3 **Noun clauses** 50
As objects 50. As appositives 51. As subjects 51. As complements 51.

4.4 **Subordination for exact statement** 52
Showing the relative importance of ideas 52. Using exact connectives 53.

4.5 **Faulty subordination** 54
Tandem subordination 55. Inverted subordination 55.

Exercises 56

5 Verbals

5.1 **Verbal phrases** 59
Subjects with infinitives 60. Subjects with gerunds 60.

5.2 **Idiomatic use of infinitives and gerunds** 62
the and *of* in gerund phrases 62. *to* with infinitives 63. Split infinitives 63.

5.3 **Misrelated modifiers** 64

5.4 **Dangling modifiers** 65

5.5 **Absolute modifiers** 66

Exercises 66

6 Agreement of subject and verb

6.1 **Verbs with compound subjects** 69
Subjects joined by *and* 69. Subjects joined by *or, nor* 70. Subjects followed by *together with* 71.

6.2 **Verbs with collective nouns as subjects** 71
Nouns referring to the group as a unit 71. Nouns referring to individuals in a group 72. Verbs with measurements and figures 72. Verbs with *data, number, public* 72. Words ending in *-ics* 73.

6.3 Blind agreement 74
Plural nouns between subject and verb 74. *one of those who* 74. *there is, there are* 74. Verb and complement 75. Inverted word order 75. *series, portion, part* 76.

Exercises 76

7 Nouns

7.1 Plurals of nouns 79
Nouns ending in *-y, -o,* or *-f* 79. Words with foreign plurals 81. Group words and compound nouns 82.

7.2 Genitive (possessive) case 83
Uses of the genitive 83. Forms of the genitive 83. *of* phrases and *'s* forms 85.

7.3 Use of *a* and *an* with nouns 85

7.4 Noun modifiers 86

Exercises 86

8 Pronouns

8.1 Reference of pronouns 89
Pronouns referring to a definite antecedent 89. Ambiguous reference 90. Pronouns referring to ideas and statements 92. Use of *who, which, that* 92. Use of *he* or *she* 92.

8.2 Agreement of pronoun and antecedent 94
Personal pronouns 94. Relative pronouns 95. Indefinite pronouns 95.

8.3 Case of pronouns 97
Subject and object pronouns 97. Possessive pronouns 99.

8.4 Reflexive and intensive pronouns 101

8.5 Choice of personal pronoun form 101
I, we 101. *you* 102. *one* 102. Avoiding shifts in pronoun form 103.

Exercises 103

9 Verbs

9.1 Tense 108
Tense forms 108. Sequence of tenses 111. Consistent use of tenses 111.

9.2 Irregular verbs and auxiliaries 112
Irregular verb forms 112. Forms of the verb *be* 114. Choice of *can* or *may* 115. *do, did, done* 115. *get, got, gotten* 116. *lie—lay* 117. *sit—set* 117. *shall—will* 117. *should—would* 118.

9.3 **Active and passive voice** 119
Appropriate passives 119. Inappropriate passives 120.

9.4 **Use of the subjunctive mood** 120
In conditions 120. In *that* clauses 121. Formulas 121.

9.5 **Idioms with verbs** 121

Exercises 123

10 Adjectives and adverbs

10.1 **Position of adjectives** 126

10.2 **Predicate adjectives** 127
good, well 128. *bad, badly* 128.

10.3 **Demonstrative adjectives** 128

10.4 **Forms of adverbs** 129
Long and short forms of adverbs 129. Bobtailed adverbs 130. *most, almost* 130.

10.5 **Position of adverbs** 130
Adverbs modifying a single word 130. Sentence adverbs 131. Misplaced adverbial modifiers 131. Position of *only* and similar adverbs 132.

10.6 **Double negatives** 133
can't hardly, couldn't scarcely 133. *can't help but* 133. *but what* 133. *irregardless* 133.

10.7 **Comparison of adjectives and adverbs** 134
Forms of comparison 134. Use of the comparative form 135. Use of the superlative form 135. Comparison of *unique* and similar words 136.

10.8 **Making comparisons idiomatic** 136
Comparing comparable things 137. Completing comparisons 137. Use of *other* in comparisons 138. Use of *like* or *as* in comparisons 138.

Exercises 139

Punctuation

11 Periods, question marks, and exclamation marks

11.1 **Periods** 142
After statements 142. After indirect questions and courtesy questions 142. After abbreviations 143. With figures 143.

11.2 **Question marks** 143
After direct questions 143. After questions within a sentence 144. To indicate a doubtful statement 144.

11.3 **Exclamation marks** 144

12 Commas

12.1 Between coordinate clauses 146
Short clauses joined by *and, or, nor* 148. Clauses joined by *but, yet* 148. Clauses joined by *for* 148.

12.2 After long introductory elements 148
Adverb clauses 149. Long modifying phrases 149.

12.3 With nonrestrictive modifiers 150
Subordinate clauses and phrases 150. Appositives 152.

12.4 To set off interrupting and parenthetical elements 152
Adverbs that compare or contrast 153. Weak exclamations 154. Names in direct address 154.

12.5 To separate items in a series 154
Words, phrases, or clauses in a series 154. Coordinate adjectives 155.

12.6 To separate for clarity 155

12.7 In conventional places 156
In numbers 157. In dates 157. In addresses 157. With titles and degrees 157. In correspondence 157. With phrases identifying direct quotations 158.

12.8 Misused commas 158
Between main sentence elements 158. Between two words or phrases joined by *and* 159. Between main clauses without a connective 159. With restrictive modifiers 159. After the last item in a series 160.

Exercises 160

13 Semicolons and colons

13.1 Semicolons 164
Between main clauses without an expressed connective 164. Between main clauses linked with a conjunctive adverb 165. With coordinating conjunctions 166. To separate elements containing other marks 166.

13.2 Colons 167
Anticipatory use 167. Between main clauses 168. Before quotations 168. Colons in conventional places 169.

Exercises 169

14 Dashes and parentheses

14.1 Dashes 171
Dashes to mark sharp turns in thought 171. Dashes to enclose parenthetical elements 172. Dashes before summaries or illustrations 172. Specialized uses of the dash 173.

14.2 **Parentheses** 173
Parentheses to enclose incidental remarks 174. Parentheses to enclose details and examples 174. Parentheses around figures 175. Parentheses with other marks 175

Exercise 176

15 Quotation marks, brackets, ellipses, and italics

15.1 **Quotation marks** 177
Quotation marks to enclose direct discourse 178. Quotation marks around quoted material 179. Quotation marks around titles 181. Quotation marks to set off words 181. Quotation marks with other punctuation 182.

15.2 **Brackets** 184

15.3 **Ellipses** 185

15.4 **Italics** 186
Italics for titles 186. Italics for words and phrases used as examples 186. Italics for foreign words 187. Italics for emphasis 187.

Exercises 188

Other conventions of writing

16 Spelling

16.1 **Overcoming spelling problems** 192
Eliminating careless mistakes 193. Using a dictionary 193. Learning to visualize words 193. Keeping a spelling list 195.

16.2 **Common spelling errors** 195
Errors caused by faulty pronunciation 196. Omission of final *-ed* 197. Confusion of words that sound alike 197. Separate words and combined forms 198.

16.3 **Some principles of spelling** 199
Final *-e* 199. *-ie-* and *-ei-* 200. Doubling the final consonant 201. Final *-y* 201. *-cede, -ceed, -sede* 202 *-able, -ible, -ance, -ence* 202.

16.4 **Variant spellings** 202

Exercises 203

17 Capital letters, hyphens, and apostrophes

17.1 **Capital letters** 208
To mark units of expression 208. For proper nouns and their derivatives 210.

17.2 Hyphens 214
In compound words 214. In group modifiers 215. With prefixes 216. Suspension hyphens 217. Unnecessary hyphens 217.

17.3 Apostrophes 218
In contractions 218. With genitive (possessive) case forms 218. For plurals of letters and figures 219. For letters dropped in representing speech 219.

Exercises 219

18 Abbreviations and numbers

18.1 Abbreviations 221
Titles, degrees, and given names 221. Government agencies and other organizations 222. Place names and dates 222. Units of measurement 223. Scientific words, technical terms, trade names 223. Other standard abbreviations 224. The ampersand 224. Capitals with abbreviations 225. Periods with abbreviations 225.

18.2 Numbers 225
Conventional uses of figures 227. Plurals of figures 228. Numbers at the beginning of sentences 228. Arabic and Roman numerals 228. Cardinal and ordinal numbers 228.

Exercises 229

Review exercises on punctuation and mechanics 230

Diction

19 Using a dictionary

19.1 Selecting a dictionary 235
Dictionaries for general use 236. Special dictionaries 237.

19.2 Learning to use your dictionary 238
Spelling and word division 238. Pronunciation 239. Meaning 242. Areas of usage and special labels 243. Synonyms and antonyms 244. Etymology 244.

Exercises 245

20 The meaning of words

20.1 Words in context and situation 249
Denotation: the core of a word's meaning 250. Connotation: the suggestion of words 251.

20.2 Fair words and slanted words 251
Words used fairly for effect 252. Slanted words 252.

20.3 Choosing the right word 254
Distinguishing words of similar spelling 255.
Distinguishing words of similar meaning 255.
Distinguishing words of opposite meaning 257.
Learning new words 257.

20.4 Concrete and abstract words 258
Effective uses of concrete and abstract words 259.
Excessive use of abstract words 261.

Exercises 262

21 The effect of words

21.1 Formal words 267
Appropriate use of Formal words 268. "Big Words"—stilted language 268. Technical words 270.

21.2 Informal words 271
Appropriate use of Informal words 271. Inappropriate use of Informal words 272.

21.3 Fresh words and lifeless words 272
Old-fashioned words 273. Trite expressions 274. Euphemisms 275.

21.4 Figures of speech 276
Types of figurative language 277. Effective figures of speech 278. Consistent figures of speech 280.

Exercises 280

Sentences and paragraphs

22 Sentence length and economy

22.1 Sentence length as a matter of style 286

22.2 Sentence length and meaning 288
Choppy (too short) sentences 288. Stringy sentences 289. Relating ideas clearly 290.

22.3 Avoiding wordiness 291

22.4 Removing deadwood 292

22.5 Avoiding careless repetition 294
Effective repetition 295. Useless repetition 295.

Exercises 298

23 Sentence variety, control, and emphasis

23.1 Sentence variety 302
Varying sentence beginnings 303. Varying S-V-O order 304. Loose and periodic sentences 304. Varying kinds of sentences 305.

23.2 Subordination to control and clarify meaning 306

23.3 Parallelism 308
Elements in series 308. Elements being compared or contrasted 309. Balanced and antithetical sentences 310.

23.4 Sentence emphasis 311
Emphasis by position in the sentence 311. Emphasis by separation 312. Emphasis by repeating key words 313. Emphasis by mechanical devices 314.

Exercises 314

24 Paragraphs

24.1 Paragraph development and length 319
Underdeveloped paragraphs 320. Typical content of paragraphs 321. Topic sentences 324. Appropriate paragraph length 325.

24.2 Patterns of paragraph development 328
Inductive and deductive development 328. Other patterns of development 329. Combining patterns of development 331.

24.3 Paragraph continuity 333
Methods of showing continuity 334. Eliminating irrelevant ideas 335. Continuity in descriptive paragraphs 336. Continuity in narrative paragraphs 337.

Exercises 338

Composition

25 Discovering and organizing material for writing

25.1 Discovering a subject 345
Narrowing the topic 347. Locating a thesis 348.

25.2 Using your resources 349
Private resources 350. Public resources 352. Your thesis and your resources 353.

25.3 Meeting your audience 354
The writer's stance 354. Adjusting to the audience 355. Style and situation 356.

25.4 Organizing your material 360
Scratch outlines 361. Thesis-sentence outlines 361 Topic outlines 363. Sentence outlines 366. Standard outline form 367. The outline in relation to the paper 371.

Exercises 372

26 Writing the first draft

26.1 **Getting started** 377

26.2 **Developing your material** 378
Kinds of development 378. Using sentences to control direction 380. Using paragraphs to control direction 381.

26.3 **Relating paragraphs in sequence** 382
Showing the connection between paragraphs 383. Showing the relation to the topic of the paper 384. Transition paragraphs 385.

26.4 **Opening paragraphs** 385
Effective openings 385. Openings to avoid 387.

26.5 **Closing paragraphs** 388
Effective conclusions 389. Endings to avoid 390.

26.6 **Framing a title** 392

Exercises 392

27 Revising and correcting a paper

27.1 **Revising the first draft** 396
Checking the content 397. Checking the organization 397. Checking the wording 398. Checking for accuracy 398.

27.2 **Manuscript form** 398
Typed papers 399. Handwritten papers 399. Margins and spacing 400. Division of words 400. Form of the title 400. Numbering pages 401. Endorsing the paper 401. Proofreading 402. Making corrections in the final copy 402. Submitting manuscript for publication 403.

27.3 **Revising a corrected paper** 403

Exercise 410

28 Writing in college and out

28.1 **Exposition** 413
Gathering information 414. Relating specialized information to your reader 415. Documenting your information 416.

28.2 **Argumentation** 416
Locating the argument 417. Using resources and evidence 418. Taking the argument to your audience 419. Testing the argument 421.

28.3 **Description** 423
Seeing your subject clearly 423. Selecting and arranging details 424.

28.4 Narration 426
Point of view 427. Use of tenses 428. Pacing a narrative 429. Including adequate details 430.

28.5 Essay examination answers 431
Reading the questions 431. Writing the answers 432. Examples of essay answers 433.

28.6 Reports 437
Class reports 437. Laboratory reports 438. Briefings and critiques 438.

28.7 Writing about literature 439

28.8 Letters 441
Business letters 441. Letters of application 445. Letters requesting recommendations 448. Letters to editors and public figures 448. Personal correspondence 449.

29 The reference paper

29.1 Choosing a topic 452
Choosing a subject area 452. Limiting the topic 453. Final definition of the topic 454.

29.2 Locating appropriate source materials 455
The library card catalog 455. Trade bibliographies 457. Periodical indexes 458. Newspaper index 461. Pamphlet index 461. General encyclopedias 461. Special reference works and encyclopedias 461. Yearbooks and annuals 469. Guides to reference materials 470.

29.3 Preparing the working bibliography 470

29.4 Taking notes 473

29.5 Evaluating your material 476
Facts to consider in evaluating 476. Primary and secondary sources 477.

29.6 Planning the paper 477
Examining and arranging your notes 478. Making a preliminary outline 478.

29.7 Writing and revising the first draft 479
Writing the first draft 479. Revising the first draft 480.

29.8 Documenting the paper 481
Where footnotes are needed 482. Using direct quotations 483. Paraphrasing 484. Plagiarism 485. Numbering and spacing of footnotes 488. Footnote form 488. Alternative forms for footnotes 494.

29.9 Assembling the completed paper 495
The final bibliography 495. Final order of contents 497. Sample reference paper 498.

Exercises 509

General bibliography

The following works give further details on many of the subjects treated in this *Handbook* and provide reliable information on other topics of English grammar, usage, and composition.

Baugh, Albert C. *A History of the English Language.* 2nd ed. New York, 1957. A readable and excellent history, considered a standard reference since its original publication in 1935.

Bryant, Margaret M. *Current American Usage.* New York, 1962. The most reliable recent work covering particular points of American usage; arranged alphabetically.

Corbett, Edward P. J. *Classical Rhetoric for the Modern Student.* New York, 1965. The most thorough modern study of the relevance of rhetoric.

Curme, George O. *Parts of Speech and Accidence.* Boston, 1935. See *Syntax*, below.

———. *Syntax.* Boston, 1931. With *Parts of Speech and Accidence*, above, one of the most complete traditional grammars of modern English, with much historical material.

Dineen, Francis P. *An Introduction to General Linguistics.* New York, 1967. A readable text on various concepts of linguistic form, including much on modern grammars.

Fowler, H. W. *A Dictionary of Modern English Usage.* 2nd ed., rev. by Ernest Gowers. New York, 1965. A standard reference first published in 1926; emphasis on British usage.

Francis, W. Nelson. *The English Language: An Introduction.* New York, 1965. An interesting introduction to the study of language.

Fries, C. C. *American English Grammar.* New York, 1940. A number of points of grammar and usage discussed with special attention to Standard and Nonstandard usage.

Hayakawa, S. I. *Language, Thought, and Action.* 2nd ed. New York, 1964. A widely read study in semantics.

Jespersen, Otto. *Essentials of English Grammar.* New York, 1933. An abridgement of Jespersen's seven-volume *Modern English Grammar on Historical Principles*, a most important description of current English.

Perrin, Porter G. *Writer's Guide and Index to English.* 4th ed., rev. by Karl W. Dykema and Wilma R. Ebbitt. Glenview, Ill., 1965. The first half of the book considers problems of composition; the second half, arranged alphabetically, discusses individual questions of grammar and usage.

Roberts, Paul. *Understanding Grammar.* New York, 1954. A good, brief, systematic English grammar.

Robertson, Stuart. *The Development of Modern English.* 2nd ed., rev. by Frederic G. Cassidy. Englewood Cliffs, N.J., 1954. Gives the background of many points of current usage.

Steinman, Martin, Jr., ed. *New Rhetorics.* New York, 1967. A collection of twelve essays dealing with different aspects of the modern revival of rhetoric.

Summey, George, Jr. *American Punctuation.* New York, 1949. An authoritative treatment of punctuation, with material bearing on sentences and traits of usage.

United States Government Printing Office Style Manual. Washington, D.C., 1959. Excellent selection of usage in the conventions of writing.

Articles and notes on specific matters of language use are frequently found in these journals: *American Speech, College Composition and Communication, College English, The English Journal,* and *Quarterly Journal of Speech.*

1 What is good English?

The language we speak, hear, read, and write is varied, alive, shifting, and often controversial. We know it long before we study it; indeed, it is such an intimate part of our lives that studying it systematically in a class may seem strange and artificial. But precisely because it *is* our voice—the voice we use in managing all our affairs, from the trivial to the noteworthy—we must learn what we can about it and work toward using it wisely and well.

Good English is something more than writing "complete" sentences, using correct verb forms, making verbs agree with their subjects and pronouns with their antecedents. Beyond these fundamentals, Good English is a matter of choosing from the broad range of our language the words and constructions that will best convey our ideas to a particular audience in a particular situation. To make the appropriate choices, we must understand something about English as a language and become sensitive to the various ways it is used in contemporary writing and speech.

1.1 The elements of language

A language consists of a system of sounds, a collection of words, some changes in word forms, and some patterns into which the words fit to convey meaning. It may or may not have a system of writing and printing.

Sounds

English has between forty and fifty sounds (about twenty of them vowel sounds and the rest consonant) and variations in pause, pitch, and stress. Each sound is used with slight modifications in actual speech; for example, some people have a full *r* and others a very slight indication of the sound. The pronunciation of words varies considerably among the different regions in which English is used, so that we can easily identify some people as Englishmen, others as Southerners, others as New Englanders.

Words

Counting everything from slang and local words to rarely used words and limited scientific terms, English has a vocabulary of well over two million words. Many of these are used in several

1.1

different senses—one dictionary gives forty different meanings for the word *check*. An unabridged dictionary has about 500,000 entries; a college dictionary has about 130,000 entries; a college student probably uses or recognizes over 50,000 basic words, not including derivatives made by adding syllables like *-ed* and *-ly*. English forms many new words by adding prefixes (*in-*, *anti-*, *re-*, *super-*) and suffixes (*-er*, *-ish*, *-ship*, *-teria*), and it makes compounds freely by putting two or more words together (*bookcase*, *streamlined*).

Word forms

Compared with highly inflected languages such as Latin or German, English uses very few changes in word forms: only a few endings, like the *-s* or *-es* of nouns (*boys*, *churches*), the *-s*, *-ed*, *-ing* of verbs (*asks*, *asked*, *asking*), *-er* and *-est* for comparing adverbs and adjectives (*hotter*, *hottest; nearer*, *nearest*), and a few internal changes, like the changes in vowels in *man-men*, *sing-sang*. These changes in form are one basis for grouping words into parts of speech.

Constructions

English has two basic ways of combining words into groups: by phrases centered on nouns or their equivalents (*in the morning; crossing the street*) and by clauses centered on verbs (*he runs the forty-yard dash; when she saw the results*). We interpret the meaning of these familiar patterns very largely from the order in which the words stand, an order that we pick up naturally as children and follow almost instinctively. Out of these simple word groups we build sentences of varying length and complexity. The study of the relationships between words and word groups in sentences is *syntax*, the principal division of *grammar*.

Writing practices

English, which like other languages first developed in speech, is represented in writing and printing by the twenty-six letters of the alphabet, a dozen or so punctuation marks, and devices like capitals and italics. The conventions of spelling, punctuation, capitalization, and the like were developed mostly by printers and serve chiefly to represent the spoken language.

These, then, are the materials of the language. This book is about the English language, especially about what is usually called Standard English, the language used by educated men in performing their public and private offices. It describes some of the qualities of English words, language patterns, and conventions, and it discusses the choices open to us as we shape the language to our hopes and needs. This chapter is about the range of possibilities available in the English language and about the process of choosing from among them for best performance.

1.2 Varieties of English usage

Living languages are systems undergoing continual growth and change. Ordinarily the changes are slow and barely noticeable—slightly different pronunciations, new shadings in the meaning of words, and gradual shifts in grammatical constructions—but their cumulative effect can be dramatic. The works of Shakespeare, written four centuries ago, present difficulties to the modern reader: many of the words are unfamiliar and the grammar often seems strange. The writings of Chaucer, who lived a few centuries earlier, are hard to read without a large glossary and a grammar guide. Still earlier works, like *Beowulf*, can be understood only by specialists who have studied Old English much as they would study a foreign language. Yet all these works are written in English and have been admired by many generations of readers.

Obviously our language has passed through many changes in the course of its history, and it will go on changing from generation to generation. Of equal interest to students of English is the fact that, at any point in its history, it also shows many internal variations. The business of everyday life includes all kinds of activities and situations, and language, both spoken and written, must serve them all. There are differences in the words and constructions typically used in different kinds of publications, even within a range no wider than that from newspapers to textbooks, and we use different language in writing or speaking to different people and in writing papers for different purposes. The following series of words, all meaning nearly the same thing, illustrates the range of expressions from which a writer or speaker must choose: *simulated*, *spurious*, *fraudulent*, *counterfeit*, *imitation*, *false*, *sham*, *pseudo*, *phony*. The first three words would most likely be found

1.2 in rather formal writing, the last three in speech or informal writing. *Counterfeit*, *imitation*, and *false* could be used anywhere.

Clearly, thoughtless trust in what we have once learned about language is not enough. Language changes in response to many needs and influences, and to use it effectively we must remain sensitive to what it *is*—be continually attentive to the language we hear in conversation, in public talks, and over radio and television, as well as the language that we read in newspapers, magazines, books, and advertisements.

We must also be sensitive to what language *should be*—our goal is to move toward effective usage, not just common practice. From the wide range of English as it is spoken and written today, we must try to select the words and forms of expression that will best serve and enlighten a particular occasion. This handbook is designed to help students choose wisely and well. It does not take the position, however, that there is always one "right" choice or that the language can be forced into a neat mold.

Until fairly recently, it was common for students of language to assume that "good" English was fixed, that departure from an inflexible set of rules governing its use was automatically "bad" English. This highly *prescriptive* approach to language study reflected the belief that there was some absolute or ideal form of English, orderly and uniform. The student had merely to learn the laws and to apply them, just as he would in studying physics or chemistry. Although the prescriptive approach often produced good results, both practical experience and modern linguistic scholarship—called *descriptive* because it studies and describes the language as it *is*—have shown it to be unsound. Whether people like it or not, our language is changing and varied.

All realistic descriptions of current English speak of different varieties of usage, although they use somewhat different names in describing them. In this book we speak of four main varieties: Formal, General, Informal, and Nonstandard. They are summarized in the table on pages 8-9. The varieties of English are not fixed compartments of the language; one shades off into another, offering the writer a range of possibilities. But in a particular piece of writing, traits of one variety will ordinarily predominate: a passage in General English may use words ordinarily found in Formal English or even an occasional Informal word, but its tone and constructions will clearly identify it as General English.

General English

Of the four main varieties of usage, General English is the hardest to describe because it is the broad range of the language so commonly used that it attracts no attention to itself. In writing, its vocabulary and sentence construction both seem natural, and its movement approaches that of speech. The punctuation in General English today is usually *open*, or relatively light. It uses the marks that are conventionally required and as many more as readers will need for ready understanding, but it generally avoids heavy or unnecessary punctuation that would slow the movement of the writing.

The following passage, from a description of a canoe trip, is in General English. The sentences average about twenty-two words and vary pleasantly from six to fifty-seven. With fifteen verbs and a number of nouns or modifiers made from verbs (*spin-casting*, *calling*, *shielded*), with the familiar pronoun reference and an easy continuity, the passage gives an active and immediately understandable picture.

> Trotlines from shore to shore get you more fish and bigger ones, but they're also more labor. After I'd finished with the line I worked along the beach, spin-casting bootlessly for bass. Four Canada geese came diagonally over the river, low, calling, and in a moment I heard a clamor at the head of the island, shielded from me by the island's duned fringe and by willows. I climbed up through them to look. At least 200 more honkers took off screaming from the sand bar at the upper end of the bare plain. The passenger ran barking after them. Calling him back, I squatted beside a drift pile, and in the rose half-light of dusk watched through the field glass as they came wheeling in again, timid but liking the place as I had liked it, and settled by tens and twenties at the bar and in the shallows above it where the two channels split.—John Graves, *Goodbye to a River*, p. 150

General English is not limited to transmitting matters of general interest; it can also be used effectively to present specialized information:

> Yet if our agriculture-based life depends on the soil, it is equally true that soil depends on life, its very origins and the maintenance of its true nature being intimately related to living plants and animals. For soil is in part a creation of life, born of a marvelous interaction of life and nonlife long eons ago. The parent materials were gathered

1.2 GE

together as volcanoes poured them out in fiery streams, as waters running over the bare rocks of the continents wore away even the hardest granite, and as the chisels of frost and ice split and shattered the rocks. Then living things began to work their creative magic and little by little these inert materials became soil. Lichens, the rocks' first covering, aided the process of disintegration by their acid secretions and made a lodging place for other life. Mosses took hold in the little pockets of simple soil—soil formed by crumbling bits of lichens, by the husks of minute insect life, by the debris of a fauna beginning its emergence from the sea.—Rachel Carson, *Silent Spring*, p. 56

The most common defect in General English is flatness, though this often comes from flat or obvious subject matter as much as from the language. (**See** §25.1, Discovering a subject.) In this passage from a short story the language is a compressed form of what we all might say (except perhaps "the world leaps into proportion"), but it has the quality of feeling that we associate with literature:

> The man who expected to be shot lay with his eyes open, staring at the upper left-hand corner of his cell. He was fairly well over his last beating, and they might come for him any time now. There was a yellow stain in the cell corner near the ceiling; he had liked it at first, then disliked it; now he was coming back to liking it again.
>
> He could see it more clearly with his glasses on, but he only put on his glasses for special occasions now—the first thing in the morning, and when they brought the food in, and for interviews with the General. The lenses of the glasses had been cracked in a beating some months before, and it strained his eyes to wear them too long. Fortunately, in his present life he had very few occasions demanding clear vision. But, nevertheless, the accident to his glasses worried him, as it worries all near-sighted people. You put your glasses on the first thing in the morning and the world leaps into proportion; if it does not do so, something is wrong with the world.—Stephen Vincent Benét, "The Blood of the Martyrs," *Thirteen O'Clock*, p. 23

Most of the English that we hear, read, speak, and write falls within the range of General English, shading off into Formal English on the one hand and Informal on the other. Because of its effectiveness and unlimited usefulness, General English is the variety used by most speakers and writers. A flexible and potentially precise language, it is the principal goal of study and practice in a composition course.

1.2

Formal English

The Formal variety of usage, found chiefly in writing, is principally a development from General English. More edited, more complex than General English, it is more influenced by reading and follows more closely the conventions built up by writers and editors in the past. It usually occurs in discussions of specialized topics and in writing addressed to somewhat limited audiences.

The vocabulary of Formal English includes most of the General words but few if any from Informal English. Necessarily, Formal English uses the specialized vocabulary of the subject matter being discussed; it also may use a good many abstract words. The grammatical constructions tend to be fuller than in General English, and ordinarily the sentences are somewhat longer and more complex. Formal writing tends to follow older practices in punctuation and to use *close* punctuation—more frequent marks than are typical in General English, and heavier ones, such as a semicolon where a comma might serve.

The Formal English used in academic, scientific, technical, and scholarly writing is usually impersonal. Good Formal writing, however, is not stilted or dull. This account of the mapping of Switzerland shows the single-minded attention to the subject, the compact and orderly statement of ideas, and the moderate use of technical terms that characterize good impersonal Formal English:

> The heroic task of making a topographic survey and map of Switzerland fell to the lot of General Guillaume Henri Dufour (1787-1875). Under his personal supervision the work was begun in 1830 and the first sheet was published in 1842. Thirty-four years later the entire survey, on a scale of 1:100,000, was finished and the last of the 25 sheets came from the press. Soon after, the map appeared in atlas form, published at Berne. Far from being a pioneering effort that would require immediate revision, the Dufour atlas proved to be a model of accuracy and artistic delineation, not only for future map makers of Switzerland, but for cartographers at large. The sheets of the atlas were used as a basis for later surveys on different scales, and on the sheets of Switzerland's new survey references were made to the corresponding sections and subsections of the original Dufour map. The art work and conventional signs on the new map were almost identical with those on the Dufour originals. The lettering and bench marks (figures denoting heights), prominent buildings, roads, boundaries and forests were printed in black. Small slopes and passes, ravines and narrow defiles that could not be shown by

1.2

gE

Summary of the principal varieties of English usage

Standard English

Formal English

Limited use. More often written than spoken.

Speaking and writing for somewhat restricted groups in formal situations. (See pp. 7,10.)

Typical uses: Books and articles dealing with special subjects for professional groups and experts • Academic writing: reference works, some textbooks, dissertations, some writing for college courses • Literature of somewhat limited circulation: essays and criticisms, much poetry, some fiction • Some editorials and business writing • Addresses and lectures to special audiences.

General English

Unlimited use. Both spoken and written.

Speaking and writing of educated people in both their private and public affairs. (See pp. 5-6.)

Typical uses: Magazine articles and books on subjects of general interest • Many college papers • Most fiction and other literature for general circulation • News and feature stories, newspaper columns • Most business letters and advertising • Conversation • Talks to general audiences.

Informal English

Limited use. More often spoken than written.

Speaking and writing of educated people in informal situations; includes slang, shoptalk, and some localisms. (See pp. 11-12.)

Typical uses: Casual conversation • Letters between people who know each other well • Diaries and personal writing • Writing close to popular speech, as in fiction and some newspaper columns.

Nonstandard English

Limited use. Chiefly spoken.

Language not much touched by school instruction; often conspicuously local; not appropriate for public affairs or for use by educated people. (See pp. 12-13.)

Typical uses: Conversations of some people at home, with friends, on the job • Representations of this speech in stories, plays, movies, comic strips, on radio and television.

Comments

1. Formal, General, and Informal English together make up Standard English. Similar subdivisions could be made in Nonstandard English.
2. The varieties are to be thought of as shading into each other—not as sharply defined and mutually exclusive. A passage might be regarded as Informal, for instance, if it had several conspicuous traits characteristic of that variety even though the greater part of the passage was in General English.
3. Usage is said to be *divided* when there is a choice between two usages in General English, both of which are in good standing (for example, the spellings *catalog* and *catalogue*, or a comma or no comma before the *and* of the last item in a series).
4. *Slovenly* (impoverished speech, often including obscenity and profanity) may be regarded as the extreme of Nonstandard: *Stilted* (pretentious and unnecessarily heavy speech or writing—"gobbledygook") may be regarded as the extreme of Standard English.
5. The varieties are characterized by some differences in word forms, in pronunciation, in vocabulary, in grammatical constructions, and by the avoidance of certain locutions (as Standard English avoids double negatives). The chief differences, and the easiest to discuss, are in vocabulary.
6. Labeling a usage as belonging to any one of the varieties is meant to indicate that it is characteristically used as the description of that variety suggests, that its connotation comes from this use, and that it is not characteristic of another variety. Such labeling is not intended to prevent a word's use under other conditions but does suggest that it may be conspicuous in another variety and that its connotation should be intended.

1.2

gE

equally spaced contour lines were printed in brown hachures. Black hachures were used to indicate rocky prominences and precipices, the general effect being a pictorial representation by oblique lighting. Horizontal surveys were shown in bronze and water was indicated by shades of blue.—Lloyd A. Brown, *The Story of Maps*, p. 273

A more personal type of Formal English is shown in the following passage. Some of the words and phrases are formal—*inert knowledge*, *radical error*, and *delicate*, *receptive*, *responsive to stimulus*. The constructions are full: note the sentence beginning *Whoever was the originator* and the following sentence, beginning *But whatever its weight of authority*. But some constructions (*I appeal to you, as practical teachers. So far, so good.*) carry an unmistakable personal emphasis and keep us aware that the writer is expressing himself as an individual.

> I appeal to you, as practical teachers. With good discipline, it is always possible to pump into the minds of a class a certain quantity of inert knowledge. You take a text-book and make them learn it. So far, so good. The child then knows how to solve a quadratic equation. But what is the point of teaching a child to solve a quadratic equation? There is a traditional answer to this question. It runs thus: The mind is an instrument, you first sharpen it, and then use it; the acquisition of the power of solving a quadratic equation is part of the process of sharpening the mind. Now there is just enough truth in this answer to have made it live through the ages. But for all its half-truth, it embodies a radical error which bids fair to stifle the genius of the modern world. I do not know who was first responsible for this analogy of the mind to a dead instrument. For aught I know, it may have been one of the seven wise men of Greece, or a committee of the whole lot of them. Whoever was the originator, there can be no doubt of the authority which it has acquired by the continuous approval bestowed upon it by eminent persons. But whatever its weight of authority, whatever the high approval it can quote, I have no hesitation in denouncing it as one of the most fatal, erroneous, and dangerous concepts ever introduced into the theory of education. The mind is never passive; it is a perpetual activity, delicate, receptive, responsive to stimulus. You cannot postpone its life until you have sharpened it. Whatever interest attaches to your subject-matter must be evoked here and now; whatever powers you are strengthening in the pupil, must be exercised here and now; whatever possibilities of mental life your teaching should impart, must be exhibited here and now. That is the golden rule of education, and a

very difficult rule to follow.—Alfred North Whitehead, *The Aims of Education*, pp. 17-18

College textbooks and other course reading are usually written in fairly Formal English. Although some writing is more Formal than it needs to be (one flaw in some technical and scholarly writing is the use of unnecessarily heavy language), intellectual growth demands mastery of Formal English. College students should be able to write rather Formal English in course papers, particularly term papers, dealing with impersonal material. They should be sufficiently familiar with good Formal English to avoid a stilted style in such papers, and they should not write Formally on matters that do not call for a Formal style.

Informal English

If we take General English as the center of Standard usage, Formal and Informal English represent its opposite ends. Typically, Informal English is the everyday language of educated people in their personal affairs, but (tidied up somewhat) it also appears in print, especially in discussions of what people do and in the work of writers who assume some intimacy with their readers.

Informal writing shows various traits of speech: rather short sentences, contractions, words and phrases that are more characteristic of conversation than of writing. The Informal vocabulary includes words like *cop*, *dead pan*, *iffy*, *phony*, *peeve*, *whodunit*. Such words are often called *colloquial* and may be so labeled in dictionaries. This means that they usually occur in speech rather than in writing, or at least that they are not commonly found in Formal writing.

Informal English is likely to make a limited use of *slang* words. These are newly made words (*peacenik*, *teeny-bopper*), or old words in extended meanings (*cool*, *straight*, *trip*, *far out*), or phrases conspicuously overused (*good deal*, *tell it like it was*). While there are almost always more conventional—and usually more precise—ways of saying the same thing, we have a continual flow of usually shortlived words fostered by a desire to be different or by a belief that new contexts require new words. Some slang proves genuinely useful and becomes part of the General vocabulary.

Also found in Informal English is *shoptalk*, words current within

1.2

gE

an occupation or sport, from bulldozing and baseball to medicine and atomic physics, especially words used in conversation (instead of specifically technical or scientific terms), the common names for materials, products, tools, operations. Shoptalk of course varies with the context and taste of its users, from the talk of a garage mechanic to that of an automotive engineer or professor of physics. Although shoptalk most naturally appears in accounts of an occupation, some of its words are used metaphorically in Informal English, like *bug*, *graveyard shift*, *huddle*, *slush fund*, *close-up*, *fade-in*, or *fade-out*.

Informal English is likely to show a good many localisms, words characteristic of a particular region, especially in names for common things (*coal oil* or *kerosene; fried cake*, *cruller*, *fatcake*, or *doughnut; sack*, *poke*, or *bag*), in special names for local occupations (*mule skinner*, *car hop*), or features of the landscape peculiar to a region (*canyon*, *coulee*, *gulley*, *hogback*, *arroyo*, *bayou*). These words often reflect the language of the early settlers, as the Dutch in New York, the Germans in Pennsylvania, and the Spanish in the Southwest. Local words appear freely in the conversation of the people of a region, in newspapers, in fiction, and in descriptions of regional life.

Informal English is of somewhat limited usefulness in writing. It is often necessary in fiction and is sometimes appropriate to vigorous and perhaps breezy discussions of contemporary life and activities, but it is out of place in most writing about serious subjects.

Nonstandard English

As generally used, the term *Standard English* refers to Formal, General, and Informal English and the term *Nonstandard English* to language that is relatively untouched by school instruction or by the traditions of printed English. Nonstandard English is not a falling off from Standard English but a variety or level of the language in its own right. Often its word forms (*ain't*, *you was*, *-s* in all persons of the verb), its vocabulary (especially the blunter words from *snot* up and down), and its constructions (such as the double negative) are actually older than those of Standard English. Nonstandard usage is gradually becoming restricted because of increased schooling and because of the leveling effect of mass communications.

At the college level, Nonstandard usage is seldom a problem, since most college freshmen have already had years of instruction in Standard English. Occasionally Nonstandard expressions may show up in rapid writing, but these as well as other careless mistakes are easily removed in revision.

The objection to Nonstandard English for college writing should be clear. It is not that its grammar is "bad," but that Nonstandard words and constructions are not appropriate to the educated readers for whom you write nor to the subjects you are likely to discuss. Questions of propriety aside, Nonstandard English also is inadequate for dealing with most abstract or complex ideas because its vocabulary is relatively limited. It may be necessary for dialog in fiction, and it can sometimes add a note of realism to character sketches of people who naturally speak it. But its use must be judged by fitness. When an expression in this book is marked Nonstandard, it should not be used in writing except for a very good reason.

1.3 The qualities of good English

An awareness of the varieties of English usage is basic to a realistic understanding of our language. The thing to remember is that Standard English encompasses a *range* of usage and thus offers you many opportunities for choice; it is not a gathering of specific practices that you must rigidly and invariably follow. You should avoid Nonstandard words and expressions and follow the accepted conventions of writing. But within the scope of Standard English you may choose selectively from a wide range of vocabulary, sentence patterns, and grammatical constructions, all equally reputable and, in certain circumstances, all equally "good."

Good English is fundamentally a matter of *appropriateness.* When we make our choices from the range language offers, we must use words in trust and place ourselves in community with others. Because it is the means we have for knowing and participating in the trivial, the practical, and the noble affairs of mankind, language *must not* be simply the plaything of our personal whim. Nor, for obvious reasons, can we use language solely to please others. If we are to use English responsibly and well, we must select language that is appropriate to us as speaker or writer, appropriate to our audience, and appropriate to the particular situation in which we find ourselves.

Appropriateness to purpose and situation

In conversation we automatically adjust our language as well as our topics to the situation. Similarly, writing, whether it is assigned or voluntary, takes on a tone. The tone of the language depends chiefly on the variety of usage.

Good judgment in choosing the variety of English appropriate to a particular occasion is one sign of a practiced writer. Slang may fit in a letter or in a popular newspaper column; it is ordinarily out of place in discussing a serious subject. Talks to most audiences are in General English, as is most fiction. Writing by and for people in the professions (teachers, doctors, lawyers, scientific and scholarly workers) is likely to be Formal.

The standards of written usage in a composition course are essentially the same standards that would be expected in similar published material. This means that papers about personal experiences, college activities, and so on would normally be in General English and that papers about ideas and perhaps most of the papers required in other college courses would be somewhat more Formal, or in what might be regarded as the General-to-Formal range, depicted thus:

Standard English

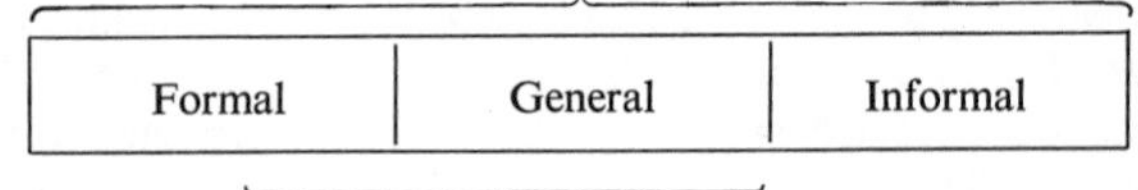

Range of college English

This expectation for college writing is *not* the result of an arbitrary decision that a given variety of language is nicer, or more correct, or more polite than others. The General-to-Formal range, because of the breadth of its vocabulary and because of its greater possibilities in sentence structure, ordinarily affords the user greater precision and more control.

If a student pays attention to purpose and situation, he should be able to treat most subjects in the language they deserve. Inexperienced writers frequently use language that is too heavy to be appropriate to them or to their subjects. For example, a student who wanted to say that he had rebelled against his parents despite having come from a happy home wrote:

> Although my domestic environment was permissive and munificent and my sibling relationships were good, I found it necessary to express my generation's mores in reaction to paternal supervision.

The student may seriously have believed that this kind of writing was better than a simple statement. He would almost certainly object to being told that his sentence was bad English, worse perhaps than if it contained some Nonstandard expressions. But Nonstandard English can be quite easily corrected, whereas inflated and pompous language must be completely rewritten to be effective. The artificial "formality" of such language is not found in good Formal writing, and it should be avoided in student papers.

Once a writer finds the tone that is right for his situation, he should stay with it unless there is some special reason for changing. Although the lines between the varieties of usage cannot be drawn precisely, conspicuous shifts from one to another should ordinarily be avoided, as in the second of these two sentences:

> In the distant pines the rising wind whined as it played among the needles. And when the storm broke, the rain came down in buckets.

Superficial consistency is not so important as fundamental appropriateness, but ordinarily one variety of English should be used throughout a piece of writing.

Reading the work of practiced writers is one good way to increase your sensitivity to language and its various uses. Before attempting to write for an unfamiliar situation, read and study some good examples of writing done for a similar purpose. Don't try to write an article for a magazine that you have never read, and don't try to write a technical report or reference paper without ever having seen one. Try to learn what is typically done and follow the accepted practices unless you have a good reason for some other usage.

Appropriateness to listener or reader

If you are trying to reach a particular type of reader, you will adjust your subject matter and your manner of expression more or less to his expectations. To communicate fully, you have to be

1.3 more than merely understandable; you have to meet your reader largely on his own ground. You do this automatically in letters, writing in somewhat different ways to different people. Trying to write without knowing who will read the words is difficult and discouraging. In writing a college paper, try to direct it to some particular audience such as the class of which you are a member. This will help you select material that will appeal to a considerable part of the group, and it will help you judge what words and what kinds of sentences are appropriate. (**See** §25.3, Meeting your audience.)

Considering the listener or reader leads to language that is clear, correct, and interesting.

Clarity. Since your aim in writing is to communicate, use clear and exact words that your readers will understand. If the subject requires terms that may be unfamiliar, try to make them clear by the way you use them or add a tactful explanation. In a few instances you may have to provide a formal definition. Clarity also calls for sentences that are not too long and that have a natural, direct movement—though you must remember the demands of your subject and situation, as well. Experienced readers can grasp more elaborate sentences than those who read little or read hurriedly. But anyone will be pleased with direct, straightforward sentences.

Careful attention to punctuation is also necessary if you are to make your statements clear to your readers. The various marks—commas, semicolons, and periods—indicate the groups of words that are to be understood as units and often show the relationship between these units. Omissions or misused marks may force a reader to go over a passage two or three times to get its intended meaning; superfluous marks may keep him from grouping words that belong together or may slow the speed of reading to the point of exasperation.

Correctness. Part of a writer's concern for his readers is meeting their expectation in language. This means following the accepted conventions of Standard English and avoiding careless and elementary errors. In language as in other matters, people tend to judge us initially by superficial traits. Elementary errors indicate that the writer just isn't bothering, that he isn't doing as well as he easily could and should. When you finish writing a paper, take time to check it carefully for errors in spelling, punctuation, and other matters of usage.

Interest. There is already enough unavoidable dullness in the world. Any reader will appreciate some liveliness in what he reads, in the writer's expression as well as his choice of material. Too many students seem to feel that serious writing requires a flat and lifeless sort of language. In striving for liveliness, you needn't try for novelty or use words that are out of the ordinary; draw on the vocabulary you might use in an intelligent, reasonably animated conversation. Avoid dragging and monotonous sentences; vary their length and pattern so that they suggest an active, alert mind. Attract your reader's interest by making reference, when appropriate, to things people have said and done, and use details to demonstrate your ideas.

One warning is needed: In gearing your writing to your reader's background and expectations, don't underestimate his intelligence, compromising yourself and insulting him. Visualize him at his best and write for him as he is then.

Appropriateness to speaker or writer

As writer, you dominate the writer-reader relationship; your judgment and sense of fitness finally controls the language you use. Whatever your purpose in writing, express your ideas in language that seems natural for you—but make sure that it also does justice to what you are trying to say. If the language you choose as being uniquely right for you is not also right for your audience and your purpose, it will fail to communicate your material. The most fitting language for you as a writer is that which gives you and your ideas fullest expression.

An important first step toward improving your language habits is studying the virtues and shortcomings of your own speech and writing. Does your language on the whole tend to be Formal or General or Informal? Are you sure of the mechanics of writing—spelling, punctuation, sentence structure? When you write a paper for a college course, do you choose the best part of your natural language or do you assume an entirely different sort of English?

In your first papers in a composition course you should write as naturally as you can, so that both you and your instructor can

1.3 analyze the present state of your language and decide together on the direction your growth should take. It is not necessary for all students in a class to write in the same way, or to write as the instructor or some particular professional writer would.

Much of the better English that we find in print is the English the writer would use in talking to his friends, tightened up some and freed of the irregularities that usually creep into speech; it is usually well within the range of the General language. In discussing "The New Way of Writing," Mr. Bonamy Dobrée, an English critic, says: "One would like to think that all of us will come to the stage of refusing to write what we would not, indeed could not, say, though that, of course, is not to limit our writing to what we actually do say."

If you approach good English with this attitude, you should have confidence in writing. Good English is not primarily a matter of rules, but of judgment. You are not struggling under a series of *don'ts* but trying to discover among the wide resources of modern English the language that best suits your purpose, your audience, and yourself.

Your motives for studying and using good English are multiple. An immediate and practical motive is to deal decently with your reader and to communicate what you have to say. A personal motive is to use and improve your present language skill. Pressures exerted by teachers or critics may have some brief effect, but in the long run you set your own standard, and in a composition course you must begin to take the responsibility for the language you use. This means commitment to an honest and precise use of the language, based on knowledge of its varieties and wide range of resources; on awareness of its possibilities stimulated by experimentation, observation, and imitation; and on discrimination in your choices.

Exercises

1. *Identifying varieties of usage.* Read the following passages and then comment on them in terms of the varieties of usage discussed in the preceding sections: Formal, General, Informal, Nonstandard. (More than one term will often be needed for a passage.) Pick out the particular words and constructions that lead you to label a passage as you do. Which expressions would you not be likely to use in your own writing?

1) The Church started its historical pilgrimage within the political framework of the Roman Empire. That multi-national and multi-religious realm embraced most of the ancient centres of Mediterranean civilization and at first offered to the Christian community a unique opportunity to unite in its fold the diverse races conquered by the Romans. A wide knowledge of the Greek tongue and the political stability of the Empire made communication easy among the early Christians, and up to the middle of the fifth century the Church was a genuinely international body in the life of such dissimilar people as the Greeks, Romans, Syrians, Egyptians, Armenians, Georgians, North Africans and the inhabitants of Spain, Gaul and Britain. They all recognized their unity and yet enjoyed considerable freedom in the management of their local affairs.—Nicolas Zernov, *Orthodox Encounter*, p. 18

2) A poet must have talent. No, this is not a joke—or rather, it is half a joke, like saying that one would like to be rich—but nevertheless it is true that most poets are a little short of talent. Don't ask me how the poet gets it. I am only making up a story. Ask God such questions. Talent is the one thing that cannot be bought, borrowed, or stolen. Many pretend to have it, but no one is deceived for long, least of all the man who is pretending. Give him a check and his face gets longer; give him a prize and he bursts into tears. For he knows that it is all a joke; inside himself he is standing without pants, naked, and the children are pointing.—Louis Simpson, "On Being a Poet in America," *The Noble Savage #5*, October 1962, p. 24

3) Ten decades have rolled around, and we meet in the first years of another century to celebrate, for the first time in the history of American colleges, the graduation of him whom most we delight to honor at Dartmouth, whose "great stone face" is carved as that of the chief orator of the new world on the walls of the academic theatre of our oldest university; and whose name was but lately selected as entitled to rank with those of Washington and Lincoln at the very top of the roll of fame of the nation, as preserved in the stately hall of learning between the Hudson and the sea.—C. F. Richardson, *Mr. Webster's College Life*, p. 22

4) In a Chicago laboratory a radiochemist stood before an oscilloscope connected to a Geiger counter. Across the oscilloscope screen, very much like the screen in a small television set, jumped a never-ending ribbon of green zigzags. The zigzags were made by the impulses coming from disintegrating atoms of radioactive carbon within the counter. The carbon had been extracted from a piece of wood, but the wood was

by no means ordinary. In fact, it was a piece of very old wood, part of a spruce tree that grew in a Wisconsin forest so long ago that when the tree was alive the Ice Age still had northern United States in its chill grip. So long ago that mastodons and mammoths still inhabited the country in force. Indeed, it is quite possible that a mastodon, crashing through the spruce forest in the chill glacial air, brushed against this very tree.—Richard Foster Flint, "Pin-pointing the Past with the Cosmic Clock," *Natural History Magazine*, May 1951, p. 200

5) At the levee which was held that night on the hillside with big bonfires, Dravot gives out that him and me were Gods and sons of Alexander, and Past Grand Masters in the Craft, and was come to make Kafiristan a country where every man should eat in peace and drink in quiet, and specially obey us. Then the Chiefs come round to shake hands, and they was so hairy and white and fair it was just shaking hands with old friends. We gave them names according as they was like men we had known in India—Billy Fish, Holly Wilworth, Pikky Kergan that was Bazaar-master when I was at Mhow, and so on and so on.—Rudyard Kipling, "The Man Who Would Be King," *Under the Deodars*, p. 210

6) A curious example of what is happening is Society, in the sense of High Society, in New York City today. Only it isn't called High Society or even Café Society anymore. Nobody seems to know quite what to call it, but the term that is catching on is Pop Society. This is because socialites in New York today seem to have no natural, aristocratic styles of their own—they are taking all their styles from "pop" groups, which stands for popular, or "vulgar" or "bohemian" groups. They dance the Jerk, the Monkey, the Shake, they listen to rock music, the women wear teen-age and even "sub-teen" styles, such as stretch pants and decal eyes, they draw their taste in art, such as "underground" movies and "pop" painting, from various bohos and camp culturati, mainly. New York's "Girl of the Year"—Baby Jane Holzer—is the most incredible socialite in history. Here in this one girl is a living embodiment of almost pure "pop" sensation, a kind of corn-haired essence of the new styles of life.—Tom Wolfe, *The Kandy-Kolored Tangerine-Flake Streamline Baby*, pp. xiv-xv

7) Some of the evil of my tale may have been inherent in our circumstances. For years we lived anyhow with one another in the naked desert, under the indifferent heaven. By day the hot sun fermented us; and we were dizzied by the beating wind. At night we were stained by dew, and shamed into pettiness by the innumerable silences of stars. We were a self-centred army without parade or gesture, devoted to freedom, the second of man's creeds, a purpose so ravenous that it devoured all our

strength, a hope so transcendent that our earlier ambitions faded in its glare.—T. E. Lawrence, *Seven Pillars of Wisdom*, p. 28

8) So it's a very important matter what college a young person attends —and not merely in terms of the cash value of a particular degree, or the equally vulgar matter of the "contacts" one can make. At stake are all the subtle dimensions that constitute a human being. How a mature man or woman will respond to a painting, or a piece of music, or another human being, what books he reads—or more to the point, *whether* he reads—all of these are molded by those four fleeting years. Even his capacity for independent thinking is created, or at least the foundation is laid, during that period. Critical thinking cannot really be taught; there is no formula for it. But the habit is something a student absorbs in an intellectual atmosphere at once bold and supportive.— David Boroff, *Campus U.S.A.*, p. x

2. *Good Formal or General usage.* Copy from a book or magazine, giving full reference to its source, a good paragraph showing either Formal or General usage. Underline the distinctive words or constructions.

3. *Appropriate usage.* Discuss the following sentences in terms of the varieties of usage and suggest how they can be improved. Translate each into General English.

1) When Ma has the miseries, it's better to lay low and let things be.

2) Fig-Mint, the Colton Stables' classiest colt, blew a ¾ workout at 1:12 yesterday.

3) The psychoanalyst who diagnosed the patient's disturbance said he was about to flip.

4) Dean Stewart has posted the lugubrious results of the examination which the prospective graduates toiled to complete yesterday.

5) After the massive encounter the annihilated were strewn like leaves upon the valley.

6) On account of him getting there that late we cancelled the appointment.

7) To be elected class president and copping the scholarship trophy in the same year was quite a feat.

8) Wayne couldn't catch the runaway dog as it ran with great celerity.

9) This slapdash paper is the work of a slothful and lazy student.

10) So perilous was the descent, so diminished the spirits of the travelers that an accident was inevitable.

4. *Analysis of current written usage.* Analyze the writing of a newspaper or magazine columnist: Eric Sevareid, Walter Lippmann, Joseph Alsop, James Reston, William Buckley, Inez Robb, Hal Boyle, or any other your instructor may suggest. Characterize the variety of usage, the columnist's attitude toward his readers, and the appropriateness of the language to the subjects discussed.

5. *Individual language background.* Keep a notebook in which you write down typical expressions, slang phrases, unusual pronunciations that you hear at home, at school, at work, or during social activities. When you have sufficient material, write a paper describing the characteristics of the different types of speech you are normally exposed to. Comment on the adaptations you need to make in moving from one situation to another.

6. *Becoming familiar with this handbook.* To help familiarize yourself with the plan of this book, use the index to look up the following debatable or divided usages and summarize what is said about each of them.

1) commas with introductory adverb clauses
2) *due to*
3) capitalizing words like *mother*, *father*, *sister*
4) hyphening compound words
5) *like—as*
6) subjects of gerund phrases
7) shorter spelling forms (*tho*, *thru*, *catalog*)
8) verbless sentences

2 Grammar of sentences

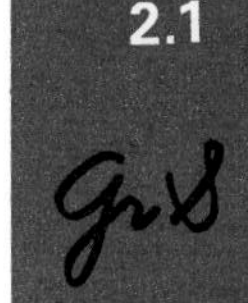

Words are symbols of ideas, but they do not begin to "say" something until we put them together. Sentences, which are syntactical units composed of words, "say" something, partly because of the lexical content *(the meaning) of the words and partly because of the* grammatical forms *that govern words put together in patterns.—Edward P. J. Corbett*

A written sentence is one or more words, punctuated as an independent unit, that *say* something. A sentence is made complete by its grammatical form and meaning or occasionally, in special circumstances, by context alone.

It looks like rain tomorrow.
Why weren't you there?
Please try to be on time.
Why not?
Good!

If a writer is to control the shape and meaning of his sentences, he must understand the importance of such matters as subject-verb agreement, coordination and subordination, the case of pronouns, and the placement of modifiers. This section reviews the basic grammatical terms he may need in analyzing and describing sentences and in discussing the relations between the words of which they are composed.

2.1 Main sentence elements

Most English sentences are made with a subject and a verb, a pattern known as the "major" or "favorite" sentence type.

The subject

The subject (s) of a sentence is a noun or noun equivalent (pronoun, noun clause, gerund, infinitive) that is the starting point of the sentence. The *simple subject* is a single word, like *women* in the first sentence below. The *complete subject* consists of the simple subject plus any words that modify it: *Talkative women.*

s
Talkative *women* often marry quiet men. [noun]

s
She talks as much as her mother does. [pronoun]

2.1

s
What she doesn't know is that no one listens. [noun clause]

s
Talking is her only exercise. [gerund]

s
To listen is to suffer. [infinitive]

The verb

A verb (v) is a word that has forms like *ask, asks, asked, asking* or *sing, sang, sung, singing* and in a sentence agrees with the subject. In the typical sentence the verb follows the subject and, like the subject, is often a nucleus for modifying words. The verb may consist of one or more words:

s v
Talkative women often *marry* quiet men.

v s v
Does he *listen* to what she says?

s v
Mrs. Jones *has driven* for twenty years without getting a ticket.

s v
Perhaps the defendent *should be given* the benefit of the doubt.

Participles, gerunds, and infinitives (*taken, taking, to take*) cannot function as full verbs in making sentences. **See** §5, Verbals, and §9, Verbs.

The *predicate* is the verb and whatever words are related to it, such as objects, complements, and modifiers. In the following sentences the complete predicate is italicized:

s v
Talkative women *often marry quiet men.*

s v
The doorbell *rang.* [The verb is the complete predicate.]

s v
After graduating from Princeton, George *spent two years serving with the Peace Corps in Latin America.*

The object

The *direct object* (o) of a verb is a noun or noun equivalent that completes the statement. It answers the question asked by adding "what" or "whom" after the verb. (Talkative women marry whom? Quiet men.)

S V O
Talkative women often marry quiet *men.* [noun]

S V O
The Sherwoods have decided *to buy a home.* [infinitive phrase]

S V O
He wondered *what he should do.* [noun clause]

The *indirect object* (IO) is used with verbs of telling, asking, giving, receiving, and so on. It names the receiver of the message, gift, or whatever, and it comes *before* the direct object:

S V IO O
He gave the *church* a memorial window.

The same meaning can usually be expressed in a prepositional phrase placed *after* the direct object:

S V O
He gave a memorial window *to the church.*

The complement

A complement (C) is a noun or an adjective in the predicate which follows a linking verb (LV). In contrast to an object, a complement is related to the subject rather than to the verb, because a linking verb (sometimes called a *copula*) expresses condition rather than direct action. A noun used as a complement is called a *predicate noun;* an adjective used as a complement is called a *predicate adjective:*

S LV C
John is a clever *designer.* [predicate noun]

S LV C
The tenor sounded a little *flat.* [predicate adjective]

The most common linking verb is *be* in its various forms: *is, are, was, were, has been, might be.* Other linking verbs include *seem* and *appear* and, in some contexts, *feel, grow, act, look, smell, taste,* and *sound.*
See also §10.2, Predicate adjectives.

Word order

In English we identify the main sentence elements chiefly by their position in the sentence—by their word order. Although the form of the words is the same, it makes a great deal of difference whether you say "the ball hit the boy" or "the boy hit the ball."

2.1 **Typical word order.** The typical order of the main elements is subject-verb-object (or subject-linking verb-complement). This is the order in which we make most statements and the means by which we understand them.

In "The class congratulated Rachel" we know through experience that *class* is the subject of *congratulated* because it precedes the verb, and that *Rachel* is the object because it follows the verb. When the verb is in the *passive voice* (a past participle preceded by some form of the verb *be*), the order of sentence elements remains subject-verb: Rachel was congratulated by the class.

So familiar is this order that we recognize it even though the statement itself may be gibberish, or "jabberwocky," as in these lines by Lewis Carroll:

> . . . the slithy toves
> Did gyre and gimble in the wabe. . . .

Whatever the meaning, most people would agree that because of the order of the words, the subject is *toves* and the verbs are *did gyre* and *gimble*.

Inverted order. The typical order of sentence elements is reversed in questions, exclamations, and emphatic statements:

V S O
Question: Have you a minute to spare?

C S LV
Exclamation: How sour these grapes taste!

O S V
Emphatic object: A better job I never had.

In sentences with *there* or *it* as an *anticipating subject* (AS), the real subject comes after the verb:

AS LV C S
It is a difficult choice.

AS LV C S
There are several reasons for the difficulty.

When the usual order of elements is reversed, you can find the subject of the sentence by locating the verb and then seeing what word answers the question formed by putting "who" or "what" before it. Thus in the expression "A lot he knows about it," *knows* is the verb, and since the answer to "*Who* knows?" is obviously *he*, *he* (rather than *lot*) is the subject.

2.2 Secondary sentence elements

In addition to the main sentence elements (subject-verb-object or subject-linking verb-complement), most sentences also contain secondary elements. Secondary elements are typically used as modifiers (M)—they describe, limit, or make more exact the meaning of main elements. The table on page 28 shows the various ways in which modifiers—single words, phrases, and clauses—might be used to qualify or expand a simple statement.

Adjectives and adverbs as modifiers

Single words used as modifiers are ordinarily related to the element they modify by means of word order. *Adjectives* relate to nouns and typically stand before the words they modify, but occasionally they come immediately after:

M M
It was a *slow*, *dangerous* climb.

M M
The steepness of the slope made the climb *slow* and *dangerous*.

Adverbs are more varied in position because often they relate to the sentence as a whole. However, when they modify a particular word (verb, adjective, or adverb) they usually stand close to it:

M
They *particularly* wanted to go.

M
He came home from the movies *quite* late.

See §10, Adjective and adverbs.

Other words and word groups as modifiers

In English a noun often modifies another noun: *glass* jar, *ski* pants, *dance* hall. These words should be called *modifiers* (not adjectives) or, more exactly, *nouns used attributively*. (**See** §7.4, Noun modifiers.)

Prepositional phrases function as modifiers in the majority of English sentences:

M M
An apartment-dweller *in a large city* can live *in the same place*
M M
for a year and never speak *to his next-door neighbor.*

2.2 Modifiers

Modifiers of the subject

M S

A word: The *local* orchestra played a selection.

S M

A phrase: The orchestra, *consisting largely of amateurs*, played a selection.

S M

A clause: The orchestra, *which had practiced hard for several weeks*, played a selection.

Modifiers of the verb

V M

A word: The orchestra played the selection *badly*.

V M

A phrase: The orchestra played the selection *with more enthusiasm than technique.*

V M

A clause: The orchestra played the selection *as if they had never rehearsed together before.*

Modifiers of the object

M O

A word: The orchestra played a *difficult* selection.

O M

A phrase: The orchestra played a selection *of old folk tunes.*

O M

A clause: The orchestra played a selection *which no one in the audience had ever heard before.*

Modifiers of the main clause

M

A word: *Nevertheless*, the orchestra played the selection.

M

A phrase: *Considering their lack of experience*, the orchestra played the selection fairly well.

M

A clause: *Since there were no other requests*, the orchestra played the selection.

Verbal phrases and subordinate clauses also can function as modifiers:

M
Finding no one at home, he scribbled a note and left it under the front door. [participle phrase modifying *he*]

M
He needed a way *to make money*. [infinitive phrase modifying *way*]

M
People *who live in glass houses* shouldn't throw stones. [subordinate clause modifying *People*]

Appositives
An appositive (A) is a noun or noun equivalent placed beside another noun to supplement or complement its meaning. It has the same grammatical function as the noun to which it relates. In speech, it is marked by a pause and a change in pitch:

A
Your lawyer, *Mr. Jenkins*, is on the telephone.

A
The story takes place in Thebes, *a city in ancient Greece.*

See §12.3, page 152, Appositives.

Modifiers of modifiers
Words, phrases, and clauses that modify the main sentence elements may themselves be modified. These expressions are called modifiers of modifiers:

MM M S V M M O
The *local* high-school orchestra played several difficult selections
MM M
very well.

2.3 Phrases and clauses

English sentences are constructed of single words, phrases, and clauses. Main (or independent) clauses form the principal grammatical units of sentences; they express completed statements and can stand alone. Phrases and subordinate clauses, on the other hand, are dependent on other sentence elements and function very much like single words.

2.3

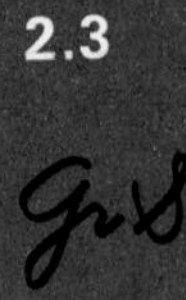

Phrases

Phrases are groups of related words connected to a sentence or to one of the elements in it by means of a preposition or a verbal. A phrase has no subject or predicate and cannot stand alone.

Prepositional phrases. A prepositional phrase consists of a preposition (*at*, *from*, *by*, *in*, *of*, *under*, etc.) followed by a noun or noun equivalent, plus whatever modifiers it may have. It functions like an adjective or adverb, depending on what element it modifies:

> He came *from a small town* [modifies the verb *came*] *in northeastern Minnesota* [modifies the noun *town*].

Verbal phrases. A verbal phrase consists of a participle, gerund, or infinitive (none of which has full verb function) plus its object or complement and modifiers. A participle phrase functions as an adjective; a gerund phrase as a noun; and an infinitive phrase as either a noun, an adjective, or an adverb. (See §5, Verbals.)

> Sentences *containing several unrelated ideas* [participle phrase modifying *Sentences*] are seldom effective.
>
> *Containing the enemy* [gerund phrase used as subject] was their first objective.
>
> The most profitable way *to understand grammatical construction* [infinitive phrase modifying *way*] is *to analyze your own sentences* [infinitive phrase used as complement].

Clauses

A *main* (or independent) clause contains a subject and predicate and is the grammatical core of a sentence. In the three sentences below, the main clauses are italicized. Each is a complete expression and could stand alone as a sentence:

> s v
> *I laughed* because I couldn't help myself.
>
> s v o s v o
> *She hated English*, but *she needed one more course to graduate.*
>
> s v o
> If I were you, *I would find a new job.*

A *subordinate* (or dependent) clause also has a subject and a predicate, but it functions as *part* of a sentence. It is related to the main clause by a connecting word that shows its subordinate relationship, either a relative pronoun (*who*, *which*, *that*) or a subordinating conjunction (*because*, *although*, *since*, *after*, *if*, *when*, etc.).

I laughed *because I couldn't help myself.*

Subordinate clauses are used like nouns (as subjects, objects, or complements), like adjectives (modifying nouns or pronouns), or like adverbs (expressing relationships of time, cause, result, degree, contrast, and so forth). The subordinate clauses are italicized in the following examples:

Noun clause (object of *confessed*): He confessed *that he loved me.*

Adjective clause (modifying *criminals*): Many of the criminals *whose cases crowded the docket each year* were third- or fourth-time offenders.

Adverb clause (of time): *When the ship approached the pier*, the band began to play.

Adverb clause (of cause): They were late *because they were held up in traffic.*

See §4, Subordinate clauses and connectives.

2.4 Sentences classified by clause structure

Sentences may be classified according to the kind and number of clauses they contain as *simple*, *compound*, *complex*, or *compound-complex.*

Simple sentences

A simple sentence contains one independent clause and no subordinate (dependent) clauses:

The man went across the street.

Although simple sentences contain only one clause, they need not be limited to a small, "simple" idea. They may contain any number of modifiers, and either the subject or the predicate (or both) may be compound:

During the long procession of later years I have lived in London for several periods, visited it countless times, and seen it in a good many different moods and stances—during the bleak agony of unemployment in the 'thirties, the prewar interval of national dilemma and

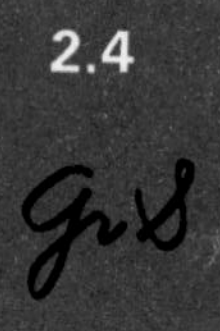

hesitation, the heroic war years themselves, and alternating times of depression and exaltation ever since.—John Gunther, "Inside London," *Harper's Magazine*, July 1967, p. 48

The finding of a kind of wonder or awe in the majesty and apparently infinite complexity of the universe has led some of the greatest scientists—among them Boyle, Hooke, Newton, and Trembley—to ascribe the value of science to its giving us an insight into the mind of God.—John R. Baker, *Science and the Planned State*, p. 33

Colleges and universities do not exist to impose duties but to reveal choices.—Archibald MacLeish, "Why Do We Teach Poetry," *The Atlantic Monthly*, March 1956, p. 51

Compound sentences

Compound sentences contain two or more main clauses and no subordinate clauses:

> The grandparents are, of course, a comic stereotype [first main clause], but the image of them "breezing on their trust funds through the world" epitomizes the character of the world of industrial capitalism, a world of wealth, power, privilege, and a breezy acceptance of privilege [second main clause].—William J. Martz, *The Achievement of Robert Lowell*, p. 7

Each clause in a compound sentence is independent and is *coordinate* (of equal rank) with the other clauses. The clauses may be joined (or separated) in one of three ways:

With coordinating conjunctions. Independent clauses are most frequently linked by the coordinating conjunctions *and*, *but*, *or*, *nor*, *for*, *yet* or the correlatives *either . . . or*, *neither . . . nor*, *both . . . and*, *not only . . . but* (*also*):

> It rained all morning, *but* it cleared up for the picnic.
> *Either* you play to win *or* you don't play at all.

Without connectives. Independent clauses not joined by coordinating conjunctions are conventionally separated by semicolons:

> They are generous-minded; they hate shams and enjoy being indignant about them; they are valuable social reformers; they have no notion of confining books to a library shelf.—E. M. Forster, *Aspects of the Novel*, p. 33

With conjunctive adverbs. The clauses in a compound sentence are sometimes linked by a conjunctive adverb such as *accordingly*, *also, consequently, however, nevertheless, therefore, then.* However, the connective function of these adverbs is weak, and a semicolon must be used before them:

> The urban renewal program has many outspoken opponents; *nevertheless,* some land has already been cleared.

See §13.1, Semicolons.

Complex sentences

A complex sentence consists of one main clause and one or more subordinate clauses:

> As far as I could determine [subordinate clause], Paris hadn't changed at all [main clause] since I last visited it ten years before [second subordinate clause].

Nearly half the sentences in current writing are complex. Complex sentences offer more variety than simple sentences, and they are generally more exact than compound sentences, because the subordinating conjunctions express more precise relationships than the coordinating conjunctions do.

Compound-complex sentences

A compound-complex sentence contains two or more main clauses and one or more subordinate clauses:

> When two men fight a duel [first subordinate clause], the matter is trivial [first main clause], but when 200 million people fight 200 million people [second subordinate clause], the matter is serious [second main clause].—Bertrand Russell, *The Impact of Science on Society,* p. 38

2.5 Sentences classified by purpose

Sentences are conventionally classified by meaning or purpose as follows:

Statements (often called *declarative sentences*):

> Jim laughed.
> Most of the sentences we speak and write are declarative.

Questions:

> At what temperature does water boil?
> Why do you ask?

2.5

Gr S

Commands (including requests and instructions):

> Write soon.
> When the liquid boils, remove it from the heat.

Exclamations (feelings, facts, or opinions expressed in an emphatic way):

> How lucky you are!
> He should be thrown out!

2.6 Minor sentence types

While the great majority of written sentences contain both subjects and verbs, some do not. In speech, we may express ourselves by a single word ("Yes." "Oh?"), a phrase ("In a minute."), or a clause ("If you say so."). Similarly, we occasionally find single words, phrases, and subordinate clauses as sentences in published material:

> And so on to Bangkok. Spit and hiss of water, the gramaphone quiet. The lights out along the deck, nobody about.—Graham Greene, *The Shipwrecked*, p. 17

We do not have to supply any "missing" words to get the author's meaning (such as "And so *the ship sailed* on to Bangkok."). Such statements are meaningful and complete as they stand. But they are minor types, exceptions to the typical English sentence with subject and predicate. When they appear in print, they are used deliberately and for a special purpose (for dialog, for emphasis, or to avoid colorless or repetitious verbs). In college writing, there is seldom occasion or reason to use such sentences. (See §3.1, Fragmentary sentences.)

Subjectless sentences

Commands and requests generally do not have subjects:

> Don't let me hear you say that again.
> Please try.

The subject is sometimes omitted in Informal writing (but never in serious writing) when it is easily carried over from the preceding sentence by the context:

> They took no interest in civilized ways. Hadn't heard of them, probably.—Clarence Day, *Life with Father*, p. 30

Verbless sentences

Several types of sentences without a main verb are used in all levels of speaking and writing. The verbs are not left out; they are not thought, spoken, or written. The statements are complete and independent without them.

Exclamations. *Ouch!*, *Oh!*, and similar words make complete exclamations, as do such phrases as *What luck!* and *How terrible!*

Answers to questions. Short answers without a main verb (*Yes. No. Not if I can help it.*) are considered complete sentences. Occasionally a writer may use a verbless construction to answer a question he has raised himself:

> What is a hero? *The exceptional individual.* How is he recognized, whether in life or in books? *By the degree of interest he arouses in the spectator or the reader.*—W. H. Auden, *The Enchafèd Flood*, p. 93

Descriptive details. In fiction especially, descriptive details are sometimes set off for emphasis or to avoid colorless verbs like *is, are, has:*

> There was one in particular of Mother looking very roguish and chic in her voluminous dress, sitting way up on top of a tall and insolent camel, with two big black men in white turbans standing off at one side. *No other member of the party around. Not a soul in sight but the black men and Mother.* Father looked at that photograph and groaned about it at night, and kept shouting things to himself about "the ends of the earth."—Clarence Day, *Life with Father*, p. 116

Thought movement. To convey the speed and pattern of mental activity, verbs are often omitted in passages portraying a character's thought:

> Getaway, no chances tonight. Down the fire escape to the next floor. No light. Another window open. Taking candy from a baby. —John Dos Passos, *Manhattan Transfer*, p. 63

Appositional sentences. A phrase that stresses the meaning of the preceding statement or looks forward to the next one is sometimes written as a complete sentence:

> So much for the contemplative aspect of a man's place in a scientific cosmos. I come now to the practical aspect.—Bertrand Russell, *The Impact of Science on Society*, p. 14

Exercises

1. *Identifying sentence elements and patterns.* The sentences below are adapted from the maxims of the seventeenth-century French writer François de La Rochefoucauld. Copy them and indicate the main and secondary sentence elements (see example below). Underline any subordinate clauses and then classify the sentences on the basis of clause structure as simple, compound, complex, or compound-complex. Use the letters in §2.1 and §2.2 or whatever other labels your instructor specifies. This example illustrates one method of analysis:

S M V M O MM
The misfortunes|of our best friends|arouse|in us|sentiments|not|

MM M
altogether|unpleasant. (simple sentence)

1) Each stage of life is new to us, and we are hampered by inexperience regardless of our age.

2) Many would never have fallen in love if they had never heard the word.

3) The jilted bachelor regrets and rejoices at his loss for the rest of his life.

4) We often find a lady who has never been guilty of an indiscretion; we rarely find a lady who has been guilty of only one.

5) When we resist temptation, it is generally true that the temptation is weak, not that we are strong.

2. *Individual analysis of sentence structure.* Make a similar analysis of the sentences in one of your recent papers. Do you use one type of sentence pattern more than another? Are the relationships between different parts of your sentences clear and reasonably exact, or do some of the statements seem merely to be tacked on? On the basis of your analysis, what particular aspects of sentence structure should you bear in mind when revising future papers?

3. *Recognizing various types of subordinate clauses.* Subordinate clauses are used like nouns, adjectives, or adverbs (see pp. 48-52). Mark the grammatical function of the bracketed subordinate clauses in the sentences below, using the abbreviations N, ADJ, ADV or other symbols specified by your instructor. If the clause functions as a noun, indicate whether it serves in the sentence as subject (s), object (o), or complement (c).

1) No poet or novelist wishes he were the only one [who ever lived,] but most of them wish [they were the only one alive,] and quite a number fondly believe [their wish has been granted.]

2) [When some obvious booby tells me that he has liked a poem of mine,] I feel [as if I had picked his pocket.]

3) Lots of people are willing to admit [that they don't understand painting or music,] but very few indeed [who have been to school and learned to read advertisements] will admit [that they don't understand English.]

4) Some writers confuse authenticity, [which they ought always to aim at,] with originality, [which they should never bother about.] There is a certain kind of person [who is so dominated by the desire to be loved for himself alone] [that he has constantly to test those around him by tiresome behavior;] [what he says and does] must be admired [not because it is intrinsically admirable,] but [because it is *his* remark, *his* act.] Does this not explain a good deal of avant-garde art?—W. H. Auden, Apothegems from "Writing," *The Dyer's Hand*, pp. 11-19

4. *Constructing sentences.* Demonstrate your ability to handle a variety of sentence patterns by constructing sentences according to the instructions below. Name the sentence type that results in each case. You may complete the sentences in any way you choose, but note that the patterns lend themselves to the construction of aphorisms such as those in Exercises 1 and 3 above.

Example: The demogogue [infinitive phrase] [verb] [noun clause].

Possible sentence: The demogogue, [to disguise his lust for power], [proclaims] [that the welfare of the people is his only concern].

1) [infinitive phrase] is [infinitive phrase].

2) The [adjective] man [compound verb] [adverb].

3) [gerund phrase] will bring [indirect object] [object].

4) Heaven [adjective clause] exists [prepositional phrase].

5) [compound subject] oppose oppression [adverb clause].

6) [participle phrase] Caesar [linking verb] [complement].

7) Confucius [appositive] said [noun clause].

8) [main clause] [adjective clause], but [main clause].

9) Beautiful women [verb] [prepositional phrase].

3 Basic sentence faults

The three most serious and conspicuous errors in sentence construction are fragmentary sentences, comma faults, and fused sentences.

A *fragmentary sentence* is an incomplete statement—a phrase or a dependent clause—carelessly punctuated as a complete sentence, as in this example:

> Fragment: The Antifederalists opposed Hamilton's economic policy. *Because they felt it tended to concentrate wealth and influence in the hands of a relatively small class.*
>
> Possible revision: The Antifederalists opposed Hamilton's economic policy because they felt it tended to concentrate wealth and influence in the hands of a relatively small class.

A *comma fault* occurs when two sentences that are distinctly separate have been joined together with a comma:

> Comma fault: The war provided the setting for many novels, three of them were especially outstanding.
>
> Possible revision: The war provided the setting for many novels, three of which were especially outstanding.

A *fused sentence* occurs when two sentences have been run together with no separating punctuation at all:

> Fused sentence: The war provided the setting for many novels three of them were especially outstanding. [The fault could be corrected as the comma fault was corrected.]

These sentence faults are considered serious because they suggest either that the writer is extremely careless about his punctuation or (if the faults appear again and again in the same paper) that he may not know what a complete sentence is.

3.1 Fragmentary sentences

Correction: Revise the fragment marked by joining it to another sentence, by making it into a complete sentence, or by rewriting the passage.

A sentence fragment can be corrected in various ways—by joining it to another sentence, by supplying a subject and a predicate, or

3.1 Frag

by rewriting the passage in which it occurs. In revising a sentence fragment, choose the most effective of the methods described in the following section. (See §2.6, Minor sentence types, for a discussion about the occasional effective use of subjectless and verbless sentences.)

Joining a fragment to another sentence

A fragmentary sentence usually should be part of the preceding sentence. If you read the passage aloud, you will notice that you pause only slightly before the sentence fragment and do not drop your voice as noticeably as you do at the end of complete sentences. This means that the fragment should be joined to the preceding sentence, usually with a comma. Sometimes it should also be rephrased.

Sentence fragment	*Revised*
The next afternoon we made our way through the harbor of Okinawa. *That island which had made history less than fifteen years before.*	The next afternoon we made our way through the harbor of Okinawa, the island which had made history less than fifteen years before.

Phrases are subordinate sentence elements and should not be carelessly punctuated as complete sentences:

Sentence fragment	*Revised*
I cite these examples to show you how interesting accounting can be. *And to give you an idea of the kind of problems an accountant has to solve.* [infinitive phrase]	I cite these examples to show you how interesting accounting can be and to give you an idea of the kind of problems an accountant has to solve.
For the past five years I have been contributing a small amount annually to the March of Dimes. *Without ever suspecting that one day a member of my own family might benefit from this foundation.* [prepositional phrase]	For the past five years I have been contributing a small amount annually to the March of Dimes, without ever suspecting that one day a member of my own family might benefit from this foundation.
Professor Brown suddenly glanced up from his notes. *His eyes twinkling with suppressed laughter.* [*Twinkling* is a participle, not a full verb.]	Professor Brown suddenly glanced up from his notes, his eyes twinkling with suppressed laughter.

3.1 Frag

Explanatory phrases beginning with *such as*, *for example*, and similar expressions belong in the same sentence as the statement they explain:

Sentence fragment	*Revised*
After the cards have been run through, the firm knows what volume of business has been done during the week in each of the departments. *Such as tobaccos, candies, canned goods, fresh produce.*	After the cards have been run through, the firm knows what volume of business has been done during the week in each of the departments, such as tobaccos, candies, canned goods, and fresh produce.

Subordinate clauses are only parts of sentences and should not stand alone without definite reason. A relative pronoun (*who*, *which*, *that*) or a subordinating conjunction (such as *although*, *because*, *if*, *when*, *while*) indicates that what follows is a subordinate clause and that it should be combined with a main clause.

Sentence fragment	*Revised*
At the time, my old rowboat with its three-horsepower motor seemed a high-speed job to me. *Although it only attained a speed of about twelve miles an hour.* [adverb clause, beginning with *Although*]	At the time, my old rowboat with its three-horsepower motor seemed a high-speed job to me, although it only attained a speed of about twelve miles an hour.
The whole area is honeycombed by caves. *Many of which are still unexplored.* [adjective clause, introduced by *which*]	The whole area is honeycombed by caves, many of which are still unexplored.

Making a fragment into a sentence

If the fragment deserves special emphasis, it can be made into a complete sentence by inserting a subject and a predicate:

Sentence fragment	*Revised*
He talked for fifty minutes without taking his eyes off his notes. *Apparently not noticing that half the class was asleep.* [*Noticing* is a participle, not a verb.]	He talked for fifty minutes without taking his eyes off his notes. Apparently he did not notice that half the class was asleep. [The subject is *he;* the predicate is the verb *did notice* plus the words related to it.]

National elections and student elections may be compared as closely as an object and its photograph. *The only difference being in size.* [*Being* is a participle, not a verb.]

National elections and student elections may be compared as closely as an object and its photograph. The only difference is in size. [*Is* is the verb, and *difference* is the subject.]

Rewriting a fragment

Sometimes involved or hopelessly snarled sentence fragments have to be completely revised. The following long "sentence" has three phrases that seem to be subjects, but there is no verb:

Sentence fragment

The people who only said "Oh, too bad," on seeing the lifeless puppy, *the small boy* who removed the dead puppy from the gutter, and the *middle-aged man* who kept saying over and over that the people were making a greater fuss about this incident than had been made over his own accident at this same corner a year ago, when he was almost run over by a taxi.

Revised

When the small boy removed the dead puppy from the gutter, some people only said "Oh, too bad." But the middle-aged man kept saying over and over that the people were making a greater fuss about this incident than they had made over his own accident at this same corner a year ago, when he was almost run over by a taxi.

3.2 Comma faults

CF | **Correction: Change the comma marked to a period or semicolon or revise the passage to make an acceptable sentence or sentences.**

A comma fault (sometimes called a *comma splice* or *run-on sentence*) is two or more independent clauses not joined by a coordinating conjunction and written with only a comma between them. The result is that one clause is simply backed up against the other:

> The card catalog is the key to the books in the library, many large libraries have separate catalogs for certain collections of books.

Each of the two clauses joined here is a main clause that could stand alone as a simple sentence. The clauses should be separated by a period or joined into a compound sentence by a semicolon or an appropriate connective.

Gaining a firm knowledge of clause structure is the surest way to avoid comma faults. If you make this error often, review §2.4, Sentences classified by clause structure. You may also find it helpful to read your papers aloud. If your voice drops or if you pause noticeably at a comma, check the sentence to see if it is actually two independent statements. For example, read this sentence aloud to see how much more marked the pause is at the comma following *past* (a comma fault) than at the comma following *six-thirty:*

> The long days of Front and Market streets were a thing of the past, the store now opened for business at ten in the morning and closed at six-thirty, including Saturdays.

The marked pause indicates that there are two separate statements here; a new sentence should begin after *past.*

Making two sentences

A comma fault may be removed by using a period instead of the comma, making two full sentences:

Comma fault	*Repunctuated*
He took a couple of steps, stopped, reached out, and turned a valve, as he did so, he told us the valves had to be checked daily.	He took a couple of steps, stopped, reached out, and turned a valve. As he did so, he told us the valves had to be checked daily.

This is usually the best solution when the ideas are clearly distinct or when commas are numerous in either or both statements. However, correcting a comma fault by putting a period between two very short, closely connected statements may result only in two weak sentences:

> I opened the door noisily, he didn't move. [Here joining the clauses by *but* is preferable to making each a separate sentence.]

Using a semicolon

Comma faults may sometimes be corrected by substituting a semicolon for the comma. This is appropriate when the ideas expressed in the two clauses are closely related:

Comma fault	*Repunctuated*
Charley then crossed the room and threw a switch which started	Charley then crossed the room and threw a switch which started

the motor, returning, he wiped the sweat from his forehead with the back of his hand.	the motor; returning, he wiped the sweat from his forehead with the back of his hand.

A great many comma faults in student papers occur with "conjunctive" adverbs (such as *accordingly*, *consequently*, *however*, *therefore*). When such adverbs appear at the junction of two independent clauses, the conventional punctuation is a semicolon. Although such words show the connection between ideas in the clauses, their connective function is weak.

Comma fault	*Repunctuated*
The person with a college education has training far beyond that which he obtained solely from books, *therefore* his chances for success are much greater than are those of a person without this education.	The person with a college education has training far beyond that which he obtained solely from books; therefore his chances for success are much greater than are those of a person without this education.

Sometimes the comma fault can be revised more effectively by substituting a connective than by repunctuating. The comma fault just given might be revised more successfully as follows:

> *Because* a person with a college education has training far beyond that which he obtained solely from books, his chances for success are much greater than are those of a person without this education.

Other uses of adverbs like *however* and *therefore* are discussed on page 165.

Revising the passage

Usually the best way to remove a comma fault is to revise the sentence, using a connective that will show the relation between the statements. The connective may be a coordinating conjunction (such as *and* or *but*), a subordinating conjunction (*although*, *because*, *if*, *since*, *when* . . .), or a relative pronoun (*who*, *which*, *that* . . .) referring to a noun in the first statement. Sometimes one statement can be revised as a phrase, as in the third example:

Comma fault	*Revised*
It is a personal matter, everyone has to cope with it sooner or later.	It is a personal matter *that* everyone has to cope with sooner or later.

3.3

FS

Comma fault	*Revised*
I bloom in the midst of a party, particularly if I feel some responsibility for its success, conversation is a stimulant more powerful than drugs.	I bloom in the midst of a party, particularly if I feel some responsibility for its success, *because* conversation is a stimulant more powerful than drugs.
Many companies are looking desperately for experts in electronics, this is a rapidly expanding field.	Many companies are looking desperately for experts in electronics, a rapidly expanding field.

See also §23.2, Subordination to control and clarify meaning.

3.3 Fused sentences

FS | **Correction: Use a period or semicolon between the two statements, or revise the passage to make an acceptable sentence or sentences.**

A fused sentence is the same kind of error as a comma fault, except that no punctuation at all appears between the main clauses. It shows plain carelessness and should be corrected in the same way as a comma fault: making two sentences of the fused sentence; using a semicolon to separate the two parts; or rewriting the passage.

Fused sentence	*Possible revisions*
Two volumes of this work are now completed the first will be published next year.	Two volumes of this work are now completed. The first will be published next year.
	Two volumes of this work are now completed, the first *of which* will be published next year.

3.4 Mixed constructions

mix | **Correction: Revise the mixed construction to make an acceptable sentence or sentences.**

When several sentence faults are combined or when a construction is not one of the standard sentence types, the result is sometimes called a mixed construction. Repunctuating cannot correct errors of this kind; the whole passage must be rewritten into acceptable sentence units. Like fused sentences, mixed constructions are usually the result of carelessness or haste.

Mixed construction	*Possible revision*
I had always admired his novels, and when I had a chance to meet him, a real delight. [independent and subordinate clauses improperly joined by *and*]	I had always admired his novels and was delighted when I had a chance to meet him.
Charles was a hard worker, but I wondered how was he going to get everything finished on time? [shift from statement to question]	Although Charles was a hard worker, I wondered how he could finish everything on time.
Of course the Haitian diet is quite different from ours, this is obvious consisting largely of beans and rice. [a comma fault and a misplaced modifying phrase]	Of course the Haitian diet, consisting largely of beans and rice, is quite different from ours.

Since mixed constructions usually involve a combination of errors, their variety is almost infinite. The only sure way to avoid them is to master all the principles of sentence construction.

Exercises

1. *Recognizing sentence units.* Read the following expressions aloud, noting where your voice drops or rises markedly and where it merely pauses slightly without much change in pitch. Then indicate what punctuation should be used at each of these intervals. Change any marks that seem incorrect. When you have finished, analyze the sentence patterns and be prepared to justify your punctuation.

1) Exposition consists of laying a thing out so that the reader can see how the parts fit together with no doubt about what follows what.

2) The first thing an expository writer ought to do is to state his subject. If he is any good.

3) Why anyone should read a writer who is confused. I could not say for the life of me.

4) The subdivisions of any topic, dealing with action, are fivefold among them are "when," "where," and "why."

5) If there are any technical terms, the writer ought to explain them as he goes along. Or include them in a glossary.

6) Is there anyone who if he is to assemble some complicated toy or mechanism does not hate blurred illustrations especially women.

7) Expository writing should be factual, however certain devices for catching attention are permissible.

8) Always keep your audience in mind, don't tell them what they already know.

9) The longer the sentence the greater the chance of confusing the reader unless relationships are made clear.

10) There are many useful devices for making abstract points clear among them analogies and comparisons.

2. *Correcting sentence faults.* Read the following passage and note whatever fragments, comma faults, fused sentences, or mixed constructions it contains. Then show how the wording or punctuation could be changed to produce acceptable sentences. Often more than one revision will be possible; choose the one you think best expresses the writer's intended meaning and emphasis. Some of the sentences need no revision.

According to Santayana religions are many, reason is one. Religion with its forms of ritual and doctrine has room for great variety; whereas reason is uniform, all students in a geometry class, for example, tend to come up with the same answer.

Religion does, of course, sometimes seek for uniformity, called orthodoxy it takes the form of a creed. To formulate creeds, generations of thinkers have hammered away at a statement of specific beliefs to which all official members of the church are expected to adhere. Creeds providing uniformity of belief even if not of reason. But creeds start with propositions that may not be self-evident, therefore they are matters of faith. Once the propositions, often called revelations, are granted, however, reason can operate on them, in fact, everything deduced from the original revelations may be perfectly logical. But logic is different from reason. When we call a man "reasonable," we generally do not mean that he is employing pure logic, instead he is adjusting logic to the conditions of reality, thus he recognizes that the context of a situation makes it necessary to give up what may be a beautiful theory if it does not fit the stubborn, irreducible facts. Faith in logic may be a kind of religion itself. Is it not reason's job to check logic from becoming a creed? Certainly for logic cannot check itself.

Yet even reason has its articles of faith, the presuppositions of science are among them. Whenever there are two explanations for a set of phenomena, both equally logical and both explain all the data, what scientist does not choose the simpler one? He has a faith in the superiority of simplicity, and in this way being like the religious person, who also accepts things on faith. Although we generally do not equate science and religion, however faith is common to both. In this respect they are alike, and only reason to help us distinguish between them. How? We appeal to common sense, that is, recognizing that nature does not ordinarily do things the hard way when a simpler one is available.

3. *Correcting sentence faults.* Several sentence faults have been introduced into the following paragraphs. Read the passage carefully and then rewrite it to eliminate the faults.

"Polis" is the Greek word which we translate as "city-state." It is a bad translation, because the normal polis was not much like a city. And was very much more than a state. But translation, like politics, is the art of the possible, since we have not got the thing which the Greeks called "the polis," we do not possess an equivalent word. From now on, we will avoid the misleading term "city-state," and use the Greek word instead. In this chapter we will first inquire how this political system arose, then we will try to reconstitute the word "polis" and recover its real meaning by watching it in action. It may be a long task but all the time we shall be improving our acquaintance with the Greeks, without a clear conception of what the polis was, and what it meant to the Greeks, it is quite impossible to understand properly Greek history, the Greek mind, or the Greek achievement.—Adapted from H. D. F. Kitto, *The Greeks*, p. 64

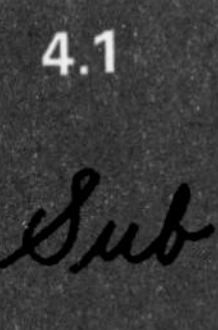

4 Subordinate clauses and connectives

A subordinate clause has a subject and a predicate, but it is shown to be an incomplete statement—a subordinate part of the sentence—by a special kind of connective that relates it to the main clause. In the following sentence, *when* and *that* are the connectives:

> *When Truman ran for re-election in 1948,* few people thought *that he could win.*

Subordinate (dependent) clauses are used in sentences as modifiers, subjects, objects, or complements. Depending on the grammatical function they serve, they are classified as adjective clauses (§4.1), adverb clauses (§4.2), or noun clauses (§4.3).

About half the sentences in most kinds of writing contain one or more subordinate clauses, for subordination enables a writer to show the relationship between ideas much more exactly than he could by stringing them out in a series of simple or compound sentences. The effective use of subordinate clauses is discussed at the end of this section. For a further discussion of subordination, see §23.2, Subordination to control and clarify meaning.

4.1 Adjective clauses

A clause that modifies a noun or pronoun is an adjective clause. The relative pronouns *who*, *which*, and *that* (p. 92) are the words most frequently used to introduce adjective clauses; these pronouns also serve as subjects or objects within the clause:

> Some people *who buy modern paintings* are interested in them primarily as investments rather than as art. [*Who* is the subject of the clause, which modifies *people.*]

> The big steam shovels, *which hold four hundred cubic yards of gravel,* can fill a flatcar in an hour. [*Which* is the subject of the clause, which modifies *shovels.*]

> The plays *that are commercially successful on Broadway* seldom qualify as serious drama. [*That* is the subject of the clause, which modifies *plays.*]

> He received a substantial inheritance from an uncle *whom he had not seen for twenty years.* [*Whom* is the object of the verb *had seen;* the clause modifies *uncle.*]

Adjective clauses may also be introduced by the relative adverbs *when, where,* and *why:*

> It was a day *when everything went wrong.* [The clause modifies *day.*]
>
> He returned to the town *where he had lived as a boy.* [The clause modifies *town.*]
>
> The reason *why these early settlements disappeared* has never been explained satisfactorily. [The clause modifies *reason.*]

See §12.3 for a discussion of adjective clauses as restrictive and nonrestrictive modifiers.

Clauses without relative words

With many adjective clauses a writer has a choice of using the relative word or not using it (the relative in such cases is never the subject of the clause):

> The only books [that] he read as a child were those [that] his teachers assigned.
>
> He is a person [whom] everyone admires.

These clauses without relatives (they are still subordinate clauses) have long been used in English and are acceptable in all varieties of writing.

and which

And is sometimes carelessly and incorrectly used between an adjective clause and the rest of a sentence. The relative pronoun *who, which,* or *that* is the only connective needed; the use of *and* or *but* is superfluous and thwarts the subordination:

Careless	*Revised*
The sea anemone is a fascinating creature *and which* looks more like a plant than an animal.	The sea anemone is a fascinating creature which looks more like a plant than an animal.

4.2 Adverb clauses

A subordinate clause that modifies a verb, adjective, adverb, or a main clause is an adverb clause. It usually expresses a relationship of time, place, direction, cause, effect, condition, manner, or concession:

He lived abroad for three years but returned to the United States *when war broke out*. [The clause modifies the verb *returned*.]

He becomes very stubborn *when he meets opposition*. [The clause modifies the predicate adjective *stubborn*.]

During her husband's absence she managed his business as well *as she could*. [The clause modifies the adverb *well*.]

Because he was a man of principle, even his opponents respected him. [The clause modifies the main statement, *even his opponents respected him*.]

English has a good many connectives for expressing adverb relationships. The following are among the most common:

after	because	since	unless
although	before	so	until
as	if	so that	when
as if	in order that	though	where
as long as	provided that	till	while

See also §4.4, page 53, Using exact connectives.

4.3 Noun clauses

Because they function as nouns, subordinate clauses used as subjects, objects, complements, and appositives are called noun clauses. Most noun clauses are introduced by *that*, but *whatever*, *whoever*, *who*, *what*, *why*, *when*, *where*, and *whether* are also used.

As objects

Noun clauses are most frequently used as direct objects:

The President said *that his meeting with Premier Kosygin had been fruitful*.

No one knows *why these early settlements disappeared*.

They wondered *what would happen next*.

Noun clauses also serve as objects of prepositions:

The poem from *which most of these quotations were taken* is Gray's "Elegy Written in a Country Churchyard."

There is a prize for *whoever gets there first*.

In the last sentence, *whoever* is the correct form rather than *whomever* because the pronoun is the subject of the clause.

As appositives

Noun clauses are quite often used as appositives:

Most people still accept the myth *that progress is inevitable.*
The fact *that he might lose* never occurred to him.

As subjects

Sentences beginning with a subject clause introduced by *that* or *whether* tend to seem rather stilted, especially if the clause is relatively long. In most kinds of writing constructions of this kind should ordinarily appear *after* the verb:

Stilted	*Revised*
That he could raise his grade by studying harder had never occurred to him.	It had never occurred to him *that he could raise his grade by studying harder.*
Whether or not we should revise our foreign policy was the principal topic of discussion.	The principal topic of discussion was *whether or not we should revise our foreign policy.*

Subject clauses introduced by other words are common in all levels of writing:

Whatever is worth doing at all is worth doing well.
Where he disappeared is a matter of conjecture.

As complements

Noun clauses sometimes occur as complements, particularly in definitions and explanations. Such constructions are likely to be awkward, however, and in Formal and General writing it is often better to substitute a different wording:

Awkward	*Better*
A common belief is *that toads cause warts.*	It is commonly believed that toads cause warts. *Or:* It is a common belief that toads cause warts.
Usually the winner is *whoever has the most endurance.*	The person with the most endurance usually wins. *Or:* Whoever has the most endurance usually wins.
Our materialism is *why some Europeans criticize us.*	Some Europeans criticize us for our materialism. *Or:* Our materialism is criticized by some Europeans.

4.3

Awkward	*Better*
A thermostat is *what controls temperature.*	A thermostat is a device for controlling temperature. *Or:* Temperature is controlled by a thermostat.

After "The reason *is* (or *was*) . . . " the preferred connective in Formal and General writing is *that* rather than *because:*

> The reason he lost the election was *that* [preferable to *because*] he lacked organized support.

4.4 Subordination for exact statement

Sub | Correction: Show the intended relationship between ideas by using appropriate subordination, or correct the faulty subordination.

Ideas that deserve equal emphasis should be grammatically coordinate (as in *My son is in high school and my daughter is in college*). But an important part of writing is discriminating among ideas that do *not* deserve equal emphasis. Statements that describe or explain another statement or tell how, when, where, or why something happened should be expressed in subordinate constructions whenever the relationship is not immediately clear from context. For example, there is no reason why three separate sentences should be made of these obviously related ideas:

> Mozart made his first trip to Italy in 1769. He was thirteen years old. His father went with him.

If the first statement is the one the writer wants to emphasize, the others could be subordinated in this way:

> In 1769, *when he was thirteen years old* [subordinate clause], Mozart made his first trip to Italy [main clause], *accompanied by his father* [verbal phrase].

Showing the relative importance of ideas

A subordinate clause usually indicates that the matter subordinated is less important to the subject being discussed than the main statement. To judge the rightness of subordination it is necessary to know what the emphasis of the passage is. For instance, in joining the two statements "The lightning struck the barn" and

"Mother was setting the table for supper," the first would be the main statement in a general account of the event:

> The lightning struck the barn [main clause] just as Mother was setting the table for supper [subordinate clause].

But if the point to be emphasized is what Mother was doing when the lightning struck, the sentence would probably be written:

> When the lightning struck the barn [subordinate clause], Mother was setting the table for supper.

The paragraph would then probably go on to tell what Mother did in the crisis.

In revising sentences, then, it is important to see that the parts are related according to their relative importance.

Using exact connectives

Subordinate clauses are exact because their connectives show a specific relationship to the main clause. Coordinating conjunctions, especially *and*, are much less definite in meaning than adverb connectives like *because*, *since*, *when*, *while* or the adjective connectives *who*, *which*, *that:*

Coordinate statements	*One statement subordinated*
Sandra was waiting for the bus and she saw a purse on the sidewalk.	*While she was waiting for the bus*, Sandra saw a purse on the sidewalk.
"Christina's World" is one of Andrew Wyeth's best paintings, and it is owned by the Museum of Modern Art.	"Christina's World," *which is owned by the Museum of Modern Art*, is one of Andrew Wyeth's best paintings.

In speaking we tend to rely on only a few of the conjunctions available for expressing adverb relationships (see §4.2), but in writing greater exactness is required. Particular care should be taken in using the overworked conjunctions *as* and *so*.

as. The conjunction *as* may introduce various kinds of adverb clauses:

> Degree or manner: I went as fast *as I could go.*
> Time: Our guests arrived *as the clock struck nine.*
> Cause: *As it was getting dark*, we made for home.
> Comparison: Lettuce is not as fattening *as avocados are.*
> Attendant circumstance: *As the fire spread*, the sky grew darker.

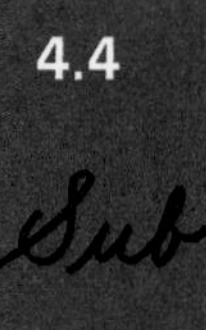

The variety of its meanings makes *as* a word to be watched in writing. In some instances it is the proper and only connective to use—to express comparisons, for example (We went as far *as the others did*), or in clauses of manner (*As Maine goes*, so goes the nation). But in many other constructions, *while*, *when*, *since*, or *because* would be more exact and emphatic:

> *While* [not *as*] we were walking, he told us stories.
> The war was almost over *when* [not *as*] he was drafted.

As is especially weak in the sense of *because*. To introduce clauses of reason, purpose, or result, *since* or *because* is better in Formal English and in most writing:

> He refused to join in the square dancing *because* [not *as*] he was afraid of making a fool of himself.

so. Like *as*, the word *so* (or *and so*) is an overworked and often inexact connective. In most writing it should be replaced by a more definite word:

Inexact	*Revised*
He couldn't find a job, *so* he decided to go to summer school.	*Since* he couldn't find a job, he decided to go to summer school.
He was new to the neighborhood, *so* he had few friends.	*Because* he was new to the neighborhood, he had few friends.

In clauses of purpose, *so that* is usually preferable to *so:*

> He went to New York *so that* [not *so*] he could find a job in publishing.

4.5 Faulty subordination

Faulty subordination is no more effective than excessive coordination. It usually results from a careless stringing together of ideas as they happen to come into the writer's mind. Consider, for example, the haphazard use of dependent constructions in the following sentence:

> Because her mother died when Barbara was five years old, and since her father lived a solitary life, Barbara had a very unhappy childhood, having no family to confide in.

The elements in this cluttered statement must be rearranged to establish some semblance of order and proportion:

> Barbara had a very unhappy childhood. She was five years old when her mother died, and since her father led a solitary life, she had no family to confide in.

When you go over the first draft of your papers, revise any subordinate elements that weaken your sentences or obscure their meaning.

Tandem subordination

Avoid statements in which a series of dependent clauses are strung together, one after another. Too many clauses beginning with similar connectives (*who, which, that; when, since, because*), each built upon the preceding one, are called tandem subordination, or "house-that-Jack-built" constructions:

Tandem subordination	*Revised*
He had carefully selected teachers *who* taught classes *that* had a slant *that* was specifically directed toward students *who* intended to go into business.	He had carefully selected teachers who specifically slanted their courses toward students intending to go into business.
The recordings *which* I bought last week were scarce items *that* are essential to people *who* are making collections of folk music *which* comes from Spain.	Last week I bought some scarce recordings that are essential to collectors of Spanish folk music.

Sentences that begin and end with the same kind of subordinate clauses are frequently awkward because of their seesaw effect:

> *When* he came home at night, Dad would always complain *when* the children weren't in bed.

Such constructions can be improved by changing one of the connectives. Usually it is possible to choose a connective that is more exact:

> When he came home at night, Dad would always complain *if* the children weren't in bed.

Inverted subordination

Putting the main idea of a sentence in a subordinate clause or phrase ("inverting" the proper relationship between statements) may result in an awkward or incongruous statement:

Inverted	*More accurate*
She was eighteen when her hands were severely burned, which meant that she had to give up her dream of becoming a concert pianist.	When she was eighteen, [main clause:] *her hands were severely burned.* As a result, [main clause:] *she had to give up her dream of becoming a concert pianist.*

Inverted or "upside-down" subordination frequently occurs in sentences that trail off into weak participle phrases:

> The road was blocked, *causing us to make a twenty-mile detour.*

Such sentences can be improved by putting the less important statement in an adverb clause:

> We had to make a twenty-mile detour *because the road was blocked.*

Exercises

1. *Functions of subordinate clauses.* List the subordinate clauses in the following paragraph and tell how each is used in the sentence (whether a noun clause is a subject, object, or complement; what word or words an adjective or adverb clause modifies).

1) In contrast, much of animal communication is instinctive rather than social. 2) That is to say, all cats mew and purr, and would do so even if they were cut off from all communication with other cats. 3) On the other hand, some animal communication seems to share the social nature of human speech and is therefore learned activity. 4) A striking example is the barking of dogs, which is characteristic only of the domesticated animal, not of dogs in the wild state. 5) Similarly, the honey dances of bees may not be altogether without an arbitrary element. 6) It is also likely that when more is known of the cries and chatterings of the great apes in the wild state, a considerable social element in their communication may be found. 7) Nor should it be thought that all human communication is social. 8) A part of our communication consists of instinctive reactions which accompany language, like the trembling of fear or the suffusion of blood which accompanies anger. 9) Yet even in the nonlinguistic accompaniments of speech, the tones of voice and the gestures, it is now clear that there is more of arbitrary and socially learned behavior than we had at one time supposed.—Archibald A. Hill, *Introduction to Linguistic Structure*, pp. 4-5

2. *Using effective subordination.* In some of the examples below, ideas expressed by main clauses should be put into subordinate constructions. In others, the subordination is not successful because it fails to show the proper relationship between ideas. Read through the examples first, and then write out your revision of each one.

1) Where words come from is what one is studying when he is studying etymology.

2) Our language has a complex history and so the study of the etymology of English words is fascinating.

3) An example is that many of the words you use carry echoes of old theories of astrology and physiology, but you may not be aware of this.

4) Because you probably did not know that you were echoing an old belief that personality is governed by the heavenly bodies, you recently called your exasperating roommate a lunatic. *Luna* means "moon" in Latin.

5) If you said, "My stars, a total disaster!" and the contents of your roommate's closet tumbled to the floor, the etymological reason is because *disaster* derives from a combination of Latin words meaning "bad star."

6) When your mercurial friend overcomes you with her quicksilver wit, remember that she is under the influence of the planet closest to the sun and so be charitable.

7) *Temperament* is a word that derives from the Latin verb *tempero*, "to mix," and recalls the old theory that the mixture of the humors that are in the body was what determined personality.

8) As you speak of an actor's spirited performance, you are probably unaware of the ancient associations of the word *spirited.*

9) *Spirited* is a word which comes from the Latin *spiritus* and which means "breath" or "air" which contains vestigially a reference to the theory which held that certains aeriform substances pass through the arteries.

10) The word *astronaut* is a very recent addition to the language. It means roughly "sailor to the stars." It derives from Greek words.

3. *Using effective subordination.* The following paragraph is written in a choppy, childish style. Rewrite it, using appropriate subordination, so that the ideas are smoothly and accurately related.

English is a queer language. Simple words have a bewildering variety of meanings. Take the word *fall.* It is a Biblical event. It is a season that follows summer. It can be followed by out. Then it conjures visions of atomic holocaust. One may fall physically. One may fall emotionally. Examples are into a pond, in love, into a brown study. Prepositions and adverbs give it additional meanings. Soldiers fall back. Jokes fall flat. Deals fall through. Night just falls. In combination with other words it may refer to a literal fall. It can also refer to a figurative fall. Consider such words as *waterfall*, *windfall*, and *landfall*.

4. *Using effective subordination.* The following passage suffers from faulty and excessive subordination. Decide what statements deserve primary emphasis and rewrite the paragraph so that the relationship between main and secondary ideas is clear.

Everyone who has studied the Bible has found some book that appeals to the sense which he has of life and that appeals to the sense which he has of great literary style. For the man who feels that he is confounded by the bewildering multiplicity of life which he finds everywhere, the book of Genesis is likely to have great appeal as it conveys a massive but simple unity which characterizes creation. Its aura of awesome mystery is what causes the book of Job to appeal to the man who is oppressed by the scientific rationalism which characterizes the modern world. The book of Matthew is able to release in the cold man great reserves of emotion and the reason is because it sets forth with such moving humility the trials and character of Christ.

5 Verbals

Verbals are non-finite verb forms that are used in sentences as nouns (subjects, objects, complements) or modifiers. Although they have many qualities of verbs—showing tense and taking objects, for example—they cannot serve as full verbs to make sentences or clauses (**see** §2, Grammar of sentences). In many sentences, however, verbal phrases function very much like subordinate clauses in showing the relationship between main and subordinate ideas:

> *When he graduated from college*, he went to New York in search of a job. [subordinate clause]
>
> *Having graduated from college*, he went to New York in search of a job. [verbal phrase, modifying *he*]

Verbals are classified by form and function as (1) infinitives (*to ask*, *to buy*), which can serve either as nouns or as modifiers; (2) participles (*asking*, *asked*, *buying*, *bought*), which modify nouns and pronouns; and (3) gerunds (*asking*, *buying*), which are verbal nouns. Although the present participle and gerund are identical in form, they can be distinguished by the way they are used in sentences, the participle as a modifier (a *dancing* figure) and the gerund as a noun (*dancing* takes skill). The forms and principal uses of verbals are illustrated in the table on page 61. **See also** §9, Verbs.

5.1 Verbal phrases

Like full verbs, verbals can take objects, complements, and adverbial modifiers. In some constructions they also take a subject, if the meaning of that term is stretched a little.

> *After accepting his invitation to dinner*, she realized that she had nothing to wear. [*invitation* is the direct object of the participle *accepting*, which is modified by the adverb *after;* the verbal phrase modifies the subject of the sentence, *she*]
>
> He avoided the accident by *running his car onto the shoulder of the road.* [*car* is the direct object of the gerund *running*, which is modified by the phrase *onto the shoulder of the road;* the verbal phrase is object of the preposition *by*]

He wanted *to be an architect or industrial designer.* [*architect* and *designer* are complements of the infinitive *to be;* the verbal phrase serves as object of the verb *wanted*]

Subjects with infinitives
An infinitive phrase often has an expressed subject:

He wanted *the whole department* [subject of the infinitive] *to be reorganized.*

If the subject of an infinitive is a pronoun, it is in the object form:

They asked *her* [subject of the infinitive] *to be chairman.*
Their mother told *them* [subject of the infinitive] *to behave.*

Subjects with gerunds
When a noun or pronoun precedes a gerund, serving as its "subject," some questions of usage arise: sometimes the genitive (possessive) form is used, sometimes the common form. The writer must depend partly on his ear in choosing the form that seems more natural, but the following principles should serve as guides:

1) When the subject of a gerund is a personal pronoun or a proper noun, the genitive form is generally used:

The less said about *his* singing, the better.
They insisted on *Bob's* playing the piano.

2) When the subject is a plural noun, the common form is usually preferred:

The manager disapproves of *women* smoking.
The staff will not tolerate *visitors* coming and going at will.

3) If the subject is abstract, the common form is used:

It was a case of *panic* getting the upper hand.
There is a danger of the *temperature* dropping suddenly.

4) When the subject is modified by other words, the common form is used:

There was something suspicious about the *daughter* of the sponsor winning the $10,000 prize.

At the outbreak of the Civil War no one in Washington foresaw the possibility of *Grant*, who had failed in so many undertakings, leading the Union forces.

Vbl

Forms and uses of verbals

Infinitives

An infinitive is (1) the base form of a verb (with or without *to*) or (2) any verb phrase that can be used with *to* to function in a sentence as a noun, an adjective, or an adverb.

Forms:	*Active*	*Passive*
Present	(to) ask, (to) be asking	(to) be asked
Past	(to) have asked, (to) have been asking	(to) have been asked

Principal uses:

Subject: *To be asked to that party* makes any girl proud.
Object: He does not like *to express his opinion.*
Modifier (adjective): I have plenty of work *to do.* (Modifies *work*)
Modifier (adverbial): The students came to *learn Russian.* (Modifies *came*)
Absolute phrase modifying the main clause: *To tell the truth,* she is a bore.

Participles

A participle is a verb form, typically ending in *-ing* or *-ed,* used as a modifier.

Forms:	*Active*	*Passive*
Present	asking	being asked
Past	having asked	asked, having been asked

Principal uses:

Modifier of a noun: a *smiling* candidate; a *clogged* drain
Participle phrase modifying a noun: The candidate *getting a majority of the votes* will be nominated.
Absolute phrase modifying the main clause: *Everything considered,* a portable typewriter seems the most practical gift.

Gerunds

A gerund is a verb form, typically ending in *-ing* or *-ed,* used as a noun.

Forms:	*Active*	*Passive*
Present	asking	being asked
Past	having asked	having been asked

Principal uses:

Gerund as subject: *Having been asked* made him happy.
Gerund phrase as subject: *Taking anthropology* opened a whole new field.
Gerund as object: She taught *dancing.*
Gerund as complement: Seeing is *believing.* (*Seeing* is also a gerund.)
Gerund as a modifier of a noun: the *dining* room, a *fishing* boat
Gerund as appositive: He had only one hobby, *collecting stamps.*

5.1

Vbl

5) When the subject is stressed, the common form is usually preferred with nouns and the object form with pronouns:

> Did you hear about the *mayor* being arrested for speeding?
> I can't imagine *him* winning the award.

6) With other noun forms, usage is divided. Formal English usually prefers the genitive form, but the common form of the noun is used in General English:

> Formal: The neighbors complained about the *dog's* barking at night.
> General: The neighbors complained about the *dog* barking at night.
>
> Formal: Jones worried about his *secretary's* taking another job.
> General: Jones worried about his *secretary* taking another job.

5.2 Idiomatic use of infinitives and gerunds

Some expressions are regularly completed by infinitives (privileged *to attend*), others by gerunds (the privilege *of attending*). When one form is substituted for the other, the result is an unidiomatic construction: for example, "anxious *to increase*" is a Standard idiom, but "anxious *of increasing*" is not. Here are typical expressions, some that call for a gerund, others for an infinitive. You will find others in your dictionary under the key (main) word of the construction.

Gerund	*Infinitive*
cannot help doing	compelled to do
capable of working	able to work
skilled in writing	the desire to write
the habit of giving	the tendency to give
successful in getting	manage to get
ignore saying	neglect to say
my object in paying	my obligation to pay
satisfaction of doing	satisfying to do

With many words, especially common ones, either a gerund or an infinitive is idiomatic: a way *of doing* it, a way *to do* it.

the and of in gerund phrases

Gerunds are more direct when they are not preceded by *the* and when they are completed by a direct object rather than an *of* phrase:

Awkward: In *the* revising *of* the first draft, the writer should check his spelling.

Direct: In revising the first draft, the writer should check his spelling.

to with infinitives

Most infinitive constructions are introduced by *to*, "the sign of the infinitive":

She needed time *to think*. They hoped *to get* home before dark. His efforts *to be promoted* failed.

To is not used, however, after auxiliary verbs (*can*, *may*, *must*, *shall*, *will*):

I can *see*. You must *try* it. We may *go* to Europe next fall.

With a few verbs (*do*, *dare*, *help*, *need*, etc.) usage varies:

I did *see* him. It did me good *to see* him.
I helped him [*to*] *learn* to drive.

Split infinitives

If an adverb comes between *to* and an infinitive (I don't want *to ever see* him again) the phrase is called a *split infinitive*. A writer should avoid split infinitives that are obviously awkward or that call undue attention to themselves:

Awkward	*Better*
I will not describe the circumstances of our meeting, or even attempt *to* physically *describe* her.	I will not describe the circumstances of our meeting, or even attempt *to describe* her physically.
After a while I was able *to*, although not very accurately, *distinguish* the good customers from the sulky ones.	After a while I was able *to distinguish*—although not very accurately—the good customers from the sulky ones.

But constructions of this sort are not always awkward. When the normal position of the adverb is after the word *to*, a split infinitive is Standard usage (The receptionist asked them *to please sit* down). Putting the adverb modifier immediately before or after the infinitive would be unnatural or misleading in some statements:

Unnatural: Autumn is the time *really to see* Europe.
Better: Autumn is the time *to really see* Europe.

5.3 MM

5.3 Misrelated modifiers

MM Correction: Revise the sentence so that the expression marked is clearly related to the word or statement that it modifies.

Verbals, either as single words or in phrases, are most often used as modifiers of individual words:

I first noticed him *sitting alone in a corner.* [present participle, modifying *him*]

The town hall, *completely renovated four years ago*, always impresses visitors. [past participle, modifying *town hall*]

He still had three years *to serve in prison* before he would be eligible for parole. [infinitive, modifying *years*]

Like other modifiers, verbal modifiers should be clearly related to the words that they modify. When a verbal construction seems from its position to refer to a word that it cannot sensibly modify, it is said to be *misrelated.* Participle phrases usually give writers the most trouble:

Misrelated	*Revised*
On the other side of the valley, *grazing peacefully like cattle*, we saw a herd of buffalo. [the participle phrase seems to refer to *we*]	On the other side of the valley we saw a herd of buffalo, *grazing peacefully like cattle.* [the phrase clearly refers to *buffalo*]

Misrelated modifiers may be momentarily confusing to the reader (or unintentionally humorous) and should therefore be avoided. Sometimes the correction can be made by putting the modifier immediately before or after the word it is meant to modify, as in the example above, but often it is better to rewrite the sentence completely:

Misrelated	*Revised*
One early-day western senator is said to have passed out campaign cards to the voters *pinned together with five-dollar bills.* [the participle phrase seems to refer to *voters*]	One early-day western senator is said to have pinned five-dollar bills to the campaign cards he passed out to voters.

Occasionally modifiers are placed so that they seem to refer to either of two elements in the sentence. These constructions (some-

times called *squinting modifiers*) can be avoided by changing the position of the modifier or by otherwise revising the sentence:

Ambiguous	*Revised*
The woman who was standing in the doorway *to attract attention* dropped her purse.	The woman who was standing in the doorway dropped her purse *to attract attention. Or:* The woman, standing in the doorway *to attract attention*, dropped her purse.

Other types of misrelated modifiers are discussed in §10.5, Position of adverbs.

5.4 Dangling modifiers

DM | Correction: Revise the sentence to include the word to which the dangling modifier refers.

Dangling modifiers refer to a word that is implied rather than actually stated in the sentence. Like misrelated modifiers, they can make a sentence confusing or ludicrous:

> *Having moved at fifteen*, his home town no longer seemed familiar.

This error often occurs when passive rather than active verbs are used:

Dangling	*Revised*
In painting four of these pictures, his wife was used as his model.	*In painting four of these pictures*, he used his wife as a model.
To find the needed information, the whole book had to be read.	*To find the needed information*, I had to read the whole book.

Usually the easiest way to correct a dangling modifier is to name the agent or the "doer" of the action immediately after the phrase, as in the revisions shown above. It is often better, however, to revise the sentence entirely, making the relationships more accurate by using other constructions. Changing the verbal phrase to a subordinate clause often improves the sentence:

Dangling	*Revised*
Having been delayed by a train accident, the leading role was played by a local girl.	*Because the leading lady was delayed by a train accident*, her role was played by a local girl.

5.5

Abs M

5.5 Absolute modifiers

A writer should distinguish clearly between verbal modifiers that obviously dangle, such as those cited above, and *absolute modifiers*—participle or infinitive phrases that modify the statement as a whole and thus do not need a specific reference word in the main clause. A number of absolute constructions are commonly used expressions:

> *Everything considered*, this plan seems best.
> *To make a long story short*, we bought the house.
> *Considering the cost of labor*, the price is reasonable.

An absolute phrase with a subject is sometimes called a *nominative absolute*. This construction is most effectively used in descriptive and narrative prose for adding details or parenthetical material:

> He stalked like the specter of a soldier, *his eyes* [subject] *burning* [participle] with the power of a stare into the unknown.—Stephen Crane, *The Red Badge of Courage*, p. 59

> On March 7 Napoleon entered Grenoble at the head of his army. With his snuffbox he rapped on the city gates, *torchlight* [subject] *playing* [participle] on his face.—C. W. Ceram, *Gods, Graves, and Scholars*, p. 99

> The Portuguese listened with his head cocked to one side, *his dark eyes* [subject] *ringed* [participle] with ash-gray circles, and now and then he wiped his damp veined dead-white hands on his stained apron.—Carson McCullers, *Member of the Wedding*, p. 71

Exercises

1. *Identifying verbals according to function.* Analyze the function of each italicized group of words and identify the verbal in it as an infinitive, participle, or gerund. If the verbal functions as a modifier, identify the word or statement it modifies; if it is not a modifier, state its use in the sentence.

My father had a small estate in Nottinghamshire; I was the third of five sons. He sent me to Emmanuel College in Cambridge, at fourteen years old, where I resided three years, and applied myself close to my studies. But the charge (1) *of maintaining me* (although I had a very scanty allowance) (2) *being too great for a narrow fortune*, I was bound apprentice to Mr. James Bates, an eminent surgeon in London, with whom I continued four years; and (3) *my father now and then sending me small sums of money*, I laid them out (4) *in learning navigation*, and other parts of the mathematics, useful to those who intend (5) *to travel*, as I always believed it would be some time or other my fortune (6) *to do*. When I left Mr. Bates, I went down to my father, where, by the assistance of him and my Uncle John and some other relations, I got forty pounds, and a promise of thirty pounds a year (7) *to maintain me* at Leyden. There I studied Physic two years and seven months, (8) *knowing it would be useful in long voyages.*—Jonathan Swift, *Gulliver's Travels*, ch. 1

2. *Idiomatic use of verbals.* Select the idiomatic form from the choices given in parentheses.

Galileo felt a keen obligation (of explaining, to explain) how things happened; his medieval-minded opponents felt bound to the necessity (to explain, of explaining) why things happened. We should consider Galileo's (conceiving of, conceiving) a new method as a revolution, an attempt (at breaking, to break) violently with the medieval custom (to see, of seeing) a purposeful reason in everything. The medieval mind's efforts (to reduce, at reducing, toward reducing) everything to pure reason grew out of the conviction that God was pure reason, and therefore everything that God had created was capable (to be, of being) made rational.

3. *Subjects with gerunds.* In the following sentences, select the form of the noun or pronoun that would be preferable in Formal usage.

1) What the average Italian thought of (Galileo, Galileo's) experimenting with falling bodies we do not know; but some churchmen viewed (his, him) working with alarm.

2) The chances of the (Church, Church's) in Rome agreeing with Galileo were small, since much of antiquity's science had been lost.

3) Galileo thought that, by patient observation, it was possible to discover the causes of (nature, nature's) functioning.

4) Romantics object to (science, science's) analyzing the emotions.

5) It is difficult to analyze (man, man's) analyzing of himself.

4. *Faulty modifiers.* Some of these sentences contain misrelated or dangling modifiers; some contain absolute constructions that need no correction. Identify those modifiers that are inaccurately used and rewrite the sentence so that its elements are properly related.

1) Being thoroughly persuaded of them myself, the beliefs I hold seem to me to be obviously true.

2) My spirits often sink in despair, however, trying to find ways to convince others of these truths.

3) After having convinced a friend against his will, both he and I find that our friendship is in doubt.

4) It does not really persuade anyone to accept my beliefs by citing authorities to prove my point.

5) To be honest about it, my friends have grown weary of my arguments and often try to avoid me.

6) After having satisfied my own mind in every detail of an argument, the decision I reach seems incontrovertible.

7) My position tends to harden very rapidly, my decision having been reached, and I am not likely to change my mind.

8) To be perfectly frank, it is unwise for you to pretend that you are convinced by what I say to be polite.

9) Above and beyond the call of mere friendship, being more important, truth is what matters.

10) To do justice to any friendship based on truth, it takes absolute candor on both sides.

5. *Revision of a faulty paragraph.* Read the following paragraph carefully, noting any inaccuracies in the use of modifying words, phrases, or clauses. Also take note of whatever weaknesses it may have in general sentence structure. Then rewrite it so that all ideas are accurately and directly expressed.

Strictly speaking, intelligent communication depends on the ability to analyze terms. Each part of a topic—each term—must be thoroughly known, it being only then possible to know what you are talking about when we mention any one of them. Therefore we can keep our eye on the topic as we proceed developing it. After getting the terms straight, the main idea then being firmly in our mind, the argument will be orderly. The principal considerations, after all, in searching for the truth.

6 Agreement of subject and verb

Agr Correction: Make the word marked agree in form with the word to which it is related: with its subject if it is a verb, with its antecedent if it is a pronoun.

In Standard English, parts of speech which vary in form for number, gender, or person must agree—that is, correspond in form—when they stand in relationship to each other. Pronouns agree with their antecedents (§8.2) and verbs with their subjects.

Subject-verb agreement is seldom a problem in English because our verbs, except for *be*, have only two forms in the present tense (which adds *-s* in the third person singular) and only one form in the past tense. (See §9, Verbs, for a full discussion of English verb forms.) Questions about the agreement of subject and verb are most likely to arise when verbs have compound subjects or collective nouns as subjects, or when the grammatical number of the subject is otherwise blurred by adjacent words in the sentence. These problems are discussed in the following sections.

6.1 Verbs with compound subjects

A compound subject is made up of two or more words, phrases, or clauses joined by *and, or, nor*. The number of the verb depends on which conjunction is used and on the meaning of the subject.

Subjects joined by and

The conjunction *and* is used to join coordinate items, to add them together. Thus subjects joined by *and* usually take a plural verb:

> *Beckett*, *Ionesco*, and *Genet have* influenced many young American playwrights.
>
> The original *draft* of the poem and the *version* finally published *differ* in several significant ways.

Exception: When the words of a compound subject refer to the same person or are considered together as a unit, the verb is usually singular:

> His warmest *admirer* and severest *critic was* his wife.
>
> *Blood*, *vengeance* and *silence is* the ancient law of the lawless Mafia throughout Sicily and southern Italy.—*Time*, July 29, 1957, p. 22

6.1

Agr

Subjects joined by or, nor

Compound subjects joined by *or, nor, either . . . or, neither . . . nor* sometimes take singular verbs and sometimes plural:

1) When both subjects are singular, the verb ordinarily is singular:

> *One* or the *other is* certainly to blame.
>
> Neither *chance* nor political *maneuvering has been* the main factor in the drift of Italy's political situation toward the Left.—Claire Sterling, "Italy: How Far Left of Center?" *The Reporter*, September 29, 1953, p. 16

Exceptions: In questions, where the verb precedes the subject, General usage tends to use a plural verb:

> *Are* [Formal: *Is*] either *Dirksen* or *Percy* supporting the bill?

In General usage a plural verb may also follow two singular subjects if they are not considered as separate:

> Neither *radio* nor *television provide* [Formal: *provides*] adequate news coverage.

2) When both subjects are plural, the verb is plural:

> No artificial *colorings* or *preservatives* are used.

3) When one subject is singular and the other plural, usage varies. In Formal writing the verb usually agrees with the nearer subject:

> One major *accident* or several minor *ones seem* to occur at this corner every weekend.
>
> Neither the *revolutionists* nor their leader *was* to blame.

In General usage a plural verb is ordinarily used even if the nearer subject is singular:

> Neither the *revolutionists* nor their *leader were* to blame.

4) When the subjects are pronouns in different persons, Formal usage requires that the verb agree in person and number with the nearer subject. In General usage (and even in Formal usage if the alternative is awkward) the verb is usually plural:

> Formal: Either *you* or *she is* likely to be elected.
> General: Either *you* or *she are* likely to be elected.
>
> Formal and General: Neither *you* nor *I are* trained for that job. [*Am* would sound unnatural.]

Such problems of agreement can usually be avoided by substituting a different, more natural construction:

> *One* of you *is* likely to be elected.
> *Neither* of us *is* trained for that job.

Subjects followed by together with

In Formal usage a singular subject followed by a phrase introduced by *together with, along with, as well as, in addition to* ordinarily takes a singular verb:

> The *treasurer as well as the president was* held responsible for the mismanagement of the company.

But a plural verb is often used in these situations when the added phrase is clearly intended as a compound subject:

> Both the *demand* for the competent serious literature, *as well as the ability* to read it intelligently, *have* seriously depreciated.—Seymour Betsky, "The Teaching of Literature," *Sewanee Review*, Autumn 1949, 47:646

A simple solution—and one that may make the statement more direct—is to use *and* wherever appropriate:

> Both *the president and the treasurer were* held responsible for the mismanagement of the company.

6.2 Verbs with collective nouns as subjects

Words that refer to a group of people or objects but are singular in form are called collective nouns: *army, audience, choir, committee, crowd, faculty, gang, group, government, jury, mob, orchestra, public, team.* Verbs and pronouns used with collective nouns are either singular or plural, depending upon the meaning of the group word.

Nouns referring to the group as a unit

Singular verbs and singular pronouns are used with collective nouns that refer to the group as a unit:

> *Class is* dismissed.
> The *committee has* already held *its* first meeting of the year.
> The *audience is* requested to remain seated during intermission.

6.2

Agr

Nouns referring to individuals in a group

When a collective noun refers to the members of the group, especially if it represents them as acting individually, a plural verb and plural reference words are used:

> The graduating *class have* all agreed to have *their* pictures taken.
> The *committee are* arguing among *themselves.*
> The *audience have* taken *their* seats.

Sentences like these often sound rather unnatural, and in most cases it is better to substitute a clearly plural subject (the committee *members*, the *members* of the audience).

Verbs with measurements and figures

Expressions signifying quantity or extent (*miles*, *gallons*, *years*, *pounds*) take singular verbs when the amount is considered as a unit:

> *Five dollars is* too much to pay for a book in that condition.
> *Four quarts* of oil *is* all the crankcase holds.
> *Three months passes* in no time at all on a dude ranch.

When the amount is considered as a number of individual units, a plural verb is used:

> *Two more dollars are* missing from the till this morning.
> There *are three quarts* of milk in the refrigerator.
> The last *three months have been* the driest in California's history.

In expressions of addition and multiplication, usage is about evenly divided:

> Five and seven *is* [or *are*] twelve.
> Five times seven *is* [or *are*] thirty-five.

A singular verb is used in expressions of subtraction:

> Twenty-five from thirty-one *leaves* six.

Verbs with data, number, public

Data is a plural form and is generally so considered in Formal, particularly scientific, writing; but since the singular *datum* is rarely used, *data* is often used for both singular and plural in General writing:

> Singular idea: The actual *data* of history [a body of facts] *consists* of contemporary facts in the form of remains and documents.—Morris R. Cohen, *Reason and Nature*, p. 381

Plural idea: When the *data* [the individual facts] *have* been secured the task is to analyze, to sift, to select and to arrange *those* data which *bear* upon each particular phase of the object or event examined until at the end the scientist has what one might call a logical construct.—G. D. Higginson, *Fields of Psychology*, p. 10

Number as a collective noun may be either singular or plural: preceded by *the*, it refers to the total sum and takes a singular verb; preceded by *a*, it refers to the individual units and takes a plural verb:

A number of pages *are* badly torn.

The number of pages assigned for daily reading *was* gradually increased to twelve.

Physicians were disturbed to find that *an* alarming *number* of bacteria *were* developing a tolerance to penicillin.

Public takes a singular verb if the writer wishes to signify the whole group (The *public is* invited); it takes a plural verb if the writer is considering the individual members (The *public are* invited).

Words ending in -ics

Physics, *mathematics*, *economics*, *civics*, *linguistics*, and similar *-ics* words that refer to a science, art, or a body of knowledge are usually considered singular; other words ending in *-ics* that refer to physical activities or qualities (*athletics*, *acrobatics*, *tactics*) are generally treated as plurals.

Singular forms	*Plural forms*
Physics was my most difficult subject in high school.	*Athletics have* been virtually abolished from some smaller schools.
Ballistics is the study of the motion of projectiles.	His motives may be good, but his *tactics are* deplorable.

Some words ending in *-ics* (*ethics*, *politics*, *acoustics*) may be used either in a singular or plural sense:

Singular idea	*Plural idea*
In almost every group, *politics is* a controversial subject.	Radical *politics were* offensive to the Federalists.
Acoustics is a branch of science that is growing fast.	The *acoustics* in this room *are* not all they might be.

When you are in doubt about the number of a word ending in *-ics*, consult a dictionary.

6.3 Blind agreement

The tendency to make a verb agree with a nearby expression rather than with its actual subject is called "blind agreement." This error occurs most frequently in the following situations:

Plural nouns between subject and verb

A singular subject followed by a phrase or clause containing plural nouns is still singular:

> Here and there a *man* [subject] such as Columbus, Galileo, and others *has* [not *have*] ventured into the unknown physical and intellectual worlds.
>
> The *lumberman* [subject] who previously sold only to carpenters and builders now *finds* [not *find*] hundreds of amateurs eager to build their own homes.
>
> I decided to see exactly how *one* of those new cars *is* [not *are*] put together.

one of those who

In Formal English, the verb in clauses that begin *one of those who* (or *that*) is plural:

> He is one of those men who never *care* how they look [The verb is plural because its subject *who* refers to *men*, not to *one*.]
>
> "The Lottery" is one of those stories that *leave* you more puzzled when you finish than when you began. [*Stories* is the antecedent of *that*.]

Although a singular verb is common in spoken English ("one of those girls who *talks* all the time") and in a good deal of published material, the plural verb is customarily used in Formal English and should therefore be used in college writing.

Exception: When *only* precedes *one of those who* the verb is singular, since the pronoun *who* then refers to a single person or thing:

> She is the only one of those women who *plays* bridge well.

there is, there are

When a sentence begins with the introductory (or "dummy")

word *there* (sometimes referred to as an "anticipating subject"), the number of the verb is determined by the subject which follows:

There *are* conflicting *opinions* [subject] about smoking in the classrooms.

There *is* great narrative and dramatic *power* [subject] in the first part of this novel.

At our camp there *were* at least a dozen *men* [subject] who were familiar with the mountain trail.

"There *was* at least a *score* [subject] of men in the place."—Michael Innes, *The Paper Thunderbolt*, p. 56

In this construction a singular verb is frequently used before a compound subject, especially if a plural verb would be unidiomatic, as in the second example below:

There *is food* and *drink* enough for everyone.
There *was nothing* he could do and *little* he could say.

Verb and complement

A verb agrees with its subject and not with its complement or its object:

Our chief *trouble* [subject] *was* [not *were*] the black flies that swarmed about us on the trip.

The *black flies* [subject] that swarmed about us on our trip *were* [not *was*] our chief trouble.

The *material* [subject] that was most interesting to me when I worked on my reference paper *was* [not *were*] the books that stated the facts forcefully.

When subject and complement differ in number, the sentence usually sounds less awkward if the subject and verb are plural, as in the second example above.

Inverted word order

When the word order is inverted, care must be taken to make the verb agree with its subject and not with some other word:

Throughout the story *appear* thinly disguised *references* [subject] to the author's own boyhood.

Is any *one* [subject] of these pictures for sale?

Accompanying the senator *were* his *secretary* and two *members* of his legal staff. [The verb has a compound subject.]

6.3

Agr

series, portion, part

Subjects like *series, portion, part, type* take singular verbs even when modified by a phrase with a plural noun:

A *series* of panel discussions *is* scheduled for the convention.

A substantial *portion* of the reports *is* missing.

The most interesting *part* of the investigations *was* the discovery and identification of the forged letters.

Exercises

1. *Finding the subject.* Find the subject of the italicized verbs in the following paragraph. If the subject is a pronoun, indicate what word or idea it refers to.

(1) *Suppose* it *were* perfectly certain that the life and fortune of every one of us *would*, one day or other, *depend* upon his winning or losing a game of chess. (2) *Don't* you *think* that we *should* all *consider* it to be a primary duty to learn at least the names and the moves of the pieces; to have a notion of a gambit, and a keen eye for all the means of giving and getting out of check? . . . (3) Yet it *is* a very plain and elementary truth, that the life, the fortune, and the happiness of every one of us . . . *do depend* upon our knowing something of the rules of a game infinitely more difficult and complicated than chess. . . . (4) The chessboard *is* the world, the pieces *are* the phenomena of the universe, the rules of the game *are* what we *call* the laws of Nature. (5) The player on the other side *is hidden* from us. (6) We *know* that his play *is* always fair, just, and patient. (7) But also we *know*, to our cost, that he never *overlooks* a mistake, or *makes* the slightest allowance for ignorance.—Thomas H. Huxley, *Science and Education*, ch. 4

2. *Selecting the appropriate verb form.* Determine the subject of each of the following sentences and select the verb form that agrees with it. If there is any problem of agreement, explain your choice of verb in terms of the points made in this section.

1) The wages of sin (is, are) death.

2) All (is, are) well.

3) Comparison of things that are unlike and that, by their uniqueness, (produces, produce) a sense of wonder in us, (show, shows) that the writer is just displaying his own cleverness.

4) Too many metaphors (is, are) a sign of a young writer.

5) "Patience and fortitude," though describing virtues, (is, are) a motto often used to counsel sloth.

6) These United States of ours (has, have) become a great nation.

7) He is one of those people who (is, are) always making trouble.

8) To have loved and to have lost (is, are) an experience most of mankind (has, have) suffered.

9) The bulk of our tax dollars (go, goes) to defense spending.

10) Neither metaphor nor simile (is, are) useful if the image is confused.

3. *Correcting errors in agreement.* Examine the following student theme for errors in agreement between subject and verb or between pronoun and antecedent. Make the necessary corrections. When you have finished, you may find it interesting to compare this writer's careless use of analogy with Huxley's use of the same literary device in the passage quoted in Exercise 1.

The faculty of a college are like a pick-up team in a sandlot game; the members will have varying degrees of competence. The inequality of their skills do not matter much, provided that each of the key players do the assigned job well.

Some faculty teams are more important than others. Thus the English department is central, for if they do not do their job well, the student body as a whole are bound to suffer. The whole curriculum depends on the abilities that the student show in reading and listening. If the students at a lecture were to fail to catch the "pitch" made by the teacher, it would be like catchers on a team which were fielding only eight men, no one of whom were behind the plate.

Committees are the staff which run such faculty teams; these are made up of both administrative officials and faculty members. Their collective jobs is to do one thing: to map the strategy for winning the student body's minds and spirits. They may seek advice from individual players on the faculty, which, after all, are in the best positions to know how the players on the student team is going to act in given situations; but overall, everyone, when the chips are down, defer in judgment to the committees.

The public are the alumni and the parents. Its job is to follow the whole complex of what is going on, to cheer when things at the school is going well, and to boo, by sending letters and criticism, when they are dissatisfied with the particulars that the management have decided on.

4. *Revising a faulty paragraph.* Read the following paragraph carefully, noting whatever errors it contains. Be alert not only to errors in agreement but also to sentence faults or weaknesses. Then revise the paragraph to eliminate errors and to make it read more smoothly.

An analogy is an extended comparison. In the hands of inexperienced writers, the use of this highly complex literary device is dangerous, for none of us, without practice, are able to keep under control all the various parts which, taken as a whole, constitutes an analogy. For example, one may begin an analogy by comparing, as does John Donne in "A Valediction: Forbidding Mourning," two lovers' souls to a pair of compasses:

If they be two, they are two so
As stiff twin compasses are two.

Immediately the phrase "twin compasses" pose a problem, thus creating two different pictures which confuses one: a compass may be either an instrument used in geometry or used in navigation. Thus the phrase "twin compasses" raise the question as to which type of compasses are meant by the poet and what does the comparison imply. If a reader gets off in the wrong direction and thinks that navigational compasses is what is being referred to, he will lose his bearings at the outset, starting to imagine perhaps a definition of love that encompasses such elements as attraction and repulsion. Whereas in completing the analogy Donne clearly has geometrical compasses in mind: the lovers' souls being like the twin legs of the instrument, which is joined together and moves in perfect harmony.

7 Nouns

Nouns are words used in sentences chiefly as subjects of verbs, objects of verbs or prepositions, as complements following a linking verb, as appositives, or as modifiers of other words. They change their form to show number (by adding *-s*, *-es*, etc.) and possession (*'s*, *s'*). A noun may designate a person (*George Washington*, *child*), place (*Spain*, *home*), thing (*pencil*, *steak*), quality (*beauty*, *rage*), action (*hunting*, *logrolling*), or idea (*justice*, *reality*).

The table on page 80 shows the forms, functions, and conventional classifications of nouns. The following sections consider the chief problems that writers have with nouns: plurals, genitives, use of *a* and *an*, and unidiomatic noun modifiers.

7.1 Plurals of nouns

Pl | Correction: Change the noun marked to a Standard plural form.

Most English nouns form the plural simply by adding *-s* to the singular form (*cats*, *girls*, *books*, *things*). If the plural makes an extra syllable, *-es* is added to the singular form (*bushes*, *churches*, *kisses*, *Joneses*).

A few nouns preserve older methods of forming the plural, adding *-en* (*children*, *oxen*) or changing the vowel (*feet*, *teeth*, *geese*, *mice*). Some nouns have the same form for both singular and plural: (1) all words ending in *-ics*, such as *athletics*, *civics*, *mathematics;* (2) the names of some animals, such as *deer*, *fish*, *mink*, *sheep;* (3) a number of words rarely or never used in the singular, such as *barracks*, *headquarters*, *measles*, *pants*, *scissors*.

The following sections consider some groups of nouns whose plurals are likely to cause trouble. There are few hard-and-fast rules, however, and the writer should learn to consult his dictionary whenever he is unsure of a plural form. If the plural of a noun is irregular, it will be shown under the entry for the singular form; if no plural is given, the plural is formed in the usual way.

Nouns ending in -y, -o, or -f

Nouns ending in *-y* preceded by a vowel form the plural regularly

7.1 Nouns: forms, functions, and classes

Forms

Singular and plural forms

Singular: boy, mother, box, child, goose, hero, baby, phenomenon
Plural: boys, mothers, boxes, children, geese, heroes, babies, phenomena

Compound nouns or group words, two or more nouns (written as one word, as two words, or hyphened) that function as a single unit: bookcase, football; pine tree, high school; father-in-law, hangers-on

Genitive or "possessive" form: boy's, Harriet's, gentleman's, girls', cats'

Gender. A few nouns in English have one form for the masculine, one for the feminine:

Masculine: actor, comedian, aviator
Feminine: actress, comedienne, aviatrix

Functions

Subject of a verb: The *tires* squealed as the *car* skidded around the corner.

Object of a verb: The new company manufactured *toys.*

Complement: A whale is a *mammal;* He became *president.*

Object of a preposition: The acrobats were performing inside the *tent.*

Indirect object: He gave the *church* a memorial window.

Appositive: Mr. McDermott, the insurance *agent*, is here.

Modifier of a noun: He thought *cigarette* holders effeminate; *Mr. Tyler's* car was stolen.

Modifier of a statement: *Each year* we make new resolutions.

Classes

Proper nouns, names of particular people, places, and things, written with capitals: Anne, George W. Loomis, London, Monday, Monroe Doctrine

Common nouns. In contrast with these proper nouns, all the other groups are common nouns.

Concrete nouns, names of objects that can be seen and touched: leaf, leaves, road, panda, manufacturer

Abstract nouns, names of qualities, actions, ideas that are perceived mentally: kindness, hate, idealism, fantasy, concept

Collective nouns, names of groupings of individuals: fleet, army, company, committee, bevy

by adding *-s* (*toys*, *bays*, *joys*). But nouns ending in *-y* preceded by a consonant change *y* to *i* and add *-es:*

apology, apologies	curiosity, curiosities	library, libraries
company, companies	ferry, ferries	study, studies

Exception: In forming the plural of proper names, the *-y* is retained and *-s* added: all the *Kellys*, both *Marys*.

Nouns ending in *-o* preceded by a vowel form the plural by adding *-s* (*folios*, *studios*, *tattoos*). If the final *-o* is preceded by a consonant, the plural is usually formed by adding *-es*, but a few nouns add *-s* only:

echoes	potatoes		pianos	sopranos
heroes	tomatoes	But:	solos	tobaccos
Negroes	vetoes		banjos	Eskimos

A few nouns ending in *-o* add either *-s* or *-es* to form the plural: *cargos*, *cargoes; hobos*, *hoboes; zeros*, *zeroes*. Because no rule can be given for adding *-s* or *-es*, a writer must either memorize the plurals or consult a dictionary.

Nouns ending in *-f* often form the plural regularly (*beliefs*, *chiefs*, *fifes*, *roofs*). But some common words ending in *-f* form their plurals by changing *-f* to *-ves:*

calf, calves	knife, knives	self, selves
half, halves	leaf, leaves	thief, thieves

The plural of a few nouns ending in *-f* may be either *-s* or *-ves: elfs*, *elves; hoofs*, *hooves; scarfs*, *scarves; wharfs*, *wharves*.

Words with foreign plurals

Some nouns have two forms for the plural: a foreign plural and the anglicized form ending in *-s* or *-es*. The foreign plural is characteristic of Formal usage, particularly in scientific and academic writing:

Singular	*Formal plural*	*General plural*
antenna	antennae (zoology)	antennas (radio, TV)
apparatus	apparatus	apparatuses
appendix	appendices	appendixes
cactus	cacti	cactuses
curriculum	curricula	curriculums
formula	formulae	formulas
index	indices	indexes

7.1

Singular	*Formal plural*	*General plural*
maximum	maxima	maximums
medium	media	mediums
radius	radii	radiuses
sanatorium	sanatoria	sanatoriums
stratum	strata	stratums
syllabus	syllabi	syllabuses
vertebra	vertebrae	vertebras

Although some dictionaries list alternate plural forms for *phenomenon* and *criterion*, *phenomena* and *criteria* are preferred in both Formal and General writing.

Certain nouns derived from Greek or Latin and ending in *-is* form their plurals by changing *-is* to *-es:*

Singular	*Plural*	*Singular*	*Plural*
analysis	analyses	neurosis	neuroses
axis	axes	parenthesis	parentheses
basis	bases	psychosis	psychoses
crisis	crises	synopsis	synopses
diagnosis	diagnoses	thesis	theses

The word for a person who has been graduated from a college has four forms:

alumnus (ə lum′nəs)	One male graduate
alumni (ə lum′nī)	Two or more male graduates or a combination of male and female graduates
alumna (ə lum′nə)	One female graduate
alumnae (ə lum′nē)	Two or more female graduates

The simplest way out of this confusion of forms is to use the term *graduate* or *graduates.*

Group words and compound nouns

Most compound words and group words form their plurals by adding *-s* to the last word of the group, whether the expression is written as one word or two:

Singular	*Plural*
baby sitter	baby sitters
cross-examination	cross-examinations
major general	major generals

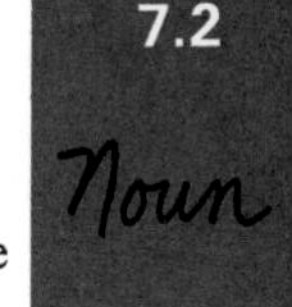

But when the significant word is the first term (as it often is in hyphened compounds), the plural sign is added to it:

daughters-in-law
men-of-war
passers-by
presidents-elect

The plural of nouns ending in *-ful* is made by adding *-s* to the last part of the word: two *cupfuls*, three *tablespoonfuls*.

7.2 Genitive (possessive) case

In English, nouns have only two case forms, the common form (*dog*, *book*, *John*) and the genitive, which is the common form plus an *s* or *z* sound (*dog's*, *book's*, *John's*) or a plural form with no additional sound (*dogs'*, *books'*). An *of* phrase (*of the dog*, *of the book*, *of John*) can function as a genitive and is usually regarded as an alternate form.

Uses of the genitive

The genitive case of nouns is commonly called the "possessive" because its most frequent function is to show possession (a *student's* book, a mannerism *of the professor*). But the genitive case also shows other relationships:

1) Description: a *day's* work, a suit *of wool*, *yesterday's* paper.

2) Doer of an act ("subjective genitive"): the *wind's* force, the *dean's* permission, the permission *of the dean*.

3) Recipient of an act ("objective genitive"): the *bill's* defeat, the execution *of a spy*.

4) Subject of a gerund (see page 60): the *doctor's* warning, the *play's* closing.

Forms of the genitive

In speech, genitive and plural forms are identical, and we can distinguish between them only by the way they are used: the genitive is followed by another noun (The *boy's work* was finished), whereas the plural is not (The *boys worked* hard). It is impossible to distinguish between the singular and plural genitive except in the larger context of what is being said.

In writing, the apostrophe signals the genitive case, and the position of the apostrophe (*boy's*, *boys'*) ordinarily tells us whether a genitive is singular or plural.

7.2

Noun

Correction: Insert an apostrophe where it belongs in the word marked or take out the unnecessary apostrophe.

Position of the apostrophe. Most singular nouns form the genitive by adding *'s*, as do the few plural nouns that do not end in *-s* (such as *men, women, children*):

the *teacher's* remarks (the remarks *of the teacher*)
a *day's* work (the work *of a day*)
the *children's* playground (the playground *of the children*)

Plural nouns ending in *-s* form the genitive by adding an apostrophe alone:

the *teachers'* meeting (the meeting *of teachers*)
the *musicians'* union (the union *of musicians*)
the *Joneses'* relatives (the relatives *of the Joneses*)

Singular nouns ending in *-s* usually form the genitive by adding an apostrophe alone, just as plural nouns do. Some writers add *'s* if an extra syllable would be pronounced, but most feel that the additional *s* looks awkward and use the apostrophe alone:

Mr. *Jones'* [or *Jones's*] business
Delores' [or *Delores's*] father
the *hostess'* [or *hostess's*] gown
the *actress'* [or *actress's*] role

Group words. With group words or compound nouns the *'s* is added to the last term:

The *Queen of England's* duties
her *mother-in-law's* address
the *attorney general's* job
someone else's responsibility

Nouns in series. When two coordinate nouns (joined by *and, but,* or *nor*) are in the genitive, the apostrophe usually is added only to the last one if there is joint possession: *Barbara and Tom's* mother. But if there is individual possession, the apostrophe is used with both nouns: *Barbara's and Tom's* bicycles, *neither Barbara's nor Tom's* teacher.

Plural nouns as modifiers. The apostrophe is not used in some expressions in which the plural noun is considered a modifier: *teachers* college, *Veterans* Administration, *United States* Post Office. Substitution of plural noun modifiers for the genitive is increasing today, and the student should carefully note letterheads, signs, official publications, and the like to determine correct usage.

of phrases and 's forms
The *'s* form of the genitive is customarily used with living things (my *uncle's* house, a *cat's* paw, a *robin's* nest) and an *of* phrase with inanimate objects (the door *of the room*, an angle *of inclination*, the beginning *of the end*). But in many instances either form may be used, the choice depending largely upon the sound and intended emphasis of the expression (the *book's* cover, the cover *of the book*). Some idiomatic expressions are usually stated in one form only (a *week's* wages, a *moment's* hesitation, an embarrassment *of riches*, the wages *of sin*).

Awkward use of 's forms. An *of* phrase is sometimes preferable to an *'s* form to avoid a clumsy or unidiomatic expression or a statement that may be ambiguous. When the modifying noun is separated from the word it refers to by a phrase or a clause, an *of* phrase should be used:

> The apartment *of the woman* who won the contest was ransacked last night. [not *The woman who won the contest's apartment* nor *The woman's apartment who won the contest*]

The *of* phrase is useful in distinguishing between the recipient and doer of an act (between the subjective and objective genitive), particularly if the meaning is unclear in context. *John's photographs* might mean either photographs *of* him or photographs *by* him, but *the photographs of John* would ordinarily mean that John was the subject of the pictures.

The double genitive. In a few statements both the *of* and *'s* forms of the genitive are used, an idiom of long and respectable standing in English: that boy *of Henry's*, some friends *of my father's*, a remark *of the author's*.

7.3 Use of a and an with nouns

The choice between *a* and *an* depends on the initial sound of the word that follows rather than the initial letter. *A* is used before words beginning with a consonant sound:

a car   a European country   a *D*   a used car

An is used before words beginning with a vowel sound:

an ape   an *F*   an hour   an honor   an oar

7.4

Noun

7.4 Noun modifiers

When an adjective is the customary form in an expression, it should be used in place of a clumsy or unidiomatic noun modifier:

> After graduating from St. Olaf, Steve took his *medical* [not *doctor*] training at Northwestern.
>
> After sparking his team to victory in the city championship, Les went on to play with a *Canadian* [not *Canada*] team.

But for words that do not have exact adjective equivalents, the noun forms are freely used as modifiers: a *murder* mystery, *kitchen* utensils, *radio* reception, *prison* walls. In some expressions either the noun or adjective form may be used: *atom* bomb, *atomic* bomb.

Noun forms used as modifiers—particularly units of measurement—are ordinarily singular: a ten-*ton* truck, a six-*foot* jump. (Used as nouns, the forms would be plural: ten *tons* of coal, a jump of six *feet*.)

Exercises

1. *Functions of nouns.* See how well you understand the grammatical terms given in the table on page 80 by identifying the function of each italicized noun in these sentences (subject of verb, object of verb, predicate noun, and so on).

1) Men fear *death* as children fear to go in the *dark*.

2) The *crown's* mounting *hostility* harried the Protestants from the kingdom.

3) Dr. Johnson called this alleged ideal, *patriotism*, "the last *refuge* of a scoundrel."

4) An extra noggin of rum was given to all *hands*.

5) A foolish consistency is the *hobgoblin* of little *minds*.

6) *Every day* Fortune showers her *smiles* upon him.

7) *Age* cannot wither her, nor *custom* stale her infinite variety.

8) *Achilles*' funeral pyre, a *mountain* of flames, gave the *sky* a garish glow.

9) As a jewel of gold in a *swine's* snout, so is a fair *woman* without discretion.

2. *Plural forms.* Read each sentence and then select the noun form you consider appropriate. If the choice is optional, explain the context in which each form would be used. Consult your dictionary if necessary to find the Standard plural form.

1) Nightly, (roomfuls, roomsful) of elegantly dressed (Negros, Negroes) listened to the blue notes from Jack's horn.

2) Delicately the proud (man-of-wars, men-of-war) dipped their masts and fired (eight-gun, eight-guns) salutes.

3) Their (enemies, enemys) stood towering on the crests of the hills and then stormed thunderously into the unprotected (valleys, vallies).

4) The (atom, atomic) blast flowered evilly behind the desert dotted with pale (cactuses, cacti).

5) (A, An) awful explosion set the (axis, axes) of the earth quivering like a slackening top.

6) (Women, Woman) preachers reminded Dr. Johnson of dogs walking on their hind legs; they seemed to one of his companions (fishes, fish) out of water.

7) The chessboard is the world; the pieces are the (phenomena, phenomenas) of the universe; the rules of the game are what we call the (laws, lawes) of nature.

8) The (tactic, tactics) for dealing with (mother-in-laws, mothers-in-law) are known to the fencer: feint, thrust, and parry—mostly the last.

9) The (alumni, alumnus, alumnae), a gaggle of ancient reactionaries, gabbled endlessly about the (syllabus, syllabi) for the new course entitled "Sex and Family Life."

10) Perfect plainness of speech is married to perfect nobleness: so much for Miss Pecunia, whose (tomatoes, tomatos) rhyme with regattas instead of (potatoes, potatos).

3. *Distinguishing between plural and genitive.* Indicate which of the italicized nouns in these sentences are correctly written with *s* endings and which should have *'s* or *s'*.

1) The *energies* of our system will decay, the *suns* glory will dim, and the earth will no longer tolerate the race which has disturbed *its* peace.

2) One of Sir James *Barries* humorous characters said, "Facts were never pleasing to him. . . . He was never on *terms* with them until he stood them on their heads."

3) As flies to wanton *boys*, are we to the *gods;* they kill us for their sport.

4) Allow not nature more than nature needs; *mans* life is cheap as *beasts.*

5) When the *childrens* laughter began to peal in the garden, the *Joneses* neighbors closeted themselves in the drawing room.

6) In the *Poets* Corner of Westminster Abbey, sleep *Englands* silver-tongued *laureates* shades.

7) This famous line of *Tennysons* is familiar to every schoolboy: "The moan of *doves* in immemorial elms."

8) But of "apt *Alliterations* artful aid" *schoolboys* and others must be wary.

9) The king was "the *peoples* prayer . . . the young *mens* vision and the old *mens* dream."

10) A *mans* life of any worth is a continual allegory. Shakespeare led a life of allegory: his *works* are the comment on it.

4. *Correcting errors in noun forms.* Read the sentences carefully, noting any errors. Then make the necessary corrections.

1) The father's-in-laws brow assumed a supercilious arch when the bride'smaid appeared in lavender organdy.

2) Matthew and Mark's gospels warn us of whited sepulchres, men of fair appearings but inner decay.

3) The kingdom of vertebrae embraces ourselfs and all beasts, birds, reptiles, efts, frogs, and fishes.

4) The family down the street's neurosis are as brightly iridescent and exotically ocellated as preening peacocks tails.

5) A dread cross which was once the scourge of innocent peoples is now an insigne of knighthood.

6) Knightes, lady-in-waitings, and even marquises limned upon the lawn an exquisite calligraphy of bright flourishs.

7) Years like great black oxes tread the world and God, the herdsmen, drives them on.

8) The doctor's last bill's effect upon the declining editor's-in-chief health was mortal.

9) One speaks of an armchairs arms often without ones being aware of the petrified metaphor.

10) Though Mephistopheles's eyes danced, Faustus's faintly distinguished the halfs of the devils cloven hoofs.

8 Pronouns

A pronoun ("for a noun") is a word similar to a noun in function, but it does not specifically name a person, place, thing, or idea. Usually it is used as a substitute for a previously stated noun, called its *antecedent*. The meaning or reference of a pronoun is generally evident from its context:

> My uncle phoned last night. *He* is coming by plane.
>
> Men over forty are invited to join. *They* may apply by mail.
>
> Ruth heard that credit cards solved all financial problems. *This* interested *her*.

Pronouns not only enable a writer to avoid an awkward repetition of nouns but also help bind clauses and statements together. Notice how the italicized pronouns in the following passage help give it continuity:

> If the history of the earth's tides should one day be written by some observer of the universe, it would no doubt be said that *they* reached *their* greatest grandeur and power in the younger days of Earth, and that *they* slowly grew feebler and less imposing until one day *they* ceased to be. For the tides were not always as *they* are today, and as with all that is earthly, *their* days are numbered.—Rachel L. Carson, *The Sea Around Us*, p. 157

Pronouns should be used more precisely in writing than they sometimes are in speaking, and they should be checked carefully in revision for proper form and reference. The following sections discuss the most common problems in using pronouns. The table on page 93 lists the various kinds of pronouns and their forms.

8.1 Reference of pronouns

Correction: Change the pronoun marked so that its reference will be exact and obvious; if necessary, substitute a noun for the pronoun or revise the sentence.

Pronouns referring to a definite antecedent

The antecedent of a pronoun should be clearly stated, not merely implied:

Inaccurate	*Accurate*
He had been vaccinated against typhoid, but *it* did not protect him. [No antecedent for *it*.]	He had a typhoid *vaccination*, but *it* did not protect him. [*Vaccination* is the antecedent of *it*.]

Instead of changing the antecedent, it is often better to substitute a noun for the inexact pronoun:

Inaccurate	*Accurate*
She couldn't understand how to make the cake until I wrote *it* out.	She couldn't understand how to make the cake until I wrote out *the recipe.*

A simple test for accurate reference is to see whether the antecedent could be substituted for the pronoun. If not, the sentence needs revision.

Inaccurate	*Accurate*
She talked a lot about the technique of horsemanship, although as a matter of fact she had never ridden *one* [horsemanship?] in her life.	She talked a lot about the technique of horsemanship, although as a matter of fact she had never ridden *a horse* in her life.

The antecedent of a pronoun should not be a noun used as a modifier or a noun in the possessive form:

Inaccurate	*Accurate*
To make an attractive tulip border, plant *them* close together. [*Tulip* is used as a modifier.]	To make an attractive border of *tulips*, plant *them* close together.
Bill provided more excitement one afternoon when he was skipping rocks across the pond and cut open a young *girl's* head *who* was swimming under water. [A noun in the possessive functions as a modifier.]	Bill provided more excitement one afternoon when he was skipping rocks across the pond and cut open the head of a young *girl who* was swimming under water.

Ambiguous reference

Sometimes the meaning of a pronoun is unclear because the pronoun could refer to two different antecedents. The writer should eliminate such ambiguity, either by substituting a noun for the pronoun or by clarifying the antecedent:

Confusing

When Stanton visited the President in February, *he* did not know that *he* would be dead within two months.

Clear

When Stanton visited the President in February, *he* did not know that *Lincoln* would be dead within two months.

Sometimes ambiguous reference may be avoided by making one of the antecedents singular and the other plural:

Ambiguous

In the nineteenth century many businessmen [plural] exploited the workers [plural] at every point, not caring whether *they* were making a decent living wage, but only whether *they* were getting a lot of money.

Clear

In the nineteenth century many businessmen [plural] exploited the workingman [singular] at every point, not caring whether *he* was making a decent living wage, but only whether *they* were getting a lot of money.

Using the same pronoun for different implied antecedents is particularly annoying to a reader and should be avoided:

Confusing

We pulled out our spare, which was under the seat, and put *it* on. *It* dampened our spirits for a while, but we decided to go on with *it*. [The first *it* refers to the tire, the second to the mishap, the third to the trip.]

Revised

We pulled out our spare, which was under the seat, and put the tire on. The flat dampened our spirits for a while, but we decided to go on with the trip.

Identifying the antecedent by repeating it after the pronoun is a makeshift practice that should be avoided:

Clumsy

Boswell first met Johnson when he (Johnson) was fifty-four.

Revised

Johnson was fifty-four when Boswell first met him.

Ambiguity sometimes results from a careless use of possessive pronouns:

Ambiguous

Mrs. Hurst was a very popular woman and *her accusation* scandalized everyone in town. [Was Mrs. Hurst the accuser or the accused?]

Revised

Mrs. Hurst was a very popular woman and *the accusation she made* [or *the accusation made about her*] scandalized everyone in town.

8.1 Pron

Pronouns referring to ideas and statements

This, *that*, *which*, and *it* are often used to refer to ideas or situations expressed in preceding statements:

> Always do right. *This* will gratify some people and astonish the rest.—Mark Twain

> Bits of thread were still dangling from the front of my gown, but we did not bother about *that*.—David Daiches, "A Matter of Degree," *The New Yorker*, May 10, 1952, p. 64

> For "human relations," unfortunately, had generally applied only to relations below that rather vague level called "management," *which* is, in a sense, going at the problem backwards.—William W. Whyte, Jr., *Is Anybody Listening?* p. 111

In such constructions, the idea to which the pronoun refers should be obvious.

Use of who, which, that

Who refers to persons, *which* generally refers to things, and *that* refers to either persons or things.

> Students *who* [or *that*] plan to enter the university in the fall quarter should forward transcripts of their records to the registrar.

> The number of men *that* [or *who*] fell within the age limits of the draft was 3,500,000.

> In five minutes he solved a problem *that* [or *which*] I had struggled with for nearly five hours.

> This is a matter about *which* more information is needed.

Restrictive clauses are usually introduced by *that* and nonrestrictive clauses by *which* or *who*. **See** §12.3.

The use of *which* to refer to persons is Nonstandard usage. *Which* is often used, however, to refer to impersonal organizations of people like groups, clubs, companies, and so on:

> The state legislature, *which* [not *who*] passed the act despite the governor's protest, had its eye on politics.

> The Maryland Company, *which* manufactured farm implements, has gone into bankruptcy.

Use of he or she

The masculine pronoun (*he*, *him*, *his*) is used when referring to a

Kinds of pronouns

Personal pronouns

	Subject	*Object*	*Possessive*
First person			
Singular	I	me	my, mine
Plural	we	us	our, ours
Second person			
Singular and plural	you	you	your, yours
Third person			
Singular			
masculine	he	him	his
feminine	she	her	her, hers
neuter	it	it	its (of it)
Plural	they	them	their, theirs

Relative pronouns

who	whom	whose
that	that	
which	which	whose, of which

Interrogative pronouns

who	whom	whose
which	which	whose, of which
what	what	

Reflexive and intensive pronouns

myself, yourself, himself, herself, itself, oneself
ourselves, yourselves, themselves

Demonstrative pronouns: this, these, that, those

Indefinite pronouns

all	both	everything	nobody	several
another	each	few	none	some
any	each one	many	no one	somebody
anybody	either	most	nothing	someone
anyone	everybody	much	one	something
anything	everyone	neither	other	such

Reciprocal pronouns: each other, one another

Numeral pronouns: one, two, three . . . first, second, third . . .

8.1 Pron

noun or pronoun that includes persons of both sexes (*student*, *teacher*, *clerk*, *everyone*, *anyone*, *somebody*):

> Each entering freshman is required to report promptly for *his* scheduled physical examination.
>
> Everyone who is eligible to vote should make certain that *he* has registered before the deadline.

When practically all of the group being referred to are women, *she* (or *her*) is used:

> A home economics major often finds that more work is expected of *her* than *she* anticipated.

The phrase *he or she* (*his or her*) is nearly always clumsy and adds nothing to accuracy, since the meaning is determined by the antecedent.

8.2 Agreement of pronoun and antecedent

Correction: Make the word marked agree in form with the word to which it is related: with its subject if it is a verb, with its antecedent if it is a pronoun.

To be clear in meaning, a pronoun must agree in number with its antecedent—the particular noun to which it refers. When a pronoun serves as subject, the number of the verb is similarly determined by the pronoun's antecedent. (**See also** §6, Agreement of subject and verb.)

Personal pronouns

Personal pronouns, like nouns, have both singular and plural forms, as listed in the table on page 93. A personal pronoun referring to a singular antecedent should be singular; one referring to a plural antecedent should be plural. Errors in agreement are most likely to occur when a pronoun is separated from its antecedent by some intervening element:

Inaccurate	*Accurate*
Although the average *American* believes theoretically in justice for all, *they* sometimes fail to practice it. [*American* is singular; *they* is plural.]	Although the average *American* believes theoretically in justice for all, *he* sometimes fails to practice it. [*American* and *he* are both singular, as are their verbs.]

Inaccurate	*Accurate*
After reading his *arguments* in favor of abolishing property, I found that I was not convinced by *it.* [*Arguments* is plural; *it* is singular.]	After reading his *arguments* in favor of abolishing property, I found that I was not convinced by *them.* [Both *arguments* and *them* are plural.]

When a pronoun's antecedent is a collective noun, the pronoun may be either singular or plural, depending on the meaning of the noun (**see** §6.2):

> The *class* planned *its* next field trip.
> The *class* had *their* pictures taken.

A pronoun referring to coordinate nouns joined by *and* is ordinarily plural:

> When *Cynthia and Barbara* returned, *they* found the house empty.

Usually a singular pronoun is used to refer to nouns joined by *or* or *nor:*

> *Dick or Stan* will lend you *his* car.

In general, the principles governing agreement between a pronoun and coordinate nouns are the same as those governing agreement between a compound subject and verb; **see** §6.1.

Relative pronouns

When a relative pronoun is used as subject, the antecedent of the pronoun determines the number of the verb and of all reference words:

> George is one of those people who *have* trouble making up *their minds.* [The antecedent of *who* is *people.*]

> George is a person who *has* trouble making up *his mind.* [The antecedent of *who* is *person.*]

Indefinite pronouns

A number of words of greater or less indefiniteness often function as pronouns: *some*, *all*, *none*, *everybody*, *somebody*, *anybody*, *anyone.* Some of these words are considered singular; others may be singular or plural, depending upon the meaning of the statement. In revising your papers be sure that verbs and reference words agree in number with indefinite pronouns.

8.2

Pron

everyone, anybody, somebody. *Everyone, everybody, anyone, anybody, someone, somebody, no one, nobody* are singular forms and are used with singular verbs (Everyone *has* left; Somebody *was* here; Nobody ever *calls*).

Spoken usage and written usage, however, often differ in the form of the pronouns used with these words. In writing, a singular reference word is Standard usage (Everyone brought *his* book); in spoken usage, where agreement is based more on meaning than on form, a plural reference word is often used.

Written	*Spoken*
Not everyone is as prompt in paying *his* bills as you are.	Not everyone is as prompt in paying *their* bills as you are.

But in some statements a singular reference word would be puzzling or nonsensical with the indefinite pronoun:

> When I finally managed to get to my feet, everybody was laughing at me, and I couldn't blame *them* [*him* would be impossible] because I was a funny sight.

all, some, none. *All, any, some, most, more* are either singular or plural, depending upon the meaning of the statement:

> All of the turkey *has* been eaten.
> All of these questions *were* answered.
> Some of the dialog *is* witty.
> Some of the farmers *have* opposed price supports.

None may be either singular or plural, depending upon the context. In current usage it is commonly used with a plural verb, but Formal usage still prefers a singular verb unless the meaning is clearly plural.

> None of our national parks *is* more scenic than Glacier.
>
> None of the charges *has* been proved.
>
> None of the new homes *are* as well constructed as the homes built twenty-five years ago. [The sentence clearly refers to all new homes.]

The emphatic *no one* is always singular:

> I looked at a dozen books on the subject, but no one *was* of any use to me.

each. *Each* is a singular pronoun and usually takes a singular verb and singular reference words:

Each of the so-called modern composers *has his* own ideas about the principles of tonality.

Every June a thousand brides wear identical gowns and *each thinks hers* is somehow unique.

Although the use of the plural form to refer to *each* is considered Informal (*Each* of the boys ran as fast as *their* legs could carry *them*), this construction is sometimes found in writing when the plural idea is uppermost:

Each of these peoples undoubtedly modified Latin in accordance with *their* own speech habits.—Albert C. Baugh, *History of the English Language*, p. 35

However, unless a writer is prepared to justify his use of plural forms with *each*, he should use singular verbs and pronouns.

See also §10.3, Demonstrative adjectives, for agreement of *this* and *that* (*this kind, that sort*).

8.3 Case of pronouns

| Case | Correction: Change the form of the pronoun marked to show how it functions in the sentence. |

Subject and object pronouns

Most personal pronouns and the relative or interrogative pronoun *who* have one form when they are used as subjects (*I, she, he, we, they, who*) and another when they are used as objects (*me, her, him, us, them, whom*). The distinction between these forms (or *cases*) is sometimes disregarded in speech (There were no secrets between Mother and *I*), but writers are expected to follow conventional use (There were no secrets between Mother and *me*). Subject and object forms are listed in the table of pronoun forms on page 93.

After prepositions. The object form of a personal pronoun is used after a preposition (a letter for *him;* among *us* three). When a pronoun immediately follows a preposition, there is seldom any question about the proper form, but when there are two pronouns, or when a noun is used with the pronoun, writers are sometimes tempted to use a subject form, as Nonstandard usage frequently does.

8.3 Pron

Nonstandard	*Standard*
After all, those men are human beings, like you and *I*.	After all, those men are human beings, like you and *me*.
The same is no doubt true of what European and Asiatic nations have heard about *we* Americans.	The same is no doubt true of what European and Asiatic nations have heard about *us* Americans.
The work was divided between *she* and *I*.	The work was divided between *her* and *me*.

After than in comparisons. In written English, *than* is considered a conjunction, not a preposition, and is followed by the form of the pronoun that would be used in a complete clause, whether or not the verb appears in the construction:

> I am older than *she* [is].
> John dances better than *I* [do].
> I like him better than *she* [does].
> I like him better than [I like] *her*.

In speech the object form is common with *than* when the pronoun stands alone (I am older than *her;* My roommate was taking more courses than *me*). It is occasionally found in General writing:

> Although he was two years older she had grown faster than *him*, and in the summer-time they used to wrestle and fight out on the plot of grass by the street.—Carson McCullers, *The Heart Is a Lonely Hunter*, p. 109

In college writing, however, the subject form is preferable in these constructions.

it is I, it's me. Formal English prefers the subject form after the linking verb *be* (It is *I;* that is *he*). But educated as well as uneducated people usually say and write "It's me" or "That's him." *Me* is more natural in this expression because the pronoun stands in the object position, immediately after a verb. All authoritative grammars and dictionaries consider *it's me* acceptable General usage. Fortunately, this construction seldom occurs in writing, except in dialog, where "It is *I*" would sound stilted.

The notion that *I* is somehow more "correct" or polite than *me* sometimes leads people to use the subject form even when the pronoun is the object of a verb: Father took Jerry and *I* to the game. The object form should be used in such constructions: Father took Jerry and *me* to the game.

who, whom. *Whom* is the Standard form when it is the object of a preposition and comes immediately after the preposition (To *whom* were you speaking? He was a man in *whom* we placed great trust). In other constructions, usage is divided:

> Formal: *Whom* are you taking to the concert? [*Whom* is the object of the verb *are taking*.]
>
> General: *Who* are you taking to the game? [Since it stands first, in the subject position, *who* seems the natural form to use.]
>
> Formal: Taxes will go up no matter *whom* we elect. [*Whom* is the object of the verb *elect*.]
>
> General: Taxes will go up no matter *who* we elect.

In college writing it is best to use *whom* in such constructions or to rewrite the sentence so that *who* may be used: Taxes will go up no matter *who* is elected.

Often *whom* is misused for *who* in a mistaken effort to be correct (*Whomever* can that be phoning at this hour?). A writer should always use *who* when it is the subject of a verb:

> He made a list of all the writers *who* [subject of *were*] he thought were important in that century.
>
> There was little doubt about *who* [subject of *contributed*] contributed most to the campaign.

The distinction between *who* and *whom* has practically dropped from speech (the *Oxford English Dictionary* says *whom* is "no longer current in natural colloquial speech"), and it may eventually disappear in writing. But here, as elsewhere in matters of disputed usage, college students should ordinarily follow Formal usage for written work.

Possessive pronouns

In writing, the chief problem in the use of possessive forms of pronouns is the apostrophe. Remember that an apostrophe is not used with the possessives of personal pronouns (a relative of *ours;* the tree and *its* leaves), nor with the possessive of the relative pronoun *who* (a boy *whose* name was Tom).

Possessive of personal pronouns. Personal pronouns have two forms for the possessive (see p. 93): one is used (as a modifier) before a noun (*my* roommate, *her* favorite hat) and the other is used (by itself or in a phrase) after a noun (That pencil is *mine;* a friend of *hers*). While either form may be used in many statements (*our* government, this government of *ours*), there are some constructions in which one form is obviously better than the other:

Clumsy	*Standard*
We decided to pool *their* and *our* resources.	We decided to pool their resources with *ours*.

its, it's. *Its* without the apostrophe is the possessive form of *it; it's* with the apostrophe is the contraction for *it is* or *it has:*

> Everything should be in *its* proper place.
> *It's* [it is] an ill wind that blows no good.
> *It's* [it has] been a long time.

One of the mistakes most frequently marked on student papers is using *it's* for *its*. If you tend to confuse these two forms you should check each instance of *its* (*it's*) when revising your papers.

Possessive of indefinite pronouns. Several of the indefinite pronouns (*all, any, each, few, most, none, some*) are used only in *of* phrases for the possessive:

> They were both happy when things were going well, but adversity brought out the best side *of each.*

The apostrophe and *s* are used with the possessive forms of other indefinite pronouns, just as they are with nouns:

> *Anyone's* guess is as good as mine.
> One man's meat is *another's* poison.
> *Somebody's* books were left in the classroom.

When indefinite pronouns are used with *else*, the apostrophe and *s* are added to *else* and not to the preceding word:

> These notes are somebody *else's.*
> Anyone *else's* offer would have been accepted.

Possessive of who and which. *Whose* is the possessive form of the relative pronoun *who. Who's*, the Informal contraction for *who is* or *who has,* is not used in most writing.

> Best known of American primitives is Grandma Moses, *whose* paintings are familiar to thousands.
>
> It is the white-collar worker *who is* [Informal: *who's*] least likely to be affected by seasonal unemployment.

Although *whose* usually refers to persons and *of which* to things *whose* is regularly used to refer to inanimate things when *of which* would be awkward.

> . . . we would cross a room in which no one ever sat, *whose* fire was never lighted, *whose* walls were picked out with gilded mouldings. . . . —Marcel Proust, *Remembrance of Things Past*, 1:55

8.4 Reflexive and intensive pronouns

The reflexive form of a personal pronoun is used to refer back to the subject in an expression where the doer and recipient of an act are the same:

> I had only *myself* to blame.
> He hurt *himself* skiing.

The same pronoun form is sometimes used as an intensive to make another word more emphatic:

> The award was presented by the governor *himself.*
> Life *itself* is at stake.

In certain constructions *myself* is mistakenly considered by some people as more polite than *I* or *me* (My wife and *myself* accept with pleasure), but in Standard English the reflexive form is not used as the subject or as a substitute for *me:*

> Another fellow and *I* [not: *myself*] saw the whole thing.
> Sam invited John and *me* [not: *myself*] to dinner.

Hisself and *theirselves* are Nonstandard English forms.

8.5 Choice of personal pronoun form

Personal pronouns indicate the person or persons speaking (first person: *I*, *we*), the person spoken to (second person: *you*), or the person or thing spoken of (third person: *he*, *she*, *it*, *one*, *they*). In writing, the choice of form may be a problem since the writer can refer to himself as *I*, *one*, or *we*. Some questions that frequently arise in using these pronouns are considered here.

I, we

There is no reason to avoid the pronoun *I* in any situation where it is needed. Some writers, perhaps through excessive modesty,

8.5 *Pron*

try to get around the natural use of *I* by devices that only call attention to themselves.

Awkward	*Revised*
After exploring the subject, *the writer* finds that mass hysteria is a rather common occurrence.	After exploring the subject, *I* find that mass hysteria is a rather common occurrence.

We is useful for general reference (*We* are living in an atomic age), but as a substitute for *I*, the "editorial" *we* is out of place in most writing.

Awkward	*Revised*
The conclusions in *our* paper are based upon information *we* obtained from the local police.	The conclusions in *my* paper are based upon information *I* obtained from the local police.

you

Overuse of the generalizing *you* (meaning people in general) should be avoided. Its implied reference to the reader may sometimes be irritating:

Awkward	*Revised*
When *you* begin reading *The Waste Land*, *you* are totally confused.	When *I* began reading *The Waste Land*, *I* was totally confused.

Use of the generalized *you* should be confined to situations which genuinely apply to everyone:

> When *you* suddenly enter a dark room, it takes a while for *your* eyes to adjust.

You can be used successfully, as in a familiar essay, when the writer seeks to establish a close relationship with the reader.

one

One is used, particularly in Formal writing, to refer either to people in general or to the writer:

> Watching the scene on television, *one* senses the drama of the situation.

But this use of *one* is impersonal, rather stiff, and often ungainly, especially when *one* is repeated several times. General English characteristically uses personal pronouns in such expressions:

Watching the scene on television, *I* [or *you*] can sense the drama of the situation.

In current American usage, it is standard practice to refer to *one* (meaning the writer or anyone) by the third-person *he* and *his* (or *she* and *her*):

One should be cautious if *he* wants to avoid offending *his* friends.

Avoiding shifts in pronoun form

Correction: Make the words or constructions marked consistent in form. Pronouns should be consistent in person and number; verbs should be consistent in tense.

In using pronouns for general reference, be consistent and do not make unnecessary shifts from singular to plural forms or from *we* to *you* or *one*.

Inconsistent	*Consistent*
After *one* has selected the boat *he* is going to learn in, it would be a good idea if *you* first learned the theory of sailing. Most of *us* have at least seen a sailing boat, but seeing one and sailing one are two different things. *One* might think that a boat can sail only with the breeze and not against it. Or *they* might think that a stiff breeze is necessary to sail a boat.	After *you* have selected the boat *you* are going to learn in, it would be a good idea if *you* first learned the theory of sailing. *You* have probably seen a sailing boat, but seeing one and sailing one are two different things. *You* may think that a boat can sail only with the breeze and not against it. Or *you* may think that a stiff breeze is necessary to sail a boat.

The pronoun *one* is more likely to lead to shifted constructions than are the other forms. Unless you intend to be impersonal and feel confident in your use of *one*, use *you*, *we*, *he*, or a noun substitute in these situations.

Exercises

1. *Selecting the appropriate pronoun form.* Select the pronoun form you consider appropriate in the following sentences. Be prepared to justify your choice.

1) Montmorency was the sort of person who took inordinate delight in studying how the words of each man, woman, or child indicate what kind of person (he, she, they) (is, are).

2) When Montmorency met anybody for the first time, he always tried to distinguish between the personality and the character of the stranger, for he knew that personality was what each man wants the public to see, and (its, their) opinion of him is too often based on appearance.

3) I was struck by what he once told (me, myself), for the remark revealed how his classical training had affected his character. The word "personality," he said, came from the Latin word for mask; once you penetrated the mask, you could decide (who, whom) you wanted to know, (who, whom) in your opinion was worthless, and (who, whom) others might be deceived by.

4) He deduced from this etymology—a sign of his logical nature—that if you look for character in a stranger and another man looks for personality, you can tell better than (he, him) whether the stranger is apt to be a true friend.

5) As an avid reader of novels, he knew that any observer of human character must be able to remember the details of appearance and habit that (he, she, he or she, they) (have, has) observed. Each of us, he characteristically used to say, must also be prepared to judge what (his, their, our) collected memories amount to as each new encounter is experienced.

2. *Agreement between pronoun and antecedent.* Rewrite these sentences, changing the words indicated. Make all other changes that would naturally follow, including those in pronoun, noun, and verb forms. Follow Formal usage throughout.

1) Change *each* to *all:* Over the course of years, I had many occasions to observe Montmorency in action; once he even lectured a novelist, pointing out that each reader must be ready to accept each detail as a fact, unless any given fact is such that each and every reader recognizes that it is impossible for such a thing to have happened.

2) Change *a person* to *people:* The novelist, who was a character in his own right, retorted that, when a person acts in such a way as to seem different from his usual self, he must expect that other persons will think he is acting out of character.

3) Change *anyone* to *everyone:* Montmorency countered by saying that novelists cannot show that what one person does is what most men do. They need only show that what most do, anyone *may* do, even if he is not normally the kind of man to act in this way.

4) Change *this* to *these:* The novelist, who was as argumentative as one of his own characters, remarked that this kind of person, i.e., one who deliberately plays a role, is the hardest to detect, for playing roles involves a deception which may be rooted in the real character that this person wishes to disguise.

5) Change *one* to *some:* I thought it out of character for Montmorency to let the argument die—but perhaps he was tired. He passed off the matter by saying that one actor may interpret the role of Hamlet one way, another another way; if one decides that the role is pathetic, another may decide that his view—the tragic one—is correct.

3. *Correcting faulty pronoun reference.* Revise each of the following sentences in which the reference of pronouns seems to you inexact, misleading, or otherwise faulty.

1) He was, I think, too pedantic to be a good novelist. For example, he would discuss points like this at length: One advantage to capitalizing pronouns which refer to God is that you can always tell when he is being mentioned, as in the sentence, "When the Lord came to Abraham, he had a grievous burden to lay on his shoulders."

2) Montmorency believed that a fictional character, as well as an actual person, tends to play an assumed role, which makes them difficult for some readers to understand.

3) When unimaginative authors let their characters repeat themselves too often, he said, they may bore readers, even though they are trying to make their characterization sharp and clear.

4) Expatiating on the point, Montmorency observed that ineffective authors often think that they need only tell their readers what their characters are like, but unless they are shown them in action they will not be credible.

5) It all depends, he added, on point of view, which is the device of the novelist that is most subtle.

4. *Correcting shifts in person and number.* Revise the following sentences to correct every needless shift in person or number.

1) My high school English teacher was a pedant; for example, he once criticized me for saying, "Creative writers often think teachers use grammar as a means to block your creative abilities."

2) He was also a stickler for consistency; if one began a sentence with "One," he had to continue using it. But this often gets one into trouble, because the number of "ones" increases until one begins to feel that one is awkward, and so he lapses into another pronoun.

3) The English is a funny race and they often speak the king's English in a funny way. My teacher was English, and when one of the English teams came over, they always were played up in his classes.

4) When a student has spent a lot of time on his compositions, they are apt to be disgruntled if all they get is grammatical criticisms. Anybody would feel the same way if you had a teacher like mine.

5) The class was so glad when the end of the term came that they gave him a present—a dictionary. One would have supposed that he would have been happy to get a dictionary, but he never cracked a smile. Maybe each of the students should not have added their sentiments after their names in the inscriptions that the class put in it.

5. *Correcting errors in the forms of pronouns.* Read the following sentences and correct any errors in the forms of pronouns. Follow Formal usage throughout.

1) Authors are a funny breed, for they are quite different from their books. The author whom you think best is often the one whom, as a person, you find is least apt to arouse your interest.

2) We feel especially disappointed when authors arouse our expectation and then do not sustain it, and I feel we are justified in complaining about them doing so.

3) A book in which a man and woman collaborate should deal accurately with human nature, for between him and her they represent the two sexes.

4) My sister and I admire Jane Austen and Charles Dickens, but she admires Austen more than me and I admire Dickens more than she.

5) Many modern detective stories do not play fair with we readers, who are, after all, the public who they are depending upon. They not only conceal clues and evidence but also leave it out altogether.

6. *Revising a faulty essay.* Read the following short essay carefully, noting whatever faults it may have in sentence construction, grammar, and general effectiveness. Be particularly alert to inaccuracies in the use of pronouns. Then rewrite the passage to eliminate its flaws.

"If everybody is somebody, then nobody is anybody" is a sentence which, if memorized, one can use to keep the social distinctions between *everybody* and *anybody* clearly in his mind. Also *somebody* and *nobody*. Persons who are somebodies do not like anybodies coming into their societies. Such an intruder is "different," and if his differences take the forms of eccentricity, they are frequently called a "character."

Now *characters* in this sense can be defined as "that which one is if one hasn't got any." That is, such persons are really not characters at all but only personalities who have substituted peculiar mannerisms for basic character. Unlike characters in books, stories about such people do not show any complexity or density of motivation. Even a consistent character can, by the multiplicity of his reactions and patterns of behavior, show us that men are never merely "flat"—to use E. M. Forster's famous term for one-dimensional instead of real. Forster's opposing term is "round," by which we mean not what it is called today—the so-called "well-rounded character." It is entirely different, being more of a three-dimensional thing whether or not you and I might consider him balanced. Hamlet is like this.

"Flat" characters make what are called "stock responses," in any given situation he will always do or say the same thing. These kind of people are absolutely predictable. And dull, as a result. As far as you and me, the ordinary type reader, is concerned, it is better to read even about round characters that are a little whacky, their being some real insight into the way such people actually are. And people like them get into even good society, as you can tell by looking in our daily paper.

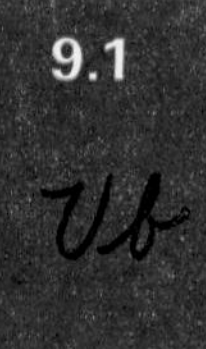

9 Verbs

Vb | **Correction: Change the verb form marked so that it conforms to Standard usage.**

The italicized words in these sentences are verbs:

The hunter *shot* a deer.
Our next speaker *will be introduced* by the chairman.
Are you ready?

Except in questions, verbs usually follow the subject. In meaning, they indicate action (*run*, *manufacture*, *write*), condition (*am*, *feel*, *sleep*), or process (*become*, *grow*). In form, they may be one word (*do*) or a phrase (*should have done*), and may add letters (prove*s*, prove*d*) or change internally (s*i*ng, s*a*ng, s*u*ng) to indicate person, number, tense, and voice. The table on page 109 lists the terms used to describe the principal characteristics of verbs.

The following sections discuss some of the most common problems in the use of verb forms. **See also** §5, Verbals, and §6, Agreement of subject and verb.

9.1 Tense

Correction: Make the tense of the verb marked conventional in form or consistent with others in the passage.

By means of the different tenses, a writer sets the time of the situation he is describing (as happening in the past, going on at present, or occurring in the future) and also shows the continuity of the action or explanation. The consistent and correct use of tense, therefore, is basic to effective writing.

Tense forms

The appropriate form of a verb should be used to indicate each of its tenses. Problems seldom arise with regular verbs, because they have only two forms: the infinitive or base form used for the present tense (*walk*, *imagine*, *sleep*) and a form ending in *-ed*, *-d*, or *-t* for the past tense and past participle (*walked*, *imagined*, *slept*). **See** §9.2 for the forms of irregular verbs.

Except for the simple present and past tenses, English verbs show distinctions of time by various phrase combinations (*have

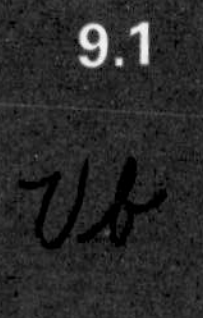

Terms used in describing verbs

Verb forms (§9.1). English verbs have three principal parts:

Infinitive (the base form)	*Past tense*	*Past participle*
ask (to ask), go (to go)	asked, went	asked, gone

Regular and irregular verbs (§9.1 and §9.2). Regular verbs add *-ed* to form the past tense and past participle (ask, asked, asked). Irregular verbs change form in other ways (sing, sang, sung; go, went, gone).

Tense (§9.1). The "time" of a verb's action as expressed in the form of the verb:
Past: I went *Present:* I go *Future:* I will go
(For other tenses, see the table on p. 110.)

Transitive and intransitive.
A verb is *transitive* when it has an object: The teacher *demanded*(V) *order*(O).
A verb is *intransitive* when it does not have an object: He *slept*(V) well.

Active and passive voice (§9.3).
A *passive* verb is a form of *be* and a past participle: *is believed, was believed, had been believed, will be believed.*
All other verbs are *active.*

Mood (§9.4). The manner in which a statement is expressed (an almost obsolete distinction now):
The *indicative mood* expresses a fact or a statement: I *am* thrifty.
The *subjunctive mood* is used in some conditions and in clauses like: It is necessary that he *be* twenty-one.

Auxiliary verb (§9.2). A verb used in a verb phrase to show tense, voice, etc.: *am* going; *had* gone; *will* go; *should have been* done.

Linking verb or copula (§2.1). A verb that "links" its subject to a predicate noun or an adjective: She *is* a teacher. The days *became* warmer.

Finite and non-finite verbs.
A finite verb (from the Latin *finis*, meaning "end" or "limit") can be limited (§6 and §9):

In *person* by a pronoun or subject (I *sing*, she *sings*)
In *time* by a tense form (she *sings*, she *sang*)
In *number*, singular or plural (he *sings*, they *sing*)

Finite verbs are full verbs in sentences and clauses: I *had gone* before he *came.*

The non-finite verb forms (participles, infinitives, gerunds) are not limited in person or number and are ordinarily used in phrases (§5): Before *leaving* I thanked our host. She needed a hat *to wear* to the party.

9.1 Vb

Verb tenses

	I	he, she, it	we, you, they
Present tenses			
Present (immediate present)	ask	asks	ask
Present progressive (continuing present)	**am** asking	**is** asking	**are** asking
Past tenses			
Past	asked	asked	asked
Past progressive (continuing period in past)	**was** asking	**was** asking	**were** asking
Perfect (past time extending to the present; past participle plus *have* or *has*)	**have** asked	**has** asked	**have** asked
Past perfect (a time in the past before another past time; past participle plus *had*)	had asked	had asked	had asked
Future tenses			
Future (future time extending from the present)	will ask **am** going to ask	will ask **is** going to ask	will ask **are** going to ask
Future perfect (past time in some future time; future tense of *have* plus past participle)	will have asked	will have asked	will have asked

Vb

walked, *had walked*, *will walk*, etc.), often supported by adverbs (for example, "he is *about* to go" as a future). The table on page 110 lists the most frequently used active tenses and the verb phrases most commonly associated with time distinctions.

Sequence of tenses

The various past tenses in English serve to distinguish degrees of past time. In necessarily simplified terms, they may be described as follows: the *past* expresses indefinite past time (he *finished*); the *perfect* expresses past time extending to the present (he *has finished*); the *past perfect* expresses past time before some other past time (he *had finished*); the *past progressive* (he *was finishing*) expresses a more extended period of past time. These tenses should be used accurately to express differences in past time.

> He *has finished* [perfect] and *is looking* [present progressive] at television.
>
> He *had finished* [past perfect] and *was looking* [past progressive] at television.
>
> He *had finished* [past perfect] when I *arrived* [past].
>
> He *finished* [past] when I *arrived* [past].

When the verb of a main clause is in the past or past perfect tense, the verb in a subordinate clause is also past or past perfect:

> They slowly *began* to appreciate what their teacher *had* [not *has*] *done* for them.
>
> Up to that time I *had* never *seen* Slim when he *hadn't* [or *didn't have;* not *hasn't*] a wad of tobacco in his mouth.

Exception: A present infinitive is usual after a past verb:

> I *would have liked* very much *to attend* [not *to have attended*] her wedding, but I was out of town.

Consistent use of tenses

Shift	Correction: Make the words or constructions marked consistent in form. Verbs should be consistent in tense; pronouns should be consistent in person and number.

Unnecessary or careless shifts in tense (as from the present to the past, or the past to the future) should be avoided:

Unnecessary shifts

I *sit* down at my desk early with intentions of spending the next four hours studying. Before many minutes *passed*, I *heard* a great deal of noise down on the floor below me; a water fight *is* in progress. I *forgot* about studying for half an hour, for it *is* quite impossible to concentrate on Spanish in the midst of all this commotion. After things *quieted* down I *began* studying again, but *had* hardly *started* when a magazine salesman *comes* into my room. [mixture of present and past]

Consistent

I *sat* down at my desk early with intentions of spending the next four hours studying. Before many minutes *had passed*, I *heard* a great deal of noise down on the floor below me; a water fight *was* in progress. I *forgot* about studying for half an hour, for it *was* quite impossible to concentrate on Spanish in the midst of all that commotion. After things had *quieted* down I *began* studying again, but *had* hardly started when a magazine salesman *came* into my room. [past tense throughout]

In single sentences inconsistencies in verb tenses often occur when a writer shifts the form of two or more verbs that should be parallel:

Shifted

For years I *have been attending* summer camp and *enjoyed* every minute of it.

Consistent

For years I *have been attending* summer camp and *enjoying* every minute of it.

9.2 Irregular verbs and auxiliaries

Some of the most commonly used verbs in English create problems in writing because of their irregular forms or optional uses.

Irregular verb forms

Errors frequently occur in the formation of certain tenses of the irregular ("strong") verbs. The most common mistakes are using a Nonstandard form (He *seen* the show last week) and confusing forms with similar spellings (*choose*, *chose*). The following list shows the principal parts of irregular verbs that sometimes cause problems. The *past tense*, second column, is used in the simple past (She *wrote* a letter). The *past participle*, third column, is used with auxiliaries to form verb phrases (The bird *had flown* away; Soon this *will be forgotten:* The chimes *are being rung*). The past participle cannot be used alone as a full verb in the past tense.

When two forms are given, both are acceptable (He *lighted* a cigarette; He *lit* a cigarette). Forms not listed are Nonstandard and should not be used in General writing. Verbs marked with an asterisk (*) are discussed in the sections following. For verbs not given here, consult a recent dictionary. Caution: If your dictionary labels a form in question *Nonstandard*, *obsolete*, *archaic*, *dialect*, or *rare* it is not suitable for college writing.

Infinitive	*Past tense*	*Past participle*
arise	arose	arisen
bear (carry)	bore	borne
bear (give birth to)	bore	born
begin	began	begun
bite	bit	bitten, bit
blow	blew	blown
break	broke	broken
bring	brought	brought
burst	burst	burst
catch	caught	caught
choose	chose	chosen
come	came	come
dig	dug	dug
dive	dived, dove	dived, dove
do*	did	done
drag	dragged	dragged
draw	drew	drawn
dream	dreamed, dreamt	dreamed, dreamt
drink	drank	drunk
drive	drove	driven
eat	ate	eaten
fall	fell	fallen
fly	flew	flown
forget	forgot	forgotten
freeze	froze	frozen
get*	got	got, gotten
give	gave	given
go	went	gone
grow	grew	grown
hang (a person)	hanged, hung	hanged, hung
hang (an object)	hung	hung
know	knew	known
lay (place)*	laid	laid
lead	led	led

9.2

Infinitive	*Past tense*	*Past participle*
lend	lent	lent
lie (recline)*	lay	lain
light	lighted, lit	lighted, lit
lose	lost	lost
pay	paid	paid
prove	proved	proved, proven
ride	rode	ridden
ring	rang, rung	rung
rise	rose	risen
run	ran	run
see	saw	seen
set*	set	set
shake	shook	shaken
shine	shone, shined	shone, shined
show	showed	showed, shown
shrink	shrank, shrunk	shrunk
sing	sang, sung	sung
sink	sank, sunk	sunk, sunken
sit*	sat	sat
slide	slid	slid, slidden
speak	spoke	spoken
spring	sprang, sprung	sprung
stand	stood	stood
steal	stole	stolen
swim	swam, swum	swum
take	took	taken
tear	tore	torn
throw	threw	thrown
wake	waked, woke	waked, woke
wear	wore	worn
wring	wrung	wrung
write	wrote	written

Forms of the verb be

The verb *be* has eight forms, three more than any other verb in English. In addition to the infinitive, there are three forms in the present tense (I *am;* he, she, it *is;* we, you, they *are*), two in the past tense (I, he, she, it *was;* we, you, they *were*), the present participle (*being*), and the past participle (*been*). The forms of *be* are not troublesome in ordinary situations, but writers should be careful not to use Nonstandard forms.

you was, you were. In the past tense, *you*, *we*, *they* are followed by *were*, not *was:*

Nonstandard	*Standard*
You *wasn't* fooling me, *was* you?	You *weren't* fooling me, *were* you?
We both joined the army when we *was* eighteen.	We both joined the army when we *were* eighteen.

ain't. *Ain't* is a Nonstandard contraction; *aren't* and *isn't* are the Standard forms. In questions with *I*, *am I not* is Formal. *Aren't I* is often used, but displeases many people. Fortunately the forms are rarely needed in writing except in dialog, where the form most natural to the speaker would be used.

Choice of can or may

In all levels of usage *can* is used for ability (This car *can* do better than 80 miles an hour; He *can* walk now with crutches), and *may* for possibility (That *may* be true; We *may* get there before dark).

To express permission, Formal English generally uses *may* (*May* I go now? You *may* have any one you like); Informal and General English increasingly use *can* in such expressions (*Can* I go now? You *can* have any one you like), but many people object to this usage. In writing it is best to use *may*.

do, did, done

The Standard forms of the verb *do* should be used in writing. Particular care should be paid to the past tense and the past participle:

Present tense: I, we, you, they *do;* he, she, it *does*

Past tense: I, you, he, she, it, we, they *did*

Past participle: I, you, we, they have (had) *done;* he, she, it has (had) *done*

Done used alone in forms like "He *done* his best to please her" is Nonstandard.

don't, doesn't. *Don't* is the contraction for *do not* (I *do not*, I *don't*); *doesn't* is the contraction for *does not* (he *does not*, he *doesn't*). The substitution of one form for the other (*Don't* she look pretty?) is Nonstandard.

9.2 Vb

Idioms with do. *Do* is used in many Standard idioms (set expressions): do without, do away with, make do, do one's fingernails. In Formal and General written English avoid Informal expressions with *do*, like these:

> When the Dean of Women arrived, she seemed *done in* [*exhausted*].
> They *did* [*cheated*] the government out of $50,000.

Expressions with *do* and *done* are so numerous in current speech that a writer should consult a dictionary whenever he is uncertain about the standing of any form.

get, got, gotten

The principal parts of the verb *get* are *get*, *got*, and *gotten* or *got*. Note that there are two forms for the past participle.

got, gotten. Both forms are used in the United States as the past participle:

> He could have *gotten* [or *got*] more for his car than that.
> In the past I have *gotten* [or *got*] good meals here.

The choice between *got* and *gotten* in such expressions depends largely upon the emphasis and rhythm of the particular sentence and on the user's speech habits. *Gotten* is perhaps the more common.

have got, have got to. *Have got* in the sense of possession (I *haven't got* a black tie) or obligation (We *have got* to finish this experiment today) is widely used in speech and is acceptable in most kinds of writing. Some writers of Formal English avoid the expression, regarding *got* as redundant and preferring *have* alone (I *haven't* a black tie; We *have* to finish this experiment today). Although *have* alone carries the meaning, it is so frequently used as a mere auxiliary of tense that we do not often consider it as a verb of full meaning. Unless your instructor tells you otherwise, you may use either *have* or *have got* except in Formal papers.

Idioms with get. In many common idioms *get* is Standard usage for all levels of speaking and writing:

get up	get along with (someone)
get away from	get over (an illness)
get ahead	get tired

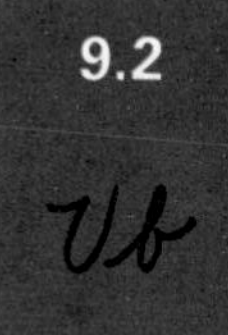

Other expressions with *get* are considered Informal and should be avoided in serious writing:

> Long-winded discussions get on my nerves.
> This modern music gets me.
> Some people seem to get away with murder.
> A stray bullet got him in the shoulder.

When you are in doubt about the standing of an idiom with *get*, consult a recent dictionary.

lie—lay

Lie, meaning to recline, does not take an object. Its principal parts are *lie, lay, lain:* You *lie* down for a rest, or *lie* down on the job; Yesterday he *lay* in bed all morning; The log had *lain* across the road for a week.

Lay, meaning to put or place, takes an object. Its principal parts are *lay, laid, laid:* He *lays* the book on the table; She *laid* her purse on the desk; The cornerstone was *laid* by the mayor a year ago. The same forms are used when *lay* means to produce an egg.

Informal and Nonstandard English use *lay* for both these verbs, but Formal and General English distinguish between them.

sit—set

The verb *sit* (as in a chair) does not take an object. Its principal parts are *sit, sat, sat:* I like to *sit* in a hotel lobby; He *sat* there an hour; I have *sat* in the same chair for three semesters.

The verb *set*, meaning to put something down, takes an object. Its principal parts are *set, set, set: Set* the soup on this pad; They *set* the trunk in the hall yesterday; She has *set* candles in the windows.

For correct uses of *set* in its many other meanings, consult the dictionary.

shall—will

In current American usage, *will* is generally used with all persons of the verb for the future tense (I *will* leave tomorrow. He *will* arrive at six. We *will* return later). To express determination or for emphasis, usage is divided about *will* and *shall* (I *will* not permit it. They *shall* pass). Some Formal writers make the following distinctions between *shall* and *will:*

9.2

Vb

Simple future

First person:	I shall ask	we shall ask
Second person:	you will ask	you will ask
Third person:	he, she, it will ask	they will ask

Emphatic future

First person:	I will ask	we will ask
Second person:	you shall ask	you shall ask
Third person:	he, she, it shall ask	they shall ask

These distinctions are seldom made today except by the most conservative Formal writers.

shall and will in questions. In questions, *will* is used in all persons, but *shall* is often used, especially in Formal English, if there is a notion of propriety or obligation:

> Will I go? Where will we go next? What will you do now?
> Obligation: Shall I go? What shall she wear?

In the negative, *won't* is the regular form:

> What *won't* they think of next?
> Why *won't* you go?

Overuse of shall. *Shall* should not be used in statements where *will* is the Standard form:

> Whether or not Congress *will* [not *shall*] pass the bill is not for me to guess.

Some people apparently think that *shall* is a more correct (or elegant) form than *will*. It isn't.

should—would

Should and *would* are used in statements that carry a sense of doubt or uncertainty:

> It *should* be cooler by evening. [Contrast with the meaning of: It *will* be cooler by evening.]
>
> I wasn't ready as soon as I thought I *would* be.

Should, like *shall*, is often used to express the idea of propriety or obligation:

> You *should* wash your hands before meals.
> I *should* answer her letter this week.

In polite or unemphatic requests, both *would* and *should* are used for the first person and *would* for the second person:

I *would* be much obliged if you could help me.
I *should* be much obliged if you could help me.
Would you please give this your earliest attention?
I wish you *would* write more often.

In indirect discourse *would* and *should* serve as the past tenses of *will* and *shall:*

Direct discourse	*Indirect discourse*
Mary said, "I will go."	Mary said that she would go.
"Shall we adjourn?" the chairman asked.	The chairman asked if they should adjourn.

9.3 Active and passive voice

We frequently have a choice of making a noun either the subject or object in a sentence, with a resulting difference in verb form:

Active verb: Jim's father *gave* him a car.
Passive verb: Jim *was given* a car by his father.

The passive consists of a form of *be* plus the past participle (*is given*, *are chosen*, *was taken*, *have been corrected*).

Appropriate passives

The great majority of English sentences use active verbs, but sometimes the passive is appropriate. Passive constructions are natural if the actor is unknown or unimportant to the statement:

The game *was postponed* because of rain.

The expressway *will be completed* by spring.

The entire fuel-handling operation *is conducted* by remote control, of course, and fresh fuel assemblies *can be delivered* to the storage rack or spent ones *removed* from it while the reactor is in operation. —T. R. Bump, "A Third Generation of Breeder Reactors," *Scientific American*, May 1967, p. 33

A passive verb may also be appropriate if the writer wants to emphasize the object or the act rather than the doer:

The fire *was discovered* by the night watchman.
The bill *is supported* by congressmen of both parties.

9.3

Vb

Inappropriate passives

|*Pass*| **Correction: Change the passive verb or verbs to active.**

Often passive constructions are weak or awkward and should be changed to the more direct active form:

Weak passive	*Active*
A distinction *is made* by sociologists between achieved and ascribed status.	Sociologists *make* a distinction between achieved and ascribed status.
All of the major Russian novelists *were studied* in my comparative literature course.	I *studied* all of the major Russian novelists in my comparative literature course.

It is sometimes awkward to combine an active and a passive verb in the same sentence:

Awkward	*Revised*
The city *needs* more money to build new schools, and it *will* probably *be raised* through a bond issue.	The city *needs* more money to build new schools and *will* probably *raise* it through a bond issue.

9.4 Use of the subjunctive mood

Certain instances of untypical verb forms are known as the subjunctive mood: He *ask* instead of *asks;* I, he, she *were* instead of *was;* I, he, she *be asked* instead of *is* or *was asked.* The use of these forms in current English is quite limited and inconsistent, even in Formal English. There is almost always an alternative construction, and writers seldom need to use the subjunctive.

In conditions

The subjunctive is sometimes used, especially in Formal English, to express contrary-to-fact, impossible, or improbable conditions:

> If I *were* in your position [I'm not], I wouldn't accept his offer.
> He said if he *were* President [he isn't], he would remove them.

The subjunctive is sometimes found in simple conditions:

> If the subject of a verb *be* impersonal, the verb itself may be called impersonal.

This use does not contribute to meaning and should be avoided.

In that clauses

The subjunctive is used in many set expressions (usually in a Formal, often legal, context) for recommendations, demands, and so on:

Formal	*General*
It is required that the applicant *be* under twenty-one.	The applicant must be under twenty-one.
It is necessary that every member *inform* himself of these rules.	Every member should inform himself of these rules. *Or:* It is necessary for every member to inform himself of these rules.
I ask that the interested citizen *watch* closely the movements of these troops.	I ask the interested citizen to watch closely the movements of these troops.

Formulas

The subjunctive is found in numerous formulas, locutions surviving from a time when the subjunctive was used freely:

If I were you	Be that as it may	Heaven forbid
Come what may	God bless you	As it were

Some of these formulas are used in all levels of the language. Some, like *Be it said*, are rather Formal. Informal English uses many petty oaths with this form: *Confound it; Psychology be hanged.*

9.5 Idioms with verbs

Correction: Change the word or expression marked so that it will be idiomatic.

Verbs and verb phrases should be both idiomatically correct and appropriate to the general level of a writer's usage. Some of the verb forms in the following list should be avoided because they are Nonstandard or clumsy. Others are acceptable in Informal or General usage but are sometimes frowned upon in Formal English.

able to: A clumsy and unidiomatic expression when used with a passive infinitive: "This shirt *can be* [not *is able to be*] washed without shrinkage."

9.5

Vb

aggravate, iritate: In Formal usage *aggravate* means to intensify or make worse; *irritate* means to vex or annoy: "The seriousness of his crime was *aggravated* by the prisoner's implication of innocent people." "Stop *irritating* me with those silly questions." Informally *aggravate* is used in the same sense as *irritate:* "I was never so *aggravated* in my life." The distinction between the two words should be observed in college writing.

being that: To introduce a dependent clause of reason or cause, *being that* is an unacceptable substitute for *because*, *since*, or *for:* "Randy decided to major in pharmacy *because* [not: *being that*] his uncle was a successful pharmacist."

contact: Many people dislike this verb as a substitute for "get in touch with someone," although it is widely used in business: "Will you *contact* our Mr. Hubble?" In General and Formal writing "call" or "see" is ordinarily used.

enthuse: Dictionaries label this verb colloquial and prefer *be enthusiastic about* or *show enthusiasm*. While *enthuse* is in fairly common use, it is generally better to use another form in college writing.

fix: In General usage *fix* commonly means repair or prepare (*fix* a broken clock, *fix* lunch for three). It also means to make fast or establish (*fix* the tent to its pegs, *fix* tariff prices). *Fix* is Informal in the sense of to *get even with* (I'll *fix* you for that).

leave, let: Leave means to depart or to abandon; *let* means to permit: "*Let* us *leave* this place." Using *leave* for *let* is Nonstandard.

predominate, predominant: Predominate is a verb: "The captain's will *predominated* throughout the voyage." *Predominant* is an adjective: "His *predominant* characteristic is laziness."

suspect, suspicion: Suspect is the verb meaning to distrust or imagine: "The police *suspected* foul play." *Suspicion* is a noun, and when used for *suspect* is a localism, inappropriate to college writing except in dialog.

try and, try to: Both are accepted idioms: *Try and* is the more common in General English (*Try and* get your work in on time), *try to* is the preferred form in Formal English (*Try to* get your work in on time).

want, want to, want that: In the sense of *ought* or *should*, *want* is Informal: "You *should* [rather than: *want to*] review your notes before the test." In statements of desire or intention, *want to* is the Standard idiom: "I *want you to get* [not *for you to get* or *that you get*] all you can from this year's work." In such constructions *want that* and *want for* are Nonstandard.

Exercises

1. *Identifying verb forms.* For each of the verb forms in the passage below provide the following information: whether the verb is regular or irregular, transitive or intransitive, active or passive, finite or nonfinite. If a verb is a linking verb, identify the predicate noun or adjective which it links to the subject.

She set the coffee on the table, just in the center. Then she dragged the newspaper by one corner in a dreamy walk across the floor, spread it all out, and lay down full length on top of it in front of the fire. Her little song about the rain, her cries of surprise, had been only a preliminary, only playful pouting with which she amused herself when she was alone. She was pleased with herself now. As she sprawled close to the fire, her hair began to slide out of its damp tangles and hung all displayed down her back like a piece of bargain silk.—Eudora Welty, "A Piece of News," *A Curtain of Green and Other Stories*, p. 22

2. *Choosing the proper verb form.* Supply the proper form of the verbs in parentheses in each of these sentences. Some of the constructions call for an infinitive, participle, or gerund (§5).

1) In the saloon the yellow-bearded cowboy pushed aside his beer and slowly (draw) his gun.

2) Tim's fear-(bite) face (whiten) sickeningly.

3) Outside a buzzard (hang) ominously just below the louring clouds.

4) At the hitching post Old Paint nervously (shake) his mane and (paw) the dusty ground.

5) Suddenly a sharp crack (rend) the air.

6) Tim's hat (spin) crazily for a moment over the bar and then (sink) languidly into a pool of (spill) beer.

7) A low moan was (wring) from Tim's quavering lips.

8) Old Paint (begin) a piteous (whinny).

9) The yellow-bearded cowboy brandished his weapon menacingly and (blow) on the smoking barrel.

10) Thereupon the care-(ride) sheriff (ride) up.

11) He had (rid) the town of many varmints heretofore.

12) He suspected that the cowboy was a drunk drover who needed to be (drive) out of town.

13) Passing the door of the saloon, the sheriff (lay) a cautious ear to the (work)-iron window grill, wondering what (lie) within.

14) The yellow-bearded cowboy (swing) his gun up again.

15) The sheriff (dive) through the swinging doors and (wrest) the gun from the cowboy's hand, saving the day.

3. *Using various tenses in sequence.* In the following passage supply the form of the verb indicated in parentheses. Be certain that you use the proper auxiliary verb as well as the correct verb form.

As the action begins, it is clear that the old man (perfect of *rise*) and (perfect of *bid*) the young soldier enter. The audience is aware that the young soldier (perfect of *know*) for a long time that it was the old man who (past perfect of *slay*) his father. When the soldier (past perfect of *return*) from the war, his mother (past perfect of *forsake*) her deathbed to tell him how the old man (past perfect of *steal*) into the house, (past perfect of *find*) the loaded gun on the night table, and, even as the mother (past of *shrink*) into the corner of the room, (past perfect of *shoot*) her husband. (Past participle of *lade*) with this heavy sorrow, her heart (past perfect of *burst*). Within the next few moments of action the young soldier (future perfect of *bind*) the arms of the old man and (future perfect of *begin*) to lead him from the room.

4. *Correcting faulty verb forms.* Correct any errors in verb form that you find in the following sentences. Some of the constructions call for verbals (§5).

1) Caesar, drest in royal robes, set his staff aside and sat upon the golden chair.

2) The people were not use to seeing their leader in this place, ordinarily reserved for special orators.

3) But the leaders of Rome had broadcasted the news that a singular event was to occur.

4) Presently Antony began to wend his way through the crowd.

5) He was following the holy course ran by so many in the past.

6) As Antony neared him, Caesar saw that he bore a diadem writhed about with laurel.

7) A tumultuous shout burst from the crowd when Antony lay the crown at Caesar's feet.

8) But Caesar refused the crown, and again twice more when Antony prest it upon him.

9) Thereupon a new outcry, as of joy, arisen from the populace and beaten upon the surrounding hills and filled the forum.

10) Having thus apparently set aside personal ambition and became a popular hero, Caesar drew nearer kingship.

5. *Using appropriate verb forms.* Which of the verb forms or phrases in these sentences would be inappropriate in college writing? Which would you consider Nonstandard and how would you revise them for General usage?

1) As I lay here on the cold floor, I do not doubt but what my host is insane.

2) Why else did he contact my wife and led me into this trap?

3) Of course, I should of suspicioned that something was amiss when he walked me straight from the front hall to this clammy cell.

4) But I have got to stop dwelling on the past and think of a way out.

5) Above, an aggravating fly keeps hurling himself futilely against the wall.

6) My situation is desperate, being that the ceiling, which is slowly descending, will do me in.

7) If only my fears will leave me be momentarily, I will try and concentrate on escape.

8) To face a situation like this, a man wants that he should be as clear-headed as if he was fresh from a long rest.

9) But I have got unnerved listening at the malicious cackling of my host beyond the door!

10) Should I get out of here alive, I aim to fix that inhuman monster.

6. *Revising inconsistent use of tense.* Read this passage carefully, noting any shifts or errors in tense. Then rewrite it to make it clear and consistent.

Pago Pago fading out of sight in the distance, a strong wind came out of the west. Suddenly, beyond the murky waves, the spout of a whale is seen and the lookout gives the signal. It seems as if the ship had been sleeping and was now suddenly awake. Orders were shouted by the mates and the men race to the whaleboats and lower them into the water. The air was full of excitement as the chase began. The long days of waiting, of carving scrimshaw and letters to be written home were over. Half a mile ahead of them the water churned angrily. The whale had sensed his danger and dove to the bottom of the sea, where he is safe from all harm. But the men in the boats will wait relentlessly until he surfaces again, their harpoons ready in their hands.

10 Adjectives and adverbs

| ad | Correction: Use the appropriate form of the adjective or adverb marked.

As parts of speech, adjectives and adverbs typically are words that are compared by adding *-er* or *-est* (*fast, faster, fastest*) or by being preceded by *more* or *most* (*luckily, more luckily, most luckily*). In sentences we identify an adjective or an adverb by finding the word or word group to which it is related: it is an adjective if it modifies (relates to) a noun or pronoun, an adverb if it modifies (relates to a verb, adjective, another adverb, or the whole sentence.

Adjective	*Adverb*
the *lucky* dog (modifies the noun *dog*)	He *luckily* won the third round (modifies the verb *won*).
The car is *fast* (modifies the noun *car*).	He drove *fast* (modifies the verb *drove*).

Other examples of use are discussed in the sections that follow.

As modifiers adjectives and adverbs describe, qualify, or make more precise the words to which they are related. These modifiers are essential in communication because the basic parts of a sentence—the simple subject, the verb, the object—seldom convey the exact or the full meaning one wishes to give. Note the difference in meaning the adjectives make in the following sentence: The *red* can on the *lowest* shelf contains a *poisonous* gas. Modifiers may add descriptive details (a scene of *pleasant* memories; he laughed *loudly*), limit or make more definite the meaning of a key word (the *first* book; he left *immediately*), or qualify statements (*Perhaps* you've had enough). **See also** §2.2, Secondary sentence elements.

10.1 Position of adjectives

Adjectives offer few problems in English because of their simple forms and relatively fixed positions. The typical position of adjectives (and of participles and nouns used as adjectives) is immediately before the words they modify, though other positions are sometimes possible:

> The coach was a relic with a *decaying* interior of *ancient red-plush* seats, *bald* in spots, and *peeling iodine-colored* woodwork. An *old-time copper* lamp, attached to the ceiling, looked *romantic* [predicate adjective] and out of place. *Gloomy dead* smoke sailed the air; and the car's *heated* closeness accentuated the *stale* odor of *discarded* sandwiches, *apple* cores, and *orange* hulls: *this* garbage, including *Lily* cups, *soda-pop* bottles, and *mangled* newspapers, littered the *long* aisle. From a *water* cooler, embedded in the wall, a *steady* stream trickled from the floor. The passengers, who glanced up wearily when Kay entered, were not, it seemed, at all *conscious* [predicate adjective] of *any* discomfort.—Truman Capote, "A Tree of Night," *Selected Writings of Truman Capote*, pp. 3-4

Two or more adjectives are often placed after the word they modify to gain emphasis or to avoid a clumsy expression:

> Except for a girl, *young* and rather *tall*, the platform was deserted.—*Ibid.*

> . . . the sailors thronged the streets in flapping blues and spotless whites—*brown*, *tough*, and *clean*.—Thomas Wolfe, *Look Homeward Angel*, p. 512

If an adjective is modified by other words, it often comes after the noun:

> The old man, exceedingly *weary* from his trip, lay down to rest.

In some set phrases or conventional expressions, the adjective always occurs after the noun (accounts *receivable*, attorney *general*, president-*elect*, battle *royal*).

10.2 Predicate adjectives

Predicate adjectives—adjectives that follow linking verbs—refer back to the subject (§2.1). The common linking verbs are *be* (*am*, *is*, *are*, *was*, *were*, *has been*), *seem*, *appear*, *become*, *grow*, *prove*, and verbs describing sensations like *taste*, *feel*, *smell*, *look*, *sound*. Sometimes these verbs are followed and modified by adverbs. (The weeds grew *rapidly*). To determine whether a predicate adjective or an adverb should be used, see whether the word modifies the subject or the verb. When it modifies or refers to the subject, use an adjective; when it modifies the verb, use an adverb:

> The children looked *unhappy*. [predicate adjective describing *children*]

10.2
ad

As the rain continued to fall, the children looked *unhappily* out the window. [adverb modifying *looked*]

He turned *abruptly* when he heard his name called. [adverb, describing the way in which he *turned*]

Overnight the weather turned *cold.* [predicate adjective modifying *weather*]

good, well

Good is an adjective (a *good* time; This cake tastes *good*). *Well* is either an adjective (He was a *well* boy; Are you feeling *well?* All is *well*), or an adverb (He writes *well*). Either *good* or *well* may be used as a predicate adjective with the verb *feel*, but with different connotations:

Don't you feel *well?* [referring to a state of health, "not ill"]

It made him feel *good* to pack his own bag and get into the front seat and drive his own car. [referring to a general attitude or bodily sensation—comfort, happiness, well-being]—John Dos Passos, *The Big Money*, p. 319

The use of *good* for the adverb *well* is Nonstandard and should be avoided in writing:

The team played *well* [not *good*] for five innings.

bad, badly

As an adjective, *bad* is the usual form after linking verbs:

She feels *bad.* The milk tastes *bad.* The situation looks *bad* to me.

But *badly* is also used when the emphasis is on the verb: I feel *badly* [or *bad*] about your troubles. Many people object to such uses of *badly*, however, and it is best to avoid them in writing.

10.3 Demonstrative adjectives

This and *that* (called demonstrative adjectives) are the only adjectives with plural forms: *this* idea, *these* ideas; *that* project, *those* projects. They are often used with *kind* and *sort*, which are singular nouns and should be preceded by singular modifiers (*this* kind of clouds, *that* sort of people). In spoken English *these* or *those* is sometimes used with *kind* or *sort* when a plural noun occurs in a following phrase (I like *these* kind of *records* best;

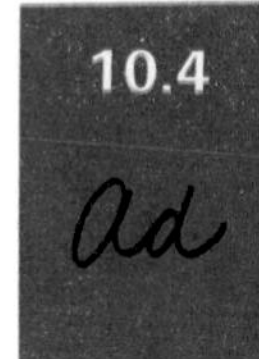

Those sort of *jokes* annoy me). But in Formal and General usage both words should be treated as singular:

> I like *this* kind of records best.
> Jokes of *that sort* annoy me.

10.4 Forms of adverbs

A number of common adverbs (*now*, *quite*, *there*, *too*) have no distinctive forms, but the majority of adverbs are made by adding *-ly* to an adjective: *accidental-ly*, *particular-ly*, *real-ly*, *sincere-ly*. A few adjectives ending in *-ly* (*early*, *likely*) are also used as adverbs.

Although adverbs can be made by adding *-wise* to a noun (*lengthwise*, *sidewise*), this practice has been greatly overused (*budget-wise*, *economy-wise*). It is better to avoid such words in General and Formal writing.

Long and short forms of adverbs

Some adverbs have two forms: one with an *-ly* ending (long form), the other without (short form): *slow—slowly*, *loud—loudly*, *tight—tightly*. Adverbs used with or without the *-ly* ending include:

bright	even	rough	straight
cheap	fair	second	tight
close	loose	sharp	wrong
deep	loud	slow	
direct	quick	smooth	

The long and short forms are often interchangeable:

> Go *slow*. Go *slowly*.
> Don't talk so *loud*. Don't talk so *loudly*.
> The rope was drawn *tight*. The rope was drawn *tightly*.

But in some situations the long and short forms are not interchangeable. The long forms are used between *to* and the base form of a verb (*to wrongly accuse*, not *to wrong accuse*) and generally between the subject and verb (They *closely* watched). The short forms are used more with short words: *new* found friends, but *newly* acquired rank. Formal writers tend to use the long forms, General and Informal more of the short forms. But since comprehensive rules cannot be given, each writer has to choose

10.4

ad

between the forms largely on the basis of the tone and sound of his sentence.

Bobtailed adverbs
When an adverb has only the *-ly* form, care should be taken not to drop the ending. Some temptations are *considerably*, *seriously*, and *differently:*

> Twenty-five dollars is *considerably* more than I want to pay. [not *considerable*]
> People often told him that he should take things more *seriously*. [not *serious*]
> He worked *differently* from the others. [not *different*]

Dropping the *-ly* in such words is a characteristic of Nonstandard usage or of extremely Informal conversation. A dictionary will tell what the Standard adverb form is.

The bobtailed adverbs most likely to be found in writing are *bad*, *real*, *sure*. In Standard English these forms are adjectives only; the adverbs have *-ly:*

> He danced *badly*.
> It was a *really* outstanding performance.
> They were *surely* enjoying themselves.

most, almost
In Formal and General English *most* is not used for the adverb *almost*, meaning "very nearly":

> I *almost* lost my mind. [adverb, modifying the verb *lost*]
>
> The train was *almost* always on time. [adverb, modifying the adverb *always*]
>
> *Most* fishermen are optimists. [adjective, modifying *fishermen*]
>
> *Almost* all fishermen are optimists. [adverb, modifying the adjective *all*]

10.5 Position of adverbs

Adverbs modifying a single word
Unlike adjectives, adverbs can have various positions in the sentence. But they should be placed in a position that clearly indicates the writer's intended meaning and desired emphasis.

When an adverb modifies a single word, its typical position is immediately before that word:

a *quite* late affair [modifies *late*]
They *never* finished the job. [modifies *finished*]

This often puts the modifier of a verb between an auxiliary and participle:

He had *quietly* withdrawn.

A modifier of a verb often follows the verb or comes after the verb and its object:

He withdrew *quietly*.
They finished(V) the job(O) *hurriedly*.

See also §5.2, p. 63, Split infinitives.

Sentence adverbs

A good many adverbial modifiers—single word adverbs, phrases, or clauses—cannot sensibly be related to another single word in a sentence. It is conventional to say that these adverbs "modify the whole sentence" and to call them *sentence adverbs*. Their position is variable:

Unfortunately they had already left.
They had already left, *unfortunately*.
They had *unfortunately* already left.

This flexibility makes it possible to shift the position of many sentence adverbs for variety as well as for emphasis.

Misplaced adverbial modifiers

Correction: Revise the sentence so that the expression marked is clearly related to the word or statement it modifies.

A writer should be careful not to misplace a modifier so that the meaning of a statement becomes ambiguous or even ludicrous:

Ambiguous: Using several pen names, the two editors have almost written every article in the magazine. [*almost* seems to modify *written*]

Clear: Using several pen names, the two editors have written *almost* every article in the magazine.

Modifiers are sometimes placed so that they could refer to either one of two elements; these are sometimes called "squinting modifiers":

> Although it was yearly said that the old boat would sink *somehow* it seemed blessed with unsinkability. [*Somehow* might modify the preceding verb *sink* or the following clause. Adding a comma after *sink* would clear up the ambiguity.]

In some constructions, misplacing the modifier may alter the intended meaning:

> The way I can stand in front of a store window and persuade myself that I need useless articles *even* surprises me. [intended meaning: *surprises even me*]

See also §5.3, Misrelated modifiers, and §5.4, Dangling Modifiers, for a discussion of the placement of verbal modifiers.

Position of <u>only</u> and similar adverbs

In Formal usage, limiting adverbs like *only*, *merely*, *hardly*, *just* are placed immediately before the element they modify:

> I need *only* six more to make a full hundred.
> The audience seemed *hardly* to breathe when the girl began speaking.

In spoken usage limiting adverbs usually stand immediately before the verb:

> I *only* need six more to make a full hundred.
> The audience *hardly* seemed to breathe when the girl began speaking.

This pattern, typical of spoken English, is usual in General writing, when no misunderstanding of the author's meaning will occur:

> When the brilliant lightweight boxer, Kid Lewis, stood for Parliament in his native borough, he *only* scored a hundred and twenty-five votes.—George Orwell, *The English People*, p. 11

> He *only* remembers one verse of the song and he has been repeating it.—Eugene O'Neill, *A Moon for the Misbegotten*, p. 72

It is possible to misplace *only* so that it seems to belong to a word that it cannot sensibly modify:

> Nonsensical: He had *only* a face a mother could love.
> Accurate: He had a face *only* a mother could love.

10.6 Double negatives

NS Correction: Change the Nonstandard expression to one that is appropriate to Standard usage.

A statement in which a second negative needlessly repeats the meaning of the first negative is called a *double negative:* "The trip will *not* cost you *nothing*." Such constructions, once acceptable in English, are now Nonstandard idioms and should be rephrased: "The trip will cost you *nothing*" or "The trip will *not* cost you anything."

Writers usually make few mistakes with obvious double negatives like *not* and *nothing*, but they need to watch the concealed ones, when *not* is combined with *but* or with adverbs of negative meaning such as *hardly*, *barely*, *scarcely*.

can't hardly, couldn't scarcely
Such Nonstandard expressions as "I can't hardly hear you" and "There wasn't scarcely enough money left to pay the taxes" are double negatives, because *hardly* and *scarcely* in this sense mean *almost not*. The Standard idioms that should be used in writing are "I *can* hardly hear you" and "There *was* scarcely enough money left to pay the taxes."

can't help but
The construction *can't help but* (or *cannot help but*) is an established idiom. Many writers, however, avoid it, using instead one of the expressions in the following sentences:

I *cannot but* feel sorry for him. [Formal]
I *can't help feeling* sorry for him. [General]

but what
The expression *but what* is Nonstandard usage in negative expressions such as "I don't doubt *but what* he will come." Standard English is "I don't doubt *that* he will come."

irregardless
Regardless is the Standard usage. The suffix *-less* is a negative ending; the addition of the negative prefix *ir-* in *irregardless* creates a double negative.

10.7

ad

10.7 Comparison of adjectives and adverbs

Comp | Correction: Make the comparison of adjectives or adverbs more accurate or more appropriate.

Most adjectives and adverbs have three different forms to indicate degrees of the characteristic they name. The positive degree (or simple form of the modifier) expresses no comparison (*red*, *slow*, *seriously*); the comparative degree represents an increase or decrease of the positive form, or makes a specific comparison between two things (*redder*, *slower*, *more seriously*, or *less seriously*); the superlative indicates the greatest (or least) degree among three or more things (the *reddest* apple of all, the *slowest* runner on the team, the *most*—or *least*—seriously presented argument).

Forms of comparison

Most adjectives and adverbs are compared in one of two ways: by adding *-er*, *-est* to the positive form, or by prefixing *more*, *most* (or *less*, *least*).

	Positive	*Comparative*	*Superlative*
Adjectives	hot	hotter	hottest
	brilliant	more brilliant	most brilliant
	expensive	less expensive	least expensive
Adverbs	near	nearer	nearest
	sincerely	more sincerely	most sincerely
	often	oftener, more often, less often	oftenest, most often, least often

In general, the *-er*, *-est* forms are used with words of one syllable (*longer*, *driest*), and *more*, *most* with words of more than two syllables (*more interesting*, *most rapidly*). With two-syllable words a writer often has a choice of either form (*abler*, *more able; easiest*, *most easy*). The sound of the expression may determine which form is used:

> His step was *steadier* and *more elastic*. Even his bloodshot eyes looked *fresher*, and his hair and beard were *softer*.—Eyvind Johnson, *Return to Ithaca*, p. 260

A few common modifiers form the comparative and superlative degrees irregularly:

bad	worse	worst
good, well	better	best
far	farther, further	farthest, furthest
little	less, lesser, littler	least, littlest
many, some, much	more	most

worse, worst. *Worst* is the appropriate form for the superlative: That was the *worst* [not *worse*] show I have ever seen.

farther, further. In Formal English a distinction is sometimes made between *farther*, referring to physical distance (It was six miles *farther* to town), and *further*, referring to abstract degree (We will study these suggestions *further*). In General English, *further* is commonly used for both distance and degree.

Use of the comparative form

The comparative form of an adjective or adverb is ordinarily used when two things are compared:

> You're a *better* man than I am, Gunga Din!
> Blood is *thicker* than water.
> She works *more diligently* than her roommate.

But in some expressions the comparative form is used when no actual comparison is mentioned (higher education, the lower depths, Better Business Bureau). In others, the reader is left to supply the comparison (Look younger, live longer). Writers of advertising copy are particularly fond of this absolute use of the comparative because of the favorable inferences the reader may draw: Smoke a *milder* cigarette; More protection for *fewer* dollars; Sudso gets clothes *cleaner*. Avoid this construction in Formal writing.

Use of the superlative form

The superlative form ordinarily indicates the greatest degree among three or more persons or things:

> He was voted the member of his class *most likely* to succeed.
>
> Many critics consider *King Lear* the *greatest* of Shakespeare's tragedies.

In spoken English the superlative is sometimes used for comparing two things (He put his *best* foot forward). The same construction is occasionally seen in writing, but this usage is regarded as somewhat Informal. In college writing, it is better to keep the superlative for comparisons among three or more.

Superlative forms also occur in expressions in which no direct comparison is implied (*best* wishes, *deepest* sympathy, *highest* praise, *most* sincerely yours). The form with *most* is frequently used as an intensive to signify a high degree:

> For example, Herbert Spencer (1820-1903), a *most* influential English philosopher. . . . —Melvin Rader, *Ethics and Society*, p. 46

The Informal use of a heavily stressed superlative to indicate nothing more than general approval (the "feminine intensive") should be avoided in serious writing:

> Hasn't she the *sweetest* voice? (Better: Hasn't she a *sweet* voice?)

Comparison of unique and similar words

Some people regard words such as *unique, perfect, dead, empty* as logically incapable of comparison or qualification because their positive forms express absolute states. But in actual usage these terms are often qualified or modified by comparative forms, as in the following examples:

> We, the people of the United States, in order to form a *more perfect* union . . . . —Preamble to the Constitution of the United States

> . . . The *more unique* his nature, the more peculiarly his own will be the coloring of his language.—Otto Jespersen, *Mankind, Nation, and Individual from a Linguistic Point of View*, p. 204

Whether words like *unique* should or should not be qualified is a matter that can be determined only by appropriateness. In college writing, they should ordinarily be used without qualification; invested with their full meaning, they are valuable words that say something precisely.

10.8 Making comparisons idiomatic

Correction: Change the expression marked so that it will be idiomatic.

In writing, expressions of comparison should be more carefully and more fully stated than they often are in speaking. Expressions that might pass unnoticed in conversation (such as *all the higher the ladder will reach* or *the slowest of any runner on the team*) are too slipshod to be used in careful writing (where the same ideas would be expressed: *as high as the ladder will reach* and *the slowest runner on the team*).

Comparing comparable things

When using comparisons in your writing, make certain that the things compared are of the same kind and actually comparable:

Terms not comparable	*Comparable terms*
The rhinoceros has a hide almost as tough as an alligator [*hide* and *alligator* are not comparable].	The rhinoceros has a hide almost as tough as that of an alligator [or *as an alligator's*].
One reviewer compared these short stories to O. Henry.	One reviewer compared these short stories to those written by O. Henry [or *to O. Henry's*].

Completing comparisons

Statements involving comparisons should be written out in full, particularly if any misunderstanding might arise through shortening one of the terms:

Ambiguous	*Clearer*
I owe him less than you.	I owe him less than I owe you. *Or:* I owe him less than you do.
He admires Eliot less than other modern poets.	He admires Eliot less than other modern poets do. *Or:* He admires Eliot less than he does other modern poets.

Double comparisons with *as . . . as, if . . . than* should be filled out in writing.

> He is *as* tall *as, if* not taller *than*, his brother. [*not:* He is as tall if not taller than his brother.]
>
> The styles vary *as* much *as, if* not more *than*, the colors.

Since the *if . . . than* construction tends to interrupt sentence movement, it is usually preferable to complete the first comparison and then add the second, dropping *than:*

> He is as tall as his brother, if not taller.
> The styles vary as much as the colors, if not more.

10.8
ad

Use of other in comparisons

Other is used when the comparison involves things of the same class, but not when the things being compared belong to two different classes:

> She is a better dancer than the *other* girls.
> She dances better than any [not *any other*] boy in school.
> *Blithe Spirit* was more successful than the *other* plays we produced.
> I think movies are more entertaining than any [not *any other*] book.

Other is not used with superlative comparisons:

> Pavlova was the best of all the [not *all the other*] Russian ballerinas.

> The Egyptians had attained the highest skill in medicine that had up to that time been achieved by any [not *any other*] nation.

Use of like or as in comparisons

To introduce a prepositional phrase of comparison, *like* is Standard usage:

> They are *like* two peas in a pod.
> He looks *like* his father.
> Bicycle riding, *like* golf, can be enjoyed at almost any age.

In college writing, *as* should not be substituted for *like* or *such as* in prepositional phrases like this:

> Some writers *like* [not *as*] Faulkner and Caldwell take their material from a particular region.

To introduce a clause of comparison with a definite subject and verb, Formal and General English both prefer *as*, *as if*, *as though* to *like:*

> He acted *as if* he didn't feel well.
> He wanted to be a doctor *as* his father had been.
> She took to cooking *as* a duck takes to water.

The use of *like* as a conjunction has increased in recent years and is slowly gaining respectable status:

> "Suddenly everybody wanted to look like he came from Harvard, or like he thought everyone looked at Harvard," says Grossman.—*Time*, Feb. 28, 1964, p. 83

However, many people are prejudiced against the use of *like* to introduce clauses, and the preferred forms *as*, *as if*, *as though* should ordinarily be used in college writing.

Exercises

1. *Functions of modifiers.* First determine what word or statement each of the italicized forms modifies. Then identify each form, according to its modifying function, as an adjective, predicate adjective, or adverb.

1) His (1) *pale* mild eyes, (2) *receding* lower jaw, and slight frame could never have expressed (3) *much* vigor, (4) *bodily* or mental. . . . His threadbare clothes were (5) *thoroughly* brushed; his soft white hair was (6) *carefully* parted and arranged; he was not a (7) *neglected-looking* old man; and at his side a fine black retriever, (8) *also* old, sat on its haunches and watched him as he went (9) *to and fro.*—George Eliot, *Felix Holt*, ch. 1

2) As I gazed (1) *out* through the (2) *mullioned* window, which was (3) *eerie* to see because of its (4) *complexly* (5) *curving* distortions, I could see, (6) *outside*, what looked like as (7) *unlikely* a garden of flora and fauna as the hand of man had ever put (8) *together*. There were (9) *silvery* birches ranged (10) *thickly* in rows with reddening sequoias, (11) *fast-growing* fields of (12) *rocket* weed interspersed with beds of roses that looked to be (13) *full-blown.*

2. *Selecting the appropriate modifier.* Select the adjective or adverb form that seems appropriate in each of these sentences and give the reason for your choice. If both forms are possible, indicate when each would be used.

A Hollywood studio presents a scene that defies description. Side by side, you can see, (clear, clearly) as day, sets from Morocco and Antarctica. Much of the construction is made so (cheap, cheaply) that it will not last (long, for long) but it looks (real, really) (good, well) at first glance. As you swing down the main street of a western town, you can imagine yourself in a two-man gunfight, drawing your six-shooter out (smooth, smoothly) as silk; you have no fears about the outcome, for you know that the (best, better) man always wins because he shoots (straighter, straightest). Around the corner you stop and stare at one of the (goldarndest, most goldarn) sights you ever saw—a great ape driving a limousine (worse, more badly) than a Keystone cop would. Past that, you come upon a grim, gaunt building set in a swamp, and you hold your arms (close, closely) to your sides in fear. It looks so real you shiver, (slow, slowly) at first, and then with (increasing, increasingly) rapid shudders. Broadway chorus girls dancing (high and mighty, highly and mightily) on a great raised stage next catch your eye and hold it (fixed, fixedly). With so much to see, it is difficult to know what to look at (most, mostly).

3. *Recognizing double negatives.* In the following sentences, point out which expressions are "double negatives" and show how they should be corrected. Explain why the negatives in other sentences are correct.

1) It is best, when you speak of a vacuum, not to refer to it as "nothing." A vacuum is not nothing.

2) A vacuum may not be the least perceptible thing in the universe, but nothing comes closer to being so, not to my knowledge.

3) Nobody can say that he has not seen something when he looks at a vacuum, disirregardless of what anybody says.

4) A vacuum hasn't hardly any properties at all.

5) I do not have any doubts but what you know that a vacuum exists even if you can't scarcely prove that it exists.

4. *Placement of modifiers.* Study the following sentences carefully and state where you would place the modifier within each sentence. If more than one position is possible, explain what change of emphasis would result from shifting the modifier.

1) Add *certainly:* The fields were carpeted with snow that had fallen in the night, for there had been none yesterday.

2) Add *scarcely:* Some had landed, oddly enough, on the back patio, where the wind was now blowing.

3) Add *almost:* Farther out in the yard, the doghouse was covered to the roof so that it looked like a small mound of cotton.

4) Add *even:* The garden walks were so obliterated by drifts that my father, who had laid out the garden, did not know where they were.

5) Add *more or less:* You could tell where one path went by following the clothesline, which had a ridge of snow that made it visible from the house.

6) Add *only:* Yesterday I had seen the yard with a few flowers growing.

7) Add *definitely:* "It's beautiful to look at," my father said, "but you'll have to shovel the walks because your mother will want to hang out the wash she did last night."

8) Add *better:* Picking up the old battered shovel, I went out into the bitter wind, knowing I would be able to get the job done before the snow hardened.

9) Add *hardly:* Although I walked on the white snow-blanket softly, I had taken a few steps when I fell in a position from which I could extricate myself.

10) Add *merely:* Because it was a moderate snowfall, I laughed and went on with my work.

5. *Modifiers in Formal usage.* Some of the adjective and adverb forms and expressions of comparisons in these sentences would be inappropriate in college writing. Revise these and briefly explain the reason for the revision.

1) The ship lay in the harbor like it was a natural fixture.

2) It had been there so long that the weather had turned it more wharf-colored.

3) Many things would be needed to refurbish it, as caulking, paint, new masts, and glass for portholes.

4) All in all, it was the most 19th-century sight in the town.

5) The ship looked as much if not more pathetic than an old hound lying forgotten-like nearby a deserted farmhouse.

6) Still, the scene was real fine artwise, and camera enthusiasts were taking pictures most every clear day of the year.

7) Picturesque as the sight was, everyone agreed it was the saddest.

8) I thought wistfully of how trim and noble the ship must have been in her heyday, what with her tall masts and most every sail stretching out to catch the wind.

9) The reason for its being there was most unique; the owner had died of a sudden before he could make it into a museum.

10) A sailing ship is the most romantic, because it pits man against the elements more than any other motorized boat does.

11) To sit on the wharf and watch the old ship rot, that's what made me feel badly.

12) Much the most dreariest of sights is watching anything lose its former beauty.

13) I only wished I could have seen her in her prime, when she was shipshape.

14) Her prow was cut sharp back, so that she could cleave the waves like a knife through hot butter.

15) She was clearly the best of all the other ships I have ever seen, bar none.

11 Periods, question marks, and exclamation marks

Good punctuation is possible only in good writing. If sentence structure is lame or stiff, punctuation is only patchwork, helping after a fashion but also showing how bad the word pattern is.—George Summey, Jr.

11.1 ⊙

Because they are used mainly as marks of termination, periods, question marks, and exclamation marks are sometimes known as *end stops.* One of these three punctuation marks is needed at the end of every complete sentence. The great majority of sentences are statements, requiring a period (.). Direct questions are followed by a question mark (?), and emphatic or exclamatory statements are terminated by an exclamation mark (!).

Periods and questions marks have several conventional uses in addition to their function as end stops.

11.1 Periods

| ⊙ | Correction: Insert a period at the place marked.

After statements

A period is used to mark the end of all sentences that are not direct questions or exclamations:

> Madagascar is an island off southeast Africa.
> Holmes was not frightened by the threats.
> "Where is he now?" she asked. "Tell me."
> "In Madagascar."
> "Oh."

After indirect questions and courtesy questions

An indirect question is really a statement *about* a question. It is always followed by a period rather than a question mark.

Indirect	*Direct*
He asked us where we got the money.	Where did you get the money?
Ask yourself if you are satisfied with your present income.	Are you satisfied with your present income?
They wanted to know what I had been doing since I graduated.	What have you been doing since you graduated?

In General usage a polite request phrased as a direct question is often followed by a period rather than a question mark:

Will you please return this copy as soon as possible.
May we hear from you at your earliest convenience.

After abbreviations
A period is conventionally used after most abbreviations:

Mr. H. L. Matthews	Mt. Blanc	Ph.D.
St. Paul, Minn.	Oct.	etc.
R.S.V.P.	D.D.S.	*ibid.*

Periods are sometimes omitted from the abbreviated names of organizations, especially if they are made from initial letters: UNESCO, GOP, VISTA. Consult an up-to-date dictionary for the preferred form of particular abbreviations. If usage is divided (U.S.S.R., USSR), follow a consistent style throughout your paper. (**See** §18.1, Abbreviations.)

With figures
A period (decimal point) is used before fractions expressed as decimals and between whole numbers and decimals:

.05	4.6	3.14159	95.6%

A period is also used to separate dollars and cents in sums of money written with a dollar sign:

$4.98	$ .98	*but* 98 cents	98¢

See §15.3 for periods used as ellipses to mark the omission of words.

11.2 Question marks

| ? | Correction: Punctuate this sentence (or sentence element) with a question mark.

After direct questions
A question mark is used after a sentence expressing a direct question:

What can we do?
Did Napoleon dislike Elba?
Really?

When a sentence begins with a statement but ends with a question, the ending determines the punctuation:

Perhaps this explanation is poor, but is there a better one?

After questions within a sentence

11.2 ?

A question mark stands immediately after a question that is included within a sentence:

Someone once remarked (wasn't it Mark Twain?) that old second-hand diamonds are better than no diamonds at all.

Thirty years ago—remember?—most people had never flown.

"Are you engaged?" he blurted.

When a question mark and quotation mark fall together, the question mark falls inside if only the quotation is a question, outside if the whole sentence is a question:

He asked himself, "Is this the best of all possible worlds?"
Do you agree that this is "the best of all possible worlds"?

To indicate a doubtful statement

A question mark is used, with or without parentheses, to show that a statement is approximate or questionable:

Geoffrey Chaucer, 1340(?)-1400
Geoffrey Chaucer, 1340?-1400

A question mark placed in parentheses to indicate humor or mild sarcasm is usually crude and better omitted:

She gave him an innocent (?) wink from behind her fan.

11.3 Exclamation marks

! Correction: Insert or remove exclamation mark at the place indicated.

An exclamation mark, or point, is used after an emphatic interjection (Oh! Ouch! Fire! Help! No, no, no!) and after statements that are genuinely exclamatory:

The building had disappeared overnight!
What torments they have endured!

Exclamation marks are far less common in factual writing than in fiction, where the dialog may require strong marks of emphasis:

> The Duke's gloved hands shook and shimmered. "I'll throw them up for grabs betwixt the Todal and the geese! I'll lock them in the dungeon with the thing without a head!"—James Thurber, *The 13 Clocks*, p. 94

Don't use an exclamation mark unless the statement itself is genuinely emphatic. An exclamation mark will not add weight to a simple statement of fact. The use of double and triple marks is the sign of an immature writer who probably has little to say:

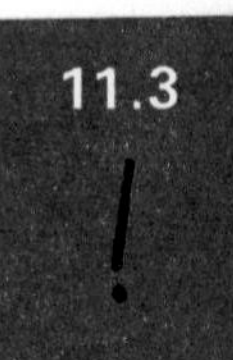

> My first job, as an elevator operator, was the most thrilling I've ever had! To me it was almost as if I was an actor, waiting my cue to speak and move!! My audience responded! (How could they help it? They had to get off!!!)

A good writer is able to command attention without resorting to such mechanical means. In student papers there is seldom a need for exclamation marks unless dialog is used.

12 Commas

Correction: Insert a comma at the place indicated.

Commas mark a slight separation between grammatical units, similar to very brief pauses in speech. They are highly important to both the meaning and the movement of all kinds of writing and account for two thirds of all punctuation marks used.

To use commas intelligently, you must know not only when to use them but also when to omit them. When units that should run consecutively are arbitrarily separated by commas or when the movement of a passage is unnecessarily interrupted, the effect can be annoying. Long sentences may be perfectly clear without any commas at all, as in this example of over fifty words:

> The manner in which their grandfather began the tremendous task of giving away substantial parts of the world's greatest fortune and the way in which their father expanded the business of philanthropy had a significant role in guiding the five brothers into new ventures intended to help make the world a better place in which to live.—Joe Alex Morris, *Those Rockefeller Brothers*, p. 133

The principal uses of the comma are described in the following sections and summarized in the table on page 147. The table also lists some constructions in which commas should *not* be used, as discussed in §12.8, Misused commas.

12.1 Between coordinate clauses

A comma is customarily used before the conjunction linking the coordinate clauses in a compound sentence, especially when the clauses are long or when it is desirable to emphasize their distinctness. Notice that the comma always comes *before* the coordinating conjunction, not after it:

> I do not deny that many departments now "permit" dissertations in the American field, but I am describing the average interest of our doctors and professors of English in the literature of their own country.—Howard Mumford Jones, *Ideas in America*, p. 6

> This is an extraordinary state of affairs, and it is only because we are used to it that we do not see how extraordinary it is.—*Ibid.*, p. 6

> Shall we leave the field to the social scientists, or shall we accept the challenge which the situation gives us?—*Ibid.*, p. 11

Commas

Commas are used:

1. Between coordinate clauses (§12.1)
   a) When they are joined by *and*, *or*, *nor* if the clauses are long or not closely related
   b) When they are joined by *but* or *yet*
   c) When they are joined by *for*
2. After long introductory elements (§12.2)
   a) When an adverb clause precedes the main clause (usually optional if the introductory clause is short and closely related)
   b) When a long modifying phrase precedes the main clause (usually optional if the phrase is short and closely related)
3. With nonrestrictive modifiers (§12.3)
   a) To set off subordinate clauses and phrases that do not limit or restrict the meaning of the term they modify
   b) To set off appositives
4. To set off interrupting and parenthetical elements (§12.4)
5. To separate coordinate items in a series (§12.5)
   a) In a series of words, phrases, or clauses not joined by conjunctions (optional before *and* joining the last item in a series)
   b) In a series of coordinate adjectives, all modifying the same noun
6. To separate constructions for clarity (§12.6)
7. In conventional places (§12.7)
   a) In numbers
   b) In dates
   c) In addresses
   d) With titles and degrees
   e) In correspondence
   f) With phrases identifying direct quotations

Commas should not be used (§12.8):

1. Between main sentence elements
2. Between two words or phrases joined by *and*
3. Between main clauses without a connective
4. With restrictive modifiers
5. After the last item in a series

Short clauses joined by and, or, nor

The comma may be omitted before the conjunctions *and, or, nor* in compound sentences if the coordinate clauses are short and closely related in thought:

> Life is short [ ] and time is fleeting.
> He had to get home [ ] or his father would be furious.
> Nancy didn't like her [ ] nor did I.

12.1

General writing often omits the comma where Formal writing would use one, as between the two independent clauses in this example:

> Nevertheless, great claims are made for him as a sensitive humanist and he is an artist much favored by teachers of art appreciation.—John Perreault, "Paul Klee: A Dissenting Opinion," *Art News*, May 1967, p. 42

Clauses joined by but, yet

In both Formal and General writing a comma is used between independent clauses joined by *but* or *yet* in order to emphasize the contrast:

> Klee's pictures have often been referred to as "poetic," but unfortunately in an art context "poetic" often means literary, precious and sentimental—a use that does an injustice to poetry, painting's sisterly art.—*Ibid.*, p. 43

> It is an imperfect system, yet it is better than none.

Clauses joined by for

A comma is necessary between clauses joined by *for* used as a conjunction, so that it won't be confused with the preposition *for*:

> He was an easy target, for anyone could pull the wool over his eyes. [*for* as a conjunction]

> He was an easy target for anyone who wanted to take advantage of him. [*for* as a preposition]

12.2 After long introductory elements

Adverb clauses and long modifying phrases are usually set off by a comma when they precede the main clause. When these elements come at the end of a sentence, a comma may or may not be necessary.

Adverb clauses

Adverb clauses (see §4.2) are often placed at the beginning of a sentence for variety or emphasis. In this position they are usually separated from the main clause by a comma:

When he said that we would be expected to write a theme every day, I nearly collapsed.

Before penicillin and other antibiotics were developed, pneumonia was often fatal.

12.2

The comma is frequently omitted when the introductory clause is short and closely related to the main clause, especially if both clauses have the same subject:

When I lived in New York [ ] I went to the theater every month.
After he seized control [ ] the situation changed drastically.

When an adverb clause *follows* the main clause, no comma is used if the subordinate clause is closely related to the meaning of the sentence:

I nearly collapsed [ ] *when he said that we would be expected to write a theme every day.*

Pneumonia was often fatal [ ] *before penicillin and other antibiotics were developed.*

If a following subordinate clause is only loosely related to the main clause and would be preceded by a distinct pause in speech, it is separated from the main clause by a comma:

The new wing will be finished by spring, *unless, of course, unexpected delays occur.*

I have known readers who find Huxley unreadable, *although they have found it impossible to explain why.*—Colin Wilson, "Existential Criticism," *Chicago Review*, Summer 1959, p. 166

Long modifying phrases

Long modifying phrases are generally punctuated in the same way as adverb clauses. When they *precede* the main clause, they are followed by a comma:

To fully understand the impact of Einstein's ideas, one must be familiar with those of Newton. [infinitive phrase]

Leaning far out over the balcony, he stared at the waves below. [participle phrase]

As a result of widespread erosion, floods are becoming more and more frequent and cause increasing devastation. [prepositional phrase]—Egon Glesinger, "The Mediterranean Project," *Scientific American*, July 1960, p. 88

When the phrases are relatively short and closely related to the clauses they modify, General writing often omits the comma:

In this context [ ] the meaning is entirely different.
To evade the draft [ ] he moved to Costa Rica.

12.2

When the modifying phrase *follows* the clause, commas are unnecessary if the thought seems to flow smoothly from one to the other. But if the phrase is only loosely related to the clause or modifies some distant expression, a comma must be used to prevent confusion:

One must be familiar with Newton's ideas [ ] *to fully understand the impact of Einstein's.*

Special treatment may be necessary [ ] *in cases of severe malnutrition.*

The local residents often saw Elgin [ ] *wandering among the ruins.*

Wilson nervously watched the man, *alarmed by his silence.* [The phrase modifies *Wilson*, not *man*.]

12.3 With nonrestrictive modifiers

Rest	**Correction: If the modifier marked is nonrestrictive, set it off with a comma or commas; if it is restrictive, do not separate it from the term it modifies.**

Subordinate clauses and phrases

A *nonrestrictive* modifier is a subordinate clause or a phrase that does not limit or define the term it modifies. In other words, it does not *restrict* the term's meaning; if it was omitted, the meaning of the sentence would not change essentially. The most persistent problems occur with clauses introduced by *who*, *which*, or *that*, but nonrestrictive phrases may also cause difficulty. Nonrestrictive modifiers are set off by commas to indicate their subordinate function in the sentence:

Last night's audience, *which contained a large number of college students*, applauded each number enthusiastically.

The people of India, *who have lived in poverty for centuries*, desperately need financial and technical assistance.

Vasari's history, *hovering between fact and fiction*, is not a reliable source of data.

Notice that the modifiers in the three preceding sentences are not essential to the terms they modify. Although some information would be lost if they were removed, the central meaning of each sentence would not change.

A *restrictive* modifier limits or defines the meaning of a term; without it, the sentence would take on a different meaning or become difficult to understand. Since it is essential to the sentence, it is *not* set off by commas:

He is a man *who thinks for himself.*
Ortiz discovered many temples *which were pre-Toltec in origin.*
The questions *that he did not answer* were the most interesting ones.

Almost all clauses beginning with *that* are restrictive. All clauses in which the relative pronoun can be omitted are restrictive (the questions *he failed to answer*, the book *I read*).

In distinguishing between restrictive and nonrestrictive modifiers, the writer must carefully consider the nature of the term modified and the context in which it occurs. If the term is fully defined in itself and cannot be confused with another, the following modifier is nonrestrictive. But if the term is vague or ambiguous without the modifier, the modifier is restrictive. Compare the function of the modifier in each of these passages:

Women *who can't drive properly* should keep off the highways.

Women, *who can't drive properly*, should keep off the highways.

Last month I read a novel and a biography. The novel, *which especially appealed to me*, was written by Hawthorne.

Last month I read several novels and a biography. The novel *which especially appealed to me* was written by Hawthorne.

While in Rome, I took photographs in the vicinity of St. Peter's. The square, *designed by Michelangelo*, is perfectly symmetrical.

While in Rome, I took photographs of squares designed by Michelangelo, Bernini, and Borromini. The square *designed by Michelangelo* is perfectly symmetrical.

A good test to apply in distinguishing between restrictive and nonrestrictive modifiers is to read the passage aloud. If your voice drops slightly in pitch and hesitates briefly before and after the modifier, the modifier is probably nonrestrictive and requires commas. If you read the passage smoothly without a pause, the modifier is probably restrictive and needs no commas.

Appositives

12.3 Appositives—nouns or noun equivalents that extend the meaning of a preceding expression—are usually nonrestrictive modifiers and are thus set off by commas:

> Thomas Malthus, *author of the first serious study of population growth*, foresaw one of our greatest modern problems.
>
> Lincoln delivered a famous address at Gettysburg, *site of a crucial Civil War battle.*

Notice that such appositives, like other nonrestrictive modifiers, must be set off by *two* commas when they occur in the middle of the sentence.

Restrictive appositives and those used as part of a person's name require no commas:

> I thought the question referred to Lewis *the novelist* rather than to Lewis *the union leader.*
>
> William *the Conqueror* invaded England from Normandy.

12.4 To set off interrupting and parenthetical elements

A word, phrase, or clause that interrupts the movement of a sentence is usually set off by commas or other appropriate marks. Whether or not the degree of interruption is sufficient to require commas depends on tone and emphasis. Formal English uses commas more frequently than General English for this purpose:

> By the end of the century, *however*, the bourgeois's world was going so strong that, *from the point of view of the poet*, it had come to seem hopeless to oppose it.—Edmund Wilson, *Axel's Castle*, p. 268
>
> Romanticism, *as everyone has heard*, was a revolt of the individual. —*Ibid.*, p. 2

To decide whether or not to set off short phrases with commas, read the passage aloud with the desired emphasis. If your voice drops and you pause slightly before and after the phrase, commas should be used. If the phrase seems to run naturally into the rest of the sentence, probably no commas are necessary:

Cybernetics, *on the other hand*, has attracted many students.
Machines are useful, *of course*, in doing complex calculations.
Machines are *of course* incapable of what we call creative thought.

Adverbs that compare or contrast

Adverbs that compare or contrast some preceding idea (*however, therefore, consequently, too, also*) are generally set off by commas when they occur within a sentence:

It was in Cholon, *too*, that the South Vietnam Premier toured a local hospital with his beauteous wife, Tuyet Mai.—*Newsweek*, June 26, 1967, p. 50

The largest single group of terms in the dictionary, *however*, is that in the general vocabulary, which belongs to all speakers of American English.—Patrick E. Kilburn, "Ruckus in the Reference Room," *Union College Symposium*, Spring 1962, p. 6

When such words appear at the beginning of a sentence, they may or may not be followed by a comma, depending on the emphasis desired:

Thus the way was cleared for further explorations.
Nevertheless, work did not always proceed according to plan.

When a clause beginning with such an adverb is joined to a preceding clause, the *semicolon* must be used, since these words are weak connectives. They relate ideas to one another but do not join them grammatically (see §13.1, page 165, Clauses linked with a conjunctive adverb):

Business recessions take place periodically; *however*, they are generally short-lived.

The natives are incredibly poor; *moreover*, they have little hope of bettering their lot.

When adverbs that closely modify the verb or the entire sentence (*perhaps, so*) begin the sentence, they should not be followed by a comma. Similarly, conjunctions are part of the clauses they introduce and should not be set off from them:

Perhaps a solution can still be found.
But the average American cannot afford such luxuries.

Weak exclamations

Weak exclamations (*well*, *oh*, *say*) and *yes* and *no* sometimes occur as modifiers, particularly at the beginning of a sentence. They are conventionally separated from the sentence they modify by commas:

> *Well*, not much can be done about it now.
>
> *Yes*, times have changed.
>
> It is doubtful whether the ordinary city-dweller is more grasping than the French peasant, *say*, or even the sturdy New Englander.—Herbert Muller, *The Uses of the Past*, p. 54

12.4

Names in direct address

Names which occur as interrupters in direct address are also set off by commas:

> I firmly believe, *fellow citizens*, that justice will prevail.
> It seems to me, *George*, that your attitude is poor.
> *Workers of the world*, unite!

12.5 To separate items in a series

Words, phrases, or clauses in a series

A comma is the mark ordinarily used to separate coordinate words, phrases, or clauses in a list or series:

> Once the great iconoclast among spectators, the baseball fan today travels in groups, performs on cue, and, as often as not, shamelessly apes the tribal customs of other fans in other cities.—Charles Einstein, "The New Breed of Baseball Fan," *Harper's Magazine*, July 1967, p. 70
>
> He remembered these feelings as precisely as he remembered the clothes, the cars, the furniture, the songs, the slang.—Arthur Mizener, *The Far Side of Paradise*, p. 116
>
> We were taught how to sit gracefully, how to walk, how to converse politely.

Formal usage requires a comma before a connective joining the last item in a series, and this practice is usually expected in college writing:

> It was left to the House of Representatives to decide whether the Presidency should go to Jackson, Adams, or Crawford.

General usage is divided, but Informal usage (especially in newspapers) usually omits the final comma if no misinterpretation is possible:

> Further tornado damage was reported in Libertyville, Barrington, Palatine and Arlington Heights.

If each of the items in a series is joined by a conjunction, commas are ordinarily omitted. The following sentence illustrates series with and without connectives:

12.6

> Scenes down on the farm *or* among raftsmen poling their flatboats *or* among the prairie schooners and Indians of the West were present in the canvasses of painters like George Caleb Bingham, William Sidney Mount, and Alfred Jacob Miller.—Holman Hamilton, "The American Renaissance," *The Democratic Experience*, p. 171

See also §13.1, page 166, Semicolons to separate elements containing other marks.

Coordinate adjectives

Commas are used to separate adjectives in a series when they modify the same noun. Since each performs the same function, such adjectives are called *coordinate*. In a coordinate series each member could sensibly be joined by *and* instead of a comma, or the order of modifiers could be reversed:

> He spoke of the *violent*, *exciting*, *challenging* era that followed the Civil War.

Commas are not used when the adjectives are arranged so that each one modifies the entire following expression. Such items cannot be joined by *and* or reversed in order:

> She made a *tasty*[ ] *Hungarian* goulash.
> He spoke longingly of the *good*[ ] *old*[ ] *prewar* days.

Notice that a comma is never used between the last adjective in a series and the noun it modifies.

12.6 To separate for clarity

Commas tend to keep distinct the constructions they separate and should be used wherever necessary to prevent misreading. They are useful in the following situations:

1) When the subject of a clause may be mistaken for the object of a verb or preposition:

As far as I can *see*, *the results* have not been promising.

When the rains are *over*, *the fields* are plowed in preparation for planting.

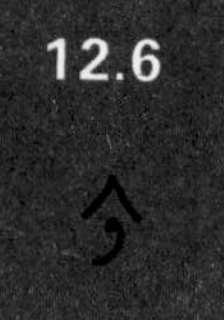

2) When a word has two possible functions, a comma can guide the reader in interpreting it properly. Words like *for*, *but*, and *however*, for example, may be used in several ways:

The surgeon's face showed no emotion, *but* anxiety and a little nervousness must have been hiding behind that impassive mask. [. . . showed no emotion but anxiety . . .]

Sharon was thoroughly embarrassed, *for* her parents treated her like a child. [. . . was thoroughly embarrassed for her parents . . .]

However, I interpreted his remarks liberally and continued my work.

However[ ] I interpreted his remarks, they made no sense.

3) A comma is sometimes necessary for clarity when one expression might be mistaken for another:

After he broke his *hand*, *writing* was very difficult for him.

4) When the same word occurs consecutively, a comma may be used, although usage is divided on this:

Whatever *is*, *is* right.

5) When the writer wishes to call attention to the second half of a compound predicate:

The underwater slopes are quite different from those of the beach face, and are usually described in a different way to take account of the substantial irregularities between the waterline and the seaward boundary.—Willard Bascom, "Beaches," *Scientific American*, August 1960, p. 83

This practice should be used only to avoid confusion in long sentences or to show contrast between the two parts of the predicate.

12.7 In conventional places

Current practices should be followed in the use of commas in conventional places. Such commas help the reader quickly recognize distinct units of information.

In numbers

Commas are conventionally used to group numbers into units of threes in separating thousands, millions, etc.:

2,853 84,962 3,542,869

Commas are not generally used in round numbers of four figures, serial numbers, or street addresses:

> There were about 2000 words in the article.
> The serial number of my typewriter is 11-6445793.
> He lives at 11085 Champagne Point Road.

In dates

Commas are used to separate the day of the month and the year:

February 8, 1928 November 21, 1962

When only the month and year are given, a comma is not necessary, although it is frequently used:

October 1929 October, 1929

The form favored in military usage—16 March 1962—is more common in British than in American writing.

In addresses

Commas are used in addresses to separate towns, counties, states, and districts:

> Toledo, Ohio
> Hamilton, Madison County, New York
> He was born in Washington, D.C., in 1937.

Notice that the final element is followed by a comma if it falls within a sentence.

With titles and degrees

> Marshall Field, Jr.
> Jerome Blum, M.A., Ph.D.
> Gen. H. L. Matthews, U.S.M.C., Ret.
> David Franklin Moore, Esq.

In correspondence

Commas are conventional after the salutation of informal letters (Dear Shirley, Dear Uncle Joe,) and after the complimentary close of most letters (Yours truly, Sincerely yours,). A colon is used after the salutation of a formal letter (Dear Mr. Miller:).

With phrases identifying direct quotations

A comma is customarily used after expressions that introduce direct quotations:

> Sherman said, "Only a fool would carry on like that."

12.7 If the phrase interrupts a sentence in the quotation, it is set off by two commas:

> "Only a fool," Sherman said, "would carry on like that."

No comma is needed with very short quotations, exclamations, or phrases closely built into the structure of the sentence:

> Father always said "Time is money."
> She began to scream "Fire!" as soon as she saw the smoke.
> One famous writer called slavery a "peculiar institution."

12.8 Misused commas

Correction: Remove the superfluous comma at the place marked.

Students frequently use too many commas because of a mistaken notion that the more punctuation, the better. Remember that too many commas are as bad as too few, and be prepared to justify every comma you use. The most common errors in using commas are described below.

Between main sentence elements

Since a comma is a mark of separation, it should not ordinarily be used between those elements of a sentence that naturally go together: subject and verb, verb and object (or complement), preposition and object. There should be no marks where the brackets stand in the following sentences:

> Subject and verb: Sometimes students who have attended expensive preparatory schools[ ] have trouble adjusting to large public universities.
>
> Verb and object: I have often noticed[ ] that a person's physical characteristics may influence his personality.

Verb and complement: Whenever he noticed that the Indians appeared[ ] restless or hostile, he took steps to pacify them.

Preposition and object: Nothing troubled her except[ ] that her friendship with Swift was causing gossip.

Between two words or phrases joined by and

Be careful to distinguish between coordinating conjunctions joining independent *clauses* and those joining other sentence elements, such as compound subjects or verbs. Except for coordinate clauses (§12.1), two items joined by *and* or by one of the other coordinating conjunctions are not ordinarily separated by a comma. Commas would be out of place in the following compound constructions:

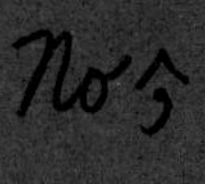

Primitive agricultural tools[ ] and bits of clay pottery were found. [compound subject]

He either talked too much[ ] or else said nothing at all. [compound predicate]

In his senior year he was captain of the football team[ ] and secretary of his class. [compound complement]

He wanted more time for study[ ] and contemplation. [compound object of preposition]

Occasionally a comma is used for clarity between the two parts of a compound predicate; see §12.6.

Between main clauses without a connective

A comma alone is an inadequate mark of separation between two main clauses. If the clauses are not joined by a coordinating conjunction, they must be separated by a semicolon or punctuated as individual sentences. See §3.2, Comma faults.

With restrictive modifiers

A restrictive modifier is one that is essential to the meaning of the sentence (see §12.3); it should not be separated from the element it modifies by a comma. The italicized elements in the following example are restrictive and should stand as they are here, without commas:

Mr. Colman proves his versatility as an actor *when he philosophizes one minute and punches his brother on the nose the next.* He portrays a man of action *if the occasion requires* and at the same time a mild-mannered, soft-spoken individual *who gives the impression of being able to think*. He has to make important decisions *when his brother and Margo tell him that this Utopia is a lot of hooey*. Mr. Colman is the only actor I have ever seen *who can show that he is thinking*.

After the last item in a series

A comma is never used between the last adjective in a series and the noun it modifies:

12.8

> He imagined himself as a *rich*, *handsome*, *successful*[ ] man of the world.

No ,

A comma is also superfluous after the last item in other kinds of lists or series:

> The work of such modern masters as Picasso, Matisse, Van Gogh, and Gauguin[ ] shocked conservative critics when it was introduced at the famous New York Armory show in 1913.

Exercises

1. *Functions of commas.* Read the following passage slowly, noting all the commas that occur. Try reading it aloud to see whether the commas correspond to natural pauses in the movement of the passage. Be prepared to discuss the reason for the use of a comma in each case (or for the omission of a comma before a relative pronoun or conjunction). The passage is taken from Jonathan Swift's "A Modest Proposal for Preventing the Children of Poor People in Ireland from Being a Burden to Their Parents or Country, and for Making Them Beneficial to the Public," a satirical pamphlet published in 1729. Does the passage contain any commas that would be considered incorrect according to modern usage?

It is a melancholy object to those who walk through this great town, or travel in the country, when they see the streets, the roads, and cabin doors crowded with beggars of the female sex, followed by three, four, or six children, all in rags, and importuning every passenger for an alms. . . .

I think it is agreed by all parties that this prodigious number of children in the arms, or on the backs, or at the heels of their mothers, and frequently of their fathers, is, in the present deplorable state of the kingdom, a very great additional grievance; and therefore whoever could find out a fair, cheap, and easy method of making these children sound and useful members of the commonwealth would deserve so well of the public as to have his statue set up for a preserver of the nation. . . .

I shall now therefore humbly propose my own thoughts, which I hope will not be liable to the least objection.

I have been assured by a very knowing American of my acquaintance in London, that a young healthy child, well nursed, is at a year old a most delicious, nourishing, and wholesome food, whether stewed, roasted, baked, or boiled; and I make no doubt that it will equally serve in a fricassee or a ragout.

2. *Deciding where commas are needed.* The following sentences provide some further examples of irony and some further practice in using commas. In which of the lettered places do you consider a comma essential? unnecessary? optional? Give specific reasons for your choice of punctuation in each instance.

1) Sir Roger told them (*a*) with the air of a man (*b*) who would not give his judgment rashly (*c*) that much might be said (*d*) on both sides.—Joseph Addison

2) We are always doing something (*a*) for Posterity (*b*) but I would fain see Posterity do something (*c*) for us.—Joseph Addison

3) Hobbes (*a*) propounder of a "great man" theory (*b*) speaks of the solitary (*c*) poor (*d*) nasty (*e*) brutish (*f*) and short (*g*) life of men.

4) It is a truth universally acknowledged (*a*) that a single man (*b*) in possession of a good fortune (*c*) must be in want of a wife.—Jane Austen

5) There never was a miracle (*a*) wrought by God (*b*) to convert an atheist (*c*) because the light of nature might have led him to confess a God.—Francis Bacon

6) Diogenes said (*a*) of a young man that danced daintily (*b*) and was commended: "The better (*c*) the worse."—Francis Bacon

7) The most melancholy of human reflections (*a*) perhaps (*b*) is that (*c*) on the whole (*d*) it is a question whether the benevolence of mankind does most good or harm.—Walter Bagehot

8) He did not think (*a*) with the Caliph Omar Ben Adalaziz (*b*) that it was necessary to make a hell of this world (*c*) to make a Paradise in the next.—William Beckford

9) To put his faith in hope (*a*) a man must have the courage of his convictions (*b*) a certain number of blind spots (*c*) and a nagging wife.

10) Disraeli (*a*) a conservative prime minister (*b*) liberal with his wit (*c*) was contemptuous of Gladstone (*d*) whom he called a sophistical rhetorician (*e*) inebriated with the exuberance of his own verbosity.

3. *Restrictive and nonrestrictive modifiers.* The following sentences contain both restrictive and nonrestrictive modifiers. Punctuate each sentence appropriately and be prepared to discuss any sentences in which choice of punctuation depends on interpretation.

1) Laws are like cobwebs which may catch small flies but let wasps and hornets break through.—Jonathan Swift

2) He put to our ears this engine [a watch] which made an incessant noise like that of a water mill; and we conjecture that it is either some unknown animal, or the god that he worships; but we are more inclined to the latter opinion.—Jonathan Swift

3) He had been eight years upon a project for extracting out of cucumbers sunbeams which were to be put into vials hermetically sealed. —Jonathan Swift

4) I said the thing which was not.—Jonathan Swift

5) His virtues were so conspicuous that his enemies unable to overlook them and his friends to whose lives they were a rebuke represented them as vices.—Ambrose Bierce

6) It is so far from being natural for a man and woman to live in a state of marriage that we find all the motives which they have for remaining in that connection, and the restraints which civilized society imposes to prevent separation, are hardly sufficient to keep them together.—Samuel Johnson

7) Read over your compositions, and wherever you meet with a passage which you think is particularly fine, strike it out.—Samuel Johnson

8) Walls which have been built for the purpose of keeping good things in often end by keeping good things out.

9) Dresses which are made out of paper may afford women a chance for more high style at low cost than cloth dresses which are more durable.

10) You are a second Shandy the father of that renowned Tristram who was annoyed half his life by a creaking door and who could not come to the resolution of removing the daily annoyance with a few drops of oil.—Goethe

4. *Recognizing errors in comma use.* Read carefully the following passage, in which some of the punctuation has been altered. Note all cases in which commas have been omitted or misused; then make the necessary corrections. If a comma is optional, be prepared to explain your reasons for using or omitting it.

Once upon a time long, long ago, I learned how to reduce a fraction to its lowest terms. Whether I could still perform that operation is uncertain; but the discipline, involved in early training, had its uses since it taught me that, in order to understand the essential nature of anything it is well to strip it of all superficial and irrelevant accretions,—in short to reduce it to its lowest terms. That operation I now venture with some apprehension and all due apologies to perform on the subject of history.

I ought first of all, to explain that when I use the term history I mean, knowledge of history. No doubt throughout all past time there actually occurred a series of events, which, whether we know what it was or not constitutes history in some ultimate sense. Nevertheless much the greater part of these events we can know nothing about not even that they occurred; many of them we can know only imperfectly; and even the few events that we think we know, for sure we can never absolutely be certain of, since we can never revive them never observe, or test them directly.—Carl Becker, "Everyman His Own Historian," *American Historical Review*, January 1932, p. 221

13 Semicolons and colons

13.1 Semicolons

Correction: Use a semicolon at the place marked to separate coordinate sentence elements.

13.1

The semicolon is a mark of separation much stronger than a comma and almost as full as a period:

> Our haunted house was not strictly in the best haunted-house tradition. It was not a ramshackle pile standing at a lonely crossroad; it was on a street inside the town and was surrounded by houses that were cheerfully inhabited. It was not tumble-down; it was a large, well-built mansion of brick, and it still stands, good as new.—Frank Sullivan, *The Night the Old Nostalgia Burned Down*, p. 133

Although the constructions requiring a semicolon are clearly defined and relatively few, many student writers have trouble with this mark of punctuation. Probably the most general fault is that of using a semicolon where a comma or other mark would be better. The semicolon is a heavy mark of separation that makes a sentence move rather slowly. It is more appropriate and more necessary in Formal writing, which is likely to use long, aggregating sentences, than it is in General writing, which usually moves quite rapidly. In deciding between a semicolon or another mark, a writer should consider the requirements of his own style and of the material he is presenting.

The few constructions in which a semicolon is required are listed below. Notice that in all its uses the semicolon marks a separation between *coordinate* elements—expressions of equal rank.

Between main clauses without an expressed connective

A semicolon must be used to separate main clauses that are not joined by one of the coordinating conjunctions (*and*, *but*, *for*, *or*, *nor*, *yet*):

> The penalty for not turning work in on time is a lowered grade; the penalty for not turning it in at all is failure.

These clauses are clearly separate in thought and structure and could be punctuated as separate sentences. A semicolon is used to combine such clauses when the writer considers them parts of one idea. Sometimes the second clause continues the thought of the first:

> Alfred Hitchcock was probably the first director to place *himself* at a slightly ironic distance from the action of his films; his own subtle mockery helped him confect high-gloss thrillers that serious people might enjoy without losing their sense of identity.—Jacob Brackman, "Onward and Upward with the Arts," *The New Yorker*, June 24, 1967, p. 49

Sometimes the second clause presents a contrasting idea:

> But however immature they are, these lovers are not dull characters; on the contrary, they are hauntingly and embarrassingly real.—Arthur Mizener, *The Far Side of Paradise*, p. 116

The use of a comma rather than a semicolon or period between main clauses without an expressed connective is considered a serious error in writing. (**See** §3.2, Comma faults.)

Between main clauses linked with a conjunctive adverb

A semicolon is used before heavy conjunctive adverbs like *however*, *therefore*, *consequently*, and *nevertheless* when they occur between clauses. Although such adverbs show a connection between the ideas, their connective function is weak and a semicolon must be used to separate the clauses:

> The investigative jurisdiction of the FBI is limited to those cases in which the stolen automobile has been transported from one state to another; however, through cost-free services provided by the FBI Laboratory and Identification Division, the FBI has been able to assist state and municipal law enforcement agencies in identifying and convicting numerous auto thieves whose operations have not yet extended across state lines.—J. Edgar Hoover, "Auto Theft Is Big Business," *Motor Trend*, December 1952, p. 17

> If the decisions or the rules of the Board permit the use of either the local official form or the conventional English form, it is the prerogative of the originating office to select the form which is most suitable for the matter in hand; therefore, in marking copy or reading proof, it is required only to verify the spelling of the particular form used.—*GPO Style Manual*, p. 62

As these examples suggest, the use of heavy conjunctive adverbs between long clauses is characteristic of a very Formal style. Students will do well to follow the practice of most current writers, who tend to use these adverbs as transitions between *sentences* rather than as transitions between clauses:

> It has a crest, a small mouth and a narrow gullet through which it draws breath or puts out its tongue. *Moreover*, its strength is not in its teeth but in its tail, and it inflicts injury by blows rather than by stinging.—T. H. White, *The Bestiary*, p. 166

13.1 ;

With coordinating conjunctions

A semicolon is sometimes used between main clauses connected by coordinating conjunctions if: (1) the clauses are unusually long, (2) the clauses are not closely related, (3) one or more of the clauses contain commas, or (4) the writer wishes to show an emphatic contrast between statements:

> The man in the street and the woman in the kitchen, confronted on every hand with new machines and devices which they owed to the laboratory, were ready to believe that science could accomplish almost anything; *and* they were being deluged with scientific information and theory.—Frederick Lewis Allen, *Only Yesterday*, p. 197

> In most cases these individualists are corporate executives, bankers, Wall Street lawyers; *but* they do not, as the economic determinists seem to believe, simply push the button of their economic power to affect fields remote from economics.—Robert Lubar, "The Prime Movers," *Fortune*, February 1960, p. 98

To separate elements containing other marks

Semicolons are often used in lists and series to separate elements that contain commas or other marks. In the following sentence, for example, the semicolons are necessary for clarity:

> Here are a few: Theodore Dreiser, of German extraction; Eugene O'Neill, of Irish ancestry; Fannie Hurst, of Jewish blood; Carl Sandburg, a Swede; John Dos Passos—his name is Portuguese; James T. Farrell, an Irishman; O. E. Rolvaag, another Scandinavian; Archibald MacLeish, and that looks Scotch; Paul de Kruif—I suppose that to be Dutch; Carl Van Doren—another Dutch name; Saroyan, an Armenian—and so on indefinitely.—Howard Mumford Jones, *Ideas in America*, p. 200

Notice that here, just as with main clauses, the semicolon separates *coordinate* elements. It is never used between elements of unequal rank, such as phrases and clauses or main and subordinate clauses.

13.2 Colons

Correction: Insert a colon at the place marked, or change the misused colon.

A colon is a mark of anticipation, directing attention to what follows:

> Molecular biologists have now provided a fairly complete picture of how genes carry out their primary function: the specification of protein structure.—William B. Wood and R. S. Edgar, "Building a Bacterial Virus," *Scientific American*, July 1967, p. 61

Students sometimes confuse colons and semicolons, but their functions are entirely different. The distinction is simple: a colon introduces or indicates what is to follow; a semicolon separates coordinate elements. The following passage illustrates the correct use of both marks (as does the sentence of the text immediately above):

> Smaller birds were less elusive: a pair of blue-winged warblers scolded us for coming so close to their nest, as the juncos had along the higher trail; a winter wren, reminiscent of the Long Trail in Vermont, lit up the woods with song; a kingfisher shot downstream with his loud rattle.—Paul Brooks, "The Great Smokies," *The Atlantic Monthly*, May 1959, p. 66

Anticipatory use

A colon may be used after a main clause to indicate that a list, an illustration, or a summation is to follow:

> A complete reading program, therefore, should include four factors: one good book each week, a newspaper or news magazine, magazines of comment and interpretation, and book reviews.—Atwood H. Townsend, "How to Use *Good Reading*," *Good Reading*, p. 97

> What made Poe particularly acceptable to the French, however, was what had distinguished him from most of the other Romantics of the English-speaking countries: his interest in aesthetic theory.—Edmund Wilson, *Axel's Castle*, p. 17

The colon is used as an anticipatory mark only after grammatically complete expressions. Do not use a colon between verbs and their objects or complements, or between prepositions and their objects.

Colon	*No colon*
He visited the following cities: Boston, Dallas, Chicago, Miami, and Seattle.	He visited Boston, Dallas, Chicago, Miami, and Seattle. [objects of verb]
The string section consists of four instruments: violin, viola, cello, and bass.	The four instruments in the string section are violin, viola, cello, and bass. [complements of verb]

13.2

Between main clauses

A colon may be used between two main clauses when the second clause is an illustration, a restatement, or an amplification of the first:

> The Great Books have about them much more, I feel sure, than mere snob appeal: they have a kind of dim religious light, a sense of the Serious Call, of the medieval scholar-saint.—Louis Kronenberger, *Company Manners*, p. 142

> The discounter's economics are simple: he buys a new car from an authorized dealer at anywhere from $50 to $150 above the dealer's cost, tacks on from $100 to $200 as his own profit.—"Autos," *Time*, February 10, 1961, p. 74

Before quotations

A colon is generally used between an introductory statement and a grammatically complete quotation, especially if the quotation is more than one sentence. If the quotation runs to several sentences, it may be paragraphed separately:

> In "A Cooking Egg," the poet demands, after a call upon a very mild, dull spinster: "Where are the eagles and the trumpets?" and himself returns the saddened answer: "Buried beneath some snow-deep Alps."—Edmund Wilson, *Axel's Castle*, p. 101

> . . . Take one of the passages I have already quoted from Yeats: "We make out of the quarrel with others, rhetoric, but out of the quarrel with ourselves, poetry. Unlike the rhetoricians, who get a confident voice from remembering the crowd they have won or may win, we sing amid our uncertainty, and, smitten even in the presence of the most high beauty by the knowledge of our solitude, our rhythm shudders."—*Ibid.*, p. 246

When a short quotation is built closely into a sentence, it may be preceded either by a comma or by a colon, depending on how it is introduced:

As Alexander Pope said, "Most women have no characters at all."

She reminded him of the words of Pope: "Most women have no characters at all."

Colons in conventional places

A colon is customary in the following places:

1) After an expression introducing examples or a large body of material (as after *places* in the preceding sentence).

2) Between hours and minutes expressed in figures: 11:30 a.m.

3) In formal footnotes and bibliographies:

Between volume and page—*The Nation*, 98:295
Between chapter and verse of the Bible—Matthew 4:6
Between the title and subtitle of a book—*China: A Modern Enigma*

4) After the formal salutation in a letter:

Dear Sir: Dear Professor Jones:

See page 209 for use of capital letter after colons.

Exercises

1. *Adding appropriate punctuation.* Add whatever punctuation is needed in the following paragraphs, and be prepared to justify the marks you use. Be particularly careful to use semicolons and colons correctly.

The principle according to which periodic sentences are constructed is simple main ideas in main clauses subordinate ideas in subordinate clauses. Such sentences are called "periodic" because their meaning which is complex and serpentine and subject to constant qualification seems to slither and slide away from the grasp until like a snake coiling its way around its subject the sentence has encircled it. The periodic sentence is the ideal sentence for certain kinds of minds such as Milton's such minds do not discover what they want to say as they say it, practicing a sort of chance analysis like those modern painters who produce design by randomness and accident instead they see the whole problem and its parts before they begin to write so that they are able to assign ideas to the kinds of clauses relevant to their nature fitting the phrase to the thought.

Such minds are by nature hierarchical in their outlook recognizing in the very prose which they write the principles of subordination of rank and to use an Elizabethan word "degree" liking neatness and order in all things including society they tend to be conservatives or at least apologists for an ennobled conservatism generally beyond the capacity of practical politicians.

Those who write short epigrammatic sentences have quite different aims and techniques using a simple structure to enable the reader at once to see the sentence as a whole and using metaphors since they are more economical and brilliant than similes to light up their ideas in memorable and pictorial phrases they try to be three things at once wittily brief flashingly comprehensive and mnemonically quotable.

2. *Recognizing faulty punctuation.* Examine the punctuation in the following paragraphs, noting especially where semicolons and colons have been misused or omitted. Then correct the faulty punctuation. Be prepared to justify your changes.

He who would write about the Civil War ought first by way of preparation: to study warfare both on land and sea, to read the records of the times as they exist in archives and newspapers and journals; to examine the history of the period preceding the war so that he can effectively explain the causes of the war and to visit wherever possible, the actual battlefields. Only if he grasps both the details and their overall patterns can the writer, with any success guide the reader through the complex and shifting movement: of men, of machines, of trends. If the reader can be convinced that the author knows his facts, which are the raw materials of history, and if the author can put the facts together in a narrative, that enables the facts to be seen in their context of action; and if the style can be a judicious mixture of the periodic and epigrammatic varied according to whether the pace of the narrative is deliberative or dramatic—only then will the result be a history worthy of the great histories of the past like those of Thucydides and Herodotus.

We have as yet in our national literature no great history of the Civil War; no book that can match even Caesar's *Gallic Wars;* though we do have some fine and solid pieces of scholarship: such as those by Douglas Southall Freeman. Too many facts are available to the modern historian, he simply cannot master them well enough to reduce them to an order at once accurate and dramatic. There is, to be sure, a great deal of historical writing being done: not only in scholarly journals such as the *American Historical Review*, and the *Journal of the History of Ideas*, but also in books, popular periodicals, and monographs. It is paradoxical that all this attention to history has in one sense produced a negative result: we have not as yet produced a great national historian, who is capable of making use of the rich materials at his disposal.

14 Dashes and parentheses

14.1 Dashes

/--/ Correction: Use a dash (or dashes) to set off the expression marked.

Dashes are used to set off parenthetical expressions and abrupt interruptions in thought. As marks of separation, they are much more emphatic than either commas or parentheses:

> All it means—but it does mean that—is that these millions of peasants are slowly putting aside their heritage of vague, mystical thoughts about the world around them (in which, for instance, an iron plow made the earth "sick") and entering the world of rational technological thinking.—Hans Koningsberger, "A Reporter at Large: China Notes," *The New Yorker*, April 30, 1966, p. 90

On the typewriter a dash is made with two unspaced hyphens. There should be no space between a dash and the words it separates:

```
Two hyphens--the hyphen is the mark on
the same key as the asterisk--are used
to make a dash in typed copy.
```

The dash is a useful mark of separation, but it should not be used to excess or in places where another mark (or none) would be more appropriate. Because dashes make an abrupt and emphatic separation, they can interfere with the flow of a passage:

> Many parts of northern Michigan—and of northern Wisconsin—were once flourishing—even booming—mining areas—but now all that has changed.
>
> Better: Many parts of northern Michigan and northern Wisconsin were once flourishing, even booming, mining areas—but now all that has changed.

There is no reason why a writer should avoid dashes if the movement or emphasis of a passage requires them, but he should not use them indiscriminately.

Dashes to mark sharp turns in thought

A dash or dashes may be used to indicate a sharp turn in the thought or construction of a sentence:

> He praised Ann's intelligence, her efficiency, her good taste—and then proposed to her sister.
>
> Cybernetics, like all young things, is inquisitive about everything, and meddles with everything—and makes its quota of blunders.—G. T. Guilbaud, *What Is Cybernetics?* p. 123

Dashes to enclose parenthetical elements

14.1 Dashes are often used to set off a parenthetical statement that is important to the meaning of the sentence. The parenthetical expressions in the following examples would carry less emphasis if they had been set off with parentheses or commas instead of with dashes:

> Every use of the past tense—"I was there. He did it."—is a bit of history.—Jacques Barzun and Henry Graff, *The Modern Researcher*, p. 8
>
> With our love of record keeping—doubtless a mark of our business society—the origin of almost everything is known or easily discoverable.—*Ibid.*, p. 189
>
> Still, we do condemn—we must condemn—the cruelties of slavery, fanaticism, and witch-burning.—Herbert Muller, *The Uses of the Past*, p. 38

For clarity, dashes are sometimes used instead of commas to set off parenthetical elements with internal punctuation:

> While Dewey, Pound, and Beard were reconstructing education, law, and history, three young humanists—Herbert Croly, Walter Lippman, and Walter Weyl—were calling for a reconstitution of politics.—William H. Harbaugh and Arthur S. Link, "The Emergence of a Modern Nation," *The Democratic Experience*, p. 344

Note that *two* dashes are necessary to enclose a parenthetical element that falls in the middle of a sentence.

Dashes before summaries or illustrations

A dash is often used to set off an expression that summarizes or illustrates the preceding statement. Such expressions are often appositives that the writer wants to emphasize:

> Hence they fostered the illusion that often inspired them—the illusion that history is or should be an exact science, free from all taint of art or philosophy.—Herbert Muller, *The Uses of the Past*, p. 28

From recording this or similar matters of passionate interest, men in various civilizations came to record other things—court ceremonies, religious sacrifices, and striking events.—Jacques Barzun and Henry Graff, *The Modern Researcher*, p. 45

Specialized uses of the dash

Dashes are sometimes used in the following conventional ways:

1) To precede a credit line, as at the end of the quoted passages in this book.

2) After introductory words that are to be repeated before each of the lines following:

We pledge—
 To uphold the Constitution
 To obey the laws of this state.

3) To separate run-in questions and answers in testimony:

Q.—Did you see him?
A.—No.

4) To indicate interrupted dialog:

"Well, I always assumed that— —"
"I don't care what you assumed," snapped John.

Notice that a *double* dash is customarily used in this case.

14.2 Parentheses

| c/ↄ | **Correction: Use parentheses to enclose the expression marked.**

Parentheses are curved marks used chiefly to enclose incidental or explanatory remarks. Although dashes and parentheses set off similar kinds of material, they are different in effect. Dashes tend to emphasize expressions, parentheses to subordinate them:

Lady Berkeley—the Queen's niece—was the leading scandalmonger at the court.

Lady Berkeley (the Queen's niece) was the leading scandalmonger at the court.

Do not confuse the use of parentheses and brackets; see §15.2, Brackets.

Parentheses to enclose incidental remarks

Parentheses are used to enclose remarks and asides that are not essential to the meaning of a passage. Sometimes the parenthetical remark falls within the sentence; sometimes it is set apart as a separate unit:

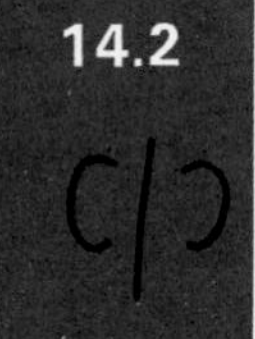

> He was adored (I have spent some time looking for the right verb, and that's it) by the members of the *Journal* staff, who greeted him each afternoon, in a sudden silence of typewriters, as if they hadn't seen him for a long time.—James Thurber, "Franklin Avenue, U.S.A.," *The Thurber Album*, p. 264

> There are still quite a few flaws in Nicklaus's game. While he now hits the ball much farther than he did as an amateur, he has become a less accurate driver. (Last year, after his victory at Augusta, he was so wild off the tee that in some tournaments his drives finished in the rough more frequently than they did in the fairway.)—Herbert Warren Wind, "The Sporting Scene," *The New Yorker*, April 30, 1966, pp. 153-154

Parentheses for added remarks should be used sparingly. Frequent parentheses may suggest that the writer is addicted to irrelevant remarks or that he is unable to construct sentences that will show the relationship between his ideas.

Parentheses to enclose details and examples

Parentheses are often used to enclose explanatory details, as in these examples:

> Barnum's "Greatest Show on Earth" anticipated the three classic elements of the put-on: the come-on (buildup), the fake-out (revelation or suspicion that things are not what they seem), and the cop-out (pulling the whole thing off without necessarily delivering the goods).—Jacob Brackman, "Onward and Upward with the Arts," *The New Yorker*, June 24, 1967, p. 40

> For seven long years (1945-1952) austerity was the key word in British economic life.

> The changes can be seen by comparing the profits made before 1929 (upper diagram) with those made after 1929 (lower diagram).

> Since there are in existence a great many "probalistic instruments" or devices for generating chance sequences (playing cards or dice, roulettes, lotteries and the like), it is not surprising that many people have toyed with the idea of throwing elements of language randomly together.—G. T. Guilbaud, *What Is Cybernetics?* p. 70

Sometimes parentheses are used to enclose contradictory or ironic details:

> Art critics, dealers, and curators must protect their identities (and jobs) as people of taste and discrimination.—Jacob Brackman, "Onward and Upward with the Arts," *The New Yorker*, June 24, 1967, p. 36

Parentheses around figures
Parentheses are sometimes used around figures or letters to enumerate points:

> The main questions asked about our way of life concern (1) the strength of our democracy, (2) our radical practices, (3) our concept of modern economy, and (4) the degree of materialism in our culture.—Vera Dean and J. B. Brebner, *How to Make Friends for the U.S.*, p. 22

In business and legal writing, figures are often repeated in parentheses after a written number:

> The payment is due in ninety (90) days.

The repetition of a figure in parentheses is inappropriate in most other kinds of writing.

Parentheses with other marks
No punctuation marks are used before a parenthetical statement that occurs within a sentence. If a comma or period is needed after the parenthetical material, it is placed *outside of* the closing curve:

> The jodhpur, because of its close fit and lack of boot (it is worn with a special pull-on shoe), is certainly not the garment for the bandy-legged man or one who can't "show a good leg."—*Amy Vanderbilt's Complete Book of Etiquette*, p. 151

When the parenthetical statement comes between sentences, the appropriate end punctuation is placed *inside* the closing parenthesis:

> The first signs of the ersatz should be treated in a relaxed manner and with some such words as these: "I see you have been smoking corn silk. It doesn't taste very good, as I remember." (Surprise on the child's part.)—*Ibid.*, p. 536

See also §17.1, p. 209, Capital letters in parentheses.

Exercise

Using appropriate punctuation. In each space in the following sentences (adapted from Longinus' *On the Sublime*), indicate which mark you would consider most appropriate in college writing: a comma, a semicolon, a colon, a dash, or a parenthesis. If no punctuation is necessary, write *O*. If more than one choice is possible, list the marks in order of your preference and be prepared to explain your reasons.

1) Strained expressions cease to be serious ____ and become burlesque ____ I mean phrases like ____ "curling torrential flames" and "vomiting to heaven."

2) The lively products of nature ____ such is the opinion of critics ____ whom I admire ____ are vitiated and debased ____ when bereft of flesh and blood by cold technicalities.

3) Now bulk ____ when hollow and affected ____ is always objectionable ____ whether in physical bodies or in literature ____ and liable to produce in us the impression of smallness ____ "Nothing" ____ it is said ____ "is drier than a man with dropsy."

4) In other respects ____ Timaeus is an accomplished writer ____ and sometimes successful in the lofty style ____ a man of wide knowledge ____ full of ingenuity ____ a bitter critic of the shortcomings of others ____ but unhappily blind to his own.

5) All glaring ____ improper use of words may be ascribed to one ____ common cause ____ it is the pursuit of novelty in style.

6) Let us always apply this principle ____ authenticity ____ to all apparent examples of the sublime in literature ____ let us ask—in all cases ____ is it merely a specious sublimity?

7) Some passions ____ far from lofty ____ are actually low ____ pity ____ grief ____ and fear ____ conversely ____ sublimity is not in the least affecting.

8) Sometimes even an unuttered thought is sublime ____ for instance ____ the silence of Ajax ____ The Odyssey, Book XI ____ is more eloquent than anything he could have said.

9) At another point ____ Ajax ____ finding himself in darkness ____ does not ask for his life ____ such a prayer would be unworthy of this hero ____ but prays for the return of light.

10) Observe how Sappho's sensations contradict one another ____ she freezes ____ she burns ____ she raves ____ she reasons ____ and these contradictions are what make her so tumultuous.

15 Quotation marks, brackets, ellipses, and italics

In general the more common punctuation marks—periods, question marks, commas, semicolons, colons, dashes, and parentheses—indicate intonation and degrees of interruption that would occur if the material was read aloud. They show how the writer wants the words grouped together for meaning and emphasis.

The four marks discussed in this section—quotation marks, brackets, ellipses, and italics—are somewhat different in purpose. They are visual guides that tell the reader at a glance such things as whether the words are a writer's own and whether they are being used in a special way. Compare the following pairs of sentences:

> He said I was a fool. [He accused the *writer* of being a fool.]
> He said, "I was a fool." [He called *himself* a fool.]
>
> He spoke of Watson's moral decline. [the moral decline of Watson]
> He spoke of Watson's *Moral Decline*. [a book by Watson]

Although quotation marks, brackets, ellipses, and italics are used less often than other punctuation, it is important to know how to use them correctly. They are often necessary in college papers, which are likely to contain references to the writing of others.

15.1 Quotation marks

Correction: Make the quotation marks and accompanying punctuation conform to conventional usage.

Quotation marks are necessary to set off direct speech and material quoted verbatim from other sources. They are also used around some titles and around words used in special ways.

Usage varies, but double quotations (" ") are the usual marks in American publications. Students should follow this convention, using single marks (' ')—made on the typewriter with apostrophes—only for a quotation within a quotation:

> "If you acted like a 'progressive' you could get food, cigarettes, the run of the camp, fewer work details—almost anything," one sergeant explained.—*U.S. News & World Report*, August 21, 1953, p. 31

Whether double or single, quotation marks are always used in *pairs*, before and after the quoted material.

Quotation marks to enclose direct discourse

15.1

Statements representing actual speech or conversation are enclosed by quotation marks. The following passage illustrates typical punctuation for direct discourse. Notice not only the quotation marks but the punctuation used with them:

> One morning when I was passing the entrance stairway, I saw Mark Twain coming in alone, with a half-smoked unlit cigar in his mouth. He called out to me, "Young man, have you got a light?"
>
> I fumbled in my pocket for a match, eager to be of service. He bent his head toward the flame, and my hand shook with anxiety, for the mustache stuck out so far, and the cigar was so short, that I feared I might go down in history as the man who burned off Mark Twain's mustache.
>
> But we got it lit, and then he looked at me sternly and barked, "Young man, do you smoke?"
>
> I said, "Yes sir; not very much sir."
>
> He said, "Don't do it; it's a filthy, expensive habit, I've got so I can smoke only dollar cigars." Then he frowned at me and turned to go to Colonel Harvey's inner office. I stood there a moment and he called back to me over his shoulder, "Dollar a barrel."—Burges Johnson, "A Ghost for Mark Twain," *The Atlantic Monthly*, May 1952, p. 65

In dialog the words of each speaker are customarily indented like paragraphs, as in the example above. But when short speeches or statements are quoted to illustrate a point in exposition, they are usually included in the paragraph where they are relevant rather than being set off:

> When he is not playing adman, businessman, referee and editor, Cerf devotes a good part of his time to keeping his authors happy. Fortunately, he enjoys it, even when his high-strung writers curl into knots. He likes to tell about the time that Sinclair Lewis spent a night at the Cerf apartment. "He had dinner," Cerf recalls, "and we were all sitting at the table. Then Bill Faulkner called up and said he was in town. I told Lewis and asked him, could Bill come over? Lewis said, 'Certainly not. This is my night!' Then at 9:30, Lewis went to bed. At 10:30, he shouted downstairs, 'Bennett!' I answered him, and he said, 'I just wanted to see if you sneaked out to see Faulkner.' "—*Time*, December 16, 1966, p. 102

Only *direct discourse*, which represents the actual words of the speaker, is enclosed by quotation marks. *Indirect discourse*, which gives the substance of what the speaker said but not his exact words, is *not* enclosed in quotes:

Direct discourse	*Indirect discourse*
The coach said, "Get in there and fight."	The coach told us to get in there and fight.
"At the present time," the senator replied, "I haven't made up my mind about the bill."	The senator replied that he had not yet made up his mind about the bill.

Quotation marks around quoted material

Words taken directly from another writer or speaker must be clearly set apart, either by quotation marks or by some other conventional typographic device such as setting them in reduced type. Whether a writer is quoting a phrase or several paragraphs, he should make certain that he follows the exact wording and punctuation of his source.

Short quotations. Quotation marks are used around quoted phrases and statements that are included within the body of a paragraph. The quoted material may be worked into the structure of a sentence or may stand by itself:

> Another immortal pun is Eugene Field's comment on the actor Creston Clarke that "he played the king as though he were in constant fear that somebody else was going to play the ace."—Max Eastman, *The Enjoyment of Laughter*, p. 111

> The attack on footnotes is direct and pointed: "It is a mean and scandalous practice in authors to put notes to things that deserve no notice."—Jacques Barchilon and Henry Pettit, *The Authentic Mother Goose*, p. 33

Long quotations. When quoted material is relatively long—more than one full sentence from the original source or more than four lines in your paper—it is usually indented and single spaced but not enclosed in quotation marks. In published material, long quotations are often set in smaller type.

A quotation within a quotation. Use single quotation marks around quoted material that appears within a quotation which is itself enclosed in double marks:

> If they depended solely on economic theory to guide them, they would be in the position of the man John Williams mentions: "About the practical usefulness of the theory, I have often felt like the man who stammered and finally learned to say, 'Peter Piper picked a peck of pickled peppers,' but found it hard to work into conversation."—C. Hartley Grattan, "New Books," *Harper's Magazine*, August 1953, p. 98

15.1 In the rare instances when a third quotation occurs within a second, double and single marks are alternated, like this:

> In the next passage he gives an example of Mill's uncontrolled temper: "Mill attacked Beaton with a poker after reading his comment that 'A work of genius is not, as Mr. Mill says, "a spontaneous outflowing of the soul"; it is the product of intellectual discipline, a quality Mr. Mill notably lacks.'"

Such a proliferation of quotation marks is confusing and can usually be avoided, either by indenting and single spacing the main quotation or by paraphrasing some of the material:

> In the next passage he gives an example of Mill's uncontrolled temper, telling how Mill attacked Beaton with a poker after reading his comment that "A work of genius is not, as Mr. Mill says, 'a spontaneous overflowing of the soul'; it is the product of intellectual discipline, a quality Mr. Mill notably lacks."

Quoted verse. A phrase or portion of a line of verse may be built into a sentence and enclosed by quotation marks, as is this phrase from *Romeo and Juliet:*

> "A plague on both your houses" was the general attitude toward the parties in any conflict, no matter what the outcome.—Percy Finch, *Shanghai and Beyond*, p. 240

If the quoted passage extends over several lines of the poem, it is best to line it off exactly as it appears in the original, single-spaced and indented. Quotation marks are unnecessary:

> Milton opens *Paradise Lost* by announcing that he will write
>
> Of Man's first disobedience, and the fruit
> Of that forbidden tree whose mortal taste
> Brought death into the World. . . .

If two or three lines of verse are incorporated into a paragraph, the passage is enclosed in quotation marks and the line breaks are indicated by diagonal lines (/):

Milton opens *Paradise Lost* by announcing that he will write "Of Man's first disobedience, and the fruit/ Of that forbidden tree whose mortal taste/ Brought death into the World."

Quotation marks around titles

Quotation marks are used to set off the titles of written works shorter than volume length, such as single poems, essays, short stories, and magazine articles. Some publications also use quotation marks around the titles of books and the names of newspapers and magazines, but in academic writing these titles and names are italicized. College writers should follow the more Formal style:

The Oxford Book of English Verse includes only two poems by Oliver Goldsmith: "Women" and "Memory."

Judith Blake and Kingsley Davis have contributed an article titled "Norms, Values, and Sanctions" to *The Handbook of Modern Sociology*, edited by Robert E. L. Faris.

See §15.4, Italics, and §29, The reference paper.

A few titles are neither set off by quotation marks nor underlined for italics: the Bible, Old Testament, the Constitution of the United States, Lincoln's Gettysburg Address, Montgomery Ward Catalog, the Denver Telephone Directory (or any other catalog or directory).

Quotation marks to set off words

Words within a sentence are often set apart by quotation marks or by italics (underlining) to show that the writer is using them in some special way.

A word used as a word. A word used as a word or as an example rather than for its meaning in a passage is either italicized (as in this book) or enclosed by quotation marks. Italics are preferred in Formal writing, but quotation marks are widely used in General writing. A writer should be consistent in following one style or the other:

Formal: People often confuse the word *allusion*, meaning "an indirect reference," with *illusion*, meaning "a misleading appearance."

General: People often confuse the meanings of words that sound alike, such as "allusion" and "illusion."

Apologetic quotes for slang and colloquial expressions. In serious writing, an expression associated with Informal or Nonstandard English is sometimes put in quotation marks to show that the writer knows it is not considered appropriate in Formal usage:

> The disheartening outcome of recent international conferences has convinced some of our statesmen that certain nations consider us as little more than "fall guys."

15.1

The trouble with apologetic quotes is that they focus the reader's attention on the expression and make him wonder why the writer chose to use it. If a writer is certain of the appropriateness of a word, he should use it without apology and without quotation marks regardless of the level of his own usage, as with the word *highfalutin* in this passage:

> I suspect that this kind of transition was easily acceptable to an Elizabethan audience, to whose ears both prose and verse came naturally; who liked highfalutin and low comedy in the same play; and to whom it seemed perhaps proper that the more humble and rustic characters should speak in a homely language.—T. S. Eliot, *Poetry and Drama*, p. 13

When a real or imaginary person is frequently referred to by his nickname, it is not set off by quotation marks:

Abe Lincoln   Huck Finn   Babe Ruth   Ivan the Terrible

In General writing there is seldom any need to use apologetic quotes about a word or expression. If the word is appropriate, use it without quotation marks. If it is not, use another.

Words used derisively. Sometimes a writer may use quotation marks around a term to show that he is using it derisively:

> This remarkable piece of "art" consists of a large canvas covered with mud and old bus transfers.
>
> She was so "genteel" that she avoided any reference to the human body.

Quotation marks to emphasize a mocking tone should be used sparingly, especially in college writing.

Quotation marks with other punctuation

The following conventions govern the use of other punctuation with quotation marks:

1) Commas and periods are always placed *inside* the closing quotation mark:

"Yes," Roger agreed, "it's too late to worry about that now."

Her watch case was described as "waterproof," but "moisture-resistant" would have been more accurate.

2) Semicolons and colons are placed *outside* the closing quotation mark:

This critic's attitude seems to be "I don't like any movie"; on a few occasions, though, he has said kind words for a travelog or a documentary film.

Fully a third of the railroad passengers were what trainmen call "deadheads": people who ride on passes and never tip.

3) Question marks, exclamation points, and dashes are placed inside *or* outside the final quotation mark, depending upon the situation. They come *inside* when they apply to the quotation only:

Mother looked at me askance and asked, "Why do you say that?"

He gave me a skeptical look which seemed to mean "Look who's talking!"

Terrence interrupted, "No, listen to this—" and proceeded to recite a poem none of us had ever heard before.

They are placed *outside* the final quotation mark when they apply to the entire statement:

Who was it who said that "good guys finish last"? [The whole sentence is a question.]

And to top it all off, she refers to her automatic dishwasher as "essential equipment for gracious living"!

End punctuation marks are never doubled; the mark within the quotation marks also indicates the end of the enclosing statement or question:

Ever since I moved to Boston to conduct symphony concerts exclusively, one of the principal questions put to me in interviews is "How much do you miss opera?"—Erich Leinsdorf, "What Makes Opera Run," *The Atlantic Monthly*, March 1966, p. 53

Notice that no period is added after the final quotation mark, even though the sentence is a statement, not a question. Occasionally it is necessary to use double marks *within* a sentence to avoid a possible misreading, as in the sentence following the one quoted above, but such instances are rare:

> Mind you, not "Do you miss opera?", because the questioner takes it for granted that it is impossible for one who has conducted so much opera to live without it, but "How much?"—*Ibid.*

15.2 [/]

15.2 Brackets

[/] **Correction: Use brackets to set off any insertion in quoted material.**

Brackets are used to insert brief editorial comments and explanations in material quoted from other writers:

> Lest it be thought that I am exaggerating, listen to Mencken: "The impact of this flood [of common-speech, non-fashionable Americanisms] is naturally most apparent in Canada, whose geographical proximity and common interests completely obliterate the effects of English political and social dominance."—Eric Partridge, *Slang Today and Yesterday*, p. 293

Comments or directions may be bracketed in conversation or in other quoted material to show that the speaker didn't actually say the enclosed words:

> For the first few minutes the practiced speaker, therefore, fills in time with his "Thank you" to the chairman introducing him. . . . Then come his formal salutations, "Mr. President, honored guests [if there are any], ladies and gentlemen."—*Amy Vanderbilt's Complete Book of Etiquette*, p. 582

The Latin word *sic* (meaning *thus* or *so*) is sometimes inserted in brackets within quoted material to mark an error in spelling, usage, or fact that appeared in the original:

> The author's next letter was headed "Danbury, *Conneticut* [*sic*] Oct. 6, 1854."

Most current writers feel that the insertion of *sic* to mark the errors of others is more snobbish than scholarly, and the practice has declined.

In this book brackets are used with examples of writing to enclose words that might better be left out of a sentence, to suggest an improved expression, and to comment on a construction. These special uses are illustrated below:

> At the end of an hour and a half we arrived at [the spot where] the red flag [was situated].
>
> He looks *similar to* [*like*] his father.
>
> *Most* fishermen are optimists. [adjective, modifying *fishermen*]

Occasionally brackets are used for parenthetical material that falls within parentheses—thus ([ ])—but such constructions are awkward and can usually be avoided. Do not confuse the normal uses of parentheses and brackets; **see** §14.2, Parentheses.

15.3 Ellipses

/.../ **Correction: Use an ellipsis to indicate any omission in quoted material.**

A punctuation mark of three spaced periods, called an ellipsis (plural: *ellipses*), indicates that one or more words have been omitted from the material that is quoted. If an ellipsis comes at the end of a sentence, the sentence period is added to the usual three, as in the second and third ellipses below:

> Fourscore and seven years ago our fathers brought forth upon this continent a new nation . . . dedicated to the proposition that all men are created equal. Now we are engaged in a great civil war . . . . We are met on a great battlefield of that war. . . .—Abraham Lincoln, Gettysburg Address

Ellipsis periods are sometimes used, especially in narrative, to indicate interruptions in thought, incompleted statements, or hesitations in speech, as in this description of the dying words of John Wilkes Booth, the assassin of Lincoln:

> Water was poured into his mouth. He blew it out feebly, opened his eyes and moved his lips to shape the words: "Tell . . . mother. . . . " Then he fainted again. When he came to, he finished his sentence: "Tell . . . mother . . . I . . . died . . . for . . . my country."—Eleanor Ruggles, *Prince of Players*, p. 194

It is best to avoid the practice of some advertising copywriters who use a series of dots in place of conventional punctuation marks: Keep your hands lovely . . . soft . . . beautiful to see . . . and to touch. . . .

15.4 Italics

Ital Correction: Underline the word or expression marked to correspond to the conventions for using italic type.

15.4 Ital

Words are set off or emphasized in most published works by printing them in slanting type called *italics*. In handwritten or typed papers, such words are underlined:

> The article first appeared in Harper's Magazine and was later reprinted in The Reader's Digest.

Italics for titles

The names of newspapers and magazines and the titles of books, plays, and other complete works published separately are conventionally italicized (or underlined):

Newsweek
The Great Gatsby
the novel *Huckleberry Finn*
Webster's Seventh New Collegiate Dictionary
The Chicago Tribune (or: the Chicago *Tribune*)
Hamlet, Act III
the movie *Ben Hur*
Dante's *Divine Comedy*

Titles of articles, short stories, poems, and other short pieces of writing that are part of a larger work are usually enclosed in quotation marks:

> "The Easy Chair" is a regular feature in *Harper's Magazine*.

See §15.1, page 181, Quotation marks around titles, and §29, The reference paper.

Italics for words and phrases used as examples

Words used as words or as examples rather than as parts of a sentence should be italicized or set off by quotation marks. In Formal writing italics are preferred:

> Even on a sophisticated level there is some variation in word usage. For instance, what in other parts of the country is called a *sidewalk* was and may still be called in my native section of Maryland a *pavement*, and what is elsewhere called a *pavement* was in our usage the *street* if in town and the *road* if in the country.—Thomas Pyles, *Words and Ways of American English*, p. 70

Italics for foreign words

Words from foreign languages that have not been absorbed into English should be italicized, not set off by quotation marks:

> It was characteristic of the *fin de siecle* writers to want to stand apart from the common life and live only in the imagination.—Edmund Wilson, *Axel's Castle*, p. 32

> Sometime soon after he arrives in Hawaii, a sweet lassitude creeps over the *malihini* (newcomer).—*Time*, December 16, 1966, p. 66

Foreign expressions that would ordinarily be underlined for italics include terms like *coup d'état*, *Weltschmerz*, *deus ex machina*, *mañana*. In most books and Formal writing, the accents and other marks are used.

Scientific names for plants, insects, and so forth are also italicized:

> The mistletoe (*Phoradendron flavescens*) is the state flower of Oklahoma.

Words from other languages that are now widely used in General English are not considered foreign terms and so are not underlined or otherwise set off:

bourgeois	debut	laissez faire	sputnik
chalet	debutante	prima donna	status quo
chic	fiancee	slalom	vice versa

Although dictionaries designate words that are now anglicized (have become part of the English language) and those that are not, their usage tends to be conservative. If a writer is certain that an expression marked "foreign" is familiar to his readers, he need not underline it.

Abbreviations of some Latin words and phrases used mainly in reference works are usually italicized (*ibid.*, *et seq.*), but Latin abbreviations in general use are not:

e.g.   et al.   etc.   i.e.   vs.   viz.

Italics for emphasis

Italics are used in printed material to indicate an emphatic word or stressed statement:

> The food, clothing, and shelter of this vast rural population add up to one fact—*poverty*.—Gerald F. Winfield, *China: The Land and the People*, p. 82

> I had never seen the play since then, but as I remember it, one of the young men dressed up as Charley's Aunt, and ran across the stage, lifting up his petticoats, and *showing his trousers underneath.* No thing since then has ever shocked me so much.—Gwen Raverat, *Period Piece*, pp. 113-114

Italics should be used sparingly for emphasis. When used excessively or with words that do not deserve stress, this device makes the writer seem affected or childish.

Exercises

1. *Quotation marks for direct speech.* All the quotation marks and indentions have been removed from the following passage from a short story. Rewrite the passage, using quotation marks and indentions to show dialog and changes in speaker.

> Hurry up, old lady, called a tall, red-haired man from an open carriage window, but grandmother didn't quicken her pace. Shove 'em on quick, shouted the guard, his green flag in his hand, his whistle hovering to his lips. But grandmother stopped and pulled at the handle of the door of an almost empty compartment where a fat old man in a black suit and a high white collar and a bowler hat sat reading his morning paper. Unlock this door, guard, she ordered. There's plenty of room in here. Have you a first-class ticket, mum? How can I say what class ticket I've got when they wouldn't sell me one?—adapted from Christine Clegg, "Picnic," *New Campus Writing*, No. 2, p. 162

2. *Appropriate use of quotation marks, brackets, ellipses, italics.* The passage that follows is part of a student paper on H. L. Mencken, the famous American journalist. The four marks discussed in this chapter—quotation marks, brackets, ellipses, and italics—have been omitted, as have typographical devices such as indention and single-spacing for quotations. The sources to which the student makes reference in this passage are reprinted on pages 190-191. Notice carefully all uses of direct quotation from the sources, omissions, and remarks or explanations interpolated by the student. Then copy the student's passage, adding appropriate punctuation and typographical devices. For the purposes of simplicity, you need not add the necessary footnotes unless your instructor asks you to do so.

To Mencken, nothing was sacred. He attacked hypocrisy and stupidity wherever he found it. In his essay on Being an American, for example, he had this to say about social life in the White House: And the current Chief Magistrate of the nation Harding--its defiant substitute for czar and kaiser--is a small-town printer who, when he wishes to enjoy himself in the Executive Mansion, invites in a homeopathic doctor, a Seventh Day Adventist evangelist, and a couple of moving-picture actresses.

In another essay from Prejudices: Third Series, Star-spangled Men, he ridiculed the pretensions of popular fraternal organizations: The Nobles of the Mystic Shrine, chiefly paunchy wholesalers of the Rotary Club species, are not content with swords, baldrics, stars, garters and jewels; they also wear red fezes. The Elks run to rubies. There is an undertaker in Hagerstown, Md., who has been initiated eighteen times. When he robes himself to plant a fellow joiner he weighs three hundred pounds and sparkles and flashes like the mouth of hell itself. Put beside this lowly washer of the dead, General Pershing newly polished would seem almost like a Trappist.

Mencken's talent for invective was enormous, and nothing pleased him more than to fill pages scourging America's buffooneries, ribaldries, imbecilities, and grotesqueries. Such forceful language was bound to arouse animosity. Frederick Lewis Allen, in Only Yesterday, reports that when Mencken denounced the residents of Dayton during the Scopes trial, the Reverend A. C. Stribling replied that Mencken was a cheap blatherskite of a pen-pusher; and to such retorts there was a large section of outraged public opinion ready to cry Amen. A few years later Mencken published a Schimpflexicon, an anthology of abusive remarks made by his critics.

Although he was an unflagging critic of America, Mencken delighted in the satirical material it provided him. He maintained that in America only the man who was born with a petrified diaphragm can fail to laugh himself to sleep every night. Many Americans apparently agreed, for the circulation of the Mercury was over 77,000 in 1927, perhaps because, as Allen says, the magazine crystallized the misgivings of thousands. At any rate, in 1927 Walter Lippmann called Mencken the most powerful personal influence on this whole generation of educated people.

Sources

And here, more than anywhere else that I know of or have heard of, the daily panorama of human existence, of private and communal folly—the unending procession of governmental extortions and chicaneries, of commercial brigandages and throat-slittings, of theological buffooneries, of aesthetic ribaldries, or legal swindles and harlotries, of miscellaneous rogueries, villainies, imbecilities, grotesqueries, and extravagances—is so inordinately gross and preposterous, so perfectly brought up to the highest conceivable amperage, so steadily enriched with an almost fabulous daring and originality, that only the man who was born with a petrified diaphragm can fail to laugh himself to sleep every night, and to awake every morning with all the eager, unflagging expectation of a Sunday-school superintendent touring the Paris peep-shows.—H. L. Mencken, "On Being an American" from *Prejudices: Third Series*, pp. 13-14

And the current Chief Magistrate of the nation—its defiant substitute for czar and kaiser—is a small-town printer who, when he wishes to enjoy himself in the Executive Mansion, invites in a homeopathic doctor, a Seventh Day Adventist evangelist, and a couple of moving-picture actresses.—*Ibid.*, pp. 21-22.

The Nobles of the Mystic Shrine, chiefly paunchy wholesalers of the Rotary Club species, are not content with swords, baldrics, stars, garters and jewels; they also wear red fezes. The Elks run to rubies. The Red Men array themselves like Sitting Bull. The patriotic ice-wagon drivers and Methodist deacons of the Ku Klux Klan carry crosses set with incandescent lights. An American who is forced by his profession to belong to many such orders—say a life insurance solicitor, a bootlegger, or a dealer in Oklahoma oil stock—accumulates a trunk full of decorations, many of them weighing a pound. There is an undertaker in Hagerstown, Md., who has been initiated eighteen times. When he robes himself to plant a fellow joiner he weighs three hundred pounds and sparkles and flashes like the mouth of hell itself. He is entitled to bear seven swords, all jeweled, and to hang his watch chain with the golden busts of nine wild animals, all with precious stones for eyes. Put beside this lowly washer of the dead, Pershing newly polished would seem almost like a Trappist.—H. L. Mencken, "Star-Spangled Men," *Prejudices: Third Series*, p. 138

The *Mercury* made an immediate hit. It was new, startling, and delightfully destructive. It crystallized the misgivings of thousands. Soon its green cover was clasped under the arms of the young iconoclasts of a score of college campuses. Staid small-town executives, happening upon it, were shocked and bewildered; this man Mencken, they decided, must be a debauched and shameless monster if not a latter-day emissary of the devil. When Mencken visited Dayton to report the Scopes trial and called the Daytonians yokels, hillbillies, and peasants, the Reverend A. C. Stribling replied that Mencken was a "cheap blatherskite of a pen-pusher"; and to such retorts there was a large section of outraged public opinion ready to cry Amen. After a few years so much abuse had been heaped upon the editor of the *Mercury* that it was possible to publish for the delectation of his admirers a *Schimpflexicon*—a book made up entirely of highly uncomplimentary references to him. Meanwhile the circulation of his magazine climbed to more than 77,000 by 1927; and in that same year Walter Lippmann called him, without exaggeration, "the most powerful personal influence on this whole generation of educated people."—Frederick Lewis Allen, *Only Yesterday*, pp. 231-232

16 Spelling

This recommendation of steadiness and uniformity [*in spelling*] *does not proceed from an opinion that particular combinations of letters have much influence on human happiness; or that truth may not be successfully taught by modes of spelling fanciful and erroneous . . . . Language is only the instrument of science, and words are but the signs of ideas; I wish, however, that the instrument might be less apt to decay, and that signs might be permanent.—Samuel Johnson*

| *Sp* | **Correction: Correct the spelling of the word marked.**

Out of decent regard for your reader, you should make certain that whatever you write is as free from error as possible. At the very least, your reader is entitled to expect that you will follow the conventions of spelling, for as long as a dictionary is readily available, you have no real excuse for submitting a finished piece of writing that contains misspelled words.

Although misspelled words seldom interfere with meaning, most people consider correct spelling a sign of literacy and even of respectability. Even those who are careless about their own spelling are quick to detect and to criticize spelling errors in the writing of others. Indeed, if you regularly misspell words you may raise suspicions about your educational background and your general ability to handle the language. More important, you may distract your reader from what you are trying to say.

16.1 Overcoming spelling problems

English spelling would be easier if each sound used in speaking were represented by a single letter or even by a combination of letters. But the way a word is pronounced and the way it is spelled do not always match. The same letter or combination of letters may represent a variety of sounds, as does the *a* in *fare*, *hat*, *many*, *lay*, *far*, *war*, *human*, or the *ou* in *though*, *bough*, *enough*, *through*. And one sound may be represented in a variety of ways: b*ee*, bel*ie*ve, prec*e*de, s*ea*, mach*i*ne. As a further complication, a number of English words are written with silent letters: lam*b*, *p*sychology, *k*nife, r*h*ythm, *w*rote. Others, called *homonyms*, sound alike but are spelled differently: *meat*, *meet*, *mete; sight*, *site*, *cite; write*, *right*, *rite; its*, *it's; peace*, *piece*.

Obviously, absolute correctness in spelling is not easy to achieve in English. Most mistakes can be avoided, however, by a writer who is willing to take the time and effort necessary to learn the spelling of difficult words, to use the dictionary when he is in doubt, and to proofread what he has written.

Eliminating careless mistakes

Carelessness undoubtedly accounts for the majority of misspelled words in student papers. It may result from too rapid writing (as in papers written in class) or from failure to proofread the finished copy carefully. Typical examples of careless misspelling are *their* for *there*, *to* for *too*, *who's* for *whose*, *it's* for *its*, *fourty* for *forty*—basic words that you learned before entering high school. Most people make careless mistakes when writing rapidly, but conscientious writers eliminate them by proofreading.

Accurate proofreading requires careful word-by-word reading. If you have difficulty checking your own writing, try following each line with a pencil point, so that you are obliged to see every word separately. Some people find it helpful to read their papers aloud, pronouncing each word distinctly. Any method is useful if it makes it easier for you to see the way that the words have actually been put down on paper.

Using a dictionary

If you are uncertain about the spelling of a word, consult your dictionary. The trial-and-error method of writing a word several ways until it "looks right" (*curiousity? couriousity? curosity?*) is unreliable.

For papers written outside class, spelling should be checked in *revision*. It is poor practice when writing a first draft to stop to look up the spelling of every doubtful word; you may lose the flow of thought or interrupt the sentence movement. Put a check in the margin or over the word as you are writing; then when you are ready to revise, look up each word you have marked.

Learning to visualize words

People who do a good deal of reading tend to be better spellers than those who read little, for seeing a word on the printed page tends to fix it in the mind. Sometimes, however, we learn to recognize a word in reading without really noticing how it is spelled. Very few Americans, for example, ever learned to spell the last name of Nikita Khrushchev, the former Soviet premier, though they saw it in their newspapers every day for years. Many people have a similar problem with such common English words as *occasion*, *occurrence*, and *precede*. When you meet a new word —or when you have to look up a familiar word—look at it carefully, noticing each syllable, and try to fix it in your mind for future use.

Writing practice. Master the spelling of troublesome words by writing them until you spell them right without hesitation. If you are uncertain about the spelling of *embarrass*, for example, write or type the word ten, twenty, or more times, in its various forms, until the spelling becomes automatic: *embarrass*, *embarrassed*, *embarrassment*, *embarrassing*.

16.1 Sp

Separate into syllables words that you find difficult to spell (consult your dictionary for the proper divisions). Stress those letters or combinations of letters that trouble you:

em baR Rass	par aL Lel
oC Ca sion al ly	preJ U dice
o MiT Ted	rep E ti tion
op tI mist	sep A rate

It helps to say the word as you write it, either aloud or to yourself. The combination of (1) seeing a word letter by letter, (2) writing it carefully, and (3) pronouncing it will overcome most spelling problems.

Learning new words. Learn to spell new words correctly as you meet them in your college courses. A new or unfamiliar expression is useless in writing until you can spell it with confidence. Make a note of the words you will probably have to write in reports or in examinations. Underline key words in textbooks and observe their spelling on the blackboard. Then write them out in syllables, pronouncing them as you do so:

ba cil lus	Gen ghis Khan
bi par tite	me tath e sis
car bon if er ous	pro pri e tar y
de men tia prae cox	u ni cel lu lar

When instructors in various courses complain that their students can't spell, they are referring either to very common words or to words that make up the essential vocabulary of their subject.

Keeping a spelling list

In your notebook, keep a list of words you have misspelled or that you have trouble spelling. The words should be spelled correctly and should be easy to find so that you can refer to them when proofreading your papers. The purpose of such a list is to prevent the same mistakes from occurring in one paper after another. When the same word occurs more than once in your list, print it in large capitals (FAS CI NATE), write it in red ink, or use any other system that will call it to your attention.

16.2 Common spelling errors

The following list contains one hundred words frequently misspelled in student papers. Each word is divided into syllables so that you can see more clearly how it is put together.

ac com mo date
ac quaint ed
a cross
a gree ment
all right
al read y
a nal y sis
ap pear ance
ar ti cle
ath let ics
at tend ance
be lieve
ben e fit ed
Brit ain
bus i ness
change a ble
choose
com par a tive
con ceive
con science
con tin u ous
de ci sion
def i nite
de pend ent
de scrip tion
de vel op
din ing room

dis ap pear ance
dis ap point
dor mi to ry
em bar rass
en vi ron ment
e quip ment
ex ag ger ate
ex ist ence
ex treme ly
fa mil iar
fas ci nate
for eign
for mer ly
for ty
gram mar
height
hin drance
im ag i nar y
im me di ate ly
in ci den tal ly
in de pend ent
in tel li gent
ir re sist i ble
judg ment [*or* judge ment]
knowl edge
lei sure
li brar y

lik a ble [*or* like able]
main te nance
man u fac tur er
mis spelled
mo not o nous
mys te ri ous
nec es sar y
no tice a ble
oc ca sion al ly
oc cur rence
o mit ted
op por tu ni ty
par tic u lar ly
pas time
per form
pre ced ing
prej u dice
priv i lege
prob a bly
pro ce dure
pro nun ci a tion
pro por tion
psy chol o gy
quan ti ty
re ceive
re fer ring
rep e ti tion
re sem blance
sched ule
sec re tar y
seize
sep a rate
sim i lar
soph o more
suc ceed
sym pa thize
tem per a ment
tend en cy
there fore
trag e dy
tru ly
un doubt ed ly
un til
u su al ly
val u a ble
writ ing

You may find this list useful in testing your spelling ability and in checking and correcting errors in your papers. A spelling list of your own, however, will be more profitable to study than lists made by others, because it will help you to concentrate on your individual problems.

Errors caused by faulty pronunciation

Although faulty pronunciation is not a major cause of misspelling, it is responsible for some very common mistakes:

Correct spelling	*Misspelling*
a*th* *l*et ics	ath*a*letics
priv *i* lege	pri*v*lege
en vi *ron* ment	envi*rom*ent
mis chie *vous*	mischiev*i*ous
pre scribe	*per*scribe
dis *g*ust	dis*c*ust

Pronounce each syllable to yourself when writing longer words (*ac-com-pa-ny-ing*, *par-tic-u-lar-ly*, *stud-y-ing*). Also notice that many longer words contain letters that are blurred or lost in speech: tem-per-*a*-men-tal, ac-ci-den-*tal*-ly, lab-*o*-ra-to-ry.

Omission of final -ed

One of the most common spelling errors is the omission of *-ed* at the ends of words. This sometimes occurs because of analogy to speech, where the *-ed* sound often is lost in rapid conversation or is assimilated by the following sound. To catch such errors in writing, you will have to rely on your eye rather than your ear. There are three principal trouble areas:

In verb forms. Regular verbs form their past tenses and past participles by adding *-ed.* Be careful not to drop these letters, especially before words beginning with *t*, like *to. Used to* and *supposed to* are perennial offenders:

> I *used to* (not *use to*) misspell words.
> He is *supposed to* be (not *suppose to* be) an authority.

In verbal modifiers. The past participle is often used as a modifier (*stewed prunes*, *raised platform*). Here too the tendency in pronunciation is to drop the *-ed*, and many such shortened forms have become established: *grade school*, *oilcloth*, *cream cheese*, *roast chicken*. Others are sometimes found in print but are debatable: *bottle beer*, *whip cream*, *advance headquarters*. In college papers it is better to use only shortened forms that are generally accepted. In less Formal writing, more latitude is allowed, but dictionaries, current written practice, and appropriateness to the paper should serve as guides.

In modifiers from nouns. Adjectives are often formed by adding *-ed* to nouns: *long-haired*, *heart-shaped*, *two-faced.* When the *-ed* is dropped in such forms—a growing tendency in current English —the result is a noun modifier (see §7.4): *king-size box*, *hard-surface road*, *high-heel shoes.* Established forms like these are appropriate in all writing, but avoid dropping the *-ed* when a noun modifier does not result: *advanced courses*, *middle-aged*, *old-fashioned*.

Confusion of words that sound alike

Be careful not to confuse words of identical or similar sound. It is easy when writing rapidly to put down *their* for *there*, *its* for

16.2 Sp

it's, *maybe* for *may be*, but a conscientious writer will check his finished work closely for errors of this sort. Substituting one form for another may suggest an idea that the writer did not intend:

> Psychiatric treatment changed Bobby from a withdrawn, unhappy child to a normal, happy boy *excepted* by his group.

The following pairs of words are often confused in writing. See if you can distinguish between them.

16.2

accept	except	lead	led
advice	advise	loose	lose
affect	effect	passed	past
aisle	isle	peace	piece
allusion	illusion	personal	personnel
birth	berth	principal	principle
capital	capitol	quiet	quite
choose	chose	stationary	stationery
cite	site	than	then
conscience	conscious	their	there
coarse	course	to	too
credible	creditable	weather	whether
desert	dessert	who's	whose
its	it's		

If you have trouble keeping any of these forms clear in mind, try making up sentences that will illustrate plainly the differences in meaning:

> Everyone *except* Sam *accepted* the invitation.
> *It's* difficult for the leopard to change *its* spots.
> The ceremonies will be held *whether* or not the *weather* is fair.

Separate words and combined forms

Observe the distinctions between expressions that are written as one word and those written as two. These forms frequently need to be checked in revision:

all ready (adjective phrase):
The girls were at last *all ready* to leave.
already (adverb of time):
It was *already* dark when they arrived.

all right (adjective phrase, conventionally written as two words):
The seats seemed *all right* to me. (The forms *alright* and *alrite* are not accepted in Standard usage.)

all together (adjective phrase):
We were *all together* at the depot.
altogether (adverb, meaning wholly):
That's *altogether* another matter.

a while (noun):
They talked for *a while.*
awhile (adverb):
Can't you stay *awhile* longer?

may be (verb phrase):
He *may be* the next mayor.
maybe (adverb, short for *it may be*):
Maybe you'll have better luck next time.

Certain phrases may be mistakenly written as one word through analogy with other forms or because they are often run together in speech:

The assignment was *a lot* more difficult than I expected. [not: *alot*]

The judge *threw out* his testimony. [not: *throughout*]

The puppy was always there at his owner's *beck and call.* [not: *beckon call*]

16.3 Some principles of spelling

Chaotic as spelling is in English, some principles are helpful for spelling common words. Listed below are guides to spelling that you have probably heard before. If you *know* that you know them, you might better spend your time on some other aspect of writing. But if you aren't quite certain about these general principles, review them and perhaps also consult the spelling section in the front pages of your dictionary for more detailed information.

Final -e

Words ending in silent *-e* generally retain the *-e* before additions (called *suffixes*) beginning with a consonant (*-ment*, *-ly*, *-some*, *-ness*), but drop the *-e* before additions beginning with a vowel (*-ing*, *-able*, *-ous*, *-ary*).

-e retained before a consonant:

arrange	arrang*e*ment	nine	nin*e*ty
awe	aw*e*some	require	requir*e*ment

definite definit*e*ly shape shap*e*less
hope hop*e*less spite spit*e*ful

Exceptions:

arg*um*ent a*wf*ul du*ly* ni*nt*h tru*ly*

-e dropped before another vowel:

argue arg*uing* imagine imagi*nar*y
arrive arri*va*l shape sha*pi*ng
conceive concei*va*ble value val*ua*ble
grieve grie*vo*us write wri*ti*ng

Exceptions: In a few words silent *-e* is retained before a vowel to avoid confusion with other forms:

dye dyeing (compare *dying*)
singe singeing (compare *singing*)

16.3

Words ending in *-ce* or *-ge* retain the final *-e* before additions beginning with *a*, *o*, or *ou* (so that the final *-c* or *-g* will not suggest the "hard" sound):

chang*ea*ble notic*ea*ble unmanag*ea*ble
courag*eou*s outrag*eou*s veng*ea*nce

-ie- and -ei-

The familiar jingle learned by most school children is helpful in spelling *-ie-* and *-ei-* words: "Write *i* before *e* except after *c*, or when sounded as *a* as in *neighbor* and *weigh*."

Words with -ie-. Words with *-ie-* are more common than words with *-ei-*. The typical sound of *-ie-* is *ē:*

achieve chief grievous niece
believe field hygiene siege

Other *-ie-* words are *mischief*, *sieve*, and *view*.

Words with -ei-. After *c*, and also to spell the sound *ā*, *-ei-* is generally used:

ceiling perceive eight reign
conceive receipt freight vein
deceive receive neighbor weigh

The long *ē* sound is spelled *-ei-* (rather than *-ie-*) in a few words: *either*, *leisure*, *neither*, *seize*, *weird*. Other sounds spelled *-ei-*: *counterfeit*, *foreign*, *height*, *heir*.

Doubling the final consonant

Double the final consonant before a suffix beginning with a vowel (*-able*, *-ed*, *-er*, *-ing*) with (1) words of one syllable ending in a single consonant after a single vowel (*brag*, *hit*, *sit*) and (2) with words of more than one syllable, ending the same way and accented on the last syllable (*commit*, *forget*, *prefer*).

One-syllable words			*Words of more than one syllable*		
bat	batter	batting	commit	committed	committing
grip	gripping	gripped	control	controllable	controlled
pin	pinned	pinning	occur	occurrence	occurred
spot	spotty	spotted	omit	omitted	omitting
wet	wetter	wettest	prefer	preferred	preferring

The consonant is *not* doubled (1) in words with two vowels before the final consonant (*daub*, *daubing; keep*, *keeper; spoil*, *spoiled*), or (2) in words ending with two consonants (*help*, *helped; peck*, *pecking; lurk*, *lurked*), or (3) when the accent of the lengthened word shifts to an earlier syllable (*infer′*, *in′ ference; prefer′*, *pref′-erence; refer′*, *ref′ erence*).

16.3 Sp

Usage is divided about doubling the final consonant of some words not accented on the last syllable, but American spelling generally favors the single consonant.

bias	biased	quarrel	quarreling
counsel	counseled, counselor	travel	traveler, traveled
diagram	diagramed	worship	worshiped, worshiping
kidnap	kidnaping, kidnaper		

Final -y

A final *-y* preceded by a consonant regularly changes to *i* before all suffixes except those beginning with *i:*

body	bodies	happy	happiness
busy	business	lonely	loneliness
carry	carried, carrying	marry	marriage, marrying
duty	dutiful	mercy	merciful
easy	easily	study	studious, studying
envy	envious	Tory	Tories

Final *-y* preceded by a vowel remains unchanged when a suffix is added:

boy	boys, boyish	enjoy	enjoyable, enjoyment, enjoying
delay	delayed, delayer	play	playful, playing, played

-cede, -ceed, -sede
Only one word ends in *-sede: supersede.* Only three end in *-ceed: exceed, proceed, succeed.* All other words of this sort end in *-cede: precede, recede, intercede, secede,* etc.

-able, -ible, -ance, -ence
Words with these endings should be carefully checked for correct spelling. Words ending in *-able* (like *advisable, desirable, improbable, suitable*) are much more common than those ending in *-ible* (such as *audible, divisible, horrible, visible*). But since no rules govern the formation of these endings, the individual words should be looked up whenever the writer is in doubt.

A few words are spelled with either *-able* or *-ible* endings. Dictionaries indicate the more common or preferred spelling by putting it first (*collapsible, collapsable; preventable, preventible*).

16.3 Sp

The spelling of words ending in *-ance, -ant; -ence, -ent* must also be watched, since pronunciation does not distinguish them (attend*ance*, confid*ence;* defend*ant*, exist*ent*).

See also §7.1, Plurals of nouns, especially page 79, Nouns ending in *-y, -o,* or *-f.*

16.4 Variant spellings

When a word is currently spelled in two ways (*extol, extoll*), it is usually a good idea to use the more common form.

Many words have secondary spellings, usually British or simplified forms generally labeled in dictionaries as *Brit., Variant, Archaic*, and so on, so that you can choose the form appropriate to your subject and style. Most people writing today, and certainly anyone who has difficulty with spelling, will ordinarily prefer:

1) The more modern of two equally reputable spellings: *draft, mold, plow* instead of *draught, mould, plough.*

2) The simpler form of a specialized word if it has attained currency among the people who use it most: *anesthetic, catalog, medieval, program, sulfur* rather than *anaesthetic, catalogue, mediaeval, programme, sulphur.*

Although it is possible to simplify the spelling of many common words (as *thoro* for *thorough, enuf* for *enough*), conventional spelling is expected in most kinds of writing. Three simplified forms are gradually gaining acceptance in General, if not in Formal, writing: *tho*, *altho*, *thru*. Other shortened forms should be avoided.

3) American rather than British spellings: *center*, *labor*, *pajama* rather than *centre*, *labour*, *pyjama*.

For the spelling of proper names (the British *Labour* Party) and for direct quotation (the Prime Minister described it as "a *humourless* situation"), British spelling should be followed, but in other situations the American forms should be used.

Exercises

1. *Current opinions about spelling.* Here are three statements about spelling, all by writers professionally interested in the often perplexing problems faced by the student. What attitude toward prescriptions for spelling will you and your instructor take?

Good spelling is a sign of literacy. We may even say that spelling and social status are related. Take the case of phonetic spelling, for example, spelling *duz* for does. This may be useful to an advertiser trying to capture and hold the attention of the buying public. But in normal situations, phonetic spelling becomes equivalent to spelling incorrectly. He who writes *neet* for neat, *ded* for dead, and *rote* for wrote will find that his friends notice such spellings. They may be amused. Or they may even be ashamed of friends who don't know how to spell. Writers do occasionally write the exact words of people whose speech is incorrect or corrupt. They even purposely misspell their words to let the reader know the speaker's social level. Mickey Spillane and John Steinbeck are authors who use this realistic spelling device in such sentences as "Elvira done tole me that nobuddy has gone to the crik." But it is one thing for a famous writer to use a special literary device; it is quite another to create the impression that you are one of the characters he's writing about.—Edna F. Furness, *Spelling for the Millions*, pp. 4-5

Because of the irregularity and inconsistency in our spelling, a most formidable task is shouldered onto all those who attempt to learn to spell. But learn to spell we must, because Americans attach high importance (a prestige factor) to being able to spell *correctly*.

Bad spelling is regarded as an infallible indication of illiteracy. It is therefore to one's advantage socially and professionally to be able to spell *correctly*.

What it amounts to is that one must have a good memory. And everyone doesn't have a good memory. Those few who have eidetic (photographic) memories are indeed fortunate. Those who have poor memories have about as much chance of staying afloat on our ocean of words (half a million of them) as a clay pigeon has in a smashing storm on the Atlantic.

Actually, there is no *correct* way to spell a word. This is very hard to get across to people, and many who read this will go away still believing there *is* a *correct* way. As if God passed along to the men who compiled spelling books and dictionaries the *right* way to spell words, as He passed the Ten Commandments on to Moses.

What the compilers did was to record the *way* certain people (who didn't know any more about it than they did) were spelling words.

What then is true, is that there has come about through *usage* a way of spelling words that ultimately was *said* to be *correct*. And is still said to be correct.

If there was an inherently correct way to spell words, spelling would not have changed over the years as it has: clerke, logyk, teche, versus clerk, logic, teach (Chaucer's time and today).—Parm Mayer, "Speling Is Strikly for the Burds," *Michigan Education Journal*, February 1, 1967, pp. 18-19

And about spelling, I do not believe in hard and fast rules, and least of all in the hard and fast rules of champions of simplified spelling, such as the late Bernard Shaw. I hold that a word is something more than the noise it makes: it is also the way it looks on the page. I am averse to simplified spelling which destroys all traces of a word's origin and history. But I think, for example, that the English would do well to omit, from a word like "labour," the superfluous U, which appears to be merely an etymological error. As to whether "centre" should be spelt "centre" or "center," that seems to me a matter of indifference. There is much to be said for the American spelling "catalog"; on the other hand I distrust simplifications of spelling that tend to alter pronunciation, as, for example, the shortening of "programme" to "program", which throws the stress onto the first syllable. And I think that the advocates of a systematic simplified spelling—such as those who recently introduced a Bill in Parliament—overlook the fact that in attempting to fix spelling phonetically, they are also attempting to fix pronunciation: and both pronunciation and spelling, in both England and America, must inevitably change from age to age under the pressure of usage and convenience.—T. S. Eliot, *American Literature and the American Language*, pp. 7-8

2. *Recognizing misspelled words*. Read the following passage carefully, noting and correcting the misspellings that have been inserted. Look especially for faulty *-ed* forms:

Nor should we be surprise that the historical record gives us this verdict. In its roots and aspirations, Western civilization is turn toward the future, not the pass; toward experiment, not the status quo; toward creation; toward "a new heaven and a new earth," not a safe and static world. It is precisely this quality of inventivness, of vision, of the courage to dream that has made Western society, for good and evil, the catalyst and prime mover in a world of magnificient but somnolent civilisations. If that quality were lost today, if no vision of the future informed its policies, no lift of hope encourage its efforts, no faith to go further and do better inspire its aims, then the hulk of its greatness might survive. But the spirit would be dead. The trial of soul we face today is to outdream the communist visionaries, outwork the communist fanatics, and outdare the voices of defeatism and discouragment within our own society. And this is precisely the challenge which Western man, again and again in his millenial record, has met and measure and triumphantly overcome.—Barbara Ward, "In Time of Trial," *The Atlantic Monthly*, February 1962, p. 37

3. *Individual spelling lists.* Keep a list of words that you will have to use in writing for the different courses you are taking. Use a different page for each subject area, so that you can add new words as you go along. To fix the spelling in your mind, divide the words into their proper syllables (consult your dictionary for this purpose).

4. *Following general principles of spelling.* Copy the words in each of the following groups, making the additions or changes indicated:

1) Supply *-ei-* or *-ie-* as required for correct spelling:

all - - d	fr - - ght	s - - ve
bel - - ve	h - - ght	s - - ze
conc - - ve	l - - sure	th - - r
counterf - - t	n - - ther	v - - l
for - - gn	p - - ce	w - - rd

2) Add *-ed* to the following verbs to show whether the final consonant is doubled or not. If there is a choice of forms, indicate both of them:

bargain	droop	quarrel
bias	drop	question
chide	kidnap	refer

clot	list	travel
dine	play	whelp

3) Add *-ing* to each of these words, making any necessary changes in the root form of the word:

become	endure	prove
control	hope	use
dine	hurry	write

4) Change each of these words to an adjective ending *-ous:*

continue	dispute	mischief
courage	glory	outrage
courtesy	grieve	sanctimony

5. *Spelling of common suffixes.* Add *-able* or *-ible* to the following words, changing letters wherever necessary to conform with accepted spellings:

accept	digest	repair
advice	force	sense
contempt	justify	train

Add *-ance, -ant* or *-ence, -ent* to these words, making any other necessary changes:

ascend	dally	provide
compete	defend	revere
confide	maintain	vigil

6. *Recognizing misspelled words.* Without referring to the text, correct the misspelled words in the following passage.

The principal that every great man is a national calamity is easily defensable. It is difficult to concieve that strong men will not irresistably impose upon thier countrymen their own eccentricities and prejadices. Napoleon, for example, beleived that he had a definate destiny to succede, a mysterous "star" guiding him and France to great heighths. He did not dream of any hinderance from the other nations of Europe. His plans were to seperate them one by one and to sieze all power and priveledge. Only Britian refused to acommodate itself to his grandiose schemes. His temperment was characteristic of his enviroment; massively fasinated by Romantic psycology, he had an exagerated consciousness of the independant existance of his charisma. Napoleon was tradgically dissappointed in his hopes, as were his spiritual forebears, Alexander the Great, Caesar, Louis XIV, and his inheritors, Hitler and Mussolini.

7. *Distinguishing between similar forms.* Compose sentences that will illustrate clearly the differences between these pairs of words of similar sound (for example: "The *morale* of the troops overseas was high"; "There seems to be no *moral* to this tale"). Pay particular attention to those words that have given you trouble in writing:

accept—except
affect—effect
angle—angel
boarder—border
desert—dessert
discrete—discreet
its—it's
loose—lose
may be—maybe
plain—plane
principal—principle
quite—quit
stationary—stationery
than—then
they're—their
to—too

17 Capital letters, hyphens, and apostrophes

17.1 Capital letters

Cap Correction: Capitalize the word marked; be consistent in use of capital letters.

lc Correction: Write the word marked with a lower case (small) letter.

Most uses of capital letters are standard conventions that every writer is expected to follow. Writing in which capitals are improperly used seems sloppy and eccentric to the reader because it focuses his attention on the wrong words and interrupts the natural flow of thought.

17.1 *Cap*

The following sections describe the most frequent uses of capital letters. A complete listing of all forms is obviously impossible, as is a description of the varying practices of different kinds of publications. In general, Formal English tends to use more capitals than General English, and newspaper usage tends to cut them to a minimum. Consult a recent dictionary or style manual if you are in doubt whether to capitalize a particular word. If usage is divided, choose the form that seems most appropriate to your paper and follow it consistently.

You may use proofreading marks to correct capitalization in your papers. Three lines under a small letter means: make this a capital. A slanting line drawn through a capital letter means: make this a lower case (small) letter.

```
march 15        He came from West of Buffalo.
```

To mark units of expression

Capital letters are conventionally used to draw the reader's attention to the beginning of a statement or to individual words in titles.

First word of a sentence. Capitalize the first word of every sentence or expression punctuated with an end stop (period, question mark, or exclamation mark):

> Has the change helped? Not much. The reason is obvious.

First word of a line of poetry. In traditional verse style, the first word of each line is capitalized:

> Yet this abundant issue seem'd to me
> But hope of orphans and unfather'd fruit;
> For summer and his pleasures wait on thee,
> And, thou away, the very birds are mute. . . .
> —William Shakespeare, Sonnet 97

First word of a quotation. The first word of a direct quotation that is in itself a complete sentence is capitalized:

> He said, "The future of mankind cannot be left to chance."
> "The crisis is here," he said. "We must act now."

But no capital is used when the quotation is fragmentary or built into the structure of the sentence, or when the second part of a quoted sentence is interrupted by an expression such as *he said:*

> According to the advertisement, it was the "most spectacular picture of the year."

> Rousseau maintained that "the love of happiness is the sole principle of all human actions."

> "The argument is based," he said, "upon a completely false premise."

In parentheses. A complete sentence enclosed in parentheses is always capitalized when it stands alone, but when enclosed *within* another sentence, it usually is not:

> The broadcast, sponsored by a local bank, was frequently interrupted by lengthy commercials. (Apparently the sponsor doesn't believe that silence is golden.)

> Fitzhugh was the member of a prominent family (his mother was the granddaughter of Sir Thomas Wyatt) and was received in the highest circles.

After a colon. A complete sentence standing after a colon is not usually capitalized when the connection with the preceding clause is close:

> We observe a great diversity of phenomena: changes in luminosity and color take place which seem to be capricious and unpredictable.
> —Philipp Frank, *Relativity: A Richer Truth*, p. 126

The sentence after the colon is often capitalized when it is distinctly separate or when the writer wants to give it emphasis:

> Quite a few teachers in the departments of science would tell the student: We scientists deliver the laws of nature to the philosopher, who has to interpret them.—*Ibid.*, p. 84

In titles of written material. The first word, the last word, all important words (nouns, pronouns, verbs, adjectives, and adverbs), and all prepositions of more than five letters are capitalized in the titles of books, magazine articles, themes, and so forth:

"The Battle Hymn of the Republic" *Of Mice and Men*
Pottery Through the Ages *A Boy and His Dog*

I and O. The pronoun *I* and the exclamation *O* are always capitalized to prevent reading them as parts of other words:

> Give a man a girl he can love,
> As I, O my love, love thee. . . .
> —James Thomson, "Gifts"

17.1

The exclamation *oh* is not capitalized unless it stands first in a sentence.

For proper nouns and their derivatives

The names of specific people, places, and things, and the words derived from them are conventionally capitalized (Karl Marx—Marxism; Africa—African sculpture; Lent—Lenten menu). Examples of the most frequent types of proper nouns are given in the following sections.

In a few cases, words originally derived from proper nouns have dropped the capital in the course of frequent use (pasteurized milk, a jersey blouse, french fries). Usage differs about the capitalization of others (diesel, levis). Up-to-date dictionaries provide a guide in such matters, as do the practices of current publications.

Names and titles of people. A person's name or nickname is capitalized:

Franklin Delano Roosevelt Walter Boyd Babe McAvoy
Teddy Roosevelt Wally Dizzy Gillespie

A title should be capitalized when it is used as part of a person's name, but not when it is used as a descriptive term. A few titles of high rank are capitalized whether or not the officeholder is named: President (of the United States), the Pope, the Queen of England, the Chief Justice of the Supreme Court. Titles referring to a position or an office rather than to the specific person holding it are not capitalized:

Capitals	*No capitals*
Professor Townsend	Francis Townsend is a professor.
Coach Elmer Fumble	Our coach is Elmer Fumble.
Sergeant David Moore	A sergeant maintains discipline.
Judge R. A. Snow	He was elected judge.
The President [of the U.S.] vetoed the bill	The president of the company resigned.
The Queen addressed the opening session of Parliament.	England has had several queens.

Names of family relationships are usually capitalized when used with a person's name or when used as proper nouns standing for the name. They are not capitalized when used as common nouns or when preceded by a possessive:

Capitals	*No capitals*
Grandma Moses	She is a grandmother.
Aunt Sarah	My aunt's name is Sarah.
I showed Mother the card.	I showed my mother the card.
Whatever Father said, we did.	His father was demanding.

Names of groups. Names referring to racial, national, linguistic, political, or religious groups are capitalized:

Negro	Swede	Democrat	Catholic
Polynesian	Italian	Republican	Jew
English	Finn	Communist	Moslem
French	Indian	Socialist	Baptist

Names of social and economic groups are not capitalized (except occasionally for stylistic emphasis):

the middle class	the intelligentsia	the bourgeoisie
the nouveau riche	theboobocracy	the proletariat

Names of organizations. Names and abbreviations of business associations, clubs, fraternities, and other voluntary organizations are capitalized:

National Association of Manufacturers (NAM)	Boy Scouts
Rotary International	League of Women Voters
Daughters of the American Revolution (DAR)	United Auto Workers (UAW)
	Phi Beta Kappa

The words *freshman*, *sophomore*, *junior*, *senior* are capitalized only when they refer to organized groups and their functions (the Freshman Class, the Junior Prom), not when they refer to an academic status (She is a sophomore; The seniors must write a thesis).

Names of places. Words that designate specific geographical divisions or particular places and areas are capitalized:

Asia	Texan
European	Boston
Latin America	Hyde Park
Ghana	the Bowery
Ireland	Third Avenue

17.1 Cap

When the names of directions are used to identify geographic areas, they are generally capitalized. When they merely indicate direction, they are not:

Capitals	*No capitals*
the old West	west of Suez
a Southerner	a southern exposure
the Far East	eastern Tennessee

Names of institutions and their divisions. The names of specific public and private institutions and their divisions and departments are capitalized. Names that apply to a whole class of institutions are not:

Capitals	*No capitals*
Chicago Public Library	a public library
U.S. Public Health Service	public health problems
Kansas City Hospital	a city hospital
Rock Falls High School	our high school
a Harvard University course	a university course
U.S. Department of Records	the records of the business
the Graduate School of Business	a business school

Specific high-school or college academic courses are capitalized; general subjects are not:

Capitals	*No capitals*
Modern French Literature	literature
Advanced Narrative Writing	composition
Chemistry 101	chemistry
Abnormal Psychology 410	psychology

Names of specific objects. Names of specific objects, such as ships, planes, structures, famous documents and artifacts, and brand-name products are capitalized:

the *S.S. Independence*	the Golden Gate Bridge	the Constitution
four-engine Constellations	the Lincoln Memorial	the Sphinx
the Super Chief	the Rosetta Stone	Cleopatra's Needle
a Rambler	Magna Charta	a Royal typewriter

Names of units in time. Capitalize words designating specific periods, events, months, days, and holidays:

the Stone Age	the Battle of Waterloo
the Renaissance	January
the Civil War	Thursday
the Norman Conquest	Labor Day

Names of seasons are not generally capitalized:

winter summer spring fall autumn

Sacred names. References to deities and to sacred texts are capitalized. Pronouns referring to the Christian Trinity are also usually capitalized:

God	Holy Ghost	Talmud
the Savior	Bible	Koran
Virgin Mary	New Testament	the Buddha

The Lord made man in His own image.

Abstractions. Abstractions like ideas, qualities, or conditions may be capitalized, especially in Formal and sentimental writing, to show that they are being discussed in some ideal or absolute state. Sometimes abstractions are personified, particularly in poetry:

> Throughout recorded history, Man has responded to the challenge of Nature.
>
> The pursuit of the Good Life is a persistent human preoccupation.
>
> Eternal Spirit of the chainless Mind!
> Brightest in dungeons, Liberty! thou art. . . .
> —Lord Byron, "Sonnet on Chillon"

In General writing, capitalized abstractions are seldom appropriate. College students should confine them to Formal papers of critical analysis or philosophical theory and follow the practices found in readings assigned in the course for which the papers are written.

Distinguishing proper and common forms. Some words can be spelled either with or without capitals. It is important to distinguish between these forms because they often have different meanings:

Capitals	*No capitals*
a Democrat (member of the Democratic Party)	a democrat (one who believes in democracy)
a Republican principle (of the Republican Party)	a republican principle (of a republic)
Orthodox beliefs (of the Greek Orthodox Church)	orthodox beliefs (conventional)
Catholic sympathies (of or with Catholics)	catholic sympathies (broad; universal)
Romantic poetry (of the Romantic Period)	romantic poetry (concerning romance or love)

17.2 Hyph

17.2 Hyphens

Hyph — Correction: Insert or remove hyphen between the words marked to conform to current usage.

Hyphens are used to connect two or more words used as a single expression (*heavy-hearted*, *will-o'-the-wisp*) and to keep parts of other words distinct (*anti-inflation*, *re-examine*).

Hyphens are needed in some instances to prevent misreading (*un-ionized*) or to differentiate between the same words used in different ways (*a drive in* the evening, a *drive-in* theater). But generally they are used as a matter of convention or for better appearance (*brother-in-law*, *hocus-pocus*).

In printed matter the use of hyphens varies considerably: newspapers and General English use relatively few hyphens; Formal English uses more. The important thing to look for in proofreading is consistency. If an expression is hyphened the first time it occurs, it should be hyphened throughout.

This section lists the most common uses of hyphens. **See also** §19.2, page 238, Spelling and word division.

In compound words

A hyphen is used between two or more words considered as a single unit in certain expressions:

Names for family relationships. Some compound names for family relationships are hyphened; others are not:

Hyphened: father-in-law, great-grandfather, sister-in-law
One word: stepson, stepmother, grandfather
Two words: half brother, second cousin

Compound numbers. A hyphen is used in numbers from twenty-one to ninety-nine. Fractions are hyphened when used as modifiers; as nouns, they are usually written as two words:

thirty-three
one hundred twenty-eight
twenty-first birthday

four fifths of a box
one-half inch
one thirty-second of an inch

In General usage, compound numbers are sometimes written without hyphens when the figure is easily understood from the context (at the age of *sixty five;* the correct answer is *thirty eight*).

In compounds with self. Most group words beginning with *self* are written with hyphens (*self-contained*, *self-pity*, *self-support*, *self-government*); some may be written with a hyphen or without (*self support*, *self government*). A very few words beginning with *self* are written as one word: *selfsame*, *selfless*, *selfhood*. Consult a recent dictionary to find out which form is preferred.

Standard compound nouns. A number of compound nouns are regularly written with a hyphen: *bull's-eye*, *good-for-nothing*, *jack-o'-lantern*, *secretary-treasurer*. Other similar compounds are written as one word (*beeswax*, *newsprint*, *policyholder*) or as two words (*intelligence test*, *labor union*, *shipping point*, *water cooler*).

Since practice is likely to vary with many of these forms, a writer often has the option of using or not using a hyphen. Where no confusion of terms is apt to arise, most writers would omit the hyphen except in conspicuously Formal style. If you are in doubt whether a hyphen is necessary, consult a good recent dictionary.

In group modifiers

When two or more words act as a closely linked modifier immediately before another word, they are often hyphened to suggest the close relationship:

gray-green eyes
a well-kept lawn

a nineteenth-century poet
an all-out effort

A hyphen should always be used to prevent a possible misreading:

a *slow-motion* picture
a *navy-blue* uniform
a *pitch-dark* room
some *reclaimed-rubber* plants

When the first word of a group modifier is an adverb ending in *-ly*, no hyphen is used after it:

richly deserved praise
openly antagonistic attitude

Compound modifiers formed with present or past participles are usually hyphened when they precede a noun:

a good-looking man
a well-planned attack

Such phrases are not usually hyphened in other positions:

Her father was good looking.
The attack was well planned.

17.2 Hyph

Long phrases or clauses used as modifiers are hyphened:

> . . . and he offers dramatic recitals about guerrillas (whom he didn't meet) and possible ambushes (which he didn't find), all of it pretty much in the gosh-we-could-even-hear-the-guns-in-the-distance school of war reporting.—G. Barrett, "Korean Scenario," *The New York Times Book Review*, July 12, 1953, p. 14

This type of construction is most likely to be found in Informal writing. It is not effective if overused.

With prefixes

Hyphens are used between certain prefixes and the root word either as a matter of convention or to prevent ambiguity. Dictionaries list most of these forms.

1) Between prefix and a proper name:

pre-Renaissance
anti-Communist
ex-President Truman
post-Civil War
un-American
pro-German

2) Between some prefixes that end with a vowel and a root word beginning with a vowel, especially if the root word begins with the same vowel:

re-elected
semi-independent
re-ink

When the parts have become merged in General use, no hyphen is necessary, though it is often still found:

cooperation
coordinate
preexistent

3) To prevent possible confusion with a similar term or when the prefix is stressed:

> to *re-cover* a sofa (to *recover* from an illness)
> a *run-in* with the police (a *run in* her stocking)
> to *re-sort* buttons (a seaside *resort*)

Stressed prefixes occur in terms like *ex-wife*, *all-American*, *do-gooder*.

Suspension hyphens

The suspension hyphen is often used to carry the modifying expression from one word over to the next:

> Two-word forms first acquire the hyphen, later are printed as one word, and not infrequently the transition is from the *two-* to the *one-word* form, bypassing the hyphen stage.—*GPO Style Manual*, p. 63

Unnecessary hyphens

Don't hyphen a term that is currently written as a single word or as two words. Even if your dictionary lists as alternatives such old-fashioned forms as *to-night* and *post-man*, use the first or preferred form. Here is a brief list of words that students are sometimes tempted to hyphen:

One word	*Separate words*
anybody (pronoun)	all right
basketball, baseball, football	class president
bookkeeping	grade curve
footnotes	high school
himself, myself, ourselves	"How do you do?"
nevertheless	motion picture
outdoor	no one
outwit	press agent
overlooked	report card
percent (or per cent)	school days
roundabout	second in command
semicolon	six o'clock
taxpayer	tax rate
today, tomorrow	water pressure
throughout	
uphold	
whatever	

17.3 Apostrophes

Correction: Insert an apostrophe where it belongs in the word marked, or take out the unnecessary apostrophe.

An apostrophe (') is used in contractions, to mark the plural form of some expressions, and to indicate the genitive (possessive) case of nouns. Although it is a minor mark that seldom affects the reader's interpretation of a statement, its omission or misuse is very noticeable.

In contractions

17.3

Contractions are an attempt to represent colloquial pronunciation in writing. They are appropriate in dialog, Informal writing, and much General writing, but they are ordinarily out of place in Formal English and in academic papers on serious subjects.

An effective Formal style cannot always be achieved simply by writing out the contractions of Informal speech. "I have not time" is stilted and thus not a good substitute for the Informal "I haven't time." In Formal writing a different idiom is often needed: "I have no time."

When a contraction is appropriate in writing, an apostrophe is used to indicate the omission of one or more letters:

can't	I'll	it's (it is)	we're
don't	I'm	o'clock	won't
haven't	isn't	shouldn't	

An apostrophe is *not* used as an apologetic mark with shortened forms:

stereo	bus	phone	photo	thru

Notice that *till* (as in "from morning till midnight") is *not* a shortened form of *until* and no apostrophe is used with it.

An apostrophe is used with dates from which the first figures are omitted (the class of '59, the spirit of '76). In Formal writing, dates should usually be written in full.

With genitive (possessive) case forms

An apostrophe is used with the singular and plural forms of nouns and indefinite pronouns to mark the genitive case:

John's car
New York's parks
a stone's throw
children's games
your parents' permission
anybody's guess

An apostrophe is *not* used with the possessive forms of the personal pronouns *his, hers, its, ours, yours, theirs:*

the city and *its* suburbs
these seats are *ours*

See §7.2, p. 83, Forms of the genitive, and §8.3, p. 99, Possessive pronouns.

For plurals of letters and figures

An apostrophe is generally used before an *s* to form the plurals of figures, letters of the alphabet, and words considered as words:

the early 1900's [*or* 1900s]
several size 16's [*or* 16s]
a .44 pistol and two .22's [*or* .22s]
There are four *s*'s, four *i*'s, and two *p*'s in *Mississippi*

17.3

For letters dropped in representing speech

An apostrophe is commonly used to indicate the omission of sounds in representing speech:

> "But J. C. he wouldn't let me be until I brought him over. Just kept on sayin', Mamie I'm not a-goin' to move until I see where I'm goin'."—Ann Petry, *The Narrows*, p. 120

It is not necessary in representing conversation to indicate all such omissions, and frequent apostrophes make for difficult reading.

Exercises

1. *Capital letters and apostrophes.* Correct any errors in the use of capital letters and apostrophes in the following paragraph.

Whether one reads the germanic prose of Carlyle or Emersons epigrammatic aphorisms, one finds a similar theory of the "great man." It is he who embodies the principle of order (Order is the supreme principle of civilization) and who imposes his shaping spirit on the shapelessness of time. "Lives of great men all remind us," as Longfellow oracularizes, that

We can make our lives sublime,
and, departing, leave behind us
footprints in the sands of time.

Did not the marching feet of Napoleon and his liberating armies beat the path to Greatness over the Continent of Europe! From the piedmontese in the South to the Northern swedish realm of count Bernadotte, the symmetries of the napoleonic code exerted a salutary influence on the dissolving chaos of the holy Roman empire. Without the chastening clarity of Napoleons conservatism, the jacobinical excesses of the French revolution would have succeeded in accomplishing what they had already begun: exporting a Universal reign of Terror. Burke in his *Reflections on the French Revolution* failed to foresee that out of the destroying flame's of the directoire would emerge Frances' immortal Phoenix.

2. *Hyphens.* Indicate which of the following expressions should be written as separate words, which should be one word, and which should be hyphened. The words in parentheses indicate the sense in which the expression is intended.

a lot (of work to do)
base ball
dark horse
every one (is present)
flame thrower
gilt edged
give and take
hydro therapy
in so far as
jet black
left overs (food)
man hunt
man of war (a ship)
may be (perhaps)
never the less
non communist
not with standing (a conjunction)
over look (to slight or neglect)
out and out (outright)
Ping Pong
re written
school board
self satisfied
semi colon
some body (is missing)
space craft
ten word (telegram)
three quarters (of an inch)
un American
where abouts (at what place)

18 Abbreviations and numbers

18.1 Abbreviations

ab | **Correction: Write in full the abbreviation marked or, if an abbreviation is appropriate, change it to the correct form.**

Abbreviations are useful and appropriate in business and legal documents, reference works, scholarly footnotes, and other places where it is important to save space. But in college papers and most other General-to-Formal writing, all but a few kinds of words should be written out in full.

Dictionaries list most current abbreviations, either as regular entries or in a separate section, but they don't indicate when these forms should be used. The following sections discuss the kinds of abbreviations that are appropriate in Formal and General writing as well as some forms that should not be used. If you are in doubt whether a particular abbreviation is appropriate, you will usually do better to avoid it.

18.1 ab

Titles, degrees, and given names

The courtesy titles *Dr.*, *Mr.*, *Mrs.*, and *Mssrs.* are always abbreviated when used with proper names, as are *Jr.* and *Sr.*: *Mrs.* Lester H. Holt, *Mr.* Claude C. Sampson, *Jr.* Academic degrees are also generally abbreviated: *M.A.*, *Ph.D.*, *LL.D.*, *M.D.*, *D.D.S.* If a degree or honorary title is added after a name, it is the only title used:

> William Carey, M.D., *or* Dr. William Carey [*not* Dr. William Carey, M.D.]
>
> James T. Holloway, Esq., *or* Mr. James T. Holloway [*not* Mr. James T. Holloway, Esq.]

In Formal writing, titles like *Reverend*, *Professor*, *President*, *Senator*, *Admiral* are usually written out in full. In most other styles they may be abbreviated *if* the first name or initials of the person are used:

Standard forms	*Forms to avoid*
The Reverend James T. Shaw	The Rev. Shaw
The Reverend Mr. Shaw	Rev. Shaw
Rev. J. T. Shaw	The Reverend delivered a sermon.

Standard forms	*Forms to avoid*
Professor John Moore Professor Moore Prof. John R. Moore	Prof. Moore John Moore is an English Prof.
General Westmoreland Gen. William Westmoreland	Gen. Westmoreland The Gen. was given a new command.

Spell out given names (sometimes called Christian names) or use initials. Avoid such abbreviations as *Geo.*, *Thos.*, *Chas.*, *Wm.*:

George Harriman *or* G. F. Harriman [*rather than* Geo. F. Harriman]

Saint is almost always abbreviated when it is used with a name:

St. Francis, *Ste.* Catherine, *SS.* Peter and Paul, Sioux *St.* Marie

18.1

ab

Government agencies and other organizations

If a government agency or other organization is known primarily by its initials (or by some other shortened name), the writer should generally use the familiar abbreviation rather than the full name:

FBI	TVA	AFL-CIO	NBC Network
CIA	GOP	SPCA	MGM Studios
FHA	ROTC	4-H Club	GPO Style Manual

Abbreviations that are pronounced as words (called *acronyms*) have become very common: UNESCO, CARE, VISTA, NATO, SETO, Amvets.

See page 225 for discussions of the use of capitals and periods in abbreviations.

Place names and dates

The names of countries, states, months, and days are usually written out except in journalistic writing and reference works:

United States	Ghent, Belgium	Wednesday, November 3
South America	Portland, Oregon	Christmas [*not* Xmas]

Words like *Street*, *Avenue*, and *Boulevard* should be written out in general writing, not abbreviated as they might be in addressing a letter.

A few unusually long place names are customarily abbreviated even in rather Formal writing: the *USSR;* Barbados, *B.W.I.* (for British West Indies); Washington, *D.C.*

Units of measurement

In consecutive writing, most expressions for time, weight, and size are customarily written out:

in a minute	*rather than*	in a min.
hour		hr.
several pounds		several lbs.
four ounces		4 oz.
weight		wt.
a half inch		½ in.
five feet six inches		5′6″ or 5 ft. 6 in.

These units are abbreviated in directions, recipes, references, and technical writing when they are used with figures: ¼ lb. butter, 16 ft. 3 in.

Scientific words, technical terms, trade names

Some scientific words, trade names, and other expressions are referred to by their abbreviations when they are familiar to readers and would be needlessly long if written out:

> DDT (in place of *d*ichloro-*d*iphenyl-*t*richloro-ethane)
> ACTH (in place of *a*drenocortico*t*ropic *h*ormone)
> Rh factor (*Rh*esus factor)
> DNA (*d*eoxyribo*n*ucleic *a*cid)
> FM radio (*f*requency *m*odulation radio)
> IPA (*I*nternational *P*honetic *A*lphabet)
> PMLA (*P*ublications of the *M*odern *L*anguage *A*ssociation)
> OED (*O*xford *E*nglish *D*ictionary)

If an abbreviation is to be used repeatedly and may not be familiar to every reader, explain it the first time it is introduced:

> The International Phonetic Alphabet, commonly known as the IPA, provides a more precise method of recording speech than does our conventional alphabet.

Measurements expressed in technical terms are abbreviated when they are used with figures:

> Tests show the car's highest speeds to be 34 mph [miles per hour] in low gear, 58.7 mph in second, and 93.5 mph in third.
>
> The turntable can be adjusted to play records at either 78, 45, or 33⅓ rpm [revolutions per minute].

Expressions of this kind are written with either three periods or none (m.p.h. or mph). They are not abbreviated when used without figures:

> The speed of a ship is usually given in knots rather than in *miles per hour.*

Other standard abbreviations

There are a few standard abbreviations that are used in all levels of writing:

a.m., p.m. The expressions *a.m.* (*ante meridiem*, "before noon") and *p.m.* (*post meridiem*, "after noon") are always abbreviated: 6:00 a.m., 12:24 p.m. Current usage prefers small letters for these abbreviations, but they may be capitalized.

18.1

The abbreviations *a.m.* and *p.m.* are used only in referring to a specific time:

> Standard: He had an appointment at 3:00 p.m.
> Nonstandard: He had an appointment in the p.m.

B.C., A.D. These expressions are used to distinguish dates in history in reference to the birth of Christ; they are always abbreviated. B.C. means "before Christ"; A.D. stands for *anno Domini*, "in the year of our Lord."

836 B.C. 76 A.D. 1962 A.D.

Commonly used Latin expressions. English has absorbed a number of Latin expressions that are conventionally abbreviated. The following are in common use and should not be italicized:

> cf. *confer*—compare (for which *see* may be used)
> e.g. *exempli gratia*—for example
> etc. *et cetera*—and so forth (never *and etc.*)
> i.e. *id est*—that is

Many writers prefer the English equivalents for these and similar expressions. In college writing, the overworked catchall *etc.* should generally be avoided. Substitute *and so forth* (*and so on, and the like*) or rephrase the list, introducing it with *such as* or a similar qualifier. **See also** §29.8, page 493, Abbreviations in footnotes.

The ampersand

In college writing the ampersand (&) should not be used as a substitute for *and* unless it appears in an expression that the writer is copying: *U.S. News* & *World Report*, Doubleday & Company, Inc.

Capitals with abbreviations

Abbreviations are capitalized when the words they stand for are capitalized or when the abbreviation represents a title:

> DAR (*D*aughters of the *A*merican *R*evolution)
> USAF (*U*nited *S*tates *A*ir *F*orce)
> Lt. Col. Brown
> St. Matthew, St. Thomas Aquinas
> 100 degrees F. (Fahrenheit)

When an abbreviation stands for words that would not be capitalized if they were written out, no capitals are needed unless the abbreviation begins a sentence.

Periods with abbreviations

A period should be put after the abbreviation of a single word and usually between the letters of abbreviations for longer terms:

p.	doz.	N.Y.	c.o.d.
ch.	Lt.	B.A.	A.T. and T.
Nov.	hp.	e.g.	P.S.

Usage is divided about the punctuation of abbreviated names made of two or more letters written as a unit. Some publications prefer periods (*P.T.A.*, *B.B.C.*), but a growing number are using the solid form (*PTA*, *BBC*), especially when the abbreviation is generally used instead of the full name. Some dictionaries list optional forms. It doesn't make much difference which form a writer uses as long as he is consistent throughout his paper.

When an abbreviation falls at the end of a sentence, only one period is used: He owned a hundred shares of A.T. and T.

18.2 Numbers

Correction: Follow conventional usage in using words or figures for numbers; be consistent in the treatment of numbers.

There are few firm rules governing the use of figures or words for numbers occurring in consecutive writing. In general, books and magazines write out all numbers through one hundred and also larger numbers that can be written in two words (*six thousand, three million*). This style is usually appropriate for college papers and for most other kinds of General and Formal writing. Newspapers and Informal writing generally use figures for all numbers over ten, and some scientific and technical publications use figures exclusively.

> General and Formal: four, ten, fifteen, ninety-four, 114, 22,500, thirty thousand, five million [but usage varies]
>
> Informal: four, ten, 15, 94, 114, 22,500, 30,000, 5,000,000 (or 5 million)

There are a few special situations (described in the section following) in which figures are always customary. In other cases, use
18.2 the form that is appropriate not only for your audience but for
your material. In general, write out all simple two-digit numbers
and round numbers that can be easily read; use figures for numbers that cannot be written in two words and for series of numbers that are to be compared.

Words appropriate	*Figures appropriate*
He shot three quail and one rabbit.	The next ship unloaded 3500 pounds of king salmon, 947 pounds of chinook salmon, and 200 pounds of crab.
Five votes were cast for the class president's proposal, twenty-one against it.	In Colorado 10,547 farmers voted for controls; in Indiana, 17,003; in Minnesota, 10,750. The nationwide total was 87.2% in favor.
If I had ten dollars for every time I've broken one of my resolutions, I would have at least a thousand dollars by now.	Dresses in the \$15-\$25 range were selling well, those from \$26-\$45 fairly well, and those over \$46 hardly at all.

Whichever form you use, be consistent. Don't change needlessly from words to figures or from figures to words in the same piece of writing:

> Inconsistent: When I was 15, I thought anyone over thirty-five was old.
>
> Consistent: When I was fifteen, I thought anyone over thirty-five was old.

Conventional uses of figures

In all levels of Standard English, figures are customarily used in the following situations:

1) Dates are always written in figures except in Formal social correspondence. The forms *1st*, *2nd*, *3rd*, and so on are sometimes used in dates, but only when the year is omitted:

October 10, 1967   Oct. 10, 1967   October 10   October 10th

2) Hours are written in figures before *a.m.* or *p.m.;* they are spelled out before *o'clock:*

7 a.m.	1800 hours (military usage)	twelve noon
11:35 p.m.	one o'clock	twelve midnight

3) Mathematical and technical numbers:

3.14159	longitude 74° 02′ E.
99.8 per cent, 99.8%	.410 gauge shotgun

Except in dates and street numbers, a comma is used to separate thousands, millions, etc., although it may be omitted in four-digit figures:

1,365 (or 1365) pounds   8,393,624   17,016

4) Page numbers and similar references:

pp. 183-186	page 12
chapter iv	Genesis 39:12
Ch. 19	Act III, scene iv, line 28 (III, iv, 28)

5) Sums of money, except sums in round numbers or, in Formal style, sums that can be written in two or three words:

Figures	*Words*
a bargain at $4.98	Can you live on two thousand a year?
The British pound was once worth $4.85.	Coffee was then selling for about a dollar a pound.

6) Street numbers (with no commas between thousands):

2027 Fairview North   Apartment 3C, 1788 Grand North

7) Statistics and series of more than two numbers, especially when the numbers are to be compared:

> The survey showed that the class contained 24 Democrats, 18 Republicans, and 3 Socialists.

Plurals of figures

The plural of a figure is written either with *'s* or *s:*

Six nines: six 9's, six 9s By tens: by 10's, by 10s

Numbers at the beginning of sentences

Numbers at the beginning of sentences are written out unless they are dates:

> Two to 3% of loading and up to 10% is common and 20 to 30% in specially surfaced papers. . . . —"Paper Manufacture," *Encyclopaedia Britannica*, p. 234

> 1960 was a year of devastating drought in China.

Arabic and Roman numerals

18.2 Num

Arabic numerals (1, 2, 17, 96) are used in almost all cases where numbers are expressed in figures. Roman numerals, either lower case or capitals (i, ii, cxlvi; I, II, CXLVI), are occasionally used to number outlines, chapters, acts of a play, or formal inscriptions. They are almost always used to number the preliminary pages of a book; a new pagination in Arabic numerals begins with the body of the book.

In Roman numerals a small number preceding a larger is to be subtracted from the larger (ix = 9, xc = 90). The following table shows the common Roman numerals (lower case):

1	i	10	x	50	l	200	cc
2	ii	11	xi	60	lx	400	cd
3	iii	15	xv	70	lxx	500	d
4	iv	19	xix	80	lxxx	600	dc
5	v	20	xx	90	xc	900	cm
6	vi	21	xxi	99	xcix	1000	m
7	vii	30	xxx	100	c	1500	md
8	viii	40	xl	110	cx	1066	mlxvi
9	ix	49	xlix	199	cxcix	1962	mcmlxii

Cardinal and ordinal numbers

Figures indicating number only are *cardinal numbers:* 1, 2, 3, 72, 135. The numbers indicating order (*first*, *second*, *seventeenth*) are *ordinal numbers*. Except in routine enumeration, ordinals should be spelled out rather than abbreviated to *1st, 2nd, 17th.*

Since the ordinals can be either adjectives or adverbs, the forms ending in *-ly* (*firstly*) are unnecessary and are now rarely used.

Exercise

Abbreviations and numbers. Read the following sentences carefully, keeping in mind the principles stated in the preceding section. Do any of them use abbreviations or numbers in a way that would be inappropriate in college writing? Rewrite faulty sentences, making whatever changes are necessary. In cases where there is a choice in usage, explain in what circumstances each form would be used.

1) When we arrived at the theater on 8th St., we found that the evening's performance would start an hr. late.

2) The University recently added 2 new members to its faculty—Jerome Blumenthal, MA, and Jos. Persons, Doctor of Philosophy.

3) Six members of the NAACP conferred recently with U.N. Representative Adlai Stevenson at his office in N.Y.

4) Fifty-five to 60% of U. of C. students approved the 10 o'clock curfew; about 30% were violently opposed.

5) His monument to St. Francis, a remarkable piece of sculpture, weighed over 2500 lbs. and rivaled his monument to Saint Peter.

6) P. 237 of the manual lists the home addresses of U.S. Senators & p. 298 lists their D.C. addresses.

7) On Dec. 23 CBS will dramatize the most celebrated Xmas story of recent times—"The Christmas Carol" by Chas. Dickens.

8) Dr. Roscoe Caries, D.D.S., reported that in an experiment involving two thousand and forty-four children, tooth decay was not significantly reduced.

9) Lee had 4 sisters (ranging in age from sixteen to 31 yrs.) and a widowed mother.

10) After 10 months the FBI agent finally tracked Groark to Ogden, Miss., where he found him suffering from d.t.'s in the barn of the Rev. John Gantry.

Review exercises on punctuation and mechanics

1. Read the following sentences and then write down what mark or marks (if any) should be used in each of the lettered spaces. Be prepared to give reasons for each mark you use, to explain possible optional marks, or to justify the omission of a mark.

1) Now (*a*) if you are to punish a man retributively (*b*) you must injure him. If you are to reform him (*c*) you must improve him (*d*) and men are not improved by injuries.—George Bernard Shaw

2) The Prison Commissioners keep them [their statements] a few pages apart (*a*) and the average reader's memory (*b*) it seems (*c*) is not long enough to span the gap (*d*) when his personal interests are not at stake. —George Bernard Shaw

3) Still (*a*) in many cases (*b*) when we don't know how to deal with an offender (*c*) we tend to put him in prison (*d*) simply to get him out of the way. To be blunt (*e*) our prisons are failures.—David Abrahamsen

4) When a policeman asks (*a*) in a contemptuous way (*b*) What is the use of psychology in treating criminals (*c*) the psychologist knows that he is dealing with a phenomenon (*d*) which (*e*) to his own way of thinking (*f*) is itself criminal.

5) Logically (*a*) the question concerning the scientific status of psychology depends upon the answer to a prior question (*b*) viz (*c*) What makes any subject scientific (*d*)—Sidney Hook

6) This is one of the chapter titles in a little 85 (*a*) cent paperback I picked up the other day (*b*) Uses and Abuses of Psychology (*c*) by Dr. H. J. Eysenck (*d*) Penguin (*e*).—Rudolf Flesch

7) When a man undertakes to deal with a complex subject (*a*) he ought (*b*) of course (*c*) to be prepared for a good deal of work, research (*d*) and activity (*e*) which (*f*) if it is to be done well (*g*) takes both time and money.

8) The relationship of crime and psychology seemed to me (*a*) after I began to read about it (*b*) just such a complex subject (*c*) and now I see that (*d*) whatever my previous ideas were (*e*) I had little right to hold them (*f*) because they were ill-founded.

9) Writers on this subject (*a*) almost always men of good will (*b*) differ so widely from each other in what they say (*c*) that it is hard for someone who (*d*) like me (*e*) is untrained (*f*) to know what view to adopt (*g*) however (*h*) I have come to some conclusions.

10) Without giving up the right to change my mind (*a*) if new evidence warrants doing so (*b*) I would now argue that the existing penal system

(*c*) bad as it may be (*d*) and with almost more defects than virtues (*e*) cannot be abandoned quickly (*f*) and it is better to try to improve things (*g*) by infusing a humane rehabilitating spirit in prison guards (*h*) wardens (*i*) and other penal officials (*j*) than to treat these men as contemptuously as we often think they treat prisoners.

2. Correct every error or inconsistency in punctuation that you find in the following sentences. Notice apostrophes, capital letters, abbreviations, and numbers as well. Follow Formal usage. If the punctuation of a sentence is satisfactory as it stands, write "C" (correct) after the number.

1) Abbreviations are a great convenience if you don't have too many of them e.g. sometimes articles about Federal agencies are so thick with clusters of initials that you cant distinguish one Agency from another.

2) A favorite device of people who have a Madison Ave. mentality is to use ACRONYMS that is abbreviations that can be pronounced as a word, like SPAR and CARE, and H.E.L.P.

3) Sometimes this device leads to trouble: as when in World war Two we invented an agency called *Allied Military Gov't. Oriental Theater;* but the acronym came out AMGOT which we discovered too late was an obscene word in Turkish.

4) These Governmental abbreviations became popular under the "new deal"; one I remember was, the *NRA*, under the control of Hugh (Ironpants) Drum.

5) Academic people often have strings of abbreviations after their names; such as Phd, F.R.S., Ll.D., and AB.

6) My view-point on this sort of title-holding is that it is pretty hoity-toity; as if I could be impressed by a lot of capital and small letters that dont mean anything.

7) Anybody who wants to go to Grad school for 5-six years can get his third degree, thats how easy it is.

8) Why do academic people have to have so many titles after all, Naval and army personnel get along with one a piece.

9) Its what a man is that counts for—as I look at the problem—no number of titles will make him any good if he hasnt got what it takes to deliver in a crisis.

10) When professors write their books are always filled with strange looking little abbreviations: like eg (meaning for example); op cit, (meaning "In the work previously quoted from"), and ibid, (which I thought was a kind of "rare bird").

3. Punctuation marks and writing conventions have been removed from the following passages. First read each selection for its meaning and general movement; then put in the punctuation you consider appropriate and necessary for an easy understanding of the passage. The statements at the beginning of each passage describe briefly the original punctuation. While the punctuation you use need not follow that of the original, be prepared to explain the marks you have put in.

1) This paragraph was written in eight sentences. Although it is by a twentieth-century author, it sometimes deviates from modern usage, and the student should study the original to see where the deviations achieve rhetorical effects.

one prisoner had been brought out of his cell he was a hindu a puny wisp of a man with a shaven head and vague liquid eyes he had a thick sprouting moustache absurdly too big for his body rather like the moustache of a comic man on the films six tall indian warders were guarding him and getting him ready for the gallows two of them stood by with rifles and fixed bayonets while the others handcuffed him passed a chain through his handcuffs and fitted it to their belts and lashed his arms tight to his sides they crowded very close about him with their hands always on him in a careful caressing grip as though all the while feeling him to make sure he was there it was like men handling a fish which is still alive and may jump back into the water but he stood quite unresisting yielding his arms limply to the ropes, as though he hardly noticed what was happening—George Orwell, "A Hanging," *Shooting an Elephant and Other Essays*

2) This paragraph by Samuel Johnson was originally written in three sentences. The original was punctuated in the manner of the eighteenth century, and the student may derive both pleasure and profit from comparing Johnson's own punctuation with modern usage.

of the passions with which the mind of man is agitated it may be observed that they naturally hasten towards their own extinction by inciting and quickening the attainment of their objects thus fear urges our flight and desire animates our progress and if there are some which perhaps may be indulged till they outgrow the good appropriated to their satisfaction as it is frequently observed of avarice and ambition yet their immediate tendency is to some means of happiness really existing and generally within the prospect the miser always imagines that there is a certain sum that will fill his heart to the brim and every ambitious man like king pyrrhus has an acquisition in his thoughts that is to terminate his labors after which he shall pass the rest of his life in ease or gaiety in repose or devotion—Samuel Johnson, "On Sorrow"

3) This paragraph was written in five sentences:

it is a curious thought that as i sit down to write this essay on the history of our species i do so in the heightened consciousness that it may never be published a holocaust may overtake it tomorrow i may lie under tons of rubble precipitated into the street along with the paper on which this history is scribbled over the whole earth this infinitely small globe that possesses all we know of sunshine and bird song an unfamiliar blight is creeping man man who has become at last a planetary disease and who would if his technology yet permitted pass this infection to another star if i write this history in brief compass it is because on the scale of the universe it is but an instant shot with individual glory and unimaginable shame man is the only infinitely corruptible as well as infinitely perfectible animal.—Loren Eiseley, "The Time of Man," *Horizon*, March 1962, p. 4

19 Using a dictionary

The writer of a dictionary is a historian, not a lawgiver—S. I. Hayakawa

Contrary to what many people think, a dictionary is not a supreme authority that can be quoted to settle all arguments about words. Rather, it is a record—necessarily incomplete—of the ways in which language is actually used. The pioneer lexicographer Samuel Johnson concluded long ago that it was folly for a man to attempt to "embalm his language," but the notion persists nevertheless that a dictionary is—or should be—a codification of linguistic law.

The question of whether a dictionary should *prescribe* or *describe* language use was brought into sharp focus by the publication in 1961 of *Webster's Third New International Dictionary.* Many people felt that the new dictionary flagrantly violated lexicographical practices, the principles of good usage, and the sanctity of the language itself. The editors had revised the familiar pronunciation key; they had avoided defining by the use of synonyms; they had chosen not to use capital letters even for proper nouns. But these were relatively minor annoyances. Certain other practices, some critics felt, were cause for genuine alarm. For example, the editors offered a variety of acceptable pronunciations for many words, and made no effort to dictate which was "best." Of the over 14,000 writers they quoted to illustrate meaning, most were from the mid-twentieth century—and some of them were not known for the splendid quality of their prose. Finally—and this caused the greatest concern—the editors had omitted most usage labels (such as *colloquial*, *vulgar*, *erroneous*) on the ground that the correctness or appropriateness of a word can seldom be determined out of context.

The furor that followed the publication of *Webster's Third* (some critics praised the new edition as loudly as others attacked it) caused many people to re-examine their own attitudes toward language and their habit of looking to the dictionary as law. Language *does* change—as evidenced by the fact that some of the words used by critics in attacking the new *Webster's* were not included, or not condoned, in the previous edition, which these same critics cited as "authoritative." A dictionary cannot control language, but can simply record the way it is actually used. The standards for determining "good English" (§1) rest in other hands.

19.1 Selecting a dictionary

A good dictionary, though not a lawgiver, is an indispensable reference tool for every college student. Dictionaries answer questions about the meanings, spellings, origins, and pronunciations of words. They also give a good deal of information about the forms of words (plurals, past tenses) and idiomatic constructions (what preposition, for example, is commonly used with a particular noun or verb). One of the most valuable habits a student can acquire in a college composition course is checking a dictionary for the meaning and spelling of words.

Dictionaries differ in size and purpose, but certain criteria apply in evaluating any dictionary for general use. First of all, it should be up to date. New words and expressions are continually coming into the language (*acrylic*, *ambience*, *apartheid*, *brainstorming*, *psychedelic*) and old words are always being used in new senses (a *crash* program, a publicity *handout*). Even spelling and pronunciation can change with time (*catalog*, *catalogue; ab′də mən*, *ab dō′mən*). In addition, most dictionaries are somewhat encyclopedic, including information about prominent people and places. There are always new names to be added (*Kosygin*, *Tanzania*) and new facts to be recorded.

In an effort to keep their entries up to date, most dictionaries make limited changes every year or so. Check the copyright dates before you buy a dictionary to find out when it was last revised. You might also want to look up some words that have recently come into use to see if they are included.

In evaluating a dictionary you should also consider the quality of its editing. A good dictionary of current English is not simply an updating of earlier word books; it reflects the research and judgment of a large staff of experts who record and analyze hundreds of thousands of examples of words in actual use. It is the responsibility of the lexicographer to make certain that he has sampled the language adequately and found all the most common uses of even uncommon words. He must then sift through his raw materials, discarding some and reworking others, until he has produced a concise, yet accurate description of the words that constitute the great bulk of our language. Whatever "authority" a dictionary has, then, depends on the scholarship, discrimination, and judgment of its editors.

Dictionaries for general use

The most complete descriptions of contemporary English are to be found in the various unabridged dictionaries. Though not practical for desk use, these large dictionaries are invaluable for reference, and at least one of them is available in every college library:

New Standard Dictionary of the English Language (Funk & Wagnalls)

The Random House Dictionary of the English Language (Random House)

Webster's Third New International Dictionary (G. & C. Merriam)

World Book Dictionary (Field Enterprises)

Two older dictionaries continue to be very useful:

The Century Dictionary and Cyclopedia (The Century Company). Although this ten-volume work, the most comprehensive dictionary ever published in the United States, has not been reprinted since before World War I, it contains much information not available in more recent dictionaries. *The New Century Dictionary* (Appleton-Century-Crofts) is basically an abridgment of this work.

19.1 Dict

Webster's New International Dictionary of the English Language (G. & C. Merriam). The second edition of the unabridged Webster, first published in 1934, is no longer in print but remains available in most libraries.

For everyday use, the most practical dictionary for a student to own is one of the shorter "college" dictionaries listed below. Your instructor may recommend that you buy a particular one, or he may leave the choice to you. Each of these dictionaries has its own special strengths, but all are well edited and adequate for college use:

American College Dictionary (Random House)

Standard College Dictionary (Funk & Wagnalls; text edition published by Harcourt, Brace & World)

Webster's New World Dictionary of the American Language (World Publishing Company)

Webster's Seventh New Collegiate Dictionary (G. & C. Merriam)

Sample entries from these dictionaries, showing the organization of their entries and some of their distinctive features, are reproduced on pages 240-241.

Special dictionaries

The general dictionaries—abridged and unabridged—are supplemented by a number of specialized word books which occasionally need to be consulted for material not to be found in general works.

Historical dictionaries. Good dictionaries for general use are based in part upon scholarly dictionaries made over long periods of time. *The Oxford English Dictionary* (twelve volumes and a *Supplement*, 1888-1928) is a historical dictionary of the words and idiomatic phrases of the English language. It traces the various forms and meanings of each word, giving the date of its first appearance in recorded English and illustrative quotations from writers to show its typical use at various times in its history (a dozen or more pages are sometimes devoted to a single word). In many kinds of study it is a basic source for research. *The Shorter Oxford English Dictionary* (two volumes) is an abridgment of the larger work and somewhat easier to use.

The Dictionary of American English (four volumes), made on the same plan as the *Oxford*, gives the history of words as they have been used by American writers from 1620 to 1900. *A Dictionary of Americanisms* (two volumes) gives the history of words that originated in the United States and brings the record of American English down to 1944. Periodicals like *American Speech* and *PADS* (Publications of the American Dialect Society) regularly publish regional and occupational vocabularies.

Dictionaries in special subjects. Most special fields have dictionaries of their specialized vocabularies. It is a good idea to know the titles of those in any fields you are going to work in. The following list merely suggests the range of such books. Most of them are revised from time to time.

Ballentine, J. A., *Law Dictionary*
Chambers's Technical Dictionary
Clark, D. T., and B. A. Gottfried, *Dictionary of Business and Finance*
Dorland, W. A. N., *American Illustrated Medical Dictionary*
English, H. B., *A Student's Dictionary of Psychological Terms*
Good, C. V., *Dictionary of Education*
Hackh, I. W. D., *Chemical Dictionary*
Henderson, I. F. and W. D., *Dictionary of Scientific Terms*
Rice, C. M., *Dictionary of Geological Terms*

19.2 Learning to use your dictionary

Dictionaries differ not only in the information they include but in the way they present it, and the best dictionary in the world will be of little value to you unless you know how to read and interpret the wealth of information it provides. Before using a new dictionary, read the front matter carefully. It will explain the organization of entries, the method of indicating pronunciation, the use of restrictive labels, and the meaning of abbreviations and symbols used in the definitions and etymologies. Then look carefully at a page of entries to see how words and phrases are handled. Test your understanding of the pronunciation guide by using it to pronounce some familiar words. Look through the table of contents to see what sections of information your dictionary provides in addition to the main alphabetical list of words. You may find a short grammar of the English language, a discussion of punctuation, a table of signs and symbols, a list of colleges and universities in the United States, and a guide to the preparation of manuscript copy.

A little time spent in learning to use your dictionary can make it immensely useful to you. The following sections describe the kinds of information found in most dictionaries, and pages 240-241 illustrate the way this information is presented in four good college dictionaries. The exercises beginning on page 245 will give you some practice in the actual use of your own desk dictionary.

Spelling and word division

Develop the habit of using your dictionary to check the spelling in your papers. If you are unable to find a word because you are uncertain of one of the beginning letters, try to think of other possible spellings for the same sound. (Is it *gibe* or *jibe?*) Remember that dictionaries give the spelling not only of the base form of a word but also of distinctive forms—the principal parts of verbs, the plurals of nouns, the comparative and superlative forms of adjectives and adverbs—that are in any way irregular.

Your dictionary may give two spellings for a word when usage is divided (*hemoglobin—haemoglobin; although—altho*). Use the spelling that the editors have indicated is the more common one. (The method of listing variants will be explained in the front matter.) Avoid spellings labeled British (such as *colour*, *gaol*) in favor of the usual American spelling.

Dictionaries divide words into units (usually corresponding to spoken syllables) by means of small dots or spaces: *de·mar·ca·tion*, *de light ful*. This device will enable you to see each part of the word clearly and to notice if you have omitted or transposed any letters. In writing, divide a word at the end of a line only where your dictionary shows a division. The word *reorganization*, for example, might be divided at the end of a line in any one of five places: *re·or·gan·i·za·tion*. Not all dictionaries divide every word in exactly the same way, but by following the practice of any good dictionary you will avoid such careless blunders as dividing *bedraggled* into *bed-* and *raggled*.

See also §16, Spelling, and §27.2, Manuscript form.

Pronunciation

Because English spelling is not consistently phonetic (there are over 250 ways to spell the forty-odd sounds in English), dictionaries use a system of special symbols to show how words are pronounced. The word *bamboozle*, for example, might be respelled this way after the entry word: *băm bōō′ zəl*. The pronunciation key at the bottom of the page will illustrate, with familiar words, the sounds represented by the symbols *ă*, *ōō*, and *ə*. Since the consonants *b*, *m*, *z*, and *l* have no special marks over them, you may assume that they are pronounced in the usual way. The accented syllable in *băm bōō′ zəl* is indicated by a heavy stress mark. Phonetic spellings also indicate secondary stress, when appropriate, usually by a lighter mark (′) but sometimes by a different symbol. Since the system for showing pronunciation varies somewhat from dictionary to dictionary, you should study carefully the explanatory notes in the front of your own book before attempting to use its pronunciation key.

Dictionaries often list two or more pronunciations for a word when usage is divided (as shown in the entries for *advance* on pages 240-241). Although the first pronunciation is usually the more common one, it is not necessarily "preferred," and you should use whichever pronunciation is customary among the educated people in your own community. *Webster's Third New International Dictionary* provides a comprehensive survey of

Sample entries from college dictionaries

ad·vance (ăd văns′, -väns′), *v.*, **-vanced, -vancing,** *n., adj.* —*v.t.* **1.** to move or bring forward in place: *the troops were advanced to the new position.* **2.** to bring to view or notice; propose: *to advance an argument.* **3.** to improve; further: *to advance one's interests.* **4.** to raise in rank; promote. **5.** to raise in rate: *to advance the price.* **6.** to bring forward in time; accelerate: *to advance growth.* **7.** to supply beforehand; furnish on credit, or before goods are delivered or work is done. **8.** to furnish as part of a stock or fund. **9.** to supply or pay in expectation of reimbursement: *to advance money on loan.* **10.** *Archaic.* to raise, as a banner.
—*v.i.* **11.** to move or go forward; proceed: *the troops advanced.* **12.** to improve or make progress; grow: *to advance in knowledge or rank.* **13.** to increase in quantity, value, price, etc.: *stocks advanced three points.*
—*n.* **14.** a moving forward; progress in space: *advance to the sea.* **15.** advancement; promotion: *an advance in rank.* **16.** a step forward; actual progress in any course of action: *the advance of knowledge.* **17.** (*usually pl.*) an effort to bring about acquaintance, accord, understanding, etc. **18.** addition to price; rise in price: *an advance on cottons.* **19.** *Com.* **a.** a giving beforehand; a furnishing of something before an equivalent is received. **b.** the money or goods thus furnished. **20.** *U.S.* the leading body of an army. **21.** *Mil.* (formerly) the order or a signal to advance. **22. in advance, a.** before; in front. **b.** beforehand; ahead of time: *he insisted on paying his rent in advance.*
—*adj.* **23.** going before: *the advance section of a train.* **24.** made or given in advance: *an advance payment.* **25.** issued in advance: *an advance copy.* **26.** having gone beyond others or beyond the average.
[ME *avaunce(n)* t. OF: m. *avancier*, g. LL *abanteāre*, der. *abante* (f. *ab* + *ante*) from before] —**ad·vanc′er,** *n.*
—**Syn. 2.** adduce; propound, offer. **5.** increase. **6.** quicken, hasten, speed up. **11.** ADVANCE, MOVE ON, PROCEED all imply movement forward. ADVANCE applies to forward movement, esp. toward an objective: *to advance to a platform.* PROCEED emphasizes movement as from one place to another, and often implies continuing after a halt: *to proceed on one's journey.* MOVE ON, a more informal expression, is similar in meaning to PROCEED; it does not, however, imply a definite goal: *the crowd was told to move on.* **12.** thrive, flourish; prosper. **13.** rise. **17.** overture; proposal.

19.2 Dict

From *The American College Dictionary.* Copyright 1947, © Copyright 1967 by Random House, Inc. Reprinted by permission.

ad·vance (ad·vans′, -väns′) *v.* **·vanced, ·vanc·ing** *v.t.* **1.** To move or cause to go forward or upward. **2.** To offer; propose: to *advance* a suggestion. **3.** To further; promote: to *advance* the progress of science. **4.** To put in a better or more advantageous rank, position, or situation. **5.** To make occur earlier; accelerate. **6.** To raise (a rate, price, etc.). **7.** To pay, as money or interest, before legally due. **8.** To lend: Can you *advance* me some money? **9.** *Law* To provide an advancement for. — *v.i.* **10.** To move or go forward: The armies *advance* on all fronts. **11.** To make progress; rise or improve: The stock market *advanced.* — *adj.* **1.** Being before in time; early: an *advance* payment. **2.** Being or going before; in front: the *advance* guard. — *n.* **1.** The act of going forward; progress. **2.** Improvement; promotion. **3.** An increase or rise, as of prices. **4.** *pl.* Personal approaches; overtures: His *advances* were rejected. **5.** The supplying of goods, money, etc., on credit. **6.** The goods or money so supplied; a loan. **7.** The payment of money before it is legally due: He requested an *advance* on his salary. **8.** *U.S.* The front or foremost part. Abbr. *adv.* **— Syn.** See PROGRESS. **— in advance** **1.** In front. **2.** Before due; beforehand: to prepare for lunch *in advance.* [ME *avauncen* < OF *avancier* < L *ab ante* from before < *ab-* away + *ante* before; the initial *a-* was later altered to *ad-* as if from L *ad-* to, toward] **— ad·vanc′er** *n.*

By permission from *Funk & Wagnalls Standard® College Dictionary,* copyright 1966 by Funk & Wagnalls, A Division of Reader's Digest Books, Inc.

ad·vance (əd-vans′, ad-väns′), ***v.t.*** [ADVANCED (-vanst′, -vänst′), ADVANCING], [ME. *avancen;* OFr. *avancer,* to forward < L. **abantiare* < *ab-,* from + *ante,* before: the *a-* was made *ad-* on the supposition that it came from L. *ad-,* to, toward], 1. to bring forward; move forward. 2. to suggest. 3. to further; help; promote. 4. to cause to happen earlier. 5. to raise the rate of. 6. to pay (money) before due. 7. to lend. ***v.i.*** 1. to go forward; move ahead. 2. to improve; make progress; develop. 3. to rise in rank, quality, importance, etc. ***n.*** 1. a moving forward. 2. an improvement; progress. 3. a rise in value or cost. 4. ***pl.*** approaches to get favor, become acquainted, etc.; overtures (*to* someone). 5. a payment made before due, as of wages. 6. a loan. ***adj.*** 1. in front: as, *advance* guard. 2. beforehand: as, *advance* information.

in advance, 1. in front. 2. before due; ahead of time.

SYN.*—advance** is used to describe assistance in hastening the course of anything or in moving toward an objective; to **promote** is to help in the establishment, development, or success of something (to *promote* good will); **forward** emphasizes the idea of action as an impetus (concessions were made to *forward* the pact); **further** emphasizes assistance in bringing a desired goal closer (to *further* a cause). —ANT.*** retard, check.

From *Webster's New World Dictionary of the American Language, College Edition.* Copyright 1968, by The World Publishing Company, Cleveland, Ohio.

19.2

Dict

[1]**ad·vance** \əd-'van(t)s\ *vb* [ME *advauncen,* fr. OF *avancier,* fr. (assumed) VL *abantiare,* fr. L *abante* before, fr. *ab-* + *ante* before — more at ANTE-] *vt* **1 :** to bring or move forward **2 :** to accelerate the growth or progress of **:** FORWARD **3 :** to raise to a higher rank **:** PROMOTE **4 :** to supply or furnish in expectation of repayment **5** *archaic* **:** to lift up **:** RAISE **6 :** to bring forward in time: **a :** to make earlier **:** HASTEN **b :** to place later in time **7 :** to bring forward for notice, consideration, or acceptance **:** PROPOSE **8 :** to raise in rate **:** INCREASE **~** *vi* **1 :** to move forward **:** PROCEED **2 :** to make progress **:** INCREASE **3 :** to rise in rank, position, or importance **4 :** to rise in rate or price — **ad·vanc·er** *n*

syn ADVANCE, PROMOTE, FORWARD, FURTHER mean to move or help to move ahead. ADVANCE stresses effective assisting or hastening a process bringing about a desired end; PROMOTE suggests an encouraging or fostering; FORWARD implies an impetus forcing something ahead; FURTHER suggests a removing of obstacles or obstructions in the way of a desired advance **syn** see in addition ADDUCE

[2]**advance** *n* **1 :** a forward movement **2 :** progress in development **:** IMPROVEMENT **3 :** a rise in price, value, or amount **4 :** a first step or approach made **:** OFFER; *also* **:** a progressive step **5 :** a provision of something (as money or goods) before a return is received; *also* **:** the money or goods supplied — **in advance :** BEFORE, BEFOREHAND

[3]**advance** *adj* **1 :** made, sent, or furnished ahead of time **2 :** going or situated before

By permission. From *Webster's Seventh New Collegiate Dictionary* © 1967 by G. & C. Merriam Co., Publishers of the Merriam-Webster Dictionaries.

American usage in pronunciation, as does Kenyon and Knott's *A Pronouncing Dictionary of American English*, available in most college bookstores.

Meaning

Dictionaries are perhaps most important for what they tell us about the meanings of words. To a reader, a dictionary is useful for finding the meanings not only of unfamiliar words but also of familiar words used in new senses. To a writer, dictionary definitions are most useful for checking the meanings of words he is not quite certain about—words, perhaps, such as *ubiquitous* or *officious*. Do these words really mean what he thought they meant when he put them down in his first draft? In revising, he should check his dictionary to make sure.

Dictionaries begin each definition, or group of definitions, with an abbreviation showing whether the word is being defined as a noun (*n.*), adjective (*adj.*), transitive verb (*v.t.*), intransitive verb (*v.i.*), or other part of speech. This information is important, for words usually have different meanings in different grammatical contexts. Sometimes the meanings are closely related (for example, the meanings of *advance* as a verb, a noun, or an adjective) but sometimes they are completely different (the meanings of *fly*, *plant*, and *court* as verbs or as nouns).

19.2 Dict

In looking for the meaning of a word in context, therefore, you must ordinarily isolate the right group of definitions before you can find the particular meaning you are looking for. Then you should look over all of the definitions included in that group. Some dictionaries give the oldest meaning first and other dictionaries the most common one. Often you will want neither of these but a more specialized meaning that comes late in the entry. At the end of the entry, or at the end of a group of definitions for one part of speech, you may also find one or more idioms listed—notice, for example, the idiom *in advance* under the entry for *advance*.

In using dictionary definitions, you should keep two general principles in mind:

1) A dictionary does not *require* or *forbid* a particular meaning or use of a word; it merely *records* the most common ways in which a word has actually been used. Therefore you must exer-

cise judgment in deciding whether a particular word will be appropriate in a particular context.

2) A dictionary definition is for the most part a record of the *denotation* of a word; at best, it can only suggest the *connotation*, which varies with context and with use. (**See** §20.1) In general, it is better not to use a word until you have heard it or read it and know at least some of its connotations.

Areas of usage and special labels

Some words (or particular meanings for some words) are labeled in a dictionary as *dialectal*, *obsolete*, *archaic*, *foreign*, *colloquial*, *slang*, *British*, *United States*, or are identified with some particular activity or field—*medicine*, *law*, *astronomy*, *music*, *sports*, *manufacturing*, *electricity*. Both kinds of labeling are illustrated in the sample entries on pages 240-241. Words unlabeled in a dictionary are considered part of the general vocabulary.

Usage labels can serve as rough guides, but a writer should bring his own observation to bear on individual words. Certainly he would ordinarily avoid words marked *obsolete* or *archaic*, but many words that carry no label (*albeit*, *perforce*) would be equally out of place in the writing of young people. On the other hand, many words marked *Dial.* or *Colloq.* (such as *prep school*, *highbrow*) might fit perfectly well into both Informal and General English. The label *colloquial*, which many people mistake to mean Nonstandard, simply suggests that a particular usage is more characteristic of speech than it is of writing. The label *U.S.* means that the usage is found in the United States but not in other parts of the English-speaking world.

Most dictionaries of the English language include frequently used words and expressions from foreign languages. Some dictionaries indicate that such terms are generally considered foreign by listing the language in parentheses: (*It.*), (*Fr.*). Some also use an identifying mark, such as a dagger or an asterisk, before all foreign-word entries. Such labels are useful to the writer because they help him distinguish between foreign words that are now considered part of the English vocabulary (*chalet*, *aria*, *mesa*) and those that are still considered distinctly foreign (*dolce far niente*, *Weltanschauung*, *enceinte*) and must be underlined in a paper. (See §15.4, page 187, Italics for foreign words.)

Synonyms and antonyms

Most dictionaries list words of similar meaning (*synonyms*) with the basic or most comprehensive word of a group and explain how these various related words differ slightly in meaning, especially in connotation. The entries reproduced on pages 240-241, for example, compare the meaning of *advance* with the meaning of such related words as *promote, forward, further*, and *proceed.* One of the dictionaries refers the reader to a synonym study that relates the meaning of *advance* to that of *progress.* Sometimes the entry for a word will also list an *antonym*, a word of opposite meaning, as *cowardly* would be an antonym for *courageous.*

There are several specialized books containing lists of related words: *Webster's Dictionary of Synonyms*, Fernald's *Standard Handbook of Synonyms, Antonyms, and Prepositions*, Soule's *A Dictionary of English Synonyms*, and Roget's *Thesaurus.* The *Thesaurus* is probably the most-used book of synonyms, but since it does not give definitions, its chief use is to remind a writer of words he recognizes but does not use regularly.

Etymology

19.2 Dict

A dictionary not only tells how a word is used and pronounced but also gives its origin, or *etymology*. Sometimes the etymology is merely a notation of the language from which the word was borrowed (as *decór* was from French and *Gestalt* was from German) or a statement of how it was coined. But often the etymology is fairly complicated; the development of the word *advance*, for example, is traced back through Middle English to Old French and finally to Latin. The explanatory notes at the front of your dictionary include a discussion of etymology and a key to the abbreviations and symbols used in tracing a word's origin.

Knowing how a word originated will often help you understand and remember it. Knowing that *philanthropy*, for example, comes from the Greek words *philein* (to love) and *anthropos* (man) may help fix its meaning in your mind. Beyond this, it may help you figure out other unfamiliar words by analogy (*philology, anthropocentric*).

Etymologies often illustrate how word meanings have changed from their original to their present use and are interesting as records of human thought and experience.

Exercises

1. *Comparing dictionary entries.* Refer to the dictionary entries on pages 240-241 to answer the following questions:

1) Where is the pronunciation given? How is the accent (stress) indicated?

2) Can *advance* be divided at the end of a line? If so, where?

3) Where is the etymology of *advance* given in the entries?

4) Do all four dictionaries list the most common meaning first?

5) As what parts of speech can *advance* be used? How do the dictionaries separate the definitions for *advance* in its various grammatical functions?

6) Are the specialized meaning labels the same in all entries?

7) Are the same synonyms listed in all entries?

8) Do the entries include sentences or phrases illustrating the use of synonyms?

9) What antonyms are listed?

10) What idiomatic phrases are given?

2. *Evaluating dictionaries.* Write out the following information about your dictionary, for discussion in class or to be handed in.

1) The title, the name of the publisher, and the most recent copyright date. This date may be found on the back of the title page.

2) A list of the sections following the introduction and preceding the dictionary entries (such as "How to Use the Dictionary," "A Guide to Pronunciation," "Usage Levels").

3) A list of the material in the appendix (if any), such as "Signs and Symbols," "Biographical Names," "Colleges and Universities in the United States."

4) Do the words appear in one alphabetical list or in separate lists (for biographical names, geographical names, abbreviations, etc.)?

5) Are derived forms (*cynical* and *cynicism* from *cynic*, for example) listed separately as main entries in the alphabetical list, or are they listed under the base word?

6) Do the etymologies come at the beginning or at the end of an entry?

7) The order of the definitions of the words. Does the older meaning or the current meaning come first in words such as: *bibulous*, *cute*, *ghastly*, *shrewd*, *liquidate*, *souse* (noun), *recession*, *fulsome*?

3. *Spelling.* What information do you find in your dictionary on the spelling of these pairs of words? Are the spellings interchangeable? If so, which form would you use and why?

aesthetic—esthetic	favor—favour
carat—karat	fiber—fibre
catalog—catalogue	gaol—jail
catsup—catchup	gray—grey
criticise—criticize	licorice—liquorice
draft—draught	sac—sack
encyclopaedia—encyclopedia	traveling—travelling

4. *Pronunciation.* To familiarize yourself with the pronunciation key in your dictionary, write out the following exercises:

1) What pronunciations does your dictionary list for each of these words? Is the first pronunciation given the one you hear most frequently? If not, tell how it differs, including the stress (accent):

address	creek	greasy	pianist
adult	decadent	herb	poinsettia
Celtic	drama	impotent	research
coupon	gibberish	leisure	Oedipus

2) How is each of these words pronounced when used as a noun? As a verb?

confine	escort	impact	misuse
conflict	exploit	import	refuse
consort	ferment		

5. *Definitions.* Answer the following questions by referring to the definitions given in your dictionary:

1) Would a professor be flattered if you called him a *pedant?*

2) Where does a *Yahoo* live?

3) Is a *ladybird* a female bird?

4) In what kind of writing would it be appropriate to use the word *gimmick?*

5) Would you be likely to find the word *lackaday* in contemporary writing?

6) In what profession would the word *dolmen* most likely be used?

7) What dialect uses of the word *fetch* does your dictionary give?

8) Where would you be most likely to hear the word *legato?*

9) When a person *rests on his laurels,* what is he doing?

10) Which of the following expressions would be underlined in a paper to indicate they belong to a foreign language?

Realpolitik de facto sarong savoir-faire toccata vice versa

6. *Definitions.* Consult your dictionary and choose the best definition for the italicized word in each of these sentences:

1) At ten he became a printer's *devil.*
2) The university allowed considerable *latitude* in dress.
3) A *shingled* bob framed her small face.
4) His *fellowship* expired at the end of the year.
5) Luther objected to the sale of *indulgences.*
6) The entrance fee was *fixed* at twenty dollars.
7) She has extremely *catholic* reading tastes.
8) Aristotle thought of virtue as the *mean* between two excesses.
9) A shift in the *fault* may cause a severe earthquake.
10) They soon discovered that the resort was a *white elephant.*

7. *Grammatical information.* Answer the following questions by consulting the grammatical information given in the dictionary entry for each word:

1) What is the past participle of *shear?*
2) What is the past tense of *bear* in the sense of *carry?*
3) What does *feign* mean when it is used intransitively?
4) What does *gull* mean when followed by a direct object?
5) What is the plural of *ghetto?*
6) What is the plural of *stratum?*

8. *Etymology.* Consult the etymologies in your dictionary to answer the following questions:

1) What is the origin of these words?

fedora Hellenic orangutan
feral lacquer robot
gerrymander lampoon sandwich

2) Which of the following words have retained most or all of their original meanings? Which have retained some? Which none?

bigot fiasco pilot
dilapidated miscegenation silly
fecund pedigree tragedy

9. *Other information.* The following questions can be answered by finding the special information they require in the dictionary. In some cases it is attached to the regular word entry; in others special sections at the back or front must be consulted.

1) Distinguish between the following similar words:

deviate—digress—diverge—swerve
slim—thin—slender—skinny
fictitious—legendary—mythical
giggle—titter—snicker—chuckle
latent—potential—dormant

2) Give antonyms for the following words: *authentic, chaste, devout, futile, venial.*

3) Who was John Huss? When did he live?

4) Where are the Carpathian Mountains?

5) How large is a lemming?

6) Is Mexico City smaller or larger than Paris in population?

7) Where is Miami University? Can a woman enroll there?

8) How long is a furlong?

9) What does the symbol B/L mean in business and commerce?

10) What does the sign ∴ mean in mathematics?

10. Collect examples illustrating the meaning of several new words used on your campus or by members of your generation: new slang words, words from the general vocabulary used in new ways, coined words. Then formulate standard dictionary entries for each, basing your definitions on four or five citations of actual use.

20 The meaning of words

Probably it is better to put off using words as long as possible and get one's meaning as clear as one can through pictures and sensations. Afterward one can choose—not simply accept—*the phrases that will best cover the meaning, and then switch around and decide what impression one's words are likely to make on another person. This last effort of the mind cuts out all stale or mixed images, all prefabricated phrases, needless repetitions, and humbug and vagueness generally.—George Orwell*

We usually take for granted that we know the meanings of the words we use, except when there is a question of accuracy (*infer* or *imply?*) or of appropriateness (*boss* or *employer?*). But if a writer is to choose the words that will best convey his meaning, and not simply accept the first ones that come to mind, he must take an active interest in words as words. What gives a particular word its special meanings in different situations? In what different ways can it be used? What impression will it make on others? Words have many possible meanings. If a writer is to choose those that best serve his purpose, he must know what the options are.

20.1 Words in context and situation

20.1 Mng

Words do not actually have "meaning" until they are *used* in speaking or writing. Then their meaning derives partly from the *context*, or the words around them, and partly from the *situation* in which they are used, which always involves the attitudes and purposes of either a speaker and listener or a writer and reader.

It is easy to see how the context limits the meaning of a word. A word like *deck*, *run*, *fly*, or *match* can be used in several senses, but usually in a particular sentence it can have only one meaning:

> You will have to *run* to catch the train.
>
> Frowning prettily, she deplored the *run* in her stocking.
>
> Mantle scored the third *run* after there were two out in the seventh.
>
> When the store opened on the morning of the sale, there was a *run* on piece goods.

The situation in which a word is used also helps clarify its meaning. The word *bill* in "The bill is too large" would mean one thing if the speaker were trying to identify a bird and another if he were discussing family finances. In writing, the situation includes both the writer and his reader. In so far as their experiences are similar, they can communicate easily; but if their experiences are different, the writer must take special pains to use words that will help the reader understand what he is trying to say.

Denotation: the core of a word's meaning

Words are arrangements of sounds or letters that we use to bring our ideas, attitudes, notions to another person's attention. These may be objects or "things" (*typewriter*, *Golden Gate Bridge*), qualities (*excellent*, *hard*), relationships (*without*, *hers*), actions or conditions (*running*, *homesickness*), or ideas (*democracy*, *truth*).

When we think first about the meaning of words, we think of their *denotation*, what they have come to represent as a result of the ways they have been used. This is the meaning that dictionaries record and try to describe for us. The thing that a word refers to or suggests is called its *referent*.

Some kinds of words have more definite denotations than others because their referents are more limited or more exact. Depending on their definiteness, words may be classified into three groups:

20.1 Mng

1) *Concrete words*, words that name specific people, places, or objects, are the most exact in meaning: *Walt Whitman*, *Lake Erie*, *my bicycle*, *the library*, *reindeer*, *a Boy Scout knife*.

2) *Relative words*, words that describe qualities, are less definite than concrete words and frequently depend for their meanings on the situation or on the writer's past experience with a term: *hot*, *pretty*, *honest*, *angry*, *silly*, *impossible*. In New York City, a *tall* building might mean any structure over twenty stories, but in a city with no skyscrapers, *tall* might refer to any building higher than five stories.

3) *Abstract words*, words that refer to general concepts—acts, situations, relationships, conditions—are the least definite: *reasoning*, *citizenship*, *education*, *intelligence*, *culture*, *objectives*, *art*. Since these words have a range of reference (think of all the activities that may be included in *education*, for example), rather than a specific referent, they are more difficult to use exactly than concrete words.

See also §20.4, Concrete and abstract words.

Connotation: the suggestion of words

Most words have been used by so many different people in such different circumstances for such different purposes that they have acquired associations and suggestions that go beyond their denotation. The qualities that words acquired from their expanded use are called *connotation.*

Very often the chief difference between words of closely related denotation is in their connotation. Both *inexpensive* and *cheap* refer to low price, but *cheap* may also connote poor quality; *average* and *mediocre* both refer to the middle of a range, but *mediocre* suggests dispraise; *belief, faith, creed, dogma* all refer to ideas held, but they differ widely in suggesting how they are held. It is easy to see why some students of language say that there are no true synonyms.

Dictionaries try to suggest the shades of meaning that words may have, but the best way to find the exact connotations of a word is to observe how it is actually used in current writing and speech. The connotation of a word often changes over time. *Sly*, for example, once meant *skillful*, but as it is generally used now it would fit into the same context as *devious* or *tricky;* it may even suggest *criminal* or, sometimes, *lecherous.* Words like *genteel* and *bucolic* have lost their favorable connotation as the values they represent have lost much of their appeal. Certain words, usually those whose referents arouse widely ranging responses, are extremely variable in connotation: *pop art*, *radical*, *socialism*, *jazz.* A writer must use such words with caution, making sure that his own attitude is clear to the reader and that he is being fair to his subject.

20.2 Fair words and slanted words

In personal writing or in persuasive writing—poetry or fiction or arguments condemning, praising, or calling for action—the connotation of a word may be quite as important as its core of meaning. Words chosen carefully for their connotative value can help the writer convey his attitude toward his subject. He can use words that honestly and fairly represent the position he has taken toward his subject, or he can assault his audience—by design or by accident—with words weighted in his favor. Words so weighted are called *slanted.*

Words used fairly for effect

It is not possible to speak or write in completely neutral, objective language about anything that has fully engaged our interest. To write well about a subject, we must care about it enough to take a position or make a judgment concerning it.

In factual as well as in imaginative writing, interest, liveliness, and effectiveness depend greatly on the successful use of connotation. Our awareness of all the values that words have enables us to represent our subject precisely, to address our audience with a varied and appealing language, and to show where we stand in relation to our material. Honestly used, our words give *shape*—as opposed to *slant*—to what we say.

The following passage, obviously part of a campaign that seeks action, is emphatic and persuasive because of the connotation of many of the words. Phrases such as *generous twinges* and *conventional charities* hit at our complacency, and many others (*slumlords, loan sharks, and clubhouse politicians*) are calculated to suggest the burden of poverty. The passage does not represent unfair slanting because we know from the writer's style that his argument is to be taken as opinion and evaluated on the basis of the evidence given and the reader's own experience.

20.2 Slant

> While most Americans have occasional generous twinges and dutifully support the conventional charities, by and large they have no exposure to the actual experience of the poor. It is hard for them to realize that there are fellow Americans today who are still being denied the right of suffrage by intimidation, fraud, and mayhem; who are suffering the condescensions of the prosperous in order to get and keep servile jobs; who are enduring the importunities of slumlords, loan sharks, and clubhouse politicians who profiteer off the poor; and who are always being admonished to patiently wait for a better day—which is virtually certain not to come if awaited patiently. Poverty in America is to be unwelcome, unwanted, and apparently unneeded in the society of one's own citizenship and birthright. It means the despair of any human hope that something will happen in the discernible future that might significantly change the day-to-day existence of those men, women, and children who are poor.—William Stringfellow, *Dissenter in a Great Society*, p. 4

Slanted words

The story is told of a harvester of prodigious appetite who shortened the legs of the dining table on the side where he sat so that the food would slide toward him for instant availability. By exploiting the suggestive power of words, writers can similarly tilt arguments and meanings in their favor.

Sometimes slanting occurs only because a writer, in his enthusiasm, allows words that are too intense to intrude in statements presented as fact. The writer who says "All television programs are designed for the twelve-year-old mind" has allowed his distaste for television programing to make him careless. Often an *all* or *most* should be a *many*, or a superlative should be reduced to a less extreme word, or an *only* or *nothing but* should be changed to allow for other possibilities.

Much unfair slanting occurs in statements of opinion where a writer, knowingly or not, assumes that he is the only reliable resource. There is nothing slanted in a simple statement of one's likes or dislikes ("I can't stand these weirdos with their long hair"). But if the same opinion is stated as a general fact in slanted wording ("Long hair and fanciful clothing are signs of decadence"), the writer implies that he expects his readers to share his opinion without thinking about it.

Just as writers who unerringly trust themselves as the only reliable resource are likely to slant their writing, so are writers who, in their enthusiasm for their own position, fail to consider more than one possibility. The following passage is from an account of anti-draft and anti-war demonstrators, whom the writer has earlier described as being "always accurate and honest."

> They never voted on anything. Like a primitive village, they seemed to know by tacit signs when they had come to a decision. This was astonishing, for in fact they were hardly acquainted. They spoke a language.
>
> Evidently they were morally fearless. They had been through the authority bit many times, with many kinds of administration. College proctors, Southern sheriffs, Feds were all of a piece. "Your generation," one said to an older man, "is all up tight about being in jail. We're not."
>
> The meeting lasted several hours during which they spoke and debated continually. I did not hear a sentence that was not intelligent, nor a tone that was not beautiful.—Paul Goodman, "We Won't Go," *The New York Review*, May 18, 1967, p. 23

Unexamined premises (such as "always accurate and honest") are the source of much slanting. For this reason, the most serious instances of slanting come in writing on social or political problems, especially when the words reflect prejudice. This type of slanted writing can be objected to on at least four grounds: it doesn't accurately represent the situation being discussed; it suggests that the writer is at the very least careless of what he says and more probably willing to distort the facts for his own purposes; it stands in the way of an intelligent and constructive approach to problems that affect the public interest; and it is likely to antagonize the reader (unless he is similarly prejudiced) and so prevent clear communication.

Not all slanted writing uses obviously weighted words. The picture that emerges in the following passage depends upon seemingly innocuous phrases (such as "air-conditioned car" and "able to whip out a poll"):

> Few things in this world appeal more to Lyndon Johnson than driving around his Texas ranch in an air-conditioned car with a sheaf of favorable polls in his pocket. Last week the President was really living.
>
> It has been some time since Johnson has been able to whip out a poll, thrust it under the nose of some startled diplomat or newsman and brandish it as evidence of his popularity. Down at the ranch, he was able to savor two samplings, one taken by Gallup before the President's Glassboro summit meetings, another by Louis Harris afterward, which showed a sharp increase in his ratings. . . . — "Music to His Ears," *Time*, July 14, 1967, p. 14

It is not enough to use words cleverly to achieve an effect. In choosing words for their connotative value, remember that you have a responsibility to deal fairly with both your subject matter and your audience. (**See also** §28.2, Argumentation.)

20.3 Choosing the right word

WW Revision: Replace the wrong word marked with one that accurately conveys your intended meaning.

In the relatively factual prose of most college writing, words should be used in their established forms and senses; if they are not, the reader may be misled or confused. An expression such as "The scene *provoked* his imagination" (in which *provoked*, commonly meaning "angered," is inaccurately used instead of *stimulated*) interferes with communication. In revising your papers, check any words that you are unsure of, especially those that are not part of your regular vocabulary. Be particularly alert to words that are easily confused.

Distinguishing words of similar spelling

In English there are many pairs of words that closely resemble each other in sound or spelling but have quite different meanings: *moral* and *morale*, *personal* and *personnel*, *historic* and *histrionic*. When writing hastily, you may carelessly substitute one word for another, but you can easily eliminate such errors by proofreading your work and by referring to a dictionary when necessary. When words of identical pronunciation, called *homonyms*, are confused in writing, the mistake may be called a spelling error (*bear* for *bare; there* for *their*). But your instructor is likely to label it WW (wrong word) if he suspects that you may not know the difference in meaning (*principal* for *principle; affect* for *effect*).

The following words are frequently confused in college papers. Learn to distinguish their spellings and meanings:

accept—except
adapt—adopt
affect—effect
allusion—illusion
censor—censure
cite—site
complement—compliment
conscientious—conscious
credible—creditable—credulous
detract—distract
formally—formerly
human—humane
imply—infer
persecute—prosecute
precede—proceed
principal—principle
respectful—respective
stationary—stationery

Distinguishing words of similar meaning

Word errors most frequently occur because the writer has failed to distinguish between words of similar meaning. A synonym is a word of *nearly* the same meaning as another:

angry—annoyed—indignant
frank—candid—blunt
multitude—throng—crowd—mob
strange—peculiar—quaint—bizarre

A few words have identical meanings and are therefore interchangeable (*flammable—inflammable; ravel—unravel; toward—*

towards). But most synonyms, while they refer to the same idea or object, differ somewhat in denotation or connotation and thus cannot be substituted for each other without affecting the sense or tone of the statement. One term may be more Formal than another (*coiffure—hair-do*); more concrete (*tango—dance*); more exact (*charitable—kind*); or more personal (*dad—father*).

Usually it is not the more subtle distinctions between closely related words that cause trouble (*necessary—indispensable; intrinsic—inherent*), but the failure to distinguish between common words in different contexts:

> The mysteries of the unknown arouse curiosity that must be *fulfilled*. [for *satisfied*]

> We may expect food consumption to increase everywhere because of the *growth in people*. [*increase in population*]

The only way to avoid such errors is to notice how words of similar meaning are used in various contexts. Connotation as well as denotation should be considered. Notice, for example, how unexpected the last word in this statement is:

> In the 1870's, Dodge City was a lawless gathering place for gun-toting cowboys, professional bad men and killers, and other *scamps*.

20.3 WW *Scamps* might be quite appropriate in referring to mischievous children, but the term is conspicuously out of place in this company of desperadoes. Some synonyms are too heavy or too flippant for the context:

> The water was rougher past the next bend, and we had *difficulty circumventing* the rapids. [too Formal: had *trouble getting around* would be more appropriate]

> I enjoyed studying Plato, because among other things I *got the lowdown on* what is meant by a Platonic friendship. [too Informal: *learned* would be better]

Writers sometimes use strings of fanciful synonyms to avoid repeating the same expression for an idea or object (*cats*, *felines*, *furry beasts*, *tabbies*, *nine-lived creatures*). Such "elegant variations" are pretentious and are usually more annoying than simple repetition. Readers expect key words to be repeated when they cannot be replaced by pronouns (*cats . . . they*). Factual synonyms (*these animals*) are also unobtrusive and will seldom strike the reader as repetitious.

Distinguishing words of opposite meaning

Some words that have contrasting or wholly opposite meanings are frequently confused, probably because the writer associates them mentally but has reversed their meanings. Among the most common antonyms or near antonyms are the following. Make sure that you know their meanings.

concave—convex
condemn—condone
explicit—implicit
famous—notorious
former—latter
inductive—deductive
physiological—psychological
prescribe—proscribe
subjective—objective
temerity—timidity

A writer who confuses such pairs may say the very opposite of what he intends. Half-knowing a word is often more dangerous than not knowing it at all.

Learning new words

Although many word errors are caused by confusion or carelessness, a writer frequently uses the wrong word (or settles for the almost-right word) simply because he does not know another one. College papers are likely to deal with complex ideas and precise distinctions that may demand a larger vocabulary than the writer has needed in the past.

It has been estimated that children enter first grade knowing about 25,000 words and add 5000 every year, so that they leave high school with a vocabulary of perhaps as many as 90,000 words. The average vocabulary for college graduates is approximately twice this size. These figures are for *recognition* vocabulary, the words that we understand when we read or hear them. Our *active* vocabulary, the words we actually use in writing or speaking, is considerably smaller.

Most people use only about a third as many words as they recognize. Thus, an obvious way for you to enlarge your working vocabulary is through conscious exercise. In making an effort to say precisely what you mean you should search not only among the words in your active vocabulary, but also among those you have learned to recognize. Frequently we find new words in reading (*cybernetics*, *rhetoric*, *apartheid*) and learn their meanings from the context or from a dictionary. Using these words in writing or speaking helps to make them more readily available for future use.

It is sometimes possible to guess the meaning of a word by knowing its parts. Many scientific words, for example, are formed with suffixes and roots from Greek or Latin:

mono- (one)	-graph (writing, written)	hemo- (blood)
bi- (two)	bio- (life)	poly- (many)
tele- (at a distance)	photo- (light)	micro- (small)

Since the combined meanings of the parts may only approximate the meaning of the whole, however, it is usually safer to use a dictionary and learn the entire word.

Ordinarily we learn and remember words not for their own sake but for the meanings they represent. We have a good stock of words in the fields that interest us because facts and ideas are retained chiefly in verbal form. Thus, anything that extends the range of your ideas or experiences will help to enlarge your vocabulary. The typical college course, for example, adds to a student's vocabulary several hundred new words and new meanings for familiar words.

When you meet a new word that is likely to be useful, learn it accurately at the start—its spelling and pronunciation as well as its usual meaning. Students often have trouble in their college courses because they only half know the specialized words essential to a subject. Using these words in conversation, when they are appropriate, or in reviewing course work with another student will fix them in your mind so that you can use them easily and accurately in examinations, papers, and class discussions.

20.4 Concrete and abstract words

Words can be classified according to the nature of their referents as *abstract* or *concrete* (p. 250). Abstract (general) words refer to ideas, qualities, acts, or relationships. Concrete (specific) words refer to definite persons, places, objects, and acts. This list demonstrates the differences between the two kinds of words:

Abstract (*general*)	*Concrete* (*specific*)
institution	Austin College
labor	running a ditching machine
men's organization	Lion's Club
a politician	the Senator from Kentucky
food	cheesecake

an educator	my history teacher
creed	Westminster Confession

Often a word cannot be labeled as abstract or concrete until it is read in context:

Abstract	*Concrete*
Honest labor never killed any man. [a generalization about all labor]	In the GM contract dispute, labor seeks a five-cent per hour wage increase. [in the context, a specific reference to the United Automobile Workers]

Effective uses of concrete and abstract words

Concrete words are essential in discussing situations, incidents, and processes that are based upon personal experience or direct observation: impressions of people or places, discussions of plans for the future, explanations of the writer's attitudes or interests. Abstract words, on the other hand, are usually necessary in discussing general ideas ("The Intangible Values of Education"), for summarizing facts or stating opinions, or for analyzing theoretical problems ("Is Specialization in Education Undesirable?").

Abstract words are more characteristic of Formal than of General or Informal English and are best used by writers with a good deal of experience in handling ideas. In this passage, for example, the writer uses very few concrete words, yet the meaning is clear to anyone who has looked closely at himself:

20.4 Abst

> It is however certain that no estimate is more in danger of erroneous calculations than those by which a man computes the force of his own genius. It generally happens at our entrance into this world, that by the natural attraction of similitude, we associate with men like ourselves young, sprightly, and ignorant, and rate our accomplishments by comparison with theirs; when we have once obtained an acknowledged superiority over our acquaintances, imagination and desire easily extend it over the rest of mankind, and if no accident forces us into new emulations, we grow old, and die in admiration of ourselves.—Samuel Johnson, *The Rambler*, No. 154

But broad ideas can also be discussed in concrete terms. For example, this discussion of "the American way of life," an extremely abstract notion, begins in language that is conspicuously specific:

> But what is the American way of life?
>
> This morning, my mail included a notice of a Rotary meeting, an appeal for funds from World Federalists, an announcement of a meeting of the state trustees of Vermont Forums, Inc., some pamphlets published by the Friends, a letter from the Institute of International Education, an invitation to join a sociological association, and a program announcement from an organization new to me—the National Cooperative School for Group Organization and Recreation. During the morning, my wife (who is active in twice as many community services as I am) was out campaigning for the Red Cross. A phone call invited me to speak at a church club, and we were notified of a square dance.—Bradford Smith, "We're Selling America Short," *The American Scholar*, Summer 1952, p. 310

Generalization is appropriate—even necessary—when a writer must summarize a large body of facts. This is frequently done in short papers on general subjects, where the writer's primary concern is to survey briefly the available facts and explain their significance. The important thing in such cases is to choose general words that *accurately* summarize the specific details examined, without distortion or unnecessary vagueness. A student
20.4 writing a paper on conservation, for example, might run across this passage:

> In the seven years from 1883 to 1890 the New South Wales Government was forced to spend not less than £1,543,000 in its attempt to control the scourge, and today rabbit control both in Australia and in New Zealand is a financial load upon every community. Many methods of eradicating this pest have been attempted. In Western Australia more than 2000 miles of fencing was erected at a cost of almost £500,000, but after it was all up it was found that some rabbits were already on the other side of the fence! Unfortunately, incidental to the compulsory use of poison for rabbits, there has been a very great destruction of wildlife as well as livestock, and phosphorus poisoning, employed for rabbit control, has been one of the principal causes of death among the marsupials and native birds.—Fairfield Osborn, *Our Plundered Planet*, pp. 161-162

In writing his paper, the student might effectively generalize from these facts as follows:

> Attempts to limit the rabbit population in Australia and New Zealand have been costly and destructive of other animal life.

It is perfectly proper to use abstract words when the material calls for them, if they can be used accurately and clearly. But writing on almost any subject gains force through the use of specific words. It is usually more convincing to generalize at the beginning or end of a paper, on the basis of a number of specific facts, than it is to pile up generalities throughout.

Excessive use of abstract words

| *Abst* | **Revision: Replace the abstract expression marked with one that is more specific.**

The most common fault in the wording of many student papers is a fondness for abstract terms where concrete words would be more meaningful and certainly more interesting. Even if an assigned topic is so worded that it seems difficult to discuss in specific terms ("The Importance of Education," "What Democracy Means"), a paper can be reasonably factual, concrete, and convincing if it is written in words that represent the writer's own experiences and beliefs.

Some students make the mistake of believing that the more general the expression, the more convincing and impressive it is. Others write without thinking, mistaking the use of abstract words for intellectual discipline. The use of a general or indefinite expression where a concrete one would fit is annoying to readers:

> I think that this quarter's work has helped me to form new physical actions and has broadened my mental ability.

If the writer means that he has learned *to swim*, or *to play baseball*, or *to dance*, he should say so; and he might also indicate just how the quarter's work has broadened his "mental ability." Has it helped him to concentrate? Taught him better study habits?

The excessive use of abstract words can become an unfortunate habit in writing. Some students never take *physics*, *history*, *economics*, or *French;* instead, they encounter *various interesting courses of study;* rather than going to a specific college, they attend *an institution of higher learning;* they do not play *golf*, *bridge*, *tennis*, or *baseball*, but *participate in various recreational activities*. Few traits of style are more boring than the unnecessary use of vague, abstract terms for ideas that could better be expressed concretely.

Exercises

1. *Words in context.* The following passage is taken from an essay on Roman architecture. What does each of the italicized words mean in this context? Write a sentence illustrating how each of these words would have a different meaning in another context.

The result is that the whole of *living* Rome is a surprisingly *contemporary* city. How many of us who photograph the Spanish Steps *realize* that the birthplace of George Washington is older? *Masons* were working on the Trevi *fountain*, into which we throw coins to *acknowledge* our nostalgia to return, while Benjamin Franklin was in London presenting the tax grievances of the *Colonies* to the British government. The great Piazza del Popolo, below our Pincian *lookout*, did not even exist when Jackson was fighting the Battle of New Orleans—it was still a blueprint in the *studios* of Giuseppe Valadier. We can find an American *parallel* even for Alexander Borgia. When the bells of Valencia were ringing out for his *elevation* to the throne of Saint Peter, the bells of Palos, in Spain, were still vibrating in the ears of the sailors aboard the little caravels *pitching* westward under the command of Columbus. And if we visit the magnificent church of Santa Maria Maggiore and look up at its gleaming, *coffered* ceiling we are sure to be told that this was the first gold brought back from the Americas.—Sean O'Faolain, "A Pontifical Splendor," *Holiday*, April 1960, p. 84

2. *Connotation.* Arrange the following groups of words into columns, according to their connotation: favorable, neutral, or unfavorable. Supply missing words wherever necessary.

1) student, scholar, bookworm
2) stubborn, firm, pigheaded
3) average, mediocre
4) counterfeit, replica, copy
5) racy, obscene, blue
6) unusual, bizarre, unique
7) tolerant, flexible, wishy-washy
8) caustic, penetrating, sharp
9) egghead, intellectual
10) reserved, aristocratic, snobbish
11) simulated, bogus
12) buffoon, wit, comic
13) officer, policeman, fuzz
14) svelte, skinny, thin
15) literary artist, hack, writer

3. *Slanted words.* Read the following passage through critically, paying particular attention to its emotional tone. What response is the writer trying to arouse? Underline all words that you consider slanted and be prepared to explain how they contribute to the writer's aim.

The leading actor was Mussolini, the strutting pygmy Caesar who marched on Rome with his Black Shirts in October, 1922, and presented Italy with twenty-two years of Fascism. It is said he made the trains run on time; those who said so believed it was a shattering triumph. Mussolini relieved Italy of its limited democracy, scorned the League of Nations and willingly played No. 1 Boy to Hitler. Old buildings were torn down to make room for his grandiose highways—the Via della Conciliazione, leading to St. Peter's, and the Via del Teatro Marcello and Via dei Fori Imperiali, flanking the Colosseum and the Forum.

From the Palazzo Venezia, close to the sleeping Forum, Mussolini thundered and boasted of Italy's coming place in the sun. But he involved the nation disastrously in a second war with Ethiopia, and in World War II brought it shockingly close to disaster. He forced Italy into an undesired war against the Allies. As defeat followed defeat, Italy was occupied by the infuriated German Army. Gradually the German Army was itself defeated and Mussolini forced to resign.—Arnold Ehrlich, "A Capsule History of Rome." *Holiday*, April 1960, p. 35

4. *Slanted words.* Bring to class for discussion examples of statements containing conspicuously slanted words. Some of these you may find in popular magazines or in newspapers, especially in the editorials or in columns written by political commentators. Distinguish between fact and opinion in the articles, and be prepared to comment upon the writer's attitude toward his information and toward his readers. Find specific examples of words you believe are intended to persuade (or mislead) the reader. Do you think that the articles would be less interesting to read if the words were more neutral in connotation?

5. *Choosing the right word.* Read each of the following sentences carefully and choose the word in parentheses that most *exactly* expresses the intended meaning.

1) He found after he had paid his tuition that he hadn't the money (requisite, necessary) to buy his dinner.

2) The latest statistics (dispute, refute, rebuke) his claim that the economy is expanding.

3) In time Einstein (convinced, persuaded, showed) most physicists that his theory was correct.

4) I admired her (poise; coolness, refinement) under the stress of a difficult examination.

5) Most states have laws that (stop, deter, prohibit) gambling.

6) We stopped in our stroll on lower Main Street to (give, donate, contribute) some money to a blind man.

7) Perhaps if you (heed, obey) the Dean of Men in this, he will relent in that.

8) No sooner had he got his own private office than he had conceived a (plan, design, scheme) to become president.

9) My instructor did not report me to the Dean, although he made it clear he did not (accept, condone, tolerate) my behavior.

10) The remarks at the end of his speech (implied, inferred, insinuated) that he had some financial support for his plan.

6. *Choosing the right word.* Examine the diction in the following sentences to determine which words are misused. Rewrite the faulty sentences, supplying more exact or more appropriate words. Be prepared to explain why you made each change.

1) Within the next few days the assassin gained considerable renown.

2) If there was any morale to the story, I did not find it.

3) I do not like to be around him, for his perpetual pessimism aggravates me.

4) A student who is writing a research paper should compulsively read through the leading works devoted to his subject.

5) How can a teacher instigate his class to write better?

6) My mother has always been a zealot of bridge and canasta and other trivial amusements.

7) If we adopt the plan, how will the changes in procedure effect the goals?

8) The course has made me familiar with new ideals in the study of genetics and things like that.

9) I found this poem extremely obtuse, and even after struggling over it for hours with a dictionary and an encyclopedia I could not decipher many of its illusions.

10) I have never been very adapt at tennis, so when the rest of the crowd wanted to go out to the courts I abstained.

7. *Increasing vocabulary.* Classify by number the words in the following list as (1) words you now use in speaking and writing; (2) words that you understand but do not generally use; (3) words that you believe you have seen before and might understand in context; (4) words totally unfamiliar to you. Look up the words that you number 3 or 4 in a dictionary. Which of these words might be useful to you?

anthropomorphic	fetish	lobotomy	sacrosanct
bibliography	feudalism	madras	scrimmage
brigantine	galaxy	malevolent	sediment
buff	gauche	metamorphosis	semantics
cabal	genocide	meteorology	shanghai
caisson	graffito	nadir	spondee
celibate	hedonist	neolithic	staccato
codicil	hoecake	opaque	tangent
context	iconoclast	paltry	tare
crustacean	ignis fatuus	parthenogenesis	teetotaler
decadent	illiterate	pedant	tovarisch
deciduous	improvise	piston	tranquilizer
demitasse	kilometer	quixotic	Uncle Tom
duenna	larva	quantum	venal
eclectic	libido	recant	versatile
ellipse	limbo	rococo	whimsy

8. *Increasing vocabulary:* Make a list of a dozen or more words of different kinds that you have added to your vocabulary in recent weeks. To refresh your memory, consult some of your recent papers, check the indexes of your textbooks, and consider the new activities you have recently enjoyed. Prepare a brief statement about the circumstances in which you met these words and the way you learned their meaning.

9. *Using concrete words.* The following paragraph is from a paper describing the advantages of living in a big city. Underline all expressions that seem to you too general, vague, or otherwise ineffective. Then rewrite the paragraph, making the language as concrete and direct as possible.

The individual who lives in an urban metropolis can engage in more leisure activities. There are many cultural institutions where he can observe wonderful artistic productions or historical artifacts; most of these require no financial contribution on his part. Then there are the commercial enterprises that present dramatic or musical arts and other interesting activities. He also has the opportunity to become acquainted with the cultural differences in the various areas surrounding him as he explores both desirable and undesirable environments within the metropolitan context. Such explorations can affect his intellectual growth and toleration. To a person who comes from a background limited in such knowledge, these experiences are factors of great importance.

10. *Accurate generalization.* Assume that you are writing a short information paper on Prohibition and wish to incorporate the information given below. How can you effectively *generalize* from the material without citing the specific illustrations? Write out your generalization.

To meet all these potential threats against the Volstead Act, the Government appropriations provided a force of prohibition agents which in 1920 numbered only 1,520 men and as late as 1930 numbered only 2,836; even with the sometimes unenthusiastic aid of the Coast Guard and the Customs Service and the Immigration Service, the force was meager. Mr. Merz puts it graphically: if the whole army of agents in 1920 had been mustered along the coasts and borders—paying no attention for the moment to medicinal alcohol, breweries, industrial alcohol, or illicit stills—there would have been one man to patrol every twelve miles of beach, harbor, headland, forest, and riverfront. The agents' salaries in 1920 mostly ranged between $1,200 and $2,000; by 1930 they had been munificently raised to range between $2,300 and $2,800. Anybody who believed that men employable at thirty-five or forty or fifty dollars a week would surely have the expert technical knowledge and the diligence to supervise successfully the complicated chemical operations of industrial-alcohol plants or to outwit the craftiest devices of smugglers and bootleggers, and that they would surely have the force of character to resist corruption by men whose pockets were bulging with money, would be ready to believe also in Santa Claus, perpetual motion, and pixies.—Frederick Lewis Allen, *Only Yesterday*, pp. 249-250

21 The effect of words

. . . no word can be judged as to whether it is good or bad, correct or incorrect, beautiful or ugly, or anything else that matters to a writer, in isolation.—I. A. Richards

Words occur in sentences and sentences occur in paragraphs and compositions. To communicate meaning, words must be used accurately in context. To be effective, they must be appropriate to the purpose and tone of the composition: the individual words should fit the subject, they should sound like the writer, and they should reach the intended reader.

Because the effect of words cannot be judged out of context, a writer must rely largely on his own judgment in choosing words that will best convey his meaning and his attitude toward his subject. A dictionary is a useful guide to meaning, but it is of little help when it comes to putting "proper words in proper places."

In the absence of specific guidelines, there are three things a writer can do to help make his word choice more effective. First, he can choose more thoughtfully from the range of his present vocabulary those words that best suit a particular purpose. Second, he can sharpen his judgment by paying closer attention to the language around him—the language of his classmates, his instructors, his parents, the people he hears speak on television and radio—and noticing the differences between Formal and Informal usage. And finally (and perhaps most important), he can read widely to familiarize himself with the range and variety of effective writing. As a writer becomes more sensitive to the uses of language, he becomes increasingly aware that his choice of words shapes not only the meaning but the effect of what he is trying to say.

21.1 Formal words

We may call a piece of *writing* Formal, even if its vocabulary is largely from General English, when its sentences are unusually complex, its organizational patterns tight and demanding. We call *vocabulary* Formal if it ranges much beyond the characteristic spoken vocabulary, from words slightly more characteristic of writing than of speaking to such specialized words as *moribund*, *educand*, *genotype*, and *ailurophobe*.

Appropriate use of Formal words

In using Formal words, an inexperienced writer runs the risk of sounding remote from his subject and from his reader. Unless he is at ease with them, he also runs the risk of seeming affected. But some situations demand and deserve the vigor and precision of good Formal usage, as illustrated in this passage:

> Again the need appears to speak up against the uncritical adulation of youth. It is anomalous that a civilization of long history and great complexity should defer to youth rather than to age. The virtues of youth are the virtues of freshness and vitality, but these are not the virtues that fit one to be the custodian of the culture that society has produced. Deferring to youth is another way of weakening oontinuity. Mark almost any young person, and you notice that he does not *see* very much, in the sense of understanding what is present to his vision. He perceives, but he does not interpret, and this is because he is too lacking in those memory traces which lead to ideas and concepts. The memoryless part of mankind cannot be the teachers of culture; they are, however, ready learners of it if the real teachers show faith in the value of what they have.—Richard Weaver, *Visions of Order*, pp. 53-54

21.1 Big W

Formal words are appropriate to writers and speakers who use them easily and naturally and to situations that require them for precision. College students should increase the number of Formal words in their active vocabulary, but these words should be the necessary ones for discussing ideas, reflecting an actual growth in intellectual scope, not an attempt to translate ordinary matters into "Big Words."

"Big Words"—stilted language

Big W | Revision: Replace the stilted word or words marked with words from the General vocabulary.

"Big Words," as the term is used here, are any and all expressions that are too heavy or too Formal for the situation. Such words sound stilted, whether they are short or long, common or uncommon. A typical fault of inexperienced writers is the use of Big Words in a misguided effort to sound profound:

> It is difficult to filter out one specific cause for a social problem. Most often there are many minute factors interrelated and closely correlated. Our conception of a social problem today possesses

more magnitude than that of two or three decades ago. We now consider the world as a unit rather than an aggregation of component entities.

Ideas are easier to understand and are more convincing if the wording is natural. It should be exact, not inflated beyond the requirements of the subject or the expectations of the reader. The language of the sentences just cited, for example, might be simplified as follows:

A social problem can seldom be traced to a single, specific cause. Today we are much more aware of the complexity of social problems than we were twenty or thirty years ago, for we have come to see that all societies are interrelated.

Students are most likely to use stilted language in papers written near the beginning of a composition course, when they aren't certain what attitude they should take toward their material or toward their readers. They may use inflated diction because they wrongly believe that a paper written for a composition course should be as Formal and impersonal as possible, or that Big Words will impress the reader, or that inflated diction is humorous ("a fair damsel garbed in the mode of the moment" instead of "a fashionably dressed young girl").

21.1 Big W

An extreme use of Big Words is sometimes called *gobbledygook* —inflated diction that seems to have lost all contact with the matter being discussed. Writing full of such jargon is often found in print today, especially in specialized journals and government publications, but this does not make it good English. Here is what James Thurber had to say of such language:

Great big blocky words and phrases bumble off our tongues and presses every day. In four weeks of purposeful listening to the radio and reading the newspapers I have come up with a staggering list, full of sound and fury, dignifying nothing: "automation," "roadability," "hummature," "motivational cognition" (this baby turned up in a series of travel lectures and was never defined), "fractionalization," "varietism," "redesegregation," "additive," "concertization" (this means giving a concert in a hall, and is not to be confused with cinematization or televisionization). . . . Ization is here to stay. It appeals to bureaucrats and congressmen because of its portentous polysyllabification. Politicians love it the way they love such expressions as "legislativewise." Lord Conesford, stout defender of the Queen's English, recently paraphrased Churchill's

> "Give us the tools and we will finish the job" by Washingtonizing it like this: "Supply us with the implements and we will finalize the solution of the matter."—James Thurber, *Alarms and Diversions*, pp. 21, 24

The remedy for too many Big Words is simple: Read aloud what you have written, preferably some time after you have written it; if you find the language conspicuously different from what you would use in conversation, look at the words carefully to see whether you can find simpler substitutes.

Technical words

In writing intended for a general audience, unfamiliar terms not made clear by the context should be defined or explained. Technical terms or unfamiliar expressions that often need explaining include:

1) Scientific terms (*isotope*, *lobotomy*, *gneiss*), and other expressions restricted to a specialized activity (*a cappella*, *heroic hexameter*, *escrow*, *chiaroscuro*, *farinaceous*, *binary*).

2) Words used in special senses rather than in the usual way (the *spine* of a book, to *justify* a line of type, the *recorder* as a wind
21.1 instrument, a *frog* as a fastener for a jacket).

3) Foreign words and phrases not customarily used by most people (*lex talionis*, *pourboire*, *eisteddfod*, *Walpurgisnacht*).

A writer should not use an inexact or wordy expression in place of a necessary technical term. If, for instance, the subject of a paper is "Mountain Climbing," it is better to define and use a word like *piton* than to say "those little metal gadgets that they tie ropes to." Do not use unfamiliar words just to show off, but use and explain those that are essential to your subject.

Often a simple definition or explanation can be worked into the sentence where the technical term is introduced, as in the following examples:

> The ability of the heart to function depends primarily on the state of the heart muscle, or myocardium, as it is technically known.
>
> In the study of rhetoric we are first to consider *inventio*, or what we now refer to as the problems of pre-writing.
>
> In cold weather the Eskimos wear mukluks (fur boots) and parkas (short fur coats with fur hoods).

As a rule, do not simply quote a dictionary definition, which may be too narrow, but compose one that fits the style and scale of your own paper. Compare a dictionary definition of *oligarchy* with this description of the term:

> I mean by "oligarchy" any system in which ultimate power is confined to a section of the community: the rich to the exclusion of the poor, Protestants to the exclusion of Catholics, aristocrats to the exclusion of plebeians, white men to the exclusion of colored men, males to the exclusion of females, or members of one political party to the exclusion of the rest. A system may be more or less oligarchic according to the percentage of the population that is excluded; absolute monarchy is the extreme of oligarchy.—Bertrand Russell, *The Impact of Science on Society*, p. 43

The crucial thing in defining a term is to give an adequate description of the way *you* are using it, with details and concrete illustrations to clarify the meaning.

21.2 Informal words

Informal words include those marked *colloquial* in dictionaries and most of those marked *slang*. They are part of Standard English but are not appropriate to all kinds of writing.

21.2

Inf

Appropriate use of Informal words

Informal words are often appropriate in discussions of sports, informal situations, and humorous material. They are also sometimes fitting in discussions of more important topics, especially by young people, where the language otherwise is typically General English. You will find such words used, without apology or quotation marks, in many of our most reputable publications. Note the italicized words in this paragraph:

> What happens to the child who is treated as an adult is that he *gets fresh*—becomes impertinent, disobedient, whiny, and a pest. Nobody enjoys him much any more, beginning with himself. Even to his loving mother he sometimes *gives a stiff pain in the neck*. But if she has read a book . . . she knows that this is because he feels anxious and insecure. Therefore she controls her impulse *to warm his tail* and send him to bed without supper; she treats him, instead, with monumental patience and slightly forced demonstrations of affection. *Daddy*, who comes home from the office pretty tired, in

> need of a drink and some peaceful home life, is likely to be less long-suffering. He may even raise the possibility of *cracking down.*—Helen Eustis, "Good-By to Oedipus," *Harper's Magazine*, June 1953, p. 46

If you are tempted to apologize for Informal words by putting them in quotation marks, ask yourself whether they are genuinely appropriate. If they are, use them without apology, but if not, replace them with words from the General vocabulary.

Inappropriate use of Informal words

Revision: Change the Informal expression to one from the General vocabulary.

It is disconcerting to a reader to encounter an Informal expression in relatively Formal writing:

> The displaced persons in Europe experienced many *tough breaks* after the end of the war. [more appropriate: *hardships*]

> The natives believe that they can expiate certain offenses against tribal customs by *throwing a feast.* [better: *giving a feast*]

21.2

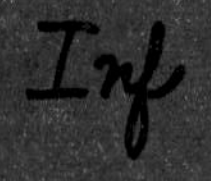

In Formal writing, Informal words not only indicate a shift in variety of usage but may also suggest that the writer has a careless or flippant attitude toward his subject:

> When Desdemona failed to produce the handkerchief, Othello began to suspect that she *wasn't on the level.*

A writer needs to be particularly careful about certain expressions so widely used that he may not realize (until the slip is called to his attention) that they are considered Informal rather than General usage:

> Plays of this sort are seldom seen *in our neck of the woods.*

> Faulkner had *a funny habit* of writing long, rather complicated sentences.

21.3 Fresh words and lifeless words

Good writing, whether factual or fictional, captures the reader's interest immediately and holds his attention throughout; other writing, concerned with similar facts or ideas, may strike him as lifeless and boring. In either instance the wording may be correct enough, but the more enjoyable and certainly more memorable reading is that in which words are fresh and direct:

> Then a tremendous flash of light cut across the sky. Mr. Tanimoto has a distinct recollection that it travelled from east to west, from the city toward the hills. It seemed a sheet of sun.—John Hersey, *Hiroshima*, p. 8

> Supper was a young squirrel who had nevertheless achieved an elder's stringiness, roasted in foil on the embers, and a potato baked in the same way.—John Graves, *Goodbye to a River*, pp. 151-152

The search for fresh and direct expression does not require that a writer should strain obviously for effect, by searching for unusual expressions or words, any more than he should by using eccentric punctuation or unconventional sentence structure. It does mean that he should take an interest in the freshness of his expression and that he should take sufficient time and thought to revise worn-out terms, incongruous figures of speech, or currently overworked expressions.

Old-fashioned words

We naturally use words that are current. In fact there is a temptation to resort too easily to "vogue words" (*bottleneck*, *breakthrough*), to allude to current activities (*getting off the launching pad*), or to add the fashionable suffix *-wise* to words that are in good use as they stand ("The play was a success *profitwise*" for "The play made a profit").

On the other hand, some writers mar their papers with old-fashioned expressions which, although they may not be obsolete or archaic, seem incongruous in contemporary writing. They may think that such words sound impressive or elegant; the reader, however, is more likely to consider the writing affected or foolish:

> One may relax on the *greensward* of a Sunday and listen to a rousing band concert.

> The game seemed to have been won, but *alas!* we failed to gain the necessary three yards in four tries.

> Little schooling was required in *days of yore* to get along in life.

Here are some old-fashioned expressions with their present-day equivalents:

amidst—among	deem—think, consider
befell—happened	supped—ate, dined
brethren—brothers	twain—two

The best way to detect old-fashioned words is to read the passage aloud and decide whether you would use such an expression in ordinary conversation.

Trite expressions

Trite | **Revision: Replace the trite expression with one that is fresher or more direct.**

Trite expressions, or clichés, are pat phrases so familiar that, given the first words, we can usually finish the expression without thinking:

This is going to hurt me more ________
He is down but not ________
Gone but ________
It isn't the heat but ________

21.3 Trite

Try to avoid the following overworked expressions that occur with relentless frequency in student papers:

Cliché	*Comment*
according to Webster	Did Webster write the dictionary you are using?
history tells us	A dubious personification, one that often leads to empty generalizations.
the finer things of life	Name two or three. No matter what they are—a good pipe, a Beethoven Quartet, a cheesecake—they'll be more convincing to the reader tnan this nebulous phrase.
last but not least	Is the last item or fact *never* of least importance?
things have come to a pretty pass	The pass is seldom pretty; better to go through the canyon.

Figurative language (§21.4) adds interest to writing when it is fresh and appropriate, but stale comparisons and personifications only serve to bore the reader. It will not make anything seem cooler, hotter, or neater if you describe it as *cool as a cucumber*, *hot as a two-dollar pistol*, or *neat as a pin*. Here is a short list of trite figures of speech; you can probably think of many similar expressions:

quick as a wink	at the drop of a hat
lost in thought	a watery grave
sly as a fox	run like a deer
rotten to the core	like a shot from a cannon
white as snow	brave as a lion
in a nutshell	Mother Nature
darkness overtakes us	spreading like wildfire
commune with nature	bull in a china shop
the rat race	the crack of dawn

Similarly, many quotations have lost their vividness through overuse:

a sadder and wiser man	all the world's a stage
stone walls do not a prison make	water, water, everywhere

So thoroughly are quotations from Shakespeare woven into our daily speech that some people, when they read or see a play such as *Hamlet* or *Julius Caesar* for the first time, are surprised to find that they have been "talking Shakespeare" all their lives:

21.3 Trite

to be or not to be
uneasy lies the head
something rotten in the state of Denmark
lend me your ears
not wisely, but too well

There are many fresh, vivid lines from less-quoted sources—in modern poetry, for instance, and in Shakespeare, too—if you wish to enliven your writing with quotations.

When you find yourself using overworked expressions, look at them closely to see if they actually mean anything to you; usually you will decide that they really mean very little, and you will make your point another way.

Euphemisms

A euphemism is a polite and often affected expression used in place of a more common term which the user fears might be offensive. Euphemisms are often used in conversation out of consideration for the listener's feelings: a teacher might tell a mother that her child is *slow* or *exceptional* rather than *dull* or *stupid;* a saleswoman is more likely to tell a customer that she has a *problem figure* than that she is *overweight* or *fat*. But although euphemisms are often necessary in social situations, they ordinarily sound evasive or affected when they are used in writing.

Euphemistic expression	*Direct expression*
a reconditioned automobile	a used car
underprivileged, disadvantaged	poor
senior citizens	old people
halitosis	bad breath
unmentionables	underwear
expecting	pregnant
pass away	die
lay to rest	bury
our statement apparently has escaped your attention	you haven't paid your bill
preferred customer	customer who pays his bills regularly

21.4 Figures of speech

21.4 Fig

Figures of speech are expressions of comparison, personification, or association that are used to intensify statements or to make them more expressive and vivid, usually by shifting from the ordinary uses and meanings of words. This is a literal, nonfigurative statement:

> The fewer words a person uses, the more quickly his meaning will be understood.

The same idea can be expressed in a more memorable way by a well-chosen figure of speech:

> . . . meaning is an arrow that reaches its mark when least encumbered with feathers.—Herbert Read, *English Prose Style*, p. 16

Notice how the use of well-chosen figures of speech enlivens this description of a summer morning in New York:

> Heat has an effect on sound, intensifying it. On a scorching morning, at breakfast in a café, one's china cup explodes against its saucer with a fierce report. The great climaxes of sound in New York are achieved in side streets, as in West 44th Street, beneath our

window, where occasionally an intestinal stoppage takes place, the entire block laden with undischarged vehicles, the pangs of congestion increasing till every horn is going—a united, delirious scream of hate, every decibel charged with a tiny drop of poison.—E. B. White, *The Second Tree from the Corner*, pp. 222-223

The use of figurative language is not limited to purely descriptive passages or to "literary" subjects. You will find figures of speech used freely and effectively in such diverse material as financial articles, literary criticism, advertising copy, sports writing, and political discussions.

Types of figurative language

Early texts in rhetoric and composition classified many figures of speech (Richard Sherry's *A Treatise of Schemes and Tropes*, published in 1550, catalogs about three hundred), but these are the ones most widely used in current writing:

Hyperbole (deliberate exaggeration for interest and emphasis):

It was a day *to end all days.*
He's the *greatest* little second baseman *in the world.*

Irony (use of a word to signify the reverse of its literal meaning):

For Brutus is an *honourable man.* . . .
That's just *great.* [expression often signifying disgust]

Litotes (deliberate understatement, often calculated to magnify the impact of what we say by its incongruity and restraint):

Hemingway was not a *bad* writer.
Golly, what a *gully!* [a description of the Grand Canyon]

Metaphor (implied comparison between unlike things that, perhaps unexpectedly, have something in common):

Out, out, *brief candle!*
Life's but a walking shadow, a poor player
That struts and frets his hour upon the stage
And then is heard no more. . . .

Metonymy (substitution of an associated word for what is actually meant):

But most by *numbers* judge a poet's song;
And smooth or rough with them is right or wrong. . . .

Suited to the *plow*, he sought to live by the *pen.*

Onomatopoeia (use of words to create a sound appropriate to the sense):

> It was a hot day in late July when I sat with Uncle Miles at Belting beside the *strippling ream.* The deliberate Spoonerism was Uncle Miles's, and it did seem to express something about the stream that rippled beside us as we sat on the spongy grass. To say strippled rather than rippled conveyed something about the movement of the water, and ream instead of stream suggested that large bream waited in it ready to be caught.—Julian Symons, *The Belting Inheritance*, p. 1

Oxymoron (coupling contradictory terms):

> At eleven, she *enjoyed the fright* of reading *Dracula.*

Periphrasis (substitution of a descriptive phrase for a name, sometimes of a name for a descriptive phrase):

> Be true to the *red, white, and blue.*

> For two consecutive holes, plus a drive on the third, he was *Ben Hogan;* then came disaster.

Personification (attribution of human qualities to nonhuman or abstract things):

> They turned and waved, and then the jungle *swallowed* them.

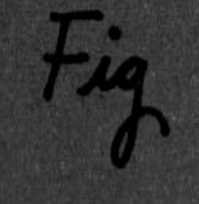

Simile (stated comparison between two unlike things that, perhaps unexpectedly, have something in common):

> My mistress' bosom is *as white as the snow, and as cold.*

Synecdoche (substitution of a term for another to which it is related in a system of classification, as in naming a part when a whole is meant, naming a whole when a part is meant):

> *Wisconsin* meets *Oregon* in the Rose Bowl.
> The poor man had twelve *mouths* to feed.

Effective figures of speech

Revision: Change the figure of speech marked to an expression that is more appropriate to your subject and your style; avoid inconsistent figures.

Although figures of speech, if they are fresh and perceptive, clearly have an appeal, they are *not* mere ornaments. Indeed, when they seem to be ornaments, we can usually conclude that they are used unnaturally and ostentatiously. If they are vivid and natural, they make writing attractive, but they can accomplish much more than this.

Each kind of figurative language has its special uses. Metaphor and simile, for example, can enlarge our perception and understanding of a subject, and can say much in little space. If a writer says, "The old cowpuncher's parenthetical legs were covered by worn brown chaps," we gain from the metaphor a pretty clear picture of the cowboy's configuration; some notion of his age and the amount of time he has spent on a horse; and some insight into his character and the writer's attitude toward him (the choice of metaphor suggests a familiar, even comic treatment). We can learn something about a subject in one area by the light cast on it from language of another area, much as we do in reading parables and allegories, which in a sense can be considered extended metaphors.

Figures of speech can help us to understand the writer's attitude toward his subject and toward his audience. Appropriate personification and periphrasis, for example, are signals of a writer's emotional involvement in his subject, and perhaps of his wish to make an emotional appeal to his audience. Litotes, hyperbole, and simile, because they show us something about the way a writer sees things, can enable an audience to know what kind of person addresses them, how perceptive he is, and how reliable he may be.

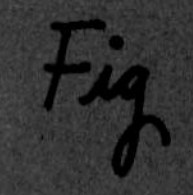

For these reasons it is obvious that figurative expressions should be in keeping with the writer's subject and his style, and that they should be accurate enough to contribute to the meaning. Expressions that are too strong or that strive too hard to be picturesque only confuse or irritate the reader:

> As fall comes in with its gentle coolness, Mother Nature *launches her chemical warfare*, changing the leaves into their many pretty colors.

> My grandfather's barn was *like a medieval fortress shrouded in legend.*

Straining for unusual expressions seldom results in effective writing. The figures to use are those that actually come to mind when you are trying to give an exact account of the subject. They should be fresh, if possible, but, even more important, they should fit their context and sound natural.

Consistent figures of speech

A figure of speech should not begin with one kind of picture and switch to another wholly unrelated one:

> The nineteenth century *became a door* opened by some of the braver authors, through which many of the earlier ideas of writing for children, which had been *crushed or discarded, again sprang to blossom*, and spread into the many branches of children's literature that we have today.

If you can look at your own writing with some degree of objectivity, you can usually determine whether a figure is consistent or not. Sometimes an expression that seemed very vivid at the moment of writing proves, upon rereading, to be confusing or even ludicrous.

Exercises

21.4 **1.** *Effective words.* Considering both the subject matter and the kind of readers that the writers had in mind, how appropriate is the diction in each of the following passages? In the examples that you consider unsatisfactory, point out specific instances of unnecessary Big Words and technical terms, of unfamiliar or far-fetched words, and of other kinds of inappropriate words. Wherever possible, show how they might be translated into more appropriate language. In the passages you consider satisfactory, explain why you think the wording is appropriate.

1) *From a sermon delivered to a predominantly middle-class congregation:* In like manner Our Lord dignifies a really simple activity of His disciples, as we have read in the pericope from The Gospel of a fishing expedition. We cannot ignore the fact that most of us live our life in the simplicities of it; the few things that come along as profundities (which we sometimes see as milestones) are not our escape from the realities, but our confirmation of these.

2) *From a freshman research paper:* Shakespeare's most individual means of expression, and a marked characteristic of his art, is his use of iterative imagery. His custom, according to Caroline Spurgeon, is to

"have before him, as he writes, some picture or symbol which recurs again and again in the form of images throughout a play. . . . " In this fashion the great dramatist develops many of his less obvious themes—ideas implied rather than stated, whose impact is heightened by the very subtlety of their presentation.

3) *From a professional journal for teachers:* This film demonstrates the progress of an idealized date, from the ideational impetus to the request, acceptance, the dating experience itself, and the final leave-taking, in the process raising some significant questions regarding dating and suggesting partial answers as discussional guides. Such questions as "How does one say good night?" aid in stimulating class discussion of the dating process and the problem areas inherent in it.

4) *From a student paper in a history course:* A lot of the Puritan temperament was due to Calvinism. Because of its emphasis on the constant temptations of the Devil, Puritans always had an eye peeled for sinful acts or thoughts in themselves and others. This produced a really morbid fascination with secret sin and guilt, and they seemed to get a sadistic thrill out of showing up sinners and making them pay for their offenses. They had a symbolical streak, too, that made them look at the most trivial happenings as signs with some theological meaning. If the wind blew shut a Bible when a man was putting in his nightly reading stint, he might take that as a sign that Lucifer was on the prowl trying to pull him from the paths of righteousness.

5) *From a student composition:* Our high school was eminently well equipped for various recreational pursuits. For those of sportive inclinations, there was the capacious gymnasium, which resounded to multitudinous roars whenever our champions engaged a challenging contingent. Here, too, were held gala affairs; as the strains of melody reverberated to the dome, the floor was inundated by swirling taffeta and a phantasmagoria of colored illuminations.

6) *From an article in a general magazine:* The radar operator aboard ship must maintain a constant vigil on the radar screen while he is on watch. The screen—usually ten to twelve inches in diameter—contains a small beam of light that constantly revolves, giving the appearance of a sweeping second hand on a wrist watch. This light works in conjunction with the radar antenna, which is constantly revolving, sending a steady stream of ultra high frequency waves over the ocean. When these waves strike a solid object, they rebound to the antenna. The wave is then relayed from the antenna to the radar screen in the form of a small spot, or "blip" as it is called. By means of a guide on the radar screen, the exact direction and the exact distance between the ship and the unidentified object can be determined.

7) *From a letter to the editor of a newspaper:* Is there no limit to the depravity to which materialistic Man can sink? Has he no regard whatever for the priceless heritage of Nature and the glory of her bounties? Despite the mayor's protestations of good intent, we now discover that Hillsdale Park is to be consigned to oblivion to make room for a redundant modern monstrosity dedicated to the perpetuation of Man's greed. For innumerable years this small Arcady has been a sanctuary for countless merchants of song. Many of us have spent untold hours basking in their melodious raptures and purveying to them what little of our store we had to share. But now the mayor plans to write Finis to these idylls. Now the celestial harmonies must cease, to be replaced by industrial cacaphony. Is this not a direct affront to Nature's plan?

8) *From the review of a musical in a newspaper:* Miss Howe is an energetic gal and can sing up a storm, but the authors haven't given her much to work with in this one. After a few hours of syrupy lyrics and Dumb Dora speeches, she looked completely beat. So did the rest of the cast. So did the audience. They all deserve a nice long breather.

2. *Technical words.* Write a short paper explaining some technical process or apparatus (a chemistry experiment, the dissection of a frog, equipment in the physics laboratory, etc.) so that it can be understood by a general audience. Be careful to define all terms that may be unfamiliar to the reader.

3. *Informal words.* The following excerpt is from a student theme on Henry Thoreau's famous essay "Civil Disobedience." This essay is one of the world's classic statements of the principles of passive resistance. Does the student's choice of words seem appropriate to the subject? Explain any objections you have to his language, and then rewrite the passage in what seem to you more appropriate words.

To me, Thoreau seems to be basically a live-and-let-live sort of person. He doesn't think you should let the government do your thinking for you or con you into going along with something you think is wrong. In fact he comes right out and says the best idea would be no government at all, if people were ready for that kind of setup. Since most of them aren't, he thinks we ought to make the best of what we have. As for himself, Thoreau thought the Mexican War and slavery were wrong, and to beef up his complaint he refused to pay his taxes. Of course this meant getting locked up, but he figured that by making a sort of model of himself he could get other people to back him up and put some pressure on the boys in Washington. I guess this isn't really as featherbrained as it sounds, because it worked O.K. in India when Gandhi tried it, even if Thoreau didn't get anywhere with it in the U.S.A. Anyway, he was mainly a sort of out-of-doors person and probably liked camping and things like that better than mixing in politics.

4. *Fresh and direct expressions.* All of the following sentences are marred by worn-out expressions or euphemisms. Be prepared to point out all such examples of ineffective diction and to suggest fresher, more direct expressions to replace them.

1) If he wins the election—and he may—we are all up the creek without a paddle.

2) Silence reigned supreme among us as the principal gave us a piece of his mind.

3) When he got to the campus post office and found his draft notice, it was a bitter pill to swallow.

4) Armed to the teeth with notes and No-Doz, he started to work on his research paper.

5) The chairman nipped the squabble in the bud and got the discussion down to brass tacks.

6) Each and every man should take out life insurance so that his loved ones will be well provided for when he goes to his eternal reward.

7) I told him straight from the shoulder that his work was no longer acceptable.

8) If it didn't mean showing my hand too soon, I would tell the newspapers that I intend to throw my hat in the ring.

9) A teacher is called upon to render services beyond the call of duty time and time again. His unselfish devotion to the youth of America goes a long way toward making this a better world to live in.

10) The investigators didn't leave a stone unturned in their relentless search for the fugitive from justice.

11) He was physically handicapped due to an unfortunate accident that deprived him of the use of his limbs.

12) The long and short of it is that an average teacher's time is taken up lock, stock, and barrel with grading papers that he cannot wash his hands of.

13) I have an uneasy feeling that we are all going to pay through the nose for the Senator's decision.

14) When for the third straight day he did not get a letter, Slade felt an aching void where his heart should have been.

15) He was on the horns of a dilemma—whether to cut class and go home to see her, or brave it out and wait for a letter.

5. *Figures of speech.* Some of the figurative expressions in the following examples are effective; others are not. If a figure is trite, strained, inconsistent, or inappropriate to the subject, explain why. If it is successful, explain what makes it so.

1) If something is not done to control the population explosion, the world will soon be overrun by starving human beings packed like sardines in a can.

2) His soaring genius and his rapier wit plumbed the depths of the American soul. Like a modern Homer, he left his imprint on the thundering tides of time.

3) A conversation is like a game of parlor leapfrog; each new speaker takes off from the back of the preceding one.

4) There is a garden in her face,
Where roses and white lilies grow,
A heavenly paradise is that place,
Wherein all pleasant fruits do flow.
There cherries grow, which none may buy
Till "Cherry ripe!" themselves do cry.

Those cherries fairly do enclose
Of orient pearl a double row;
Which when her lovely laughter shows,
They look like rose-buds filled with snow.
Yet them nor peer nor prince can buy,
Till "Cherry ripe!" themselves do cry. . . .

Thomas Campion

5) We've kicked around some of the ideas from last week's brainstorming session and have decided to send up some trial balloons. As you know, our competitive position needs some firming up and we can't afford to lay a bomb with the pack snapping at our heels. So let's all put our backs into it and wipe the egg off our faces.

6) The forest was emerald green, calm, and as quiet as a clam at low tide.

7) Satirist Swift would, however, hardly be amused by this film, which, with commerce aforethought, scissors his plot and ruthlessly modernizes his ironic allegory of Lilliput and Brobdingnag into a monster movie freckled with psychiatric footnotes.

8) I'm afraid that in those days I was a pretty mousy type, but I began to bloom under the influence of my swimming coach. He was the first to show me how to light a fire under myself instead of wallowing in daydreams.

9) If we are to build a stable cultural structure above that which threatens to engulf us by changing our lives more rapidly than we can adjust our habits, it will only be by flinging over the torrent a structure as taut and flexible as a spider's web, a human society deeply self-conscious and undeceived by the waters that race beneath it, a society more literate, more appreciative of human worth than any society that has previously existed.

22 Sentence length and economy

There is a natural emphasis in his style, like a man's tread, and a breathing space between the sentences.—Henry David Thoreau

Good sentences are varied in length and in pattern. Sometimes they are leisurely, unfolding slowly and gradually rounding out the idea; sometimes they are direct and emphatic. They may be balanced, or curt, or loose. They may be accumulating, piling up facts or ideas to achieve a stated meaning, or they may be discriminating, distinguishing grammatically among facts and ideas to achieve a stated meaning. In other words, they have qualities of style that make them readable and sensible.

The stylistic qualities of sentences are matters of choice rather than of rule. A writer can write short, grammatically correct sentences almost indefinitely, but if he wishes to say what cannot be said in that way—to expand his meaning or to vary it—then he must choose from among the various correct grammatical constructions those that will be effective for his situation. This means that critically reading and revising first-draft sentences is extremely important in developing a good writing style.

This section is concerned with the stylistic features of sentence *length*, including economy of wording. Section 23 considers the variety of forms, or *patterns*, that sentences may take to communicate meaning.

22.1 Sentence length as a matter of style

22.1 SL

Written sentences vary in length according to the writer's purpose, the way in which he typically expresses his ideas, and the type of material he is presenting. Longer sentences generally occur in rather Formal discussions of complex ideas, shorter ones in rapid narrative, easy exposition, and other General writing.

Sentence length varies somewhat according to the fashion of the times. Early nineteenth-century writers built their ideas into sentences that averaged thirty to forty words. Current writing uses somewhat shorter sentences, averaging between twenty to thirty words. These figures are only averages, of course; the individual sentences may vary greatly in length.

There is no special virtue in either long sentences or short ones. More important is the total effect of a passage in which the sentences are characteristically long or short. In the following paragraph by a well-known scholar and teacher, the sentences are considerably shorter than the average for professional writers. Yet the form is appropriate because the statements—many of them directives or suggestions for action—are intended to be emphatic. (The one long sentence near the middle varies from the pattern, but it is itself a series of brief statements):

> Concentration must be learnt. It should be learnt in school. A good teacher can teach it to his pupils. It should not be imagined as nothing but an effort of the will. Concentration is also an intellectual process. It is choice. Take the same boy who reads his book slowly, grudgingly, five lines at a time, and increase the urgency of his study—somehow, anyhow—make the choice clearer to him, and the importance of his study paramount—put him to work on the prize essay—and then watch. "Turn that radio off!" he shouts. He clears the table, except for one photograph. He sits fixed in one position till he is cramped. Sometimes, when he is really intent, he will miss meals and forget about sleep. All this because he has chosen one aim and discarded others. And that, after all, is what we learn to do throughout life.—Gilbert Highet, *The Art of Teaching*, pp. 68-69

But in another work, Mr. Highet uses a longer, more complex and leisurely sentence pattern, appropriate both to the subject matter and to the kind of audience he is addressing:

> Are these shadows on so many of our horizons the outriders of another long night, like that which was closing in upon Sidonius? We cannot yet tell. But modern scholars must regret that they have to work during a time when instead of that general supranational comradeship which helped to build the learning and culture of the sixteenth and nineteenth centuries, it is becoming more and more difficult to exchange opinions across the world, to bring from distant countries books where new and vital points of view are freely expressed, to carry on many-sided correspondences with far-off scholars and encounter no difficulties other than those involved in the common search for truth, and to feel oneself part of a world-wide structure of art and learning, greater than all the things that divide mankind: nationalities and creeds, fear and hate.—Gilbert Highet, *The Classical Tradition*, p. 472

The problem of length in most student sentences is seldom a matter of the average number of words per statement. More often it is variety and appropriateness: the ability to use the form, long or short, that best suits the writer's purpose and his material and that will give variety and liveliness to his writing.

22.2 Sentence length and meaning

SL — Revision: Rewrite the passage marked to eliminate choppy or stringy sentences and to show the relationship of ideas.

Appropriate sentence length is determined less by the number of words in a sentence than by what a sentence contributes to the total meaning of a paragraph. Self-evident or extremely obvious statements contribute nothing to writing:

> These scientific theories came into being only after definite steps had been taken.

Of course definite steps were taken. This statement is so general that one could substitute for *scientific theories* almost anything that comes to mind—the Brooklyn Bridge, the United Nations, a college dance, or a term paper.

Choppy (too short) sentences

Some sentences say too little because a simple idea has been broken up unnecessarily into two or more statements, as in this example:

> I took my first course in mathematics at Riverdale High School. This was first-year or elementary algebra.

A reader will not feel any need to invest his time in these individual sentences, which might better be combined:

> I took my first course in mathematics, elementary algebra, at Riverdale High School.

A succession of very short sentences tends to give a piece of writing a halting, jerky effect. Such sentences also impede the flow of thought, for they fail to show how ideas are related:

> We arrived at the induction center that afternoon. We were divided up. We were sent to barracks. They were reserved for draftees. The barracks were old. The floors were scrubbed almost white. Vague scars of cigarette burns marked them. I wondered how many wars had brought draftees here.

The choppy movement of this passage gives an effect the writer did not intend. The passage could be made smoother by combining related statements:

> When we arrived at the induction center that afternoon, we were divided up and sent to the old barracks reserved for draftees. The floors were scrubbed almost white, but the vague scars of cigarette burns marking them made me wonder how many wars had brought draftees here.

Short sentences are useful in various writing situations—in dialog, for emphasis, for creating a feeling of rapid action or of tension—but the writer must exercise judgment if he is to use them successfully. In the following passage, for example, the writer's intention was probably to convey a feeling of excitement, but the breathless style defeats this purpose because it is continued too long, with no break in sentence pattern:

> It was my senior year in high school. Our basketball team had won the trophy the year before. This year the team was considered even stronger. Nearly every member of the pep club was seated. It was the final game. We had come all the way through the tournament without a defeat. This game would determine which team would be the champion. I looked toward the end of the gym. The referees were talking. They, too, were excited. Would that starting gun never go off! My hands were clammy. My checks burned.

Examine closely any passage in your own writing that contains a noticeable number of consecutive sentences under eighteen words. Try reading the passage aloud to see whether it conveys the effect you intended or whether the writing is simply careless or hasty.

Stringy sentences

Avoid stringing together (with *and*, *but*, *so*, *and then*) statements that should be written as separate sentences or as subordinate elements. Sentences carelessly tacked together in this manner are not only monotonous to read but lose all their emphasis because every idea seems to be of equal importance:

> About fifty feet away I saw a buck deer running for safety *and so* I kneeled on my right knee *and then* I brought the rifle to my right shoulder. He was still running, *so* I fired one shot at him, *but* I missed, *but* he stopped and looked at me, *and then* I had a much better target to shoot at.

Reading such flabby sentences aloud should reveal their weaknesses and help you to revise them for better organization:

> About fifty feet away I saw a buck deer running for safety. Kneeling on my right knee and bringing the rifle to my shoulder, I fired once, but missed. He stopped to look at me, providing a much better target.

Stringy sentences often result from linking too many main clauses together (*Most people know that our productive system is the world's best* and *they have grown to expect great things from this system*, and *they should*). The cure lies in cutting down the number of coordinating conjunctions (*and*, *but*, *so*) and in subordinating ideas of lesser importance.

Relating ideas clearly

Avoid combining unrelated ideas in the same sentence. If there is a relationship between the ideas, so that they can reasonably be combined, show what it is. Don't leave it to your reader to puzzle out:

> As Byron is the poet of youth, it is appropriate that the new and completely reset edition of his poems should be published on March 1. [What is the relation between *youth* and the date of publication?]
>
> Nassau has a delightful climate that attracts hundreds of tourists every year, and some historians think that Columbus landed in this area in 1492. [If there is any relationship between Nassau's climate and Columbus, it should be stated.]

22.2 SL

Sentences that are haphazard or contain contradiction can be improved by clarifying the intended relationship:

Haphazard	*Revised*
There is no evidence to support the fact that her marriage to another writer may have had some influence on her style.	Although her marriage to another writer may have had some influence on her style, there is no evidence to support this.
I consider *The Old Man and the Sea* one of the literary masterpieces of our time, but many people have disliked Hemingway's other novels.	Even those who have disliked Hemingway's other novels are likely to enjoy *The Old Man and the Sea*, which I consider one of the literary masterpieces of our time.

A sentence should be constructed so that the most important idea receives greatest emphasis; the relationship of other ideas can usually be shown in subordinate constructions.

See also §23.2, Subordination to control and clarify meaning, and §23.4, Sentence emphasis.

22.3 Avoiding wordiness

Revision: Make the sentence or passage marked less wordy and more direct; avoid unnecessary predications.

Sentence economy means wording statements so that their meaning can be grasped by the reader without unnecessary effort. No one likes to listen to a speaker who talks too much and says too little, and no reader likes to cut his way through a tangle of useless words or constructions to get at a relatively simple idea. Phrases, clauses, or other constructions that use many words to say what can be said more directly are called *circumlocutions.*

Practicing sentence economy doesn't mean that you should strip your sentences down to the bare minimum, as you might in composing a telegram or writing a classified ad. The shortest words and simplest constructions are not always the most economical, for they may fail to convey your exact or complete meaning. Economy of expression requires rather that you state your ideas in the most accurate and direct way possible.

Often it is possible to make a statement more direct by reducing a complete predication (a sentence or a clause) to a shorter construction (a phrase or a single word):

> Sentence: *The snow lay like a blanket.* It covered the countryside. [two predications]
>
> Clause: The snow, *which lay like a blanket*, covered the countryside. [two predications]
>
> Phrase: The snow covered the countryside *like a blanket.* [one predication]
>
> Word: The snow *blanketed* the countryside. [one predication]

Since each clause you use increases the number of predications, one way to tighten sentence form is to eliminate unnecessary and ineffective verbs and their modifiers:

Two predications	*Reduced*
He crawled slowly over the river bank, looking for the flint chips which would mean that he had found a campsite.	He crawled slowly over the river bank, looking for flint chips marking a possible campsite.

The two verbs that can most frequently be eliminated without any loss of meaning are *be* in its various forms and *have:*

Excessive predication	*More economical*
He is a native of the plains and knows the value of water conservation.	*A native of the plains*, he knows the value of water conservation.
A few of the fellows *who were less serious* would go into a bar *where they would* have a steak dinner and a few glasses of beer.	A few of the *less serious* fellows would go into a bar *for* a steak dinner and a few glasses of beer.
There is only one excuse *that is acceptable*, and *that is* "I have a class this hour."	*Only one excuse is acceptable:* "I have a class this hour."

If a large number of your sentences begin with *There*, see if some of them couldn't just as well start with another word:

Wordy	*More direct*
There are two plays in our anthology and I like them both.	I like both plays in our anthology.
There is a suggestion box in almost all big business houses where employees may put ideas.	Most big business houses provide suggestion boxes for their employees.

22.3 Wdy While a writer's style and the general movement of his sentences determine to a large degree whether shorter or longer constructions are more appropriate, the careless habit of consistently using two or more statements where one would be just as effective should be avoided in all styles of writing.

22.4 Removing deadwood

| Dead | Revision: Revise the sentence or passage marked to eliminate deadwood.

Deadwood is a term for a particular kind of wordiness: lazy words and phrases that clutter up a statement without adding anything to its meaning.

> Anyone acquainted with violin construction knows that the longer the wood is seasoned, the better *the result will be as far as* the tone of the instrument *is concerned.*

Empty expressions like those in italics above are excess baggage and do nothing to further communication. They often find their way into first drafts because they come so handily to use, but a writer should take care to prune them out in revision. Eliminating deadwood will make a statement neater and more direct without changing its meaning in the least, as these examples illustrate (deadwood in italics):

> Every thinking person these days seems to agree *with the conception* that the world has gone mad.
>
> Because *of the fact that* she had been ill, she missed the first two weeks of classes.
>
> After a delay of forty-five minutes, the audience *got to the point that it* became restless and noisy.

The wordy formulas that serve as fillers in casual conversation are more noticeable and annoying in writing than they are in speech. Roundabout expressions should be replaced in revision by terms that say the same thing more directly:

get in touch with	means	*call* or *see*
due to the fact that	means	*because* or *since*
in this day and age	means	*now* or *today*
at the same time that	means	*while*

Certain words, generally in stereotyped phrase combinations, account for much of the deadwood found in student writing. This list, while not exhaustive, illustrates phrases built upon the most common of these words:

Word	*As deadwood*	*Deadwood eliminated*
case	*In many cases* students profit from the research paper.	Many students profit from the research paper.
character	Her gossip was *of a sordid and ugly character.*	Her gossip was sordid and ugly.
exist	The crime conditions *that existed* in Chicago became intolerable.	The crime conditions in Chicago became intolerable.

Word	*As deadwood*	*Deadwood eliminated*
fact	In spite of *the fact that* he is lazy, I like him.	In spite of his laziness, I like him.
factor	Speed is also *an important factor.*	Speed is also important.
field	Anyone interested in *the field of* American history should take his course.	Anyone interested in American history should take his course.
instance	*In many instances*, students write their papers just before the deadline.	Often students write their papers just before the deadline.
line	He always thought he would be successful *along agricultural lines.*	He always thought he would be successful in agriculture.
manner	He glanced at her *in a suspicious manner.*	He glanced at her suspiciously.
nature	She seldom talks on any subject *of a controversial nature.*	She seldom talks on any controversial subject.
seem	*It seems that* we have not lost a daughter, but gained another icebox-raider.	We have not lost a daughter, but gained another icebox-raider.
tendency	When I am supposed to be working, I *have a tendency to* clean my pipes and dawdle.	When I am supposed to be working, I clean my pipes and dawdle.
type	His father had an executive *type of* position.	His father had an executive position.

These words have definite meanings in some expressions (a *case* of measles, a minor *character* in the play, a *field* of clover, and so forth), but as used here, they are meaningless and unnecessary deadwood.

22.5 Avoiding careless repetition

Revision: Eliminate the ineffective repetition of words, meaning, or sound.

Unless repeated for a definite reason, a word or a phrase should not be made conspicuous by too frequent use in the same passage.

Effective repetition

Sometimes repetition is essential for meaning or for sentence structure:

> Try as we may, we cannot, as we write history, escape our *purposiveness.* Nor, indeed, should we try to escape, for *purpose* and meaning are the same thing. But in pursuing our *purpose*, in making our *abstractions*, we must be aware of what we are doing; we ought to have it fully in mind that our *abstraction* is not perfectly equivalent to the infinite complication of event from which we have *abstracted.*—Lionel Trilling, *The Liberal Imagination*, pp. 185-186

Intentional repetition may also be effective for emphasis:

> There is no way of becoming *inaccurate* by industry, and if you deliberately try to be *inaccurate* you fail. *Inaccuracy* is perhaps the most *spontaneous* and the *freest* of *gifts* offered by the Spirit to the wit of man. It is even more *spontaneous* and more *free* than the *gift* of writing good *verse*, or that rarer *gift* which I have also written of here—the *gift* of writing abominably *bad verse;* exceptionally *bad verse;* criminally *bad verse;* execrable *verse.*—Hilaire Belloc, *On*, pp. 125-126

Some kinds of words must of course be used over and over again: articles (*a*, *an*, *the*), conjunctions (*and*, *but*, *or*), prepositions (*of*, *in*, *at*), and pronouns (*it*, *that*, *my*, *which*). Because their purpose is strictly functional, these words are usually not noticed.

Useless repetition

Unintentional, unnecessary, and ineffective repetition of words is illustrated in these passages:

22.5 Rep

> The bonfire was sparkling and *gay*. Here and there the light from the fire showed a *gay* homecoming pennant. Then the cheerleaders dashed through the crowd, their *gaiety* infecting everybody.
>
> When I was in high school, I would take a book home once or twice a week and maybe read it two or three hours at a *time*. *Most of the time* I would read *most* of my homework just in *time* to have it ready before class began. It was very easy *most of the time* to read the assignment and have it prepared when my *time* came to be called upon for recitation.

Repetition of this kind is obviously bad, for it focuses attention on words rather than on ideas. It also suggests that the writer is careless and unconcerned with what he is saying.

Repetition of words. Repeat words in a passage only when you have good reason for doing so. Key words (such as the subject) may sometimes be repeated for clarity or emphasis, but less important terms should not be used more often than necessary.

Careless repetition	*Revised*
The *problem* of feeding her ever-increasing population is one of India's most acute *problems.*	Feeding her ever-increasing population is one of India's most acute problems.
Many people think *that* if a *product* is endorsed by a prominent person *that* it is a good *product* to buy.	Many people think that a product endorsed by a prominent person is a good one to buy.

Especially to be avoided is repetition of the same word in two different meanings:

If I *run*, I'll get a *run* in my stockings.	If I run, I'll *tear* my stockings.
Astrology is so popular in Hollywood that many movie *stars* won't sign a contract unless the *stars* are favorable.	Astrology is so popular in Hollywood that many of the movie stars won't sign a contract unless their *horoscopes* are favorable.

It is not always possible to correct careless repetition by striking out a word or substituting another of similar meaning. When a passage becomes badly cluttered like this one, complete rewriting is the only way to clear it up:

22.5 Rep

Annoying repetition	*Revised*
There has been a *theory* advanced that the Vikings were here long before Columbus. As time goes on, more evidence is found to substantiate this *theory*. After reading several *articles* about *this*, I ran across some *articles* on the first discovery of America by people other than the Vikings. *This* interested me greatly, and I decided to investigate *this* as my topic for the research paper.	I began looking for a topic by reading several articles on the discovery of America by the Vikings, a theory that is being substantiated by increasing evidence as time goes on. Then, more or less by accident, I found that the Vikings may not, after all, have been the first people to visit America. This idea interested me greatly, and I decided to make it the topic of my research paper.

Repetition of meaning. Adding an expression that repeats the meaning of another (called *tautology*) is one of the most common forms of unprofitable repetition. The italicized expressions in the following sentences are a form of deadwood (§22.4). They should be omitted because they merely repeat ideas that are sufficiently expressed in other words in the sentences:

> In the modern world *of today*, time has a meaning different than it had when transportation was slower.
>
> It is believed that the age of the earth is about two billion years *old*.
>
> She decided to trim the kitchen in bright red, but the *resultant* effect was not what she had anticipated.

Words like *color*, *size*, and *shape* often needlessly repeat a meaning that is already clear:

Unsatisfactory	*Revised*
His hair was brick red *in color*.	His hair was brick red.
The length of the locks is about two thirds of a mile *long*.	The locks are about two thirds of a mile long.
Behind the house was an enclosed court which was rectangular *in shape*.	Behind the house was an enclosed rectangular court.

The abbreviation *etc.* (*et cetera*) means "and so forth." To write "*and* etc." is equivalent to saying "and and so forth." Avoid this Nonstandard expression.

Repetition of sounds. A sound should not be made conspicuous by careless repetition. The cumulative effect of certain suffixes like *-ly*, *-ment*, and *-tion* may be unfortunate:

> The concept of such sanctuar*y* immunit*y* unquestionab*ly* predominant*ly* influenced the ene*my* to enter into the conflict.
>
> Written permis*sion* of the administra*tion* is required for re-registra*tion* of those students who are on proba*tion*.

Alliteration—the repetition of the same sound at the beginning of words in a series—is out of place when it attracts attention to the words at the expense of the ideas:

> I am looking for a shop that still has *p*leated *p*ants for *p*oor and *p*aunchy *p*rofessors.
>
> He then made himself comfortable in a *r*ather *r*ickety *r*attan *r*ocker.

Even though your papers are not usually written to be read aloud, you should try to avoid unintentional sound patterns that may be momentarily irritating or distracting to a reader who has a sensitive ear:

> The enemy was re*port*ed to have seized this im*port*ant *port*, and reinforcements were hurrying up in sup*port*.

Exercises

1. *Choppy sentences.* The following paragraph is composed of short, choppy sentences. Rewrite it so that it reads more smoothly and so that its ideas are more effectively grouped and subordinated.

I went to Brunhilde High School before I came here. I can remember doing many foolish things there. Some of them can probably hurt me in years to come. I was allowed to select the teachers I wanted. This was an entirely new experience for me. I was always selecting the easiest teachers. Then there would be no challenge, and I would play around too much. This was, of course, my biggest problem. Since I played around so much, I really don't know how to study now. But I always made somewhat good grades. I was always finding ways to get out of doing what had to be done. Then came my senior year. Then I realized how important it was to study. I learned to hunt the good teachers. Everything I learned was in my senior year at Brunhilde.

2. *Stringy sentences.* The following paragraph is awkward and difficult to follow because it is composed of stringy and sprawling sentences. Rewrite it so that its ideas are clearly related in sentences of appropriate length.

One of the rare cases in which public opinion has succeeded in influencing the quality of mass entertainment is that of comic books which are sold by the millions to young children. Until a few years ago, most of these books were filled with material that was highly objectionable and it was growing steadily more violent and gruesome to the point that even the more hardened adults who examined them were shocked and had fears that they might be dangerous to young, unformed minds. Some of these books depicted nothing but a long succession of sadistic crimes that were pictured in great detail, and on several occasions it was found that delinquents who had committed crimes admitted that they deliberately imitated brutalities they had seen in comic books which obsessed them. Finally parents and educators decided that the situation was a dangerous one and had to be brought under control before it became a permanent threat to the community and to the mental health of young Americans, whose early ideals influence their adult lives.

3. *Relating ideas clearly.* Examine the following passages and be prepared to discuss them from the standpoint of meaning and effectiveness of communication. Which statements are obvious? ambiguous? contradictory? Wherever possible, suggest revisions that would make the meaning clear.

1) My high-school days are over and I realize I cannot turn back time, so I must now make the best of my future. Now that I am continuing my education, I am also trying to improve on the mistakes I made in high school. One by one I am ironing out the deep wrinkled problems and solving them.

2) There is a lot of evidence that great scientific discoveries do not happen by chance, but usually involve thinking on the part of the scientist.

3) There are two major factors that help a person mature, heredity and environment. Although my heredity was good, my environment was a different matter. The friends I had were by no means juveniles, nor were they scholars. Since I spent most of my spare time with my buddies, I adopted the same habits they had concerning studying. We did not excel or fail in school, but we could have done a lot better.

4) As time passes, many complexities in our environment result from scientific and technological advancements which create new branches in every field of activity, thus causing the youth of today to seek out a more thorough education.

5) The body goes through certain changes between youth and old age, whether a person realizes it or not.

4. *Economy of expression.* Tighten the following paragraph wherever possible by substituting words and phrases for clauses; eliminate all unnecessary words.

There were so many things to do and the summer was so short. We could go and chase rats in the barn, which was a dangerous and slightly sickening enterprise; we could teach a kitten how to play circus. We could climb to the roof of the corridor where we could watch the ducks file out to the pond, and crack dry mirthless jokes to one and another. We could help with the cider press, where all the apples with a rotten spot, those that had been claimed and contended for by the yellow jackets, disappeared into the hopper and gushed out the sides in a seethe of liquor that was brown and bubbly. There were so many things to do and the summer was so short.

5. *Removing deadwood.* Read the following sentences carefully, looking for roundabout expressions and deadwood. Then rewrite them into direct and economical statements.

1) In college one must put away the childish thoughts of his boyhood and begin thinking of the future that lies ahead with adult ideas and responsibilities.

2) Throughout my previous school days I have been the type of person who hasn't had to study a great deal to get grades above those obtained by the average student.

3) One of my bigger excuses was the fact that I claimed there were too many social activities currently in progress.

4) The method used to detect the approach of other ships is radar.

5) One lady aroused my indignation when she claimed that her son, who was six feet in height, was under twelve years of age.

6) Habits can be classified into two distinct types: one is the useful, progressive, uplifting kind while the other is of the nature that deteriorates character and often damages the physical body.

7) My scholastic averages show, in my opinion, a rather distorted picture of my true knowledge.

8) I have chosen this road of higher education to reach my goal, which is that of teaching children.

9) To reach this goal I must be well educated and have a thorough understanding of my subject.

10) The income from the tourist business is an important source of revenue for people who own businesses in Florida.

6. *Avoiding careless repetition.* Revise the following sentences to eliminate careless or ineffective repetition of words, meaning, or sounds. If the repetition in any statement seems intentional and effective, explain what purpose it serves.

1) The hazy figures in the background are vague and indefinite, and they add a sinister note to the painting.

2) The advantage of getting a broader perspective through travel is only one of the advantages of spending a summer traveling through the United States.

3) Many people live so compulsively by the clock that they have a fixed time for eating, a fixed time for bathing, and a fixed time for everything but enjoying life.

4) An application of lotion to the area of inflammation should relieve the pain.

5) Concrete and steel have both been used successfully in skyscraper construction, but buildings of concrete must have much thicker walls at the lower levels than those of steel. On the other hand, concrete has a far greater decorative potential than steel.

6) The shock of discovering that someone you trust is not worthy of your trust can have a traumatic effect on the mind that lasts for years.

7) Most reasonable teachers are rational and do not grade papers on the basis of personal feelings or emotions toward the students.

8) In a serious discussion, the participants cannot let unimportant matters interfere with subjects they must discuss thoroughly and seriously.

9) When Bob went to a party, his mother brought him and his mother picked him up. When he had a homework problem, his mother solved it. And if he failed an exam, his mother called on the teacher personally.

10) In 1959 he led an expedition to Sumatra to study sacred rites seldom witnessed by outsiders.

23 Sentence variety, control, and emphasis

. . . the effective speaker and writer of prose is he who does not merely catch *his sentence-patterns but who* grips *them and wields them with well-controlled purpose.—Simeon Potter*

Language incorporates a range of possibilities from which the writer chooses according to his needs. It is possible to write without making choices, but not to write well.

We can put words together to say something because we have a range of grammatical patterns that we can use to link words in meaningful ways. Just as a good writer presumably does not accept the first *words* that come to mind, but rather chooses the best, so he also chooses the *sentence patterns* that best enable him to communicate his meaning. By varying the construction of his sentences, he is able to control and emphasize his meaning and to ensure his reader's interest and understanding.

23.1 Sentence variety

Var	**Revision: Vary the sentence patterns in the passage marked to avoid monotony and to make your meaning clearer or more emphatic.**

23.1 *Var*

When reading good writing we are usually unaware of the pattern of the sentences; it is only when the pattern becomes monotonous, either in length or in arrangement, that it forces itself to our attention. Consider these two paragraphs, the first a rephrasing of the second:

> We hear that Russia emphasizes foreign language and so we have suddenly increased our own offerings in these fields. Our schools have not analyzed our needs, though. There is one school that has re-established Latin and another school that has introduced conversational French for infants. These schools haven't asked whether Latin or conversational French are as imperative as knowledge of Moslem customs or religion. The same schools haven't asked what languages are needed and for what ends.

> Hearing that Russia emphasizes foreign language, we have suddenly increased our own offerings. But too seldom have our schools analyzed our needs. One school has re-established Latin; another has introduced conversational French for infants. Seldom have they

asked whether Latin and French are as imperative as knowledge of Moslem customs or religion, or what languages are needed and for what ends.—Lou LaBrant, "The Dynamics of Education," *The Saturday Review*, September 12, 1959, p. 28

The ideas in both versions are identical; so too are most of the words. What makes Professor LaBrant's original paragraph more readable, more understandable, is the movement of the statements—a movement casual and natural, with variety in sentence structure.

Varying sentence beginnings

When several consecutive sentences begin the same way—with a noun subject, for example—the passage is likely to be monotonous and to lack impact:

> *Meteorology* has made many advances in recent years. *Weather observation balloons* have been developed to gather data from the upper stratosphere. *Time-lapse photography* has improved the study of cloud formations and patterns. *Barometric instruments* of greater sensitivity are widely used. *Radar* is useful in detecting the approach of storms and precipitation.

Sentence beginnings can be varied and made more interesting by occasionally starting with a modifier—a word, phrase, or clause—as in this passage from an essay on the Grand Canyon:

> *We* have almost come full circle. *Once* those who had seen the Canyon thought of it as useless. *Then came* those who thought it might be useful because of the river which flowed through it. *They* were in turn followed by men like Theodore Roosevelt, who saw the Canyon as a precious heritage of wonder and beauty. *Now, today*, it is threatened again by men interested only in exploitation, men who unfortunately have the means to destroy what no age before ours was "technologically advanced" enough to transform and mar.
>
> "*Human needs come first*" is the all too specious slogan of those for whom the words of Theodore Roosevelt carry no weight. *They* do not like to admit that those primary needs in which they happen to be interested are the "human needs" of temporary economic advantage. *That the Grand Canyon, the sublime "great unknown" of John Wesley Powell*, might fall victim to the manipulations of sloganeers should be unthinkable; that it is not unthinkable should be our shame.—Joseph Wood Krutch, "The Eye of the Beholder," *The American West*, May 1967, p. 20

To begin sentence after sentence with the same kind of modifier is no less monotonous, of course, than to begin every sentence with the subject. Deliberately inserting or shifting modifiers to gain variety is a makeshift or affected practice, hence an ineffective one. The emphasis you wish to make and the general movement of the passage should determine your sentence beginnings. Professor Francis Christensen has noted that professional writers place an adverbial modifier or other secondary element before the subject in about 20 per cent of their sentences.

Varying S-V-O order

A less common means of varying sentence patterns is changing the usual order of subject-verb-object or subject-verb-complement in declarative statements. This is called *inversion:*

> Supplementing the guitars and drums are a solo cello, a ragtime piano, an Indian sitar, sound effects of barnyard animals, and a complete symphony orchestra.—Peter Schrag, "Facing the Music," *The Saturday Review*, August 19, 1967, p. 61

Except in questions and requests, inversion should ordinarily be used only when the words put first really deserve special emphasis by withholding the subject. Inversion used solely for variety may have painful results, as in this reversal:

> A garden city, with one of the most delightful climates in the world, is Victoria.

Loose and periodic sentences

23.1 Var

Sentence patterns may also be varied by using both loose and periodic sentences.

Loose sentences. In a loose sentence the main statement comes first, followed by subordinate elements that explain or amplify its meaning. This pattern is the one most commonly used both in conversation and in writing, for we characteristically make our points by accumulating meanings:

> For especially in the fourth and third centuries B.C., new cults were brought into the religious practice of the state, though as regards myth and ritual they were stamped with the Roman mark. But the influx of ideas never penetrated to the heart of the old Roman religion, which was fixed in its essential nature. It continued both in the city and in the countryside, as is abundantly clear when the

> evidence of literature and inscriptions becomes more plentiful.—R. H. Barrow, *The Romans*, p. 17

One particular kind of loose construction, called *prolepsis* in early rhetoric texts, can be particularly useful. Prolepsis is the expression of a general statement, which is then followed by amplifying details:

> Once on the mound, he was a most unlikely looking pitcher, slouching, tangle-footed, absent, with the aspect of a lost goose.

Such a construction can set the subject for a paragraph or short essay and determine its content. A writer could, for example, amplify the statement above by describing particular occasions to illustrate each characteristic.

Periodic sentences. A periodic sentence is one in which the main statement is not completed until the end or near the end of the sentence:

> And around the sunken sanctuary of the river valley, stretching out in all directions from the benches to become coextensive with the disc of the world, went the uninterrupted prairie.—Wallace Stegner, "Quiet Earth, Big Sky," *American Heritage*, October 1955, p. 23

Although periodic sentences were characteristic of much writing before this century, they are now much less common than loose sentences. They require careful planning and are more typical of a Formal than of a General style. The very fact that periodic sentences are not widely used, however, gives the pattern all the more value as a means of achieving emphasis.

When framing a periodic sentence, the writer should make certain that the suspension is not awkward or unnatural, as it is in this example:

> The reader will probably agree after reading this essay *that Pearl Buck's example* of the woman who, after being married for a number of years and raising a family, gradually loses interest in most of her former outside activities, *is true*.

Varying kinds of sentences

If a writer discovers in scrutinizing his first draft that he has written an essay in which most of the sentences have the same kind of clause structure, he should consider combining, dividing, or reshaping his sentences. Quite aside from the question of variety, different kinds of sentences—simple, compound, complex—are ordinarily necessary for meaning and for emphasis.

Sometimes a question or directive makes an effective variation from the usual declarative sentence:

> Only by resurrecting our own memories can we realize how incredibly distorted is the child's vision of the world. *Consider this, for example. How would Crossgates appear to me now, if I could go back, at my present age, and see it as it was in 1915? What should I think of Bingo and Sim, those terrible, all-powerful monsters?* I should see them as a couple of silly, shallow, ineffectual people, eagerly clambering up a social ladder which any thinking person could see to be on the point of collapse. I would be no more frightened of them than I would be frightened of a dormouse.—George Orwell, *Such, Such, Were the Joys*, p. 61

Questions and commands can be effective if they serve a legitimate purpose, but like other sentence patterns they should not be used solely for the sake of variety. Unless the answer is self-evident ("Who would trade freedom for tyranny?"), don't raise a question without answering it. Never conclude a paper with a pointless, blunt question such as "What do *you* think?"

23.2 Subordination to control and clarify meaning

Sub	**Revision: Show the intended relationship between ideas by using appropriate subordination, or correct the faulty subordination.**

By bringing related ideas together, a writer gives continuity to his writing and signals the direction of his thinking to his reader. But even when ideas are so closely related that they belong in the same sentence, they do not necessarily deserve equal weight. A writer must decide, in every case, how contributing ideas can best be arranged around a major idea, or how minor points can best accumulate to help make a major point. This means that every sentence is *composed.*

An indiscriminate clustering of ideas in a sentence or paragraph is a disservice to the writer, to the subject, and to the reader. Ideas are *not* all the same: some are antecedents to others, some are conditions of others, some are less important than others. The writer who fails to show the relationship of one idea to another—whether in a single sentence or in a series of sentences—informs his reader, in effect, that all his ideas are equally important or that he is too lazy to bother making his meaning clear:

Failure to subordinate in a single sentence	*Ideas effectively related*
I worked hard and I turned out a first-rate manuscript, and I missed my deadline and my publisher was angry.	Although I worked hard and turned out a first-rate manuscript, my publisher was angry because I missed my deadline.
Failure to subordinate in a series of sentences	*Ideas effectively related*
That, I think, is our ancient mission. Sometimes we have deserted it. Then we have failed. You must help us. Then there will be no desertion. I do not want to mislead the people. I would rather lose the election. I do not want to misgovern the people. I would rather lose the election.	That, I think, is our ancient mission. Where we have deserted it we have failed. With your help there will be no desertion now. Better we lose the election than mislead the people; and better we lose than misgovern the people.—Adlai Stevenson, Speech accepting the Democratic nomination for President, 1952

Subordination serves the writer in several ways. A writer can put minor ideas into grammatically dependent constructions in order to stress his major point in an independent construction. And at the same time, if he is judicious, he can precisely relate the major and minor ideas. The key statements in the following passage occur at the first of each sentence. Because the author does not move slowly toward his main points but chooses to announce them bluntly at the start of each sentence, they form a dramatic list of predictions for the future:

> *Houses will be the natural environment*, not formally specified, since there the individual will want to express himself. *Normal multistory residence buildings will need much greater areas per floor* so that a whole community will be able to operate at each level—a community with its shopping center, playgrounds, and public squares. *Automated factories will be placed within the earth*, especially in hills and mountains.—C. A. Doxiadis, "The Coming Era of Ecumenopolis," *The Saturday Review*, March 18, 1967, p. 14

In each sentence in this passage, contributing points follow the major statement. In the first two sentences they are arranged to establish cause-effect relationships.

Thoughtful subordination also allows the writer to move easily from sentence to sentence, using dependent constructions as transitions. Notice, for example, the subordinate clause introducing the last sentence of this passage:

> When you write, you make a point, not by subtracting as though you sharpened a pencil, but by adding. When you put one word after another, your statement should be more precise the more you add. *If the result is otherwise*, you have added the wrong thing, or you have added more than was needed.—John Erskine, "A Note on the Writer's Craft," *Twentieth Century English*, p. 254

Because grammatical constructions are important signals of meanings, a writer should make certain in checking his first draft that he has not put major ideas into minor constructions, or minor ideas into major constructions—a fault known as inverted or "upside-down" subordination.

See also §4, Subordinate clauses and connectives, especially §4.5, Faulty subordination.

23.3 Parallelism

Paral (//) | **Revision: Make the sentence elements marked parallel in form.**

Ideas of equal value in a statement should be made *parallel*—that is, they should be expressed in the same grammatical form. Putting coordinate ideas in parallel constructions helps the reader see in which direction the statement is going and makes for smoother writing, since it helps prevent unnecessary shifts in person and number and in the tense and mood of verbs.

Elements in series

Words, phrases, and clauses in series are best stated in parallel form. The italicized words in the following sentence are parallel because each is the object of the preposition *with:*

> His mind was filled with artistic *projects*, *schemes* for outwitting his creditors, and vague *ideas* about social reform.

The compound predicates in this sentence are also parallel:

> His dramatic attempt to take over the conduct of his own case *alienated* him from his counsel, almost *broke up* the trial, and probably *helped* to cost him his life.—Joseph Kinsey Howard, *Strange Empire*, p. 516

When coordinate ideas are not stated in parallel form, the statement is likely to seem awkward and unpolished:

Not parallel

We were told *to write* in ink, *that we should* use but one side of the paper, and *we should* endorse our papers in the proper manner. [an infinitive phrase and two clauses]

Parallel

We were told *to write* in ink, *to use* but one side of the paper, and *to endorse* our papers in the proper manner. [three infinitive phrases]

A preposition or a conjunction should be repeated between the items of a series when necessary for clarity:

Preposition not repeated

These problems are currently of great concern *to* the school system, teachers, and many parents.

Clearer

These problems are currently of great concern *to* the school system, *to* teachers, and *to* many parents.

Conjunction not repeated

The opposing citizens argued *that* the increased tax rates were exorbitant and the commissioners should find some other way to raise the money.

Clearer

The opposing citizens argued *that* the increased tax rates were exorbitant and *that* the commissioners should find some other way to raise the money.

23.3

Elements being compared or contrasted

Elements that are compared or contrasted through the use of pairs of conjunctions such as *either . . . or*, *neither . . . nor*, *not only . . . but* (or *but also*) are usually clearer and more emphatic when they are stated in parallel constructions:

> It is not always easy to select, at your bookshop or library, the particular book which will best serve your purpose, but if, before deciding, you give a little attention to certain points, you are less likely *either to buy one* which will not give you full return *or to take home* from the library one which will cause you disappointment, delay or inconvenience.—Lionel McColvin, "How to Use Books," *The Wonderful World of Books*, p. 180

> This is the life of a musician in which are recorded *not only the events* of his life, *but also details* of all his works, which are analyzed and described fully.—Ibid., p. 176

Since a reader expects similar constructions to follow pairs of conjunctions, he may be momentarily confused or side-tracked if the pattern is shifted:

Shifted	*Parallel*
You may go to the ski jump either *by special train* or a *chartered bus may be taken.*	You may go to the ski jump either *by special train* or *by chartered bus.*
He admired the Senator not *for his integrity*, but *because of his political cunning.*	He admired the Senator not *for his integrity*, but *for his political cunning.*

Making related ideas parallel is one of the jobs of revision. Similar forms for similar ideas help hold a sentence together.

Balanced and antithetical sentences

When parallel constructions, especially clauses, are noticeably equal in length and similar in movement, the sentence is called *balanced.* Balance is useful for emphatic statements, for comparing and contrasting ideas:

> Abbé Dimnet, in *The Art of Thinking*, was teaching the American how to think in a few easy lessons, just as ten years later Mortimer J. Adler was to teach him how to read in a few somewhat harder ones. —Leo Gurko, *The Angry Decade*, p. 25

> The best model of the grand style simple is Homer; perhaps the best model of the grand style severe is Milton.—Matthew Arnold, *On Translating Homer*

23.3 Paral

When contrasting clauses occur in parallel constructions in a single sentence, the sentence is called *antithetical.* Such a construction fittingly emphasizes a striking or important contrast:

> You may eat without danger our canned food, fresh and hot from your own campfire, but you will drink in peril the dirty water, polluted and foul from the nearby stream.

Antithetical sentences can easily be overused, but they are occasionally effective to mark turning points in an essay—the first half of the sentence pulling together what precedes, the contrasting second half forecasting what follows.

23.4 Sentence emphasis

Revision: Rewrite the passage marked so that the position and expression of the ideas will show their relative importance.

In composing your sentences you should help your reader to see your ideas in the same relative importance as you do—to distinguish among the most important, the less important, the incidental. Although the emphasis given to particular ideas depends in large part upon the way the whole paper is put together, from the beginning to the final paragraph, individual sentences can weaken or strengthen this effect. The sentences in the following paragraph, for example, are unemphatic because they are haphazardly constructed. They are wordy, the beginnings are weak, and each ends in a flabby construction:

> There are some interesting points about contemporary American life in "The Mobile Society" by Herman Matthews. Some of the things he notes are the paradoxes in it. The way a person often reduces his independence by relying more on mechanical devices is one example the author gives. A man may actually become the machine's slave instead of its master, as he thinks he is.

To make the statements more forceful and concise, the writer might have revised the sentence structure in this way:

> In his essay "The Mobile Society," Herman Matthews points out some of the paradoxes in contemporary American life. He notes, for example, that increasing reliance on mechanical devices often reduces a person's independence. Thinking he is the machine's master, he may actually become its slave.

Emphasis by position in the sentence

Important ideas can be stressed by putting them in emphatic positions in the sentence. In longer statements the most emphatic position is usually at the end, the next most emphatic position at the beginning:

> If it was the workings of our democracy that were inadequate in the past, *let us say so.* Whoever thinks the future is going to be easier than the past *is certainly mad.* And the system under which we are going to have to conduct foreign policy is, I hope and pray, *the system of democracy.*—George F. Kennan, *American Diplomacy, 1900-1950*, p. 73

Sentences—particularly those that introduce or sum up the main points of a topic—should end strongly. Statements that are qualified by a phrase or a word at the end are usually weak:

Unemphatic	*Improved*
The work at the mill was hard and often dangerous, but the mill hands didn't complain, *or at least very seldom.*	The work at the mill was hard and often dangerous, but the mill hands seldom complained.
These songs are dull and unoriginal, *with few exceptions.*	With few exceptions, these songs are dull and unoriginal.

Because the main statement is not completed until the end, periodic sentences are frequently more emphatic than loose sentences:

Loose	*Periodic*
Sociology 101 should interest every thoughtful student with its discussion of the theoretical as well as the practical aspects of human behavior.	Sociology 101, with its discussion of the theoretical as well as the practical aspects of human behavior, should interest every thoughtful student.

A particular kind of periodic sentence, the *climax* sentence, directs the reader through phrases and clauses arranged in ascending order to the most important element at the end:

> We shall fight on the beaches, we shall fight on the landing-grounds, we shall fight in the fields and in the streets, we shall fight in the hills; we shall never surrender.—Winston Churchill, Speech following Dunkirk, 1940

23.4 Sentences that begin with *There is* or *There are* tend to be unemphatic as well as wordy; frequent use of these constructions will make your writing seem flat and uninteresting.

Flat	*Improved*
There were several people who objected to the commission's plan.	Several people objected to the commission's plan.

Emphasis by separation

Ideas can be emphasized by setting them off from other parts of the sentence with strong internal punctuation—semicolons, colons, or dashes (§13 and §14):

> It is one thing to read *Time;* it is another to pronounce the words correctly.—E. B. White, *Quo Vadimus?* p. 94

He needed the support of the Princeton seniors and graduates, of Dean West of Princeton, of Harvey the political manager, of Colonel House, of the people of Europe, of the people of America—and he got it.—Edward Ryerson, "The Leadership of Woodrow Wilson," *The American Scholar*, Summer 1952, p. 305

When the ideas warrant it, the most emphatic separation is into individual sentences:

Adolescence is a kind of emotional seasickness. Both are funny, but only in retrospect.—Arthur Koestler, *Arrow in the Blue*, p. 82

Emphasis by repeating key words

Statements can be made emphatic by repeating important words or phrases:

These and kindred questions *need* discussion, and *need* it urgently, in the few years left to us before somebody presses the button and the rockets begin to fly.—George Orwell, *The Orwell Reader*, p. 334

His highest hope is to *think* first what is about to be *thought*, to *say* what is about to be *said*, and to *feel* what is about to be *felt*.—Bertrand Russell, *Unpopular Essays*, p. 67

In your reading you will sometimes see a word or phrase repeated deliberately for effect at the beginning of consecutive clauses or sentences:

I believe this government cannot endure permanently half slave and half free. *I do not expect* the Union to be dissolved—*I do not expect* the house to fall—but *I do expect* it will cease to be divided.—Abraham Lincoln, "House Divided" speech, 1858

The light has gone out, I said, and yet I was wrong. For *the light* that shone in this country was no ordinary light. *The light* that has illumined this country for these many years will illumine this country for many more years, and a thousand years later *that light* will still be seen in this country and the world will see it and it will give solace to innumerable hearts.—Jawaharlal Nehru, Speech on the death of Gandhi, 1948

The Declaration of Independence illustrated this same kind of repetition. Occasionally you will also see a word or phrase repeated at the *end* of consecutive clauses, as in Psalm 136, where each verse concludes "for his mercy endureth forever." In the hands of a skilled writer, these techniques can be highly effective, but they should be used very sparingly, and only when a serious subject can be honestly and appropriately conveyed in the deliberate manner they suggest.

Effective (and intentional) repetition should be distinguished from careless repetition, as discussed in §22.5.

Emphasis by mechanical devices

The least effective way to emphasize ideas is by underlining or capitalizing words, by setting them off in quotation marks, or by using emphatic punctuation marks (!!!). Certain kinds of advertising rely heavily on such devices:

> "Oh, of course," you may reply, "it's just a matter of calories." But IS it? Suppose you had to choose between a larger glass of orange juice and half a sirloin steak? You would probably reach for the orange juice. Actually, *the steak would give you 15 times as many ENERGY-stimulating calories. Yet the total number* of calories in each is roughly the same! So, you see, it ISN'T "just a matter of calories." It's the KIND of calories that makes the big difference.

In college writing, mechanical devices for emphasis should ordinarily be avoided; the wording of the statement or its position in the sentence should give it the emphasis it deserves.

Exercises

1. *Sentence patterns.* To gain practice in using different sentence structures, write two imitations of each of the following sentence patterns. Use ideas or information that you are familiar with, but preserve the structure of each example. The first, for example, might be converted into a comparison of two kinds of automobile.

1) If of Dryden's fire the blaze is brighter, of Pope's the heat is more regular and more constant. Dryden often surpasses expectations, and Pope never falls below it. Dryden is read with frequent astonishment, and Pope with perpetual delight.—Samuel Johnson

2) He bowed his head in the dust before his Maker, but he set his foot on the neck of his king.—Thomas Macaulay

3) A student unacquainted with the attempts of former adventurers is always apt to overrate his own abilities; to mistake the most trifling excursions for discoveries of moment, and every coast new to him for a new-found country.—Joshua Reynolds

4) We know that a few strokes of the axe will lop a cedar, but what arts of cultivation can elevate a shrub?—Samuel Johnson

5) I returned, and saw under the sun, that the race is not to the swift, nor the battle to the strong, neither yet bread to the wise, nor yet riches to men of understanding, nor yet favor to men of skill; but time and chance happeneth to them all.—Ecclesiastes 9:11

2. *Sentence variety.* Make a close study of at least twenty consecutive sentences in one or more of your recent papers. Take notes on the following points:

1) The kind of sentences you have used: simple, complex, compound, compound-complex; statements, questions, exclamations; loose, periodic, balanced.

2) The pattern of your sentence structure. Compare the number of sentences that follow the typical subject-verb-object order with the number of sentences in which you have varied this order.

3) The economy of the statements in your sentences. Put brackets around each word, phrase, or clause that adds nothing to the meaning of a sentence and around every sentence that does not actually advance the thought. Estimate the amount of material that you might have omitted without changing either the meaning or the effectiveness of the paper.

On the basis of the preceding analysis, write a report telling what you have discovered about your sentences. Mention the good features of your sentences as well as those that need improving.

3. *Controlling sentence structure.* Using whatever parts of the following sentences you need, compose a sentence according to each of these patterns: (1) balanced coordinate construction; (2) antithetical construction; (3) periodic construction; (4) one subject and several verbs; (5) one verb serving more than one clause. For example, sentences 6 and 7 can be converted into one periodic construction: Knowing our frame, pitying them that fear him as a father pities his children, he remembers that we are dust.

1) The Lord is merciful and gracious, slow to anger and plenteous in mercy.

2) He will not always chide: neither will he keep his anger for ever.

3) He hath not dealt with us after our sins; nor rewarded us according to our iniquities.

4) For as the heaven is high above the earth, so great is his mercy toward them that fear him.

5) As far as the east is from the west, so far hath he removed our transgressions from us.

6) Like as a father pitieth his children, so the Lord pitieth them that fear him.

7) For he knoweth our frame; he remembereth that we are dust.

8) As for man, his days are as grass: as a flower of the field, so he flourisheth.

9) For the wind passeth over it, and it is gone; and the place thereof shall know it no more. *Psalm 103:8-16*

By reducing clauses to words and phrases, combine the first three sentences above into a single sentence that is periodic.

4. *Parallel structure.* Rewrite the following sentences, eliminating unnecessary words and making related elements parallel in form:

1) To touch the heart of his mystery, we find in him one thought, strange to the point of lunacy: the thought of duty, the thought of something owing to himself and to God and his neighbor: an ideal of decency, to which he would rise if it were possible; a limit of shame that he will not stoop below if possible.

2) I wrote because it amused me, and I enjoyed correcting the work, too.

3) I told him to report to the principal's office and that he was to bring me a note from his mother.

4) The town turned out to be hard to reach, a bore, and very chilly in the evening.

5) The squirrel in our front yard is a playful sort, and who mocks us from his tree.

6) He trudged his way through his homework, and finished off his notes, then turning on the TV.

7) The house was charming and a real buy, but it was not near enough public transportation nor quite large enough for our family.

8) People who haven't been to Alaska ask questions about the prices how cold it gets in winter, and what is worth seeing.

9) I am tall and bald and have an ungainly gait.

10) This report is exceptionally complete and a fine example of concise writing.

5. *Sentence emphasis.* Rewrite any of the following sentences that seem too loose, unemphatic, or generally weak.

1) Television programs today are very adolescent in content, at least most of them.

2) There were two magnificent volcano peaks which towered over the valley.

3) Theoretically, the plan seemed flawless; its results, however, were disastrous.

4) Students on the campus were completely unaware that under the abandoned stands of Stagg Field, scientists had produced, through concentrated day-and-night effort under rigid security precautions, the first controlled atomic chain reaction.

5) There is something the average voter doesn't realize—that his ONE vote really *can make a difference;* in fact, it can change the outcome of the WHOLE ELECTION!

6) Thumbing frantically through his catalog and clutching his registration cards in his sweaty hands while he stands in line is the typical freshman.

7) Sculpture is an excellent hobby, although it can be expensive and not everyone has the skill to pursue it.

8) Outside his office, there were several customers waiting and they insisted there were other matters they had to attend to.

9) The recent civil defense drill—like all the preceding ones—showed that public apathy toward survival methods is immense.

10) Many juvenile delinquents (you'd be surprised *how* many) have parents who refuse to try to *understand* them.

6. *Review exercise on sentence effectiveness.* Read the following passage through carefully, keeping in mind all the sentence weaknesses discussed in §22 and §23. Then, without changing its content or organization more than is necessary, revise the passage so that the sentences are economical, varied, and generally effective:

Countless are the beauties and wonders of nature, and also countless are the pleasures that I have experienced in the study of nature. With a feeling of awe for the principles of geometry, I have examined the intricate design of a snowflake. Caught in the curved arm of a stem, a violet's perfect grace has been a source of wonder to me. While studying an ant lion's method of survival, I have gained a new respect for nature's skilled engineering. With a feeling of envy I have watched a monarch butterfly in soaring flight, or in a tranquil seance on a sunlit leaf.

The respect and admiration I have felt for nature have been important parts of my thinking since childhood. As an explorer in my grandmother's garden, I was delighted by the feel of damp corn silk against my cheek, and hypnotized by the rhythmic movements of a dirt dauber building its mud cocoon. Never failing to check for tonsils, I was ecstatic over each snapdragon's rainbow-hued throat.

24 Paragraphs

Paragraphs and other structural elements are no mere superficial devices; they are fundamental methods by which the writing fulfills its purpose. If a bridge is to support the stresses and strains to which traffic subjects it, its builder must combine the hardness of the stones with the structure of the arches. In writing, quite solid substance will lose some of its effect if it is not properly ordered. Good structure emphasizes meaning and helps to create it.—Robert W. Daniel

¶ No ¶	Revision: Check the paragraph or paragraphs marked for development, length, and continuity. Make your paragraph divisions correspond to clear-cut divisions of the topic.

The structure of a piece of writing, which a writer must control if readers are to understand his meaning, is shaped by the larger elements of the work, such as paragraphs. When effectively controlled, every paragraph in a paper discusses a slightly different aspect of the subject, its indention redirecting the reader's attention. But at the same time that it separates units of thought for reading ease, a good paragraph is smoothly related to the paper as a whole and sometimes serves the paper additionally by providing transition or by emphasizing key points. These aspects of paragraphs are explored in §26, Writing the first draft, which discusses the use of paragraphs to control the direction of a paper, the techniques for relating paragraphs in sequence, and the special requirements for paragraphs that open or conclude a paper. The present section is concerned with the general problems of paragraph development and paragraph continuity.

24.1 Paragraph development and length

¶ dev	Revision: The paragraph marked is not adequately developed. Add enough explanation or illustration to make the central idea clear and complete.

A fully developed paragraph is one in which the central meaning is clear and complete. Some ideas can be fully expressed in a few simple statements; others may require from a hundred to two hundred words or more of explanation or illustration in order to be fully developed.

Underdeveloped paragraphs

The effect of underdeveloped paragraphs is illustrated by the following student narration of a trip:

> Two years ago I took my first trip to Alaska. On this particular voyage there were only forty-five passengers. I learned from the steward that the usual number of weekly passengers ranged from seventy-five to two hundred.
>
> The fruit basket in each cabin was filled daily with apples, oranges, and other kinds of fruit. Since meals were included in the price of the ticket, we could choose anything we wanted from the menu without worrying about the price.
>
> We arrived at our first port, Sitka, on a rainy day. We were told that the ship would be there for about four hours unloading cargo and that we could go ashore if we so desired. After taking a good look at the town, I decided that I would very much prefer to be on board ship.

These paragraphs are unsatisfactory because they raise questions that the writer fails to answer: Why were there so few passengers on this trip? (This should be explained in the first paragraph or else not mentioned.) What is the point of the second paragraph, which jumps so abruptly from the introductory statements? the abundance of food? how cheap it was? how much the writer enjoyed it? Some statement is needed at the beginning of this paragraph to link it with the preceding one and to express the main idea ("Because there were so few passengers, we were offered more food than we could eat. . . ."). The third paragraph leaves the reader wondering what Sitka looked like, what unpleasant things the writer saw that made him prefer to stay on his ship.
24.1 Three or four explanatory sentences would have cleared up this point and would have made the paragraph more interesting.

¶ dev The following paragraph is similarly underdeveloped. It is too brief to convey adequately the writer's ideas:

> Man has been faced lately with many different ideas and systems of government. Each has tried to win the majority to its side, frequently by force or by unscrupulous propaganda. Each man thinks of himself as being representative of the majority.

This paragraph could be improved by listing some specific examples after the second sentence (Russia? China? Spain?) and by using a separate paragraph to explain the third sentence.

A good way to avoid underdeveloped paragraphs is to explore all your ideas fully in the first writing, putting down everything that occurs to you. If the paragraph turns out to be too long or to contain irrelevancies, it is easy enough to trim it in revision. To do the reverse—to fill out an underdeveloped paragraph with details and explanations—takes much more time. (See §26, Writing the first draft.)

Typical content of paragraphs

Most fully developed paragraphs are composed of three sorts of statements:

1) *General statements* in a paragraph may range from attitudes and opinions (This is the better plan; You are wrong) to large generalizations (Everyone needs some form of artistic expression; There is no such thing as a universal truth).

2) *Specific statements* are generally sub-topics of general statements. In a paragraph opening with the general statement "This is the better plan," the specific statement that followed (not yet a detail) might be something like "It has three particular advantages."

3) *Details* are particular observations and facts (He is eleven years old; This lily is a Henryi; In two years the city's population increased by 11,460) and summaries of facts (All day the planes had been running late).

Generalizations and statements of opinion are most convincing when supported by details, because details can usually be checked for accuracy. Most effective writing, in fact, is made up largely of *details*, with occasional *general statements* to hold them together and show their meaning, and with occasional *specific statements* to direct the reader's attention. The details, specific statements, and general statements in the following paragraph are labeled:

One is appalled by the lack of historical dimension in so much modern sociology as well as urban studies.	General statement
This is particularly true of the American Institute of Planners' conference.	Specific statement, which focuses attention
Often they express themselves with warm-hearted rhetoric.	Detail, as illustration
They know	Detail, as illustration

slums and ghettos exist and that they should not. They realize the social tensions of cities, the hatred and fear between the rich and the poor: the splendor of the former's environment, the ugliness of the latter's.	Detail, as illustration
At no place, however, does the conference discuss the nature of political action required to effect change.	Contrasting detail, as illustration
In many ways these planners are like generals deep in the tactics and strategy of war without an army to fight it.	Contrasting detail, as illustration
Social progress and the improvement of cities have been due to two fundamental processes: one, technological advance, which could be quickly exploited for private profit; the other, radical political protest.—J. H. Plumb, "The Future Without the Past," *The Saturday Review*, July 29, 1967, p. 23	Contrasting general statement

Whether a paragraph is basically expository or argumentative in purpose, its full development generally depends on adequate use of both details and general statements. An *expository* paragraph is a unit of facts (details) and ideas (general statements) to *explain*. This is the way a doctor begins an explanation of coronary thrombosis, a term unfamiliar to many readers:

24.1

> The diagnosis of "heart disease" is feared by all of us, and not without reason. As long as the heart beats there is hope, but we all realize that if the heart stops beating we will die.
>
> The ability of the heart to function depends primarily on the state of the heart muscle or myocardium, as it is technically known. Our existence, therefore, depends largely on the state of the blood vessels that bring nourishment to the myocardium—the coronary arteries. The heart can, of course, be damaged by other disease processes. For instance, the heart may fail because it is irreparably damaged by an infection as in rheumatic heart disease, or by poisons, or toxins, as in diphtheria.—William A. R. Thompson, M.D., "Coronary Thrombosis," *Today's Health*, September 1952, p. 30

The first paragraph makes contact with the reader's common knowledge and concern. The second begins the actual exposition, explaining the meaning of the technical word *myocardium* and rapidly adding other facts that expand the reader's understanding of coronary thrombosis.

An *argumentative* paragraph is a unit of facts (details) and ideas (general statements) to *persuade*. The following paragraphs open an argumentative essay that calls for changes in our colleges by pointing out present weaknesses. The first paragraph begins with a general statement that is explained by the details following. The second paragraph contains two general statements—the first announcing the existence of problems, the second announcing more clearly the nature of the problems. The third paragraph opens with a question that guides the development of the paragraph, which is filled with details:

> It is understandable that there should be so little fundamental criticism of our colleges and universities. Most original thinking still comes from them, but this is less because they are such good places for it than because there is hardly any place else with even the minor advantages they afford. Few students are unbiased or competent critics. Journalists too often today reproduce others' views rather than develop their own—and the views they would reproduce on colleges and universities would be naturally of the "expert"—presidents and admissions officers and professors. Perhaps most important, most people are too worried about getting their children into college to be concerned much about what goes on once they get there.
>
> But there are extremely serious problems in the colleges. And despite the millions of dollars now being spent on research in higher education, we are not doing much to make college education much more than a huge boondoggle—which is what most of it is today.
>
> From where do I draw my evidence for this view? Aside from my own experience as a student (City College in New York, the University of Pennsylvania, Columbia University), I have been a college teacher: I taught sociology for a year at the University of California in Berkeley, a year at Bennington College in Vermont, a half-year at Smith College—a crude sampling of our better universities and colleges. I have lectured or engaged in research at a half-dozen more colleges and universities, and have friends with whom I have talked about teaching and its problems at almost every important university in the country. Of course I am aware of exceptions, but I am confident that my general conclusion about

> college holds.—Nathan Glazer, "The Wasted Classroom," *Harper's Magazine*, October 1961, p. 147

Developing paragraphs by full use of details removes a frequent worry of student writers—"getting the required length." An assignment of "about six hundred words" means that the student is to take a subject and select from his information and thinking about it what can be conveyed in about that number of words. The bulk of the space in most papers should be taken up with specific details, with occasional general statements to interpret or summarize their meaning. A final test question for either a paragraph or a paper is "Have I put in enough of what I know and believe about this subject to lead a reader to see it as I do?"

Topic sentences

Both the clearness and completeness of a paragraph can generally be enhanced by stating its main idea in what is called a *topic sentence:* a key sentence to which the other statements in the paragraph are related. The topic sentence typically comes at the start of the paragraph, as in this example:

> *All the while, in other parts of the world, the terrors of the second World War were being foreshadowed by a series of ominous and bloody events.* In the north of Spain, a revolt of the Asturian miners was being ruthlessly suppressed through the importation of Moorish troops from Africa. Hitler was carrying out his "blood purge" against a cadre of former associates. Dollfuss, after slaughtering the socialist working class of Vienna, in February, was himself murdered by the Nazis in July. In October, King Alexander of Yugoslavia and Foreign Minister Barthou of France were assas-
> 24.1 sinated by Croatian terrorists in the pay of Mussolini, and in December, Kirov, a close associate of Stalin, met a similar fate on a street in Leningrad. Meanwhile, in the Chaco jungles far to the south, the unpublicized but sanguinary war between Bolivia and Paraguay was dragging on without headlines and seemingly without end.—Leo Gurko, *The Angry Decade*, pp. 106-107

Another method is to work *toward* the topic sentence, using it as a summary or a conclusion for the details in the paragraph, as in this passage from an argumentative work:

> Behold the fowls of the air: for they sow not, neither do they reap, nor gather into barns; yet your heavenly Father feedeth them. Are ye not much better than they? / Which of you by taking thought

can add one cubit unto his stature? / And why take ye thought for raiment? Consider the lilies of the field, how they grow; they toil not, neither do they spin: / And yet I say unto you, That even Solomon in all his glory was not arrayed like one of these. / *Wherefore, if God so clothe the grass of the field, which to day is, and to morrow is cast into the oven,* shall he *not much more* clothe *you, O ye of little faith?*—Matthew 6:26-30

The purpose of a topic sentence is twofold: (1) to help the writer focus his ideas on one central thought to which every statement in the paragraph is directly related, and (2) to make it easier for the reader to see what the paragraph is about, by specifically stating its controlling idea. Topic sentences are most typically found in expository and argumentative writing, but often even in descriptive paragraphs a single sentence will state a dominant impression that is borne out by the remaining sentences. (**See also** §24.2, page 328, Inductive and deductive development.)

Appropriate paragraph length

Remember that a fully developed paragraph should embody a clear-cut division of the topic. A paragraph indention is a mark of separation, indicating to the reader that one stage in the development of the topic has been completed and that another is about to begin.

A paragraph that attempts to cover more than one stage of the topic should be divided:

> About three years ago when I started my junior year in high school, a neighbor who was the captain of the local National Guard unit paid me a visit. He started talking about the wonderful possibilities the Guard had to offer—training in radio, electronics, and other technical subjects. Evidently he must have been a good recruiting officer, for after he talked for an hour, I fell for his argument and joined, thinking I might learn something. I did. [*Next sentence starts a new stage of the topic.*] After attending a few drills, I was able to draw some conclusions about this outfit and my place in it. All the fancy talk I had heard was just propaganda, for as soon as I got my uniform, they hustled me down to the anti-aircraft installation. From then on, for two and a half years, I spent most of my weekly drills wiping the guns while the NCO's stood around talking baseball and women to each other. Occasionally they would look busy when they saw an officer coming, but most of the time they loafed while I worked.

Since the discussion of recruiting clearly stops with "I did," the next sentence should begin a new paragraph.

Perhaps a more common fault of inexperienced writers is breaking up related statements into too many paragraphs. This distracts the reader and gives the writing a choppy effect:

> The day of the game finally arrives and the first thing you do is look out the window to check on the weather.
>
> As the paper predicted, it is a beautiful sunny morning with very little wind—real football weather. You try to pass the morning by reading about the game, while you are counting the hours and the minutes until the game starts.
>
> Finally you start for the game, only to find the nearest parking lot over a mile from the stadium. You begin the long walk across the campus, joining the thousands of people all as eager as you are, all hurrying in the same direction.
>
> As you pass the impressive Gothic buildings, memories of your college days come back to you, and you wish for a moment at least that you were back in school again.

The first two paragraphs concern the morning of the game and should be written as one; the last two paragraphs also deal with one topic—the trip to the stadium—and should similarly be combined.

To get an idea of how your paragraphs compare in length with those of experienced writers, examine some articles in several recent publications. Students beginning a writing course generally write paragraphs averaging from forty to seventy-five words, but as they learn to develop their ideas more fully their paragraphs approximate those in books and magazines—seventy-five to a
24.1 hundred words. Paragraphs in newspapers are usually considerably shorter, but they are deliberately abbreviated for fast reading
¶ dev and are not typical of General writing. Ordinarily if there are more than two or three indentions on a single page of one of your papers, you should look at your writing carefully to determine whether or not you have separated things that belong together in the same paragraph.

This does not mean that a short paragraph is automatically a poor one: even a one-sentence paragraph can sometimes be used to good effect. In the following passage, for example, a single short sentence conveys a dramatic moment and hence deserves to stand alone as the second paragraph:

And it was wild. The wind, whistling out of the south at 25 knots, the most that *Tinkerbelle* could stand up under reefed main, built up menacing seas that threatened to bowl her over on her beam ends. She had to be swerved around periodically to meet the biggest of the cross waves almost head-on or she'd have gotten into serious trouble. Yet on we swooshed like the proverbial scalded cat, reeling off a fraction less than two nautical miles every fifteen minutes.

"England, here we come!" I yelled at the stars.

But it was no time for exuberance; we were perched too precariously on the thin line between maximum speed and minimum safety. To remain on that perch demanded senses tuned to their greatest receptivity. It called for unwavering alertness, instant detection of the slightest change in conditions, and swift, appropriate responses. A moment's inattention could be disastrous.—Robert Manry, "Crossing the Atlantic in a 13-foot Sailboat," *Harper's Magazine*, June 1966, p. 47

In the next example, so much is packed into a single long sentence that it too fully deserves to stand as a paragraph:

But to bring us entirely to reason and sobriety, let it be observed, that a painter must not only be of necessity an imitator of the works of nature, which alone is sufficient to dispel this phantom of inspiration, but he must be as necessarily an imitator of the works of other painters: this appears more humiliating, but is equally true; and no man can be an artist, whatever he may suppose, upon any other terms.—Joshua Reynolds, *Discourses upon Art*, No. 9

Single-sentence paragraphs that serve as transitions between one part of the discussion and another are fairly common in papers that have several main divisions. The sentence below follows a four-paragraph introduction and clearly forecasts the development of the rest of the essay:

There are, I found, three main sources of waste in college teaching: the classroom system, the examination system, the departmental system.—Nathan Glazer, "The Wasted Classroom," *Harper's Magazine*, October 1961, p. 147

The real test of paragraph length is not the number of words or lines but rather the answer to these questions: Why was indention necessary? Should any one of the paragraphs be written as two, for clarity and emphasis? Are two so closely related that they should be combined? Appropriate paragraph length follows almost automatically from effective paragraph development.

24.2 Patterns of paragraph development

Much of the labor of writing consists in managing general statements and details, arranging them in sequences that move toward a point, or support a point, or move toward a transition, or achieve some other effect.

Inductive and deductive development

The two basic patterns for developing the main idea in a paragraph are *deductive development*, supporting a main point made at the beginning of the paragraph, and *inductive development*, moving toward a main point at the end. Deductive and inductive development are often referred to as the methods of *support* and *climax*.

In the following paragraph, inductive in pattern, the early sentences provide the data on which the conclusion—the last sentence—is based:

> Puffing heavily, I flopped into the cockpit and lay clutching the handhold above the compass as my breathing slowly returned to normal. The situation, to state the case mildly, could have been a lot worse. I had been given a bad scare and was soaked through, but nothing really calamitous had happened. *Tinkerbelle* was still right side up and clear of water, and neither she nor I had suffered so much as a scratch. And, best of all, I now had evidence of exactly how stable she was. That one piece of empirically gained knowledge transformed the whole harrowing experience into a blessing in disguise. There would be no more torturous nights in the cockpit; from now on I would sleep in comfort in the cabin, even in the foulest weather, with the assurance that my boat would remain upright. No longer did I need to fear being trapped there by a capsize. This discovery made the remainder of the voyage immensely more enjoyable than it would otherwise have been.—Robert Manry, "Crossing the Atlantic in a 13-foot Sailboat," *Harper's Magazine*, June 1966, p. 49

The more common deductive pattern, illustrated in the following paragraph, has the primary assertion or main point first, followed by supporting details:

> Junior colleges come in all sizes and kinds. There are the private ones for fashionable young ladies in pleasant rural settings, outgrowths of what once were called "finishing schools." They are

likely to have a somewhat boarding-school air about them, a well-bred, ivy-covered look and manner and sometimes (though by no means always) negligible academic standards. By contrast there are vast city junior colleges teeming with several thousand students jammed into barely adequate old brick public-school buildings. Indeed a great many community colleges have been started in outmoded high-school buildings and later moved, when the community could raise the money by floating a bond issue and getting state aid, to a campus on the outskirts of town. I visited one college in upstate New York where I was shown the stables and carriage house in which it had held its first classes. In Philadelphia a new community college at present occupies what was once Snellenberg's department store.—Russell Lynes, "How Good Are the Junior Colleges?" *Harper's Magazine*, November 1966, p. 54

Notice that the central thought in both of these paragraphs is focused in a topic sentence, its position depending on the pattern the writer has used to develop his main idea.

Other patterns of development

Some texts spell out a number of specific "methods" for developing paragraphs. The catalog of methods usually includes deduction (support) and induction (climax) as well as these patterns:

1) *Illustration*, ordinarily another name for the overall method of elaborating a general statement by illustrative details

2) *Definition* (frequent in exposition and argument), the explanation of a term by logical definition, that is, by assigning the term to an appropriate species or class and then distinguishing it from other members of the class

3) *Comparison* and *analogy*, the explanation of a particular subject by pointing out its similarities to another subject, usually one that is better known or more easily understood

4) *Contrast*, the explanation of a particular subject by pointing out how it differs from another subject

5) *Cause-effect*, the arrangement of a paragraph according to cause-effect sequence, such as beginning a paragraph with a general statement giving a cause and filling out the paragraph with specific effects, or beginning a paragraph with a series of specific statements naming separate causes and concluding with a general statement that gives the effect

6) *Classification*, the explanation of a subject either by putting it into the class it belongs to and then examining the characteristics of the class, or by dividing the subject in order to consider its individual parts

7) *Chronological order* (characteristic of narrative writing and of expository writing concerned with explaining a process), the arrangement of events in temporal order

8) *Spatial order* (probably most characteristic of descriptive writing), the arrangement of objects in some systematic spatial sequence, as near to far, far to near, high to low

It is possible to write good paragraphs by deliberate use of any one of these patterns, and you can probably find examples of each in the magazines you read. The pattern of development in the following paragraphs is indicated in the margin:

Development by definition

I am interested in driving as a sort of art, a challenge to my wit and abilities.	First step of definition: *driving* classified as *art*
By driving I do not mean knowing how to shift from first to second or how to turn around in the back yard or how to get over a stretch of deserted country road.	Negative distinctions
I am talking about the sort of thing you do if you try to make good time between, say, New York and Boston or between Kansas City and Seattle, running around forty to sixty miles an hour on the open road and pushing through lines of traffic as quickly as common sense will let you.	Differentiation: driving specified as distinct from other member of the class
Nothing that I write will apply to the snail-paced progress in a traffic-jammed city street.	Negative distinction
Let's consider a few simple truths about getting from here to there in a car.—Lincoln Dryden, "How to Drive a Car," *Harper's Magazine*, June 1952, pp. 82-83	Transition to following paragraphs

Cause-effect development

Overpopulation would drive wildlife to the wall; the eagle and the elk would become memories;	Single cause stated: *overpopulation* Effect No. 1
the smell of pine already is synthesized and marketed in pressurized cans for use in deodorizing our apartments and—who knows—perhaps someday our cities.	Effect No. 2
Many would eat fish-flour, but	Effect No. 3
few would know the taste of brook trout or fresh-caught salmon.—Stewart L. Udall, "Our Perilous Population Implosion," *The Saturday Review*, September 2, 1967, p. 13	Effect No. 4

All of these methods, or patterns, of development are good, but as Professor Francis Christensen has pointed out, they are no more relevant to paragraph development than to writing sentences or long papers. A single sentence may state a complete analogy, and an entire paper may be structured as a definition. The methods are really no more than characteristic ways of thinking, operations we go through as we mull things over and work them out.

Combining patterns of development

You should notice too as you read that the various methods or patterns of development often converge in a single paragraph. For example, the paragraph below, quoted on pages 321-322 to illustrate the management of general statements and details, depends also on the contrast stated in the sixth sentence *(At no place, however, . . .)*, the comparison in the seventh sentence *(these planners are like generals)*, and the implied contrast in the last sentence (progress *should* come from urban planners, but instead it has come from two other sources):

> One is appalled by the lack of historical dimension in so much modern sociology as well as urban studies. This is particularly true of the American Institute of Planners' conference. Often they express themselves with warm-hearted rhetoric. They know slums and ghettos exist and that they should not. They realize the social

> tensions of cities, the hatred and fear between the rich and the poor: the splendor of the former's environment, the ugliness of the latter's. At no place, however, does the conference discuss the nature of political action required to effect change. In many ways these planners are like generals deep in the tactics and strategy of war without an army to fight it. Social progress and the improvement of cities have been due to two fundamental processes: one, technological advance, which could be quickly exploited for private profit; the other, radical political protest.—J. H. Plumb, "The Future Without the Past," *The Saturday Review*, July 29, 1967, p. 23

The following paragraph illustrates the pattern of classification in the second sentence (introducing the three constituent elements of society) and of definition in the fourth sentence (defining *discovery* and *invention*):

> It is the function of the scholar to evoke into life wisdom and beauty which, apart from his magic, would remain lost in the past. A progressive society depends upon its inclusion of three groups—scholars, discoverers, inventors. Its progress also depends upon the fact that its educated masses are composed of members each with a tinge of scholarship, a tinge of discovery, and a tinge of invention. I am here using the term "discovery" to mean the progress of knowledge in respect to truths of some high generality, and the term "invention" to mean the progress of knowledge in respect to the application of general truths in particular ways subservient to present needs. It is evident that these three groups merge into each other, and also that men engaged in practical affairs are properly to be called inventors so far as they contribute to the progress of society. But any one individual has his own limitation of function, and his own peculiar needs. What is important for a nation is that there shall be a very close relation between all types of its progressive elements, so that the study may influence the market place, and the market place the study. Universities are the chief agencies for this fusion of progressive activities into an effective instrument of progress. Of course they are not the only agencies, but it is a fact that today the progressive nations are those in which universities flourish.—Alfred North Whitehead, *The Aims of Education*, pp. 102-103

24.2
¶ dev

A paragraph, like a full paper, should follow the form of development that best suits the subject and that will be clearest to the reader.

See also §26.2, Developing your material.

24.3 Paragraph continuity

¶ con	Revision: Rewrite the paragraph marked to make the relationships between ideas clear.

A paragraph represents a chain of thought; it is a series of statements that are associated in your mind and that you want the reader to see in the same relationship. The elements in most paragraphs should be related as closely as the elements in a sentence, where presumably the parts fit each other to make a whole. In the following paragraph, notice that the pattern is deductive: a general statement (the topic sentence) opens the paragraph and is followed by specific statements clearly developed from the general statement. Note, too, that the opening sentence illustrates the same kind of relationship, its second clause developing out of its first (*If . . . , then*).

> If the scheme of things is purposeless and meaningless, then the life of man is purposeless and meaningless too. Everything is futile, all effort is in the end worthless. A man may, of course, still pursue disconnected ends, money, fame, art, science, and may gain pleasure from them. But his life is hollow at the center. Hence the dissatisfied, disillusioned, restless spirit of modern man.—Walter T. Stace, "Man Against Darkness," *The Atlantic Monthly*, September 1948, pp. 54-55

In the paragraph below, the relationships between successive statements are shown in the margin:

Have you got termites? In your house, I mean. It is the newest and most fashionable house disease.	Three sentences presenting the subject
It used to be called "ants" and no one was interested.	Contrast
Also sinus used to be called catarrh. But "sinus" made the old disease under another name popular.	Comparison
Last summer in the fashionable country places the talk was all about termites.	Repetition of idea in third sentence
How so and so suddenly stepped on her floor and went right through.	Example of the "talk"
And, my dear, they had to call an exterminator and it cost hundreds and hundreds of dollars	Example continued

> to get rid of the things; the whole house was almost torn apart and they had to treat the floors with the most awful smelling stuff! If you hadn't termites, you just weren't in Society.—Roy Chapman Andrews, *This Amazing Planet*, p. 101

Repetition of idea in third sentence

It is not so important to be able to name the relationships as it is to make sure that they will be clear to the reader. He should not have to "read between the lines" to supply missing connections.

Methods of showing continuity

The most common ways of showing continuity between statements are: (1) *repetition* of an important word from a previous sentence, (2) use of a *synonym*, a different word of much the same meaning as one already used, (3) use of a *pronoun* referring to a word or idea in the preceding sentence, (4) use of a *connecting word*, an adverb or a conjunction that points out the thought relationship. These signs of the relationship between statements are italicized and labeled in brackets in the following paragraph:

> An instructive example of the failure of a people to take advantage of available materials is afforded by the Onas of South America. *In this respect* [synonym: failure to take advantage of available materials] *they* [pronoun: the Onas] may be contrasted with the Eskimos. *Here* [adverb: connecting with preceding two sentences] are *two peoples* [synonym: the Onas and the Eskimos] living in cold environments, the one to the north, the other to the south. *The Eskimos* [repetition] have made a most satisfactory adjustment to their environment. *They* [pronoun: the Eskimos] have good houses and a complete wardrobe. *Indeed* [adverb: connects and emphasizes], *the latter* [pronoun: a complete wardrobe] surpasses that of most civilized peoples of the past. *The Onas* [repetition], *on the other hand* [connective: shows contrast with preceding statements], go practically naked, and lacking adequate shelter, seek unsuccessfully to keep warm before an open fire. *Yet* [connective: contrast] *the Onas* [repetition] hunt the guanaco, the skin of which is suitable for clothing. In trying to account for the backwardness of *these people* [synonym: the Onas], *then* [connective: result], geographic conditions are not to be emphasized.—William F. Ogburn and Meyer F. Nimkoff, *Sociology*, p. 110

The thought of this paragraph is a unit, and each statement follows the other clearly. You cannot start reading it after the first sentence without realizing that something has gone before. (The sentence "The Eskimos have made a most satisfactory adjustment to their environment" could start a paragraph, but if it did, the paragraph would be about Eskimos, not about Eskimos and Onas.)

We are inclined to overlook the absences of guides to the reader in our own writing, because the relationship of ideas is already clear to us, but we notice immediately when other writers forget to show the connection between ideas. Consider how the following unconnected paragraph is improved by showing the relationship between the statements:

Unconnected version

Many people today believe that objectionable movies should be censored by federal or local agencies. The recent emphasis in American films on immorality and violence is outrageous. They are undermining our nation's morals and our prestige abroad, according to many people. There may be some truth here. I agree with the diagnosis, but I cannot accept the cure. Censorship poses a greater threat to a democracy, in my opinion.

Relationships shown

Many people today believe that objectionable movies should be censored by federal or local agencies. *These critics* have been outraged by the recent emphasis in American films on immorality and violence. *Such films*, according to *them*, are undermining our nation's morals and our prestige abroad. *This* may be true. *However*, although I agree with *their* diagnosis, I cannot accept *their* cure. It seems to me that censorship poses a greater threat to a democracy *than objectionable entertainment*.

Eliminating irrelevant ideas

Paragraph continuity is damaged by the introduction of irrelevant and unrelated ideas. These break the chain of thought and make a paragraph seem ragged:

> Among the oddities of the plant world, Venus's-flytrap is one of the most interesting. *Venus is the mythological goddess of love.* It is a carnivorous plant that catches and devours insects and occasionally even small birds. This is done by means of paired lobes that resemble the halves of an oyster or clam, *scientifically known as bivalves.* When the lobes are open, they expose a colorful

> interior that attracts insects in search of nectar. Once it is disturbed, the powerful lobes snap shut, and strong digestive juices go to work to break down and assimilate the body. *Some people have successfully grown these plants in their homes.*

The italicized statements in this example are not directly related to the subject of the paragraph, and in revision they should be omitted or transferred to another paragraph. The last sentence above, for example, might be appropriate in a paragraph telling how to grow Venus's-flytrap, but it is out of place in a description of the plant's physical qualities.

Continuity in descriptive paragraphs

The details in a descriptive paragraph should give the reader a clear, unified impression. Descriptive writing is more than simple enumeration. You need to choose the most effective details and arrange them so that the more important ones stand out. The following paragraph illustrates a lack of selection and focus. Too much attention is given to minor details, and as a result no single impression emerges:

24.3 ¶ con

> We entered the Roundup Room through a curtained entrance just past the check room on a right turn. The Roundup Room was a long ell-shaped affair with the end of the ell angling off to the left. It was about two-hundred feet long and probably fifty feet wide. Along the wall on the left ran a long bar made of dark wood. Behind the bar five bartenders were busily filling orders and giving them to a dozen or so waitresses ranging in age from about twenty to forty-five. Above the bar mirror on the wall were paintings of western scenes and cartoons, like those I described on the outside of the building. Down the aisle in front of us there seemed to be a beehive of activity, with couples coming and going to the small dance floor. I say "small" because it couldn't have been more than twenty-five feet square. On our right were small tables, all filled with customers, and on the right wall, farther down, were a number of small booths. We threaded our way through the smoky haze to an empty table.

If the writer intended to emphasize the overcrowding and confusion in this room, he should have concentrated on those features and omitted or briefly summarized such unnecessary details as the shape and dimensions of the room, the paintings above the mirror, and so on.

In writing a descriptive paragraph, decide what main impression you want to achieve; then arrange your material so that all the statements contribute to this central impression. **See also** §28.3, Description.

Continuity in narrative paragraphs

When you are relating an experience, describing an incident, or summarizing the plot of a story or play, keep the action moving in one direction and avoid unnecessary interruptions. The italicized sentences in the following paragraph destroy the continuity of the narrative because they stop the action:

> It was the seventh of August, 1959. My friend and I were hitchhiking from a small town in the northern part of the state. Unlike most adventurers I did not notice the sky nor did I feel the impending danger. *I guess I don't make a very good hero. Now I must get back to my story.* After waiting by the side of the road for some time, we were picked up by two men in an old Chevy.

Later events in this narrative should show whether or not the writer is "a very good hero." This unnecessary remark not only slows down the story, but also suggests the outcome of the incident before it is unfolded.

The connection between statements in a narrative paragraph is usually simple, since it is controlled by time. Events follow each other as they happened in time or as they are imagined to have happened. The verbs usually carry this movement, and the continuity is made stronger by the repetition of the same grammatical subject from one sentence to another. Time may be emphasized and made more obvious by adverbs—*then, next, before, soon, later, presently*—or by adverbial phrases or clauses: *When he got to the corner . . . , After the last dance . . . .* The italicized verb forms and adverbs of time in this passage show how large a part words of action and time play in giving continuity to a narrative paragraph:

24.3 ¶ con

> They *ran* for three hours. *Finally, avoiding* hummocks and *seeking* low ground, they *intercepted* the rain squall. *For ten minutes* they *ran* beneath the squall, *raising* their arms and, *for the first time, shouting* and *capering. Then* the wind *died* and the rain squall *held* steady. They *were studying* the ground. *Suddenly* one of them *shouted, ran* a few feet, *bent forward* and *put* his mouth to the ground. He *had found* a depression with rain water in it. He *bent*

down, a black cranelike figure, and *put* his mouth to the ground.—Eugene Burdick, "The Invisible Aborigine," *Harper's Magazine*, September 1961, p. 70

To maintain continuity in narrative paragraphs, keep the tense of verbs consistent. If you start with one tense—the past or the present—don't shift without reason to another. **See also** §28.4, Narration.

Exercises

1. *Paragraph analysis.* Study the paragraphs in one of your recent papers in light of the elements discussed in this section. Are they developed with enough details to make your points effectively? Is the relation between all the statements clear? Is there any special reason why your paragraphs are developed in the way they are? How long are the longest and shortest paragraphs? What is the average length? Compare these figures with the averages given on page 326. Can you justify the length of any paragraphs that are unusually long or short? Revise your least effective paragraphs.

2. *Paragraph development.* Examine the following paragraphs. Which of them are not adequately developed? How could they be improved (more details, addition of general statements, clearer relationships between ideas, a different method of development)? Revise the paragraphs, making whatever additions or changes you feel are necessary.

1) Over the years motion picture producers have flooded the country with a stream of "monster" and "space" movies. In so doing, they have created a distorted image of science fiction in the minds of most Americans, a conception of science fiction that causes the average person to assume that any book labeled as science fiction must be the story of a gigantic monster intent on destroying the world or that of a race of intelligent beings equally intent on destroying mankind.

2) There are a few highly industrialized cities in Mexico even today. Scattered along both coasts are oil-refining centers like Tuxpan, Tampico, and Minatitlán. Monterrey has its brewery industry, Pachuca its mining, and Orizaba its textiles. Mexico City is surrounded by a ring of diversified industries. But outside of these, Mexico remains largely agricultural.

3) Horror movies are not as good as they used to be. In the old days make-up experts spent half a day getting an actor ready to play Frankenstein or the Wolf Man. In a recent science fiction picture all the monsters were wearing cheap rubber masks. The scientific background is not as carefully prepared either.

4) We have not attained by any sense or means of reckoning any form of Utopia as men seek to dwell together with other men. Instead, we are, as Bunyan says, in progress in pilgrimage, in which every day becomes both a teaching and a learning mechanism. We are those who can look back to where we have been; we are those who can look forward to a goal which we pursue; but we have to live day by day. What we yearn for is not yet accomplished, but this merely means we do not cease working as well as yearning for its accomplishment.

5) Many current science fiction movies are ridiculously indifferent to elementary science. In *Konga* a scientist injects a young chimpanzee with a growth hormone and is delighted when it more than doubles in size. Neither he nor his assistant seem to notice, however, that the chimp has changed into a gorilla in the process. In *Untamed Women*, shipwrecked Americans find an uncharted island inhabited by a tribe of women descended from ancient Celtic seafarers; dinosaurs periodically emerge from the jungles to harass them. But the women wear modern foundation garments and speak English, and the dinosaurs are iguanas and gila monsters vastly magnified.

6) Another reason for the great migration to cities was the educational opportunities they offered. Some rural high schools were quite good, but others were small, one-room buildings in which a barely educated local mother tried to teach a dozen young people of different ages and abilities. The distance from the farm to the school was often five miles or more. In the city there were trolleys and buses to take people quickly and easily wherever they wanted to go. Besides, the student was less likely to be burdened by after-school chores, and he could have a wider circle of friends.

3. *Paragraph development, division, and length.* Examine the following passage from a student paper. Do the paragraph divisions correspond to shifts in ideas? Should some of the shorter paragraphs be combined? Should the long paragraph be divided? Be prepared to justify any changes you suggest.

J. D. Salinger's *The Catcher in the Rye* bears many resemblances to Mark Twain's *Adventures of Huckleberry Finn.*

Both are first-person narratives full of comic irony, colloquial language, picaresque structure, and themes of anti-phoniness.

The patterns of the two plots are closely parallel. There is the inspiration of their honesty against sham, release provided by rebellion against society, and the sympathetic awareness of melancholy roles. Holden and Huck travel a common trail of the quests of youth in an unfriendly adult world. Their journeys are separated by a hundred years and several hundred miles, and their standards and societies vary greatly, but their ultimate goals are basically the same—peace. Nearly every society has had a tradition of the Quest—a seeking after that which is tremendous. There are two main types of quests that individuals pursue. The first type is one of acceptability and stability in society. It is a life based on what is known and can be trusted.

The second quest seeks not stability, but rather a society where Truth is unwarped by society, where the individual is more important than the group. It is this second quest in which Holden and Huck are engaged.

4. *Patterns of paragraph development.* Analyze the development of each of the following paragraphs. Does it follow one of the patterns of development discussed in §24.2? What use does it make of details and general statements? Does it have a topic sentence?

1) On the river the wind wasn't strong, but high up it was doing violence. The El Greco clouds suddenly, as though consciously, coalesced into a gray overcast that turned the day ominous. Two long skeins of big birds flapped across that grayness toward the south—snad-hill cranes, grating out their castle-gate croak—and I knew what the air's muggy edge meant. Geese confirmed it, the first I'd seen, four snows in a little disciplined V, winging solemnly and soundlessly south. The wind on the river died, and paddling I began to sweat. It was the kind of day that usually, in the Texas fall, is full of a kind of waiting; things are moving, the year is changing, a norther is coming.—John Graves, *Goodbye to a River*, p. 98

2) Every great war has two sides, the glorious and the terrible. The glorious is perpetuated in multitudinous pictures, poems, novels, statues: in Meissonier's canvases of Friedland and Austerlitz, Byron's stanzas on Waterloo and Tennyson's on the Light and Heavy brigades, St. Gauden's Sherman riding forward victory-crowned, Freeman's "Lee." The terrible is given us in a much slighter body of memorabilia: Jacques Callot's gruesome etchings of the Thirty Years War, Goya's paintings of French atrocities in Spain, Zola's "The Debacle," Walt Whitman's hospital sketches, and the thousand-page novels that drearily emerged from the Second World War.—Allan Nevins, "The Glorious and the Terrible," *The Saturday Review*, September 2, 1961, p. 9

3) In the fine arts, then, the experience becomes intensified by the arresting of sensations. We become aware with tingling pleasure of the colors and shapes on a canvas, of the sounds of a voice or a violin. The other senses, too, have their possible aesthetic exploitation, but touch, taste, and smell are not as finely manipulable, not as easily incorporated in objects or detached from practical biological interests as are sight and sound. The peculiar function of the fine arts lies, therefore, chiefly in the realm of these two subtle and finely discriminated organs, the eye and the ear. Color, which for practical purposes is usually the most negligible aspect of an object, is the painter's special material. Differences in rhythm and tone, negligible in practical communication, become for the musician the source of all his art, for the music lover the source of all his pleasure. The senses from being incitements to action are turned into avenues of delight.—Irwin Edman, *Arts and the Man*, pp. 27-28

4) It would not be difficult to come to an agreement as to what we understand by science. Science is the century-old endeavor to bring together by means of systematic thought the perceptible phenomena of this world into as thoroughgoing an association as possible. To put it boldly, it is the attempt at the posterior reconstruction of existence by the process of conceptualization. But when asking myself what religion is, I cannot think of an answer so easily. And even after finding an answer which may satisfy me at this particular moment, I still remain convinced that I can never under any circumstances bring together, even to a slight extent, all those who have given this question serious consideration.—Albert Einstein, *Out of My Later Years*, p. 24

5. *Paragraph continuity*. Each of the following three paragraphs lacks continuity. Rewrite them, making whatever rearrangements, additions, or omissions are needed to make the continuity clear.

1) My grandparents still follow many of their national customs. They have lived in the United States for almost forty years. The traditional ceremony of the eggs begins on the night before Easter, when my grandmother prepares a dozen elaborately decorated eggs. Despite her age, she still has a very firm hand. The eggs are passed from hand to hand around the table, where the whole family has gathered. My grandfather chants a prayer meanwhile. The eggs are taken outside and buried in the garden, and everyone goes to bed for the night. Then everyone takes the candle he has left lighted in his window and returns to the garden. As dawn is breaking, the eggs are dug up and placed in a basket decorated with flowers. There is a sumptuous breakfast to celebrate the successful recovery, and man's redemption by Christ has been acted out.

2) By 1937 Americans began to grow aware of the menace of fascism. The United States government extended the Neutrality Act to cover the war in Spain. This prevented the republicans from getting American guns and supplies. Up until 1937 Americans had paid more attention to domestic than to foreign problems because they had not been dramatized. But tensions were mounting in Europe, and the Spanish Civil War attracted a great deal of interest. A Gallup poll taken in 1937 showed that 65 per cent sided with the republican forces against the fascist Franco. It was 75 per cent in 1938. Of course Hitler represented fascism at its worst, as we all know.

3) When I got about thirty feet out into the lake, I saw that the water was rougher than I had thought. Several large breakers hit me full in the face, and I took in too much water for comfort. There are techniques good swimmers use to avoid getting swamped by breakers, but I had never learned them because I didn't think it was important at the time. I decided to head back toward the rocks, but I couldn't see the flat shelf where I had entered. In desperation, I headed toward a jagged group of rocks nearby. Just as I got close to it and was groping for a foothold, a large breaker threw me against a sharp edge and knocked me breathless. Being thrown against rocks in rough waters is a danger many inexperienced swimmers overlook.

6. *Paragraph continuity.* Assume that the following list is a collection of notes you have jotted down on the subject of land problems in the Mediterranean area. Incorporate the information into an orderly, unified piece of writing, using appropriate paragraph divisions. Add whatever words or phrases are necessary to make the relationships between ideas clear.

Mediterranean countries were once prosperous.

Their population is rising fast.

Many trees were cut down in past centuries.

The Mediterranean basin used to be the center of Western civilization.

The land is becoming less productive every year.

Much of the land today is arid or semi-arid.

The United Nations has started a project there to improve land use.

Grass and trees help water soak down into the soil.

Poverty is widespread in Mediterranean countries.

Desert areas cover 1.25 billion acres and are increasing every year.

Trees are essential to prevent erosion.

Restoring all the forests would take too long.

The United Nations is financing increased fertilization.

The land has been overgrazed, so that much grass and forest have been destroyed.

The topsoil is being washed away.

Floods are becoming widespread.

The United Nations wants to restore balanced land use.

Irrigation would be a help.

The sizes of grazing herds must be reduced.

Agriculture and animal husbandry must be integrated.

25 Discovering and organizing material for writing

You see, freedom has nothing to do with lack of training; it can only be the product of training. You're not free to move unless you've learned to walk, and not free to play the piano unless you practice. Nobody is capable of free speech unless he knows how to use the language, and such knowledge is not a gift: it has to be learned and worked at.—Northrop Frye

A good sentence or a good paragraph (the topics of the last three sections) is a pleasure to read, whether found in the middle of another writer's dull page or favorably formed in panic in the middle of one's own essay examination. But not even a collection of good sentences or of good paragraphs will make a good essay, unless they conspire happily together. Ordinarily a writer cannot expect this to happen by accident.

If an essay is to be *for* something, to answer a need, a writer must expect to spend more time and effort on *pre-writing* tasks than on the writing task itself. Well before starting his first draft (and while he is writing it and revising it), a writer must consider such questions as the following: What is the subject, what kind of proposition is being stated, and what is the purpose in stating it? What kinds of resources are available for treating the subject, and how may they be used to best advantage? How can the material be most effectively presented to a particular audience? In what ways can the material be arranged, and if there are several options, which form of development is most likely to unite situation, writer, and audience?

It is often said in books about writing that most of us have a lot to say—the problem lies in *learning how to say it*. But it is unrealistic to think that a writer's only chore is finding *how* to say something: all of us can remember floundering and scrambling *prior* to writing, in the pre-writing time, to find what exactly we want to say. If it is true that most of us have a lot to write about, it is also true that most of us have first to *discover* that we do. What we have to say is not always impelling, there, ready to be said: more often than not we have to find it, know it, discover it. This means examining our personal resources, weighing our judgments and our whimsy, and evaluating our information.

25

Even after we discover that we do have something to say, we must still consider whether it *needs* to be said. Any student, given an assignment to write a five-hundred-word theme and turn it in on Monday, can obviously argue that something needs to be said if he is to satisfy the course requirements. But even the most routine subject ("My Summer Vacation," "Why I Came to College") given in a conventional assignment should be examined for its needs: Do I have resources that enable me to say something on this subject? If I have something to say, can I make it worth saying? Can I propose something and offer support for it? Remember that in a sense all writing is persuasive. This does not mean that it is necessarily controversial, or that it must urge an audience to action. It means rather that all good writing *proposes* something —perhaps a program of reform, perhaps honest self-examination, perhaps simply a way of seeing a landscape.

25.1 Discovering a subject

The task of determining what to write about is much simpler when the topic is determined by the occasion—for instance, when a businessman answers a letter, when a scientist reports an experiment he has completed, or when some specific, relevant topic grows out of a discussion in a composition class. But the occasion will not always determine your topic. For a class assignment you may be given several subjects from which to choose, or you may be given a single subject that did not develop from class discussion, or you may be left free to select your own topic. When this happens, you may have to spend considerable time on the project even before you can begin making scratch notes. It is always best to think about the subjects offered (or about the situation—your class—if no subject is offered) before making a final decision. Topics chosen at random or out of desperation at the last possible moment seldom make satisfactory papers.

The problem is that a topic alone does not ordinarily give you a *purpose* for writing. If you are assigned a topic such as "Why I Came to College" or if you choose for yourself a topic such as "A Freshman Views the Draft," you must still determine why it is worth while to explain your reasons for coming to college or to present your judgments of the draft. In other words, you have to investigate the situation in which you and an audience are to come together. What does it require? What can you achieve by

presenting your reasons and judgments? Of what concern will they be to an audience?

When you are asked to select your own subject, choose one that actually interests you—a subject that you would like to talk about and one that you feel reasonably qualified to discuss. Not all assigned topics will arouse immediate interest, but even conventional topics can, with time and thought, yield you an interest and a purpose.

Whether working with an assigned subject or one of your own choosing, you will need to explore the topic's *potential.* How many different themes could you write from the same topic? Of these, which is most likely to propose something of worth to your audience? The author of the following essay clearly has not considered the many possibilities his topic offers; he has not used the resources available to him; he has not considered the interests and needs of his audience. He has not, in other words, discovered a proper subject in the case before him:

My Theater Experience

I worked at a theater before coming to college. When my parents started managing the drive-in, they drafted me to do the odd jobs there.

While working in the cafeteria, box-office, and the projection booth, I met many new people. I found that people come to a movie for different reasons. One man said that he came to get away from his wife and kids. Many boys and girls came to have dates. A few people, however, actually came to watch the movie.

At the drive-in, I experienced different emotions due to the actions of my customers. One lady aroused my indignation when she claimed that her son, who was six feet in height, was under twelve years of age. A boy eleven years old does not have to pay admission; therefore her son was admitted free. I was amused when one boy tried to hide in the back floor of a car, under a quilt, while the driver drove into the theater. I am aware of such tricks, and the boy was caught. One girl caught her slacks on the barbed wire while climbing over the fence at the back of the theater. I helped her off the fence, and I sold her a ticket. She never came over the fence again.

I experienced new and enlightening experiences at the theater. At the drive-in, I found that real people are often more entertaining than people in the movies.

In his last sentence the writer arrives finally at a statement that could give purpose and shape to an essay, but it is a statement he has not seriously developed. Unrealized possibilities cluster both within and without this theme. Within the theme in its present form, several things are barely mentioned that might have become interesting propositions: What is different about working in a drive-in? Who are the "new people"? What are the different reasons for attending drive-in theaters? What is the range of emotions aroused by the customers (here, the range runs only from A to B)? What about that girl hanging on the fence? Most of all, how could the last sentence be developed into an amusing account of human folly?

The topic also has other possibilities not explored in this theme. A student who has spent a considerable time working in a drive-in theater *does* have something to say, and it *could* have merit. The possibilities of "My Theater Experience" include an interesting, specific, concrete survey of taste and manners; a critical judgment of the movies themselves; an interesting commentary on the peripheral conveniences added to theaters; a thoughtful consideration of leisure life, or of waste, or of dating practices. But the writer of "My Theater Experience" clearly did not discover a subject worth writing about.

Narrowing the topic

As you are thinking about topics assigned to you or about other possible topics, consider whether any of them can be developed into an essay that is *for* something, an essay that will involve you in working out a subject in the company of an audience. There is seldom any danger that the topic you select will be too narrow. It is the large subjects like "American Foreign Policy," "The Aims of Higher Education," and "The Role of Women in Contemporary Society" that lead to difficulty. On such ambitious subjects most writers can only repeat commonplace judgments and empty generalities, and after writing a paragraph or two, they find that they have nothing more to say.

Limit the topic you select so that you can develop it fully in the required number of words. Most college themes are short—even a thousand-word theme would fill only one newspaper column. Because even ten thousand words would not be enough to cover most large general subjects ("Justice," "Crime Prevention," "Forestry"), break down such subjects into topics you can handle. "TV Westerns," for example, might be limited to "The Effect of TV Westerns on Children." But since there are many children and many TV Westerns, you might write a more interesting paper and offer more interesting judgments by focusing specifically on your little brother and TV Westerns.

Concentrate on a single, well-defined aspect of the subject rather than on the subject as a whole:

Too General	*Specific*
Voting as an Obligation of Citizenship	Arousing Student Interest in College Politics
Sportsmanship	How Sportsmanship Differs in Tennis and Baseball
Smog Control	Anti-Smog Devices for Cars

As you gather information your topic may change slightly—and it may continue to change slightly through all the preliminary stages of your thinking. The important thing to remember at first is to keep the topic specific and to avoid falling back on a general subject, saying less and less about more and more.

Locating a thesis

When you have gone far enough in your thinking and planning to select a specific topic, then you can begin to see what position you may want to take toward it. A definite statement of the main point or central idea of your paper (usually best given in a single declarative sentence) will help you to see just where you are going and why, and it will also help you to select the material you are going to use in the paper.

This *thesis statement*, or *thesis sentence*, is not the topic of your paper nor its title (which is usually no more than four or five words); it is a sentence that answers the question "What is the main idea that I am trying to present to the reader?" A statement of the central or controlling idea of a paper titled "The Honor System" might read "The honor system works only as well as the students want it to work" or "The honor system at this college is popular with the faculty but not with the students." In a paper explaining a process or activity, the thesis statement might be "Learning to play the violin demands patience as well as talent" or "Performance is more important than appearance when you are buying a used car."

One way to bring a subject into clearer focus and to locate a thesis is to examine the subject by asking some long-used and still relevant questions. In *Classical Rhetoric for the Modern Student*, Professor Edward P. J. Corbett records the questions like this:

An sit (whether a thing is)—a question of fact
Quid sit (what it is)—a question of definition
Quale sit (what kind it is)—a question of quality

These questions, as Professor Corbett says, will not immediately provide a thesis, but they will help you to decide what feature of the subject you are going to treat. For example, in the theme titled "My Theater Experience" (page 346), the first question probably does not need answering—presumably there is no doubt that the writer has had some theater experience. But either of the other questions might have directed the writer to a thesis statement and a more interesting paper. For example, an answer to the question of "*what* it is" would entail a complete record of the various kinds of experience the writer had in the theater. To define these experiences completely might still be too much for a single theme; if so, the writer could focus on a particular feature of his experience and formulate a thesis statement such as "Some of the things I learned while working in the drive-in theater prepared me for other jobs later in life." Or the writer could just as easily turn to the question of "what *kind* it is" and concentrate on the *meaning* or *quality* of his experience, with a thesis statement like this: "Eighteen months of work in a drive-in theater taught me something, I think, about the difference between public and private manners."

Formulating a thesis statement will help you determine just exactly what you want to say and, by forcing you to stick to your subject, will help unify your work. It will also help you to determine what resources you will need (perhaps only your own present knowledge and beliefs, perhaps additional information) to handle the topic adequately.

25.2 Using your resources

Rhetoric, Professor Donald C. Bryant has said, is the "energizer of truth." That is to say, the resources and techniques of speech and writing give truth its vitality and relevance. Good writing and good speaking rest on the discovery of the possible means of presenting a subject to an audience. In the early stages of preparing a paper, this means, in addition to locating your thesis, considering what your thesis needs and exploiting the resources available to you.

The following essay was written for a composition class:

Habits

Habit is an occurrence of a certain act or deed so frequent as to become a matter of course. Habit can be classified in two distinct types. One is the useful, progressive, uplifting kind while the other is of the nature that deteriorates character and often damages the physical body.

Every individual has a choice of deciding on the high or low road to follow in creating habits. If young people were vividly aware that early life determines their destiny, a definite change of attitude would be prevalent today. As a general rule, men do not become truly successful when held down by evil and destructive habits. The idle, careless youth most often becomes the profligate, worthless man while in contrast the temperate, industrious youth leads to the strong, reliable, and trusty man.

The young person who allows an evil habit to fasten itself upon him may not understand why in later years it cannot be defied. Life is too short to be spent in the grip of habits that are contrary to man's ultimate destiny.

It would be possible to compile an interesting (and long) catalog of flaws and inadequacies in this short theme. Foremost in the catalog would be the author's failure to focus on a specific, usable topic and his failure to exploit the possible resources for such a theme. It appears that he has not examined his own knowledge (if he has, he has not bothered to record it), and it also appears that he has not gained much from observation. Neither has he considered and used possible supplemental resources, reading and other kinds of investigation beyond his own present knowledge.

Two kinds of resources—what we might call *private resources*
25.2 and *public resources*—should be considered in developing a paper.
Some subjects require one, some the other, some both.

Plan

Private resources

For some papers that you will write you already know enough to treat the subject well. Your own experiences will provide subjects and material for many college themes: what you have done in school and out, the jobs you have held, your hobbies, the people you know, the places you have visited, the courses you are taking in college. Consider this brief list of topics and see how many you could write on from your own experience:

Overcoming Self-Consciousness	Considerations in Buying a Car
A Job I Disliked	A Successful Amateur Play
Advice to a High-School Student About to Enter the University	The Perils of Teen-Age Marriage
	Building a Record Collection
Living Within a Budget	Planning a Vacation
Baby-Sitters Earn Their Pay	Hero Worship Among Teen-Agers
How to Handle Firearms Safely	

You need not feel that a paper based upon your personal experiences will be boring to others. Some college freshmen, particularly when writing their first themes, are afraid that their own experiences have been too limited, or that their opinions and attitudes are too commonplace to be of interest to anyone but themselves. But much published material is based upon incidents and attitudes that are in no way unique or sensational ("Making Your Hobby Pay," "The Most Unforgettable Character I Have Met," "Diary of a City-Bred Farmer," "Should Eighteen-Year-Olds Vote?") If a writer is interested in what he has to say, his readers probably will be too. A fresh and lively account of the experiences of a baby-sitter is more readable than a dull description of a journey up the Amazon. The problem in writing a personal experience paper, as demonstrated earlier by the analysis of the theme on "My Theater Experiences," is to discover a thesis worth writing about.

If you are far enough along in your thinking and planning to formulate a thesis, you will be able to tell whether or not your present knowledge, opinions, and attitudes are sufficient material. For papers based on personal experience, ask yourself as many questions as you can think of about the subject. If you are going to explain how a person should apply for a job, recall and analyze your own experiences in looking for work. How did you find out what jobs were available? How did you decide which jobs to apply for? Did you apply in person or by letter? If you were not

hired, what were the probable reasons? What mistakes, if any, did you make either during an interview or in your letter of application? If you were going to apply for another job, would you go about it in the same way?

A similar analysis will help you gather material for papers presenting personal opinions or attitudes. If you decide to enumerate the qualities of a good teacher, think of two or three of your teachers who were outstanding and try to discover what qualities they had in common: a sound knowledge of their subject? a genuine interest in students? a willingness to help the slower students? fairness in grading? a sense of humor? You could extend your analysis by considering also one or two teachers who were definitely unsatisfactory, to see what qualities they lacked.

At this stage of thinking about your subject, jot down on paper every idea that occurs to you, whether you are sure you will use it or not. One idea often suggests another and better one, and may help you to reshape or clarify your thesis. After a reasonable amount of reflection, you will usually have more than enough material to write a paper of the assigned length.

Public resources

Not all papers can be written entirely from personal opinion or experience. Many subjects call for information that must be gathered by reading, by observation, or through personal interviews. Some subjects will demand thorough research and formal presentation. Others may require only the addition of your casual reading as support. Still others—such as some of the interpretive essays you will be asked to do in English courses—may require that you gather additional information (for example, information about literary techniques), even though the paper is going to be an informal expression of your response to meaning in something you have read. It is perfectly permissible to use your reading casually for any subject that requires it—that is, not as in a formal report with documentation, but as the natural supplement to what you wish to say.

25.2

In using outside resources to develop material for a paper, read critically, and think about what you read. Be careful to distinguish between verifiable *facts* (the cost of living index in New York City and in Chicago) and *opinions* (the reasons why the Republican Party lost the 1964 election). On controversial subjects, read and weigh the opinions on all sides of the question before arriving at a firm opinion of your own.

Make the effort to understand and assimilate material from published sources before using it in a paper. Instead of copying an author's words, think about the ideas he is expressing. Do you agree or disagree with them? Why? Proper acknowledgment should always be made for borrowed material—in a footnote if the paper requires formal documentation, or informally if the situation seems to warrant, as for the quotations opening the sections of this handbook. (See §29.8, Documenting the paper, for details on using materials from printed sources.)

Your thesis and your resources

Your thesis statement and your resources work reciprocally. The thesis statement will help determine what resources are necessary, and the available resources will help sharpen the thesis. Suppose that for a paper on folk singing you have jotted down these preliminary ideas:

1) My interest in folk songs began in high school
2) Learn a lot about American history from them
3) European countries have native songs too
4) Some early folk songs have been lost
5) Most people prefer popular music
6) The lyrics reflect the interests of the people who made them up
7) You need no special musical training to sing folk songs
8) Unusual folk songs I have heard
9) My grandmother has taught me several songs
10) My mother sang songs when I was young that I later discovered were old folk songs

From these random notes you could frame several central ideas. If you formulated a thesis such as "Folk singing is both entertaining and educational," you would be able to concentrate on items 2, 6, 7, and 8 (and possibly 9 and 10), and you could develop the thesis adequately with your present knowledge of folk songs. If, on the other hand, item 6 attracted you, it could stand as your thesis sentence. It might be possible, if you were observant and were familiar with many folk songs, to develop this thesis too

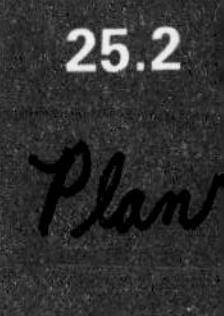

without using outside resources; but if the thesis engaged your interest further, it might require research to trace folk songs to their point of origin. Your own interests and the needs of your subject, in other words, will help to determine what resources you turn to.

25.3 Meeting your audience

There is no clear-cut, step-by-step process for settling all the problems of writing: they intermingle and work on each other. Your thesis, for example, helps determine what resources you will use, and your resources, in turn, may cause you to modify your thesis. Your thesis and your resources together may suggest a particular style (formal, for example, or informal, familiar, or detached), just as the needs of a particular style may call for particular kinds of resources. And your thesis, resources, and style will all be partly determined by the needs and interests of your particular audience. Well before you begin to write a paper, you should begin to see how these various considerations will affect one another, shaping not only what you say but how you say it.

There is a reciprocal relationship between subject and form, and if a writer focuses on either at the expense of the other, his writing will suffer. This relationship depends, as Professor Wayne Booth has put it, on a just and careful balance among the arguments available on the subject; the interests, needs, and peculiarities of the audience; and the character of the writer.

The writer's stance

It is possible—even common—for a writer to busy himself so at winning his audience that he does scant service to his subject and to himself. Taking what Professor Booth calls the "entertainer's stance," a writer can temporarily win his audience, like a *Time* movie reviewer, with wit and whimsy and sentences that seem well turned even if they have no serious context.

Good writing, by contrast, requires honesty of the writer—an honest, serious approach to his subject and to his audience, and an honest critical understanding of his own capabilities. We are all *partial* when we write, in that we cannot say all that is to be said on any subject; the demands of space and time, the interests and patience of our readers, and the inadequacies of our own character and knowledge make it unlikely that what we write can ever express an entire truth. But that does not mean that our piece of writing is by definition a poor thing. Indeed, it is the character of good writing that it is a single, limited voice speaking to think things out.

To say that a writer is necessarily partial and limited is not to say that he must be phony. He can *seem* to escape his incompleteness by resorting to standardized responses, stereotyped phrasing, and concepts uncritically accepted. And, in doing so, he can sometimes sound impressive: he can use elevated generalities, for example, or stereotyped impersonal language that allows him to pretend he is being totally objective. But it won't do.

Before you begin writing the first draft of a paper, you must discover where *you* stand with regard to your subject and to your audience. Have you engaged yourself in the subject enough to make it interesting to others? Have you weighed it to give it worth? What position will you take toward your subject in presenting it to your audience? Must you address the audience in strictly logical and impersonal fashion? Or does the subject justify a more emotional presentation? Or should you concentrate rather on the impression of yourself that will emerge through your writing? Can you combine these tactics in such a way that you and your audience will come together and share an idea?

Adjusting to the audience

"That book is good in vain," John Dryden said, "which the reader throws away." As you are planning a piece of writing, you must keep in mind the interests and needs of your particular audience. It is easy, of course, to forget your readers and to think only about your subject in some of the writing you will do in college. The announcement of an assigned subject, as has already been suggested, does not necessarily give you a purpose for writing; but unless you *discover* a purpose and relate it to your audience—usually, your class—even a dutiful fulfillment of the assignment will amount to little. If you ignore your audience, your work is bootless, no matter how correct.

Your audience will feel ignored if your writing seems aimless. Did you write *only* to count the images in a Shakespearean sonnet? To list the causes of an economic depression? To enumerate as expected the reasons you came to college? To describe six varieties of repression? To tell in meek conventionality how you spent your summer vacation? If so, why did you bother? Why are those Shakespearean images relevant to your audience? Why is it worth your audience's time to share your understanding of repression? What is the purpose of your writing?

Keeping your potential audience in mind will also help you to select the material you will use. How much do your readers already know about the subject? What information and explanation will they need? What kind of material are they likely to find most interesting?

If your subject is familiar to most readers—local architecture, for example, or traffic problems—eliminate obvious statements and develop the ideas that are most likely to arouse interest. Perhaps the majority of your class does not know that fashions in local architecture have changed three times in the last forty years, or that the building in which the class now meets was once considered radical in design. If it is common knowledge that the traffic situation in your city is deplorable, concentrate on other points: plans for traffic control that have been considered and rejected; the experience of other cities with one-way streets; the method of selecting and training traffic officers; the effect of traffic congestion on drivers' nerves or on local business.

When you are writing on a subject that most people know little about (operating a switchboard, taxidermy, Aztec religion), consider your material from the viewpoint of the general reader. What terms should be defined? What technical material should be explained or perhaps left out? What kinds of illustrations and examples will help make the subject as clear to the reader as it is to you?

Style and situation

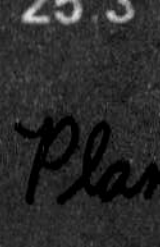

For a *reader*, the study of style is an effort to discover the qualities of language in a particular story or essay that give rise to his impressions of it, especially his response to those aspects of meaning that would be lost in a summary or paraphrase. But to a *writer*, style is something more than the character of his work after he has left it; it is a resource he brings to his task. A good writer knows, for example, that there are times to be taut and restrictive and times to be loose and expansive, and he knows that there are options in word choice, sentence pattern, and paragraph construction that can help him to achieve either end. He uses style, in other words, as one means for controlling the shape of his writing and making it relevant to his audience and situation.

Earlier in this section it was suggested that all writing, in the last analysis, is meant to be persuasive. An argumentative essay is clearly intended to persuade, of course, but even descriptive and narrative writing are persuasive in the sense that the writer wants his audience to see something as he has seen it or to understand a sequence of events as he has understood it. The means of persuasion vary, however, according to the writer's purpose and the situation in which he writes.

If a writer's purpose is to demonstrate or celebrate something in the *present* (in what was called *demonstrative* writing by earlier rhetoricians), his work is likely to be somewhat emotional in tone and to rely heavily on connotative and figurative language. President Kennedy's Berlin speech is an example of this use of language, its repeated refrain "Let them come to Berlin" gaining more fervor and emotional weight with each repetition. If, on the other hand, a writer's purpose is to effect policy and bring about change for the *future* (in what was formerly called *deliberative* writing), an honest weighing of the facts calls for a quieter language, a more thoughtful tone. If his purpose is to evaluate the *past* (in what was formerly called *judicial* or *forensic* writing), still other language may be appropriate—typically, language that is firm and forthright, judicious and unweighted.

Over the centuries rhetoricians have been concerned with classifying the different stylistic techniques that writers have used for these different kinds of writing. Although terminology has varied, most classifications of style have recognized the polarities of the *heightened* or *grand* style, which is elaborate and contrived and tends to make use of emotional connotations, and the *plain* style, which is literal and direct. Between these extremes is a range of *middle* or *mixed* styles, built on a conversational base but using some of the devices of the more elaborate grand style.

A writer can do few things worse, of course, than adopt a certain tone and style arbitrarily. But a writer who understands something about different styles can often adapt particular techniques to achieve particular purposes. (**See also** §23, Sentence variety, control, and emphasis.) Some of the techniques of sentence structure that characterize the *grand* style, for example, can be especially effective in building an emotional appeal. One such technique is a parallel sequence that moves toward an emotional climax:

> But in a larger sense we cannot dedicate, we cannot consecrate, we cannot hallow this ground.—Abraham Lincoln, Gettysburg Address

Another technique inverts normal sentence structure to make a long, building, periodic sentence (page 305):

> It is rather for us to be here dedicated to the great task remaining before us,—that from these honored dead we take increased devotion to that cause for which they gave the last full measure of devotion; that we here highly resolve that these dead shall not have died in vain; that this nation, under God, shall have a new birth of freedom; and that government of the people, by the people, and for the people, shall not perish from the earth.—*Ibid.*

Ending sentences with the same word or phrase (a device known as *epistrophe*) helps to give a compelling rhythm, a refrain-like character, to a group of sentences or to a whole paragraph. In Mark Antony's funeral oration, for example, the ironic repetition of "Brutus is an honourable man" works on the crowd and helps the speech build to its climax. Omitting connectives in a parallel series of phrases or clauses (*asyndeton*) can cause a sentence to seem filled with ideas that, because of their weight, cannot be delayed in expression, as in Caesar's famous "I came, I saw, I conquered."

The *middle* or *mixed* styles, perhaps most common in argumentative writing, depend on other techniques, appropriate for quite different effects. For example, the sobriety of the balanced sentence (page 310) suggests that the writer has considered the possibilities, weighed them carefully against each other, and made his judgment. The use of a connective between all parallel phrases or clauses in a series (*polysyndeton*) slows the pace of the work and gives it a deliberate, thoughtful tone:

> He is immortal, not because he alone among creatures has an inexhaustible voice, but because he has a soul, a spirit capable of compassion *and* sacrifice *and* endurance. The poet's, the writer's, duty is to write about these things. It is his privilege to help man endure by lifting his heart, by reminding him of the courage *and* honor *and*

> hope *and* pride *and* compassion *and* pity *and* sacrifice which have been the glory of his past.—William Faulkner, Speech accepting the Nobel Prize

Style, of course, is a personal thing, and techniques associated with one level often appear in other levels as well. Balanced and antithetical sentences, for example, may have their uses even in the *plain* style, though it commonly depends on simpler constructions. For a practiced writer, style is not a conscious concern but a by-product of his effort to make the language carry out his purpose in a particular situation.

A good deal of varied reading will help you become increasingly aware of the possibilities of the language and see how they may be adapted to your own material, purpose, and individual temperament. You can also work to improve your style by analyzing your own writing critically and experimenting with different ways of expressing the same idea. In the long run, however, an effective style depends on your purpose and integrity as a writer. The passage below is the first paragraph from a freshman theme titled "Censorship." The author's manner of writing —the form of the piece—defeats his meaning, which is wobbly enough anyway:

> As our society grows more sophisticated, more questionable topics are openly discussed in books, which enjoy wider distribution in our more literate age and culture. In reaction to this trend toward liberality there is arising a vocal group of citizens advocating censorship. It is really not surprising to find the same upright citizens, who were known as prohibitionists in the 1920's, indignantly calling for the banning of books whose subject matter and treatment they determine to be detrimental to the morals of our fair land. In the 1920's they believed that demon rum would corrupt the people and drive goodness from our American way of life. Today these same moralists argue that the literature which they condemn as lewd, if allowed to circulate freely, will eventually drive out good books and weaken the morals of our society.

Several things in this paragraph indicate that the writer has put down words without coming to grips with his subject and without concern for his reader. In the first sentence he refers to "questionable topics," which in no way informs the reader what he is talking about, since almost anything can be questionable. A few lines further on, he associates these "questionable

topics" with a "trend toward liberality," which a reader might mistake for compassion and generosity. Later still he carelessly identifies the people he is criticizing with the prohibitionists of the 1920's, though he must mean simply that they are the same kind of people. He does a disservice to both himself and his reader by continually using clichés ("upright citizens," "fair land," "demon rum," "American way of life") as a substitute for thinking. This writer, like all writers, has a style—but it is the lackadaisical, conditioned-reflex style of someone who is writing for no purpose.

25.4 Organizing your material

Before you begin to write, plan the order in which you intend to present your material. With some subjects the material itself will determine organization. For example, narratives (§28.4) and papers that describe personal experiences usually follow the order of events: first this happened, then this, then something else. An explanation of a process follows a similar step-by-step pattern of presentation. In descriptive writing ("Manhattan at Dawn," "A Trip Through the Carlsbad Caverns") the normal order may be from one point to another (entering the Caverns, going to the first level, arriving at the Big Room) or from a general impression to the specific details that give rise to it, arranged more or less in the order of prominence. (**See** §28.3, Description.)

The order of presentation may require more thought with other subjects, such as "A Criticism of Olivier's *Hamlet*" or "Repression and Rationalization as Defense Mechanisms." Whether you select the topic or your instructor assigns one, in most instances you will have to examine the material carefully to find the best order for your special purpose. (**See** §26.2, Developing your material, for suggestions about choosing a pattern of development.)

In organizing most papers, you will find it useful to make an outline. Four kinds of outlines are widely used: the scratch outline, the thesis-sentence outline, the topic outline, and the sentence outline. Sometimes your instructor will tell you which form he wants you to use. When he does not, select the form that best suits your method of working and the kind of paper you are writing. In planning a long paper, especially one involving research, you will probably want to make a topic or sentence outline. For short papers and extemporaneous writing, informal notes or a scratch outline will generally serve the purpose. Even for long papers, you may find it useful to work informally for some time before committing yourself to a final, detailed plan. It is not uncommon, for example, for writers at work on long projects to draft key passages—an opening paragraph, a closing paragraph, a passage developing the central idea—and then to fit these bits of writing into a more formal plan, along with jotted notes, sentences, and other scraps of ideas. Whatever techniques you use, the important thing is to develop a plan that will guide you in writing your paper.

Scratch outlines

A scratch outline is a series of notes—single words or phrases—jotted down to refresh your memory as you write. An outline of this sort is useful when time is limited, as when you are writing examinations or brief papers in class. The following is a sample scratch outline for a theme on the subject "The Value of Summer Jobs":

Earning money for clothes and school
Sense of responsibility
Learning to budget own time and money
Opportunity to learn about different kinds of jobs
Develop good work habits and maybe learn practical skills

The exact form of a scratch outline is not particularly important, since ordinarily you will be the only one who sees it. If the list is longer than five or six items, you will need to arrange the entries in some logical order (or number them) before beginning to write.

Thesis-sentence outlines

If you have developed a thesis sentence (page 348), you may be able to use its parts as the terms of your outline. This can be especially helpful for short papers and essay examinations. Suppose, for example, that upon arriving in class you are given an assignment to write a short theme during the class period, and that one of the possible topics is "Campus Fashions." Suppose further that your experience and observation enable you within

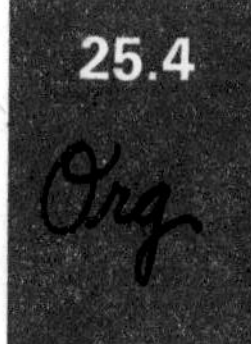

a few moments to jot down the following ideas on this general subject:

> Something like hippie dress is fairly common
> Standard fraternity-sorority dress is just as common
> There are some variations
> Most people dress pretty much alike
> It's getting harder to tell the two styles apart

It is possible to arrange these notes as a scratch outline, as suggested above. Another moment's reflection, however, might enable you to exercise tighter control over your theme by formulating a thesis sentence such as this:

> While there are some interesting variations in fashion here and there on campus, the dominant modified hippie and standard fraternity dress, which draw closer together every day, give our campus a near-homogeneous appearance.

If you can get this far quickly, you can use the thesis sentence as your outline. The sentence above, for example, could forecast a fairly brief, six-paragraph theme, each paragraph developing in sequence the structural units of the thesis sentence:

> Paragraph 1: a brief introduction that ends with the thesis sentence
>
> Paragraph 2: the interesting variations in fashion (this, judging from the form of the thesis, is an interesting but minor part of the theme)
>
> Paragraph 3: the modified hippie style
>
> Paragraph 4: the standard fraternity style
>
> Paragraph 5: recent illustrations that show the two coming together
>
> Paragraph 6: a conclusion on the homogeneity of style on your campus

One particular advantage of this method of organizing is that you can plan the shape and emphasis of your theme by planning the shape and emphasis of your thesis sentence. Your observation might lead you to revise the thesis sentence above in this way:

25.4

> While the dominant modified hippie and standard fraternity dress (which draw closer every day) give our campus a near-homogeneous appearance, some very interesting variations have appeared here this year.

A short theme developed from this sentence would have a totally different emphasis from the one suggested above.

Topic outlines

The topic outline, the most frequently used kind of formal outline, is helpful in organizing papers of more than five hundred words. It consists of brief phrases or single words (not sentences) which are numbered or lettered to show the order and relative importance of the ideas.

The first thing to do is to get all your ideas down on paper. On the subject "The Army as a Career," your preliminary thinking might produce this rough, unsorted list of ideas:

Security
Promotion slow but steady
Many different branches appeal to different men
Low pay
Depression won't bother you
Can't be fired
Cost of uniforms
Discipline often annoying
Frequent moves hard on soldier's family
See interesting places and people
Social life restricted to small circle
Good retirement benefits
Annual vacation with pay
Many military men later successful in politics and business

Determining the central idea. A quick glance at the list above reveals that some points stress the advantages of an army career; others, the disadvantages. The next step then is to divide the notes into two columns:

Advantages	*Disadvantages*
Security	Low pay
Promotion slow but steady	Cost of uniforms
Many different branches appeal to different men	Discipline often annoying
Depression won't bother you	Frequent moves hard on soldier's family
Can't be fired	Social life restricted to small circle
See interesting places and people	
Good retirement benefits	
Annual vacation with pay	
Many military men later successful in politics and business	

In this form the relationship between the various ideas is not shown (What is the relationship between "Promotion slow but steady" and "Many different branches appeal to different men"?) and there is no clear balance between the two columns (Is "Security" supposed to balance "Low pay"?). In analyzing the columns, however, you can see that there are two main ideas in each—the financial aspect of an army career and the living conditions that go with army life. You might then balance the notes in this way:

I. Financial aspect
    A. Disadvantages
        1. Low pay
        2. Cost of uniforms
    B. Advantages
        1. Security
        2. Slow but steady promotion
        3. Depression won't bother you
        4. Can't be fired
        5. Good retirement benefits
        6. Annual vacation with pay
        7. Many military men later successful in politics and business
II. Social aspect
    A. Disadvantages
        1. Discipline often annoying
        2. Frequent moves hard on soldier's family
        3. Social life restricted to small circle
    B. Advantages
        1. Many different branches appeal to different men
        2. See interesting people and places

When the notes are arranged in some system, decide on the main point you want to make in your paper. "The Army as a Career" doesn't tell what you are going to *say* about the subject; it is a title, not a central idea.

At this stage you can see that there is more and stronger material on the financial advantages of a military career than on its disadvantages. On the other hand, the disadvantages of living conditions seem to outweigh the advantages. But assuming that you want to treat the subject fully and in a favorable light, you could frame a tentative statement of purpose: "Although there are definite disadvantages to an army career, the advantages outweigh them." This statement will now govern the reworking of

the outline. At this stage it is still tentative and can be changed as the purpose becomes clearer in your mind.

Revising the outline. With the central idea as your guide, arrange the outline so that every part of it contributes directly to the purpose of the paper. Examine each heading separately to see if it needs to be strengthened or elaborated upon, if it repeats or overlaps another heading, or if it is unrelated to the central idea.

In the first part of the outline "Cost of uniforms" seems to be a weak point. Aren't officers given allowances for their uniforms? Possibly "Expense of frequent entertaining" is a stronger point, so substitute it for "Cost of uniforms."

The financial advantages of an army career seem to stand out, but looking at these entries closely, you will see that some overlap or are actually minor parts of other points. The heading "Security" obviously covers "Slow but steady promotion" and "Can't be fired." The third heading, "Depression won't bother you," is probably superfluous, since it really is part of "Can't be fired." Closer examination reveals that "Annual vacation with pay" is an aspect of living conditions rather than of finances; it should therefore be shifted to the second main heading.

Under "Advantages" in the second main heading, the first entry "Many different branches appeal to different men" seems out of place or else incorrectly phrased. Perhaps the point is that military men can find the jobs they like or are best fitted for.

As the plan now stands, the first part seems to be the stronger. To make the argument more convincing, it would be a good idea to reverse the present order: begin with "Living conditions," and then end the paper on an emphatic note—the training that the army affords for success in other fields. After these changes have been made, and after some headings have been reworded to make them parallel in form, the final outline might be:

Thesis sentence: From the standpoint of finances and living conditions, there are some disadvantages to an army career, but the advantages outweigh them.

I. Living conditions
  A. Disadvantages
    1. Discipline often annoying
    2. Frequent moves hard on soldier's family
    3. Social life restricted to a small circle

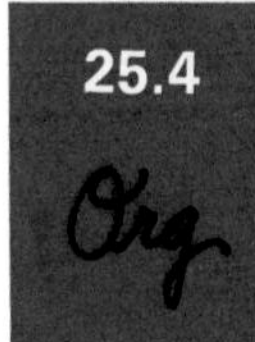

B. Advantages
   1. Opportunity to find the job one is best fitted for
   2. Annual leaves with pay
   3. Chance to travel, to see new places, and to meet new people

II. Financial considerations
   A. Disadvantages
      1. Low pay
      2. Frequent entertaining expensive
   B. Advantages
      1. Security
         a. Slow but steady promotion
         b. Permanent employment
         c. Good retirement benefits
      2. Preparation for success in business or politics after retirement

The outline now can be the basis for an orderly paper that makes a definite point.

Sentence outlines

A sentence outline is developed in exactly the same way as a topic outline, but the ideas are more fully expressed. Each heading is expressed as a complete sentence, usually consisting of just one main clause:

Thesis sentence: From the standpoint of finances and living conditions, there are some disadvantages to an army career, but the advantages outweigh them.

I. Living conditions are a major consideration in choosing a career.
   A. Army life has several shortcomings in this respect.
      1. The strict discipline imposed is often annoying.
      2. Frequent moves are hard on a soldier's family.
      3. Social life is usually restricted to a small circle of army families.
   B. On the other hand, there are certain advantages to life in the army.
      1. The military, with its wide range of occupations, gives one an opportunity to find the job he is best suited for.
      2. There are generous annual leaves with pay.
      3. Wide travel opportunities can introduce one to new places and people.

II. Financial considerations are also of major importance.
   A. Two disadvantages are apparent.
      1. Army pay is low compared to that in many civilian jobs.
      2. Officers are burdened with the cost of frequent entertaining.

B. The advantages, however, are more striking.
   1. The army offers a high degree of job security.
      a. Promotions are slow but steady.
      b. There is almost no danger of dismissal.
      c. Retirement benefits are good.
   2. An army career is an excellent preparation for success in business or politics after retirement.

Each heading is a complete sentence, and only one sentence—not two or three. Each sentence is also in the form of a statement, not a question.

The chief advantage of a sentence outline is that the ideas will have to be clear and fully thought out before they can be stated in complete sentences. For that reason it is sometimes assigned for training in writing long formal reports such as the reference paper.

Standard outline form

Numbering, indention, punctuation, and other physical aspects of outlines follow certain conventions, particularly when the outlines are to be read by someone other than the writer. When you are required to turn in an outline with your paper, use the type of outline your instructor specifies and put it in standard form.

Numbering and indention. Make the numbering of your headings consistent throughout. This is the typical method for numbering and indenting a topic or sentence outline:

Thesis sentence: ______________________________

______________________	(Sentence statement)
I. ____________________	(Roman numeral for main head)
A. ____________________	(Capital letter for subhead)
1. ____________________	(Arabic numeral for second sub-
2. ____________________	head)
a. ____________________	(Lower case letter for third sub-
b. ____________________	head)
B. ____________________	
II. ____________________	

The main heads (I, II, III . . .) are set flush with the left-hand margin. The subheads are indented four or five spaces in typed copy and about three quarters of an inch in longhand, or they may be indented so that they are directly under the first word of the preceding heading, as shown in this book.

25.4

When a heading runs over one line, the second line is indented as far as the first word of the preceding line:

I. The photoelectric cell, known as the "electric eye," has been put to a variety of practical uses.
   A. It is used in elevator floors to enable the elevator to stop at exactly the right level.

When you make an outline, avoid overelaborate and confusing systems. There is rarely any need to go farther than the third subhead (a, b, c . . .). Two levels of headings are often enough for a short paper.

Punctuation and capitalization. In a topic outline, capitalize only the first letter of the word beginning the heading (and all proper nouns), and do not put any punctuation at the end of the entry, because these headings are not complete sentences.

I. Present need for physicists
   A. In private industry
   B. In government projects
   C. In colleges and universities

Punctuate every heading in a sentence outline just as you would punctuate the sentences in your paper: begin with a capital letter and end with a period or other end stop. Except for proper nouns, other words in the heading are not capitalized (a heading is not a title).

I. The advantages of specialization in college are numerous.
   A. The student is able to set a goal for himself.
   B. He can obtain more knowledge about his subject.

Content of headings. Each heading in an outline should be specific and meaningful:

Vague and useless	*Specific*
The Profession I Want to Follow	The Profession I Want to Follow
I. Introduction	I. Lifelong interest in veterinarian's work
II. Why I prefer this work	A. Grew up with animals on a farm
III. What the opportunities would be	B. Saw importance of veterinarian's work
IV. The chances for success	C. Worked with a veterinarian last two summers
V. Conclusion	

II. Many opportunities in veterinary work today
  A. In rural areas
  B. In cities
III. Worth-while and well-paid profession

Headings like "Introduction," "Body," and "Conclusion" aren't useful unless you indicate what material belongs in the sections. Instead of using general labels such as "Causes" and "Results," indicate what the causes or results are; it will save time later.

Putting headings in the form of questions or in statements that will have to be filled in later is not an efficient practice. The necessary information will have to be supplied when you write, so you might as well supply it in the planning stage.

Indefinite

I. The Wars of the Roses
  A. When they began
  B. Why?

Definite

I. The Wars of the Roses
  A. Started 1455
  B. Caused by rivalry between Houses of Lancaster and York

Dividing the material. If a heading is to be divided at all, it should be divided into more than one part. This practice is based upon the principle that nothing can be divided into fewer than two parts. For every heading marked *I*, there should be at least a *II*, for every *A*, there should be a *B*, and so on.

Inaccurate division

The Three Branches of the Federal Government
I. The executive branch
  A. President and Cabinet
II. The legislative branch
  A. The House of Representatives
  B. The Senate
    1. Functions
III. The judicial branch
  A. The Supreme Court

Accurate division

The Three Branches of the Federal Government
I. The executive branch
  A. President
  B. Cabinet
II. The legislative branch
  A. The House of Representatives
  B. The Senate
    1. Special functions
    2. Special privileges
III. The judicial branch
  A. The Supreme Court
  B. Lower courts

When there is only one heading under a topic, it usually repeats what is in the topic and should therefore be included with it:

Unnecessary division

The Smithsonian Institution
I. Established by an Englishman
  A. James Smithson
    1. In 1846

Accurate division

The Smithsonian Institution
I. Established by James Smithson, an Englishman, in 1846

The main heads of an outline should represent equally important divisions of the subject as a whole.

Unequal headings

Growing Roses
I. Preparing the soil
II. Planting
III. Growing the plant
IV. Mildew
V. Insect pests
VI. Using a spray gun

Equal headings

Growing Roses
I. Preparing the soil
II. Planting
III. Watering
IV. Fertilizing
V. Spraying

Similarly the subdivisions should designate equally important divisions of one phase of the main divisions:

Unequal subheads

I. Job opportunities in Wisconsin
  A. Raising crops
  B. White-collar work
  C. Dairy farms
  D. Factory jobs
  E. Breweries

Equal subheads

I. Job opportunities in Wisconsin
  A. Agriculture
  B. Business
  C. Industry

Headings of equal rank should not overlap: what is in *II* should exclude what is covered in *I; B* should be clearly distinct from *A*.

Overlapping

Ways of transporting freight
I. Water
  A. Ships
  B. Freighters
II. On the ground
  A. Trucks
  B. "Piggyback" in trucks
III. Railroads
IV. In the air

Accurate

Ways of transporting freight
I. Ship
  A. Passenger ships
  B. Freighters
II. Truck
III. Railroad
  A. Loaded into cars
  B. "Piggyback" in trucks
IV. Airplane

Making headings parallel. Headings in the same series are put in the same grammatical form. In a topic outline, if *I* is a noun, *II* and *III* are also nouns; if *I* is a prepositional phrase, so are *II* and *III*. The same principle applies to subdivisions: when *A* under *I* is an adjective, *B* and *C* are also adjectives. A sentence outline should use complete sentences throughout and not lapse into topic headings. The following examples show how headings can be made parallel in form:

Headings not parallel	*Parallel headings*
The Art of Putting	The Art of Putting
I. The stance is fundamental	I. The stance
II. The grip	II. The grip
III. Importance of the backswing	III. The backswing
IV. Stroking the ball	IV. The contact with the ball
V. Follow through with care	V. The follow-through
The Selective Service System	The Selective Service System
II. Four reasons for deferment	II. Four reasons for deferment
A. Because of occupation	A. Occupation
B. Dependents	B. Dependents
C. Some are physically unfit	C. Physical disability
D. Because of age	D. Age

The outline in relation to the paper

The usefulness of an outline depends on the material in it. No matter how correct the form—in numbering, punctuation, and parallel structure—if the outline doesn't help in writing your paper, its main purpose has been defeated.

From the main divisions in a good outline you can estimate the number and the relative length of the paragraphs in your paper, although usually the paragraphs will not correspond exactly to the headings. You can frequently construct topic sentences for these paragraphs by rephrasing or expanding the headings. The divisions will show where transitions are needed within and between paragraphs and suggest the kind of development: contrast, comparison, additional illustration, summary, and so fōrth. (See §24.2, Patterns of paragraph development, and §26.2, Developing your material.)

An outline should be long enough to suit your purpose, and no longer. It should be no more complex than the material demands. The number of main headings for most papers ranges from three

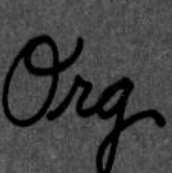

to five. A larger number of main heads for a thousand-word paper suggests that the division is haphazard or that the organization is faulty. The same principle applies to subheadings. Outlines that run from *A* through *J* or *K* need revision, for no single topic needs such minute subdivision. And except for very complex material, there is seldom any need to go beyond the third subhead.

When you are asked to submit an outline with your paper, it should represent the plan of the paper as it actually has been written, not as it *might* have been written. In other words, your outline serves as the table of contents. If you have found it necessary in writing the paper to depart from your original plan, make the corresponding changes in the final outline before handing it in.

Exercises

1. *Limiting the subject.* Select three of the following *general* subjects and for each one write down two *specific* topics that would be suitable for a paper of 500 words and two topics for a 1000- to 1200-word paper.

Campus fashions
Campus protest movements
College architecture
Prestige symbols
Modern heroes
School discipline
Academic freedom
Machines in education
Current music
Science fiction
Population growth
Study abroad
Student summer work
Television standards
Automobile safety
Student power
Automation
Grading practices
The older generation
Popular myths
Sunday school
The hippie movement

2. *Topics based on personal experience.* Make up a list of topics, based upon your past experiences, of specific matters that you would like to write about and that might interest others. Make an inventory of places you have lived in or visited; people you know; jobs you have had; sports, hobbies, reading, plays, movies; subjects you like to talk or argue about. If you do this early in the course, you will have a ready supply of material for papers in which the choice of subject is left up to you.

3. *Topics for investigation.* Prepare a list of topics for investigation. They may range from some aspects of aeronautics to voodoo practices in the West Indies—any matter that interests you or about which you would like to know more. When your list is complete, select two subjects you think would make good papers of 500 words each, two for papers of 1200 words each, and one suitable for a 2500-word paper.

4. *Sticking to the central idea.* Examine the controlling idea for each of these three topics. What points listed should be changed or eliminated? How would you group the remaining ideas?

Salmon Fishing: Salmon fishing is a thrilling and inexpensive sport.

1) Requires skill
2) Prizes offered for biggest fish
3) Equipment need not be expensive
4) Boats can be rented cheaply
5) Salmon fight to the last breath
6) Columbia River and Puget Sound two of the best areas
7) Conservation efforts have paid off
8) Baked salmon is a delectable dish
9) How the Indians prepare salmon
10) No thrill equals that first strike
11) A sport for young and old

Regulating Children's TV Habits: Although some TV programs are undesirable, parents should not regulate what children watch.

1) There are some excellent educational programs
2) Developing good judgment depends on practice in choosing
3) TV often takes place of baby-sitter
4) Children want to watch what playmates watch
5) Some TV programs bad for immature minds
6) Children resent too much discipline
7) Outdoor exercise also important
8) Free play of curiosity develops intellect
9) Violence fascinates children
10) Many sponsors aim programs at children
11) Parents should set good example for children
12) Overprotection in youth produces distorted ideas of reality

Mexico and the United States: Despite obvious differences, Mexico and the United States have much in common.

1) Both are in North America
2) Mexico has little industrial development

3) Populations are mixtures of many nationalities
4) Private enterprise basic to both
5) Mexico still not largely middle class, like U.S.
6) Poor transportation in much of Mexico
7) Both are republics with two-party systems
8) Mexico had great Indian civilization before Spanish conquest
9) Many Mexicans live in southwestern U.S.
10) Mexico revolted against the Spanish
11) Both provide extensive public welfare and free education
12) Great variety of natural resources in each

5. *Analysis of planning.* The following essay was written as an assignment for a freshman composition class. Write a critique of the essay with respect to the matters discussed in this section. Does it have a specific, manageable subject? Does the author seem to have a purpose in writing about it? What resources does the subject call for? Which has the author used? Might he have done better with other resources? What is his attitude? How does he seem to approach his audience? Does he accommodate his audience in his writing? Does his manner of writing seem appropriate for the subject and the situation? Is it natural to him? These are some of the matters you might consider. How you consider them, and in what order, is another problem of planning for you.

The Motion Picture Industry and Science Fiction

Science fiction has become stereotyped in the minds of the American public as juvenile and escapist literature through the greed of the Hollywood film industry.

Over the years, motion picture producers have flooded the country with a stream of "monster" and "space" movies. In so doing, they have created a distorted image of science fiction in the minds of most Americans, a conception of science fiction which causes the average person to assume that any book labeled as science fiction must be the story of a gigantic monster intent on destroying the world or that of a race of intelligent beings intent on destroying mankind.

The American public cannot be blamed for believing this to be a true picture of science fiction; for the great mass of evidence upon which they have had to base their judgment has been overwhelmingly of the trashy type. This is not to say that "monster" and "alien" movies must always be of this inferior type, but that they must remain so only so long as Hollywood can make two bad ones for the price of one good.

If we ignore the movies based, more or less, on the novels of Jules Verne and H. G. Wells because of their dated themes, we find that there have been very few films written by science fiction authors. I am personally familiar with only four such movies. "Voyage to the Bottom of the Sea," by Theodore Sturgeon, was so unlike his usual style of writing as to cast doubt on his authorship. George Orwell's "1984" was terribly cut and rewritten for the screen. "Out of the Cold," by John Campbell, was retitled "The Thing" and was turned into an ordinary "monster" movie by Hollywood. Finally, Robert A. Heinlein's "Destination: Moon" was hailed by many people as the finest science fiction movie ever made.

The last of these four movies, "Destination: Moon," has been widely acclaimed, but it contained not a single monster or extra-terrestrial creature and in addition won an Academy Award in one of the Academy's technical divisions. "Destination: Moon" should have shown Hollywood that science fiction movies could be more than just another "monster" movie. A glance at today's movie listings which contain an advertisement for "Ghidrah, the Three-Headed Dragon" will show that even concrete evidence cannot shake the Hollywood mentality.

Because of this unreasoning attitude, only the power of the dollar can ever force Hollywood to produce science fiction films that deal with man's destiny and the problems that will confront him in the years to come instead of its usual fare of monsters and aliens. This could only be brought about by action on the part of the general public, but because the public has been convinced it knows all about science fiction, this is impossible. Science fiction readers thus faced with an insoluble problem are reduced to a vague and uncertain hope that the future will bring a change for the better. The movie industry has prevailed, and science fiction must remain stereotyped.

6. *Scratch outlines and topic outlines.* Write a scratch outline on any one of the following topics that appeals to you. When you have jotted down all your notes, frame a thesis sentence and put the notes in the form of a topic outline. Use accurate subdivisions.

Learning to Dance
Why Writing Is Difficult
Why People Watch Excavations
A High Fidelity System
Secrets of Good Cooking
Should Physical Education Be Required in College?
Income Is Not the Primary Goal of Education
Managing a Rummage Sale
Speaking in Public
Fraternity and Sorority Rushing
Hot Rods
Unusual Place Names
Forecasting Election Results
I Prefer Bach
Our Local Parking Problem

7. *Outline form.* Study the following outlines from the standpoint of effective and useful planning. Then state specifically what you consider to be the unsatisfactory aspects of each one, either in form or content. Revise the outlines.

1) Types of American schools
    I. Schools open to everyone
        A. Elementary schools
        B. There are many colleges and universities
        C. Secondary or high
        D. Providing technical instruction
        E. Private schools

2) Why everyone should be able to swim.
    I. Everyone should learn to swim.
        A. As early as possible.
            1. Children have been taught as young as three years
    II. The ability to swim may save your life.
        1. never swim alone
        2. don't show off in the water
        3. Many schools require students to pass swimming tests.
            a. my experiences
            b. Red Cross lifesaving test.

3) Increasing automation in industry presents many problems.
    I. Unemployment
        A. Permanent layoffs
        B. Shorter working hours
        C. Decreases job opportunities
    II. What is automation?
        A. Definition
        B. Uses
            1. Where it cannot be used
        C. There are many advantages to automation
    III. Increased leisure time
        A. Recreation
            1. Hobbies
            2. Traveling
            3. Adult education classes
    IV. New skills are required.
        A. Trained technicians
        B. The unskilled workers are laid off.
            1. Providing government benefits
            2. Providing added training
    V. Is automation here to stay?

26 Writing the first draft

The only reason I can think of for the somewhat higher average of good writing in France is that the brouillon *is a national institution. The* brouillon *(literally: scrambled mess) is the first draft, and even the concierge writing to the police about anarchists on the third floor begins with a* brouillon, *later found by his heirs.—Jacques Barzun*

When you are reasonably satisfied with your preparations and your scheme for organizing your material, you are ready to begin the actual writing. Papers composed outside the classroom should always be written out in rough draft first, then revised and copied. No matter how certain you are about the material and the order of presentation, a complete first draft is essential if the final paper is to represent your best work.

Up to this point you have been dealing with ideas in abbreviated or shorthand form as notes or outline headings, though you may have written bits and pieces in complete form. Now you are ready to put it all down in full sentences and paragraphs, to see the whole paper as your reader will, and to make whatever changes may be necessary for continuity and effectiveness.

26.1 Getting started

Begin writing the first draft as soon as you have decided on the contents and organization of the paper. Don't wait for "inspiration" or for the proper mood. For almost everyone, writing is work, and just as with other tasks, you must often begin writing when you would much prefer to do something else. If you wait until the last minute, your first draft may have to serve as your final paper.

The beginning of a paper is often the most difficult part to word effectively. If you can't think of a good opening sentence, begin with some other part; if the wording of a good first paragraph doesn't come to you at once, start with a part that comes more easily. You shouldn't waste time trying to get an ideal opening; as you work, a good start will usually occur to you. Many beginnings are actually written last. (See §26.4, Opening paragraphs.)

Once you have broken the ice by writing two or three sentences, you will find it easier to go on, even without that elusive "inspiration." Writing, like many other activities, calls for a warm-up.

As a rule, write the first draft as rapidly as you can. Your paper will have more life if you put your ideas down one after the other without pausing to worry about correctness. This is the stage at which you should concentrate on getting down the gist of what you have in mind. You are the only one who will see your first draft, and matters of spelling, punctuation, and wording will be taken care of in revision. (See §27.1, Revising the first draft.)

Plan to spend at least an hour at uninterrupted writing. When you are working on a paper that is too long to be written in one sitting, stop in the middle of a paragraph or a passage that is going easily and well, perhaps even in the middle of a sentence. This ordinarily makes it much easier to get started again when you come back to your work. Take time to read over what you have already written before you begin writing again.

Leave plenty of space in the first draft for making corrections and changes. There should be ample margins on both sides of the page and space between lines for insertions and corrections.

26.2 Developing your material

Make the first draft as complete as possible. Write down more than you will probably use in your final paper; be generous with explanations and illustrative examples. It is much easier to cut out material in revision than it is to look for more to satisfy the requirements of length or completeness of presentation. Papers that are heavy with material added at the last moment always seem disjointed. Those that have been pruned down from, say, fourteen hundred to a thousand words are more compact and to the point.

Put in any good ideas that occur to you when you are writing the first draft, even though they may not have appeared in the original plan. In this stage an outline does not need to be followed down to the last minor sub-division. Frequently a sentence written on paper will bring to mind an aspect of the topic that you overlooked when your material was in the form of notes. If the new idea turns out to be irrelevant, it can be omitted in revision; but if it is important, you can alter your outline to include it.

Kinds of development

As the full paper grows from the organization plan you have decided on, it should follow the form of development that best suits the subject and that will be clearest to the reader. The patterns of development discussed in the section on paragraphs (§24.2) are applicable to whole papers as well, but often adequate development of a paper requires a combination of different kinds of paragraphs. Which kind predominates is determined by the plan of the paper. These are some of the most commonly used types of order:

1) *Time:* describing events in the order of their occurrence. This is appropriate in narrative writing (the story of a hike, a report of an athletic contest, an account of an incident in history) or in describing a process (the construction of a log cabin, the application of stage make-up, stages in the development of a frog).

2) *Space:* describing spatial objects in expository writing (a description of a city from outskirts to center, of a ship from bow to stern, of a mural from left to right).

3) *Increasing complexity:* beginning with the simple or familiar and proceeding to the more complex or unfamiliar (discussing wind instruments beginning with the toy whistle, continuing to simple flutes, and ending with orchestral instruments like the oboe and bassoon).

4) *Comparison and contrast:* discussing all the features of one idea or situation, then all the features of another, and ending by drawing a conclusion about the two ("The Radio and Newspapers As Sources of News," "Popular Heroes of Two Generations," "Public Schools and Private Schools"). If such a plan seems to make the paper break in the middle, present a sequence of comparisons and contrasts on each major point—not all the features of public schools and then of private schools, but some order like this: 1. Cost of attendance, 2. Curriculum, 3. Facilities.

5) *Support:* beginning with a general statement or impression and then supporting it with specific examples, details, reasons. This method is useful for such topics as "The Value of Studying Foreign Languages," "The Problems of Increasing Automation," "Freshman Composition Courses Should Be Abolished."

6) *Climax:* beginning with a specific fact or situation and unfolding the subject until it stands completed at the end. A paper about the development of the polio vaccine might begin with the need for the vaccine, then take up the problems facing researchers, go

on to explain how solutions were found, and end with the production of an effective vaccine.

7) *Cause to effect* or *effect to cause:* beginning with an analysis of causes, culminating in a statement of effect, or stating the effect first, then moving to the analysis of cause. The subject should determine which pattern is better: if you are writing about your city's traffic mess, for example, you might want to describe that problem briefly at the beginning as an effect already known, then proceed to an analysis of the causes, which are probably less well known.

The working outline should represent the kind of development most appropriate to your subject. For example, the topic outline for the paper on the army as a career (page 365), with its grouping of advantages and disadvantages, lent itself naturally to the comparison-and-contrast method. Often two kinds of development are used in combination: a narrative could follow both the order of time and that of climax; the method of support might be used effectively with comparison or climax. The essential thing is that you present your material in some sensible order.

Using sentences to control direction

One way to get into your draft and develop your meaning—especially if you are having trouble starting your paper or a particular section of it—is to use a sentence to direct the development. In your opening, for example, you can use your thesis sentence to forecast the development of your theme as a whole. (See §25.4, page 361, Thesis-sentence outlines.) And in the body of your paper, you can similarly work with sentences to direct the development of each section.

Suppose that you have developed this topic outline as the basis for a paper:

The Profession I Want to Follow

Thesis sentence: I want to become a veterinarian because of my lifelong interest in veterinary work, because of the many opportunities it offers, and because it is a worth-while and well-paid profession.

26.2

I. Lifelong interest in veterinarian's work
  A. Grew up with animals on a farm
  B. Saw importance of veterinarian's work
  C. Worked with a veterinarian last two summers

II. Many opportunities in veterinary work today
    A. In rural areas
    B. In urban areas
III. Worth-while and well-paid profession

The thesis sentence is a guide, directing the development of the outline and the theme. It could be used, for example, to forecast a climactic development that places increasing stress on the series of three factors.

The separate sections of the theme could also be directed by opening sentences. For example, we can assume that Section I will require at least three paragraphs. To control the relationships among them, the writer could introduce the section like this:

> Although I grew up with animals on a farm and saw the importance of the veterinarian's work, I didn't really understand all that a veterinarian does until I worked with one the last two summers.

This sentence, which might be used to open the first paragraph of the first section or might be used alone as an introduction, shows how the ideas in Section I are related and gives the writer a direction: there is a time sequence which suggests that he might make the three paragraphs of this section narrative; the last paragraph should probably get the dominant stress.

The first section closes with the idea that the writer is aware of the value of the veterinary profession. Section II, then, might open with a sentence like this:

> The needs for veterinary work are great in the country and surprisingly varied in the city.

This sentence, which makes the rural and urban needs coordinate, could forecast a balanced treatment by the method of comparison. The section would probably be developed in two paragraphs. Section III might then be directed in this way:

> Because the needs for veterinary medicine are great, the work is worth while; because the work is needed, the pay is good.

This balanced introductory sentence could lead the writer into a balanced, judicious paragraph stating an effect—the causes having been analyzed in Sections I and II.

Using paragraphs to control direction

Sometimes a writer can also use particular patterns of paragraph development (§24.2) to determine a means of expanding his material. For example, given the thesis sentence and outline just discussed, he might find it helpful in developing his material to think of the three paragraphs of Section I as statements of cause. He could then develop all three paragraphs by illustration, which is one of the methods for explaining cause. He could do the same thing with Section II. This would give the writer five illustrative paragraphs stating causes; the paper could then culminate in a final paragraph stating the effect. By planning a theme in this way, a writer can know beforehand what should be accomplished in each paragraph.

Using paragraph patterns can be especially helpful in writing short themes. Suppose you arrive in your composition class some Monday morning to find an assignment on the blackboard for an in-class theme. One of the suggested subjects invites your response to the idea of an honor system. If you are familiar with the patterns of paragraph development, you might be able very quickly to settle on a design, a means of developing your paper. Not everyone has participated in an honor system; not everyone knows what it is. You might therefore decide that the purpose of your paper would be to explain what an honor system is. Knowing the pattern of definition, you could develop your explanation like this:

> Paragraph 1: entirely *illustration*, describing an honor system in action
>
> Paragraph 2: *comparison* of honor system with similar things, such as codes of behavior in clubs
>
> Paragraph 3: *contrast*, an account of how honor system is unlike other codes

The sequence of three paragraphs forms a definition: the first by illustration identifies the *term;* the second by comparison puts the term in a *class;* the third by contrast shows how it *differs* from other members of the same class. With this three-paragraph definition, you might then be able to write a fourth, concluding paragraph of evaluation.

26.3 Relating paragraphs in sequence

As you write your first draft, remember that you are going to have to take a reader with you. Your individual paragraphs should represent a progressive development of the subject. If there is too wide a gap in ideas between the end of one paragraph and the beginning of the next, the reader may not be able to follow your line of thought.

Showing the connection between paragraphs

Link paragraphs together by connecting the topic of a new paragraph with the topic of the preceding one. Usually the easiest way to do this is to phrase the opening statement of a paragraph so that it grows out of what you have just said. This method of continuity is illustrated in the following sentences from the first five paragraphs of an essay comparing the matrimonial prospects of girls in women's colleges with those of girls in coeducational institutions:

. . . Yet surely a woman has as much—or as little—natural right to spurn matrimony as a man has.	End of 1st paragraph
Nevertheless not many of us today care to sing the praises of celibacy. . . .	Start of 2nd paragraph
. . . Today we as a people set more store on marriage than ever before in our history.	End of 2nd paragraph
This growing sense of the value of matrimony has boosted the prestige of coeducation among us. . . .	Start of 3rd paragraph
. . . By contrast it is suspected that separate colleges for women . . . by supposedly cloistering the girls and reducing their contacts with men to social events, cut down chances of marriage.	End of 3rd paragraph
In defense, the advocates of women's colleges have been a bit sniffy and condescending about the "matrimonial bureaus" which they say are operated on coeducational campuses. . . .	Start of 4th paragraph
. . . At times they have even implied that . . . only college girls of	End of 4th paragraph

relatively feeble intellect will let themselves lapse into domesticity.	
The American public has enough common sense to see that most of this is an elaborate whistling in the dark. . . . —Lynn White, Jr., "Do Women's Colleges Turn Out Spinsters?" *Harper's Magazine*, October 1952, p. 44	Start of 5th paragraph

This example shows that paragraphs are connected by the same methods used to link sentences within a paragraph (§24.3): by repetition of an important word (paragraph 4: *women's colleges*), by a pronoun or a synonym (paragraph 5: *this;* paragraph 3: *this growing sense of the value of matrimony*), or by a connective word (paragraph 2: *Nevertheless*).

Showing the relation to the topic of the paper

Whenever possible, show the relation between the paragraph and the topic or thesis of the paper. This is a good way to keep your paragraphs going in the same direction. For example, in this discussion of the games played by primitive peoples, the author begins each paragraph by introducing a different kind of sport:

Wrestling is probably universal....	1st paragraph (four sentences follow)
Races are far more common	2nd paragraph (three sentences follow)
Ball games are also widespread, but vary greatly in type. . . .	3rd paragraph (six sentences follow)
Frequently the ball games are played in a more elaborate way....	4th paragraph (fourteen sentences follow)
In the Plains and Southwest of our country the "hoop and pole" game enjoyed great popularity....	5th paragraph (six sentences follow)
Compared with such sports rope-skipping seems simple, but the Australian Euahlayi make an art of it. . . .	6th paragraph (two sentences follow)
Polynesians lead in aquatic sports. . . .	7th paragraph (four sentences follow)

Maori stilt-walkers raced one another across streams, and also tried to upset one another's balance. . . . —Robert H. Lowie, *An Introduction to Cultural Anthropology*, pp. 164-166	8th paragraph (two sentences follow)

Transition paragraphs

For major transitions, such as from one main section of a long paper to another, a brief self-contained paragraph will often serve to prepare the reader for what is coming next. This is a typical transition paragraph:

> No such startling change in the habits of a people could have taken place without far-reaching social effects. Let us glance at a few of them.—Frederick Lewis Allen, *The Big Change*, p. 125

Ordinarily the subject matter of successive paragraphs is so closely related that separate transition paragraphs are not needed, and in short papers they are usually out of place.

26.4 Opening paragraphs

The first paragraph of a paper has two functions: to introduce the subject and to arouse the reader's interest. Plan your paper so that you can get into your subject as quickly as possible. Don't begin too far back: if your topic is the assassination of Lincoln, there is no need to start with an account of Lincoln's early career or even of his presidency. The shorter the paper, the more direct your beginning should be.

If, after finishing your first draft, you find that you have written an obviously weak beginning, see if the second or third sentence, or even the second paragraph, may not provide a better starting point. Often the first few lines of writing are simply a warm-up for the writer, and the paper actually begins a few sentences later.

Effective openings

No matter what you are writing about, the beginning of your paper should catch the reader's interest and get him into the subject. Some of the ways to accomplish this are discussed below:

A statement of purpose or point of view. This need not be a mechanical statement ("In this paper I am going to give you my reasons for majoring in business administration.") or a flat rewording of the assignment, but a natural leading into the topic:

> When I decided to enter the university, like most freshmen I had only the vaguest notion of what subject I intended to major in. But now after two quarters of haphazardly chosen course work, and after a good deal of self-analysis, I have decided that *there are at least four good reasons why I should major in business administration.*

If your purpose is to discuss one aspect of some general topic, the first paragraph should make the limits of your paper clear:

> The Great Lakes are one of the major lake systems of the world. Through the centuries many large cities have grown up along their perimeter as people recognized their value for inland navigation, water supply, and recreation. Pollution of their waters by industrial wastes has also inevitably increased through the years, until now it presents a serious threat. *The pollution problems in Chicago are typical of those of the Great Lakes area as a whole.*

A definition. If your paper deals with some subject which has a variety of meanings for different readers, it is good to make your definition clear at the outset. There is no need to start with a flat and stereotyped statement like "According to Webster, a hobby is 'an engrossing topic, occupation, or plan, etc., to which one habitually returns.' " Give a definition that fits your own approach to the subject:

> A hobby, as I see it, is an activity that takes up most of your spare time and all of your spare money. At least that has been my experience since I became interested in photography. . . .

An important fact. One of the quickest and clearest ways to open a paper is with the statement of an important fact that will lead to the general topic. This is a natural opening for a narrative and can also be good for a discussion of ideas:

> There have been two downright attempts by government to curb freedom of the press in America since Plymouth Rock. The first took place when John Peter Zenger, a New York publisher, was jailed in 1735 for criticizing the British colonial governor, but through a brilliant defense by Andrew Hamilton, a salty old Philadelphia lawyer, was acquitted. In the second instance, 63 years later under our own young Constitution, the accused was less fortunate.—Alvin Harlow, "Martyr for a Free Press," *American Heritage*, October 1955, p. 42

A reference to personal experience. If your subject is one with which you have had some personal experience, a reference to your connection with it provides an appropriate beginning. In an article on the problems of medical care, for example, the author, a physician, begins in this way:

> There is a hospital bill on my desk. On October 10, Mrs. A———, a Boston resident, aged 66, fell and broke her hip. Her hip was operated upon and nailed, and she left the hospital on November 18. Excellent care contributed to her recovery. The hospital bill was $2949.38. The surgeon's fee is not known. It is this problem of paying the cost of medical care that the Forand Bill and its many rivals, including a reluctant Administration's proposal, have been attempting to solve. And yet there is more, much more, to the problem than the question of how, and how much, the government will pay.—Osler Peterson, M.D., "How Good Is Government Medical Care?" *The Atlantic Monthly*, September 1960, p. 29

A lively detail or illustration. A good way to arouse the reader's interest and curiosity is to begin with a lively detail—perhaps with an anecdote, an apt quotation, or an allusion to some current topic. Such material should of course be related to the subject of the paper, as is this beginning of an article on the conservation of natural resources:

> There may be more truth than humor in the cartoon of two cave men wearily dragging the carcass of a saber-toothed tiger to the mouth of the home cave, surrounded by a number of drooling cave babies. One provider is saying to the other, "They get further and further away each year, and scarcer and scarcer." Certainly the impact of man upon nature has been recognized from earliest times. —Samuel Ordway, Jr., "Plunder or Plenty?" *The Saturday Review*, April 15, 1961, p. 13

Openings to avoid

The opening paragraph should mark the actual beginning of the paper and be clearly related to the subject. If it does not create interest in the subject or get it under way, it probably does not belong in the paper. These common mistakes make poor beginnings:

Beginning too far back. If you are discussing the organization of the United Nations, there is no need to begin with the reasons for the failure of the League of Nations, nor is there any reason to begin a paper on Kennedy as President with an account of his legislative career. The shorter your paper, the more direct should be your beginning. A statement of your purpose or a rewording of your central idea is the simplest way to begin a paper written in class.

An apology or a complaint. A statement such as this is discouraging to most readers: "Being a lowly freshman, I'm afraid that what I have to say on this topic won't be of much value . . . ." Complaints are also better left unwritten: "Before I started to write this theme, I thought I could find some interesting material on it in the library, but there wasn't any . . . ." Remember that readers are interested only in the ideas that you present, not in the difficulties or disappointments you may have had while writing the paper.

Too broad a generalization. "Science in the last fifty years has made more progress than any other branch of knowledge" is a generalization far too sweeping to explain or prove in a five-hundred-word or even a five-thousand-word paper. Statements such as this are likely to be more impressive to the writer than they are to the reader. Wherever possible, begin with a specific statement: "Though smaller than your thumb, an electronic device called the transistor has had a tremendous effect on radio and television sets."

A self-evident statement. Avoid starting a paper with a remark so obvious that it need not be mentioned: "America has a great number of resorts situated in her many scenic localities." And resist the temptation to open your topic with some commonplace observation that gives no hint of your subject: "It has been said that the only thing constant in life is change." If you have started your paper with a self-evident remark, see if the sentence immediately following may not mark the actual beginning of the subject.

26.5 Closing paragraphs

The beginning and ending of your paper—the point at which you meet your reader and the place at which you leave him—should be the most forceful parts of your paper. Make the ending definite and emphatic. Plan your conclusion so that it won't trail off or leave your reader up in the air. The final paragraph should round out your discussion in such a way that the reader will know you have said all you intended to say and that you have not stopped because you were tired of writing or because time ran out. Remember that the total effect of your paper will depend largely upon the way you end it.

Effective conclusions

Your final paragraph should tie together the ideas you have been developing and emphasize the main point of the paper. Some suggestions for effective conclusions follow:

A climax. Make your final paragraph the culmination of the ideas you have been developing, or save the most important idea for the last. The concluding paragraph thus becomes the climax of the paper. A student paper of about a thousand words, which has described in detail the operation of a large used-car lot, brings all the details to a focus in this conclusion:

> This used-car lot was sponsored by an organization which sells over a million cars a year, so it was by no means a fly-by-night affair. Although no sloppy repairs were done, and no highly crooked deals were tolerated, there was just a slight suspicion that the company was getting the best of every customer on every deal. This company, however good or bad, is representive of many similar organizations in the United States.

A suggestion for action. If you have been criticizing some situation (parking on the campus, the price of textbooks, daylight-saving time), end your paper with a positive suggestion for action. Make the statement definite, as in this ending of an article about gambling laws:

> The underworld is thriving on our hypocrisy and stupidity. So long as we persist in our efforts to end gambling by prohibitory legislation, we promote police corruption. Police honesty can never be a relative matter. Police corruption erodes the average citizen's respect for the law and makes him cynical about all law enforcement. We cannot continue to tolerate a partnership that invites corruption. And, yes, we owe it to the judiciary to end the existing judicial farce. —John Murtagh, "Gambling and Police Corruption," *The Atlantic Monthly*, November 1960, p. 53

A summary statement. Longer and more formal papers are sometimes concluded by restating the main points of the discussion.

This final paragraph, for example, sums up the author's assessment of Nigeria's future:

> Nigeria has the leadership; it has the assets, material and human, to become possibly the most dynamic nation on the continent. It has its problems. There may even be times of crisis. Yet Nigeria should achieve the momentum of a free people operating under a free system of economics that should carry it to the forefront of prosperous and stable nations.—Thomas Melady, "Nigeria: Potential for Stability," *Current History*, February 1961, p. 97

But for most papers written in composition courses, it is seldom necessary or advisable to summarize what has been said. The result is often a weak and mechanical ending.

Tying in the ending with the beginning. The final paragraph may repeat, in different wording, the opening idea. This method is particularly useful for longer papers, both to remind the reader what the main subject is and to give it final emphasis. Or it may return to some figure of speech or point of view used to introduce the subject. For example, an article surveying recent changes in education begins and ends with the same analogy:

> Anyone who attempts to survey the effects of five years of change on American public education must feel great kinship with the photographer who attempts a snapshot of a moving subject, because the changes are unceasing. My survey was predictably outdated before its results could be received, tabulated, and published....
>
> With all the shortcomings of the box-camera approach, one must still draw the conclusion that, if another type of photograph were possible—an aerial shot of the entire American public school system—it would show perceptible and generally consistent activity everywhere, a scurrying directed toward augmenting the "product" of public schools in quantity, and especially in quality.—Richard Kleeman, "Five Years of Change," *The Saturday Review*, March 18, 1961, pp. 50, 63

Endings to avoid

Avoid unemphatic, inconclusive, or contradictory endings. Here
26.5 are some typical pitfalls to avoid in your closing paragraphs:

An apology. Ending a paper with an apology for its shortcomings only serves to emphasize them:

> I am sorry this paper is so short, but I always have a difficult time putting my ideas on paper.

If you carefully work out your ideas before writing and then present them as effectively as you can, you will not need to apologize for your efforts.

A qualifying remark. If the last sentence of a paper is an exception or a qualifying remark, it weakens everything that has been said before:

> Although I haven't answered why some people refuse to face facts, I have come to the conclusion that not facing facts may be a natural part of human nature. Of course this can be carried to extremes.

There may be two sides to every subject, but when the purpose or scope of your paper is limited to the arguments for one side only, don't suddenly shift to the other side in your conclusion. If, for example, you have been presenting every argument you can think of in favor of universal military training, don't end like this: "Of course, there is much to be said for the other side also." If you feel such a qualifying statement is necessary, make it earlier in the paper.

Minor details or afterthoughts. A paper describing the role of the pitcher in baseball shouldn't end with a remark about other aspects of the game:

> Baseball is one of America's favorite sports, and to spend an afternoon at the Yankee Stadium or Polo Grounds watching two great pitchers battling for a victory is an exciting experience. What I have said about pitching gives you an idea what a pitcher must keep in his mind while out there on the mound, or as a substitute on the bench. *There are eight other players on the team besides the pitcher and the same can be written about each individual player and his position.*

Some concluding statements make a reader wonder whether the writer actually finished his paper or abandoned it in the middle of an idea:

> I could go on and on for pages and pages describing the other interesting people I met on the ship, but the length of this paper doesn't permit it.

Instead of putting a sentence such as this at the end of your paper, round out the description fully, or if the topic is already developed sufficiently, see if the next to the last sentence wouldn't make a respectable conclusion.

26.6 Framing a title

Word the title of your paper so that it gives a definite and accurate idea of the subject matter in as few words as possible. A title need not mystify or startle the reader, although it may perhaps arouse his curiosity or appeal to his sense of humor. Interesting titles are always appreciated, but one that is brief, simple, and exact will serve the purpose.

A title should not suggest more than the paper actually covers. If you are discussing your tastes in music, avoid such sweeping titles as "Modern Jazz" or "Music of Today"; use instead "Music I Like" or "Why I Prefer Thelonius Monk." A report on the experiences of a baby-sitter scarcely deserves the title "Child Psychology" or "The Care of Infants"; "Experiences of a Baby-Sitter" will be good enough if you cannot think of a better title.

Unnecessarily long titles are not satisfactory, especially those that merely repeat the assignment: "An Experience in Childhood That Left a Lasting Impression on Me." The thesis sentence of your paper is not intended to serve as a title. Instead of writing "Reading Taught by Sound Should Replace Sight Reading," name the subject: "Reading by Sound."

The title is not part of the paper, and it should not be referred to by a pronoun in the first sentence. If you want to mention the title in your opening, rephrase it slightly.

Unsatisfactory	*Satisfactory*
Becoming a Citizen	Becoming a Citizen
This is not a difficult process in the United States. . . .	It is not difficult for an immigrant to become a citizen of our country. . . .

Exercises

1. *Kinds of development.* Examine the following list of subjects for papers. What kind of development would be most appropriate to each? If more than one kind is possible, explain why.

Lecture or seminar?

San Francisco at dawn

James Bond, the culture hero

The growth of suburbs

Divorce is increasing

How to keep college relevant

Revising the curriculum for the students

The Indian and civil rights

Our useless student congress

A trip through the southwestern desert

The discovery of King Tut's tomb

Recession in the churches

2. *Sentences and paragraphs as directors of development.* Below is the first paragraph from the *rough draft* of a student paper called "Why Go to College":

Many entering freshmen who have just recently graduated from high school are still a little naive in their way. In high school the student is constantly guided by an invisible rope tied to their necks by the teachers. So many times the student is told what to do and how to do it, the teacher is always by the students side, coaxing him a little by telling the student that if he doesn't draw any more pictures of her on the blackboard, she might give him an A instead of a B grade which the student deserves. There is still a lot of "teachers pets" in high school. When the immature high school students gets to college, he finds that he is going to have to make a big adjustment. It is a gradual process but when the student completes this process, he will become an independent thinker, learn to make his own decisions, and be able to handle the responsibilities put upon him.

Read the paragraph carefully and then revise it in different ways according to the suggestions that follow, making whatever other changes are necessary for smoothness and correctness. Some of the suggestions may require slight additions in content:

1) Rewrite the end of the paragraph so that it concludes with a sentence of appropriate parallel construction, the parts of which might become topics for succeeding paragraphs.

2) Rewrite the opening of the paragraph as a periodic sentence, the form of which might then be used to forecast a narrative development to a climax through the rest of the essay.

3) Rewrite the opening of the paragraph as a balanced sentence to forecast a balanced contrast through the rest of the essay.

4) Convert the paragraph into a support paragraph that opens with the dominant idea.

5) Rewrite the paragraph so that it will fit into the opening of a cause-and-effect sequence.

3. *Paragraphs in sequence.* Select a recent magazine article that seems to you clear and direct in its development. How does the author relate paragraphs to each other and to the central idea of the article? Point out all words, phrases, and clauses that relate a paragraph to the one preceding it. Does the author use any short transitional paragraphs to move from one major idea to another? Would the article be as easy to follow if all transitional devices were removed?

4. *Good beginnings and endings.* Examine the following beginnings and endings from student papers. Which seem to you weak or unemphatic? Why? Be prepared to point out the good qualities of those you consider effective.

1) *Beginning paragraph from a paper called "Good Neighbors or Bad":*
Since I myself have never been outside of the United States, it may be foolish of me to think I can make any useful suggestions about our Latin-American policy. However, I have read about recent events in the Caribbean and South America with great interest, and, if you will bear with me, I would like to comment at some length on our present policy.

2) *Beginning paragraph from a paper called "The Utility of Cats":*
When the California Gold Rush was at its height, grain supplies were so devastated by rats that prospectors eagerly paid $100 and up for cats. One enterprising merchant is said to have made a fortune by bringing a shipload of stray cats from New York to San Francisco via Cape Horn. Although the cat has not always been so highly prized, its usefulness to man has been recognized since the days of the Pharaohs. Its continuing popularity in the United States is certainly due to its utilitarian as well as to its decorative qualities.

3) *Beginning paragraph from a paper called "Modern Chicken Farming":*
The world today is not what it was fifty years ago. Just think of all the amazing technological changes that have taken place. The automobile

has replaced the horse and buggy; radio and television have revolutionized communications; modern medicine has conquered disease. And in 1945 the atomic age was born. Chicken farming, too, has changed drastically from what it was in 1910. I would like to describe some of those changes in the pages that follow.

4) *Closing paragraph from a paper called "What a Liberal Education Means to Me":*

But the greatest value of a liberal education is a personal one; it goes beyond politics and economics. Besides helping the individual to live in his world, it helps him to live with himself. Liberal studies stimulate a love of reason and a flexible, inquiring attitude toward the great questions of mankind. They keep the mind strong and alert and stimulate a well-rounded intellectual development which is as essential to a full life as physical development. A liberal education, in the deepest sense, is an education for life.

5) *Closing paragraph from a paper called "The Population Explosion":*

All the statistics indicate that the future is bleak for the human race if the population explosion is not checked. Food, water, and other essential resources are even now inadequate. Living space is dwindling fast. Of course the picture may not be as dark as it looks. Maybe science will find a solution before long, or maybe the explosion will just taper off.

6) *Closing paragraph from a paper called "Population Pressures":*

An architect recently suggested that cities could be built in the sea to house the extra millions. They would consist of concrete buildings like silos attached to pontoon islands, and could extend as far below the water as they do above. People who lived on the lower levels could then watch the fascinating underwater world through their living-room windows! Man has never even begun to exploit the sea and knows very little of its hidden wonders.

5. *Good beginnings and endings.* Look at the opening and closing paragraphs of your own recent papers and criticize them in terms of the points made in §26.4 and §26.5. Rewrite two or three that are unsatisfactory.

27 Revising and correcting a paper

The business of letters, howsoever simple it may seem to those who think truth-telling a gift of nature, is in reality two-fold, to find words for a meaning, and to find a meaning for words. Now it is the words that refuse to yield, and now the meaning, so that he who attempts to wed them is at the same time altering his words to suit his meaning, and modifying and shaping his meaning to satisfy the requirements of his words.—Walter Raleigh

When you have finished the first draft of a paper, put it aside for a while before revising it. Most people find it difficult to look at their own writing objectively while the ideas they have expressed are still fresh in mind. For this reason, the first draft should be written as early as possible, so that you can wait a day or two (or at least several hours) before examining it for faults. The purpose of revision is to check major as well as minor matters: to tighten and improve the organization, the content, and the expression, as well as to correct the mechanics of writing.

27.1 Revising the first draft

You can save time and improve the quality of your writing by going over the first draft systematically looking for specific faults. The hit-or-miss approach to revision is a waste of time, since at best only the most glaring faults will be caught.

Your papers will be evaluated on the basis of the following points. Keep them in mind when you revise:

1) The *content:* the ideas, facts, examples used to support the central point of your discussion

2) The *organization:* the pattern by which your ideas are developed, from beginning to end

3) The *wording:* the way in which ideas are expressed, including grammar, word choice, sentence structure, and general effectiveness of expression

27.1 Rev

4) The *mechanics*, or conventions, of writing: spelling, punctuation, division of words at ends of lines, and so forth

It is not expected that you will re-read your paper four times to check for each kind of fault. The four categories overlap; usually, for instance, content and organization can be checked at the same time. The purpose of a systematic method of revision is to help you concentrate on your individual problems.

Checking the content

Read the first draft thoughtfully to make sure you have put in enough material to make the subject clear, convincing, and interesting to your readers. Here are five questions that may help you to judge the effectiveness of the material:

1) Are more (or better) details, examples, illustrations needed?

2) Is the information sufficiently clear so that the reader who knows little or nothing about the subject can readily understand it?

3) Are there general statements that need to be supported by facts? If you say, for example, that Texas has the best flying weather in the United States, have you presented facts and figures to support this idea?

4) Do the opinions or attitudes you have expressed represent your own convictions on the subject, or have you merely repeated what you have read or have heard other people say? It is easy for a writer to use the expression "the American way of life"; it is much more difficult for him to explain what it means.

5) Have you included any statements that do not have direct bearing on the subject you are discussing? If so, remove them in revision.

Checking the organization

Study the first draft to see if the subject advances from one section to the next and if the emphasis falls where you want it to. As you revise the paper, ask yourself these questions:

1) Is it clear from the beginning (or near the beginning) what the paper is about? Avoid wordy and irrelevant introductions.

2) Does each paragraph advance the subject, or is there some skipping back and forth?

3) Do the important ideas stand out clearly from the minor points and details?

4) Will the ending leave the reader with the impression that you want to make?

Checking the wording

Read your paper aloud (or have someone else read it to you) to see if it sounds the way you intended it to sound. Awkward repetition, clumsy constructions, and involved sentences will be easily detected this way.

1) Are there any words whose meanings you are not quite sure of? In case of doubt, consult your dictionary.

2) Have you used any technical term or unfamiliar expression that needs explanation?

3) Do you notice any unnecessary repetition, either of individual words or of ideas, that should be omitted?

4) Is the level of usage consistent throughout? Watch for any unintentional lapses from one variety to another, as from Formal to Informal usage.

5) Are any of the sentences too involved? If you stumble over a passage while reading it, revise it for greater clarity.

Checking for accuracy

Most of the common errors marked on student papers (spelling, punctuation, fragmentary sentences, omission of words, and so forth) result from carelessness or haste. You can eliminate many such mistakes from your writing by looking carefully for the specific kinds of mistakes that have occurred most frequently in past papers.

If you aren't quite certain about the spelling of a word, don't trust to luck or rely on a friend's opinion; find the correct spelling in your dictionary. If fragmentary or run-on sentences give you trouble, take time to analyze any sentence you suspect may be incorrectly punctuated. If you have used too many commas in previous papers or have failed to paragraph properly, study the sections in this handbook that deal with these matters.

27.2 MS

27.2 Manuscript form

MS | Revision: Correct the form of your manuscript so that it is consistent with the instructions given.

If you have selected an interesting subject and have developed it to the best of your ability, you will take pride in the final form of your paper. Make a neat and accurate copy of your revised paper to submit to your instructor. Follow the directions he gives you for the form; the size and the kind of paper; margins and spacing; numbering of pages; endorsement. Typical manuscript form is described in the following pages.

Typed papers

If you have a typewriter and know how to use it, it is a good practice to type all papers written outside class. Typed manuscript is easier to read than most handwriting and is generally preferable for written work in all college courses.

In typing your final draft, use unlined white 8½ by 11 inch paper of good quality bond. It is discourteous to a reader to use onion skin or other transparent sheets that let the type show through. Never use colored paper. Use black ribbon and change it before it gets pale. Keep the type bars clean by frequent brushing.

Type everything double spaced except long quotations and footnotes. These should be set off appropriately and single spaced, as shown in the sample reference paper printed on pages 498-507.

Follow standard conventions in typing. For the figure 1 use lower case l (not capital I). For a dash use two hyphens with no space between the words:

```
The book--a first edition--was missing.
```

Before you hand your paper in, check it carefully for typographical errors. Uncorrected typing mistakes are counted as errors in composition courses.

Handwritten papers

If you cannot type, you need not worry that your grade will suffer. With reasonable care, handwritten papers can be made just as acceptable as those that are well typed.

Use lined white paper 8½ by 11 inches, with lines at least one half inch apart. Themes written on closely lined paper are hard to read and difficult to correct. Do not use pages torn from spiral-bound notebooks, because their rough edges stick together. Use black or dark blue ink.

Handwritten papers should be easy to read. If a word looks misspelled or is difficult to decipher, it will probably be marked as an error. Handwriting that is too small puts an unnecessary strain on the eyes of the reader; handwriting that is excessively large is no less difficult to read. Try to strike a happy medium in size. If you have developed what you consider to be an individual style of penmanship, make certain that it will be as legible to others as it is to you.

Margins and spacing

Leave ample margins on both sides of the page. An inch and a half on the left and an inch on the right are customary margins in both handwritten and typed papers. Leave at least an inch and a half at the top and an inch at the bottom of every page.

Indent paragraphs uniformly. Five spaces from the left-hand margin is the customary indention for typed papers, and about an inch for those written in longhand. Don't indent any line that is not the beginning of a paragraph, even though it is the first line on a page. The last line on a page should not be left partly blank unless it is the end of a paragraph.

Don't crowd your writing at the bottom of a page. Start a new page, even if it will contain only a line or two.

Division of words

| *Div* | Revision: Divide the word marked according to the syllabication given in a reliable dictionary.

If you leave plenty of room at the right-hand side of your page, you will not have to divide many words at the ends of the lines. It is a good idea to divide words only if writing them out or putting them on the next line would make the lines conspicuously uneven.

Words of one syllable should not be divided at all: *through, played, bright*. Also avoid breaking a word if a single letter will be left at the beginning or end of a line. There is no point in dividing a word like *a-lone;* the single letter at the end of the line is less attractive than leaving space and carrying the whole word over to the next line. See §19.2, page 239, Spelling and word division.

27.2 MS

Words spelled with a hyphen *(mother-in-law, self-confidence)* should be divided only at the hyphen.

Form of the title

The title appears on the first page of your paper. On unlined paper, place it in the center and about two inches from the top of the page; on lined paper, write the title on the top line. Leave a blank line between the title and the first line of the text.

Capitalize the first and last words in your title and all others except short words like *and*, *the*, *a*, *an*, and prepositions less than five letters long.

Breaking and Training a Horse
The Art of Making Friends
How Not to Become Overweight
Victory Through Airpower

No period should be put after a title. However, if the title is expressed as a question or as an exclamation, it should be followed by the proper end punctuation.

Why Not UMTC?
Man Overboard!

Titles are not enclosed in quotation marks. Even when familiar quotations are used as titles, no marks are needed:

Blood, Sweat, and Tears
The Home of the Brave

Numbering pages

The first page of a manuscript is not numbered. Begin with the second page, using Arabic numerals (2, 3, 4 . . .) for paging. Numbers are customarily put at the top of the page in the right-hand corner or in the center. Make certain that the pages of your paper are in the right order before you turn the paper in.

Long tables, diagrams, charts, and other material supplementary to the words of the text are usually put on separate pages, placed near the part that refers to them, and numbered consecutively with the other pages.

It is not correct to write "more" at the bottom of each page or to put "Finis" or "The End" at the conclusion.

Endorsing the paper

Endorse your papers as your instructor directs. Include all the information he asks for, and put it in the right order. Clear and uniform endorsement is a real convenience to the teacher who must handle the papers.

Ask your instructor how he wants papers submitted, whether folded, flat, or otherwise. Sheets should be held together by paper clips that can be slipped off, not by fasteners or staples that pierce the paper, or by pins, bobby pins, or string. Use binders only for longer papers.

Proofreading

When you finish your final draft, put it aside for a while and then proofread it carefully before handing it in. No matter how perfect the finished product may appear, it will pay to give it one final check. Errors somehow creep into even the most careful writing. To find them, you will have to get away from the paper for a time so that you can look at it with a fresh eye.

Look for slips of the pen or typing errors, for the omission of words and marks of punctuation. And look particularly for the kind of mistakes that have been marked on your previous papers.

Making corrections in the final copy

Changes and corrections should be kept to a minimum, particularly on important papers. When you have to make major changes in the final copy (rewording sentences, revising paragraphs), do the page over. For minor changes (spelling, punctuation, adding or striking out a word), make the corrections as neatly as possible and according to standard practices.

To add a word, use a caret (∧) and write the missing word directly above it:

```
                    be
Manuscript should ∧ easy to read.
```

To strike out a word, draw a straight line through it (don't use parentheses or brackets):

```
Final copy should be as ~~as~~ accurate as possible.
```

To indicate the beginning of a new paragraph where you have failed to indent, write the symbol ¶ immediately before the first word of the new paragraph:

```
So ended my first day away from home.¶The second day . . . .
```

To correct a misspelled word, draw a line through it and write the correct form directly above. This makes a neater and more legible correction than an erasure:

```
                                   quantity
Quality is more important than ~~quanity~~.
```

27.2

MS

To indicate in typed copy that two letters should be reversed in order (transposed), use a curved line:

```
bewteen          recieve          Smiths' novel
```

Submitting manuscript for publication

Manuscript that is to be submitted for publication, in a campus magazine or elsewhere, should be typed and should follow the directions already given.

The writer's name and full address should be typed in the upper left-hand corner of the first page. A stamped, self-addressed envelope should be enclosed for the possible return of the manuscript. It is not necessary to write a letter to a publisher when submitting a manuscript unless there are facts to be given about the sources of material used, its accuracy, or possibilities for illustration.

27.3 Revising a corrected paper

In composition, as in other areas of experience, you often learn by making mistakes. No matter how conscientiously you have applied yourself to a written assignment, you are likely to find that the instructor has marked a number of corrections on the returned paper. To improve your writing skills, you must give serious attention to these corrections.

Many instructors require their students to revise all corrected papers and resubmit them. But even if the instructor does not ask for revisions, he expects students to make a careful analysis of all correction marks and to revise or rewrite the paper accordingly. A cursory glance down the margins is not enough—if errors and weaknesses are not studied and corrected they will undoubtedly recur in other papers.

Some papers, of course, may contain only minor errors, requiring the change of a few words or punctuation marks on the original. Often, though, a satisfactory revision means sentences or even whole paragraphs must be rewritten or rearranged. For passages that require extensive changes, experiment with different versions. Then read the revisions through several times to determine which is the best one.

In correcting a paper, it is important to understand *why* the corrections are necessary. If the instructor's mark is not immediately clear to you, consult the correction symbol key at the back of this handbook and then read the relevant section in the text, noting the examples and comparing them with the passage marked.

Compare the original and corrected versions of the student paper reprinted on pages 404-407. This paper was used because it

Good Study Habits

It is important for every college student to develop good study habits. A lucky few have already developed them in high school, but for the majority of students the greater demands of college work requires some adjustment. Good study habits consist primarily of two things: a mature mental attitude and appropriate physical techniques.

Everyone should remember that being a college student is a demanding full-time job, and they should be prepared to spend about forty-five or more hours a week at it. Like any other job, it requires effort and concentration. Some students are indifferent toward required courses, which they feel are uninteresting or cannot see how they are related to their chosen course of study. Students should remember that if colleges require certain courses, usually of a general nature, this means that they present basic knowledge that every educated person is expected to acquire while in coll-ege. If you are indifferent to such courses, you are condemning yourself to a lopsided intellectual development, which you will probably regret later on in life.

Whether attending class or studying at home, full concentration is essential. Students sometimes complain that they do poorly in courses even though they spend many hours studying everyday. "Studying" means inattentively running their eyes over a page between frequent distractions from the radio, conversing with their roommates, and daydreams.

Good Study Habits

It is important for every college student to develop good study habits. A lucky few have already developed them in high school, but for the majority of students the greater demands of college work require some adjustment. Good study habits are based on two things: a mature mental attitude and appropriate physical techniques.

Everyone should remember that being a college student is a demanding full-time job, and he should be prepared to spend about forty-five or more hours a week at it. Like any other job, it requires effort and concentration. Some students are indifferent toward required courses because they consider them uninteresting or unrelated to their chosen field. They should remember that such courses are required because they provide general knowledge expected of every college graduate. Students who neglect these courses are limiting their intellectual growth and usually regret it later.

Full concentration is essential both in the classroom and in the study room. Students sometimes complain that they do poorly in courses even though they spend many hours studying every day. But to many of them "studying" means inattentively running their eyes over a page between frequent distractions from the radio, conversations with their roommates, or daydreams. Five hours of this kind of studying is worth less than an hour of uninterrupted concentration. The

Five hours of this kind of studying is worth less than an hour of uninterrupted concentration on the material. A student who goes to a lecture without having done the assigned reading and without having reviewed his notes from the last lecture, is not really in a good mood to acquire new information and relate it to what he already knows.

An erratic and undisciplined approach to study is usually disasterous. Many students ignore course assignments until just before an examination. Then they frantically do all the required reading in one or two nights, try to decipher sloppy, disorganized notes, and stay up all night over black coffee cramming hundreds of facts into their heads. The result is usually that he comes to the examination fatigued and stupefied by a plethora of chaotic data. All of this could have been avoided if the student had kept up with his assignments and had gotten into the habit of taking neat, orderly notes which were reviewed by him regularly. Studying for an examination should involve only glancing over his notes and readings and planning how to organize related facts to answer the questions most likely to be asked.

A student should not be afraid that his room mates and friends will call him a square if he sets aside regular times for daily study and refuses to be interrupted. On the contrary, most good students are respected by their fellow students and popular because they devote more time to social activities than students with poor study habits.

same principle applies to class attendance. A student who goes to a lecture without having done the assigned reading and without having reviewed his notes from the last lecture is not concentrating on acquiring new information and relating it to what he already knows.

An erratic and undisciplined approach to study is usually disastrous. A student with poor study habits ignores course assignments until just before an examination. Then he frantically does all the required reading in a day or two, tries to decipher his sloppy, disorganized notes, and stays up all night over black coffee cramming hundreds of facts into his head. The result usually is that he comes to the examination not only exhausted but also confused by a mass of unrelated facts. He could have avoided all this by keeping up with his assignments, making orderly notes, and reviewing his notes regularly. Studying for an examination then would involve no more than glancing over the material and mentally organizing it in terms of the questions most likely to be asked.

A student should not be afraid that his roommates and friends will make fun of him if he sets aside regular times for daily study and refuses to be interrupted. On the contrary, good students are usually respected for their scholastic achievements and, because they use their time more efficiently, are usually freer to participate in social activities than are students with poor study habits.

exhibited a variety of faults. (The most serious fault was pointed out in the instructor's overall comment: "Your general approach is vague and unrealistic. What do you actually *do* when you are studying your best?") Study the instructor's marks on the original version and determine their meaning. Then examine the changes (underlined) made in the corrected paper. In working out his revision, the student has learned such things as the following:

MS Titles of papers are not enclosed in quotes or underlined. They should be set off from the body of the paper by extra space.

Agr Blind agreement should be avoided. Despite intervening words, subject and verb must agree: *demands* (S) *require* (V).

WW Words should be chosen for their exact meaning.

Agr Pronouns must agree in number with their antecedents: *Everyone* is singular and should be referred to by a singular pronoun (*he* rather than *they*).

// Constructions joined by coordinating conjunctions should be equivalent in rank and meaning.

Wdy Ideas should be expressed as directly and economically as possible.

Ref Pronouns should refer clearly to a definite antecedent. The pronoun *they*, marked for faulty reference in the original version, might seem to refer to *colleges* or *students* as well as to *courses*.

Div A word should be divided at the end of a line according to the syllabication shown in a dictionary.

Shift Shifts in person (*they* to *you* in the second paragraph, *they* to *he* in the fourth paragraph) should be avoided.

DM The sentence should include the word to which the modifier refers.

¶ con The relationships among ideas in a paragraph should be made clear to the reader.

No , Subject and verb should not be separated by a comma: *A student* (S) *is* (V).

Awk Awkward passages should be smoothed out when revising a first draft.

Big W Stilted, unnecessarily heavy language is out of place in all kinds of writing.

Pass	The awkward use of the passive voice should be avoided, especially an unnecessary shift to passive from active.
Inf	A writer should be consistent in his level of usage. The Informal *call him a square* is conspicuously out of place in this relatively Formal paper.
Log	The logic of a statement must be made clear to the reader. Devoting a large amount of time to social activities does not necessarily make a student popular; neither do good study habits. The writer's intended meaning is made clear in his revision.

In writing his next paper, this student should profit from his mistakes and do a better job. He will probably be particularly concerned about the instructor's general comment on the importance of dealing directly and realistically with his subject matter. There is no particular reason why a reader should pay much attention even to the corrected version of this paper. Although it eliminates most of the specific faults in the original version, it is still conventional, commonplace, irrelevant, and dull—the kind of paper that anyone can write without thinking and that arouses no thought in the reader.

In correcting this paper, the student should also have observed that there are two large categories of weaknesses in his writing: faulty diction and awkward sentence construction. The instructor has called his attention to poor word use in four instances: the inaccurate *consists of;* the vague and inappropriate *a good mood;* the inflated *fatigued and stupefied by a plethora of chaotic data;* and the Informal *call him a square.* In addition, the passages marked for sentence economy (Wdy) and awkwardness (Awk) are marred by poor word choice as well as faulty sentence construction. In short, the student generally lacks skill in selecting accurate, appropriate, and forceful language to express his ideas. If he wants to avoid word errors in future papers, he will have to read the text sections on diction thoroughly, become more alert to other writers' use of words, consult his dictionary frequently, and study his first drafts critically to eliminate wordiness and pretentiousness.

The instructor has also marked several passages for sentence and paragraph weaknesses. The second paragraph concludes with two long, clumsy sentences (Wdy). The third paragraph lacks continuity (¶ con), because the student has omitted certain words and expressions necessary to indicate connections and transitions between his ideas. The fourth paragraph contains two jumbled, awkward sentences (Awk). In the corrected version, the student has made each of these passages more clear and direct, and has gained valuable practice in expressing his ideas as economically as possible. To avoid sentence weaknesses in his future papers, he should practice reading his sentences and paragraphs aloud to see whether they are difficult to follow, repetitious, or ambiguous. And to assure continuing improvements, he should become more alert to sentence patterns used by other writers, particularly in published material.

Any student who analyzes his errors and revises his papers as carefully as the writer of the sample paper did will soon find that even his original drafts are improving.

Exercise

Revising a paper. Study the following student paper carefully and then revise it, keeping in mind the check points mentioned in this section. Is the material clear and well organized? Does the paragraphing make sense? Are the beginning and ending paragraphs effective? Does the paper contain errors in grammar and diction? Did the student overlook any errors in mechanics during the final proofreading?

Jayville News

Jayville does not have a television or radio station or even a weekly newspaper. It does have several ladies' clubs and auxiliaries. They perhaps do an even better job of spreading local news. Chief among these is the so-called Sewing Club, whose members meet every Friday afternoon to sip coffee and exchange gossip ranging from the opinion that Joe Webster's new baby has an ugly profile to subjects like the Profumo affair, not to sew. Since this club has a maximum membership of twelve and since there is always a bunch of women wanting to get in, to become a member entitles a lady to a high place in Jayville society. It also allows here to hear the latest gossop before most others do. I remember vividly a Friday when the cackling twelve were meeting at our house. I was pretending to study in my room. Then there arose a chatter in the front parlor that could have easily brought down the walls of another Jericho. Upon investigation, I learned that Maurine Harwell had disclosed information indicating that Jake Smith had been meeting Mary Belle Ransom at a tavern in the city every Saturday night for months. All the while his wife sat at home caring for their three children. When the ladies recovered from the initial shock caused by this announcement, they resolved to "not breath a word of this to anyone". Within a week each resolve was borken. The tales was being whispered all over town. Every woman in Jayville who does not belong to the Sewing Club condemns its gossip. But each of them wish secretly that she was a member.

The social power of the Sewing Club stems from its members belonging to other clubs such as the Methodist W.S.C.S., the PTA and the Baptist Womens Auxiliary. By having its tentacles in each of these organizations, the Sewing Club is able to control a good portion of the community's social life. Also, by attending all these other functions, the Sewing Club members are able to disseminate their latest tales and pick up new ones for next Friday's meeting.

Generally, news is gathered in bits at the club meetings of lesser importance. Then it is shared at the Friday Sewing Club meeting, and then distributed to all of the other clubs. For example, Maurine had learned of the Smith-Ransom affair at the Wednesday gathering of the P.T.A. If this tale had spread from here directly to all of the other clubs in town, it might have taken weeks to get around. But by being told at the Sewing Club, it's rate of transmission was greatly increased.

28 Writing in college and out

Since, therefore, there has been placed equally at our disposal the power of eloquence, which is so efficacious in pleading either for the erroneous cause or the right, why is it not zealously acquired by the good, so as to do service for the truth.—St. Augustine

The long and short papers that you will write for your composition course are not so different from the reports and term papers that you will write for your other college courses, and these in turn are not so different from the practical, business, or technical writing that you may do outside of college. A letter of recommendation, for example, is both informative and persuasive. It offers information about a person's past (usually narrative) and about his present (often descriptive) in order to make an argument for his future. The argument may be developed by any of the methods you might use in developing an argumentative paper.

All that has been said in the preceding sections of this handbook about planning and writing papers for a composition course applies equally well, then, to most of the writing you will do in college or out. The location of your thesis (§25.1)—your decision about what you wish to say—will ordinarily determine whether your writing is primarily informative or persuasive. Knowing that, in turn, will help you to know what kind of resources you will need (§25.2), what attitude you will take toward your audience (§25.3), and what methods of development will be most useful (§24.2 and §26.2).

Your basic task as a writer—whether you are writing a short story, a research paper, an essay examination, or a letter to a friend—is to discover what you want to say and then to say it well, so that your reader will see your subject in the same way you do. The particular techniques you will use may vary, however, depending on your immediate, practical goals. This section will consider some of the special problems involved in different kinds of writing: exposition, argumentation, description, narration, answers to essay examinations, reports, literary analyses, and letters.

28.1 Exposition

The purpose of exposition is to *inform* the reader, to carry his knowledge of something beyond its present point, to help him understand a situation or a process, to give him information about an idea or belief. It ranges from the explanation of small personal matters ("How to Select a College Wardrobe") to erudite scientific treatises ("The Effect of Ultraviolet Light on Steroids").

Skill in exposition is essential in all college work. Most of the writing you will do, except in creative writing courses, will be designed to inform your reader or to explain a point of view. Most of the reading required in college, except in literature courses, is also expository. Increasing skill in expository writing, then, is a major aim of beginning composition courses.

Most of the suggestions about writing in §25, Discovering and organizing material for writing, and §26, Writing the first draft, are especially relevant to exposition. You will also find it helpful to study §24.2, Patterns of paragraph development. Definition, comparison, contrast, and the other methods of development discussed there are useful, even necessary means of explanation.

Gathering information

Whatever your subject and whatever the length of your paper, you will have to exercise judgment in deciding what resources to use and in gearing your information to your particular audience and situation. (**See** §25.2, Using your resources.) Some of the short expository papers you will be assigned in college can be based entirely on your own knowledge and experience. Other papers will require that you gather and evaluate information from various sources in order to develop your subject adequately.

Even when you base your paper on a personal experience, such as building a boat or working in a drive-in theater, you may find it useful to add to your information by reading in the library or by talking to people who have had similar experiences. It is a good idea in planning such a paper to make a list of points about which your memory is hazy or about which you lack adequate information. Then, to fill in the gaps, you can extend your observations or read what others have reported about the subject.

For typical information papers on subjects such as "The Electoral College" or "Devices for Controlling Air Pollution," you will usually need to consult a variety of printed sources—books, magazines, newspapers—to find information you cannot gather first-hand. Some of these sources may be course textbooks or assigned outside readings which provide basic facts and figures to use as a nucleus for the paper. Others may be books of your own that supply information on subjects that interest you, like sports, hobbies, or history. Or you may find relevant information in current magazines and newspapers, either those you subscribe to or those in the college library.

Relating specialized information to your reader

In gathering and selecting additional facts to use in an expository paper, be particularly careful to consider your audience. If you are writing a paper for a group of bridge fanciers, you probably need not define terms like *point count* and *slam* or explain how a *finesse* is made, since your readers would be familiar with such fundamentals. But if you are writing on bridge for an English class, you cannot expect the typical student to have this knowledge; to make sure that your audience understands, you must take the time to insert brief explanations. If you omit them, the whole paper may be puzzling or even incomprehensible to a general reader. Remember that you are writing the paper in hopes of telling him something new, of adding to his knowledge in an area where he does not have your background. Put yourself in his place: what words or ideas might be unfamiliar to him? How can you explain these things so that he will understand them?

The following passages show effective and ineffective ways of relating specialized information to a general reader:

Ineffective	*Effective*
There are various ways to bridge the gap from one solo to the next. The trumpeter may play a series of riffs accompanied only by the rhythm section. This is probably the most common method.	There are various ways to bridge the gap from one solo to the next. Probably the most common method is for the trumpeter to play a series of short, conventional jazz phrases, called "riffs," accompanied only by the rhythm section—piano, bass, and drums.
If the bleeding becomes severe or there is a chance of infection, you may have to cauterize the wound.	If the bleeding becomes severe or there is any chance of infection, you may have to cauterize the wound by searing it with a piece of metal that has been held over a flame until it is red-hot.

Documenting your information

When your own observations form the basis of the paper, be sure to tell the reader why you consider your statements to be fairly authoritative. Otherwise he may not be sure how much value to attach to them. Somewhere near the beginning of the paper, state the circumstances under which you gathered your facts:

> Since I was sixteen I have spent my summer vacations working in a local department store, first as a stock clerk and later as an assistant display manager. During that time, I have become familiar with the typical organization of a large retail store. . . .

> My home is only nine miles away from the Menominee Indian reservation, and I have had frequent opportunities to meet and talk to members of the Menominee tribe. . . .

> In gathering examples for this paper, I spent ten hours listening to radio programs featuring rock-and-roll records and copied down the lyrics of a dozen of the current favorites. . . .

When you incorporate published material into your paper, be sure to reproduce it accurately and to credit the sources, whether you quote them directly or not. It is not fair to present someone else's experiences or observations as if they were your own. In a research paper, credit is given formally by means of footnotes (§29.8, Documenting your paper), but in a general paper mention may be made informally. The following are some typical examples of how such acknowledgments can be handled:

> Franklin Soames, the author of *Zapotec Culture*, found that . . . .

> At a recent medical convention, H. L. Matthews, the noted urologist, was quoted as saying . . . .

> But according to Jean Lafontant, in a recent article in *The Saturday Review* . . . .

Sources which have been used extensively may be given in a note at the beginning or at the end of a paper:

> Much of the material for this paper was taken from Ralph L. Winters, *Land Problems in Latin America* (Chicago, 1959).

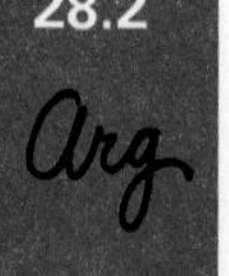

28.2 Argumentation

Whereas the purpose of exposition is to *inform* the reader, the purpose of argumentation is to *convince* him. The two kinds of writing have much in common, and both are based on facts or impressions gathered from various sources. But expository writing simply *presents* information, while argumentative writing *uses* it to support or test a belief. A paper describing current fashions in clothing, the social habits of bees, or the history of the slave trade invites the reader to share the writer's knowledge of his subject; a paper attacking campus rules for dress, on the other hand, expresses an opinion and tries to convince the reader of its validity. Like exposition, argumentative writing ranges widely, from matters close at hand ("Down with Large Classes") to those of major public concern ("Let's Get Out of Vietnam").

Locating the argument

An argumentative paper *proposes* something. Whether it calls for action or simply asks for the recognition of a point of view, it centers on a proposition that the writer must be prepared to prove.

An argument from a proposition, as Professor Edward P. J. Corbett has said in *Classical Rhetoric for the Modern Student*, is similar to a factual report in that it can ordinarily be judged as true or false; but a statement of fact is not in itself an occasion for argument, since presumably facts can be checked. An argument is also similar to a statement of opinion, in that it represents a judgment the writer has made; but an opinion is not an occasion for argument unless it is based on *facts* instead of mere preference, for only then can its validity be proved.

In planning a persuasive paper, you must take the time to formulate your proposition carefully. As your thesis statement, your proposition gives direction and unity to your argument. Ordinarily it needs to be simple—composed ideally, perhaps, of a single subject and a single predicate. If you argue, for example, that "County government must be put into new hands on election day and reformed to keep state and federal agencies from encroaching on local authority," you have, by using a double predicate, introduced two arguments, both of which must then be proved.

You should find the suggestions in §25.1, Discovering a subject, helpful in formulating an arguable proposition. If your work in college or out will require considerable work in formal argument, you would do well to consult basic studies of argumentative discourse such as the rhetoric texts of Aristotle and Cicero. Modern texts on logic and argumentative technique will also be valuable.

Using resources and evidence

When we state our opinions in informal situations, we often give little or no evidence to support them: "John is a reckless driver"; "The cost of living is going up every day"; "Divorce is the main cause of juvenile delinquency." This does not mean that we have no good reasons for believing as we do, but simply that our reasons are usually known and accepted by our listeners. On occasions when our opinions are questioned, we may attempt to support them with facts drawn from our experience and reading: "John had two accidents last month, and he always drives too fast." "Steak is up twenty cents a pound, and a refrigerator costs almost twice as much today as it did six years ago." "Psychologists say that emotional stability depends on a secure family life." Such evidence is considered acceptable or even convincing in informal situations, usually because the listener's personal regard for the speaker determines how much weight he attaches to the evidence.

In writing, however, the relationship with your audience is far more impersonal; authority must rest much more on the facts themselves. The reader who knows neither John nor you will want to know what kind of accidents John had and who was at fault; he will wonder whether "too fast" means in excess of speed limits; he may suspect that "always" is an exaggeration. Before accepting your opinion in regard to the relation between divorce and delinquency, he may want to hear what psychologists say in their own words, to be sure you are not misinterpreting their remarks or ignoring opposed opinions.

The more facts supporting your opinion that you can gather from experience or from the written statements of others, the more reason you can give the reader to accept that opinion. You will probably not be able to present absolute *proof*, but the greater the weight of your evidence, the more probable it will seem to him that your belief is the best one.

Some traditional kinds of argument may suggest certain ways of thinking about your material that will lead you to the evidence you need. One is the *argument from nature*. Not long ago on a college campus a young man who wished to call attention to inadequacies in the campus guidebook petitioned to have his name placed on the ballot in an election for homecoming queen. He maintained that he was eligible on the grounds that the guidebook stipulated only that candidates should be students under twenty-one; sex was not mentioned in the body of the rules. The young man's petition was denied through an argument from nature. Pointing out that the rules came under the heading "Eligibility requirements for homecoming queen," his opposition seized on the meaning of the word *queen*—by nature a female—to deny his eligibility. An argument from nature may be developed by a number of techniques: by defining the nature of a thing; by studying the meanings attached to the key words in a proposition; by classifying the subject in order to establish a frame of reference in terms of which it can be discussed.

Men cannot always agree on the nature of things, of course, and for that reason they have often turned to other kinds of argument. The *argument from analogy* brings a subject and argument into a reader's knowledge by suggesting its similarity to something better known to him, as in the fairly common—but usually ineffective—analogy of government and business. The evidence you bring to this kind of argument must show that the comparison is both meaningful and accurate.

The *argument from consequence* enforces a proposition by examining cause and effect, antecedent and consequence. This is a useful kind of argument, but it is limited by the fact that human affairs are not ordered by certain laws of causality. Poverty *sometimes* breeds crime; prolonged tyranny *frequently* leads to revolution; honesty is *occasionally* rewarded. Before expressing an opinion about the outcome of some course of action, or about the cause of some event, make sure that the weight of evidence lends probability to your statement.

The *argument from authority* depends upon the testimony of respected men, the authority of institutions, the weight of important documents. This is probably the least popular of the traditional kinds of argument, for most audiences prefer to feel that the truth is *discovered* in the course of an argument, rather than that it has been *pronounced* by authority.

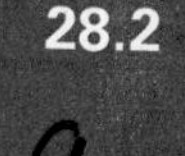

Taking the argument to your audience

Whatever kind of argument you use, remember that your reader has some confidence in his own intelligence and judgment and is likely to resent a writer who attempts to make up his mind for him. State your facts as specifically as possible—so that your reader can check them for himself if he wants to—and give your reasons for whatever conclusions you draw. Compare the following statements for effectiveness:

Vague	*Specific*
A couple of years ago, the president of a big corporation said that taxes were too high.	In a speech to the Toledo Chamber of Commerce on April 14, 1960, Oscar Winslow, president of the Winslow Steel Corporation, said, "Corporation taxes today are so high that they are destroying business incentive."
In many of his newspaper articles, H. L. Mencken made slighting references to democracy. Anyone can see that he despised it.	In his articles for the Baltimore *Sun*, H. L. Mencken frequently referred to democracy in terms such as these: "the domination of unreflective and timorous men, moved in vast herds by mob emotions" (July 26, 1920); "it may be clumsy, it may be swinish, it may be unutterably incompetent and dishonest, but it is never dismal" (July 14, 1924).

In trying to persuade the reader to accept your opinion, you will naturally want to gather facts that will support your position. It is not fair to your reader, however, to suggest that *all* evidence reinforces your belief. He may be familiar with contrary evidence; even if he is not, its absence may make him suspect that you are stacking the deck in your favor. In a court of law, an attorney who deliberately suppresses evidence damaging to his case may be disbarred from future practice. The consequences to a writer are usually not so serious, but he also may lose his case.

When you come across facts that do *not* support your opinion, give them as careful consideration as those that do. Is their source authoritative and relatively free of bias? Do they offer serious and relevant reasons to question your present opinion? Do they outnumber the facts you can find to support it? It may be that you will want to alter or modify your proposition after taking opposing facts into account. You may decide that your original opinion was wrong; many writers are unaware of the flimsy basis of their beliefs until they begin trying to substantiate them.

28.2

Even if the facts you gather do not change your opinion, it is unfair to simply discard those that fail to support it. In fact, it will strengthen your position in the reader's eyes if you frankly admit unfavorable evidence along with your reasons for being unpersuaded by it. Remember that the reader is your jury. If you have arrived at an opinion by weighing opposing evidence sensibly, he should be able to do the same.

Testing the argument

One way to test your argument, or to examine the argument of another writer or speaker, is to scrutinize it for flaws in reasoning and in the use of evidence. Probably the most common flaws are these:

Hasty generalization. In informal situations, we often overgeneralize from the facts: "She's *never* on time"; "*Everybody* likes him"; "Advertising is *only* a pack of lies." A little consideration shows us that in reality all-or-none, black-or-white situations are rare; reality is more accurately described in terms of finer shadings and degrees. The average reader is aware of this, and although he will accept and make statements like the above uncritically enough in conversations, he is suspicious of them in writing.

Be especially cautious in using terms like *all*, *always*, *everybody*, *nobody*, *never*, *none*, *only*, and *most*. Before making such all-inclusive statements, make sure that they are justified. If there are any exceptions to some assertion you make, modify your language to make it more accurate. Don't say that *all* women want a home and family: *almost all*, *most*, or *many* might be more accurate. Before you say that *most* early marriages end in divorce, ascertain from some reliable source whether more than 50 per cent actually do; otherwise you are not justified in using *most*. Keep in mind that the English vocabulary provides you with a wealth of qualifying terms (*some*, *few*, *frequent*, *rare*, *often*, *occasional*, *slight*, to name only a few) and choose those that most accurately describe the number, extent, and frequency of the facts you are asserting. Compare the two statements on page 422 for precision of expression. Both are based on the same facts (Of the delinquents in the State Training School, 75 per cent come from low-income families, 45 per cent have used narcotics at some time, and 20 per cent have IQ scores over 100):

Overgeneralization	*Accurate statement*
Almost all delinquents in the State Training School come from homes *on the verge of starvation. Most* of them are dope *addicts*, and *very few* are *brilliant.*	*Three out of four* delinquents in the State Training School come from *low-income homes. Almost half* of them have *at least experimented* with narcotics. A *significant minority* are *above average mentally.*

False analogy. Comparison and analogy are effective means of arguing, but only if there is really a basic similarity between the compared terms. If, for example, a university administrator sets out to argue for new rules and economies in his school on the basis that it should be run like a business, we should probably reject his argument on the grounds that his analogy is not valid, for similarities between a business and a university seem only incidental, not essential.

Post hoc, ergo propter hoc. This fallacy (literally, "after this, therefore because of this") is the fairly common one of assuming that two events or things are causally related simply because they are related in time. The young lady who gets a marriage proposal a week after becoming a blonde probably owes her success to something else.

Non sequitur. The label *non sequitur* ("does not follow") applies to errors of reasoning in which the conclusion does not follow from the evidence presented. Sometimes a step in reasoning has been omitted, and the fallacy can be corrected by supplying the missing link. But sometimes the conclusion is drawn from evidence that has no bearing on the issue: that Bart Starr uses a particular shaving cream has nothing to do with its quality; that a man does not beat his wife has nothing to do with whether he is a good husband; that the army teaches useful skills has nothing to do with the wisdom of sending troops to Vietnam.

28.2 Arg

Begging the question. This term applies to an argument that assumes the truth of what needs to be proved. A politician who argues "Our feeble county government, desperately in need of reform, must be placed in new hands on election day" is begging the question unless he *proves* that the present government is feeble and in need of reform.

Ignoring the question. This is a broad term that applies to all arguments that are irrelevant, as when a governor argues that his administration is not corrupt because the state budget is balanced. Another way he might ignore the issue would be to resort to an *argumentum ad hominem* ("argument against the man"), attacking the integrity of his opponents rather than the charge of his own corruption. Or he might use *glittering generalities* such as "my devotion and dedication to the fine people of this great state" to draw his audience into acquiescence by the weight of good words. All arguments that use emotional means to persuade an audience to arrive at a judgment without examining the evidence are ways of ignoring the question.

When you have finished the first draft of an argumentative paper, examine it carefully for flaws. Have you weighed the available evidence? Are your generalizations supported by fact? Are your inferences valid? Make sure that your argument is both honest and sound.

28.3 Description

The purpose of descriptive writing is to make a reader see an object, person, or scene as you have seen or imagined it. This requires an eye for significant details as well as a knack for putting sense impressions into words. Description is often written for its own sake, as a form of artistic expression, and it may also be an important part of other kinds of writing, from long research papers to technical reports and case histories.

Seeing your subject clearly

To make a description vivid to a reader, you must first of all know where you stand, physically and mentally, in relation to the thing you are writing about. How did you see your subject? From what angle? Under the weight of what mood? How can you define your subject, distinguishing it from similar things in the same class? What makes this particular sunset, for example, different from all others?

Descriptive writing succeeds only when you show your audience the specific, identifying details of object or scene. This requires that you see it clearly yourself, that you understand what you see, and that you say *precisely* what you see, as the writer has done in this passage:

> I know how a prize watermelon looks when it is sunning its fat rotundity among pumpkin vines and "simblins"; I know how to tell when it is ripe without "plugging" it. I know how inviting it looks when it is cooling itself in a tub of water under the bed, waiting; I know how it looks when it lies on the table in the sheltered great floor-space between house and kitchen, and the children gathered for the sacrifice and their mouths watering. I know the crackling sound it makes when the carving knife enters its end and I can see the split fly along in front of the blade as the knife cleaves its way to the other end; I can see its halves fall apart and display the rich red meat and the black seeds, and the heart standing up, a luxury fit for the elect.—Mark Twain, *Autobiography*

No two persons look at a scene in exactly the same way. What makes one writer's description more vivid than another's is the kind of details he selects and the way he arranges them.

Selecting and arranging details

Good descriptive writing is precise. If in describing a person you write "I first noticed this lady because she was wearing a funny hat," your description won't mean much to the reader because there are many kinds of funny hats. State in specific terms what the hat looked like: perhaps it was a black velvet beret covered with sea shells or perhaps it was a miniature merry-go-round.

Notice how lifeless the description is in this paraphrase, from which the specific expressions have been removed:

> After Lincoln became a lawyer, he started to pay more attention to his appearance. But even though he wore his hair in the accepted fashion of the time, he still wasn't well dressed. As a result, he acquired the reputation of being one of the most careless dressers in town, along with another local man, who was a judge, and who was equally careless about the way he looked.

By way of contrast, compare the description as it was written:

> And though Lincoln had begun wearing broadcloth and white shirts with a white collar and black silk cravat, and suggestions of side-burns coming down three-fourths the length of his ears, he was still known as one of the carelessly dressed men of Springfield, along with Stephen Logan, who wore unbleached cotton shirts and had sat two years as a circuit court judge wearing an unbleached cotton

shirt with no cravat or stock.—Carl Sandburg, *Abraham Lincoln: The Prairie Years*, I, 302-303

Being specific in descriptive writing doesn't mean that you should overload your sentences with adjectives and adverbs. While such words are used to "describe" or qualify other words, too many of them can be disastrous to any piece of descriptive writing. To refer to the Grand Canyon as "*absolutely* the *most marvelous* sight I have *ever* seen in my *entire* life" may give the reader some hint about your emotions, but it won't tell him much about the Canyon or help him re-create your impression of it.

The details you select for a descriptive passage should contribute to a central impression. (See §24.3, page 336, Continuity in descriptive paragraphs.) Often a few well-selected details will give a sharper picture than a large number of ill-assorted ones:

> The Pompeian Barber Shop was in the basement of the Hotel Thornleigh, largest and most dynamically modern hotel in Zenith. Curving marble steps with a rail of polished brass led from the hotel-lobby down to the barber shop. The interior was of black and white and crimson tiles, with a sensational ceiling of burnished gold, and a fountain in which a massive nymph forever emptied a scarlet cornucopia. Forty barbers and nine manicure girls worked desperately, and at the door six colored porters lurked to greet the customers, to care reverently for their hats and collars, to lead them to a place of waiting where, on a carpet like a tropic isle in the stretch of white stone floor, were a dozen leather chairs and a table heaped with magazines.—Sinclair Lewis, *Babbitt*, pp. 284-285

If you are writing a character sketch, remember that what a person does or says may be more revealing than his physical appearance. This brief paragraph tells the reader more about what kind of person Mrs. Matson is than would a good many lines of purely personal detail:

> A blind Negress, a tray of pencils hung about her neck, a cane monotonously tapping the pavement before her, came down the street. Mrs. Matson swerved sharply to the curb to avoid her, wasting a withering glance upon her. It was Mrs. Matson's immediate opinion that the woman could see as well as she could. She never gave to the poor on the streets, and was distressed if she saw others do so. She frequently remarked that these beggars all had big bank accounts.—Dorothy Parker, "Little Curtis," *Laments for the Living*, p. 128

To give focus to a description, you may find it useful to adopt one of the methods for developing material discussed in §26.2. For example, a spatial arrangement that takes you from left to right in picturing your subject, or from high to low, or from near to far, or from far to near, may help you to create order in your description. Professor Leo Rockas has said in *Modes of Rhetoric* that description is writing that aspires to be painting—its order is determined by space. Professor Rockas suggests, indeed, that when a writer sets out to enliven description with active verbs (part of a time order), he converts it into narration.

Often objects attract attention to themselves and deserve to become subjects for description because of some special impression they make. Thus, an interesting way to organize description is to focus attention on the dominant impression, subordinating all else. In the following passage the impression of quiet laziness, idleness, dominates the scene:

> After all these years I can picture that old time to myself now, just as it was then: the white town drowsing in the sunshine of a summer's morning; the streets empty, or pretty nearly so; one or two clerks sitting in front of the Water Street stores, with their splint-bottomed chairs tilted back against the walls, chins on breasts, hats slouched over their faces, asleep—with shingle-shavings enough around to show what broke them down; a sow and a litter of pigs loafing along the sidewalk, doing a good business in watermelon rinds and seeds; two or three lonely little freight piles scattered about the levee; a pile of skids on the slope of the stone-paved wharf, and the fragrant town drunkard asleep in the shadow of them.—Mark Twain, *Life on the Mississippi*

Good descriptive writing demands restraint and discrimination. It also takes practice to get the exact effect that you want. One way to get additional practice is to study published examples of descriptive writing that appeal to you, observing what kinds of details the writers use and how they present them.

28.4

28.4 Narration

The purpose of narrative writing is to recreate an experience or event, usually without expository comment. Like description, narration depends upon particulars, but unlike description, it moves through a time period:

> It was almost midnight when they slipped between the frigate *Emerald* and the southern tip of Prudence Island. Close to the shore, they suddenly heard horses running. As his men weighed their oars, Barton had the chilling thought that he had been decoyed into a trap. But the sound died away; it was apparently nothing more sinister than a few horses frolicking in a pasture. Running ashore in the cove, Barton left a man to guard each boat while the five squads made their way up the gulley.—Leonard Falkner, "Captor of the Barefoot General," *American Heritage*, August 1960, p. 31

Point of view

The particulars of narrative writing are reported to an audience selectively through a given point of view. Ordinarily it is neither possible nor desirable to present every action, trivial and noteworthy, in a sequence of events. Rather the writer focuses on those aspects of an experience that, from his point of view, make it worth preserving.

Most of the narrative writing you do will be presented as the narrative of either a first-person observer or participant or of a third-person observer. Personal narratives and autobiographical sketches are ordinarily told in the first person, but it will depend on the story you tell whether you present yourself as participating or observing. In historical writing, reports, and case histories, you will ordinarily present the action in the third person, letting the events speak for themselves.

Whether you report an action as a participant or observer, try to focus attention directly on what went on. In the following passage the narrator draws attention to *himself* rather than to the event he is narrating:

> I was riding with a friend late one night, returning from a long weekend trip. I was extremely tired, and I am sure he was too, and as a result we weren't very observant about traffic lights. I did notice in the distance one very red blinker light, though. I also saw a car directly in front of ours, like a slow moving ship in a submarine's sights. I knew immediately that we were going too fast to stop, so my natural reaction was to brace myself for a crash. It seemed to me that I could hear the tires squealing for minutes before anything happened. I was surprised to find during those actually few short seconds that I was seeing a variety of vivid colors that I hadn't even noticed before. I was aware of the yellow dividing strip of the highway, and still off in the distance, the brilliant red flashes

> of the traffic signal. There were also the browns and grays and whites of the surrounding buildings, that I hadn't seen a few moments before, but now were things of sharp beauty.

This narrative could be tightened up, and the *I's* made less conspicuous, by revising some of the sentences:

> Late one night I was riding with a friend. We were both extremely tired after a long weekend trip and not very watchful of the traffic lights. But I was dimly aware of one very red blinker light in the distance. Suddenly a car loomed up in front of us, like a slow moving ship seen through a submarine's sights. We were going too fast to stop, and instinctively I braced myself for the crash. Our tires squealed for what seemed minutes. Actually only a second or two passed, but in that brief instant, all the color of the scene jumped into view—the bright yellow dividing strip of the highway, the brilliant red flashes of the traffic light, the browns, grays, and whites of the nearby buildings. For one sharp moment everything took on a strange and fearful beauty.

A reader will understand your experience more clearly if you concentrate on the events as they happened instead of on your feelings about them.

Use of tenses

In narrative writing events are typically written down in chronological order, with verbs and adverbs controlling the movement:

> . . . *After a long half hour*, the rain *eased* a bit and the clouds *rose.* I *relaxed* a little. I *was showing* them that a rookie *could get through.* *Just then*, the engine *stopped* cold. As a rule, *when* an engine *fails*, it *will give* some warning. The water temperature *will rise*, or the oil pressure *will drop*, or there *is a knocking or clanking*. Even if it *is only for a minute or two*, it *gives* the pilot a chance *to look around* and *head for* a field or open place. However, *when* the timing gear in a Liberty engine *failed*, *one second* it *was roaring along* even and strong, and *the next* there *was* a tremendous silence. I *quickly twisted* all the knobs and gadgets in the cockpit, but there *was* no response, and the engine *stayed* dead. *While* my hands *were trying to restart* the engine, my neck *was stretching* and my eyes *searching* for some sort of field *to land in.* I *was surrounded* by heavily forested, sharply rolling hills. To my left *was* a cuplike basin with a small clearing. It *was* downwind, but my gliding radius *didn't allow* much choice. I *went* for it.—Dean C. Smith, "Flying by Guess and by God," *The Atlantic Monthly*, September 1961, p. 42

Most narrative writing uses the past tense, but the present (or "historical present") is sometimes used to create a sense of events actually happening, as in this paragraph:

> Our ship is hooting for all she's worth. An important last-minuter comes surging up. The rope hawsers are being wound clankily in. Seagulls—there are never very many in the Mediterranean—seagulls whirl like a few flakes of snow in the upper chill air. Clouds spin. And without knowing it we are evaporating away from the shore, from our mooring, between the great *City of Trieste* and another big black steamer that lies like a wall. . . . —D. H. Lawrence, *Sea and Sardinia*, p. 41

Whether a narrative is written in the present or past, one tense should be kept throughout. This paragraph illustrates unnecessary and confusing tense shifts:

> As I *hop* [present tense] on the city transit that will take me to the University, I notice that as always the bus is filled past capacity. As I *turned* [past] around, I saw a blind man sitting directly behind me with a dog lying at his feet. I *watch* [present] the dog, sitting there perfectly still, looking through the glass doors. Suddenly the dog *got up* [past], nudged his master, who pulled the cord above his head and with no difficulty got off the bus and proceeded up the street. I *wondered* [past] how a dog could be trained to know when to get off the bus, when to cross the street, and when to wait for a signal. Dogs seem to have more sense than some humans.

Pacing a narrative

Because its order is temporal, narration presents some problems not found in description. Foremost among these is the problem of pacing. Whether a series of events that you are narrating covers three years, three weeks, or three hours, you cannot reproduce the entire sequence—nor should you want to, for much of the time in any sequence of events is filled with action that has no particular bearing on the experience you are relating. The problem is to pace the telling of your story so that thorough attention goes to the significant actions and less attention to actions that have less immediate impact for your narrative.

28.4

If you study any example of effective narrative writing you will see, as Professor Rockas has noted, a balance of "remote" narration and "minute" narration. We *do* something just about all the time, but it may be that only a small portion of our doing is directed toward an end that is central to the experience we are trying to preserve in narrative. Still, if the significant actions that warrant narration are to have any context and continuity, they must be seen as part of a continuing stream of events. What a writer must do, then, is find a way to suggest a considerable amount of time in a relatively short space (remote narration) and so create a context for his slower, more detailed account of the significant actions (minute narration). If you are a reader of comic strips, you will remember that in a strip such as *Steve Canyon* or *Terry and the Pirates* the cartoonist-narrator will occasionally use a picture or two to show the heroes at their regular work; but when some dramatic episode nears its climax, he may use the full strip for several weeks to present a single, climactic action. Similarly in a television program such as *Gunsmoke*, we sometimes get brief glimpses of the hero going about his daily routine, but the dramatic action demands most of the time.

Including adequate details

If your narrative is to come alive for your reader, you must include enough details to make it interesting and understandable. Avoid any statement that might leave the reader wondering "What?" or "Why?" or "When?" or "Who?" In this paragraph, for example, the narrator fails to tell *what* his teacher said or *why* "the results of the contest were disappointing":

> On the night of the final judging, I was so nervous I could hardly move my fingers. As I waited backstage for my turn to appear, I was sure I had forgotten the opening notes of my number completely. I began thinking of ways to escape; maybe I could faint or pretend to be violently ill. But then at the last minute my piano teacher came by to wish me luck and *said something that suddenly changed everything*. When my turn came, I played with ease and confidence. *Although the results of the contest were disappointing*, I was pleased that I had conquered one of my major enemies—stage fright.

28.4 Nar

In selecting details, choose those that illuminate or enliven significant actions. A narrative should not be loaded down with minute and unimportant details. You can usually make your point and still keep the action moving by selecting two or three lively incidents, as in this example:

Grandmother didn't need reasons for fussing at Grandpa. She told everyone that he wouldn't chop wood or carry water for her. If he did bring wood to her, she would throw it out the window, stick by stick, not caring where it landed. If he brought her water, carrying it from the spring, several hundred feet away, she would pour it out —over him, if possible. Then she would take the empty pail and her cane, and trudge painfully down the long slope to the spring and back again, though it might take her half the morning, the time depending upon her mood and strength. "If I want fresh water, I have to carry it myself, because George is walkin' to Marionville or sittin' on his behind somewhere," she would say to anyone she chanced to see. "And if I want wood, I have to get my boy Jake to come over and chop it for me."—Bertie Johnson, "The Never-Ending Time," *The New Yorker*, October 4, 1952, pp. 86-87

See also §24.3, page 337, Continuity in narrative paragraphs.

28.5 Essay examination answers

Answering an examination question in essay form is similar to writing a short expository or argumentative paper. In studying for the course, you have become familiar with a fairly wide range of information; to answer a specific question you must recall the relevant material, organize it, and present it in essay form.

Reading the questions

Because most examinations have a time limit, students often begin writing feverishly after no more than a glance at the questions. The results of such frantic haste are usually disappointing. You can use the allotted time far more profitably if you take a few minutes at the start to read all the questions and directions. If a choice is offered, decide which question you are best prepared to answer and cross out the others. If the questions have different values, plan the amount of time to spend on each: a question worth 10 per cent, for example, should not take up 30 per cent of your time. Try to save a few minutes at the end to check your answers.

Before beginning to write, be sure to read the question thoroughly. Many answers are unsatisfactory simply because the student misinterpreted or forgot the question in his hurry to fill the paper with words. The instructor has deliberately planned his questions to test your knowledge in specific areas; he is not asking you to improvise and answer questions of your own making. Examine each question carefully and decide what kind of answer it requires. Don't misread or overlook key words. Notice in the following questions how a change in one word would affect the whole question:

> Explain the effect [causes] of the Spanish-American War.
> Describe the reproduction [digestion; development] of the frog.
> Discuss the structure [sources; significance] of *Moby Dick*.

Since the verb often determines the nature of the answer, take particular care to interpret it properly. Here are some of the verbs instructors commonly use in essay questions.

> *analyze:* give main divisions or elements, emphasizing essentials
> *classify:* arrange into main classes or divisions
> *compare:* point out likenesses
> *contrast:* point out differences
> *criticize:* give your opinion as to good and bad features
> *define:* explain the meaning, distinguish from similar terms
> *describe:* name the features in chronological or spatial order
> *discuss:* examine in detail
> *evaluate:* give your opinion of the value or validity
> *explain:* make clear, give reasons for
> *illustrate:* give one or more examples of
> *interpret:* give the meaning or significance
> *justify:* defend, show to be right
> *review:* examine on a broad scale
> *summarize:* briefly go over the essentials

To make sure that in writing you do not stray from the question, repeat its key word or words in your opening sentence.

Writing the answers

Before beginning to write an answer to a question, remember that the instructor expects you to demonstrate *specific* knowledge on the subject. A succession of vague generalities will not be ac-
28.5 ceptable. Even if you are discussing a fairly broad general topic, support whatever generalizations you make with specific illus-
Exam trations. Do not omit essential particulars because you assume the instructor is familiar with them already. Of course he is; the main purpose of his examination is to find out what knowledge *you* have acquired.

A scratch outline (§25.4, page 361) of the main points you plan to develop in your answer may be useful as a guide in writing. But whether you make an outline or not, make a concentrated effort to set your thoughts down in some logical order: all the sentences should relate to the question asked, and each should lead to the next in an orderly fashion. Many essay answers are unsuccessful because the student, although well-informed, presents information in a haphazard, unrelated fashion, giving the impression that he is thoroughly confused on the subject. Remember that the *length* of the answer is not the criterion of its worth: choosing the right facts and organizing them sensibly will impress the reader far more. Avoid throwing in unrelated material just to demonstrate your knowledge or to disguise your ignorance of more pertinent information. Since the time you have to write your answer is limited, you should confine yourself strictly to what you know about the specific question asked. Your instructor is not likely to give you much credit for a short essay on the wrong subject, no matter how good it may be.

Examination answers should be written in acceptable General English. Although the instructor will not expect an essay written in class to be as fully developed and as polished in style as one written at home, he will expect it to be adequate in grammar, usage, and the mechanics of writing. Even if a paper is otherwise accurate, frequent misspellings do much to lower the reader's opinion of it. Take particular care to spell and use correctly any technical terms or names that have been used in the course: *myosis*, *mercantile*, *assize*, *neurosis*, *imagery*, *Lamarck*, *Malthus*, *Schopenhauer*. An instructor will be understandably disturbed if he thinks you have paid scant attention to terms you have heard in class and read in the text numerous times. Careful proofreading of the answers will help you eliminate any careless errors you may have made and will also give you a chance to fill in gaps in information.

Examples of essay answers

Reproduced on the following pages are essay answers in biology, history, and American literature. Read each question carefully, decide what sort of answer is required, and compare the two student answers. Then read the criticisms that follow. The sentences in the answers are numbered to facilitate discussion.

Question: Define *dominant* as it is used in genetics.

Answer A:

(1) In genetics, dominant is the opposite of recessive. (2) Different characteristics are inherited by the individual by means of genes acquired from the male and female parents. (3) These genes are arranged, or carried, on chromosomes, and are paired, one from each parent. (4) A good deal is still unknown about the behavior of genes, although the science of genetics is making rapid progress. (5) Gregor Mendel, a monk, made discoveries in heredity by doing experiments with sweet peas. (6) He found that certain traits are stronger (dominant) and others are weaker (recessive). (7) Therefore, if two genes carry the same characteristic, one will be dominant over the other. (8) Examples of this are dark eyes, normal color vision, etc.

Criticism: Answer A contains irrelevant general information (sentences 2-5) and does not give a clear definition of *dominant*. You cannot explain the meaning of a word simply by naming its opposite (sentence 1). "Stronger" and "weaker" (sentence 6) are poor synonyms because they have such a variety of meanings. The answer also misleads by oversimplification: sentence 7 implies that complete dominance occurs in *all* pairings of genes. It is also not clear to what species of life the two examples in the last sentence (dark eyes and normal color vision) refer.

28.5

Answer B:

(1) The term *dominant* as used in genetics refers to that situation in which one gene in a pair takes precedence over another in determining a given characteristic in the individual. (2) For example, if a child inherits a gene for blue eyes from one parent and for brown eyes from the other, he will have brown eyes. (3) This is because the brown-eyed gene is *dominant;* the blue is *recessive.* (4) He still carries both genes and may transmit either to his offspring, but one has masked the effect of the other in his physical appearance. (5) Clear dominance does not occur in all pairings, however. (6) Sometimes *mixed dominance* occurs, as in the case of sweet peas, where a cross between a red and a white parent produces pink offspring. (7) Some cases of dominance are *sex-linked;* the gene for color blindness in humans, for instance, is dominant in the male and recessive in the female.

Criticism: Answer B is satisfactory. The term is clearly defined in the first sentence. Sentences 2-4 give an example of its use, distinguish it from its opposite, and add an important qualification. Sentences 5-7 note two important variants in the meaning of the term. There is no irrelevant material.

Question: Compare and contrast English and Spanish colonial methods in the New World.

Answer A:

(1) The Plymouth colony suffered many hardships in the early years of its existence. (2) This was also true of the Roanoke colony, but it eventually failed and did not survive. (3) The climate was more promising there, but it seemed as if the kind of people it included, like gentlemen unused to work, adventurers, and renegades, did not have the patience and religious fervor of the New England settlers. (4) The same was true of the Spanish colonies in Florida and elsewhere—the climate was good, but the men were selfish and had no direction. (5) The Spanish were more cruel toward the Indians than the English, and there was nothing constructive in their aims.

Criticism: More than half the answer (sentences 1-3) contrasts *two English colonies* rather than *English and Spanish colonial methods.* Mention of climate in sentences 3 and 4 is also irrelevant to a question dealing with methods. "Selfish" and "had no direction" need further explanation, as do "cruel toward the Indians" and "nothing constructive."

Answer B:

(1) The Spanish generally thought of the New World as a reservoir of riches to be tapped. (2) The great Spanish conquerors, like Cortez and Pizarro, were explorer-adventurers whose main aim was to subjugate the native population and wrench from them whatever riches and power they possessed. (3) The Spanish method was usually to impose a military dictatorship upon a restive populace; the domination depended on military force. (4) The English, on the other hand, thought of the New World colonies as a *permanent* extension of English civilization. (5) Their methods were not to immediately extract native riches, but to plant the seeds of English life in the new continent. (6) Unlike the Spaniards, the English generally emigrated in family units, placated rather than subdued the native inhabitants, invested labor and capital in the New World soil, and awaited long-term fruits. (7) Settlement was their aim rather than exploitation.

Criticism: This answer is much more satisfactory than A. The basic differences in aim and the consequent differences in method are fairly well stated. The first section of the answer (sentences 1-3) describes Spanish methods; the second (sentences 4-7) presents the significant differences in English aim and method.

Question: Explain the significance of Walt Whitman's *Leaves of Grass* in the development of American literature.

Answer A:

(1) *Leaves of Grass,* by Walt Whitman, was published in 1851, more than a hundred years ago. (2) It was a long personal poem in free verse. (3) At first it did not get a very favorable reaction, although some critics liked it, but today it is widely praised. (4) It was important because

1) free verse
2) celebrated America
3) democratic
4) realism

(5) Carl Sandburg, in poems like "Chicago," (1920?) writes in the tradition established in *Leaves of Grass.* (6) Among Sandburg's contemporaries were Vachel Lindsay and William Vaughn Moody and Hart Crane. (7) *Leaves of Grass* brought new freedom to American poetry because it broke from many of the old traditions in poetry like that of Longfellow and Whittier. (8) Therefore, it is truly significant.

Criticism: Sentences 1-3 and 6 do not specifically relate to the question. The heart of the answer seems to be sentence 4, but the unexplained list of headings conveys nothing. If these points are important, each should be developed in a separate sentence or two. Sentences 5 and 7 also seem to be relevant but are vague. *What* tradition did *Leaves of Grass* establish? *What* old traditions did it break? Was "Chicago" written in 1920 or not?

Answer B:

(1) Although Whitman's *Leaves of Grass* has many characteristics of nineteenth-century Romantic literature, it is an important landmark in American literature. (2) At a time when American poetry was rigidly conventional in meter and rhyme, Whitman boldly experimented with varying line lengths and free verse. (3) In subject matter, too, *Leaves of Grass* explored new frontiers. (4) A disciple of democracy and modern technology, Whitman made frequent reference to common trades and people, machinery and the less savory details of urban life: all considered "low" subjects unfit for poetry by such traditionalists as Longfellow and Whittier. (5) In his choice of such subjects and in the frankness with which he discussed human behavior, Whitman was preparing the way for the Realistic movement which was to emerge toward the close of the century. (6) Twentieth-century celebrants of industrial America like Sandburg and Hart Crane were poetic descendants of Whitman; even today, poets like Allen Ginsberg are indebted to Whitman in style and attitude.

Criticism: In this essay the points merely listed in A are developed and made specific. The relation of the poem to both earlier and later poetic traditions is explained. All sentences are relevant and are well related to each other.

28.6 Reports

The various kinds of reports you will be asked to prepare in school or on a job may require special forms of presentation, but the problems of gathering, organizing, and developing materials for reports are about the same as for expository papers. Usually the assignment of a report will define your subject for you and suggest the kind of resources you will need. For example, if a committee of the Student Congress wants to propose changes in the campus rules concerning dress, it may first ask a member of the committee to prepare a report on how the problem has been handled at other colleges and universities. Thus, the member's task is clearly defined for him: he must accumulate statements of policy regarding dress from the catalogs and guidebooks of other schools and then give an impartial account of his findings to the rest of the committee.

Usually the subject of a report will determine how you should approach your audience. Some reports, such as sales reports and progress reports, can appropriately include opinions, but most call for a straightforward presentation of factual information.

Class reports

The oral or written reports you may be asked to prepare for some of your classes are not drastically different from committee reports and other work you may engage in outside school. Ordinarily the purpose of a report is to bring before an audience (a class, a committee, one's employer) information that it might not receive otherwise. Class reports are often intended to acquaint class members with a book, an experiment, a field experience, or some other kind of information which is important to them but which they do not have time or opportunity to gather for themselves. Here is a fairly typical plan for a class report:

An introduction setting the limits to your report and explaining the topic

A brief note on the sources of your information

A chronological presentation of any background material

A transitional passage identifying your main point and any contributing minor points

A discussion of each minor point

A discussion of your major point

A conclusion discussing the pertinence of your report to the work in which your audience is engaged

Laboratory reports

Laboratory reports present information only. Typically, they describe the specific methods used in research as well as the results obtained. Most science courses have a guide that prescribes the form of laboratory reports, as do most companies that depend on laboratory work.

Briefings and critiques

Ordinarily a *briefing* is intended to prepare a group of people to do a particular piece of work; a *critique* is an evaluation of the work once it has been done. These types of reports are becoming increasingly important because of the trend in most institutions to involve more and more people in planning and decision-making. A briefing and a critique might typically follow these patterns:

Briefing:

A brief introductory account of the circumstances bringing you together (a program, a project, a piece of work to be done)

A brief account of the origin, nature, and goals of the program

A brief account of the various separate programs and goals that form the total program

An account of the goals of each specific part of the program

An account of how each of the specific programs integrates with the others

A presentation of the schedule that must be followed

A conclusion reiterating the importance of each separate program to the whole program

Critique:

An introduction discussing the success or failure of the program as a whole

An evaluation of each of the separate programs, with criticism of their accomplishments and suggestions for future programs

An evaluation of the whole program, with recommendations for change or shifted emphasis in the future

An evaluation of practical planning, schedules, deadlines, with recommendations for change if necessary

A summary of the achievements of the program

28.7 Writing about literature

In your college English courses you will frequently be called upon to write about literature—to examine, interpret, and discuss fiction, poetry, drama. Although students sometimes think that such assignments call for a special set of skills, literary analysis and interpretation is not radically different from the analytical reading and interpretive writing you might do in history, philosophy, and sociology courses or from your critical response to an editorial, magazine article, sermon, or letter to the editor. We read an editorial, presumably, not just to discover the overt statement it makes, but also to discover the writer's motivation, the choices and assumptions he has made in selecting and presenting his material, the values he has expressed and those he has implied through the connotative impact of his words. In much the same manner, we examine a piece of literature critically and sort out our thoughts about it in order to understand it more fully.

In writing about literature, as in all kinds of writing, you must first discover a definite subject (§25.1). An assignment to write about a particular literary work such as *Gulliver's Travels* does not necessarily give you a topic or a thesis to work from: you must still find a reason for writing, a point you wish to make about the book. The following classification of types of criticism may help you to focus on a subject when you are planning a paper about a work of literature. This classification is based largely on a list of areas for literary research compiled by Professor B. Bernard Cohen in his *Writing About Literature.*

1) *Textual analysis.* One kind of literary criticism is devoted to a close examination of the text itself—preparation and publication, revisions, errors or misprintings, various editions, and so forth. Part of the meaning of Book III of *Gulliver's Travels* was clarified, for example, with the discovery—some 175 years after initial publication—of a short passage that had been printed in the first edition but had been deleted thereafter. It is unlikely that you will do highly specialized textual research for the papers you are assigned in undergraduate courses, but you can often find a subject in existing textual problems (such as the effect on the meaning of Keats' "Ode on a Grecian Urn" of the punctuation of the last two lines).

2) *Relationships among the author's works.* It is sometimes useful to examine the work in hand by considering it in the light of the author's other works. For example, it may be possible to understand the manner of *Gulliver's Travels* better by considering it along with "A Modest Proposal" and some of Swift's other satires.

3) *Relevance to biography.* Some papers on literary subjects can profitably examine the particular circumstances in the author's life that helped give shape to his work.

4) *Study of the creative process.* If primary sources such as letters and diaries are available, it is possible sometimes to study a given work for what it reveals about the creative process. Why did Swift write the four books of *Gulliver's Travels* in an order other than that in which they are printed?

5) *Relation of the work to literary theory.* It is also possible to develop fruitful explorations of a work by examining it in the light of theories about art and literature current when the work was written.

6) *Impact of the times on the work.* Sometimes it is interesting to approach a literary work as an artifact, to determine how it records and reflects the ideas and events of its own time.

7) *Relationship of the work to literary tradition.* A work of literature can be studied in terms of the literary habits, assumptions, and techniques the author has inherited from other writers. You might examine *Gulliver's Travels*, for example, to see how Swift adopted, rejected, or refined the techniques of satire that were already in use.

8) *Relationship of the work to a particular subject area.* Sometimes you can find a worth-while subject for a paper by looking at a literary work for what it reveals about a particular field of interest or idea. You could, for example, increase your understanding of *Gulliver's Travels* and write something of interest about it by focusing on what it says about English politics.

9) *Reception of the work.* You can often learn a great deal about a work by discovering how it was received in its own day or at any later time.

10) *Interpretive essay.* An interpretive essay calls for you to work out your own response to a literary work. In developing your

ideas for such a paper, remember that you will not know enough about the work to write a thoughtful interpretation after one cursory reading. You should read through the entire work rather quickly at first to get a sense of its whole development, but then you will ordinarily need to return to it for closer readings. Don't feel that you must read complicated implications in every line or on every page, but read carefully enough to know the work well, so that you can synthesize your interpretation from the details you observe in character development, structure, choice of language, and the like. In interpreting a literary work you will find it useful to examine the work to see what artistic problems it posed for the author and what choices he made in solving them.

28.8 Letters

Although letter-writing is not ordinarily taught in composition courses, it is one of the most important forms of written expression. In many situations, letters are the only means you have to make yourself heard. They deserve your best effort.

What you say in a letter and the way you say it will depend upon your purpose, the person you are writing to, and, above all, upon the way you customarily express yourself. Beyond that, you should be familiar with the conventions of correspondence, so that the form and appearance of your letters will make the intended impression. The form established for business letters is standard for most kinds of formal correspondence.

Business letters

Neatness, clarity, and directness are the chief virtues of a business letter. It should include all relevant information (such as dates, prices, description of merchandise) and should be as brief as is consistent with clarity. The tone should be courteous, even if you are complaining about an error.

The sample letter on page 443 illustrates the content and form of a typical business letter. Notice the position and punctuation of the heading, inside address, greeting (salutation), and close.

Spacing and general appearance. Select stationery of appropriate size and good quality, with envelopes to match. Good stationery costs little more than an inferior grade, and it will make a much better impression on the person who receives your letter. For business letters the standard sheet is 8½ x 11 inches, the same size as ordinary typing paper.

Typed letters are expected in business correspondence, and they are becoming increasingly popular for personal correspondence. In typing your letter, leave generous margins and center the body of the letter so that the page will be well balanced in appearance. Space paragraphs distinctly, using either block or indented form. Block paragraphs are set flush with the left margin of the letter; they are separated by a line space, as shown in the sample on page 443. For indented paragraphs, begin five spaces from the left-hand margin. Be consistent in form. If a letter runs to more than one page, use a separate sheet of paper for each page and number the pages at the top.

The heading. A heading should be typed in the upper right-hand corner, giving the writer's complete address and the date. The standard form is the block pattern, with end punctuation omitted. The name of the city, the state, and the month are generally written out in full:

902 Luther Place
Duluth, Minnesota 55804
January 5, 1968

If you use a letterhead which includes the address, type the date below it, flush with the right-hand margin or centered, depending on the design of the letterhead.

Inside address and greeting. The inside address of a business letter gives the full name and address of the person or firm to whom it is directed. It appears flush with the left-hand margin, at least one line below the last line of the heading. No punctuation is used at the ends of the lines. If you wish to mention the person's title or position in the firm, put the designation immediately below his name in the inside address:

Mr. Robert Cunningham
Personnel Director
Allen, Swift and Company
4863 Commercial Street
Dallas, Texas 75222

1512 Moore Street
South Bend, Indiana 46556
September 11, 1966

Matthews Camera Company
5412 S. Kenwood Avenue
Chicago, Illinois 60637

Gentlemen:

The Odyssey Camera, Model 2-S, that I ordered from you (Invoice No. 7343) came yesterday.

In examining it I found that the shutter is stuck fast and will not open when I push the release. In addition, two of the lens attachments are scratched and the third does not fit the camera. I am returning the entire order with this letter and hope that you will replace it promptly.

Can you tell me when the telephoto attachment for this model will be available?

Yours very truly,

Robert St. Clair

Robert St. Clair

The greeting, or *salutation*, appears below the inside address, separated from it by a line of space. In business letters it is followed by a colon. If the letter is addressed to a particular individual in a firm, you may use either his name or an impersonal greeting:

Dear Mr. Keiser: [*or* Dear Sir:]
Dear Miss Jenkins: [*or* Dear Madam:]

If it is addressed to the firm as a whole or to an individual whom you do not know by name, use the masculine form of address:

Gentlemen:
Dear Sirs:
Dear Sir:

Close and signature. A conventional expression called the *complimentary close* is used at the end of the letter. Only the first word of the close is capitalized and a comma customarily follows. The general tone of the letter will suggest how formal the close should be:

Formal	*Less formal*
Yours truly,	Sincerely yours,
Yours very truly,	Sincerely,
Respectfully yours,	Yours sincerely,

The signature is always written in longhand below the close. For clarity, however, you should type your name below your signature. In business letters a woman indicates in parentheses whether she is *Mrs.* or *Miss* by one of these formulas:

(Miss) Cynthia R. Holt

(Mrs.) Cynthia H. Adamic

Cynthia H. Adamic
(Mrs. Edmund B. Adamic)

Addressing the envelope. Both the address of the person to whom you are writing and your own address should be clear and complete on the front of the envelope. A block style—with the left-hand margin even—is the standard form for both addresses.

No punctuation is used at the end of the lines in this form. A comma is used between the name of a city and the state if they are put on the same line, but not between the state and the ZIP code: Chicago, Illinois 60611.

Barbara Stewart
1421 College Avenue
Iowa City, Iowa 52240

Mr. Robert Cunningham
Personnel Director
Allen, Swift and Company
4863 Commercial Street
Dallas, Texas 75222

When you abbreviate street designations, use the standard forms (*St.* for *Street*, *Ave.* for *Avenue*, *Blvd.* for *Boulevard*). For names of states, use only those abbreviations given in your dictionary (*Penn.*, *Okla.*).

Use an envelope that matches your stationery and fold the letter to fit. With long business envelopes, a standard sheet (8½ x 11 inches) is folded horizontally into three sections. With short business envelopes, it is folded once across the middle and then twice in the other direction.

Letters of application

Among the more important—and most difficult—kinds of letters that you may have occasion to write are letters of application. When you apply by letter for a job, or perhaps for admission to a school, you are in effect trying to "sell yourself" through your writing. In such situations you may be torn between undue modesty and an understandable desire to present yourself in the most favorable light. The best thing to do is to express yourself simply and sincerely, to give all pertinent information, and to put your letter in attractive and suitable form. A sample letter of application is shown on page 446.

The form of most letters of application—the heading, spacing, close, and so on—follows that of a typical business letter. To get the proper arrangement on the page, type an experimental draft of your letter. Before you mail the letter, be particularly careful to check for mechanical errors. A prospective employer will not

856 East Oceanside Drive
Los Angeles, California 90016
June 5, 1967

Dr. Hamilton Caine
Director of Research
Roan-Settering Foundation
780 West Augusta Boulevard
Los Angeles, California 90004

Dear Dr. Caine:

Your classified notice in the current Journal of Pathology states that there is an opening for a bacteriologist on your staff. I would like to apply for the position.

I have a B.S. degree in bacteriology from Midwestern University in Green Bay, Wisconsin, where I graduated in 1965. I have also attended one summer session at the University of Chicago, where I took a special seminar in microbiology and statistical techniques. While a student at Midwestern, I worked for two summers as a part-time laboratory assistant in the Department of Bacteriology. I also worked one summer for the late Dr. Joseph Roth at the Froude Institute in Chicago, helping him prepare the statistical tables for his recently published Tropical Diseases. Since October 1965 I have been a bacteriologist for the Los Angeles Board of Health. I am twenty-four years old, single, and in good health.

A transcript of my academic work will be supplied on request by the Registrar at Midwestern University. The following persons have consented to furnish letters of reference:

Dr. Donald Fenton, Chairman, Department of Bacteriology, Midwestern University, Green Bay, Wisconsin 54312

Mr. Burton Powers, Froude Institute, 5116 S. Kimbark Avenue, Chicago, Illinois 60637

Dr. George Komer, Los Angeles Board of Health, 212 Vine Street, Los Angeles, California 90017

If my qualifications are satisfactory, I would appreciate an interview at your convenience. My phone number is 267-1927.

Yours sincerely,

Nancy Wallace

(Miss) Nancy Wallace

1734 Hilltop Road
Hartford, Connecticut 06118
May 16, 1967

Professor Robert Lawson
5142 S. University Avenue
Pittsburgh, Pennsylvania 15007

Dear Professor Lawson:

Since my graduation from the university two years ago I have been working as a claims adjustor for the Equity Life Insurance Company here in Hartford. I have found this job very satisfying and have gained valuable experience from it, but now I hope to obtain an even better position with a firm in New Orleans: Williams, Le Sage, and Company. This is one of the largest accounting firms in the South, and it offers excellent opportunities for advancement.

The personnel office of Williams, Le Sage has asked me to obtain several letters of recommendation from persons familiar with my academic background. Since you were my advisor and supervised the writing of my Honors paper, I believe you are particularly well qualified to judge my abilities. I would be very grateful if you would send a brief assessment of my work and personal qualifications to the following address:

Mr. Charles Smith
Personnel Director
Williams, Le Sage, and Company
912 Bourbon Street
New Orleans, Louisiana 70102

I hope to see you and thank you personally when I return to the campus for the Alumni Weekend next month.

Sincerely,

Stanley Seidman

Stanley Seidman

be favorably impressed if you misspell his name or any common words.

Give all the information the prospective employer requires (age, previous experience, education) and any other details you believe might be useful: why you want the job, what special qualifications you possess, and so on. Be careful, however, that you do not include irrelevant material. A letter that is brief and to the point will be better received than one that is long-winded.

Notice in the sample letter on page 446 that the writer begins by telling what job she is applying for. The body of the letter then lists the writer's previous experience and education, personal data, and references. In closing she suggests a personal interview and tells where she can be reached.

Always ask the permission of people you list as references. Give their complete addresses and correct titles (Professor, Dr., Mrs.). *Mr.*, *Mrs.*, and *Dr.* are the only titles that are abbreviated. All others are written in full.

If you are asked to include documents (such as photographs, transcripts of academic records, or photostats), use a crushproof envelope. If you want the enclosures returned to you, include a self-addressed, stamped envelope.

Keep a carbon copy of your letter. If you don't get the job, study the letter and try to improve on it next time.

Letters requesting recommendations

Some employers may ask you to supply letters of recommendation from former teachers or employers. Like application letters, requests for recommendations should be brief and courteous. Notice that in the sample letter on page 447 the writer begins by telling his former professor why he needs the recommendation. He then explains what kind of information the company requires and where the letter should be sent. He closes with an expression of personal gratitude. In writing such requests, be sure to remind the teacher or employer when you were his student or employee and where (which class or company department). It is difficult for a person to write a useful recommendation if he only vaguely remembers the writer.

Letters to editors and public figures

People in a democratic society often wish to express their

opinions to newspapers, magazines, or influential public figures. Such communications should be written in standard business letter form and should be brief and pointed. Even if you are expressing disagreement with some opinion or policy, try to be reasonable and courteous. Your letter is much more likely to have the desired effect if it relies on facts and sound logic than if it presents an impassioned subjective reaction. The more formal greeting and close (*Dear Sir: Yours very truly,*) are usual in these letters.

Consult the appropriate section of a dictionary or an etiquette book for the proper forms of address for senators, cabinet members, and other high government officials.

Personal correspondence

The types of correspondence discussed in the preceding sections present the major letter-writing problems for students. The form and manner of expression are crucial in making a favorable impression on a distant person or on an impersonal business organization. Other types of letters and notes, especially those written to friends, are relatively easier to compose.

Familiar correspondence is like conversation between friends: the tone is cordial and relaxed, the form less rigid than in other types of letters. This does not mean, however, that letters written to friends should be sloppy; they should be neat and legible as well as interesting. Taking some pains with the appearance of a letter and with such matters as spelling and punctuation is a courtesy you owe the reader. Revising an occasional personal letter will perhaps raise the level of all your correspondence.

Whether you should type a personal letter or write it in longhand depends upon the purpose of the letter and the person to whom you are writing. Typing is appropriate for many kinds of personal correspondence, but handwriting is always better for invitations and replies and for letters that convey sentiment or sympathy.

No heading except the date is needed between regular correspondents, but it never hurts to include your address in the heading, particularly when you write someone infrequently. The envelope with your return address is often discarded long before your letter is answered.

28.8

The greeting between friends is usually *Dear Bob* or *Dear Ruth*, followed by a comma. If you are writing to an older person, someone you do not call by first name, either of these forms will serve (the colon is more formal):

Dear Miss Breckenridge,
Dear Professor Brown:

The complimentary close ranges in warmth from *Love*, through *Yours* and *Sincerely*, to *Yours very truly* for persons whom you know only slightly.

Consult an etiquette book for the established forms used in issuing and replying to formal social invitations and announcements.

29 The reference paper

For it may be laid down as a maxim that he who begins by presuming on his own sense has ended his studies as soon as he has commenced them.— Joshua Reynolds

Planning and writing a reference paper (also called a library paper, a research paper, or a term paper) is an important part of most freshman composition courses. This project, often assigned in the middle or later part of the course, is a record of intelligent reading in several sources—books, magazines, encyclopedias, and other reference works. The preparation of a reference paper has much in common with other writing assignments, but in addition it provides:

1) Practice in exploring the possibilities of a subject and limiting it so that it can be treated adequately in a paper of a given length —typically from 1500 to 3000 words.

2) An introduction to the resources of the library and training in the most efficient ways of locating information.

3) Practice in using source material intelligently—choosing between what is useful and what is not, evaluating the ideas of others, organizing and interpreting the information.

4) Acquaintance with documentation and manuscript form typically expected in academic work and in reports and papers prepared for publication.

5) An opportunity to learn something new about a subject and to gain specialized, thorough knowledge of it.

Because the reference paper is longer and more complex than most other compositions you may be asked to write, it is discussed in terms of successive steps: choosing a topic (§29.1), locating appropriate source materials (§29.2), preparing the working bibliography (§29.3), taking notes (§29.4), evaluating your material (§29.5), planning the paper (§29.6), writing and revising the first draft (§29.7), documenting the paper (§29.8), and assembling the completed paper (§29.9). The actual task of preparing a reference paper, however, can seldom be divided into such neat categories. The steps overlap and certain operations must be repeated as work progresses. For example, as you get into your reading you may decide that your chosen topic needs to be modified; and as you write your paper you may discover gaps in your information that must be filled in by further reading. The best advice, perhaps, is to start on the assignment early and to take particular care in choosing and defining your topic, so that both your research and your writing will have a clear focus.

29.1 Choosing a topic

One important prerequisite for writing a good reference paper is that you should have a genuine interest in the subject you are going to investigate. In some courses, the subject field may be limited by the instructor's general assignment (perhaps to various aspects of the United Nations, or to the history of a specific geographic area, or to an author or work of literature you have studied); but more often the choice of a subject will be left up to you.

In either instance, you should be reasonably certain that the specific topic you select will be one that you will like to read about, to think about, and then to write about. Since a reference paper may take as much as five or six weeks to prepare, it can easily become a chore—and be largely a waste of time—unless you feel that what you are doing is of some interest and importance. The suggestions in §25.1, Discovering a subject, are as relevant to the reference paper as they are to other kinds of writing.

Choosing a subject area

Before making a definite decision on your topic, consider your various interests in and out of school. These general subjects may suggest particular topics that you might want to investigate:

1) A subject related to one of the courses that you are now taking or that you intend to take. For example, if you are going to major in business administration and you intend to take American economic history next year, you might investigate the beginning of child labor laws or early life insurance companies in the United States.

2) A subject related to your reading interests (biography, history, science fiction, detective stories) or one related to your favorite hobby or sport (music, dress design, mountain climbing, baseball).

3) A subject about which you now have an opinion but little actual information. Does capital punishment help prevent crime? Are children with high IQ's generally successful in later life? Is hazing in fraternities declining? Do rapid readers retain more than slow readers?

4) A subject that has aroused your curiosity but that you have never had time or opportunity to investigate. Of what value are computers in education today? Do sun spots actually affect the weather? How has the popularity of television affected book sales? Can rain be made by cloud seeding?

You will be likely to find a real purpose in writing if you select a topic that ties in with one of your current interests.

Limiting the topic

As soon as you know what general subject area you would like to concentrate on, find a specific topic within that area that can be treated adequately and profitably in a paper of the assigned length. Keep these considerations in mind when you are narrowing your topic:

1) *Length of the reference paper.* A freshman reference paper is not expected to be the last word on a topic; neither is it intended to be a disconnected enumeration of commonplace facts or a superficial summary of a complex topic. Limit your topic enough so that your treatment of it can be reasonably thorough. The danger of selecting a topic that is too narrow is far less than the danger of choosing one that is too broad and lacks focus. (See §25.1, page 347, Narrowing the topic.)

2) *Availability of source material.* Before you begin to read and take notes, find out whether the more important books and periodicals that you will need are available in your college library. Since half-a-dozen or more sources are usually required for a reference paper, you should be certain that enough material is available before you begin your research.

3) *Complexity of the source material.* For some subjects (chemical structures of synthetic rubber, for example), the available material may be too technical for a general reader to understand—and perhaps too complicated for you to interpret without a good deal of study.

If you have only a hazy notion about the approach you might take to the general subject you have selected, explore its possibilities by spending a few hours doing some preliminary background reading in one or more general or special encyclopedias (many are listed in §29.2, pages 461-469), in some magazine articles, and perhaps in some newspaper articles, if the subject you have chosen is one of current interest and likely to be covered by the daily press.

Next, look through the library card catalog and the guides to periodical literature (§29.2) to see how the general subject you have selected may be broken down into smaller units. A broad subject like *aviation* might first be limited to *commercial aviation*, then to *the functions of the CAA*, and then still further to *recent safety measures suggested by the CAA.*

Final definition of the topic

Before you begin to take notes, define your topic as precisely and clearly as possible. At this early stage in your planning, you are not expected to make a final statement of the central or controlling idea of your paper; but if you have decided to write on *rural electrification*, for example, you should certainly know whether you intend to discuss *the progress of rural electrification in the South* or *changes in farming methods brought about by electricity.* Unless you have a reasonably accurate idea of what the focus of your paper will be, your reading will be without direction and a great deal of the material you gather may later have to be discarded as useless. It is a good idea to check your topic with your instructor before you begin your research.

Avoid drastic last-minute changes in your topic unless it has proved completely unsuitable. A sudden switch, two or three weeks after the paper has been assigned, wastes precious time and usually indicates that the original topic was chosen hastily and without enough thought.

It is often advisable, however, to make minor changes in a topic. As you are gathering and evaluating your material, you may decide that you should narrow your topic further or shift its emphasis slightly, perhaps changing *the process of making oil paints* to *sources of pigments for oil paints.* Consult your instructor about any changes you would like to make in your topic before you continue extensive reading.

29.2 Locating appropriate source materials

One purpose of the reference paper is to acquaint you with the resources of your college library so that you can locate the information you need quickly and efficiently. On most subjects, the material in the library is so extensive and so varied in form (books, periodicals, encyclopedias, newspapers, pamphlets) that a writer about to begin his research would be hopelessly lost unless he knew something about the essential works in his subject, the methods used to index and catalog material, and the quickest way to obtain this information.

This section deals with library facilities and the various aids that will help you find the material for a reference paper. Librarians are always willing to help a student with his research problems, but every student should also be willing to help the librarians, too, by showing some knowledge of the standard sources of reference.

The library card catalog

The card catalog is an alphabetical card index of the items in the library. The cards, filed in drawers or trays, are located in the main reading room or other central spot. Most card catalogs, in addition to listing all books in the library, give the titles of periodicals (and indicate what copies the library has), encyclopedias, government publications, and other works.

Almost all books are listed in three places in the card catalog of most libraries, alphabetized by author, by subject, and by title. The cards issued by the Library of Congress, like those reproduced on the next page for *Forty Acres and Steel Mules* by Herman Clarence Nixon, are almost universally used for cataloging.

You can save yourself many hours of thumbing through books that are not relevant to your subject by learning to interpret and evaluate the information given in the card catalog. The subject card reproduced on page 456, for example, includes the following information (keyed to the circled numbers on the card):

1) *Subject.* The subject heading on the catalog card tells in general what the book is about. In this instance, the general subject is agricultural administration. Also listed on the card (in item 7) are the other subject headings under which the book is cataloged.

Subject card

① AGRICULTURAL ADMINISTRATION

②
309.175 **Nixon, Herman Clarence, 1886–** ③
N65f ④ ... **Forty acres and steel mules. Chapel Hill, The University of North Carolina press, 1938.**

⑤ vii, 98 p. front., plates. 27 cm.

⑥ "Selected bibliography": p. 97–98.

⑦ 1. Agriculture—Southern states. 2. Southern states—Soc. condit. 3. Southern states—Econ. condit.—1918– 4. Agricultural administration—U. S. I. Title.

⑧ HD207.N5 630.975 38—17363

Library of Congress [73k½]

Author card

309.175 **Nixon, Herman Clarence, 1886–**
N65f ... **Forty acres and steel mules. Chapel Hill, The University of North Carolina press, 1938.**

vii, 98 p. front., plates. 27 cm.

Title card

Forty acres and steel mules

309.175 **Nixon, Herman Clarence, 1886–**
N65f ... **Forty acres and steel mules. Chapel Hill, The University of North Carolina press, 1938.**

vii, 98 p. front., plates. 27 cm.

2) *Call number.* The call number in the upper left-hand corner tells where the book is located in the library. In most libraries, borrowers obtain books by filling out a slip with the call number, author, title, and the borrower's name and address. If you have access to the stacks, the call number will enable you to locate the book you are looking for.

3) *Author's name and birthdate.* If you are already familiar with the subject you are investigating, the author's name may tell you whether the book is likely to be authoritative.

4) *Title and facts of publication.* The date of publication is sometimes an important clue to the usefulness of a book. For example,

if you are looking for more recent information on agricultural administration in the South than would have been available in 1938, you will not waste time examining this book.

5) *Number of pages, illustrations, height.* The number of pages in the book suggests how extensive its coverage is. This book is brief—98 pages of text, plus seven (vii) pages of introductory material. Notice, however, that it contains illustrations (plates) that may be useful. (The indication of height—27 cm.—is for librarians.)

6) *Special information.* The catalog card indicates that the book contains a two-page bibliography that might prove helpful in directing you to other sources. None of the books listed, however, would be later than 1938, the year in which this particular book was published.

7) *Other subject headings.* The list of other subject headings under which the book is cataloged may provide a further clue to its content. The subject headings for this book show that it is concerned with agricultural administration in the South but also has more general bearing (4. Agricultural administration—U.S.).

8) *Facts for librarians.* The information at the bottom of the catalog card—the Library of Congress classification (HD207.N5) and so on—is for the use of librarians and need not concern you.

See §29.3, page 470, Preparing the working bibliography, to see what information from the library catalog card should be included on your own bibliography card.

Trade bibliographies

The bibliographies published for booksellers and librarians should be consulted to locate books that are not listed in the card catalog of your library or to learn if a book is still in print. The most important trade bibliographies are:

Books in Print. New York, 1948-date. A listing by author and by title of books included in *Publisher's Trade List Annual* (New York, 1847-date), which lists—by publisher—all books currently in print.

Cumulative Book Index. New York, 1900-date. Gives complete publication data on all books published in the English language, listing them by author and by title. Published monthly, with cumulative volumes issued periodically.

Paperbound Books in Print. New York, 1955-date. Especially useful since some important books are available *only* in paperback. Published monthly, with cumulative volumes issued three times a year.

Subject Guide to Books in Print. New York, 1957-date. An invaluable index to the titles listed in *Books in Print.*

Periodical indexes

A great deal of essential material, particularly on current topics, is available only in periodicals, which may range from popular magazines and newspapers to technical journals and learned publications. This material is cataloged in various guides and indexes, some of them published monthly, others annually. Knowing how to use periodical indexes will not only simplify the task of research but will also enable you to make your reference paper more authoritative and up to date.

Readers' Guide. The most generally useful of all periodical guides is the *Readers' Guide to Periodical Literature* (New York, 1900-date), which indexes the articles in more than 120 magazines of general interest. It is published monthly in paperbound volumes which are afterwards gathered in large cumulative volumes covering a year or more.

The entries in the *Readers' Guide* are listed alphabetically both by subject and by author. The abbreviations used in the listings—for the titles of periodicals, the month of publication, and various facts about the article itself—are explained on the first page of each volume. On page 459 is a reproduction and explanation of five consecutive main entries from a monthly issue.

Other periodical indexes. In locating sources for a reference paper you may find it useful to refer to one of the specialized periodical indexes listed below. Most of them appear annually; the year after the title shows when publication began. The indexes are listed alphabetically.

29.2 Ref

Applied Science and Technology Index. New York, 1913-date. Subject index to periodicals on science, technology, and related subjects.

Art Index. New York, 1929-date. Author and subject index for fine-arts periodicals and museum bulletins.

Bibliographic Index: A Cumulative Bibliography of Bibliographies. New York, 1938-date.

Sample entries from the Readers' Guide

(1) **GUEST, Barbara**
Travel talk; poem. Nation 192:487 Je 3 '61
(2) **GUIDANCE.** See Vocational guidance
(3) **GUIDANCE systems for space vehicles.** See Space vehicles—Control systems
(4) **GUIDEBOOKS**
Potluck on the road; Mobil travel guide. il Time 77:44+ Je 2 '61
(5) **GUIDED missile bases**
Featherbedding on the pads. Time 77:78-9 My 5 '61
$500 a week, strikes, and delays for missile bases. il US news 50:103-4 My 8 '61
Goldberg ready to move against work stoppages. Miss & Roc 8:54 My 22 '61
Lessons from the labor hearings. W. J. Coughlin. Miss & Roc 8:54 My 22 '61
Missile base labor rules face overhaul. G. C. Wilson. Aviation W 74:77+ My 22 '61

Explanation: The heading for (1) is an *author* entry. Barbara Guest is the author of a poem entitled "Travel Talk" published on page 487 in volume 192 of the magazine *Nation* for June 3, 1961. The number before the colon in each entry refers to the volume of the periodical; the number after the colon refers to the page.

Entries like (2) and (3) that are followed by *See* are cross references to articles listed elsewhere in the *Guide.*

Items (4) and (5) are subject entries. In this particular volume of *Readers' Guide* only one article on "Guidebooks" (4) is listed. This is an illustrated (il) article on the Mobil travel guide entitled "Potluck on the Road" in volume 77 of *Time* for June 2, 1961. It begins on page 44 and is continued elsewhere in the issue.

"Guided missile bases" (5), a subject entry, is followed by a list of *titles* of articles on this subject found in various magazines issued during the period which this particular *Readers' Guide* covers. The wording of the title and the information thereafter are often useful in determining whether an article may be helpful or not in gathering material for a reference paper. A quick glance will indicate that all of the articles under (5) are written about the labor issues arising on guided missile bases.

Biography Index: A Cumulative Index to Biographical Material in Books and Magazines. New York, 1946/47-date.

Book Review Digest. New York, 1905-date. Author, subject, and title index to published book reviews; gives extracts and exact references to sources.

Business Periodicals Index. New York, 1958-date. Subject index to periodicals on all phases of business, including particular industries and trades.

Catholic Periodical Index: A Guide to Catholic Magazines. Scranton, Pa., 1930-date.

Dramatic Index. Boston, 1909-1949. Index to articles and illustrations concerning the American and English theater.

The Education Index. New York, 1929-1964. Author and subject index for educational periodicals, books, and pamphlets.

Poole's Index to Periodical Literature. Boston, 1802-1881. Subject index to American and English periodicals, many of which are no longer published but are still important; supplements cover the years 1882-1906; precedes coverage of *Readers' Guide.*

Public Affairs Information Service. New York, 1915-date. Subject index to books, periodicals, pamphlets, and other material on economics, government, and other public affairs.

Social Sciences and Humanities Index. New York, 1907-date. Author and subject index to periodicals from various countries; devoted chiefly to the humanities and social sciences; formerly titled *International Index to Periodicals;* supplements *Readers' Guide.*

United States Government Publications Monthly Catalog. Washington, D.C., 1895-date. Lists various publications of the government in all fields.

29.2 **Directory of periodicals.** *Ulrich's International Periodical Directory* answers the question "What periodicals are available in this field?" It classifies both American and foreign periodicals by subject area and also tells which periodical indexes cover them. Volume I of this periodical directory (12th ed. New York, 1967/68) covers scientific, technical, and medical periodicals. Volume II (11th ed. New York, 1965/66) covers the arts, humanities, business, and social sciences. At the start of each volume is a list of publications devoted primarily to abstracting articles in different fields. Earlier editions of *Ulrich's* (first published in 1932) do not include foreign periodicals.

Newspaper index

The New York Times Index (New York, 1913-date) is a monthly index to articles appearing in *The New York Times*, with annual volumes. This index will help you find articles of general interest in local papers as well as in the *Times*, because it gives the dates of events, speeches, and important documents that presumably would be covered in all papers of the same date.

Pamphlet index

The *Vertical File Index: A Subject and Title Index to Selected Pamphlet Material* (New York, 1932/35-date) describes each pamphlet listed, tells how to purchase it, and lists the price.

General encyclopedias

The following general encyclopedias are authoritative and include many bibliographies and cross references. All are regularly revised; several are supplemented annually with yearbooks (see pages 469-470).

Chambers's Encyclopaedia. 15 vols. Volume 15 contains a general index.

Collier's Encyclopedia. 24 vols. Volume 24 contains a general index and bibliography. Supplemented annually.

Columbia Encyclopedia. A single-volume encyclopedia, but remarkably useful.

Encyclopaedia Britannica. 24 vols. Volume 24 contains a general index. Supplemented annually.

Encyclopedia Americana. 30 vols. Volume 30 contains a general index. Supplemented annually.

Special reference works and encyclopedias

The following reference works go into more detail than do general encyclopedias, and their coverage is more specialized. An early acquaintance with those related to your subject will be valuable in your research.

Art

Chamberlin, Mary W. *Guide to Art Reference Books.* Chicago, 1959.

Encyclopedia of World Art. 15 vols. New York, 1959-date.

Fielding, Mantle. *Dictionary of American Painters, Sculptors and Engravers.* New York, 1945.

Myers, Bernard S., ed. *Encyclopedia of Painting*. New York, 1955.

The Praeger Picture Encyclopedia of Art. New York, 1958.

Atlases

Atlas of World History. Ed. R. R. Palmer. Chicago, 1957.

Columbia-Lippincott Gazetteer of the World. Ed. Leon E. Seltzer. New York, 1962.

Encyclopaedia Britannica World Atlas. Chicago, 1963.

National Geographic Atlas of the World. Ed. M. B. Grosvenor. Washington, D.C., 1963.

Biography

Chambers's Biographical Dictionary. London, 1961. [General]

Current Biography. New York, 1940-date. [General]

Dictionary of American Biography. 20 vols. New York, 1928-1937. [American]

Dictionary of National Biography. Ed. Leslie Stephen and Sidney Lee. 63 vols. London, 1885-1901. Reissued in 22 vols., London, 1908-1909. Supplements to 1950. [British]

A Dictionary of Universal Biography of All Ages and People. Ed. Albert M. Hyamson. New York, 1951. [General]

International Who's Who. London, 1935-date. [General]

Webster's Biographical Dictionary. Springfield, Mass., 1966. [General]

Who's Who. London, 1849-date. [British]

Who's Who in America. Chicago, 1899-date. [American]

Business

Munn, G. G., ed. *Encyclopedia of Banking and Finance*, rev. F. L. Garcia. Boston, 1962.

Nemmers, Erwin E., and C. C. Janzen, eds. *Dictionary of Economics and Business*. Paterson, N.J., 1959.

Winser, Marian (Manley). *Business Information: How to Find and Use It*. New York, 1955.

Chemistry

Rose, Arthur, and Elizabeth Rose. *The Condensed Chemical Dictionary*. New York, 1961.

Thorpe, Jocelyn F., and M. A. Whiteley. *Thorpe's Dictionary of Applied Chemistry*. 12 vols. New York, 1937-1956.

Drama

Baker, Blanch M. *Theatre and Allied Arts: A Guide to Books Dealing with the History, Criticism, and Technic of the Drama and Theatre, and Related Arts and Crafts.* New York, 1952.

Fidell, Estelle A., and D. M. Peake, eds. *Play Index, 1953-1960: An Index to 4592 Plays in 1735 Volumes.* New York, 1963.

Harbage, Alfred. *Annals of English Drama, 975-1700: An Analytical Record of All Plays, Extant or Lost, Chronologically Arranged and Indexed by Authors, Titles, Dramatic Companies, Etc.* Philadelphia, 1964.

Hartnoll, Phyllis. *The Oxford Companion to the Theatre.* London, 1957.

Nicoll, Allardyce. *A History of English Drama, 1660-1900.* 6 vols. Cambridge, 1952-1959.

Ottemiller, John H. *Index to Plays in Collections: An Author and Title Index to Plays Appearing in Collections Published Between 1900 and 1962.* New York, 1964.

Van Lennep, William, et al. *The London Stage, 1660-1800: A Calendar of Plays, Entertainments & Afterpieces, Together With Casts, Box-Receipts and Contemporary Comment. Compiled from the Playbills, Newspapers and Theatrical Diaries of the Period.* Carbondale, Ill., 1960-. (In progress.)

Economics

Horton, Byrne J., et al. *Dictionary of Modern Economics.* Washington, D.C., 1948.

Education

Alexander, Carter, and A. J. Burke. *How to Locate Educational Information and Data.* New York, 1958.

Monroe, Paul, ed. *A Cyclopedia of Education.* 5 vols. New York, 1911-1913.

UNESCO. *World Survey of Education.* 3 vols. Paris, 1955-date.

Geography

Cox, Edward Godfrey. *A Reference Guide to the Literature of Travel, Including Voyages, Geographical Descriptions, Adventures, Shipwrecks and Expeditions.* Seattle, Wash., 1935-1949.

Sealock, Richard B., and Pauline A. Seely. *Bibliography of Place Name Literature: United States, Canada, Alaska and Newfoundland.* Chicago, 1948.

Wright, John Kirtland, and Elizabeth T. Platt. *Aids to Geographical Research: Bibliographies, Periodicals, Atlases, Gazetteers, and Other Reference Books.* New York, 1947.

History (American)

Adams, James Truslow. *Dictionary of American History.* 6 vols. New York, 1942-1961.

Beers, Henry P. *Bibliographies in American History: Guide to Materials for Research.* New York, 1942.

Handlin, Oscar, et al. *Harvard Guide to American History.* Cambridge, Mass., 1954.

Morris, Richard B., ed. *Encyclopedia of American History.* New York, 1961.

Schlesinger, Arthur M., and Dixon R. Fox, eds. *A History of American Life.* 13 vols. New York, 1927-. (In progress.)

History (General)

Bury, J. B., et al. *The Cambridge Ancient History.* 12 vols. Cambridge, 1923-1939.

Gwatkin, Henry M., et al. *The Cambridge Medieval History.* 8 vols. Cambridge, 1911-1936.

Langer, William L., ed. *An Encyclopaedia of World History.* Boston, 1952.

Ward, A. W., et al. *The Cambridge Modern History.* 13 vols. Cambridge, 1902-1911.

Woodcock, Percival G., ed. *Concise Dictionary of Ancient History.* New York, 1955.

Literature (American)

Cambridge History of American Literature. 4 vols. New York, 1933.

Gohdes, Clarence. *Bibliographical Guide to the Study of the Literature of the U.S.A.* Durham, N.C., 1963.

Hart, James D. *The Oxford Companion to American Literature.* New York, 1965.

29.2 Haywood, Charles. *A Bibliography of North American Folklore and Folksong.* New York, 1961.

Kunitz, Stanley J., and Howard Haycraft, eds. *American Authors, 1600-1900.* New York, 1938.

Richards, Robert F., ed. *Concise Dictionary of American Literature.* New York, 1955.

Spiller, Robert E., et al. *Literary History of the United States.* New York, 1964.

Woodress, James L. *Dissertations in American Literature, 1891-1961.* Durham, N.C., 1962.

Literature (Classical)

Gray, Louis H., and John A. Macculloch, eds. *Mythology of All Races.* 13 vols. Boston, 1916-1964.

Harvey, Sir Paul. *The Oxford Companion to Classical Literature.* Oxford, 1940.

Larousse Encyclopedia of Mythology. London, 1959.

Literature (English)

Baker, Ernest A. *The History of the English Novel.* 10 vols. New York, 1961-1964.

Bateson, F. W., ed. *Cambridge Bibliography of English Literature.* 4 vols. New York, 1941-date.

Baugh, Albert C. *A Literary History of England.* London, 1948.

Cambridge History of English Literature. New York, 1939.

Courthope, William J. *A History of English Poetry.* 6 vols. New York, 1895-1910.

Harvey, Sir Paul. *The Oxford Companion to English Literature.* Oxford, 1946.

Kunitz, Stanley J. *British Authors Before 1800.* New York, 1952.

——————. *British Authors of the Nineteenth Century.* New York, 1936.

Wilson, Frank P., and Bonamy Dobree, eds. *The Oxford History of English Literature.* New York, 1945-. (In progress.)

Literature (General)

Baldensperger, Fernand, and Werner P. Friederich. *Bibliography of Comparative Literature.* New York, 1960.

Bernhardt, William F., ed. *Granger's Index to Poetry.* New York, 1962.

Cook, Dorothy E., and Isabel S. Monro. *Short Story Index.* New York, 1953-date.

Eastman, Mary Huse. *Index to Fairy Tales, Myths, and Legends.* Boston, 1926. Supplement, 1937.

English Association. *The Year's Work in English Studies.* Oxford, 1919-1921-date.

Harvey, Sir Paul, and Janet E. Heseltine. *The Oxford Companion to French Literature*. Oxford, 1959.

Hornstein, Lillian H., ed. *Reader's Companion to World Literature*. New York, 1956.

Kunitz, Stanley J. *Twentieth Century Authors*. New York, 1942. Supplement, 1955.

Magill, Frank N., ed. *Masterplots*. 6 vols. New York, 1960.

Modern Humanities Research Association. *Annual Bibliography of English Language and Literature, 1920-*. New York, 1920-1921-date.

Morgan, Bayard Q. *A Critical Bibliography of German Literature in English Translation, 1481-1927*. New York, 1965.

Shipley, Joseph T., ed. *Dictionary of World Literature*. New York, 1943.

Smith, Horatio, ed. *Columbia Dictionary of Modern European Literature*. New York, 1947.

Steinberg, S. H., ed. *Cassell's Encyclopaedia of Literature*. 2 vols. London, 1953.

Thompson, Stith. *Motif-Index of Folk Literature*. 6 vols. Bloomington, Ind., 1955-1958.

Thrall, William F., and Addison Hibbard, eds. *A Handbook to Literature*. New York, 1960.

Music

Apel, Willi. *Harvard Dictionary of Music*. Cambridge, Mass., 1947.

Baker, Theodore. *Biographical Dictionary of Musicians*, rev. Nicolas Slonimsky. New York, 1958.

————. *Dictionary of Musical Terms*. New York, 1923.

Ewen, David. *Encyclopedia of Concert Music*. New York, 1959.

Grove, Sir George. *Grove's Dictionary of Music and Musicians*, ed. Eric Blom. 10 vols. London, 1954-1961.

Loewenberg, Alfred. *Annals of Opera, 1597-1940*. 2 vols. Geneva, 1955.

New Oxford History of Music. London, 1954-. (In progress.)

Sachs, Curt. *History of Musical Instruments*. New York, 1940.

Scholes, Percy A. *The Oxford Companion to Music*. London, 1955.

Thompson, Oscar. *International Cyclopedia of Music and Musicians*, rev. Robert Sabin. New York, 1964.

Westrup, Jack A., and F. L. Harrison. *The New College Encyclopedia of Music*. New York, 1960.

Philosophy

Baldwin, James Mark. *Dictionary of Philosophy and Psychology.* 4 vols. New York, 1940-1949.

Runes, Dagobert D., ed. *The Dictionary of Philosophy.* New York, 1942.

Russell, Bertrand. *A History of Western Philosophy.* New York, 1945.

Urmson, J. O., ed. *The Concise Encyclopedia of Western Philosophy and Philosophers.* New York, 1960.

Political Science

Burchfield, Laverne. *Student's Guide to Materials in Political Science.* New York, 1935.

McLaughlin, Andrew C., and Albert B. Hart, eds. *Cyclopedia of American Government.* 3 vols. New York, 1914.

Plano, Jack C., and Milton Greenberg. *The American Political Dictionary.* New York, 1962.

Smith, Edward C., and Arnold J. Zurcher, eds. *New Dictionary of American Politics.* New York, 1955.

Theimer, Walter. *Encyclopedia of Modern World Politics.* New York, 1950.

Psychology

Baldwin, James Mark. *Dictionary of Philosophy and Psychology.* 4 vols. New York, 1940-1949.

English, Horace B., and Ava C. English. *A Comprehensive Dictionary of Psychological and Psychoanalytical Terms.* New York, 1965.

Grinstein, Alexander. *The Index of Psychoanalytic Writings.* 5 vols. New York, 1956-1960.

Harriman, Philip L., ed. *Encyclopedia of Psychology.* New York, 1946.

Quotations

Bartlett, John. *Familiar Quotations.* Boston, 1955.

Harbottle, T. B. *Dictionary of Quotations* (Classical). London, 1906.

The Oxford Dictionary of Quotations. Oxford, 1953.

Stevenson, Burton E. *Book of Quotations, Classical and Modern.* London, 1956.

Religion

Barrow, John Graves. *A Bibliography of Bibliographies in Religion.* Austin, Texas, 1955.

Butler, Alban. *Lives of the Saints.* 4 vols. New York, 1956.

The Catholic Encyclopedia. 16 vols. New York, 1913. Supplement, 1922.

Cross, F. L., ed. *The Oxford Dictionary of the Christian Church.* London, 1957.

Ferm, Vergilius T. A., ed. *An Encyclopedia of Religion.* New York, 1945.

Frazer, Sir James G. *The New Golden Bough*, ed. Theodor H. Gaster. New York, 1959.

Gibb, H. A. R., and J. H. Kramers, eds. *Shorter Encyclopedia of Islam.* Leiden, 1953.

Hastings, James, ed. *Dictionary of the Bible.* 5 vols. New York, 1963.

———. *Encyclopaedia of Religion and Ethics.* 7 vols. New York, 1951.

Miller, Madeleine S., and J. Lane Miller. *Harper's Bible Dictionary.* New York, 1952.

Nelson's Complete Concordance of the Revised Standard Version of the Bible, comp. J. W. Ellison. New York, 1957.

Oxford Bible Atlas, ed. Herbert G. May, et al. London, 1962.

Roth, Cecil, ed. *The Standard Jewish Encyclopedia.* New York, 1962.

The Universal Jewish Encyclopedia. 10 vols. New York, 1939-1944.

Zaehner, Robert C., ed. *The Concise Encyclopedia of Living Faiths.* London, 1959.

Science (Applied)

Applied Science and Technology Index. New York, 1913-date.

Ballentyne, D. W. G., and L. E. Q. Walker. *A Dictionary of Named Effects and Laws in Chemistry, Physics, and Mathematics.* New York, 1961.

Besserer, C. W., and H. C. Besserer. *Guide to the Space Age.* Englewood Cliffs, N.J., 1959.

McGraw-Hill Encyclopedia of Science and Technology. 15 vols. New York, 1966.

Michels, Walter C., et al. *The International Dictionary of Physics and Electronics.* Princeton, N.J., 1956.

Tweney, C. F., and L. E. C. Hughes, eds. *Chambers's Technical Dictionary.* New York, 1958.

Science (Biological)

Henderson, Isabella F., and W. D. Henderson. *Dictionary of Scientific Terms.* Princeton, N.J., 1960.

Howard, A. V., ed. *Chambers's Dictionary of Scientists.* New York, 1951.

Jenkins, Frances B. *Science Reference Sources.* Champaign, Ill., 1965.

Stedman, T. L. *Stedman's Medical Dictionary.* Baltimore, 1953.

Van Nostrand's Scientific Encyclopedia. Princeton, N.J., 1958.

Social Sciences

Basler, Roy P., et al. *A Guide to the Study of the United States of America.* Washington, D.C., 1960.

Clarke, Jack A., ed. *Research Materials in the Social Sciences.* Madison, Wis., 1959.

Fairchild, Henry Pratt, ed. *Dictionary of Sociology.* New York, 1944.

Hoselitz, Berthold F., ed. *A Reader's Guide to the Social Sciences.* Glencoe, Ill., 1959.

Seligman, Edwin R. A., and Alvin Johnson. *Encyclopaedia of the Social Sciences.* 15 vols. New York, 1930-1935.

Zadrozny, John T., ed. *Dictionary of Social Science.* Washington, D.C., 1959.

Speech

Brigance, William N., ed. *A History and Criticism of American Public Address.* 2 vols. New York, 1943.

Haberman, Frederick W., and James W. Cleary, comps. *Rhetoric and Public Address: A Bibliography: 1947-1961.* Madison, Wis., 1964.

See also §18.1, page 237, Special dictionaries.

Yearbooks and annuals

The following annuals provide up-to-date facts and figures on a wide variety of subjects, particularly those of current interest.

The Americana Annual: An Encyclopedia of Current Events. New York, 1923-date. Annual supplement to the *Encyclopedia Americana* with a chronology of events of the preceding year.

Britannica Book of the Year. Chicago, 1938-date. Annual supplement to the *Encyclopaedia Britannica*, with cumulative index.

Collier's Year Book. New York, 1939-date. Annual supplement to *Collier's Encyclopedia.*

Information Please Almanac. New York, 1947-date.

Social Work Year Book. New York, 1929-date. Biennially since 1929; social work and related fields.

The Statesman's Year-Book: Statistical and Historical Annual of the States of the World, 1864-. London, 1864-date. Covers historical and statistical events throughout the world.

The World Almanac and Book of Facts. New York, 1868-date. This is one general reference that any student can afford to own, and one that anyone with a serious interest in current affairs can hardly afford to be without. The index is in the front of each volume.

Yearbook of the United Nations. Lake Success, N.Y., 1947-date. Activities of the United Nations.

Guides to reference materials

Many other specialized reference works can be found by consulting the following guides:

Barton, Mary N., comp. *Reference Books: A Brief Guide for Students and Other Users of the Library*. 4th ed. Baltimore, 1959.

Murphey, Robert W. *How and Where to Look It Up*. New York, 1958.

The Reader's Adviser: An Annotated Guide to the Best in Print in Literature, Biographies, Dictionaries, Encyclopedias, Bibles, Classics, Drama, Poetry, Fiction, Science, Philosophy, Travel, History. Rev. and enl. by Hester R. Hoffman. 10th ed. New York, 1964.

Shores, Louis. *Basic Reference Sources: An Introduction to Materials and Methods*. Chicago, 1954.

Walford, Arthur J., ed. *Guide to Reference Material*. London, 1959. Supplement, 1963.

Winchell, Constance M. *Guide to Reference Books*. 7th ed. Chicago, 1951. Supplements, 1952-1962.

29.3 Preparing the working bibliography

A working bibliography is a list—on note cards—of the books, magazine articles, and other published works that you intend to consult when gathering material for your reference paper. The number of references you should collect will depend upon the nature of the assignment, but it is always best to begin with more than you will probably need. If your working bibliography includes only a bare minimum of sources, you will probably have to take time later to find more: a book you want from the library may already be out on loan; one article on your list may prove to be too technical; another may merely repeat material you have already collected.

Whether your initial bibliography contains many sources or relatively few, you will probably want to add others as you get into your research and find new avenues you want to explore.

Each entry in your working bibliography should be written on a separate card. Use either a 3 x 5-inch or 4 x 6-inch card or slip of paper. Cards are sturdier and easier to work with than odd slips of paper. With only one reference on each, they can be rearranged quickly for alphabetizing; new ones can be inserted in the proper places and useless ones discarded. (You may want to use 3 x 5 cards for the working bibliography and 4 x 6 cards for taking notes, since the larger cards will obviously hold more data and will also be readily distinguishable from your bibliography cards.)

Bibliography cards for different types of references are illustrated on page 472. Each card should include all the facts you will need to identify the reference and obtain it from the library. It should also have all the information you will need in preparing the final bibliography. The punctuation suggested here is a standard form for bibliographies:

1) *Author's name*, with the last name first (followed by a period). If the book is edited, use the editor's name (followed by a comma), followed by *ed.* If the article or pamphlet is unsigned, write the title first on the card.

2) *Title* of the book (underlined and followed by a comma) or of the article (in quotation marks and followed by a comma).

3) *Facts of publication:*

a) *For a book:* the place of publication (followed by a comma) and the date (followed by a period). If your instructor asks you to include the name of the publisher, insert it after the place of publication: New York: The Macmillan Company, 1966.

b) *For a journal article:* the name of the journal (underlined and followed by a comma), the volume number (in Roman numerals), the date (in parentheses, followed by a comma), and the pages covered by the article (followed by a period).

c) *For a magazine article:* the name of the magazine (underlined and followed by a comma), the date of the issue (followed by a

Sample bibliography cards

For a book by one author	327.73 P719C	Plische, Elmer. Conduct of American Diplomacy. New York, 1950.
For a book, edited	820.9 B3261	Baugh, Albert C., ed. A Literary History of England. New York, 1948.
For a signed article in an encyclopedia	Reference room shelf 12	Bear, Donald. "Painting," Encyclopedia Britannica (1957), XVII, 36-68C.
For a journal article	Periodical desk	Pearsall, Robert Brainard. "The Presiding Tropes of Emily Brontë," College English, XXVII (January 1966), 266-273.
For a magazine article	051 For V. 49 pt. 1	Rossa, Robert V. "The Central Bank in a Market Economy," Fortune, March 1961, pp. 124-127, 168-181.
For an unsigned newspaper article	Periodical desk	"Bar Association Insists on Trial News Curbs," Chicago Sun-Times, January 12, 1968, p. 18, col. 1.

comma), and the pages covered by the article (followed by a period).

d) *For a newspaper article:* the name of the newspaper (underlined and followed by a comma), the date (followed by a comma), the page on which the story appeared (followed by a period). The column number may be added after the page number (separated from it by a comma).

4) *Library call number*, or the location of a reference work in the library. This information, placed in the upper left-hand corner, should be written just as it appears in the card catalog, so that you can relocate the reference if the need arises.

See also §29.9, page 495, The final bibliography.

29.4 Taking notes

Accurate and full notes are essential for writing a good reference paper. You can save time when taking notes if you approach the problem in a workmanlike manner. Don't try to take down everything you read; instead, spend a little time looking over the book, the article, or the pamphlet to see if it contains the information you want. If you have given enough thought to formulating and narrowing your topic, you will have a pretty clear idea of what you are looking for.

When examining a book, look first at the index and the table of contents to see in what sections your subject is treated. See also if there are any tables, graphs, bibliographies, or further references that might be useful. Skim each chapter or article to find out what it covers. Then go over it again carefully, taking down the notes you will need.

Notes should be taken on either 3 x 5-inch or 4 x 6-inch cards so that you can later arrange the material according to the plan of your paper. It is usually a waste of effort to try to take notes in numbered outline form since you probably won't know the final plan of your paper until you have finished your research. What is important is to make each note card accurate, clearly written, and clearly labeled. Each note card should contain these essential parts, as illustrated by the sample cards shown on page 475:

1) The *heading* at the top of the card, showing what material it contains.

2) The *source* (just enough information, usually author and title, to identify it) and *page number*, accurately noted.

3) The *content*, facts or opinions (summarized in your own words or directly quoted) accurately recorded.

Notes that cannot be readily interpreted a week or a month after they have been recorded are obviously of little use to a writer; so too are incomplete or carelessly written notes. You can avoid a good deal of tedious, unnecessary work, including rereading and rechecking, by following these simple rules:

1) Use *one side* of each card only. Your material will then be easier to classify and arrange, and you won't run the risk of overlooking a statement on the back of a card.

2) Include only *one major point* or a few closely related facts from the same source on a single card. If the information is too extensive to write on one side of a card, use two or three cards and number them in sequence.

3) Get all the information accurately the first time you consult a source so that you won't have to make extra trips to the library.

4) Put all *direct quotations* (statements, including single sentences and phrases, that you copy word for word from any published source) in quotation marks. If you omit a word or words in a direct quotation use ellipsis periods (§15.3) to indicate the omission (. . .). If you are paraphrasing the source, state the idea in your own language. (See §29.8, page 485, Plagiarism.)

5) Write your notes legibly in ink (penciled notes may become blurred with frequent handling) so that you won't have to recopy them. When you use abbreviations, be sure that you will know later on what they mean.

It isn't necessary to write out all your notes in complete sentences; practical shortcuts such as the omission of *a*, *the*, *was*, and other such words are good for summarizing material. If the method you use for taking notes in lecture courses or on your textbooks has proved successful, use it also for your reference paper.

29.4

Accurate notes are one of the chief tools of scholarship. Early and careful practice in taking them is excellent training that may be useful in later college courses and in a great many positions after graduation.

Sample note cards

Direct quote

Origins of Parliament — Maurois, *Hist. of Eng.*, 146

"The convoking of the different 'Estates' of a Kingdom (military, priestly and plebian), in order to obtain their consent to taxation, was not peculiar to England in the fourteenth century."

Summarized material

Incidence of neurosis among the poor — Harrington, *Other Amer.*, 119

Though there is a myth that the richer you are the more neurotic you are likely to be, the truth is just the opposite: poor people suffer from mental illness more often than people in any other social class.

Statistical data

Enrollment in institutions of higher education (1000's) — *Stat. Abstract*, (1966) 107

	1930	1940	1950	1960	1962
Total	1101	1494	2659	3216	3726
Public	533	797	1355	1832	2213
Private	568	698	1304	1384	1514

29.5 Evaluating your material

Since writing a reference paper is in part an exercise in critical judgment, it is important that you learn to evaluate the sources you use. The statement "I found a book in the library that said . . . " is a confession of uncritical work. It is your responsibility to find and use the most informative books and the most authoritative material available to you.

Facts to consider in evaluating

A freshman engaged in writing his first reference paper on a subject that is unfamiliar to him is not expected to know offhand that a work by author A is wholly worthless or that author B is considered the foremost authority on the subject. He can, however, arrive at a fairly accurate estimate of his sources by considering these facts about them:

1) *Date of publication.* If your subject is one for which recent facts are important, see that the sources are up to date. The most recent edition of a book or an encyclopedia will generally be more useful and authoritative than an earlier one. (There are, of course, exceptions. Though the most recent edition of *Encyclopaedia Britannica*, for example, would obviously be most up to date, the earlier editions are more useful on most literary topics, since the treatments are fuller. Similarly, later editions of *Bartlett's Quotations* have dropped many of the quotes included in earlier editions.)

2) *Completeness.* With magazine articles, it is better to read the original article as it was printed in full instead of a condensation or reprint of it. Similarly, an article in a one-volume encyclopedia that you happen to have at home may not be as thorough or as reliable as one in the *Britannica* or other major reference work.

3) *Facts and opinions.* Distinguish carefully between an author's facts and his opinions. Label the opinions "So-and-so thinks that . . . ." In general, pay more attention to *facts* (unless your paper is about various opinions), since you will need facts to support your own opinions.

4) *Objectivity of the source.* A book or an article based in large part upon an author's opinions or his biases—particularly when the subject is controversial—should not be used as your sole

authority on the matter. Read material on the other side of the question before reaching a conclusion.

When you are in doubt about the reliability of a source, a librarian or your instructor may be able to give you advice. Reviews in the more specialized journals review and evaluate books in their own fields. *Book Review Digest* (New York, 1905-date) may also prove helpful. And, of course, after you have worked a while on your subject, you will be in a better position to evaluate the material yourself.

Primary and secondary sources

A *primary* source is an original document or a first record of any fact or event. A *secondary* source is another writer's discussion of such material. For example, the Constitution of the United States is a primary source; an article or a book written *about* the Constitution is a secondary source. A scientist's report of his experiments with penicillin therapy in the *Journal of the American Medical Association* is a primary source; a newspaper or magazine comment on these results is a secondary source.

While many undergraduate reference papers must rely heavily on secondary references, a student should use primary sources whenever they are available so that he can get as close to the facts as possible and form his own conclusions. In preparing a biographical study, for instance, the actual letters, diaries, and other writings of a person provide excellent material and are often more helpful than the comments someone else has written on them. With other subjects, you may be able to use lecture notes taken in one of your courses, or you can perhaps get first-hand information through personal interviews with persons who are authorities on the matter—college professors, city officials, or other informed people in the field of your investigation.

29.6 Planning the paper

The central or controlling purpose of a reference paper should be clear in your mind long before you have finished investigating all your resources. You know, for instance, whether you are trying to reach a conclusion about two opposing viewpoints or whether you are trying to explain an event or situation. When you have gathered a sufficient amount of material to put your topic in focus, it is time to formulate a thesis sentence (§25.1, page 348) that will state your controlling purpose and to outline the order in which you will develop your material.

Examining and arranging your notes

First read through all your notes to refresh your memory and determine the general order in which you will arrange your material. Then arrange the notes in piles, grouping together all the notes on a particular aspect of your subject. The headings at the top of each card will be useful in helping you sort and arrange your material. At this stage you should note any gaps in your material that will have to be filled in with further reading before you start your first draft.

If any of the notes you have taken no longer seem relevant to your purpose in writing, put them aside in a tentative discard pile. Almost anyone engaged in research finds that a good deal of carefully recorded material has to be discarded. Don't succumb to the temptation to include material that has no bearing on your thesis simply because it is interesting or because you worked hard to find it.

Making a preliminary outline

When you have arranged your note cards to your satisfaction, state the central idea of your paper in a thesis sentence (not in two or more sentences nor in the form of a question). Then make a rough outline showing the order in which you intend to present your material. Each point in the outline should contribute in some way to the development of your central idea or thesis. To crystallize your plan and to make it possible for your instructor to examine it and make suggestions, you should follow standard outline form. At this stage a topic outline is generally sufficient; if necessary, you can later expand the entries into complete sentences. (See §25.4, Organizing your material, for a discussion of outlining and outline form.)

Neither your preliminary outline nor your thesis sentence needs to be considered as final. It is better, in fact, to make a reasonably flexible outline so that you can make whatever changes seem desirable as you write and revise your first draft.

29.7 Writing and revising the first draft

A reference paper should represent your writing at its best—in terms of organization, sentence structure, wording, and emphasis. The most convincing proof that you have actually learned something new from your research is the way you have evaluated, organized, and expressed your material. Instructions concerning the proper form of footnotes (§29.8) and bibliography (§29.9) should be followed to the letter. The paper should be as neat as you can possibly make it, with each part in its proper order and all errors in spelling and punctuation carefully corrected.

Writing the first draft

Make certain that you are thoroughly familiar with your material before you begin to write. You should have the information on your note cards so well in mind that you can write rapidly and with confidence once you start. For this reason, it is a good idea to review your notes once more just before you begin writing.

This draft should be written in the same way you would write the first draft of any other important assignment (as discussed in §26, Writing the first draft), but with ample room left for documentation. You can leave spaces between the lines or at the bottom of the page to insert the necessary footnotes. Some writers put the documentation in the text of the first draft:

The theory reserved the most desirable characteristics for northern people. Those of the south were pictured as jealous, superstitious, cowardly, lascivious, cruel, and inhuman.[3] Because of this belief, Shakespeare's choice of

----

[3]Philip Butcher, "Othello's Racial Identity," Shakespeare Quarterly, III (July 1952), 246.

----

a black Othello as the victim of Iago's plot makes it especially convincing to the audience.

In the first draft, the footnotes may be put all together on a separate page or handled in any other way that will be convenient when you make the final copy.

If a passage seems to need more facts or further documentation, don't interrupt your writing to do the necessary additional research. Put a question mark or some other notation in the margin, continue with your writing, and look up the material after you have finished the first draft.

Most reference papers are written in a rather Formal, impersonal style. Usually the writer does not need to refer to himself at all, but if he does, the reference should be brief. Remember, however, that impersonal writing does not have to be flat or lifeless. The information itself will provide the interest if you express it clearly and directly.

Revising the first draft

Revising a reference paper means more than merely putting the footnotes in proper form and order. To do a thorough job—one that will satisfy you as well as your reader—you should examine your paper from these viewpoints:

1) *The material or content.* See if the main parts in your paper relate directly to the central idea. Omit any sentences or passages that are repetitious or irrelevant and, wherever necessary, make your points clearer by additional illustration, either from your own knowledge or from one of your sources. Examine closely every direct quotation (particularly the longer ones) to see whether you might better put the statement in your own words. Check each technical or unfamiliar term: Is the meaning clear from the context or should you define it?

2) *The structure and the expression.* First look at the introduction of your paper to see if it actually gets the subject started quickly or is just an unnecessary preamble. Then consider the transitions between paragraphs, watching for any abrupt shifts in thought or
29.7 lack of relationship between the main divisions of the paper. Finally, read the conclusion: Is it as definite and emphatic as the facts will permit? After checking the structure, go over the paper carefully to correct all the errors you can find in wording, punctuation, and spelling (pay particular attention to the spelling of proper names and technical terms).

3) *The outline and thesis sentence.* The outline should be an accurate table of contents for your reference paper in its final form. Make certain that it is stated in the way your instructor has requested (either in topics or complete sentences), and that you have followed the conventional numbering system. Generally the first outline, made before the first draft is written, contains too many divisions or misleading and overlapping headings; the central idea (thesis sentence) is also likely to be vague or inexact. Both should be revised at this point for greater accuracy, following the form described on pages 367-371.

4) *The documentation.* When revising your first draft, you should ask yourself whether you have used too many or too few footnotes. A full page without any references may need further documentation; on the other hand, a great many footnotes on each page may indicate that some of the material could better be combined or rephrased to eliminate unnecessary references. When you are satisfied that your material is properly documented, check the form of each footnote in detail to make certain that it is complete, accurate, and consecutively numbered. Standard footnote form is described in the following section. Be sure to follow any special directions that your instructor may give you regarding the use of abbreviations, punctuation, and similar matters of footnote style.

29.8 Documenting the paper

Any paper based upon the writing of others should acknowledge each and every source from which an idea or statement is taken. In a reference paper the acknowledgments are made by footnotes —notes at the bottom of the page (numbered to correspond to numbers in the text) that show exactly where the information was obtained. The method of documentation recommended by most English instructors is described on pages 488-494 and illustrated in the student paper beginning on page 498. (Some style guides for research writing recommend putting all footnotes in proper sequence and numbering them in the usual way at the end of the paper, following the last page of the text and preceding the bibliography. This style should not be followed, however, unless your instructor specifically recommends it.)

Where footnotes are needed

When drawing on the work of another writer or researcher, you owe him the courtesy of giving credit where credit is due. You also owe your *reader* the courtesy of providing the sources of your information so that he can judge them for himself. Failure to document borrowed information is at best carelessness; at worst, it is plagiarism, which means offering material written by someone else as your own work (see page 485). Footnotes are essential in two situations:

1) *After direct quotations.* Each statement taken word for word from a printed source should have a reference number at the end of the quotation and be properly identified in a footnote. The only exceptions to this rule are well-known expressions, such as familiar Biblical quotations ("Blessed are the poor"), famous lines from literature ("Something is rotten in the state of Denmark"), and proverbs ("A bird in the hand is worth two in the bush").

2) *After all important statements of fact or opinion taken from written sources and expressed in your own words.* These include figures, dates, scientific data, descriptions of events and situations about which you have no first-hand knowledge (what happened at a session of the United Nations, how coffee is cultivated in Brazil, the role of Madagascar in World War II, and so on), and all opinions and interpretations that are not actually your own (such as one writer's reasons for the popularity of baseball in the United States, or an opinion on foreign policy from a newspaper editorial).

In some publications, footnotes are also used for comments or additional information that the writer does not wish to include in the text. In freshman reference papers, however, this practice should be kept to a minimum; if a statement is worth making, it usually belongs in the text.

Footnotes are *not* needed for statements that would pass without question. These include obvious facts ("Certain chemicals cannot be used in the preservation of foods in the United States."), matters of common knowledge ("Hiroshima was devastated by an atomic bomb in August 1945."), general statements and expressions of the writer's own opinion ("The medical and biological sciences have made unbelievable progress in the last twenty years.").

The following sections discuss some things to consider in integrating footnoted material into the text of your paper.

Using direct quotations

In incorporating material from sources into your reference paper, you will often have to decide whether to quote directly or to restate the material in your own words. In general, direct quotations are preferable only in these situations:

1) *Interpretations of literary works.* When a statement or opinion in your paper is based on a passage in a poem, essay, short story, novel, or play, quote from the passage so that the reader can see the basis for your interpretation:

> The closing passages of *Moby Dick* also suggest that the whale represents some omnipotent force hostile to man. Ishmael says that Moby Dick rushed at the ship with a "predestinating head," and that "retribution, swift vengeance, eternal malice were in his aspect . . . in spite of all mortal man could do."[1]

When you are writing a paper that requires frequent references to a literary work, however, you need to footnote the edition of the text you are using only once, the first time you use a quotation. Thereafter, you may identify quotations by giving (immediately after the quotation, in parentheses) the page numbers for fiction; the line numbers for poetry; the act and scene for drama (followed by the line numbers if the play is in verse):

> Man, who once stood at the center of the universe, confident that he was the end of Creation and could claim kinship with the angels, is now—to use the playwright's favorite figure—shrouded in a "mist" that isolates him from God and shuts off all his questioning about the problems of ultimate order. As Webster says of the Cardinal in *The Duchess of Malfi*, Man
>
> which stood'st like a huge pyramid
> Begun upon a large and ample base,
> Shalt end in a little point, a kind of nothing. (V.v.96-98)

2) *Important statements of information, opinion, or policy.* Whenever the *exact* wording of a statement is crucial in its interpretation, it should be quoted in full:

> President Kennedy told Khrushchev that Russia could not expect to spread Communism abroad without opposition: "What your gov-

ernment believes is its own business; what it does in the world is the world's business."[2]

3) *Distinctive phrasing.* If your source states some idea or opinion in a particularly forceful or original way that would be weakened by paraphrasing, quote the exact words:

Russell does not believe that our age lacks great ideas because religion has declined: "We are suffering not from the decay of theological beliefs but from the loss of solitude."[13]

A quotation should be smoothly integrated into the text of your paper. Even though its source is given in a footnote, it should be preceded by some brief introductory remark like "a leading educator recently said that . . ."; "as Edmund Wilson points out . . ."; "an editorial in the *Chicago Tribune* argued that . . . ." If you inject a quotation without explanation, the reader is forced to interrupt his reading by looking for the footnote.

See §15.1, page 179, Quotation marks around quoted material, for a discussion of ways to set up long and short quotations from both prose and verse.

Paraphrasing

Although a reference paper relies heavily on the writings of others, it should not consist simply of a long string of word-for-word quotations from sources. Like any other paper, it should represent your own characteristic style. Except in the situations described in the preceding section, information from a source should ordinarily be *paraphrased*—restated or summarized in your own words. Otherwise your paper will have a jumbled, patchwork effect that may distract or confuse the reader. Compare the two following passages for effectiveness:

Too many direct quotations: Authorities disagree about the dating of these pyramids. Professor Sheldon Muncie says, "The preponderance of evidence collected by investigators in recent years points to a date no earlier than 1300 A.D. for the construction of the lowest level."[1] Professor William Price basically agrees with him: "Bricks of this type were not used in the surrounding areas until the late fourteenth century."[2] But Robert McCall found that "The radiocarbon readings are completely out of line with the standard textbook dates; the original substructure is at least 700 years older than Muncie's earliest estimate."[3]

Paraphrase: Authorities disagree about the dating of the pyramids. Professors Sheldon Muncie and William Price concluded, on the basis of the type of brick used and other evidence, that they were begun no earlier than the fourteenth century.[1] But Robert McCall's radiocarbon readings indicate a date earlier than 600 A.D.[2]

The best way to write a smooth paraphrase is to absorb the content of the source passage and then, without looking at it, to write its information down in your own words. When you have finished, you should check it for accuracy and any unconscious borrowing of phrases and sentences. Remember that even though the words are your own, the information or ideas are not; you will still have to use a footnote to identify the source.

Plagiarism

Most college writers know that copying another's work word for word without giving him credit is considered plagiarism. But they often assume that this practice is frowned on only when long passages are involved—whole pages or paragraphs. Consequently, they feel free to copy phrases and sentences without using quotation marks and footnotes. Actually, any uncredited use of another's information, ideas, or wording is plagiarism. Under the mistaken notion that he is paraphrasing, a student often reproduces his source almost exactly, changing only a word here and there. An honest paraphrase, however, is one in which the student states the ideas of his source in his own language, using original sentence patterns and words. The examples on the following pages show the difference between genuine paraphrase and plagiarism of source material:

Original source (from Alexis de Tocqueville, *Democracy in America*, I, 248-249): No political form has hitherto been discovered that is equally favorable to the prosperity and the development of all the classes into which society is divided. These classes continue to form, as it were, so many distinct communities in the same nation; and experience has shown that it is not less dangerous to place the fate of these classes exclusively in the hands of any one of them than it is to make one people the arbiter of the destiny of another. When the rich alone govern, the interest of the poor is always endangered; and when the poor make the laws, that of the rich incurs very serious risks. The advantage of democracy does not consist, therefore, as has sometimes been asserted,

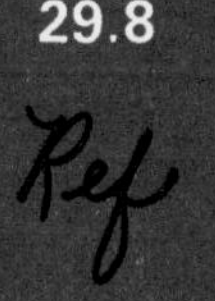

in favoring the prosperity of all, but simply in contributing to the well-being of the greatest number.

Student version A:

Hitherto no one has found a political form that favors equally the prosperity and development of all the different classes of society. Experience has shown that it is just as dangerous to place the fate of these classes in the hands of one class as to let one nation dictate the destiny of another. Government by the rich endangers the poor; and the poor make laws that often harm the interests of the rich. Therefore, the advantage of democracy does not consist in raising general prosperity, but simply in adding to the well-being of the majority.

[**Plagiarism.** By omitting any reference to De Tocqueville, the writer implies that these ideas are his own. In organization the paragraph follows the source very closely—same order of ideas, same number and structure of sentences. Many of the words and phrases are lifted bodily from the source without quotation marks to indicate that they are not the writer's. In other cases, he has simply rearranged word order and substituted synonyms (*found* for *discovered*, *nation* for *one people*, *adding* for *contributing*, *majority* for *greatest number*).]

Student version B:

DeTocqueville says that no form of government in history has been uniformly beneficial to all classes of society. He maintains that both the rich and the poor, when in control of the government, pass laws favorable to their class and repressive toward the other. According to him, the virtue of a democracy is that it benefits the majority, not that it benefits the whole.[1]

[**Paraphrase.** The writer admits, both in the text and in a footnote, that the ideas in the paragraph are De Tocqueville's. He states them in his own words and does not slavishly follow the source. Quotation marks are unnecessary, since none of the phrases are De Tocqueville's.]

Original source (from Lionel Trilling, "F. Scott Fitzgerald," *The Liberal Imagination*, p. 42): Thus, *The Great Gatsby* has its interest as a record of contemporary manners, but this might only have served to date it, did not Fitzgerald take the given moment of history as something more than a mere circumstance, did he not, in the manner of the great French novelists of the nineteenth century, seize the given moment as a moral fact. . . . For Gatsby, divided between power and dream, comes inevitably to stand for America itself.

Student version A:

Of course the one thing that makes The Great Gatsby interesting is its picture of the life of the twenties, but if it were only this it would by now be out of date. Instead, like the great French novelists, Fitzgerald made the particular moment a moral symbol. Gatsby, the main character, divided between power and dream, represents the American dilemma.

[**Plagiarism.** This version does not reproduce the source as closely as version A of the De Tocqueville passage; it more subtly plagiarizes the original. Again, the writer gives no indication that the ideas expressed are not his own. The wording, except for "divided between power and dream," is largely original. The comparison between Fitzgerald and the great French novelists is not original, and implies a critical breadth suspiciously beyond the range of most undergraduate writers.]

Student version B:

As Lionel Trilling points out, The Great Gatsby is much more than a record of the manners of the twenties. In miniature, Gatsby represents America, "divided between power and dream."[1]

[**Paraphrase.** The writer credits Trilling as the originator of the ideas he presents. He also puts quotation marks around the one phrase he uses verbatim.]

Numbering and spacing of footnotes

In the text of the paper, the footnote number is placed *at the end of the quotation or statement* for which the source is being given; it is never placed before the borrowed material. The number is raised slightly above the line and is placed outside the end punctuation of the statement to which it refers: ". . . nearly 400,000 in 1953."[13]

Footnotes are generally numbered consecutively throughout the paper in Arabic numerals beginning with 1. If the last footnote on the first page is numbered 3, the first footnote on the second page will be numbered 4, and so on. It is impossible to say how many footnotes should appear in a paper of a given length because the number varies with the type of subject and the kind of sources used; however, the typical student reference paper contains from two to four footnotes on a page. Studying some footnoted articles or books will help you see how the system works.

In typed manuscript, footnotes are single spaced (but separated from each other by an extra line of space) and the first line of each is indented as for a paragraph. It is a good idea to separate footnotes from the text with a short line extending about one inch from the left margin, as shown in the sample paper on pages 498-507.

Footnote form

Generally, each footnote should contain at least four essential facts (the information a reader would need if he were locating the source himself): the author's name, the title of the work, the facts of publication (place and date), and the specific page or pages of the source used.

29.8 Ref

Practices in footnote form vary, chiefly in punctuation and kinds of abbreviations. This section follows the form recommended by the *Style Sheet* of the Modern Language Association (MLA), the form most often used in academic writing. Alternative systems are frequently used in scientific papers (see p. 494). Follow carefully any changes your instructor may want you to make in the form described here.

Footnotes for books. The *first time* you refer to a book in a footnote, put the information in this order, including as much as is relevant in each case:

1) The author's name, first name or initials first: Austin Beard; I. A. Richards

2) When appropriate (as in footnote 5 on page 490), the title of the chapter or section of the book, in quotation marks: "The Conversion of the Anglo-Saxons"

3) The title of the book, underlined (to indicate italics): *A History of England*

4) When appropriate (as in sample footnotes 4 and 6), the name of the editor, compiler, or translator (first name or initials first), preceded by *ed.*, *comp.*, or *trans.*: trans. Hamish Miles

Exception: If the editor's or translator's name is more relevant to your citation than the author's, put his name at the beginning of the footnote, followed by *ed.* or *trans.* The author's name then comes *after* the title: Samuel Butler, trans. *The Iliad*, by Homer

5) When appropriate, the edition number (if other than the first edition) or the series name and number: 3rd ed.; Univ. of Washington Pubs. in Lang. and Lit., XVI

6) The place and date of publication, in parentheses: (London, 1937). If your instructor asks you to include the publisher's name, put it between the place and date: (Chicago: University of Chicago Press, 1949)

7) When appropriate (as in sample footnote 3), the volume number, in Roman numerals. But if the volumes were published in different years, the volume number *precedes* the place and date: Ronald Smith, *Autobiography*, I (New York, 1913), 12

8) The page reference, using the abbreviations *p.* for *page* and *pp.* for *pages*. But if the footnote includes the volume number, the abbreviation *p.* or *pp.* is omitted: I, 80; I (New York, 1913), 12

If part of a reference is included in the text of the paper, it need not be repeated in the footnote. If the author's name is in the text, the footnote begins with the title; if both author and title are in the text, only the publication data and the page reference need be in the footnote. This is sometimes called a *split note*.

Sample footnotes—first reference to a book. Study the sample footnotes given below, noting the order of information and the punctuation: a comma between the author's name and the title; no comma between the title and the opening parenthesis; a comma between the place of publication and the date; a comma after the closing parenthesis; a period at the end of the footnote.

[1]Walter Gellhorn, *American Rights: The Constitution in Action* (New York, 1960), p. 178. [one author]

[2]Giles W. Gray and Claude M. Wise, *The Bases of Speech*, 3rd ed. (New York, 1959), p. 322. [two authors; a revised edition]

[3]Walter Blair and others, *The Literature of the United States*, 3rd ed. (Chicago, 1966), I, 80. [more than three authors; a two-volume work, both volumes published in the same year; the Latin abbreviation *et al.* may be used instead of *and others*]

[4]*Letters of Noah Webster*, ed. Harry R. Warfel (New York, 1954), p. 352. [an edited book]

[5]Harry Levin, "Literature as an Institution," *Literary Opinion in America*, ed. Morton Dauwen Zabel (New York, 1951), pp. 658-659. [a signed article in an edited book of selections written by various authors]

[6]Paul Valéry, *Monsieur Teste*, trans. Jackson Mathews (New York, 1947), p. 47. [a translated book]

[7]*A Manual of Style*, 11th ed. (Chicago, 1949), p. 37. [a book for which no author is given]

[8]David Fowler, *Piers the Plowman*, Univ. of Washington Pubs. in Lang. and Lit., XVI (Seattle, 1961), p. 23. [a book in a series; because the series number is considered part of the title, the abbreviation *p.* is kept before the page reference]

Subsequent references to a book. For subsequent references to the same work that do not immediately follow the original reference, a short form should be used: the author's last name only (if not more than one book by the same writer is being cited) and the page number, thus:

29.8 [9]Gellhorn, p. 150.

If two sources by the same author have previously been cited, the short form must also include the title, to make clear which work the note refers to. A shortened form of the title may be used:

[10]Gellhorn, *American Rights*, p. 150.

If the book has no author, the title should be used:

[11]*A Manual of Style*, p. 92.

See page 493 for the use of *ibid.* in footnotes.

Footnotes for magazine and journal articles. The first time you footnote a magazine article, give (1) the author's name, (2) the title of the article, in quotation marks, (3) the name of the magazine, underlined to indicate italics, (4) the date of the publication, and (5) the page or pages. The volume number is used in footnoting an article from a scholarly journal and may also be included for a magazine.

[12]John Pearce, "Kentucky's Quiet Revolution," *Harper's Magazine*, January 1961, p. 45.

When a volume number is used, it is expressed in Roman numerals and precedes the date (which is then in parentheses). The abbreviation *p.* or *pp.* is omitted if the volume is given:

[13]Ernest W. Kinne, "Reading Improvement for Adults," *College English*, XV (January 1954), 224-227..

If the author's name is not given, begin the footnote with the title:

[14]"The New Old Heidelberg," *Time*, June 9, 1961, p. 49.

Sometimes an issue number (or name of the issue) is needed. It follows the volume number:

[15]William Thomson, "Hindemith's Contribution to Music Theory," *Journal of Music Theory*, IX, Spring (1965), 53-55.

Subsequent references to a magazine or journal article may be shortened in the same way as those for books.

Footnotes for encyclopedia articles. These are handled in much the same manner as references to books and magazine articles When the author's name is given, put it first in the footnote:

[16]Donald Culross Peattie, "Trees of North America," *The Encyclopedia Americana* (New York, 1962), XXVII, 36.

If the article is unsigned, begin with the title:

[17]"Rhetoric," *Encyclopaedia Britannica* (Chicago, 1964), XIX, 247.

Notice that the volume number follows place and date of publication and that the abbreviation *p.* or *pp.* is omitted.

Footnotes for newspaper articles. Unless the article is signed, the reference to a news story consists of the name of the paper, underlined; the date; and the page. The headline is usually omitted, since it may change from edition to edition:

[18]*Chicago Tribune*, June 13, 1967, p. 28.

If the newspaper has sections that are paged separately, the section number should be included. The column number may also be given:

[19]*Chicago Tribune*, Dec. 10, 1967, Sec. 2, p. 4, col. 3.

If the section of the paper has a title, that title should be indicated:

[20]Sanche de Gramont, "Jerusalem: Experiment in Coexistence," *The New York Times Magazine*, July 30, 1967, p. 14.

Footnotes for pamphlets, documents, unpublished material. The form is similar to that for a book, but the footnote may include added identification taken from the title page of the source:

[21]Ella B. Ratcliffe, *Accredited Higher Institutions 1944*, U.S. Office of Education Bulletin 1944, No. 3 (Washington, 1954), pp. 87-88.

[22]Unpubl. thesis (Univ. of Washington, 1950) by Wallace Joseph Smith, "The Fur Trade in Colonial Pennsylvania," p. 19. [titles of unpublished works are usually enclosed in quotation marks]

As with a book, the citation begins with the title when the author's name is not given:

[23]*Higher Education for American Democracy*, Report of the President's Commission on Higher Education, I (Washington, 1947), 26.

Footnotes for Biblical citations. Unless the quotation is very familiar ("Thou shalt not steal"), citations from the Bible should be identified by book, chapter, and verse:

[24]Matthew 6:26-30.

Often the identification is given in parentheses immediately following the quotation instead of in a footnote. Notice that the name of the book is neither underlined nor placed in quotation marks. A colon separates chapter and verse.

Footnotes for material at second hand. When the material used is taken at second hand from another work, give both the original source and the source from which it was taken:

[25]Ronald Bryden, "Pseudo-Event," *New Statesman*, Oct. 4, 1963, p. 460, in *The Deputy Reader: Studies in Moral Responsibility*, ed. D. B. Schmidt and E. R. Schmidt (Chicago, 1965), p. 78.

Use of ibid. in footnotes. As used in a footnote, the abbreviation *ibid.* (for the Latin *ibidem*, "in the same place") means that the reference is to the same book or article as the preceding footnote. It can be used only to refer to the work listed in the footnote *immediately* preceding:

[26]B. Bernard Cohen, *Writing About Literature* (Chicago, 1963), pp. 86-87.

[27]*Ibid.*, p. 93.

When it stands first in a footnote—as it almost always does—*ibid.* is capitalized; because it is an abbreviation, it is always followed by a period. Usage varies on putting *ibid.* in italics (underlining it) or leaving it in Roman type; follow the recommendation of your instructor.

The use of *ibid.*, and of Latin abbreviations in general, is decreasing in academic writing. Usually it is just as simple to use a shortened reference to author and title (as illustrated on page 490) as it is to use *ibid.* As a convenience to the reader, a short form of the footnote should always be used instead of *ibid.* for the first footnote on a new page.

Other abbreviations in footnotes. Standard abbreviations such as those for states (*Menasha, Wis.; Norwood, Mass.*) are commonly used in footnotes (but *New York* rather than *N.Y.* in reference to the city). The following abbreviations may also be used to save space. Follow the recommendation of your instructor about whether to underline those from Latin.

anon.	anonymous
ca. or *c.* (*circa*)	about a given date (*ca.* 1490)
ch., chs.	chapter, chapters
col., cols.	column, columns
ed.	edited by or edition (2nd ed.)
et al. (*et alii*)	and others (used with four or more authors); you may also simply write "and others"
e.g. (*exempli gratia*)	for example (preceded and followed by a comma)

ibid. (*ibidem*)	in the same place (explained on page 493)
i.e. (*id est*)	that is (preceded and followed by a comma)
l., ll.	line, lines (in typewritten copy it is better to write these out, to avoid confusion with the figures 1 and 11)
MS., MSS.	manuscript, manuscripts
n.d.	no date of publication given
n.p.	no place of publication given
p., pp.	page, pages (the word *page* is never written out in footnotes)
rev.	revised edition or revised by
sic	thus (placed in brackets after an error in quoted material to show that you are aware of the error; seldom used by contemporary writers)
trans. or tr.	translated by
vol., vols.	volume, volumes

Alternative forms for footnotes

Research papers in the sciences often use systems of reference to sources quite different from the system just described, which is the one generally used in the humanities and social sciences. The references have the same purpose—giving the author, title, and facts of publication of articles and books used, to acknowledge the source of materials and to make it possible for a reader to go directly to a source if he wishes further information. The details of form vary considerably among the different scientific and technical fields and often among the books and journals within a field. If you are writing a paper for a course in the sciences, you will need to follow your instructor's specification of which system to use or study the form of a particular journal and follow its practice. For more complex systems and variations in footnotes for scientific fields, see the special guides listed in the sample bibliography, page 496. Whatever system you follow, do not shift
29.8 from one system to another in your paper: consistency in form is essential in the use of footnotes.

Any description of footnotes makes their use seem much harder than it really is. If you have good notes with the exact sources of the facts clearly recorded, it is relatively simple to keep track of the necessary sources in the first draft and to place them in the final paper in the proper form.

29.9 Assembling the completed paper

In preparing the final copy of your research paper, refer to the suggestions given in §27.2, Manuscript form. You will also find it useful to study the sample student paper on pages 498-507. Proofread your final copy carefully before turning it in. A well-researched paper can be seriously marred by careless errors and inconsistencies.

The final bibliography

The finished reference paper concludes with a bibliography of the sources used in the paper. This is an alphabetic list of all books, magazine articles, or other publications that have been documented in the footnotes. Occasionally it may also include references that you have explored in depth but have not cited directly in your paper. The principal purpose of a bibliography is to help the reader identify the sources you have used.

Your bibliography cards (§29.3) should contain all the information you need to compile the final bibliography. The form for a bibliography (which differs somewhat from footnote form) is illustrated on page 496. Follow these general guidelines:

1) All entries are listed in alphabetical order, by the author's *last name* or, if the author is unknown, by the first *significant* word of the title (disregarding *A* or *The*). When two or more works by the same author are listed, a line of dashes, followed by a period, may be used instead of the author's name for all but the first work.

2) It isn't necessary to give the page numbers you cited in a book or the number of pages the book contains. You should, however, list the inclusive pages for articles in periodicals or newspapers.

3) Do not separate the list according to kinds of publications. Since the bibliography for most student papers is short, all sources should appear in the same list.

4) Do not number the entries.

Punctuation varies in different bibliography styles, mainly in the use of commas, colons, and parentheses. The form shown here illustrates one style that can be followed without difficulty. Be sure to note carefully any different practices your instructor may want you to follow.

The sample bibliography that follows lists books, articles, and pamphlets on various aspects of writing and documenting research papers:

Bleifuss, William W. "Introducing the Research Paper Through Literature," *College English*, XIV (April 1953), 405-406. [article in a scholarly journal]

Campbell, William G. *Form and Style in Thesis Writing*. Boston, 1954. [book; one author]

Cooper, Charles W., and Edmund J. Robins. *The Term Paper*. Stanford, Calif., 1934. [two authors; notice that only the first author is listed last name first]

Coyle, William. *Research Papers*. New York, 1960.

Handbook for Authors of Papers in the Journals of the American Chemical Society. Washington, D.C., 1967. [author unknown]

Hilbish, Florence M. A. *The Research Paper*. New York, 1952.

Lester, James D. *Writing Research Papers: A Complete Guide*. Glenview, Ill., 1967.

A Manual of Style. 11th ed. Chicago, 1949. [a revised edition]

Publication Manual of the American Psychological Association. Rev. ed. Washington, D.C., 1967.

Seeber, Edward D. *A Style Manual for Authors*. Bloomington, Ind., 1965.

————. *A Style Manual for Students*. Bloomington, Ind., 1964. [second work listed for same author]

Style Manual for Biological Journals. Washington, D.C., 1960.

Sypherd, W. O., Alvin M. Fountain, and V. E. Gibbens. *Manual of Technical Writing*. Chicago, 1957. [three authors; for four or more authors, give the name of the first author only, followed by *and others* or *et al.*]

29.9

If your instructor asks you to include the publisher's name for books, the usual form is this:

Lester, James D. *Writing Research Papers: A Complete Guide*. Glenview, Ill.: Scott, Foresman and Co., 1967.

Final order of contents

The reference paper, usually submitted in a manila folder, should contain all the parts in the order your instructor has assigned. Typically, the completed paper has the following units. Make sure that you include any other material (such as your first outline or first draft) that your instructor asks for.

1) *Title page*. The title of the paper should be centered; your name, the date, the course number, and any other information your instructor requests should be put in the lower right-hand corner.

2) *Outline*. The thesis sentence and the outline in the form assigned (topic or sentence outline). The revised outline should correspond to the organization of the final paper.

3) *Text of the paper*. The final copy of the paper, complete with footnotes, charts, and diagrams wherever needed. The numbering of the text usually begins on the second page, with Arabic numerals centered at the top or at the top right-hand corner.

4) *Bibliography*. The final bibliography should follow the last page of the text, starting on a separate page.

This extended explanation may suggest to you that writing a reference paper is an impossible task to accomplish in a mere five or six weeks of work. It isn't. Done carefully, with due attention to each of the stages outlined in this section, it may be accomplished with no more effort than you would put forth for your other courses. And if your reference paper represents your best work, you will find the assignment a satisfying one and good training for later college work.

The following pages present a sample student paper, complete with outline, text, and bibliography. See pages 508-509 for a key to the symbols in the margin of the text. Exercises on the reference paper begin on page 510.

F. Scott Fitzgerald: Spokesman of the Jazz Age

Thesis sentence: As an honest commentary on his own life and on the era in which he lived, F. Scott Fitzgerald's work represents a valuable contribution to American literature. [A]

I. Fitzgerald grew up with a desire for wealth but also with a poor person's distrust of the rich. [B]

  A. His family was proud of its background but had little money.

  B. He was educated in expensive schools, where he felt at a disadvantage among his rich classmates.

  C. His early feelings about wealth are seen in "The Diamond as Big as the Ritz" and "Winter Dreams."

II. World War I brought optimism, then disillusionment.

  A. Fitzgerald enlisted in 1917 and, while stationed in Alabama, met and became engaged to the wealthy and luxury-loving Zelda Sayre.

  B. His hopes for marriage and for a writing career were both temporarily dashed after the war.

III. Fitzgerald's writing and life during the twenties made him a symbol of the Jazz Age.

  A. Publication of <u>This Side of Paradise</u> (1920), a novel of the postwar generation, made him rich and famous overnight.

  B. He married Zelda and plunged into an irresponsible, pleasure-seeking life, first in New York and later in Europe, where the couple's continued extravagances forced him to resort to commercialized writing.

C. While in Europe he also wrote his best novel, The Great Gatsby, whose hero reflects Fitzgerald's conflicting feelings toward his own life.

IV. The end of the twenties brought a tragic decline in Fitzgerald's personal life and in his literary career.

A. Zelda had a mental collapse from which she never recovered.

B. Fitzgerald's writing became discredited along with the values of the twenties, and he began a progressive physical and mental decline.

C. Fitzgerald's disillusionment during this period is reflected in "Babylon Revisited."

V. Though thoroughly discredited at the time of his death in 1940, Fitzgerald made a lasting contribution to American literature.

A. He epitomized the ideals of the Jazz Age but at the same time remained critically detached from them.

B. He honestly portrayed a way of life that was his personal ruin.

F. Scott Fitzgerald: Spokesman of the Jazz Age C

In the closing lines of <u>This Side of Paradise</u>, the novel that made him rich and famous overnight, F. Scott Fitzgerald described his generation as one that had "grown up to find all gods dead, all wars fought, all faiths in men shaken."[1] D With the war over, America was settling back to Harding "normalcy" with reckless abandon. Money was plentiful, and material pleasures were wantonly pursued. This was the era E of the flapper and the Charleston, of the raccoon coat and the speak-easy, an era when playing the stock market was a kind of national Bingo. More than any other writer, Fitzgerald became the literary spokesman of the Jazz Age. And, because he embodied so many of its characteristics himself, his writings were a chronicle of his personal life as well.

Francis Scott Key Fitzgerald was born in St. Paul, Minnesota, on September 24, 1896, the only son of Edward and Mary Fitzgerald. The father was a weak, pleasant man who had little success in business, and the family was for some time supported by a small inheritance of Francis' mother.[2] F Mrs. Fitzgerald, an eccentric, domineering woman, and her

----

29

[1]<u>This Side of Paradise</u> (New York, 1920), p. 304.

[2]Arthur Mizener, "Francis Scott Key Fitzgerald," <u>Dictionary of American Biography</u>, XXII (New York, 1958), 189. Unless otherwise noted, all biographical data in this paper are from this source.

-2-

family made the boy feel that he was of well-to-do stock, an assurance belied by the family's straightened circumstances. A maiden aunt paid to send him to Newman, an expensive prep school, where he was painfully conscious of being "one of

G the poorest boys in a rich boys' school."[3] Although he tried hard to win praise, his aggressiveness and occasional unwillingness to conform made him unpopular. As was to be true of him throughout life, he was drawn to the rich, but he maintained a proletarian's distrustful attitude toward them. A story written in 1922, "The Diamond as Big as the Ritz," expressed these early feelings in fantasy form: a young man, spending the holidays with a wealthy schoolmate, learns that the mountain on which the estate stands covers the largest diamond in the world and that he will never be permitted to return to the outside world to reveal the secret. The story ends with a romantic escape as the moun-

H tain is blown up.[4]

When the time came to enter college, Fitzgerald chose Princeton, traditionally a social, rich boys' school. Again he strove to be accepted, to become part of their world. Like Dexter Green, the hero of "Winter Dreams," Fitzgerald

----

[3]Interview by Peggy Mitchell, The Atlanta Journal, 1924, in Arthur Mizener, The Far Side of Paradise: A Biography (Boston, 1951), p. 22.

[4]The Stories of F. Scott Fitzgerald, ed. Malcolm Cowley (New York, 1951), pp. 5-38.

-3-

wanted "not association with glittering things and glittering people--he wanted the glittering things themselves."[5] He joined numerous organizations, became a member of a fashionable fraternity, and acquired a moderate campus renown by writing two musical comedies for the Triangle Club. His dream of being elected president of the club and becoming top man at school was shattered, however, when failing grades forced him to withdraw. I J

The war came in 1917, and Fitzgerald was among the first to enlist. Perhaps, like Dexter Green, "he was one of those young thousands who greeted the war with a certain amount of relief, welcoming the liberation from webs of tangled emotion."[6] While stationed outside Montgomery, Alabama, he met and became engaged to Zelda Sayre, the daughter of a justice of the Alabama Supreme Court. Like most of Fitzgerald's heroines, she was beautiful, restlessly intelligent, and addicted to a life of luxury. After being discharged in 1919, Fitzgerald optimistically set out for New York to become a famous writer, but had to settled for a ninety-dollar-a-month advertising job. Zelda, after some wavering, broke their engagement, causing Fitzgerald the second major disappointment of his life. Distraught, he went back to St. Paul to resume writing a novel he had begun at Princeton. K

----

[5]Stories, p. 130.

[6]Ibid., p. 143.

-4-

The publication in March 1920 of This Side of Paradise, a novel about the pleasure-seeking postwar generation, brought Fitzgerald immediate success. Suddenly, popular magazines were clamoring for the short stories they had previously rejected, and money seemed to pour in. In April, Zelda, having reconsidered Fitzgerald's proposal, came to New York to marry him. At once the couple plunged into the giddy, irresponsible whirl of café society, as if determined to be living symbols of the Jazz Age:

L

> They rode down Fifth Avenue on the tops of taxis because it was hot or dove into the fountain at Union Square or tried to undress at the Scandals, or, in sheer delight at the splendor of New York, jumped, dead sober, into the Pulitzer fountain in front of the Plaza. Fitzgerald got in fights with waiters and Zelda danced on people's dinner tables.[7]

M

From 1920 to 1925 Fitzgerald's income was $113,000,[8] and practically the entire amount was spent on extravagances, leaving him with his old feeling of financial insecurity. In 1924 he and Zelda moved to Europe, where expenses were lower. But Paris and the Riviera were as drunk with spending as New York, and Fitzgerald was forced to turn out a good deal of hasty, commercialized writing to pay off a mounting pile of bills. Now that he was on the merry-go-round, he found it impossible to get off.

----

[7]Mizener, The Far Side of Paradise, p. 117.

[8]Katherine Brégy, "F. Scott Fitzgerald--Tragic Comedian," The Catholic World, May 1951, p. 87.

-5-

During his stay in Europe, Fitzgerald also wrote what is generally considered his finest work, The Great Gatsby. The hero of this novel, a tragic victim of romantic illusions, in many ways resembles Fitzgerald. Born James Gatz in North Dakota, he seeks association with the rich, apes their manners, and creates the glittering Jay Gatsby from "his Platonic conception of himself."[9] Stationed in the [N] South during the war, he falls in love with Daisy, a wealthy, irresponsible belle, but his poverty stands between them, and Daisy marries Tom Buchanan, a rich profligate. Gatsby is unwilling to give up his dream: grown rich through bootlegging and convinced that money can buy anything, he lavishes a fortune in winning Daisy back. But in the end he is destroyed by the "vast carelessness" of the rich and his false dream of "the orgiastic future."[10] As Lionel Trilling [O] points out, Gatsby, "divided between power and dream," represents not only the anomaly in Fitzgerald's character, but in the American character as well.[11] [P]

As the dream world of the twenties abruptly ended with the stock market crash of 1929, Fitzgerald's own life entered a tragic decline. In 1930 Zelda suffered a mental

----

[9] The Great Gatsby (New York, 1953), p. 29.

[10] Ibid., pp. 180, 182.

[11] Lionel Trilling, "F. Scott Fitzgerald," The Liberal Imagination (New York, 1950), p. 251.

-6-

collapse from which she never fully recovered; the rest of her life was spent in mental hospitals. Both critics and public turned angrily on the ideals of the orgiastic twenties and everything associated with them. Publishers began to reject Fitzgerald's writings, and he started drinking heavily. Still in his early thirties, he found himself an overnight has-been, as he had once been an overnight success.

The pathos of his life at this period is reflected in "Babylon Revisited," in which the central character, a reformed alcoholic, has lost his wife and the custody of his child. Returning to Paris after the crash, he finds the gay crowds of the twenties gone, except for a few dissipated cronies. He sees in retrospect the illusory life of his youth, where "the snow of twenty-nine wasn't real snow. If
Q you didn't want it to be snow, you just paid some money."[12]

Fitzgerald's despair and heavy drinking resulted in a complete physical and mental breakdown in 1935. In 1940 he died in Hollywood, where he had been trying to extricate himself from debt by writing hack scripts for movies. When he died, the obituaries made it clear that most people regarded him as a relic from a discredited age, the leader, as West-
R brook Pegler put it, of a "cult of juvenile crying-drunks."[13]

----

[12] Stories, p. 402.

[13] The New York World Tribune, December 26, 1940, in Mizener, Far Side of Paradise, p. xvii.

-7-

Although Fitzgerald was tragically deluded by wealth and bogus ideals, he was also a critic of them. Edmund Wilson, a lifelong friend, observed as early as 1922 that "Fitzgerald is romantic, but also cynical about romance. . . . He casts himself in the role of the playboy, yet at the playboy he maliciously mocks."[14] As Fitzgerald himself once wrote, "the test of a first-rate intelligence is the ability to hold two opposed ideals in the mind at the same time, and still retain the ability to function. One should . . . be able to see that things are hopeless and yet be determined to make them otherwise."[15] Because he was so deeply committed to the ideals of the twenties, their ruin became his personal ruin; because he portrayed them honestly and unsentimentally, he left a valuable contribution to American literature. S T

----

29 Ref

[14]Edmund Wilson, "F. Scott Fitzgerald," A Literary Chronicle: 1920-1950 (Garden City, N.Y., 1956), p. 33.

[15]The Crack-Up, ed. Edmund Wilson (New York, 1945), p. 69.

-8-

U Bibliography

V Allen, Frederick Lewis. *Only Yesterday*. New York, 1957.

Brégy, Katherine. "F. Scott Fitzgerald--Tragic Comedian," *The Catholic World*, CLXXIII (May 1951), 87.

Fitzgerald, F. Scott. *The Crack-Up*, ed. Edmund Wilson. New York, 1945.

W ------------. *The Great Gatsby*. New York, 1953.

------------. *The Stories of F. Scott Fitzgerald*, ed. Malcolm Cowley. New York, 1951.

------------. *This Side of Paradise*, New York, 1920.

Mizener, Arthur. *The Far Side of Paradise: A Biography*. Boston, 1951.

------------. "Francis Scott Key Fitzgerald," in *Dictionary of American Biography*. New York, 1958, XXII, 189-191.

Trilling, Lionel. "F. Scott Fitzgerald," in *The Liberal Imagination*. New York, 1953.

Wilson, Edmund. "F. Scott Fitzgerald," in *A Literary Chronicle: 1920-1950*. Garden City, N.Y., 1956.

(See pages 508-509 for comments on this reference paper, keyed to the symbols in the margins.)

Key to symbols

[A] The thesis sentence shows clearly the direction this paper will take. The careful formulation of a thesis statement helps a writer to keep the focus on a central idea and to avoid the temptation of introducing irrelevant material. (A consideration of Fitzgerald's literary technique, for example, would probably contribute nothing to the support of this writer's thesis.)

[B] This sentence outline follows standard outline form and, like the thesis sentence, focuses on the development of a central idea.

[C] Although the title of the paper has been given at the start of the outline, it should be repeated on the first page of the text.

[D] Direct quotation. Since the author's name is given in the text, it need not be repeated in the footnote. The title of the source, also mentioned in the text, might similarly be omitted, but its inclusion makes the note immediately clear.

[E] General information requiring no footnote.

[F] Biographical information from a specific source, requiring a footnote. The covering statement at the end of footnote 2 eliminates the need for further footnoting of simple biographical data.

[G] A direct quotation borrowed indirectly, as the footnote shows, from another source. In cases of indirect borrowing, both the primary and secondary sources must be given in the footnote.

[H] Summary of a short story. Since the author and title are given in the text, both may be omitted from the footnote. Thus, footnote 4 begins with the name of the collection in which the story can be found.

[I] Direct quotation from a different short story, with author and title given in the text. Although footnotes 4 and 5 refer to the same collection of short stories, the writer has used a shortened form of the title (*Stories*) instead of *ibid.* in footnote 5 because the note falls on a new page. This saves his reader the inconvenience of having to turn back to the earlier note.

[J] This biographical information is covered by the comprehensive footnote to the *DAB* on page 1; no footnote is required here.

[K] Direct quotation from the same short story cited immediately above. Although *ibid.* is correctly used in footnote 6, a shortened form of the reference would be equally appropriate: *Stories*, p. 143.

[L] A long quotation set off by indention and single spacing, with no quotation marks. Because the source was previously cited, a shortened reference is used in footnote 7. Both author and title are necessary since the writer has used two different sources by Mizener.

[M] Biographical information from a source other than the *DAB* and therefore requiring a footnote.

[N] A direct quotation from a novel. It is necessary to include the novel's title in footnote 9 so that the source of the actual quotation will be absolutely clear; the author, however, is adequately identified in the context of the paper.

[O] Direct quotations from two different pages in the novel cited immediately above. The writer might have used a shortened reference instead of *ibid.: The Great Gatsby*, pp. 180, 182.

[P] Direct quotation and paraphrase of critical judgment. (A footnote would be necessary for the paraphrase even if the direct quotation had not been used.) Although the author's name is given in the text, it is repeated in the footnote to show that Trilling is author of the entire work (*The Liberal Imagination*) as well as the particular essay cited.

[Q] Direct quotation from a short story, with author and title made clear in the text. *Stories* must be used here rather than *ibid.* because the footnote immediately preceding refers to a different work.

[R] Direct quotation from a newspaper article quoted in a book. The original source of the quotation is given in full, but a shortened form is used for the secondary source, which has been cited previously (footnote 3).

[S] Direct quotation from an essay in a book of collected essays. The author's name, though given in the text, is repeated in the footnote to make it clear that he is author of the entire collection.

[T] Direct quotation, with the author's name but not the title given in the text.

[U] This bibliography follows the style recommended in the MLA *Style Sheet*, which does not include the publisher's name. If your instructor asks you to add this information, insert it between the place and date of publication, preceded by a colon and followed by a comma: Garden City, N.Y.: Doubleday & Company, Inc., 1956.

[V] Source not cited in a footnote but used for background reading.

[W] Several works by the same author, alphabetized by title (disregarding *The*, *A*, or *An*). A line, followed by a period, is substituted for the author's name for all but the first work.

Exercises

1. *Limiting a subject.* From this list of general subjects, select one that you know something about or that you are interested in, and show how it might be progressively narrowed down to a specific topic suitable for a reference paper of the length assigned in your course. If necessary, consult the card catalog or one of the periodical indexes to see what subdivisions of the subject are listed:

Architecture in America
Current problems in advertising
Child psychology
Contemporary music
Acting
Fashions in dress
Foreign diplomacy
A historical figure
A religious leader
Journalism
Juvenile delinquency
Literature
Mathematics
Modern art
Motion pictures
Photography
Recent contributions of science
Sports and their importance

2. *Judging topics.* These are some preliminary subjects submitted by students for reference papers of about 1500 words, before they had begun to investigate their sources. As stated here, which ones do you think would be unlikely to result in satisfactory papers, and for what reasons?

1) Revolutionary movements in Mexico
2) Is limited war possible?
3) Recent changes in stage design
4) The problem of smog in large cities and how to control it
5) The future of advertising in America
6) Some great moments in American sports
7) Origins of modern furniture design
8) The Dow-Jones average
9) Hitler
10) A history of jazz in America

3. *Evaluating source materials.* Read two articles in general encyclopedias on your topic and at least one other reference—a special reference work (see lists in §29.2, pp. 461-469), a book, or a periodical. Then contrast or compare these articles as to (1) the most recent dates of publication, (2) completeness of their discussions, (3) emphasis or possible bias, (4) approach, whether popular or technical, (5) the general value of the article for your purpose.

4. *Preparing to write.* After you have decided on a specific topic and have made a preliminary investigation of your sources, prepare brief notes on these topics:

1) Your reasons for choosing the subject

2) Your present knowledge about the subject and what further reading you will have to do

3) The information you assume your readers already have about this subject (consider the members of your composition class as your potential readers)

4) The reference works—general and specialized—that you think will prove most useful to you in finding material

5) The main point or points you hope to make in your paper

5. *Using reference works.* In what reference works would you look *first* for information on these matters?

1) A speech made by the Secretary of State in New York four or five weeks ago

2) The college degrees held by a prominent contemporary American

3) Attendance at professional football games last season

4) The full title of *Don Quixote* as translated by Samuel Putnam and given in the two-volume edition of 1949

5) An extended discussion of the Quaker Church in America

6) A good discussion of the beginnings of opera

7) A reliable article on Oliver Cromwell

8) The title and date of an article on the coronation of Queen Elizabeth that appeared in the *New Statesman*, an English magazine

9) An account of Custer's last stand in 1876

10) A useful summary of a political event of a year ago

6. *Using footnotes.* If any of these statements appeared in your reference paper, which would you footnote, and why?

1) The War Between the States came to an end at Appomattox courthouse in 1865.

2) Perhaps the most famous of the early "how to" books was Dale Carnegie's *How to Win Friends and Influence People.*

3) Discussing the problem of good and evil, Dr. Einstein stated in his book, *The World as I See It*, that "one does people the best service by giving them some elevating work to do"—a statement with which I agree.

4) Very little is known about Shakespeare's early life.

5) Some scientists, however, do not believe that bacterial cells have a nucleus in the strict sense, since they consider the entire cell to be a nucleus.

6) The Nobel prizes are awarded under the provisions of the will of Alfred Bernhard Nobel, Swedish chemist and engineer, to persons who have made outstanding contributions in the areas of physics, chemistry, physiology or medicine, literature, and world peace.

7) Grantland Rice was the most famous modern sports writer.

7. *Making footnote form consistent.* Put the following references to source material in consistent footnote form as they would appear in a reference paper. Use the system described in this section, or one assigned by your instructor. Number the entries consecutively, as they appear here.

1) To page 107 of a book titled Science: The Glorious Entertainment, written by Jacques Barzun and published by Harper and Row, Publishers, in New York in 1964.

2) To pages 53 and 68 of an article in The Saturday Review for August 19, 1967. The title of the article is The Chinese University, Target of the Cultural Revolution, and the author is C. T. Hu. The magazine is published in New York.

3) To page 208 of this handbook.

4) To pages 147 to 150, inclusive, of the book mentioned in item 1.

5) To page 13 of a pamphlet published by the University of Illinois, Urbana, Illinois, in 1952. The title of the pamphlet is Preparing Technical Material for Publication, and three authors are listed on the title page: Lisle A. Rose, Elmer F. Heater, and George R. Foster. The pamphlet is further described as University of Illinois Bulletin Volume 50, Number 32; the price is sixty cents.

6) To a direct quotation by John F. Kennedy printed on page 81 of the magazine U.S. News & World Report for June 5, 1961. This is Volume L, Number 23 of the magazine.

7) To the same source and the same page given in 6.

8) To an unsigned article called Jamaica in the 1962 edition of the Encyclopedia Americana, a thirty-volume work published in New York by

Americana Corporation. The article appears on pages 599-600 of Volume 15.

9) To figures cited on page 600 of the same source given in 8.

10) To pages 52 and 59 of a pamphlet titled Raising the School Level Age, published in Paris in 1951 by UNESCO. The author is Isaac Leon Kandel.

8. *Correcting footnote and bibliographical form.* In the following exercise containing sample footnotes and a sample bibliography, identify and correct the improper forms.

Footnotes:

[1]Gilbert Highet, *The Classical Tradition* (New York, 1949), p. 315.
[2]See footnote 1 above, p. 278.
[3]Philip Siekman, *Winterset in the Canadian Economy*, FORTUNE, (January 1961), page 94.
[4]Mason, Alden F. *The Ancient Civilizations of Peru.* Baltimore, 1957, p. 79.
[5]*Ibid.*, p. 33.

Bibliography:

Patrick Suppes, *Axiomatic Set Theory* (Princeton, 1960).
Cox, Richard. "The Strong Man of Katanga," *The Reporter*, XXIV (March 30, 1961), 22.
Pooley, Robert C. *Teaching English Grammar.* New York, 1957.
Porter G. Perrin, George H. Smith, Jim W. Corder, *Handbook of Current English*, Glenview Illinois, 1968.
Gray, James, "Three Audiences for Criticism," THE SATURDAY REVIEW, August 5, 1961, p. 17.

9. *Using source material.* This exercise provides practice in distinguishing between plagiarism and paraphrase and in evaluating the effective use of an original source. Examine the source material below and the three student uses of it. Then answer the questions that follow the student versions.

Original source (from Dorothy Bethurum and Randall Stewart, *Classics of the Enlightenment* [Chicago, 1954], p. 5): The stiff brocades and the coffee houses of the eighteenth century were far from anything we know in our life, as were many eighteenth-century habits of thought. But in the satiric attacks on contemporary ills we understand the period. The satiric touch is our best weapon today, too. Our satire expresses itself best in drawing and in painting rather than in literature, but if we were to change the medium, we could see many parallels to eighteenth-century writers. Rouault is at times as mordant as Swift. Feininger, Klee, Thurber, Helen Hokinson, and the cartoons of *The New Yorker* bring home to us the follies and the moral confusion of today.

Student version A: Although many eighteenth-century customs and ideas are unfamiliar to us, we use satire in much the same way. As Bethurum and Stewart point out, "Rouault is at times as mordant as Swift . . . and the cartoons of *The New Yorker* bring home to us the follies and the moral confusion of today."

Student version B: We are far removed from the brocades, coffee houses and beliefs of the eighteenth century. But we understand its use of satire to attack contemporary ills. Our best satire is in drawing and painting rather than in literature. Rouault, Feininger, Klee, Thurber and *The New Yorker* cartoons attack contemporary foolishness and moral chaos.

Student version C: Literary satire is not as common today as it was in the eighteenth century, but it is still very much alive in other art forms. Look at the paintings of Levine, the cartoons of Lichty, the comic dialogues of Mike Nichols and Elaine May.

Evaluate each student's use of the source material:

1) Student version A: (a) is an honest use of direct quotation and requires a footnote; (b) is an honest use of direct quotation that does not require a footnote; (c) is a misleading use of direct quotation, since some material is left out; (d) is a case where quotation marks and a footnote are not necessary, since the passage is so short.

2) Student version B: (a) is a skillful summary of the original source and requires no footnote since no direct quotation is involved; (b) is a good paraphrase that requires no footnote; (c) is a statement of personal opinion based on general information and requires no footnote; (d) is so close to the original source that it is plagiarism, whether a footnote is added or not.

3) Student version C: (a) completely distorts the original source and is therefore dishonest; (b) is a paraphrase of actual information and requires a footnote; (c) repeats only a common fact from the source and is otherwise original; it requires no footnote; (d) illustrates poor research technique because it does not use exact phrases from the source.

10. *A report based on your work in writing your reference paper.* Prepare to write a brief report in class on one of the following topics. Bring your bibliography and note cards with you for reference, if necessary.

1) A summary of your reference paper, giving the essential ideas and the emphasis of the original

2) The sources which you found most useful and why

3) Some problems you encountered in organizing your paper and how you solved them

4) The material you omitted from your rough draft and your reasons for eliminating it

5) What you have learned from the assignment, such as methods of organizing complex material, how to find material in the library, or possible areas for future investigation

Index

This index lists words, phrases, and affixes discussed in the text as well as general topics. In looking up a particular point of usage (use of *shall* or *will,* agreement with *one of those who,* choice of *good* or *well),* look first under the individual word or phrase.

Page references in **boldface** refer to the most important discussions of a topic. The page numbers of appropriate exercises are listed in *italics* after the other references.

A

A, an, when to use, 85
A while, awhile, 199
Abbreviations, 143, **221-225**; *ex. 229*
academic degrees, 221
addresses, 222, 445
appropriateness of, 221
capitalization of, 211, 225
dates, 222
explanation of, first time used, 223
in footnotes, 489-493, **493-494**
measurement, expressions of, 223
names of organizations, 143, 222
names of persons, 221-222
place names, 222, 445, 493
punctuation of, 143, **225**, 493-494
scientific and technical words, 223
titles, 221-222
trade names, 223
-able, -ible,
spelling changes with, 199-201
words formed with, 202
Able to, for *can,* 121
Absolute modifiers, 61 (table), **66**; *ex. 67-68*
Absolute use of the comparative degree, 135
Absolute words, comparison of, 136
Abstractions, capitalization of, 213
Abstract words,
defined and illustrated, 80 (table), 250, **258-259**
effective and ineffective use of, **259-261**; *ex. 266*
Academic degrees, 157, 221
Accent, shown in dictionaries, 239
Accept, except, 198, 255
Accordingly, 32, 43
Accusative case. *See* Objective case *and* Objects.
Acknowledgement of borrowed material, 416, **481-495**. *See also* Bibliography *and* Footnotes.
Acronyms, 222
Act, as a linking verb, 25
Action,
in narrative, 337-338, 426-431
verbs indicating, 108
Active voice,
defined, 109 (table), 120
uses of, 119-120
of verbals, 61 (table)
A.D., B.C., 224
Adapt, adopt, 255
Addresses,
envelope form, 444-445
letter headings, 442
punctuation of, 157, 442-444
street numbers, 227, 444, 445
ZIP codes, 444
Adjective clauses, 31, **48-49**; *ex. 56*
and or *but* misused before, 49
connectives used with, 48-49, 53
defined and illustrated, 48-49
misused as sentences, 40

Adjective clauses (continued)
restrictive and nonrestrictive, 150-152, 159-160
See also Subordination.
Adjectives, 27, 28 (table), **126-129, 134-138**; *ex. 139-141*
comparison of, **134-136,** 136-138
compound, hyphen with, **215-216**
coordinate, 155
coordinate, 53, 155
degrees of, 134-136
demonstrative, 128-129
in description, 425
forms of, compared to adverbs, 129, 134-135
functions of, 27, 28 (table), 126-128
modified by other elements, 29, 127
position of, 27, 126-127
predicate adjectives, 25, **127-128**
proper, capitalized, 210-214
in series, punctuation of, 155
See also Modifiers.
Adverb clauses, 31, 48, **49-50,** 56; *ex. 56*
connectives used with, 50 (list), 53-54
defined and illustrated, 49-50
misused as sentences, 40
punctuation with, 147 (table), 148-149
time sequence emphasized by, 49-50, 337
See also Subordination.
Adverbs, 27, 28 (table), **129-138;** *ex. 139-141*
bobtailed, 130
comparison of, **134-136,** 136-138
conjunctive, **32-33,** 43, 153, **165-166**
degrees of, 134-136
double negatives, 133
forms of, **129-130, 134-135**
functions of, 27, 28 (table), 126, 130-131, 337; *ex. 139*
hyphening of, in group modifiers, 215-216
as interrupting elements, 153
long and short forms of, 129-130
misplaced, 131-132
misused for predicate adjectives, 127
in narrative, 334
position of, 27, **130-132;** *ex. 140-141*
punctuation with, 153, 165-166
relative, 49
Advice, advise, 198
Affect, effect, 198, 255
After, introducing subordinate clauses, 31, 50
Afterthoughts, avoidance of, in ending paragraph, 391
Aggravate, irritate, 122
Agreement of pronoun and antecedent, 71, **94-97;** *ex. 104-105*
indefinite pronouns, 95-97
personal pronouns, 94-95
pronouns referring to coordinate nouns, 95
relative pronouns, 95
Agreement of subject and verb, **69-76;** *ex. 76-78*
after *one of those who,* 74, 95
after *there is, there are,* 74-75
errors caused by blind agreement, 74-76
verbs with collective nouns as subjects, 71-74
verbs with compound subjects joined by *and,* 69
verbs with compound subjects joined by *or, nor,* 70
verbs with indefinite pronouns *(some, all, none)* as subjects, **95-97**
verbs with relative pronouns *(who, which, that)* as subjects, 95
Ain't, 115
Aircraft, names of, 213
Aisle, isle, 198
All,
agreement with, 95-96
possessive form of, 100
All ready, already, 198
All right, alright, alrite, 198
All together, altogether, 199
Alliteration, 297
Allusion, illusion, 198, 255
Almost, most, 130
Along with, agreement of verb with subjects joined by, 71
Alphabet, 2
Already, all ready, 198

Also, as conjunctive adverb, 33, 153
Altho, although, 203
Although, introducing adverb clauses, 31, 40, 43, 50
Alumnus, forms of, 82
A.M., P.M., 224, 227
Am, ain't, 115
Ambiguity,
incomplete comparisons, 137
position of modifiers, 64-65, 130-132
punctuation to avoid, 155-156
reference of pronouns, 90-91
Ampersand (&), 224-225
An, as article, 85
An sit, 349
Analogy,
as method of paragraph development, 329
as technique of argument, 419, 422
Analysis, plural form, 82
-ance, -ence, 202
And,
agreement of pronoun with nouns joined by, 95
agreement of verb with subjects joined by, 69
ampersand (&) as substitute for, 224-225
to correct comma fault, 43
joining main clauses, punctuation with, 148, 159, 164, 166
joining a series, punctuation with, 154
joining two words or phrases, omission of comma with, 159
misused before *who* or *which,* 49
repetition of, in a series, 295, 358-359
semicolon in place of, 164-165
And which, and who, 49
Anglicized words, 187
Announcements, formal, 449-450
Annuals and yearbooks, 467-470
Answers, omission of verb in, 35
Answers for essay examinations, 431-436
-ant, -ent, 202
Antecedent,
agreement of pronoun with, 94-97; *ex. 104-105*
clear reference of pronoun to, 89-94; *ex. 105*
Anticipating subjects (expletives), 26, 74-75
Antonyms, 244, 257; *ex. 248*
Any, anybody, anyone,
agreement with, 95-96
masculine pronoun used to refer to, 94
possessive form of, 100
Anyone else, possessive form of, 100
Apologetic quotation marks, 182, 272
Apology, avoidance of, in beginnings and endings, 388, 390-391
Apostrophe, **218-219;** *ex. 219-220*
in contractions, 218
in dates, 218
for letters dropped in representing speech, 219
misused with possessive pronouns, **99-100,** 219
for plurals of letters and figures, 218-219
for possessive of nouns, **83-84,** 218-219
for possessive of some indefinite pronouns, 100
Apparatus, plural forms, 81
Appear, as linking verb, 25, 127
Appendix, plural forms, 81
Application letters, 445-448
Applied science, reference works in, 458, 468
Appositional sentence, 35
Appositives,
defined, 29
gerunds and gerund phrases as, 61 (table)
noun clauses as, 51
punctuation of, 152
Appropriateness as quality of good English, **13-18;** *ex. 21*
Arabic numerals, 228
for footnotes, 489-491
for numbering manuscript, 401, 497
for outline subheads, 367
See also Numbers.
Archaic words, 202, 243, 273-274
Are, aren't, ain't, 114-115
Argue, arguing, argument, 200

Argumentation, 323-324, **416-423**
argument from analogy, 419
argument from authority, 419
argument from consequence, 419
argument from nature, 418-419
fallacies in logic, 421-423
finding an arguable proposition, 417
testing the argument, 421-423
use of details, 323-324
use of evidence, 418-419
Argumentum ad hominem, 423
Arise, principal parts of, 113
Arrangement of material. *See* Development of ideas *and* Outlining.
Arrive, arrival, 200
Art, reference sources in, 458, 461-462
Articles *(a, an, the),*
capitalization of, in titles, 401
choice of *a* or *an,* 85
disregarded in alphabetizing, 459, 509
use of *the* to introduce a gerund phrase, 62-63
As,
adverb clauses introduced by, 50, 53-54
inexactness of, 53-54
or *like* to introduce comparisons, 138
similes introduced by, 278
As . . . as, construction of double comparisons with, 138
As, as if, as though, to introduce clauses of comparison, 138
As long as, introducing adverb clauses, 50
As well as, agreement with subjects joined by, 71
Asides, parenthetical, 174
Asyndeton, 358
Atlases, listed, 462
Attorney general, 84, 127
Attributive nouns, 27, 86
Author, form for citing,
in bibliography, 471-473, 495-496
in footnotes, 488-491
Auxiliary verbs, 109 (table), 114-119
Awkward constructions,
bracketed material within parentheses, 185
choppy or stringy sentences, 288-290
genitive forms, 85, 101
inverted subordination, 55-56
noun clauses as complements, 51-52
of which, 101
passive verbs, 120
tandem subordination, 55
wordy sentences, 291-294

B

Bad, irregular comparison of, 135
Bad, badly, 128, 130
Balanced sentences, 310, 358
Barely, in double negatives, 133
Basic (common) form of nouns, 80, 83
Basic sentence faults, **38-45;** *ex. 45-47*
comma faults, 38, 41-44
fragmentary sentences, 38-41
fused sentences, 38, 44
mixed constructions, 44-45
Bat, forms of, 201
B.C., A.D., 224
Be,
as a linking verb, 25, 98, 109 (table), 127
case of pronoun after, 98
complement after, 25, 127-128
forms of, **114-115,** 119
in passive verbs, 119
Bear,
confused with *bare,* 255
principal parts of, 113
Because,
as and *so* misused for, 53-54
being that misused for, 122
due to the fact that misused for, 293
for correcting comma faults, 43
for exact subordination, 31, 40, 50, 53-54
Become, as linking verb, 109 (table), 127
Before, introducing adverb clauses, 50
Begging the question, 422
Begin, principal parts of, 113
Beginning paragraphs, 377, 378, **385-388;** *ex. 394-395*

effective beginnings, 385-387
ineffective beginnings, 387-388
use of thesis sentence, 380-381
Beginnings of sentences,
numbers written out, 228
variation in, 303-304
Being that, for *because,* 122
Berth, birth, 198
Between, case of pronoun after, 97-98
Bi-, 258
Bible, references to, 181, 482, **492**
Bibliographies for the book trade, 457-458
Bibliography, preparation of, **470-473, 495-496**; *ex. 513-514*
cards, information to include, 471-473
final form, 169, 495-496
preliminary list, 470-473
samples, 472, 496, 507
sources for compiling (listed), **455-470**
Big Words, **268-270**; *ex. 280-282.* *See also* Diction.
Bio-, 258
Biographical dictionaries, 460, 462
Biological sciences, sources of reference, 469
Birth, berth, 198
Bite, principal parts of, 113
Blind agreement, **74-76**
Block form,
for addressing envelopes, 444
for letter headings, 442
for paragraphs, 442
Blow, principal parts of, 113
Bobtailed adverbs, 130
Book reports, 437-438
Book Review Digest, 477
Books, form for citing,
in bibliography, 471-473, 495-496
in first footnote, 489-490
in subsequent footnotes, 490-491
Both . . . and, as correlatives, 32
Brackets, **184-185,** 402
Brand names, capitalization of, 213
Briefings, 438
Break, principal parts of, 113
Bright, brightly, 129
Bring, principal parts of, 113
British usage, 202, 203, 239
Buildings, capitals for names of, 213
Burst, principal parts of, 113
Business, reference works in, 460, 462
Business letters, 175, 221, **441-445**
But, as coordinating conjunction, 32, 43, 164
comma used with, 147 (table), **148,** 156
in double negatives, 133
semicolon used with, 166
But what, misused for *that,* 133
But which, but who, misused in introducing subordinate clause, 49

C

Cactus, plural forms, 81
Call numbers, library, 456, 473
Can, able to, 121
Can, may, 115
Can't hardly, couldn't scarcely, 133
Can't help but, 133
Capital, capitol, 198
Capitals, **208-214**; *ex. 219-220*
abbreviations, 225
abstractions, 213
after colon, 209-210
close of letters, 444
deity, references to, 213
dictionary as guide to, 208
directions, 212
emphasis gained by, 314
family relationships, 211
geographical divisions, 212
outlines, 368
parenthetical sentences, 209
place names, 212
proper nouns and their derivatives, 210-214
time, units of, 213
titles of books, etc., 210, 401
titles of people, 210-211
Card catalogs, library, 455-457
Cardinal numbers, 228
Cards, bibliography, 471-473

Cards, for notes, **475,** 478
Caret, for insertion, 402
Case forms,
of nouns, 60, 62, 80 (table), **83-85;** *ex. 87-88*
of pronouns, 93 (table), **97-101;** *ex. 103-104, 106*
See also Genitive case, Objective case, *and* Subject.
Case, as deadwood, 293
Catalog, library, 455-457
Catch, principal parts of, 113
Catchall expressions, 224
Cause, adverb clauses to show, 40, 50, 53
Cause-effect, as method of development, 329, 331, 380, 419
-ce, words ending in, 200
-cede, -ceed, -sede, words formed with, 202
Censor, censure, 255
Center, centre, 203
Central idea. *See* Pre-writing, Subjects for papers, *and* Thesis statement.
Cf., 224
Character, as deadwood, 293
Character sketch, detail for, 425
Charts and tables, position of, 401
Cheap, cheaply, 129
Chemistry, reference works in, 462
Choose, chose, 113, 198
Choppy sentences, **288-289;** *ex. 298*
Christian names, abbreviation of, 222
Chronological order,
as method of development, 330, 379
in narrative, 337-338, **426-430**
Circumlocutions, 292. *See also* Economy of expression.
Citations, form of,
in bibliography, 470-473, 495-496
in footnotes, 488-495
Cite, sight, site, 192, 198, 255
Clarity,
commas used for, 155-156
dashes used for, 172
essential to business letters, 441
explaining specialized information, 270-271, 415-416
good English characterized by, 16
parallelism of coordinate ideas, 308-310
relating ideas in paragraphs, 333-338
relating ideas in sentences, 290-291, 306-308
relating paragraphs in sequence, 382-385
repetition of key words, 256
sentence emphasis, 311-314
subordination of less important ideas, 52-54, 306-308
supporting details, 321-324
topic sentences, 324-325
Class reports, 437-438
Classification, as method of paragraph development, 330, 372
Clauses, **29-33;** *ex. 36-37*
adjective, 31, **48-49;** *ex. 56*
adverb, 31, **49-50;** *ex. 56*
compared with phrases, 29
coordinate, defined, 32
incorrectly joined, 39, **41-44;** *ex. 45-47*
incorrectly used as sentences, **38-41;** *ex. 45-47*
main (independent), defined, 29-30
noun, 31, **50-52;** *ex. 56*
punctuation between, 146-152, 164-168
reduced to words or phrases, 291-292
restrictive and nonrestrictive, punctuation of, 150-152, 159-160
sentences classified by kind and number of, 31-33; *ex. 36-37*
subordinate (dependent), defined, 29-31, **48-56;** *ex. 56-58*
See also Main clauses *and* Subordinate clauses.
Cliches, **274-275;** *ex. 283-284*
Climax, as a method of development, 328-329, 379-380
Climax sentence, 312
Close, closely, 129
Close, complimentary,
for business letters, 444
for personal letters, 450
Close modifiers. *See* Restrictive modifiers.

Close punctuation, 7
Closing paragraphs, **389-391**; *ex. 394-395*
Closing punctuation, 142-145
Coarse, course, 198
Coherence. *See* Continuity.
Coined words, 244; *ex. 248*
Collective nouns, **71-74,** 80 (table), 95; *ex. 75-78*
College dictionaries, 236, 240-241
College writing, usage appropriate to, 14-16
Colloquial expressions, 11, 234, **243,** 271-272
apologetic quotes for, 182
contractions, 218
See also Informal English.
Colon, **167-169,** 183; *ex. 169-170, 230-233*
anticipatory use of, 167-168
clauses separated by, **168,** 312
conventional uses of, 169
greeting or salutation followed by, 158, 169, **444, 450**
quotations preceded by, 169
semicolon distinguished from, 167
series preceded by, 167-168
use of capital after, 209-210
with quotation marks, 183
Combined forms, distinguished from separate words, 198-199
Come, principal parts of, 113
Comma, **146-160,** 147 (table), 164-166; *ex. 160-163, 230-233*
appositives set off by, 152
comma faults, 39, **41-44,** 159, 165
conventional uses of, **156-158,** 227, 444, 449, 490
coordinate clauses separated by, 146-148
distinguished from dash, 171
distinguished from semicolon, 164-166
interrupting and parenthetical elements set off by, 152-154
introductory clauses and phrases set off by, 148-150
lists and series punctuated with, 154-155, 160
misuses of, 158-160
necessary for clarity, 155-156
nonrestrictive modifiers set off by, 150-152
optional uses of, 147 (table), 148, 149-150
with parentheses, 175
with quotation marks, 158, 168-169, 183
Comma fault (comma splice), 38, **41-44,** 159, 165; *ex. 45-47*
Commands (imperative sentences), defined, 34
for sentence variety, 306
Commit, forms of, 201
Common (basic) form of nouns, 80 (table), 83
formation of plurals, 79-82
preceding a gerund, 60, 62
Common nouns, defined, 80 (table). *See also* Proper nouns.
Comparative degree, 134-135
Comparison of adjectives and adverbs, **134-136**
Comparison-contrast, as method of development,
in a paper, **379,** 380-382
in a paragraph, **329,** 331, 333
See also Analogy.
Comparisons, construction of, **136-138,** 309-310; *ex. 139-141*
figurative comparisons (metaphors and similes), 277-278
form of pronoun after *than,* 98
incomplete comparisons, 137
parallelism in comparisons, 309-310
use of *like* or *as,* 138
use of *other,* 138
Complement,
blind agreement with, 75
defined, **25**
position of, 25
subordinate clauses as, 48, 50-52
with verbals, 59-60
See also Predicate nouns *and* Predicate adjectives.
Complete subject, defined, 23-24
Complex sentence, defined, 33; *ex. 36*
Complexity, materials arranged by degree of, 379

Complimentary close, 444, 450
Composition, **319-515**
argumentation, 323-324, 416-423
description, 336-337, 423-426
developing ideas, 319-332, 378-382; *ex. 338-341, 392-395*
discovering a subject, 344-349, 452-454
exposition, 322-323, 413-416
first draft, 377-392, 479-480; *ex. 392-395*
letters, 441-450
literary analyses, 439-441
manuscript form, 398-410, 488-507; *ex. 410-412, 511-512*
narration, 337-338, 426-431
organization, 367-371, 478-479; *ex. 375-376*
paragraphs, 319-338, 381-391; *ex. 338-343, 393-395*
pre-writing, 344-360
reference papers, 451-509
reports and critiques, 437-438
resources, 349-354, 414-415, 418-419, **455-470** (list)
revision, 396-410, 480-481; *ex. 410-412*
sentences, 286-298, 302-314, 380-381; *ex. 298-301, 314-318, 393-394*
style, 356-360
See also individual entries for the sub-headings listed above.
Compound adjectives (group modifiers), 197, 215-216
Compound-complex sentence, defined, 33
Compound nouns (group words), defined, 80 (table)
genitive (possessive) form of, 84
hyphens with, 214-215
plurals of, 82-83
Compound predicate,
comma misused in, 159
defined and illustrated, 31-32
separated for clarity, 156
Compound sentence, **32,** 33
punctuation of, 146-148, 164-166
See also Main clauses.
Compound subject, 31, 159
agreement of verb with, **69-71,** 75
comma misused in, 159
Compound words. *See* Compound adjectives *and* Compound nouns.
Compounding elements from Greek and Latin, 258
Conceive, conceivable, 200
Concession, adverb clauses of, 49
Conciseness. *See* Economy of expression.
Conclusions, for a paper, **389-391,** 480
Concord. *See* Agreement.
Concrete words,
defined and illustrated, 80 (table), 250, **258-259**
effective use of, **259-261**; *ex. 265-266*
Condition,
adverb clauses of, 49
subjunctive to express, 120
verbs indicating, 108
Conjugation. *See* Verbs.
Conjunctions,
comma faults corrected by, 43-44
coordinating, listed, 32
correlative, 32, **70-71,** 309-310
for paragraph continuity, 334
repetition of, for clarity, 295
repetition of, for effect, 358-359
subordinating, 31, 43, **50** (listed), 53-54
See also Coordinating conjunctions *and* Subordinating conjunctions.
Conjunctive adverbs,
function and effect of, 32-33, 165-166
punctuation with, 33, 43, 165-166
Connectives,
choice of, for exactness, 50, **53-54**
comma faults corrected by, **43-44**
conjunctive adverbs, weakness of, 32-33, 43, 165-166
for continuity, 334, 384
misused in tandem subordination, 55
repetition of, for clarity, 295
repetition of, for effect, 358-359
semicolon substituted for, 32, 42-43, **164-165**
See also Coordinating conjunctions, Correlative conjunctions, Relative

adverbs, Relative pronouns, *and* Subordinating conjunctions.
Connotation of words, **251**; *ex. 262*
slanted words, **252-254**; *ex. 263*
synonyms, 255-256
See also Diction.
Conscientious, conscious, 198, 255
Consequently,
as conjunctive adverb, 33, 43
punctuation with, 153, 165-166
Considerably, considerable, 130
Consistency,
in abbreviations, 225
in figures of speech, 280
in footnote form, 494-495
in parallel constructions, 308-310
in person and number of pronouns, **103**; *ex. 105-106*
in tense, **111-112**, 338, 429; *ex. 125*
in tone and level of usage, **15**, 249-250, 259-260, **267-272**
in use of hyphens, 214
in use of quotation marks and italics, 181
in writing number with words or figures, 226
Consonants, doubling of final, 201
Constructions, grammatical,
comparisons, 137-138
main clauses, 30
parallel structures, 308-310; *ex. 316*
prepositional phrases, 30
sentences, 23-35, 38-45; *ex. 36-37, 45-47*
subordinate clauses, 30-31, 48-56; *ex. 56-58*
verbal phrases, 30, 59-66; *ex. 66-68*
Contact, for *call* or *see,* 122
Context, meaning determined by, 234, 242, **249-251**, 258
Continuity,
among ideas in a paragraph, **333-338**; *ex. 341-343*
between paragraphs, 383-384
in descriptive paragraphs, 336-337
in narrative paragraphs, 337-338
related to sentence length, 288-291
subordination to improve, 52-54, 306-308
Contractions, 218
Contrast. *See* Comparison-contrast.
Conventions of writing, 2, 3, **142-238**; *ex. 232-233*
abbreviations, **221-225**, 493-494; *ex. 229*
apostrophes, 83-85, 99-100, **218-219**; *ex. 219-220*
bibliography form, 470-473, **495-496**; *ex. 513*
brackets, **184-185**, 402
capital letters, **208-214**; *ex. 219-220*
colons, **167-169**; *ex. 169-170*
commas, **147-160**, 164-166; *ex. 160-163*
dashes, **171-173**; *ex. 176*
ellipses, **185**, 474
exclamation marks, 144-145
footnote form, **488-495**; *ex. 513*
hyphens, **215-217**, 239, 400; *ex. 220*
italics, **186-188**, 489-491; *ex. 188-191, 512*
manuscript form, **398-403**; *ex. 410-412*
numbers, **225-228**; *ex. 229*
parentheses, **173-175**; *ex. 175*
periods, 142-143
question marks, 143-144
quotation marks, **177-184**, 314, 401; *ex. 188-191*
semicolons, **164-166**; *ex. 169-170*
spelling, **192-203**, 238-239; *ex. 203-207*
See also individual entries for the sub-headings listed above.
Conversation. *See* Dialog.
Coordinate adjectives, 155
Coordinate clauses,
defined, 32
overuse of, 54, 289-290
punctuation of, 146-148, 164-166
See also Main clauses, Subordinate clauses, *and* Subordination
Coordinate elements,
comma misused between two, 159
commas to separate a series of, **154-155**
coordinate adjectives, 155
coordinate nouns, agreement of verb or pronoun with, **69-71**, 75, 95
coordinate nouns, possessive of, 84

Coordinate elements (continued)
semicolon used only with, **164-166**
See also Coordinate clauses.
Coordinate ideas, parallel structure for, 308-310
Coordinating conjunctions, 32
comma faults corrected by, 43-44
joining clauses, 32, 43-44, 53, 146-148, 166
joining items in a series, 154-155
overuse of, 53, 290
punctuation with, **146-148,** 154-155, 166
Copula, defined, 109 (table). *See also* Linking verbs.
Correcting a paper, **403-410.** *See also* Revision.
Correlative conjunctions,
agreement of verb with subjects joined by, **70-71**
coordinate clauses joined by, 32
parallel constructions with, 309-310
Correspondence. *See* Letters.
Counsel, forms of, 201
Countries, abbreviations for, 222
Courses, academic, capitalization of, 212
Courtesy questions, 142-143
Courtesy titles, 157, 221
Credible, creditable, credulous, 198, 255
Critiques, 438
Curriculum, plural forms, 81

D

-d, -ed, -t,
endings for regular verbs, 108, 109 (table)
omission of, as spelling error, 197
Dangling modifiers, **65;** *ex. 67-68. See also* Misrelated modifiers.
Dare, use of *to* with, 63
Dashes, **171-173;** *ex. 176*
for emphasis, 171-172, 312-313
with quotation marks, 183
Data, agreement with, 72-73
Dates,
abbreviations of, 222
at beginning of sentence, 228
contracted form of, 218
form and punctuation of, **157,** 219, 227
form for citing, in footnotes, 489
Dead, modified by comparative forms, 136
Deadwood, elimination of, **292-294,** 297; *ex. 300. See also* Wordiness.
Declarative sentence, defined, 33
Decimals, period with, 143
Declension. *See* Case *and* Number.
Deduction, as pattern of paragraph development, 328-329
Deep, deeply, 129
Definition, as method of paragraph development, 329, 330, 332
Definitions,
in dictionaries, 242-243; *ex. 246-248*
in a paper, 270-271, 415-416
Degree, adverb clauses of, 53
Deity, references to, 213
Degree, of adjectives and adverbs, **134-136**
Degrees, academic, 157, 221
Deliberative writing, 357
Demonstrative adjectives, 128-129
Demonstrative pronouns, 92, 93 (table)
Demonstrative writing, 357
Denotation of words, **250,** 255-256
Dependent clauses. *See* Subordinate clauses.
Descriptive writing, **336-337, 423-426**
paragraph continuity in, 336-337
selecting and arranging details in, 336-337, 424-426
spatial order in, 330, 379, 426
use of modifiers in, 126, 425
verbless sentences in, 35
Details,
in description, 336-337, 423-426
in exposition and argumentation, 222-224
for interest and support of general statements, 321-324
in narration, 430-431
in opening and concluding paragraphs, 321, 387, 391
parentheses enclosing, 174-175
use of specific and abstract words, 258-261

Detract, distract, 255
Development of ideas in writing, **319-332, 378-382**; *ex. 338-341, 392-395*
answers to essay questions, 432-436
argumentation, 323-324, 416-423
beginnings and endings, 385-386, 388-391
checking development and organization, 396-398
details and general statements, **321-324**
exposition, 322-323, 413-416
organizing the paper, 360-372, 377-392, 477-478
paragraph development, **319-332**
paragraphs in sequence, 382-385
patterns of development, **328-332, 378-382**
See also Outlining, Paragraphs, *and* Pre-writing
Diagrams, position of, in a paper, 401
Dialectical words, 243
Dialog,
paragraphing and punctuation of, 158, 173, **178-179**
short sentences for, 34, 289
Diction, **249-261, 267-280,** 409; *ex. 262-266, 280-285*
abstract and concrete words, 250, 258-261
confusion of similar or opposite words, 254-257
connotation of words, 251
context, importance of, 234, 242, **249-251**, 258
deadwood, 292-294, 297
denotation of words, **250,** 254-258
economy of expression, 291-297
euphemisms, 275-276
figures of speech, 276-280
foreign words, 270
Formal words, 267-271
Informal words, 271-272
meaning of words, 242-243, 249-261
old-fashioned words, 273-274
repetition, careless, 294-298
slang, 8, 11, 271-272
slanted words, 251-254
stilted language, 268-270
technical words, 7, 8, 11, 270-271
trite expressions, 274-275
wordiness, 291-292
Dictionaries, **234-244**; *ex. 245-248*
college, 236, 240-241 (samples)
definitions in, 242-243
etymology in, 244
foreign words in, 243
grammatical information in, 242
historical, 237
listed and described, 235-237
pronunciation in 239, 242
spelling in, 193, 202-203, 238-239
synonyms and antonyms in, 244
unabridged, 234, 236
usage labels in, 234, **243**
word division in, **239,** 400
Dictionary of American English, 237
Different, differently, 130
Dig, principal parts of, 113
Direct, directly, 129
Direct address, commas with, 154
Direct discourse, form for, 158, **178-179**
Direct expression. *See* Economy of expression.
Direct object, defined, 24. *See also* Objects.
Direct questions, 142-144
Direct quotations,
footnotes for, 482
integrated with text, 179-181, 482-484
punctuation with, 158, 168-169, **179-181**, 474
when to use, 482-484
Direction, adverb clauses of, 49
Directions (*north, south,* etc.), 212, 223
Directive sentences. *See* Commands.
Dissertation, unpublished, footnote for, 492
Distract, detract, 255
Dive, principal parts of, 113
Divided usage,
in abbreviations, 223
in irregular verb forms, 113-114
in pronunciation, 239
in spelling forms, 82-83, 202-203, 238-239
Division of content. *See* Outlining.

Division of words, **239**, 400
Do,
idioms with, 116
principal parts of, 113, 115
Documentation of a paper, 416, **481-495.** *See also* Bibliography *and* Footnotes.
Documents, footnotes for, 492
Doer of an act, genitive to show, 83, 85
Done, don't, Nonstandard uses of, 115
Double comparisons, 137
Double genitive, 85
Double negatives, 133; *ex. 140*
Draft, draught, 202
Drag, principal parts of, 113
Drama,
citation of, 483
reference works in, 460, 463
Draw, principal parts of, 113
Dream, principal parts of, 113
Drink, principal parts of, 113
Drive, principal parts of, 113
Due to the fact that, 293
Dummy words, 74-75
Dye, dyeing, dying, 200

E

-e, final, before suffixes, 199-200
Each,
agreement with, 96-97
possessive of, 100
Eat, principal parts of, 113
Economy of expression, **291-297**; *ex. 299-300*
careless repetition, 294-297
deadwood, 292-294, 297
wordiness, 291-292
-ed,
doubling of consonant before, 201
ending for regular verbs, 108, 109 (table)
omission of, as spelling error, 197
Education, reference works in, 460, 463
Effect, adverb clauses of, 49
Effect, affect, 198, 255
Effect-to-cause. *See* Cause-effect.
Effective word choice. *See* Diction.
E.g., 187, 224, 493
-ei- or *-ie-,* 200
Either . . . or, 32
agreement with elements joined by, **70**
parallel construction with, 309-310
Elliptical sentences, 34-35
Ellipses, **185**, 474
Else, following indefinite pronouns, 100
Emphasis, **311-314**; *ex. 317*
balanced sentences, 310, 358
climax sentences, 312
exclamatory sentences, 142, 144-145, 314
inverted word order, 304
mechanical devices, 187-188, **314**
periodic sentences, 305, 312, 358
punctuation, 144-145, 171-173, 186-188, 312-313
reflexive pronouns, 101
repetition, intentional, 295, 313-314
shall and *will,* 117-118
short sentences, 289
subordination, 52-54, 306-308
word order, 26, 127, 131, 311-312
Empty, modified by comparative forms, 136
-en, as plural ending, 79
-ence, -ance, words formed with, 202
Encyclopedia articles, footnotes to, 491
Encyclopedias,
general (listed), **461**
specialized (listed), **461-470**
End stops, **142-145**
position of, with quotes, 183-184
Ending paragraphs, **389-391**; *ex. 394-395*
Endorsement of papers, 401, 497
English language. *See* Language.
Enthuse, 122
-ent, -ant, 202
Envelope form, **444-445**
Epistrophe, 358
-er, -est,
doubling of consonant before, 201
to form comparisons, 134-135
-es, -s, as plural endings, 79-82, 201
Essay examination answers, 431-436
Et al., 187, 490, **493**
Etc., 187, **224**

Etymology, 244; ex. *247-248*
Euphemisms, **275-276**; *ex. 283-284*
Euphony. *See* Sound, repetition of.
Evaluation,
of an argument, 421-423
of resources, 350-354
Even, evenly, 129
Everybody, everyone,
agreement with, 95-96
masculine pronoun referring to, 94
possessive of, 100
Evidence, use of, in argumentative writing, 418-419
Exactness,
choice of connective for, 50, 53, 54
sentence economy and, 291-292
subordination for, 52-54, 306-308
word choice for, 249-262
Examples,
colon to set off, 167-168
enclosed in brackets, 184-185
enclosed in parentheses, 174
italicized or set off by quotation marks, 186
used for paragraph continuity, 334
See also Details.
Except, accept, 198, 255
Exclamation marks, 142, **144-145**, 183, 314
Exclamations, 34
inverted word order in, 26
O, oh, 210
omission of verb in, 35
punctuation of, 142, 144-145
Exist, as deadwood, 293
Explanatory phrases,
enclosed in brackets, 184
enclosed in parentheses, 173
misused as sentences, 40
Expletives. *See* Anticipating subjects.
Exposition, **413-416**
Expository paragraphs, 322-323

F

-f, nouns ending in, plurals of, 79-81
Fact, as deadwood, 294
Factor, as deadwood, 294
Fair, fairly, 129
Fair use of words, **251-252**
Fall, principal parts of, 113
Fallacies in reasoning, 421-423
False analogy, 422
Familiar correspondence, 449-450
Family relationships, names of,
capitalization of, 211
hyphening of, 215
Far, irregular comparison of, 135
Farther, further, 135
Feel, as linking verb, 25, 127
Feminine intensive, 136
Feminine nouns, 80
Feminine pronouns, 92-94
Few, possessive of, 100
Field, as deadwood, 294
Figures. *See* Numbers.
Figures of speech, **276-280**; *ex. 284-285*
consistency of, 280
defined and illustrated, 276-278
effectiveness of, 278-280
trite figures, 274-275
Final bibliography, 495-497
Final draft,
manuscript form for, **402-410**; *ex. 410-412*
preparation of, **398-401**, 495-497
See also Revision.
Final paragraphs, **389-391**; *ex. 394-395*
Finite verbs, defined, 109 (table)
First draft, **377-392**, 479-481; *ex. 392-395*
beginning and ending paragraphs, 385-388
development of thesis, 378-382
relating paragraphs in sequence, 382-385
revision, **396-398**
selecting a title, 392
See also Composition *and* Pre-writing.
First names, abbreviation of, 222
First person pronouns, **93** (table)
appropriateness of, in writing, 101-102, 427-428
I or *me,* 97-98
possessive forms of, 99-100
use of reflexive and intensive forms of, 101

Fix, as a verb, 122
Fly, principal parts of, 113
Footnotes, **479-495**; *ex. 511-513*
 abbreviations, 221, 489-493, **493-494**
 alternative forms, 494
 Biblical citations, 492
 books, **489-491**
 encyclopedia articles, 491
 in first draft, 480
 magazine and journal articles, 491
 newspaper articles, 492
 numbering, 488
 pamphlets, 492
 punctuation, 169, 489-491
 second reference, short form or *ibid.* for, 490-491, 493
 secondary sources, 492-493
 spacing, 488
 split, 489
 unpublished material, 492
 when to use, **482-488**
For, 32, 164
 being that misused for, 122
 comma with, 148, 156
For example, 40
Foreign words,
 appropriateness of, 270
 italics for, **187,** 493
 plurals of, 81-82
Forensic writing, 357
Forget, principal parts of, 113
Formal correspondence, 449-450
Formal English, **7-11**; *ex. 18-21*
 punctuation style, 7, 148, 164, 208, 214, 221
 word choice, 259-261, **267-271**, 272
Formula, plural forms, 81
Formulas for use of subjunctive, 121
Forty, fourty, 193
Fractions, hyphening of, 215
Fragmentary sentences, **38-41**; *ex. 45-47*
Freeze, principal parts of, 113
-ful, plural of nouns ending in, 83
Further, farther, 135
Fused sentence, 38, **44,** 45; *ex. 45-47*
Future perfect tense, 110 (table)
Future tense, 110 (table)
 use of *shall* or *will,* 118
 See also Tense.

G

Gender,
 of nouns, 80 (table)
 of pronouns, 92-94
General English, **5-6,** 7, **8-9**; *ex. 18-21*
 punctuation style, 5, 148, 152, 208, 214, 221
 word choice, 14, 243, 259-261, 267-272; *ex. 280-282*
Generalizations,
 details in relation to, 321-324
 meaningless, 261, 388
 unsupported, in argument, 421-422, 423
Genitive (possessive) case,
 apostrophe, position of, **83-84,** 218-219
 choice of *-'s* form or *of* phrase to show, 83, **85,** 100
 of coordinate nouns, 84
 defined, 83
 double genitive, 85
 of group words, 84
 idiomatic use of, 85
 of indefinite pronouns, 100
 of nouns, 79, 80 (table), **83-85**; *ex. 87-88*
 of personal pronouns, 93 (table), **99-100**
 of plurals and nouns ending in *-s,* 84
 subjective vs. objective genitive, 83
 subjects of gerund phrases, 60, 62, 83
 uses of, listed, 83
 of *who* and *which,* 100-101
Geographic areas, names of,
 abbreviation, 222
 capitalization, 212
Geography, reference works in, 462, 463-464
Gerunds, **60-63**; *ex. 66-68*
 forms and typical uses of, 61 (table)
 idiomatic use of, 62-63
 as non-finite verb form, 109 (table)
 participles identical in form to, 59
 subjects of, 60, 62
Get,
 idioms with, 116-117
 principal parts of, 113, 116

Give, principal parts of, 113
Given names, abbreviation of, 222
Glittering generalities, 423
Go, principal parts of, 113
Gobbledygook, 9, 269-270
Good, irregular comparison of, 135
Good, well, 128
Got, gotten, 116
Government agencies, abbreviations for, 222
Grammar of sentences, **23-35**; *ex. 36-38*
  basic sentence faults, **38-45**; *ex. 45-47*
  clauses, functions of, 29-31, **48-56**; *ex. 56-58*
  main sentence elements, 23-26
  minor sentence types, 34-35
  modifiers, kinds of, 27-29
  phrases, functions of, 29-31
  secondary sentence elements, 27-29
  sentences classified by clause structure, 31-33
  sentences classified by purpose, 33-34
  subject-verb agreement, **69-76**; *ex. 76-78*
  word order, 26
Grand (heightened) style, 357
-graph, 258
Greek, compounding elements from, 258
Greeting (salutation), 169
  in business letters, 442, 444
  in personal letters, 449-450
Grip, forms of, 201
Group words. *See* Compound adjectives *and* Compound nouns.
Grow,
  as a linking verb, 25, 127
  principal parts of, 113

H

Hackneyed (trite) expressions, 274-275; *ex. 283-284*
Had, tenses formed with, 110 (table)
Handwritten papers, form for, 399-400
Hang, principal parts of, 113
Hardly,
  in double negatives, 133
  position of, as limiting adverb, 132
Have,
  omitted, to avoid wordiness, 292
  tenses formed with, 110 (table)
Have got, have got to, 116
He, him, his, 92, 94, 101, 103
He or *she, his* or *her,* 92, 94
Headings, for letters, 442
Headings for outlines, 367-371
Heightened (grand) style, 357
Hemo-, 258
Her, hers, 101, 103
Himself, herself, 101
Historic, histrionic, 255
Historical dictionaries, 237
Historical present tense, 429
History, reference works in, 464
Homonyms, 192, 255
Honorary titles, form of, 157, 221
Hours,
  figures or words for, 227
  and minutes, colon between, 169
However,
  between main clauses, 33 43, **153, 165-166**
  as an interrupting element, 153
  punctuation with, 33, 43, **153, 156,** 165-166
  at the start of a sentence, 153, 156, 166
Human, humane, 255
Hyperbole, 277
Hyphen, **214-217**; *ex. 220*
  in compound modifiers, 215-216
  in compound nouns, 214-215
  plural of words containing, 80 (table), 82-83
  with prefixes, 216-217
  word division, at end of line, 239, 400

I

I, capitalization of, 210
I, me, after forms of *be,* 98
I, we, appropriate use of, 101-102
Ibid., 143, 187, **493,** 494
-ible, -able, words formed with, 202
-ics, nouns ending in, 79
  as subjects, agreement of verb with, 73-74

Idioms,
choice of genitive form, 85
choice of infinitive or gerund, 62
in comparisons, 136-138
dictionary as guide to, 242
use of *to* with infinitives, 63
verbs and verb phrases (listed), **121-122**
with *do,* 116
with *get,* 116-117
I.e., 187, 224, 494
-ie- or *-ei-,* 200
If, introducing subordinate clause, 31, 40, 43, 50
If . . . than, construction of double comparisons with, 137
Ignoring the question, in argument, 423
Illogical arguments, 421-423
Illusion, allusion, 198, 255
Illustration, as method of development, 329, 382. *See also* Details.
Illustrative words or phrases, set off, 172, 174
Imagery. *See* Figures of speech.
Imperative sentences. *See* Commands.
Impersonal use of *one,* 102-103
Imply, infer, 255
In addition to, agreement with subjects joined by, 71
In this day and age, as deadwood, 293
Incomplete comparisons, 137
Incomplete (fragmentary) sentences, **38-41**; *ex. 45-47*
Indefinite pronouns,
agreement with, 95-97
listed, 93 (table)
possessive form of, 100
Indentions,
outlines, 367-368
paragraphs, 178-179, 325
quotations, long, 179, 399
Independent clauses. *See* Main clauses.
Index, plural forms, 81
Indicative mood, 109 (table)
Indirect discourse,
omission of quotation marks, 179
use of *would* and *should,* 119
Indirect objects, defined, **25.** *See also* Objects.
Indirect questions, punctuation of, 142
Induction, as pattern of paragraph development, 328
Infer, imply, 255
Infinite (non-finite) verb forms, 108, 109 (table)
Infinitives, 59, **60-63**, 109 (table); *ex. 66-67*
as absolute modifiers, 66
comma with, as modifying phrases, 149-150
forms of, **61** (table)
idiomatic use of, 62-63
infinitive phrase, defined, 29, 59, **61** (table)
objective case with, 60
position and reference of, as modifiers, 64-66
sequence of tenses with, 111
split, 63
subjects of, 60
to with, 63
uses of, 24, 25, **61** (table)
Inflammable, flammable, 255
Inflated diction, 269
Inflection. *See* Case, Number, *and* Tense.
Informal English, **8-9** (table), **11-12,** 14; *ex. 18-21*
contractions, 218
subjectless sentences, 34
word choice, 11-12, 271-272
Information papers. *See* Exposition *and* Reference papers.
-ing, spelling changes before, 187, 199-200
Inserts,
caret to indicate, 402
in quoted material, enclosed in brackets, 184
Instance, as deadwood, 294
Institutions, capitalization of, 212
Intensive form of personal pronouns, 93 (table), **101**
Interest,
details used for, 321, 387, 424-425, 430-431
importance of, in selecting a topic, 345-349, 452-454

importance of, in writing, 17
in opening paragraphs, 385-387
Interjections, punctuation of, 144
Internal punctuation. *See* Colons, Commas, Dashes, Parentheses, *and* Semicolons.
Interrogation point. *See* Question mark.
Interrogative pronouns, listed, 93
Interrogative sentences. *See* Questions.
Interruptions,
in dialog, indicated by dash or ellipsis, 173, 185
in thought, set off by punctuation, 152-154, 171-172, 173-174
Intransitive verbs, defined, 109
Introductions. *See* Beginning paragraphs.
Introductory sentence elements, punctuation of, 148-150, 153, 154
Invention. *See* Pre-writing.
Inverted subordination, **55-56**
Inverted word order, 26, 304
agreement of subject and verb in sentences with, 75
Investigative papers. *See* Reference papers.
Invitations, 449
Irony, 175, 160-162, **277**
Irregardless, for *regardless,* 133
Irregular (strong) verbs, 109 (table), 112-119
Irritate, aggravate, 122
-is, changed to *-es* in plurals, 82
Is, isn't, 114-115
Isle, aisle, 198
It, possessive form of, 100
It, vague reference of, 92
It is, there is, 26, 74-75
Italics (underlining),
conventional uses of, **186-188**; *ex. 188-191*
for foreign words or abbreviations, 187, 224, 493
or quotation marks, for titles, 177, **181,** 186, 401
or quotation marks, for words used as words, **181,** 186
Its, it's, **100,** 197-198
Itself, 93, 101

J, K

Jargon, 269-270. *See also* Shoptalk.
Joint possession, use of apostrophe to show, 84
Jones,
genitive of, 84
plural of, 79
Journal articles, citation of,
in bibliography, 471, 496
in footnotes, 491
See also Magazine articles.
Judicial writing, 357
Key sentences. *See* Topic sentences.
Key words,
in essay examination questions, 432
repeated for continuity, 256, 334
repeated for emphasis, 313-314
Kind, agreement of demonstrative adjectives with, 128-129
Know, principal parts of, 113

L

Labor, labour, 203
Laboratory reports, 438
Language,
effective use of, 13-18
elements of, 1-3
prescriptive approach to, 4, 234
varieties of usage, 3-13; *ex. 18-22*
Languages, names of, capitalized, 211
Latin words and phrases,
abbreviations of, 224, 493-494
compounding elements from, 258
italics for, 187, 493
Lay,
distinguished from *lie,* 117
principal parts of, 113
Lead, principal parts of, 113
Lead, led, 198
Leave, for *let,* 122
Lend, principal parts of, 114
Length,
of paragraphs, **325-327**; *ex. 339-340*
of sentences, **286-298**; *ex. 298-301*
-less, negative suffix, 133
Less, least, to form comparisons, 134

Let, misuse of *leave* for, 122
Letters, **441-450**
application letters, 445-448
business letters, 441-445
complimentary close, 444, 450
envelope form,
formal social correspondence, 449-450
greeting (salutation), 442, 449-450
letters of recommendation, 447, 448
personal correspondence, 449-450
Letters (of the alphabet),
omission of, indicated by apostrophe, 218, 219
plural form of, 219
Levels of English usage. *See* Usage, varieties of.
Library card catalogs, **455-457**
Library facilities, 455-470
Library papers. *See* Reference papers.
Lie,
distinguished from *lay,* 117
principal parts of, 114
Lifeless words, **272-276**; *ex. 283-284*
Light, principal parts of, 114
Like or *as,* in comparisons, 138
Limiting adverbs, placement of, 132
Line, as deadwood, 294
Linking verbs, **25** (listed), 109
predicate adjective with, **127-128**
Lists (series),
colon before, 167-168
parallel form for, 308-309
punctuation between items in, 154-155, 166
Literature,
citation of, 483, 492
papers about, 352, **439-441**, 483
sources of reference, 465-466
Litotes, 277
Little, irregular comparison of, 135
Localisms, 8-9 (table), 12
Logic,
errors in, **421-423**
inductive and deductive development of ideas, 323-324
kinds of argument, 418-419
See also Argumentation.
Long form of adverbs, 129-130
Look, as linking verb, 25, 127
Loose, loosely, 129
Loose, lose, 198
Loose modifiers. *See* Nonrestrictive modifiers.
Loose sentences, 304-305
Lose, loose, 198
Lose, principal parts of, 114
Loud, loudly, 129
Lower case. *See* Capitals.
-ly, as adverb ending, **129-130**
final *-e* retained before, 199-200
no hyphen after, 216

M

Magazine articles,
bibliography form for, 471, 473, 495-496
footnote form for, 491
indexes to, 458-460
quotation marks with titles of, 181, 491
Main (independent) clauses,
connectives to join, **32-33**, 43-44, 165-166
defined, **30**
inverted subordination, 55-56
joined incorrectly, **41-44**
modified by adverb clauses, 49
modifiers of, 66
punctuation between, 146-148, 159, 164-166, 168
sentences classified by their use of, 31-33
stringy sentences, 290
See also Subordinate clauses.
Main sentence elements,
defined, **23-26**
misuse of comma between, 158-159
modifiers of, 27-29
See also Sentence elements.
Manner, adverb clauses of, 49, 53
Manner, as deadwood, 294
Manuscript form, **398-403**; *ex. 410-412*
bibliography, 169, 470-473, **495-496**; *ex. 513*
corrections in the final copy, 402

division of words, 239, 400
endorsing the manuscript, 401, 497
footnotes, **479-495**; *ex. 511-513*
handwritten papers, 399-400
margins and spacing, 400
numbering of pages, 401
outlines, final, **367-371**, 497
proofreading, 402
reference papers, 479-497
sample papers, 404-407, 498-507
title, 400-401
typed papers, 399-401
Many, irregular comparison of, 135
Margins,
on letters, 442, 444
on manuscripts, 440
Masculine pronouns, referring to mixed groups, 92-94
Mass nouns, 80 (table)
Maximum, plural forms, 82
May, can, 115
May be, maybe, 198-199
Me, after forms of *be,* 98
Meaning,
abstract words, 250, **258-261**
antonyms, 244, 257
concrete words, 250, **258-261**
connectives, choice of, 50, 53-54
connotation, 243, **250,** 255-256
context, importance of, **249-250,** 258
denotation, 243, **250,** 255-256
dictionary as guide to, **242-243**
modifiers, accurate use of, 27-29, 64-65, 126-132
punctuation to emphasize and clarify, 144-145, **155-156,** 171-173, 186-188
repetition of, careless, 296-297
sentences as units of, 23, **288-291**
subordination to clarify, **52-54, 306-308**
synonyms, 244, 255-256
See also Emphasis.
Measurement, units of,
abbreviations for, 223-224
agreement of verbs with, 72
noun forms designating, 86
Mechanics. *See* Conventions of writing.
Medium, plural forms, 82
Merely, as limiting adverb, 132
Metaphor, 277, 279
Metonymy, 277
Micro-, 258
Middle (mixed) style, 357-358
Minor sentence types, 34-35
Misrelated modifiers,
adverbs, **131-132;** *ex. 140-141*
verbal phrases, **64-65;** *ex. 66-68*
Miss, Mrs., with signatures, 444
Misspelling, causes of, **195-199;** *ex. 204-206. See also* Spelling.
Mixed construction, **44-45**
Mixed (inconsistent) figures, 280
Mixed (middle) style, 357-358
Mode. *See* Mood.
Modifiers, **27-29,** 126
absolute, 66
adjectives and adverbs, 27-29, **126-138**
appositives, 29, 152
comma misused after, 150
compound, hyphening of, 215-216
dangling, 65
kinds of, 27, **28** (table), 29
misrelated, **64-65,** 131-132
of modifiers, 29
nouns used as, 27, 79, 80 (table), **86**
position of, 27, 64-66, 126-127, 130-132
predicate adjectives, 24, **127-128**
prepositional phrases, 27, 28 (table), 30
restrictive and nonrestrictive, **150-152,** 159-160
squinting, 65, 132
subordinate clauses, 28 (table), 29, 31, **48-50**
verbal phrases, 27, 28 (table), 30, **59-66**
Money, form for writing sums of, 143, 227
Mono-, 258
Months, form for names of, 213, 222
Mood, of verbs,
defined, 109 (table)
imperative, in commands, 34, 306
subjunctive, uses of, 120-121

More, most,
agreement of verbs with, 96
to form comparisons, 126, **134**
Moreover, punctuation with, 153, 166
Most,
agreement of verbs with, 96
as intensive, 136
misused for *almost,* 130
possessive form of, 100
to form comparisons, 126, **134**
Movement, narrative, 337, **430-431**
Mrs., Miss, with signatures, 444
MS., MSS., 494
Much, irregular comparison of, 135
Music, reference works in, 466
My, mine, 99-100
Myself, correct use of, 101

N

Names, proper,
abbreviations for, 221-222
capitalization of, 210-211
Narrative writing, **337-338, 426-431**
detail in, 430-431
dialog, form for, 178-179
movement of action, 429-431
paragraph continuity, 337-338
point of view, 427-428
sentence length, 286-288
tenses, use of, 338, 428-429
Nature, as deadwood, 294
Negative, double, 133
Neither . . . nor, 32
agreement with elements joined by, 70
parallel constructions with, 309-310
Nevertheless, punctuation with, 33, 153, 165
New York Times Index, 461
Newspaper articles, form for citing,
in bibliography, 473
in footnotes, 492
Nicknames, capitalization of, 210-211
No one, agreement with, 96
Nobody, agreement with, 96
Nominative absolute, 66
Nominative case. *See entries beginning with* Subject.
Non sequiturs, 422
None,
agreement with, 95-96
possessive of, 100
Non-finite (infinite) verbs, defined, 109
Nonrestrictive (loose) modifiers,
comma with, **150-152;** *ex. 162*
introduced by *which* or *who,* 92
Nonstandard English, **9, 12-13**
Nor, 32
agreement with elements joined by, 70, 95
comma with, 146-148, 154-155
in *neither . . . nor* constructions, 70, 309-310
Not, in double negatives, 133
Not only . . . but also, 32, 309-310
Notes for reference papers, **473-474,** 478
Noun clauses, 31, 48, **50-52;** *ex. 56*
Noun equivalents. *See* Appositives, Gerunds, Infinitives, Noun clauses, *and* Pronouns.
Noun modifiers, 79, 80, **86**
Nouns, **79-86;** *ex. 86-88*
a or *an* with, 85
classes of, 80 (table)
collective, agreement with, **71-74**
compound, hyphening of, **214-215**
defined, 79
forms and functions of, 80 (table)
gender of, 80 (table)
genitive (possessive) form of, 80 (table), **83-85**
modifying other nouns, 79, 80 (table), **86**
plural forms of, **79-83**
predicate nouns, 25, 80 (table)
proper, capitalization of, 210-214
reference of pronouns to, 89-91
Number,
of collective nouns, 71-74
of compound subjects, 69-71
of indefinite pronouns, 95-97
of personal pronouns, 94-95
shifts in, 103
See also Agreement.
Number, as subject, agreement of verb with, 72-73

Numbering,
of footnotes, 488
of letter pages, 442
of manuscript pages, 401, 497
of outline headings, 367-368
Numbers, **225-228**; *ex. 229*
abbreviations used with, 223
agreement of verbs with, 72
Arabic and Roman, 228
beginning a sentence, 228
cardinal, 228
commas used in, 157
compound, hyphening of, 215
figures or words for, 225-226
ordinal, 228
parentheses around, 175
plurals of, 218-219
Numeral pronouns, 93 (table)

O

-o, plurals of nouns ending in, 79-81
O, oh, 210
Object clauses, 25, 50
Objective case,
with infinitives, 60
of pronouns, 62, 93 (table), 97-99
who, whom, 99-101
Objective genitive, 83, 85
Objects, **24-26**
direct, defined, 24
gerunds used as, 61 (table)
indirect, defined, 25
infinitives used as, 25, 61 (table)
modifiers of, 28 (table)
noun clauses as, 25, 50
position of, 24-25, 26
of prepositions, 97-99
pronouns used as, case of, 93 (table), 97-99
of verbals, 59, 63
Obsolete words, 243, 273-274
Occur, forms of, 201
O'clock, hours spelled out before, 227
Of course, punctuation with, 153
Of phrases,
misused with gerunds, 62-63
to show genitive, 83, **85,** 100
Of which, whose 100-101
Oh, 154, 210
Old-fashioned words, **273-274**
Omissions,
of letters and sounds, apostrophe for, 218, 219
of words, ellipses to indicate, 185, 474
On the other hand, punctuation with, 153
One, impersonal use of, **102-103**
One of those who (or *that*), 74, 95
Only, as limiting adverb, 132
Onomatopoeia, 278
Open punctuation, 5
Opening paragraphs, 377, 378, **385-388**; *ex. 394-395*
Opinion, expressions of. *See* Argumentation, Fair use of words, *and* Slanting.
Or, 32
agreement with elements joined by 70, 95
comma with, 146-148, 154-155
in *either . . . or* constructions, 70, 309-310
Order of words. *See* Word order.
Ordinal numbers, 228
Organization, of a paper, **360-372,** 377-392, 477-478. *See also* Development of ideas *and* Outlining.
Organizations, names of, 222
Other, in comparisons, 138
Our, ours, 99-100
Outlining, **360-372,** 478, 481, 497, 498-499 (sample); *ex. 374-376*
division of materials, 369-370, 481
form, standard, **367-371**
parallel headings, 371
revision of outline, **365-366,** 371-372, 481, 497
scratch outlines, 360-361
sentence outlines, 360, 366-367
thesis-sentence outlines, 360-362
topic outlines, 360, 363-366
working from an outline, 360-362, 364, 371-372, **380-382,** 478
Overpunctuation, 158-160
Oxford English Dictionary, 237
Oxymoron, 278

P

Page numbers,
 Arabic vs. Roman numerals for, 228
 in bibliography, 495
 in footnotes, 489, 491
 of manuscript, 201, 497
Pamphlet index, 461
Pamphlets, cited in footnotes, 492
Papers. *See* Composition *and* Reference papers.
Paragraphs, **319-338, 382-391**; *ex. 338-343, 394-395*
 argumentative, 323-324
 beginning and ending a paper, 385-391; *ex. 394-395*
 continuity between, 383-385
 continuity within, 333-338; *ex. 341-343*
 deductive, 328-329
 descriptive, 336-337
 details in, 321-324
 development, adequacy of, 319-327; *ex. 338-340*
 development, patterns of, 327-332, 381-382; *ex. 340-341*
 dialog, 178
 direction of paper controlled by, 381-382; *ex. 393-394*
 division of, 178, 319, 325-327; *ex. 339-340*
 expository, 322-323
 general statements in, 321-324
 indention of, 325, 402, 442
 inductive, 328
 length, 319-327; *ex. 339-340*
 links between, 383-385
 narrative, 337-338
 opening and closing, 385-391; *ex. 394-395*
 outline in relation to, 371, 380-382
 sequence of, 382-385; *ex. 394*
 topic sentences in, 324-325, 329
 transition between, 383-385
 transitional, 327, 385
Parallelism,
 for expressing coordinate ideas, 308-310
 in outlines, 371
Paraphrase,
 compared with plagiarism, **485-488**; *ex. 513-514*
 effective use of, 484, 507
 in taking notes, 474, 475
Parentheses, **173-175**; 489-491; *ex. 176*
 brackets distinguished from, 184-185
 capitals within, 209
 dashes distinguished from, 173
 punctuation with, 175
Parenthetical expressions,
 initial capital in, 209
 set off by brackets, 185
 set off by commas, 152-154
 set off by dashes, 171-172
 set off by parentheses, 173-175
Part, agreement with, 76
Participles and participle phrases, 30, **59, 61** (table)
 as absolute modifiers, 66
 forms and typical uses, **61** (table), 108, 109 (table)
 gerunds distinguished from, 59
 as infinite (non-finite) verb forms, 109 (table)
 misused as sentences, 39-41
 position and reference of, as modifiers, **64-66**; *ex. 67-68*
 weak, at end of sentence, 56
 See also Past participle.
Parts of speech. *See* Adjectives, Adverbs, Conjunctions, Interjections, Nouns, Prepositions, Pronouns, *and* Verbs.
Passed, past, 198
Passive voice, **119-120**
 formation of, 109 (table), 119
 ineffective use of, 120
 of verbals, 61 (table)
 word order with, 26
Past participle,
 defined, 108, **109** (table)
 of irregular verbs (listed), 112-114
 spelling errors with, 197
 tenses formed with, 110 (table). *See also* Participles.
Past perfect tense, 110 (table), 111
Past progressive tense, 110 (table), 111

Past tense,
of irregular verbs (listed), 112-114
in narrative, 429
of regular verbs, 108, 109 (table), 110 (table), 111
spelling errors with, 197
of verbals, 61 (table)
Pay, principal parts of, 114
Peace, piece, 192, 198
Perfect, comparison of, 136
Perfect tenses, 110 (table), 111
Perhaps, punctuation with, 153
Periodic sentences, **305,** 312, 358
Periodicals,
citation of, in bibliography, 471-473, 495
citation of, in footnotes, 491
indexes to, 458-460
Periods,
conventional uses of, **142-143,** 225
ellipses shown by, 185
with parentheses, 175
with quotation marks, 183
Periphrasis, 278
Persecute, prosecute, 255
Person, of pronouns. *See* Personal pronouns.
Personal, personnel, 198, 255
Personal correspondence, 449-450
Personal experience, papers based on,
discovering a subject, 344-349
resources, 350-352, 353-354, 416
See also Description, Exposition, *and* Narration.
Personal pronouns, 92, 93 (table), 94-95, 97-103; *ex. 103-107*
agreement of, with antecedent, **94-95**
apostrophe misused with, **99-100,** 219
avoiding shifts in person of, 103
changes in form for, **93** (table), 97-100
choice of first, second, or third person, **100-103**
he or *she,* in referring to groups, 92-94
intensive form, use of, 101
listed, 93 (table)
possessive form, 60, 62, **99-100,** 219
reflexive form, use of, 101
subject or object form, 60, **97-98**
with gerunds, 60, 62
with infinitives, 60
Personification, 278
Persuasion. *See* Argumentation.
Philosophy, reference works in, 467
Phrases,
absolute, 66
clauses reduced to, for economy, 291-292
of comparison, introduced by *like,* 138
dangling or misplaced, **64-65**
deadwood, 293-294
defined, **29-30**
deliberately used as sentences, 34-35
function of, as modifiers, **27, 28** (table), 30
introductory, punctuation of, 148-150
misused as sentences, **39-41**
parallel form for, in series, 308-309
parenthetical, punctuation of, 152-154, 171-172, 173-175
prepositional, 25, 27, 30
restrictive and nonrestrictive, **150-152**
verb tenses formed with, 110 (table), 111
verbal, 29, 30, **59-66**
Piece, peace, 192, 198
Pin, forms of, 201
Place, adverb clauses to show, 49
Place names,
abbreviations for, 222
capitalization of, 212
Place of publication, citation of,
in bibliography, 471, 496
in footnotes, 489
Plain style, 357, 359
Plagiarism, 482, **485-488;** *ex. 513-514*
Planes, names of, 213
Planning papers. *See* Pre-writing *and* Reference papers.
Plays, citation of, 483
Plurals of letters and figures, 228
Plurals of nouns, **79-83;** *ex. 87-88*
collective nouns, 71-73
compound nouns and group words, 82-83
foreign plurals, 81-82
genitive of plurals, 83-84
irregular plurals, 79

Plurals of nouns (continued)
  nouns ending in *-ics,* 73
  nouns ending in *-y, -o,* or *-f,* 79-81, 201
P.M., A.M., 224, 227
Poetry,
  citation of, 483
  style for quoting, 180-181
Point of view,
  in narrative writing, 427-428
  shift in, 103
Polite requests,
  punctuation of, 143
  would and *should* in, 119
Political groups, names of, 211
Political science, reference works in, 467
Polysyndeton, 358
Poole's Index to Periodical Literature, 460
Portion, agreement with, 76
Position of modifiers,
  adjectives, 27, 126-127
  adverbs, 27, 130-132
  verbal phrases, 64-66
Positive degree, of adjectives and adverbs, 134-135
Possessive forms. *See* Genitive case.
Possessive pronouns, 93 (table), **99-100,** 219
Post hoc, ergo propter hoc, 422
Precede, proceed, 194, 255
Predicate, defined, 34. *See also* Complement, Objects, *and* Verbs.
Predicate adjectives, 25, **127-128;** *ex. 139*
Predicate nouns, 25, 80 (table)
Predication, excessive, 291-292
Predominate, predominant, 122
Prefer, forms of, 201
Prefixes, hyphen after, 216-217
Prepositional phrase, 25, **27,** 28 (table), **30,** 138. *See also* Phrases.
Prepositions,
  case of pronouns after, 97-98
  linking gerund phrases, 62-63
  repetition of, to clarify parallelism, 295
Present infinitive, 61 (table)
  with past verb, 111
Present participle. *See* Participles and participle phrases.
Present progressive tense, 110
Present tense, 110
  historical present, 429
  See also Tense.
Pre-writing, **344-360;** *ex. 372-375*
  discovering a subject, 344-349, 439
  locating a thesis or proposition, 345, 348-349, 417
  narrowing the topic, 347-348, 453-454
  personal experience as resource, 346-347, 350-352
  potential of the topic, 344-345, 354-357
  purpose in writing, 344-345, 354-357
  resources, related to thesis, 350, 353-354
  style, related to subject and purpose, 354, 356-360
  thesis statement, 348-349, 361-362
  writer's stance, 354-355
  See also Development of ideas *and* Organization.
Principal, principle, 198, 255
Principal clauses. *See* Main clauses.
Principal parts of verbs, 109 (table)
  of irregular verbs (list), 112-114
Procede, precede, 194, 255
Process, verbs indicating, 108
Prof., Professor, 221-222, 448
Progressive forms of verbs, 110 (table)
Prolepsis, 305
Pronouns, **89-103;** *ex. 103-107*
  agreement of, 94-97
  case forms, 93 (table), **97-101**
  choice of personal pronoun, 100-103
  defined and classified, 89, **93** (table)
  demonstrative, 92, 93 (table)
  indefinite, 93 (table), 95-97, 100
  intensive, 101
  interrogative, 93 (table)
  number of, **94-97**
  paragraph continuity through use of, 334
  personal, 92, 93 (table), **94-95, 97-103**
  possessive, 93 (table), 99-101, 219

reference of, **89-94**
reflexive, 101
relative, 30-31, 92, 93 (table), 99, 100-101
repetition of, for continuity, 334
shift in person or number of, 103
subject or object form, 60, 97-98
Pronunciation,
dictionary as a guide to, 239, 242; *ex. 246*
divided usage in, 239
of homonyms, 192, 197-198, 255
spelling in relation to, 192, 196-197
Proofreading, 193, 208, 402
Proper adjectives, 210-214
Proper nouns, 80 (table)
abbreviations for, 221-222
capitalization of, 210-214
prefixes with, 216
as subjects of gerund phrases, 60
Prosecute, persecute, 255
Prove,
as linking verb, 127
principal parts of, 114
Provided that, introducing adverb clauses, 50
Psychology, reference works in, 467
Public, agreement with, 72-73
Public Affairs Information Service, 460
Publication, form of manuscripts for, 403
Publisher, citation of,
in bibliography, 496, 509
in footnotes, 489
Punctuation, **142-191**; *ex. 230-233*
abbreviations, 143, 225, 493-494
addresses and letter headings, 157-158, 442-444
ambiguity corrected by, 155-156
bibliographies, 471-473, 495-496
close or open, 5, 7
comma faults and fragmentary sentences corrected by, 38, 41-44;- *ex. 45-47*
emphasis shown by, 151-152, 171-173, 186-188, 312-313
footnotes, 489-492
See also individual marks listed under Conventions of writing.
Purpose, adverb clauses of, 54
Purpose in writing, 344-345, 354-357. *See also* Pre-writing *and* Thesis statement.

Q

Quale sit, 349
Qualifiers. *See* Modifiers.
Qualifying statement, as an ending to avoid, 312, 391
Quantity, agreement of verb with expressions of, 72
Quarrel, forms of, 201
Question marks, **143-144**
position of, with quotes, 183
Questions, 33,
agreement of verb with compound subjects in, 70
courteous, punctuation of, 143
direct vs. indirect, 142-143
interrogative pronouns, 93 (table)
inverted word order of, 26
punctuation of, 143-144
for sentence variety, 306
shall and *will* in, 118
Quick, quickly, 129
Quid sit, 349
Quiet, quite, 198
Quotation marks, **177-184**; *ex. 188-191*
apologetic, 182, 272
double or single, **177-178**, 179-180
for emphasis, 314
or italics, for titles, 177, **181**, **186**, 401
or italics, for words used as words, **181**, 186
other punctuation marks with, 178, 182-184
Quotations,
acknowledgment of, 494
capitalization of, 209
comma or colon before, 158, 168-169
dialog, form and punctuation of, 178-179
direct and indirect, 178-179, 482-484
ellipses for omissions in, 185, 474
errors in, marked by *sic,* 184, 494
form for setting off, 179-181

Quotations (continued)
inserts within, enclosed in brackets, 184
long, form for, 179
poetic, form for, 180-181, 483
punctuation of, 158, 168-169, **177-184,** 474; *ex. 188-191*
short, form for, 179
sources of, 467
trite, 275
when to use, 482-484
within quotations, 179-180
See also Footnotes *and* Paraphrase.

R

Radius, plural forms, 82
Readers' Guide to Periodical Literature, 458-459
Real, really, 130
Reason, clause of, 54
Reason is because, reason is that, 52
Reciprocal pronouns, 93
Recommendation, letters requesting, 447-448
Redundancy. *See* Repetition *and* Wordiness.
Reference, of modifiers. *See* Position of modifiers.
Reference, of pronouns, **89-94;** *ex. 105*
Reference books and aids, 235-237, **455-470** (listed)
dictionaries, 235-237
encyclopedias, general, 461
encyclopedias, specialized, 461-469
guides to reference materials, 470
library card catalog, 455-457
newspaper index, 461
pamphlet index, 461
periodical indexes, 458-460
specialized reference works, 461-469
trade bibliographies, 457-458
yearbooks and annuals, 469-470
Reference papers, **451-497,** 498-508 (sample); *ex. 510-515*
bibliography, 470-473, 495-497
evaluating the material, 476-477
final form, 495-497, 498-507 (sample)
first draft, 479-480
footnotes, 479-495
notes, 473-475, 478
outlines, **360-372,** 478-479, 481, 497, 498-499 (sample)
planning, 477-478
primary and secondary sources, 477
revision of first draft, 480-481
sources of reference, 455-470
style and level of usage, 479-480
topic, choice of a, 452-454
See also Development of ideas, Exposition, *and* Pre-writing.
Referents, of words, 242, 250, 258
Reflexive pronouns, 93 (table), **101**
Regardless, irregardless, 133
Regular (weak) verbs, 108, 109 (table). *See also* Verbs.
Relative adverbs, introducing adjective clauses, 49
Relative pronouns,
agreement with, 95
and or *but* misused before, 49
introducing subordinate clauses, 30-31, 40, **48**
listed, 93 (table)
optional, with some adjective clauses, 49
possessive form of, 99, **100-101**
sentence faults corrected by adding, 40
who or *whom,* 99
who, which, or *that,* 92, 101
Relative words, defined, 250
Relatives, names of, 211
Religion, reference works in, 460, 467-468
Repetition,
careless, of words, meaning, and sounds, **294-298;** *ex. 300-301*
for emphasis or effect, 295, 313-314, 358, 390
for paragraph continuity, 334
Replies, omission of verb in, 35
Replies to invitations, 449-450
Reports, **437-438**

Requests,
omission of subject in, 34
use of *should* and *would* in, 119
Research papers. *See* Reference papers.
Respectful, respective, 255
Responsible use of words, 251-254, 421-423
Restrictive (close) modifiers,
comma omitted with, 150-152, **159-160**
defined, 151, 159
introduced by *that,* 92
Result, clause of, 54
Reverend, The Reverend, Rev., 221
Revision, **396-410**; *ex. 410-412*
of corrected papers, **403-410**
corrections, method of indicating, 402
of first drafts, **396-398**, 480-481
manuscript form, **398-403**
of outlines, **365-366**, 371-372, 481, 497
of paragraphs, 319-328, 333-338
of reference papers, 480-481
of sentences, 38-45, 288-297, 302-314
Rhetoric, 349. *See also* Composition, Paragraphs, Sentences, *and* Style.
Ride, principal parts of, 114
Right, rite, write, 192
Ring, principal parts of, 114
Rise, principal parts of, 114
Roman numerals, **228**
for main heads of outlines, 367
for volume number, in footnotes, 489-491
Rough, roughly, 129
Rough draft. *See* First draft.
Run, principal parts of, 114
Run-on sentences. *See* Comma faults.

S

-'s to form genitive case, **83-85**, 100
-s, -es ending for plural nouns, **79-83**
exception to, 79
genitive of nouns ending in, 84
Saint, abbreviation of, 222
Salutation,
for business letters, 442, 444
for personal letters, 449-450
Sanatorium, plural forms, 82
Sacred names, capitalization of, 213
Say, punctuation with, 154
Scarcely, in double negatives, 133
Science, reference works in, 462, 468-469
Scientific words, 270
abbreviation of, 223
italics for, 187
suffixes and roots forming, 258
Scratch outlines, **360-362**; 433; *ex. 375*
Seasons, names of, 213
Second, secondly, 123
Second person pronouns, 93 (table), 102, 103
Secondary sentence elements, **27-29**; *ex. 36-37*
misused as sentences, **39-40**; *ex. 45-47*
See also Modifiers, Phrases, *and* Subordinate clauses.
See, principal parts of, 114
Seem,
as deadwood, 294
as linking verb, 25, 127
Self-, hyphening of compounds beginning with, 215
Semicolon, **164-166**; *ex. 169-170*
between coordinate clauses, 32-33, **42-43**, 153, **164-166**
distinguished from colon, 167
position of, with quotation marks, 183
to separate elements containing commas, 166
to separate statements, for emphasis, 312-313
Sentence,
defined, 23
grammar of, **23-25**; *ex. 36-37*
See also Sentence elements *and* Sentences.
Sentence adverbs, 131
Sentence economy. *See* Economy of expression.

Sentence elements, **23-45**; *ex. 36-37*
appositives, 29, 152
clauses, 29-31, 48-52
complements, 25, 127-128
main, comma misused between, 158-159
main, defined, 23-27
modifiers, defined, 27-29
objects, defined, 24-25
order of, 26, 304
phrases, 29-30, 59-62
predicate, defined, 24
secondary, defined, 27-29
secondary, misused as sentences, 39-40; *ex. 45-47*
subjects, defined, 23-24
verbs, 24, 108-121
See also Sentences.
Sentence emphasis. *See* Emphasis.
Sentence faults, **38-45**; *ex. 45-47*
Sentence length, **286-298**; *ex. 298-301*
choppy sentences, 288-289
economy of expression, 291-297
stringy sentences, 289-290
style, 286-288
Sentence outlines, 360, **366-367**, 498-499 (sample)
Sentences, **23-35**, 38-48, 286-298, 302-314, 380-381; *ex. 36-37, 45-47, 298-301, 314-318*
antithetical, 310
appositional, 35
balanced, 310
choppy, 288-289
classified by purpose, 33-34
classified by clause structure, 31-33; *ex. 36-37*
climax, 312
coherence in, 52-56, **288-291**, 306-308
comma faults, 38, **41-44**; *ex. 45-47*
commands, 34
complex, 33
compound, 32-33
compound-complex, 33
declarative (statements), 33, 304
defined, 23
direction of writing controlled by, 380-381
economy in, 291-297; *ex. 298-301*
elliptical, 34-35
emphasis in, 311-314; *ex. 317*
end punctuation of, 142-145
exclamatory, 34-35, 144-145
fragmentary (incomplete), 38-41; *ex. 45-47*
fused, 44
grammar of, **23-35**; *ex. 36-37*
imperative (directive), 34
incomplete (fragmentary), 38-41; *ex. 45-47*
interrogative, 33, 143-144, 306
inverted, 26, 75, 304
length of, **286-298**; *ex. 298-301*
loose, 304-305
meaning, as units of, 23, 288-291
minor types of, 34-35
patterns, 33-34, 302-306; *ex. 314-315*
periodic, **305**, 312, 358
run-on, 41-44; *ex. 45-47*
simple, 31-32
stringy, 289-290
subjectless, 34
subordination to clarify meaning of, 52-56, 306-308; *ex. 56-58*
thesis sentences, 348-349
topic sentences, 324-325
types of, 31-35
variety in, 302-306; *ex. 314-315*
verbless, 35
wordiness in, 291-297; *ex. 298-301*
word order of, 25-26, 304
See also Sentence elements.
Sequence, paragraphs in, **382-385**; *ex. 394*
Sequence of tenses, 111-112
Series (lists),
colon before, 167-168
genitive form of nouns in, 84
parallel form for, 308-309
punctuation between items in, 154-155, 160, 166
Series, agreement with, 76
Seriously, serious (as adverb), 130
Set,
distinguished from *sit,* 117
principal parts of, 114
Shake, principal parts of, 114

Shall, will, 118-119
Shape, shapeless, shaping, 200
Sharp, sharply, 129
She or *he,* 94, 101, 103
Shifts (inconsistencies),
in figures of speech, 280; *ex. 284-285*
in parallel constructions, 310
in person and number of pronouns, 103; *ex. 105-106*
in point of view, 103
in tense, **111-112,** 338, 429; *ex. 125*
in thought, 335-336, 382-385, 480
in tone and level of usage, 272
Shine, principal parts of, 114
Ships, names of, 213
Shoptalk, 8-9 (table), 11-12. *See also* Jargon.
Short form of adverbs, 129-130
Short form of footnotes, 490-491, 493
Short quotations, manuscript form for, 179
Shortened spelling forms, 202-203, 238
Should, would, 118-119
Show, principal parts of, 114
Shrink, principal parts of, 114
Sic, 184, 494
Sight, site, cite, 192
Signature, for business letters, 444
Silent letters, 192
Similes, 278, 279
Simple sentence, 31-32
Simple subject, 23-24
Simplified spellings, 202-203
Since,
introducing subordinate clauses, 31, 43, 50, **53-54**
misuse of *as* and *so* for, 54
misuse of *being that* for, 122
misuse of *due to the fact that* for, 293
Sing, principal parts of, 114
Single quotation marks, **177,** 179-180
Single-sentence paragraphs, 327
Single-word modifiers, **27, 28** (table)-
adjective and adverb forms, **126-138**
position of, 126-127, 130-131
Single-word sentences, 34-35
Singular nouns, 80 (table)
genitive form of, 83
noun modifiers, 86
of same form as the plural, 86
See also Plurals of nouns.
Singular verbs, agreement, 69-76
Sink, principal parts of, 114
Sit,
distinguished from *set,* 117
principal parts of, 114
Site, cite, 198, 255
Size, abbreviations for words of, 223
Slang,
apologetic quotes for, 182
appropriateness of, 8-9 (table), 11, 271-272; *ex. 248*
Slanted words, **252-254;** *ex. 263-264.* *See also* Connotation.
Slide, principal parts of, 114
Slow, slowly, 129
Smell, as linking verb, 25, 127
Smooth, smoothly, 129
So,
inexactness of, 53-54
introducing adverb clauses, 50
punctuation with, 153
sentences strung together with, 289
So that, introducing clauses of purpose, 50, 54
Social correspondence, 449-450
Social sciences, reference works in, 460, 469
Some,
agreement of verb with, 95-96
irregular comparison of, 135
possessive of, 100
Somebody, someone, somebody else,
agreement of verb with, 96
possessive of, 100
reference to, by masculine pronoun, 94
Sort, agreement of demonstrative adjective with, 128-129
Sound,
careless repetition of, 297-298
consonant and vowel, 1
omitted, apostrophe to show, 219
words similar in, 192, 197-198, 255
Sound, as linking verb, 25, 127
Sources for reference papers. *See* Reference books and aids *and* Reference papers.

Spatial order of development, 330, 379, 426
Speak, principal parts of, 114
Speech, reference works in, 237, 469
Specific words, 250, **258-261**; *ex. 266*
Spelling, **192-203**; *ex. 203-207*
  -able, -ible, -ance, -ence, 202
  British, 202-203, 239
  -cede, -ceed, -sede, 202
  combined forms, 198-199
  common errors, 195-197
  compound words, hyphening of, **214-216**
  confusion of similar and opposite words, 197, 254-257
  dictionary as guide to, 193, 238-239
  doubling the final consonant, 201
  -ei- or *-ie-,* 200
  final *-e,* dropped or retained, 199
  final *-y,* changed to *-i-,* 79, 81, 201
  genitive forms, 83-85, 99-101
  methods for improving, 192-197
  plural forms of nouns, **79-83**; *ex. 87-88*
  prefixes, hyphen after, 216-217
  principles of, 79, 81, 199-202
  suffixes, rules for adding, 79-83, 199-202
  variant forms, 202-203, 238-239
Splice, comma. *See* Comma faults.
Split footnote, 489
Split infinitives, 63
Spot, forms of, 201
Spring, principal parts of, 114
Squinting modifiers, 65, 132
Stand, principal parts of, 114
Standard English, **3, 8-9** (table), 14, 16-17. *See also* Formal English, General English, *and* Informal English.
States, abbreviations for, 222, 445
Stationary, stationery, 198, 255
Statistics, figures for, 227
Steal, principal parts of, 114
Stilted language, 9, 218, **268-270**
Straight, straightly, 129
Stratum, plural forms, 82
Street addresses, form for, 157, 227, 442, 444-445
Stress, shown in dictionaries, 239
Stressed prefixes, hyphen after, 217
Stringy sentences, **289-290**; *ex. 298-299*
Strong verbs. *See* Irregular verbs.
Style, **356-360**
  classifications of, 357-358
  figurative language, 276-280; *ex. 284-285*
  paragraph development, 328-332; *ex. 340-341*
  related to purpose, 356-357
  sentence length, 286-288
  sentence variety and emphasis, 302-314; *ex. 314-318*
  word choice, 267-280; *ex. 280-285*
  See also Formal English, General English, *and* Informal English.
Subject of a gerund, 60-62, 83; *ex. 67*
Subject of an infinitive, 60
Subject of a participle phrase (nominative absolute), 66
Subject of a sentence, **23-24**
  agreement with verb, 23, **69-76**; *ex. 76-78*
  anticipated by *there is, it is,* 26, 74-75
  complement linked to, 25, 127-128
  compound, 31, 69-71, 75
  defined, 23-24
  omitted, 34
Subject clauses, 24, 51
Subject pronouns, 93 (table), 97-99
Subjective genitive, 83
Subjectless sentences, 34
Subjects for papers, **344-349**, 452-454; *ex. 372-374, 509-510*
  discovering a subject, 344-349, 417
  limiting the subject, 347-348, 453-454
  locating a thesis, 345, 348-349, 417
  subjects for literary papers, 439-441
  subjects for reference papers, 452-454
  thesis statement, 348-349, 361-362
  See also Pre-writing.
Subjunctive mood, 109 (table), **120-121**
Subordinate (dependent) clauses, 29-31, **48-56**, 306-308; *ex. 56-58*
  adjective clauses, 31, **48-49**, 150-152
  adverb clauses, 31, **49-50**, 56, 149

and or *but* misused before, 49
in comparisons, introduced by *as,* 138
misused as sentences, 39-40; *ex. 45-47*
noun clauses, 31, **50-52**
restrictive and nonrestrictive, **150-152,** 159-160
See also Subordination.
Subordinating conjunctions, 33, 43, **50,** 53
Subordination, 23, 29-31, **48-56, 306-308;** *ex. 56-58*
faulty, 54-56
inverted, 55-56
meaning clarified by, 52-54, 306-308
sentence faults corrected by, 38-45; *ex. 45-47*
stringy sentences corrected by, 54, 289-290
tandem, 55
thwarted by *and* or *but,* 49
See also Subordinate clauses.
Substantives. *See* Noun equivalents.
Subtitle, preceded by a colon, 169
Such as, introducing phrases, 40, 138
Suffixes, 2, **199-202,** 258; *ex. 205-206*
Summarizing expression, set off by dashes, 172-173
Summary statement, in concluding paragraph, 389-390
Superlative degree, of adjectives and adverbs,
forms of, 134-135
uses of, 138
Superlatives, careful use of, 253
Support, as a method of development, 328-329, 379
Support of generalizations. *See* Generalizations.
Sure, surely, 130
Suspect, suspicion, 122
Suspension hyphen, 217
Swim, principal parts of, 114
Syllables,
accented, 239
as aid in spelling, 194
as a guide to word division, 239, 400
number of, determining form of comparison, 134
Syllabus, plural forms, 82
Synecdoche, 278
Synonyms, 255-256
in dictionaries, 244; *ex. 248*
for paragraph continuity, 334
Syntax, 2. *See also* Sentence elements.

T

-t, -ed, or *-d,* endings for regular verb forms, 108, 109 (table)
Tables and charts, position of, in a paper, 401
Take, principal parts of, 114
Tandem subordination, 55
Taste, as linking verb, 25, 127
Tautology, 296-297
Tear, principal parts of, 114
Technical English,
abbreviations, 223-224
appropriate word usage, 7, 8 (table), 11, **270-271**
numbers written in figures, 227
simplified spellings, 202-203
Tele-, 258
Tendency, as deadwood, 294
Tense, **108-112;** *ex. 124, 125*
consistent use of, 108, **111-112,** 338
forms, regular, **110** (table)
of infinitives, participles, and gerunds, 61 (table)
of irregular verbs and auxiliaries, **112-119**
in narrative writing, 337-338, 428-429
sequence of, 111
Term papers. *See* Reference papers.
Terminal punctuation, **142-145**
Tests. *See* Essay examination answers.
Textual analysis, 439
Than, case of pronouns with, 98
Than, then, 198
That, as demonstrative adjective, with *kind* or *sort,* 128-129
That, as demonstrative pronoun, reference of, 92
That, as relative pronoun, 30
introducing adjective clauses, 48
introducing noun clauses, 50-52

That (continued)
introducing restrictive clauses, 92, **150-151**
reference of, compared to *who* and *which,* 92
That clauses, subjunctive in, 121
That kind, those kind, 128-129
The, to introduce a gerund phrase, 62-63
Their, theirs, 93 (table), 100
Their, there, 193, 197-198, 255
Themselves, theirselves, 101
Then,
confused with *than,* 198
conjunctive adverb, 33
There is, there are,
as anticipating subject, 26, 74-75
overuse of, 312
Therefore,
between main clauses, 33, 43, **153, 165-166**
as interrupting element, 153
punctuation with, 33, 43, **153, 156,** 165-166
at beginning of sentence, 153, 156, 166
Thesaurus, as source of synonyms, 244
These, those, 128-129
Thesis-sentence outlines, 360, **361-362**
Thesis statement (thesis sentence),
development directed by, 362, **380-381,** 417
formulation of, **348-349,** 454, 478, 481, 497
outline built on, **361-362,** 365
resources determined by, **353-354**
See also Pre-writing.
Third person pronouns,
forms of, 93 (table)
he or *she,* 92, 94
uses of, 101, 103, 427
This,
as demonstrative adjective, 128-129
as demonstrative pronoun, 92, 93 (table)
This kind, these kind, 128-129
Tho, though, 203
Thoro, thorough, 202
Though, introducing adverb clauses, 50
Throw, principal parts of, 114
Thru, through, 203
Thus, punctuation with, 153
Thwarted subordination, 49
Tight, tightly, 129
Till, until, 50, 218
Time,
adverbs used to emphasize, 337, 428
chronological pattern of development, 330, 337, 426-430
shown by adverb clauses, 49, 53
shown by tense, 111, 428-429
Time, expressions of,
abbreviation of, 223
capitalization of, 213
punctuation of, 169
figures or words for, 223, 227
Title of a paper,
manuscript form for, 400-401, 497
selection of, 392
Titles (of articles, books, etc.),
bibliography form for, 471-473, **495-496,** 507
books cataloged by, 455-457
capitalization of, 210, 401
footnote form for, **488-491**
italics or quotation marks for, 177, **181,** 186
Titles (of people),
abbreviation of, 221-222, 448
address form, 442
capitalization of, 210-211
honorary, 221
punctuation of, 157, 221-222, 225
To, with infinitives, **63,** 129
To, too, 193, 198
Together with, agreement with subjects joined by, 71
Tone,
appropriateness of, **13-18,** 259, 267-272
consistency in, 15, 249-250, **267-272**
Too, punctuation with, 153
Topic. *See* Pre-writing, Subjects for papers, *and* Thesis statement.
Topic outlines, 360, 478
development of, **363-366**
standard form for, **367-371**
See also Outlining.

Topic sentence, **324-325**, 329, 333
Toward, towards, 255-256
Trade bibliographies (listed), 457-458
Transitions. *See* Continuity.
Transitive verbs, 109 (table)
Travel, forms of, 201
Trite expressions, **274-275**; *ex. 283-284*
Try and, try to, 122
Type, as deadwood, 294
Typed papers. *See* Manuscript form.

U

Ulrich's International Periodical Directory, 460
Unabridged dictionaries, 234, 236 (listed)
Underdeveloped paragraphs, 319-327; *ex. 338-340*
Underlining. *See* Italics.
Unique, comparison of, 136
Units of measurement, 223
Unity. *See* Continuity.
Unless, introducing adverb clauses, 50
Unpublished material, footnotes for, 492
Until, till, 50, 218
Upper case. *See* Capitals.
Upside-down subordination, 55-56
Usage, varieties of, **3-13**, **8-9** (table); *ex. 18-22*
  appropriateness of, 13-18, 259, 267-272
  consistent use of, 15, 249-250, 267-272
  dictionary as a guide to, 243
  See also Divided usage.
Used to, use to, 197

V

Vague reference, of pronouns, 90-92
Vague words, 258-261
Variant spellings, 202-203, 238-239
Variety,
  in sentence length, 286-288
  in sentence pattern, **302-306**; *ex. 314-315*
Verbals and verbal phrases, 30, **59-66**; *ex. 66-68*
  defined, 30, 59, 109 (table)
  forms, **61** (table)
  idiomatic use, 62-63
  position and reference, 64-66
  uses, 28, 30, **61** (table)
  See also Gerunds, Infinitives, *and* Participles.
Verbs, **108-122**; *ex. 123-125*
  agreement with subject, **69-76**; *ex. 76-78*
  auxiliary, 63, 109 (table), 114-119
  be, forms of, 114-115
  consistent tense of, 111-112, 338
  defined, 24, 108, 109 (table)
  finite and non-finite, 109 (table)
  forms, 109 (table), 110 (table), 112-119
  idiomatic use of, 116-117, **121-122**
  irregular (strong), 109 (table), **112-114** (listed)
  linking, **25**, 109 (table), 114-115, 127
  modifiers of, 27-29, 49-50, 126
  mood of, 109 (table), 120-121
  number of, 69-76, 109 (table)
  objects of, 24-26
  omission of, 35
  position of, 24, **26**, 75, 304
  principal parts of, 109 (table), 112-114
  regular (weak), 109 (table), 110 (table)
  shall and *will,* 117-118
  subjects of, 23-24, 69-76
  subjunctive mood of, 109 (table), 120-121
  tenses of, **108-112**, 110 (table)
  terms describing, 109 (table)
  transitive and intransitive, defined, 109
  voice of, 109, **119-120**
  See also Verbals.
Verse. *See* Poetry.
Vertebra, plural forms, 82
Vertical File Index, to locate pamphlets, 461
Viz., 187
Vocabulary, methods for increasing, 194, **257-258**; *ex. 265. See also* Diction *and* Dictionaries.

Vocative (direct address), commas with, 154
Voice, active and passive,
of infinitives, participles, and gerunds, 61
of verbs, 26, 109, **119-120**
Vogue words, 273-274
Volume number,
in bibliography, 471-472, 496
in footnotes, 489-491
Vowels, 1
changed in irregular verbs (table), 113-114
changed in plurals of special nouns, 79
See also Spelling.
Vs., 187
Vulgarisms. *See* Nonstandard English.

W

Wake, principal parts of, 114
Want, want to, want that, 122
Was, were, Standard usage of, 114
We, I, appropriate use of, 101-102
We, us, 97-98
Weak connectives. *See* Conjunctive adverbs.
Weak verbs. *See* Regular verbs.
Wear, principal parts of, 114
Webster's Third New International Dictionary, 234, 236, 239
Weight, expressions of, 223
Well,
as adjective or adverb, 128
irregular comparison of, 135
as predicate adjective, 128
as weak exclamation, 154
What, introducing noun clauses, 50, 52
Whatever, introducing noun clauses, 50
When, 40, 43
as exact connective, 53-54
introducing adjective clauses, 49
introducing adverb clauses, 50
introducing noun clauses, 50
Where,
introducing adjective clauses, 49
introducing adverb clauses, 50
introducing noun clauses, 50
Whether, introducing noun clauses, 50, 51
Which, 31
and or *but* misused before, 49
introducing adjective clauses, 40, 48
introducing nonrestrictive clauses, 92, 150-151
possessive of, 100-101
reference of, compared to *who* and *that,* 92
While,
as exact connective, 53-54
for *at the same time that,* 293
introducing adverb clauses, 40, 50, 53-54
Who,
and or *but* misused before, 49
introducing adjective clauses, 48
introducing nonrestrictive clauses, 92, 150-151
introducing noun clauses, 50
object form of, 99
possessive of, 100-101
reference of, to persons, 92
Who, whom, 99
Who's, whose, of which, 100-101
Why,
introducing adjective clauses, 49
introducing noun clauses, 50-51
Will, shall, 118-119
-wise, added to nouns to form adverbs, 129, 273
With, agreement with subjects joined by, 71
Women, genitive of, 84
Won't, 118
Word forms, in English, 2
Word order,
inverted order, 26, 75, 304
position of single-word modifiers, 27, 126-127, 130-132
typical S-V-O pattern, 25-26
variations in sentence pattern, 26, 75, 304-306
Word use. *See* Diction.
Wordiness, **291-292**; *ex. 299-300. See also* Deadwood *and* Repetition.
Words used as words, italics or quotation marks for, **181,** 186

Worse, worst, 135
Worship, forms of, 201
Would, should, 118-119
Wring, principal parts of, 114
Write, principal parts of, 114
Write, right, rite, 192
Write, writing, 200
Writing, conventions of. *See* Conventions of writing.
Writing papers. *See* Composition, Pre-writing, *and* Revision.
Wrong, wrongly, 129

X, Y, Z

Xmas, for *Christmas,* 222
-*y,* final, changed to -*i*-, 79-81, 201
Yearbooks and annuals, 469-470
Yes, 154
Yet, punctuation with, 148, 164-165
You, overuse of, 102
You was, you were, 115
Your, yours, 93 (table), 99-100
Yourself, 101
ZIP codes, 444

2 3 4 5 6 7 8 9 10 11 12 13 14 15 16 17 18 19 20 21 22 23 24 25 PI 74 73 72 71 70 69 68

Correction symbols

This list of correction symbols and abbreviations covers the most common errors in writing. Refer to the section number indicated for information regarding revision.

Ab Improper abbreviation §18.1

Abst Too abstract §20.4

Ad Incorrect form of adjective or adverb §10

Agr Error in agreement
- of subject and verb §6
- of pronoun and antecedent §8.2

Amb Ambiguous

Awk Awkward

Big W Big Words—stilted §21.1

Cap Use capital letter §17.1

No cap No capital letter §17.1

Case Wrong case form of pronoun §8.3

CF Comma fault §3.2

Coh Lacks coherence (continuity)
- within paragraph §24.3
- between paragraphs §26.3

Comp Mistake in comparison of adjective or adverb §10.7 and §10.8

D Error in diction §20 and §21
- connotation §20.1
- slanted §20.2
- wrong word §20.3
- too abstract §20.4
- stilted §21.1
- too Informal §21.2
- trite §21.3
- poor figure of speech §21.4

Dead Deadwood §22.4

Div Word division §19.2 and §27.2

DM Dangling modifier §5.4

Ec Economy of expression §22

Emph Sentence emphasis §23.4

Fig Figure of speech inappropriate or inconsistent §21.4

Frag Fragmentary sentence §3.1

FS Fused sentence §3.3

Gr Error in grammar §2

Id Unidiomatic §9.5

Inf Expression too Informal §21.2

Ital Italics (underlining) §15.4

lc Use lower case letter §17.1

Log Error in logic §28.2

Mix Mixed construction §3.4

MM Misrelated modifier
- verbal phrase §5.3
- adverb §10.5

Mng Meaning not clear

MS Error in manuscript form §27.2

NS Nonstandard usage §1.2

Num Use of words or figures for numbers §18.2

Org Faulty organization §25.4

Par / *¶* Paragraph unsatisfactory in development, continuity, or length §24

¶ con Paragraph continuity §24.3

¶ dev Paragraph development §24.1